microeconomics

H

microeconomics

Stephen Dobson
University of Hull

G. S. Maddala
Ohio State University

Ellen Miller
University of North Carolina

McGRAW-HILL BOOK COMPANY

London · New York · St Louis · San Francisco · Auckland
Bogotá · Caracas · Lisbon · Madrid · Mexico
Milan · Montreal · New Delhi · Panama · Paris · San Juan
São Paulo · Singapore · Sydney · Tokyo · Toronto

Published by
McGRAW-HILL BOOK COMPANY EUROPE
Shoppenhangers Road, Maidenhead, Berkshire SL6 2QL, England
Telephone: 01628 23432   Fax: 01628 770224

British Library Cataloguing in Publication Data
Dobson, Stephen
  Microeconomics
  I. Title
  338.5

ISBN 0-07-707870-5

12345 BP 98765

Typeset by P&R Typesetters Ltd
and printed and bound in Great Britain
by The Bath Press, Avon.

Printed on permanent paper in compliance with
the ISO standard 9706

to
my parents   S.M.D.

---

to
Kameswari, Tara and Vivek   G.S.M.

---

to
my father   E.M.

Contents

List of Applications and Examples

Preface

With all the acceptable books on microeconomics available, why have we produced yet another one? The reason is that no one book develops the core topics patiently and clearly, while also giving students a sense of microeconomics as a field of study that is vibrant and always evolving. In addition to an exposition of the core topics that is more painstaking than most, to help students develop the foundation so critical to economists' thinking, we include references to the specific theorists and developments of the past. We also give a sense of the 'interesting edge' topics that involve the thinking of today's (and tomorrow's) microeconomists. These topics can be dealt with depending on the time available and the needs of instructors.

Special Features of the Book

The following are some of the special features of this book:

1 The book offers exceptionally patient and careful coverage of the core topics in microeconomics. Some examples are Chapters 2 and 3 (Theory and Analysis of Demand), Chapters 9 and 10 (Monopoly) and Chapter 16 (Externalities and Public Goods). In our opinion, this degree of care not only sets this book apart, but also helps students establish the strongest possible foundation in microeconomic analysis.

2 The book also features in-depth coverage of many topics from current microeconomic research. Topics such as the rigidity of prices, advertising and market structure, the economics of uncertainty, the economics of information, and intertemporal choice and risk provide students with a sense of the dynamic nature of contemporary microeconomics. These topics can, however, be treated as optional, and the instructor can pick and choose among them, as time permits, according to his/her and the student's interest.

3 The book presents microeconomics in the context of its historical development, both in giving the development of core topics and explaining modern research. Numerous references to the classic economic literature help students understand the fabric of economic thought.

4 The book features many innovative examples and applications of microeconomic theory. The applications in the book are both numerous and detailed. They are designed to be of interest to both specialists and non-specialists, and serve to demonstrate the relevance of the theory to the analysis of current issues and problems. The applications also cover a wide range of areas—education economics, energy economics, environmental economics, health economics, transport economics, urban economics, and many others. Some applications worked out in detail include: cash subsidies versus subsidies in kind (Chapter 2), VAT on domestic energy (Chapter 2), social security and negative income tax (Chapter 3), empirical cost curves (Chapter 5), private and social health insurance (Chapter 7), transport improvements and land values (Chapter 7), rent control (Chapter 8), the Common Agricultural Policy (Chapter 8), energy conservation (Chapter 9), import fees on oil (Chapter 10), the effects of minimum wage laws (Chapter 13), monopsony and minimum wages (Chapter 14), the economics of professional sport (Chapter 14), land use restrictions in agriculture (Chapter 15), a profit tax on oil producers (Chapter 15), optimal road pricing (Chapter 16), estimating lifetime earnings (Chapter 17), and the market for durable goods (Chapter 17).

The Importance of Microeconomics

In microeconomics we study the economic behaviour of individuals and firms, the different types of market organization, and how individuals and firms interact with government. Although generalizations cannot be taken literally, many economists argue that it is in courses in microeconomics that students learn the fundamental principles of economic theory. The principles that are most important to the economists' way of thinking include the fundamentals of supply and demand, the distinction between accounting and opportunity cost, the relationship between the margin and the average, and so on. In this book we present the basic principles of microeconomics in a thorough manner, and introduce numerous applications and policy problems throughout. Students thus learn both the tools of analysis and how to apply them to practical problems.

Who Can Use the Book?

This text is appropriate for undergraduate intermediate-level microeconomics courses. It is also ideal for undergraduate courses in business studies, business administration, management, and social science. The book is also appropriate for MBA courses and postgraduate conversion courses that include economics. This text covers all the basic material required for courses in microeconomics and also several supplemental topics so that instructors can choose the ones they consider most appropriate. Knowledge of calculus is not required of the reader, so this text can be used in more basic courses as well. We have paid careful attention to the figures that illustrate the arguments. The details of the figures are explained in the text so that the arguments flow in a logical way. For instructors who would like to adopt an algebra-based coverage, we have included a mathematical appendix.

Chapters 6, 7, 12, 18, and some sections of the other chapters might be omitted in more basic courses. The book permits considerable flexibility in the choice of topics, particularly because the applications are included in each chapter.

Pedagogical Aids

The book contains a wide variety of pedagogical learning aids, including the following:
- Chapter introductions
- Numerous diagrams and illustrations
- Detailed chapter summaries
- A list of key term in each chapter
- Questions and problems
- A glossary of the more important key terms (those marked with an asterix (*) in 'Key Terms' lists)
- Numerous examples of current topical interest

Supplemental readings are provided in the footnotes when the particular topic is discussed in the book. Students can thus refer to the supplemental readings that are of interest to them.

In addition to the many applications in the text, specially highlighted examples of particular interest are often used to illustrate the theory in more depth. They include: paying for retirement pensions (Chapter 1), Christmas gifts (Chapter 2), valuing the countryside (Chapter 3), the costs of health care (Chapter 5), pricing admissions to EuroDisney (Chapter 7), collusion in the market for white salt (Chapter 11), advertising and alcohol consumption (Chapter 12), valuing a human life (Chapter 15), and the optimal level of transport safety (Chapter 16).

Stephen Dobson
G. S. Maddala
Ellen Miller

Acknowledgements

In the preface to the original US edition. Maddala and Miller thank friends, colleagues and reviewers for their comments and suggestions. In preparing this edition, I have also benefited greatly from the help and advice of a number of people. Stephen Trotter read through the entire manuscript and made many helpful suggestions and comments. Thanks are also due to Jon Atkins, Chris Hammond, Gerry Makepeace, Mike Turner and Simon Vicary for providing information and help in particular areas.

I must also thank Brendan Lambon, Business and Economics editor at McGraw-Hill, for his encouragement, keen interest and enthusiasm. A number of my heroes make appearances in the book. I thank them for contributing to the project. Apologies to the many others I have had to leave out!

Stephen Dobson

Introduction to Microeconomic Analysis

The basic problems of economics are simple; the hard part is to recognise simplicity when you see it. The next hardest part is to present simplicity as common sense rather than ivory tower insensitivity.

H. G. Johnson[1]

Common sense is not so common.

Voltaire

1-1 The Nature of Microeconomics

Microeconomics studies the decisions of individuals: individual consumers and individual firms. Knowledge of microeconomic principles enables us to explain how and why individual consumers and firms make decisions. For example, in microeconomics we study how the choices of consumers are affected by changes in the prices of goods and in the level of consumer income. Microeconomics also considers how firms decide how much of a good to produce and how many workers to employ. We can also use microeconomic theory to examine how markets operate by studying the interaction of consumers and firms.

Let us look more closely at the sort of decisions that individuals and firms may make. An *individual* has many decisions or choices to make: (1) whether to go into further and/or higher education after school; (2) whether to buy or rent a house or flat; (3) whether to marry. In fact, our whole life is a complex multiple-choice problem. Similarly, *firms* also have many choices to make: (1) whether to expand output; (2) whether to close down a plant; (3) whether to produce output in the home country or in an overseas plant.

Not all choices are economic. For example, whether to marry is not usually considered an economic choice. However, some economists such as Becker analyse even this as a pure economic problem. Becker talks of couples separating when the utility expected from staying married falls below the utility expected from divorce, of people marrying when the utility expected from marriage exceeds the utility expected from remaining single, and so on.[2] We are mostly concerned with more conventional economic choices involving the allocation of scarce resources.

Choices are dictated by *scarcity*: scarcity of the resources at our command. Productive resources are

[1] H. G. Johnson, 'The Study of Theory', *American Economic Review*, 64 (Papers and Proceedings) (1974): 324.

[2] G. Becker, 'A Theory of Marriage', *Journal of Political Economy*, 81 (1973): 813–46, and *Journal of Political Economy*, 82 (1974): S11–26. See also G. Becker, E. Landes, and R. Michael, 'An Economic Analysis of Marital Instability', *Journal of Political Economy*, 85 (1977): 1141–87, and G. Becker, *A Treatise on the Family*, Harvard University Press, Cambridge, Mass., 1981.

usually classified under the following categories:

1 *Natural resources*: land, water, air, minerals, forests
2 *Human resources*: skilled and unskilled labour
3 *Capital resources*: machines, equipment, buildings
4 *Entrepreneurial resources*: a special category of human resources, consisting of people who combine natural, human, and capital resources to produce output, take risks, etc. Entrepreneurs are the ones who make the decisions about the organization of production.

We discuss these resources as factors of production.

Firms must decide how to combine these scarce productive resources to produce goods and services. The goods and services produced are also scarce and must be allocated among society's consumers. Most allocation of goods and services, under capitalism, is through markets. Here, consumers must decide how to allocate their limited (or scarce) purchasing power among the various scarce goods and services.

Economics has sometimes been referred to as the 'science of scarcity' because it focuses on the allocation of society's scarce resources. The emphasis in this book is on the analysis of individual decisions made by consumers, firms, and, to a much lesser extent, by government which affect the ultimate allocation of society's scarce resources.

Example 1-1   Paying for Retirement Pensions

One example of economic choice on a large scale concerns government decisions on public (i.e. government) spending. At times of economic recession the government invariably runs up a large budget deficit. One way to reduce the size of the deficit is to cut public spending. The government has to make the following choices: (1) which part of its spending to cut (on education, health, defence, social security, and so on) and (2) which part of its spending not to cut.

The obvious way to reduce public spending in the UK is for the government to cut its spending on social security, since this currently accounts for about one-third (or £80 billion) of total public spending. The obvious area of social security spending to cut is the basic state (retirement) pension, as this absorbs about

one-third of the £80 billion. The solution seems straightforward. To reduce the size of the budget deficit, the government should reduce public spending. To cut public spending, it should cut spending on social security; and to do this, it should reduce the basic state pension.[3]

The nature of the basic pension is under review because of the growing proportion of old-age pensioners in the UK. Not only is the proportion of elderly people increasing, but also the proportion of working-age people is falling. It is estimated that in the UK the number of people over 65 years of age will increase from 10 million to 15 million by the year 2030. There are now 4.3 people aged 15–64 for every 1 person over 65; by 2030 there will be 3.2. In the United States this ratio is expected to fall from 5.4 to 2.8, and in Japan it is expected to fall from 6.2 to 3.1. The worry for the UK government is that the public finances will not be able to support so many pensioners. The fact that there will be fewer working people to support each pensioner has prompted the government to review the basic pension.

One possible solution is to raise the taxes of those of working age. This is unlikely, however, given that the Government Actuary calculates that national insurance contribution rates would have to increase by about 7.5 per cent by 2030 to maintain the value of the state pension in relation to earnings. Alternatively, the government could hold pensioners' living standards at their current level by continuing the policy of allowing the pension to grow in line with prices but not average earnings. (The basic pension is worth twice as much today relative to prices as it was 30 years ago, but it is worth the same relative to earnings.) This would eliminate the need to raise tax rates but it would widen the gap between the level of pensions and the incomes of the working population. Moreover, there would be a continued decline in the relative income of those pensioners who are exclusively dependent on the state pension.

Perhaps the most likely development is for the government to encourage more people to join private pension schemes. Already, about one-half of all 22- to 26-year-olds have private pensions. However, the government has to consider the economic consequences of such action. The basic pension is funded out of the national insurance contributions of the

---

[3] Further discussion of this can be found in the article, 'Old Problem', *The Economist* (13 February 1993): 28–9.

working population. If people opt out of the basic pension and join private schemes, it still means that the government has to pay for the pensions of those already retired. But the better off would now be saving for their own private schemes and would not be paying state contributions. The public finances would almost certainly worsen in the short run, so defeating the object of the exercise.

1-2 Positive and Normative Analysis

The answers to many problems in microeconomics depend on whether we are conducting positive or normative analysis. It is common knowledge that economists often disagree. These disagreements can be reconciled if we know whether they result from different assumptions or working hypotheses, or from different views about how things ought to be. The former is a difference of opinion about what is, and the latter is a difference of opinion of what ought to be.[4] It is possible that two economists starting with the same premises would come to different conclusions because of differences in opinion about what ought to be done. This conflict is extremely prominent when it comes to analysing the different policies of the government.

Positive economics deals with the question of what is, and *normative economics* deals with the question of what ought to be. Normative economics involves prescriptive statements; for example, the statement that the government should guarantee a minimum income for every individual is a prescriptive statement. Another such prescriptive statement is that the government should stop all overseas aid programmes. These are statements in normative economics.

Statements in positive economics are statements that start with assumptions and derive some conclusions (which can be checked with data). For example, 'a minimum wage law increases youth unemployment' is a statement in positive economics because it can be verified or refuted with actual data. A statement such as 'a profit-maximizing firm will set its price equal to its marginal cost' is a statement in positive economics. Positive statements do not involve values or opinions.

Note, however, that we have given only a simple description of positive and normative economics. There is, actually, considerable dispute as to what is positive and what is normative. For example, if positive economics is 'what is', then we should talk about how consumers actually do behave when they go shopping, or how firms actually do price their products, and so on. But to study this we have to observe the actual behaviour of individuals and firms and study their psychology. In this book, we start with some assumptions, such as 'consumers maximize utility', 'firms maximize profits', and then derive some implications from these assumptions. Some call this normative economics, arguing that in essence we are saying that consumers *ought to* maximize utility, producers *ought to* maximize profits, and so on.

All these assumptions are considered by economists as *rational*. However, in real life many consumers are *partly irrational*, and so are many firms.[5] There are two reasons for this:

1 Real world-problems are much more complicated than those that we study in microeconomics texts, and it is impossible to be as rational as is assumed in the texts. In real life you have to make many approximations, rough-and-ready calculations, etc., and the human mind is capable of assimilating only a limited amount of information.

2 The decisions made by consumers and firms are not all based on pure economic reasoning. There is a lot of psychology involved.

This area of studying individuals and firms at the actual decision-making level comes under what Leibenstein calls 'micro-microeconomics'.[6] Since this is a book on microeconomics, not micro-microeconomics or psychological economics, when we talk of an individual or a firm we are talking of a rational individual (maximizing utility) or a rational firm (maximizing profit), except for a digression in Chapter 6.

There are two reasons why we discuss only rational economic behaviour:

1 Individuals can be rational in only one way, but they can be irrational in several ways. Furthermore, it is hard to predict the actions of irrational individuals.

---

[4] We are assuming that there are no mistakes in logic. Those economists that make mistakes in their arguments are excluded from our discussion.

[5] Simon calls this 'bounded rationality'. See H. Simon, *Models of Man*, John Wiley, New York, 1957.
[6] H. Leibenstein, 'The Missing Link: Micro-Micro Theory', *Journal of Economic Literature*, 11 (1979): 477–502.

2 Many of the important conclusions we derive in microeconomic theory are not substantially altered by irrational behaviour.[7]

In summary, this book discusses the behaviour of economically rational consumers and firms. Furthermore, we derive conclusions about the behaviour of consumers and firms from some simple assumptions, without imposing value judgements.

1-3 Microeconomic Models: Assumptions and Reality

Economic analysis begins with models. What is a model? It is simply a description of the economist's view of how things work. Economists first construct simple models and then progressively complicate them. Given that the real world is complicated, the economist's task of constructing a simple model is not an easy one. In constructing a simple model, the economist has to make some 'simplifying' assumptions, such as: there is no uncertainty; all consumers have the same tastes; there is only one homogeneous product. None of these assumptions is, of course, realistic, but there are always some aspects of reality that are irrelevant or of negligible importance for any problem. Thus, some of the 'unrealistic' assumptions made by the economist are justified on the grounds that they enable us to concentrate on the essential aspects of the problem while ignoring irrelevant detail.

For instance, suppose we want to analyse the demand for cars. We may say that the price of cars, family income, the price of petrol, and so on are the important factors to consider. Of course, in a remote sense the demand for cars also depends on the price of ice cream, because if the price of ice cream rises people can substitute cars for ice cream. But no one considers this a realistic or important factor.

We might, therefore, say that *a model is a simplified representation of the real world*. Many scientists have argued in favour of simplicity, because simple models are easier to understand, communicate, and test with data. For instance, the philosopher Popper says: 'simple statements, if knowledge is our objective, are

to be prized more highly than less simple ones because they tell us more; because their empirical content is better, and because they are testable'.[8] Friedman also argues: 'a hypothesis is important if it "explains" much by little, that is, if it abstracts the common and crucial elements from the mass of complex and detailed circumstances surrounding the phenomena to be explained and permits valid predictions on the basis of them alone'.[9]

The choice of a simple model to explain complex real-world phenomena often leads to two criticisms: (1) the model is oversimplified; (2) the assumptions are unrealistic. To the criticism of oversimplification, we can argue that it is better to start with a simplified model and then progressively construct more complicated models. This is the approach we follow in this book.

To the criticism that the assumptions are unrealistic, it has been argued, most notably by Friedman, that the assumptions of a theory are never descriptively realistic. Friedman says:

> To be important, therefore, a hypothesis must be descriptively false in its assumptions ... the relevant question to ask about the 'assumptions' of a theory is not whether they are descriptively 'realistic', for they never are, but whether they are sufficiently good approximations for the purpose at hand. And this question can be answered by seeing whether the theory works, which means whether it yields sufficiently accurate predictions.[10]

The statement that the assumptions *must* be descriptively false is a provocative statement (and it provoked a lot of controversy), but there is a point here. What we should mean by 'realistic' assumptions is that they take all the relevant variables into account but are descriptively inaccurate in the sense that they simplify and idealize rather outrageously. If simplicity is a desirable criterion, then the assumptions have to be descriptively inaccurate. But this does not mean that we can make any assumptions that we like. All it means is that we can make assumptions that do not flatly

---

[7] G. Becker, 'Irrational Behaviour and Economic Theory', *Journal of Political Economy*, 70 (1962): 1–13.

[8] K. Popper, *The Logic of Scientific Discovery*, Hutchinson, London, 1959, p. 142.

[9] M. Friedman, 'The Methodology of Positive Economics', in *Essays in Positive Economics*, University of Chicago Press, 1953, p. 14.

[10] Ibid., pp. 14–15.

contradict anything observable and then proceed to test the predictions.

Not all economists agree with this irrelevance-of-assumptions thesis. The major criticism of this argument is that you cannot use accuracy of predictions as the only test of economic theories, because there can be many spurious correlations. The fact that one theory (A) gives better predictions than another theory (B) does not necessarily imply that theory A is a better theory. As an illustration, Hendry compared two theories that try to explain movements in the UK price level over the period 1964–75.[11] The first theory uses money supply as an explanatory variable, and the other uses a variable C. The latter theory does much better in predicting movements in the price level, except that variable C is simply the *cumulative rainfall in the UK!*

Of course, not all competing theories contrast variables such as money supply and rainfall. But if one is arguing that economic theories are to be judged on the basis of predictions alone, there ought to be some stringent definitions laid down concerning what 'accuracy of predictions' means.

Many economic theories do not generate any predictions. (We discuss this in Chapter 11 when we consider monopolistic competition.) This does not mean that these theories are useless; such theories suggest new avenues of approach and focus attention on problems that were ignored earlier. Some other economic theories are just exercises in pure deductive logic. If assumptions A, B, C, etc. are made, then conclusions X, Y, Z, etc., follow. There are many examples of these exercises in mathematical economics.

In the following chapters of this book we make some assumptions to enable us to start with simple models that are easy to understand. To understand the basic principles of microeconomics, we cannot start with a huge model with all the complications built into it. We have to go step by step, starting with the simplest models and many simplifying assumptions.

The propensity of economists always to start with some assumptions is the butt of a popular joke narrated by economists themselves at social gatherings. The story is about three men on a desert island, and all they have is one huge can of tuna. The three men are starving and are discussing how to open the can. The

first man, a physicist, suggests a way to make a fire hot enough to melt the can. The second, an engineer, suggests a slingshot that will hurl the can against a rock with enough force to puncture it. The third, an economist, suggests that they 'assume a can opener' and proceed from there.

For the remainder of the chapter we briefly describe the best-known microeconomic model: the demand and supply model. Many of you will have already met this material in your introductory course. Nevertheless, it provides a useful overview of important principles in microeconomic analysis.

1-4   Demand and Supply Analysis*

Before considering the interaction of buyers and sellers in the market-place, it is useful to examine the two sides of the market independently. We begin arbitrarily by looking at the behaviour of buyers, or the demand side.

Individual Demand

By way of definition, *demand* simply indicates the quantities of a good (or service) that an individual or group of individuals is willing to purchase at various prices, as long as other things remain the same. This is what is known as the '*ceteris paribus*' condition. The words '*ceteris paribus*' are Latin for 'other things remaining the same'. Demand is thus composed of many price and quantity pairs for a given set of circumstances.

It is frequently useful to illustrate demand graphically through a demand curve as in Figure 1-1. To an economist, *demand* refers to the entire relationship between price and quantity, *ceteris paribus*. For any single price there is a corresponding *quantity demanded*. So the term 'quantity demanded' refers to a particular point on a demand curve. As long as the *ceteris paribus* condition holds, we can move along a demand curve; we are merely changing quantity demanded. If the *ceteris paribus* condition is violated, then an entirely new demand curve results; we say that there is a change in demand, and the demand curve shifts.

---

[11] D. Hendry, 'Econometrics—Alchemy or Science?' *Economica*, 47 (1980): 387–406.

---

* A mathematical treatment of some of this material is given in the Mathematical Appendix at the end of the book.

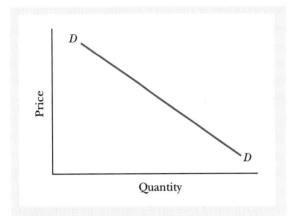

Figure 1-1   Demand curve of an individual consumer

An important question concerns the slope of a demand curve. Why is it downward-sloping (negatively sloped)? The answer is because of the law of demand. The *law of demand* says: the quantity demanded of a commodity is smaller at higher market prices and larger at lower market prices, *ceteris paribus*. If quantity increases as price falls, then the curve illustrating this relationship must slope downward from left to right. (Recall, however, from your introductory course that in the case of Giffen goods the demand curve is upward-sloping (positively sloped).) There is, incidentally, no

reason to believe that a typical demand curve has a constant slope or that the relationship between price and quantity is a linear relationship. Demand curves are sometimes drawn this way merely for simplicity.

As we said above, if something other than price changes so that the *ceteris paribus* condition is violated, then an entirely new demand curve results. The following changes result in a *shift* in a demand curve: changes in tastes, changes in incomes, changes in the price of other commodities, and changes in expectations. If more of the commodity is demanded at every price, then the demand curve shifts to the right as shown in Figure 1-2(a). This is called an *increase* in demand. If less of the commodity is demanded at every price, then the demand curve shifts to the left, as shown in Figure 1-2(b). This is called a *decrease* in demand.

Individual Supply

The supply side of the market is similar in some ways to the demand side. By way of definition, *supply* indicates the quantities of a good (or service) that the seller is willing and able to provide at various prices, *ceteris paribus*. Supply can be illustrated through a supply curve, as in Figure 1-3. *Supply* refers to the entire relationship between price and quantity, *ceteris paribus*. So an entire supply curve illustrates supply. And

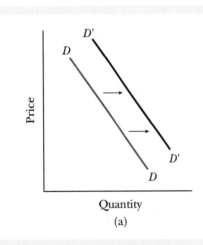

(a)

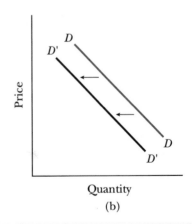

(b)

Figure 1-2   Shifts in the demand curve

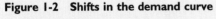

(*a*) A shift to the right (or increase in demand)
(*b*) A shift to the left (or decrease in demand)

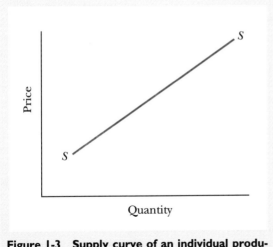

Figure 1-3   Supply curve of an individual produ-cer

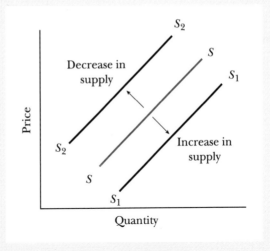

Figure 1-4   Shifts in the supply curve

corresponding to any single price, there is a single *quantity supplied*. So the term 'quantity supplied' refers to a particular point on the supply curve.

Examining the supply curve, a pattern again appears. As the price of the product rises, the quantity supplied increases as well. Thus, a supply curve has a positive slope, or slopes upward from left to right. That is, price and quantity supplied vary directly. Our supply curve obeys the law of supply. The *law of supply says*: *ceteris paribus*, the quantity supplied of a commodity is larger at higher market prices and smaller at lower market prices. The law of supply is analysed in greater detail in future chapters when we look behind the supply curve at the cost structure of the firm.

As long as the *ceteris paribus* condition is satisfied, we can move along a single supply curve, merely changing quantity supplied. But if something other than the price of the product changes, then an entirely new supply curve results; we say that there is a change in supply, and the supply curve shifts.

As with the demand curve, there are several factors that produce shifts in the supply curve. These are new discoveries, availability of a new technology, changes in the supply of inputs, changes in the weather, and so on. If more of a commodity is supplied at every price, then we say there is an increase in supply. The supply curve shifts to the right. If less of a commodity is supplied at every price, then we say that there is a decrease in supply. The supply curve shifts to the left. This is shown in Figure 1-4.

Market Equilibrium and the Impact of Changes in Demand and Supply

So far we have examined each side of the market separately. It is now time to put the two together. Marshall (1842–1924) compared demand and supply to the two blades of a pair of scissors: there is no point in arguing which of the two blades is doing the cutting. Similarly, prices are determined by the interaction of demand and supply, and one cannot ignore either element.

We assume that the market is *competitive*. This means that there is a large number of buyers and sellers and, hence, no one buyer or seller has control over the market price. In this case the point of intersection of the demand and supply curves gives the price that prevails in the market. This is shown as the price P^* in Figure 1-5. This is the price that every buyer pays. The corresponding quantity Q^* is the total quantity transacted by the buyers and sellers.

The price P^* is determined by the intersection of the demand and supply curves and is called the *equilibrium price*. The quantity transacted Q^* is called the *equilibrium quantity*. The word 'equilibrium' denotes a state of rest from which there is no tendency to change. In Figure 1-5 point C describes a position of equilibrium because this is the point where all buyers and all sellers are satisfied.

If the price is higher than P^*, say P_1, then buyers can buy what they want to buy at that price, but sellers

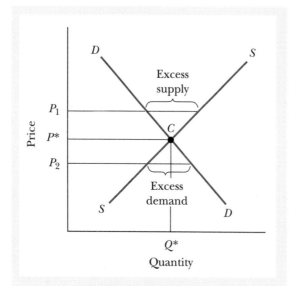

Figure 1-5 Determination of equilibrium price and quantity (competitive market)

cannot sell all they want to sell. This is a situation of *excess supply* or *surplus* in the market. The suppliers are dissatisfied. This situation cannot be sustained and the market price has to come down. If the price is lower than P^*, say P_2, then sellers can sell what they want to sell at that price, but buyers cannot buy all they want to

buy. This is a situation of *excess demand* or *shortage* in the market. The buyers are dissatisfied. This situation cannot be sustained and the market price has to go up. When prices are above or below the equilibrium level, we say the market is in *disequilibrium.*

We can now discuss the effects of changes in demand and supply on the equilibrium price and quantity. What we are doing falls in the area of *comparative statics.* This is the branch of economics that compares equilibrium positions when external circumstances change. That is, we study the effect on equilibrium positions if the demand and supply curves shift.

Let us consider an increase in demand. What happens to the equilibrium price and quantity depends on whether (1) the supply curve is unchanged, (2) there is an increase in supply, or (3) there is a decrease in supply. These situations are described in Figure 1-6. In all three cases $D_0 D_0$ is the initial demand curve and $S_0 S_0$ the initial supply curve. $D_1 D_1$ is the new demand curve and $S_1 S_1$ is the new supply curve. The initial equilibrium price and quantity are P_0 and Q_0 respectively, and the new equilibrium price and quantity are P_1 and Q_1 respectively.

In Figure 1-6(a), when supply remains unchanged, the effect of an increase in demand is that both the equilibrium price and equilibrium quantity increase. In Figure 1-6(b), when there is an increase in supply,

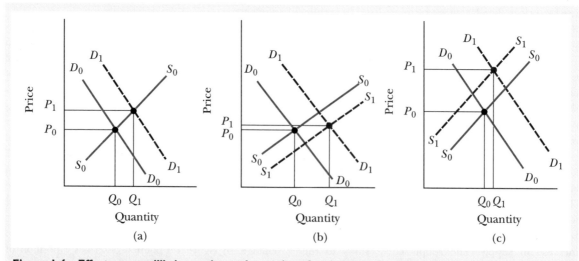

Figure 1-6 Effects on equilibrium price and quantity of an increase in demand

(a) Supply unchanged
(b) An increase in supply
(c) A decrease in supply

Table 1-1 Effects of shifts in the demand and supply curves on equilibrium price and equilibrium quantity

Supply	Demand		
	Increase	No change	Decrease
Increase	P(?) Q(+)	P(−) Q(+)	P(−) Q(?)
No change	P(+) Q(+)	No change	P(−) Q(−)
Decrease	P(+) Q(?)	P(+) Q(−)	P(?) Q(−)

equilibrium quantity increases but we cannot say anything about equilibrium price. This is because the increase in demand puts upward pressure on price while the increase in supply puts downward pressure on price. Price can go up, stay the same, or come down; it all depends on the relative magnitudes of the shifts in the demand and supply curves. In Figure 1-6(b) we see that the equilibrium price goes up, but we can derive the other conclusions by changing the magnitudes of the shifts in the demand and supply curves.

In Figure 1-6(c), when there is a decrease in supply, the equilibrium price goes up, but we cannot say anything about the equilibrium quantity. This time, the decrease in supply puts downward pressure on output while the increase in demand puts upward pressure. The net effect can be either an increase or a decrease. Again, it all depends on the relative magnitudes of the shifts in the demand and supply curves. Only one of the three possibilities is illustrated in Figure 1-6(c), but it is easy to show the other cases by simply changing the magnitudes of the shifts in the demand and supply curves.

We can analyse the case of a decrease in demand in a similar fashion. All these cases are shown in Table 1-1. For compactness, we use the following notation: P(+) means the equilibrium price goes up; P(−) means the equilibrium price goes down; and P(?) means we cannot say whether the equilibrium price goes up, stays the same, or goes down. Q(+), Q(−), and Q(?) are defined similarly and refer to equilibrium quantities. The results can be verified by drawing the demand and supply curves.

Example 1-2 Winter Freezes and the Price of Coffee[12]

The market for coffee is a good example of how changes in supply and demand can lead to volatile prices and quantities in a market. The volatile nature of this market stems primarily from changes on the supply side, since the supply of coffee depends greatly on whether producers face favourable or unfavourable weather conditions. The chief weather hazard that producers face is severe frost. A poor harvest, due to frost, can have a significant global impact if it occurs in large coffee-producing countries. This was the case in 1977, when a severe frost in Brazil produced a bad harvest and the impact was widely felt.

The effect of the Brazilian frost on the coffee market was that the supply curve shifted sharply to the left. This resulted in a price increase and a significant fall in the quantity traded. Frequent changes in world coffee prices are of particular concern to those coffee-producing countries that rely heavily on coffee exports to help finance economic development. For instance, in the 1980s coffee accounted for more than 90 per cent of total exports from Uganda.

A detailed analysis of the coffee market requires a discussion of the factors shifting the demand curve as well as the supply curve. Also, we may wish to examine how the actions of commodity speculators affect the coffee market and to consider how we can identify a single price when there are many different types and grades of coffee. This is left as an exercise for interested readers.

1-5 Government Intervention in Markets: Price Controls

We can also use our basic demand and supply model to consider the effect of government *price regulation* in a market. In the case of controls on maximum prices, the government has in mind the idea that low-income

---

[12] This example is adapted from the *Economic Review*, 10 (September 1992): 7–8.

consumers are likely to suffer a great hardship if prices are 'too high'. Government controls on maximum prices prevent prices rising to their market-clearing level.

One example of controls on maximum prices is rent controls, designed to keep private-sector housing rents below their market-clearing level. As can be seen from a simple demand and supply diagram, such as the one in Figure 1-5, rent controls, in fixing the price below the equilibrium level, create an excess demand or shortage in the market. The excess demand goes into alternative housing arrangements. Furthermore, it is likely that some of the excess demand will generate a *black market*. In other words, some transactions take place at the controlled rent and some others take place above the controlled rent in an illegal market often called the 'black market'.

This situation is shown in Figure 1-7. At the controlled price of P_c, Q_1 is the legally available quantity of accommodation. At Q_1 some tenants are prepared to pay P_1 for accommodation, as shown by the height of the demand curve at Q_1. Landlords benefit if they rent housing at a price above P_c, and so there is scope for transactions to take place. Thus, black markets are likely to occur. The extent of the black market depends on the nature of any penalties imposed on the parties carrying out the transactions and on the chances of getting caught.

Since one of the major objectives of rent controls is to transfer income from landlords to consumers, it might be interesting to see under what conditions this is possible. Consider the case where the quantity supplied is fixed and equal to Q_0. The effects of rent controls in this situation are illustrated in Figure 1-8. The supply curve SS is vertical at the quantity Q_0. DD is the demand curve. The equilibrium price is P_0 and, of course, the quantity supplied and demanded is Q_0.

Suppose the price is controlled at P_c which is less than P_0. Then the quantity supplied is still Q_0, as before. There is, of course, an excess demand equal to BC, but this remains unsatisfied. Assuming the quantity of housing to be fixed, we see that there is an income transfer equal to the shaded area shown in Figure 1-8 from landlords to the tenants currently occupying the accommodation. Before, tenants spent $P_0 Q_0$ for the amount of Q_0. Now they spend only $P_c Q_0$ for the same amount Q_0.

Of course, the rent control draws new consumers into the market, and this is what causes the excess demand. But since the quantity supplied is fixed in the short run, they cannot get any rental housing at the price P_c. Remember, however, that, because quantity supplied is fixed only in the short run, the above arguments may not hold good in the long run. However, the argument about income transfers is based on an implicit assumption of fixed supply.

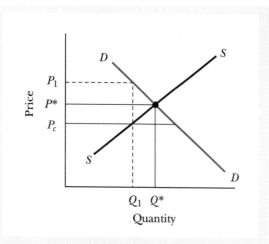

Figure 1-7 Rent controls: paying the 'black market' price

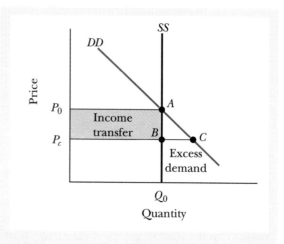

Figure 1-8 Effect of rent controls under conditions of fixed supply

I-6 Summary

Microeconomics is concerned with the study of the choices of individuals and firms. It considers how their decisions are co-ordinated through interactions in markets.

The choices made by individuals and firms are dictated by scarcity. Firms must decide how to combine scarce productive resources to produce goods and services, and consumers must decide how to allocate their limited purchasing power among the various scarce goods and services.

The solutions to many problems in microeconomics depend on whether we are conducting positive or normative analysis. Positive economics deals with questions concerning what *is*, and normative economics deals with questions about what *ought to be*. Individuals and firms are assumed to behave rationally since this enables us to derive conclusions about their behaviour from some simple assumptions.

Microeconomics makes use of theories or models that enable us to focus on the essential aspects of the problem while ignoring irrelevant details. Many models may not be realistic, but the important test of any theory is whether it helps explain the phenomenon under investigation.

The most frequently used model of resource allocation is the demand and supply model. The demand curve relates price to the desired quantities of purchase; other conditions remaining the same, quantity demanded falls as price increases. Similarly, the supply curve relates price to the desired quantities of sale; other things remaining the same, quantity supplied rises as price increases.

It is important to distinguish between the terms 'demand' and 'quantity demanded'. In common conversation they may be used interchangeably, but in economics they mean two different things. 'Demand' refers to the entire relationship between price and quantity. 'Quantity demanded' refers to the quantity that buyers are willing to purchase at a particular price. Thus, when we say there is an increase in demand, we mean that the demand curve shifts to the right so that quantity demanded increases at every price. Similarly, a decrease in demand means a shift of the demand curve to the left. The terms 'increase in supply' and 'decrease in supply' are similarly interpreted as shifts in the supply curve.

Market equilibrium occurs at the point of intersection of the market demand and supply curves. Market equilibrium changes when there is a change in one or more conditions that influence the behaviour of either buyers or sellers so that there is a shift in the demand and/or supply curves.

Shifts in the demand curve occur when there is a change in tastes or income or the prices of related goods. Shifts in the supply curve occur with changes in input supply, the state of technology, new discoveries, and changes in the weather.

Controls on maximum prices produce a situation of excess demand. In the case of rent controls, the excess demand leads to the creation of a 'black market'.

Key Terms

Black market
Ceteris paribus
Change in demand
Change in quantity demanded
Change in quantity supplied
Change in supply
Comparative statics
Demand
Disequilibrium
Economic model
Equilibrium price and quantity
Excess demand or shortage
Excess supply or surplus
Law of demand
Law of supply
Normative economics
Positive economics
Price controls
Rational behaviour
Scarcity
Supply

Questions

I Classify the following propositions as positive or normative statements:

(a) The government should spend more money on education.

(b) The universe is only 10 000 years old.

(c) Defence spending should be reduced to a more acceptable level.

(d) Inflation is primarily a monetary phenomenon.

(e) Extra-terrestrials exist and have visited the earth.

(f) Rich people should pay more tax.

(g) Low inflation stimulates economic growth.

(h) The distribution of income in society should be more equal.

(i) George Best should be the manager of the England football team.

2 In what sense do economic models abstract from reality? Are unrealistic models of no use? Why do economic models make use of behavioural assumptions?

3 Indicate which of the following statements is an increase or decrease in demand, an increase or decrease in quantity demanded, an increase or decrease in supply, or an increase or decrease in quantity supplied:

(a) Lufthansa reduces its average air fare by 30 per cent in order to attract more passengers.

(b) Wheat farmers decide to withhold some of their product from the market because prices are too low.

(c) The public begin to take seriously news that fatty foods cause ill health.

(d) Firms desire to produce more because of a reduction in raw material costs.

4 What does the term 'ceteris paribus' mean? How does it relate to the distinction between a change in quantity demanded and a change in demand?

5 Consider the market for video cassette recorders (VCRs). How do each of the following changes affect demand, supply, and equilibrium price and quantity? Discuss why.

(a) Consumer incomes increase dramatically.

(b) Penalties on the recording of copyrighted materials are imposed and enforced.

(c) Cinemas reduce their prices.

(d) An improvement in technology dramatically reduces production costs.

(e) It is rumoured that prices of VCRs will rise sharply next year.

6 The accompanying table is a demand and supply schedule for apples. The quantity is measured in boxes of 48 apples each.

Price per box (48 per box)	Quantity demanded (millions of boxes per year)	Quantity supplied (millions of boxes per year)
£6	25	125
5	50	100
4	75	75
3	100	50
2	125	25
1	150	0

(a) What is the equilibrium price and quantity in this market?

(b) At a price of £6 per box, does a surplus or shortage exist in the market? What is the magnitude of this disequilibrium condition?

(c) If the government controlled the price of apples at £3 per box, what would happen in the market for apples?

7 If the equation for the market demand curve is $Q_D = 10 - 4P$, and the equation for the market supply curve is $Q_S = 4P$, find the market equilibrium price and quantity. Verify your answer graphically.

8 From January 1979 to January 1980, the price of gold nearly tripled. Yet as the price of gold rose, sales of gold increased as well. Does this imply that the demand curve for gold is upward-sloping? Why or why not?

9 For each of the following statements, answer 'true' or 'false', and then provide a reason for your answer.

(a) An increase in demand and a decrease in supply always results in a higher equilibrium price and a lower equilibrium quantity.

(b) Ceteris paribus, if the government sets a product's price below its equilibrium price, neither a surplus nor a shortage exists.

(c) An increase in the price of designer-label coats causes the quantity demanded to fall.

(d) An increase in demand and an increase in supply have an indeterminate effect on product price, but equilibrium quantity increases.

10 From time to time, the European Union gives away surplus agricultural commodities (cheese, butter, and so on), and retail grocers often complain that the 'giveaways' reduce their sales. Is this complaint valid? Is there a change in demand or quantity demanded? Explain your answer.

11 Every year there is a shortage of tickets at the 'official' price for the tennis finals at Wimbledon. What does this imply about the official price relative to the equilibrium price? Generally, a black market then develops in which tickets are sold for £100 or more. If instead tickets were auctioned to ensure that they sold for the equilibrium price, how would the average price paid be affected? If stiff penalties were imposed on black marketeers, how would the current black market price be affected? Show your results using demand and supply analysis.

2 Theory of Consumer Behaviour

2-1 Introduction

In the previous chapter we reviewed the idea of an individual's demand curve. In this chapter, we look behind the demand curve and examine how the consumer decides what quantities of various commodities to consume.

We argue that consumers choose the commodity bundle that provides them with the greatest satisfaction. In economics we call this satisfaction *utility*. Of course, consumers are not free to select any commodity bundle they like. They must choose from among the bundles which they can afford, and whether they can afford a particular bundle depends on their income as well as on the prices of the various commodities.

We begin the chapter by introducing the concept of utility and the notion that consumers attempt to maximize their utility. Many a student has argued that utility functions do not exist and, hence, the consumer cannot possibly seek to maximize utility. The question of the existence of utility functions or the realism of the conscious weighing of utility by the consumer is somewhat immaterial. These theoretical tools provide a useful model which can be employed to explain and accurately predict consumer behaviour in a variety of settings. In other words, we can argue that consumers behave as though they were seeking to maximize utility.

After introducing the concept of utility, we develop a graphical representation: the consumer's indifference curve map. The next step is to depict graphically the consumer's budget limitations. We then combine the indifference curves and the budget line to determine the commodity bundle that is optimal.

In the final part of the chapter we demonstrate the applicability of our new tools. We use indifference curve analysis to compare the impact of an income tax with that of a selective excise tax on consumer well-being. We extend this example to examine the relative benefit of a cash subsidy as opposed to an in-kind subsidy. We study the issue of whether, and when, quantity allotments are preferable to price rationing. All these issues and many others can be analysed using our basic theory of consumer behaviour.

2-2 The Concept of Utility and its Relation to the Value of Goods and Services

The satisfaction a consumer derives from the consumption of commodities is termed *utility* by economists. Suppose a consumer eats a pizza. The total satisfaction she gets from this is called *total utility*. Suppose she now consumes an extra pizza. The extra satisfaction she gets from consuming the pizza is called the *marginal utility* of the second pizza. We assume that the consumer compares the utility of different commodity bundles and chooses the one giving her the highest utility from among all the bundles she can afford.

The term 'utility' is associated with the philosopher Bentham (1748–1832). However, neither he nor the economists of the time understood the relationship between the value of goods and the utility derived from their consumption. Smith (1723–1790) distinguished between *value in use* and *value in exchange* and gave the famous example of diamonds and water.[1] Diamonds have a high price (a high value in exchange), but they are unnecessary for life (they have a low value in use). Water, on the other hand, has a low price (low value in exchange), but is necessary for life (has a high value in use).

It was Jevons (1835–1882) who pointed out the relationship between utility and price (or value in exchange). In a paper read to the British Association for the Advancement of Science in 1862, he introduced the concept of marginal utility. He argued that it is marginal utility, not total utility, that is related to price.[2] His book, *Theory of Political Economy* (1871), contains a systematic development of the marginal utility concept. Returning to the example of diamonds and water, the result he derived can be written as

$$\frac{\text{Marginal utility of diamonds}}{\text{Price of diamonds}} = \frac{\text{marginal utility of water}}{\text{price of water}}.$$

This is the connection between utility and value. The relationship makes intuitive sense; consumers who purchase both commodities distribute their expenditure so that the last pound spent on each commodity yields the same extra utility. Otherwise, consumers could increase total utility, without additional expenditure, by consuming more of the good with the higher marginal-utility-to-price ratio and less of the other product. We return to this point later in this chapter.

There are two questions we need to ask at this stage:

1   How do you measure utility?
2   What is the relationship between prices of goods and their utility?

---

[1] This is commonly known as the 'Diamond–water paradox', as described in his book, *The Wealth of Nations*, written in 1776.
[2] Menger (1840–1921) and Walras (1834–1910) are said to have discovered the same independently. Menger is widely known as the founder of the 'Austrian School of Economics'. Schumpeter (1883–1950) called Walras the greatest of all economists.

2-3   Cardinal and Ordinal Utility*

Is utility measurable? Cardinal utility theory says that it is measurable just as prices and quantities are. That is, we can assign a number of *utils* to each commodity. For example, a pizza = 5 utils and a bottle of lager = 6 utils.

Ordinal utility theory says that utility is not measurable like prices and quantities. But one can *order* the utilities from different goods. That is, we can say whether the utility of a pizza is less than, equal to, or greater than the utility of a bottle of lager.

In cardinal utility theory, total utility and marginal utility are both measurable. As we defined earlier, total utility for *n* units of a commodity is the total satisfaction derived from the consumption of *n* units, and marginal utility of the *n*th unit is the *additional* utility obtained from consuming the *n*th unit. Table 2-1 gives a hypothetical example.

One thing we notice in Table 2-1 is that marginal utility decreases as more and more units are consumed. This is the *law of diminishing marginal utility*. The assertion that products are characterized by diminishing marginal utility as consumption rises is an empirical one. This assertion is widely believed, despite the absence of a generally accepted measuring device for utilities. It corresponds to our common-sense notion that the first pizza or lager gives more satisfaction than the second, that the first million a person makes gives more thrill than say the tenth million, and so on.

Total utility increases as long as marginal utility is greater than zero. At the point of maximum utility,

Table 2-1   Total and marginal utility

Number of pizzas	Total utility	Marginal utility
0	0	
1	20	20
2	35	15
3	45	10
4	50	5
5	53	3
6	55	2
7	56	1
8	56	0
9	55	−1
10	53	−2

---

*A mathematical treatment of some of this material is given in the Mathematical Appendix at the end of the book.

marginal utility is zero.[3] If the consumer whose total utility is as shown in Table 2-1 is maximizing her utility, she consumes eight pizzas because she consumes until her marginal utility is zero. We will see later that she consumes fewer if she has to pay a price.

Note that, although we illustrated the law of diminishing marginal utility with an example that assumes cardinal utility (utility measured in absolute magnitudes), the law does not depend on cardinal utility. Even if utility were to be measurable only on an ordinal scale, we could still make statements like 'the marginal utility of the first pizza is greater than the marginal utility of the second pizza which is greater than the marginal utility of the third pizza', and so on.

Economists who believed in cardinal utility can be divided into two groups: those who believed in cardinal *and* additive utility, and those who believed in cardinal but not additive utility.

Nineteenth-century economists such as Jevons, Walras, and Marshall belonged to the first group. They considered utility to be not only *measurable* but also *additive*; that is, if a pizza gives 5 utils of utility and a bottle of lager gives 6 utils of utility, then the utility of both a pizza and a bottle of lager is $5 + 6 = 11$ utils.

Economists such as Edgeworth (1845–1926) and Fisher (1867–1947) belonged to the second group. They argued that utility is measurable but not additive, that it depends simultaneously on all the amounts of the different goods consumed. In the above example, the utility of both a pizza and a bottle of lager could be less than 11 utils. This approach assumes some amount of interdependence in the satisfaction derived from each good. The marginal utility a consumer derives from another gram of butter normally depends on the consumer's current rate of consumption of other commodities such as margarine or bread. With additive utility, the marginal utility of any commodity is independent of the amounts consumed of other commodities. Clearly, the assumption that utility is additive is not a reasonable assumption to make, given the interdependencies that exist in the consumption of several goods.

In mathematical terms, we say that utility is a function of the quantity consumed of all the commodities. If there are two commodities, we write this function as

$$U = U(x_1, x_2),$$

where $U =$ utility, and x_1 and x_2 are the quantities consumed of the two goods. With additive utility, we can write

$$U(x_1, x_2) = U_1(x_1) + U_2(x_2),$$

where $U_1(x_1)$ is the utility derived from the consumption of the first good alone, and $U_2(x_2)$ is the utility derived from the consumption of the second good alone.

If the commodities are substitutes in consumption, $U(x_1, x_2)$ is less than $U_1(x_1)$ plus $U_2(x_2)$. Examples are butter and margarine and tea and coffee. If the commodities are complements, so that when used together the consumer derives more satisfaction than when used separately, then $U(x_1, x_2)$ is greater than $U_1(x_1)$ plus $U_2(x_2)$. An example is tomato ketchup and french fries.

Until now we have discussed cardinal utility. Next, we consider ordinal utility. As we said earlier, the law of diminishing marginal utility is valid whether utility is measured on a cardinal scale or on an ordinal scale.

It was Pareto (1848–1923) who laid the foundations for the modern theory of consumer behaviour by removing the measurability associated with cardinal utility theory. It is assumed that the consumer need not be able to assign numbers that represent utility, but can rank commodities in order of preference. For example, the consumer may prefer a bottle of lager to a pizza but cannot say that the lager gives 6 utils of utility and the pizza 5 utils of utility. Similarly, with reference to Table 2-1, the consumer can say that the marginal utility of the first pizza is greater than the marginal utility of the second but cannot give 20 utils to the marginal utility of the first pizza and 15 utils to the marginal utility of the second one.

The modern theory of consumer behaviour, based on ordinal utility, uses the technique of *indifference curves*. Indifference curves are curves that show combinations of goods that give the same total utility to the consumer. We now examine these curves.[4]

---

[3] In mathematical terms, if $U(x)$ is total utility, dU/dx is marginal utility. $U(x)$ is maximum where $dU/dx = 0$ and $U(x)$ is an increasing function of x if $dU/dx > 0$.

[4] As a historical note, although it was Pareto who argued in favour of ordinal utility, indifference curves were derived by Edgeworth, who believed in cardinal utility theory. Fisher also used indifference curve analysis, although he, too, believed in cardinal utility.

2-4   Indifference Curves

An *indifference curve* shows combinations of two commodities that a consumer is indifferent between. It gives the combinations from which the consumer derives the same total utility or level of satisfaction. Thus, it can also be called an *iso-utility curve* ('iso' means same).

Figure 2-1 illustrates an indifference curve. It shows the combinations of pizzas and bottles of lager from which the consumer derives the same level of satisfaction (i.e. is indifferent between). For example, point E represents a bundle containing 5 bottles of lager and 5 pizzas; point F depicts a combination of 3 lagers and 8 pizzas. Because these two points lie on the same indifference curve, we know that this consumer derives the same satisfaction from either combination of the two goods.

We consider only two commodities. With more than two commodities we have to talk of *indifference surfaces*. It is hard to show indifference surfaces on paper (which is two-dimensional). Furthermore, almost all the principles of consumer behaviour can be discussed in terms of two commodities and illustrated in two-dimensional diagrams.

First, why have we drawn the indifference curve as downward-sloping? (We discuss the curvature toward the origin in the next section.) If bottles of lager and pizzas both give positive satisfaction to the consumer, then increasing the number of lagers while holding the number of pizzas constant increases the consumer's total utility. So, if we want to hold utility constant, as the number of bottles of lager increases, some pizzas have to be taken away. Thus, as we move along an indifference curve, the quantity of one commodity rises and the other falls. This, of course, implies a negatively sloped indifference curve.

One more thing to note is that every point, and hence every commodity bundle, lies on some indifference curve. In Figure 2-1 all points above the indifference curve correspond to combinations where the consumer has more bottles of lager and no fewer pizzas, or more pizzas and no fewer lagers, than the points on the indifference curve. So these points represent higher levels of satisfaction. Thus, they lie on higher indifference curves.

For instance, consider point C above the indifference curve. The vertical line from C intersects the indifference curve at point A, and the horizontal line from C intersects the indifference curve at B. Compared with A, at point C the consumer has the same number of pizzas but more bottles of lager, and hence is better off at C than at A. Similarly, compared with B, the consumer has the same number of lagers but more pizzas, and hence is better off at C than at B. Thus, C is a point on a higher indifference curve.

By similar reasoning, we can show that point D below the indifference curve has to be a point on a lower indifference curve. Compared with point E, the consumer has the same number of pizzas and fewer bottles of lager at D. Or compared with F, the consumer has the same number of lagers but fewer pizzas. Thus, D has to lie on a lower indifference curve than E and F.

Of course, with some commodities the individual gets less total utility by having more of the commodity (see the example in Table 2-1). Thus, the 'good' becomes a 'bad'. In this case, the consumer is better off having less of the commodity than more. Such a commodity might be household rubbish or pollution.

Indifference curves for goods versus bads are shown in Figure 2-2. The curves are upward-sloping, as they should be. If the consumer is given more of a bad, then the consumer needs more of the good to keep him or her on the same indifference curve. As for the curvature of the curves, we again encounter this problem in the next section, where we discuss the marginal rate of substitution concept.

We can also consider indifference curves between two bads. For instance, if we assume that unemployment is bad, and inflation is bad, then the indifference

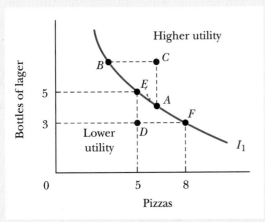

Figure 2-1   An indifference curve for two goods

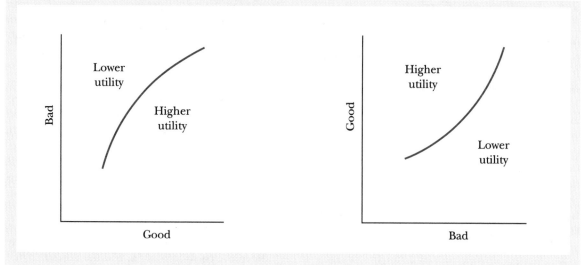

Figure 2-2   Indifference curves for goods versus bads

curves of consumers are as shown in Figure 2-3. The indifference curve is downward-sloping like the indifference curve for two goods shown in Figure 2-1. It has the opposite curvature, but this too is discussed in the next section.

In the cases of the indifference curves presented in Figures 2-2 and 2-3, the points of higher and lower utility shown in the figures can be verified as we have done earlier with the points in Figure 2-1.

Finally, two fundamental assumptions are usually made that translate into some properties of indifference curves: (1) *completeness* of the ordering of preferences, and (2) *transitivity* (or consistency) in the ordering of preferences. Completeness implies, in our example, that, given any two combinations A and B of pizzas and bottles of lager, the consumer is able to rank them. For instance, if

A = 2 pizzas and 3 bottles of lager and
B = 4 pizzas and 2 bottles of lager,

then the consumer is able to say whether he prefers A to B, prefers B to A, or is indifferent between A and B. This assumption means that there is an indifference curve passing through every point in the positive quadrant of Figure 2-1.

To illustrate transitivity, suppose there are three combinations, A, B, and C, of goods:

A = 4 bottles of lager and 3 pizzas
B = 5 bottles of lager and 1 pizza
C = 2 bottles of lager and 5 pizzas

We illustrate a little of our own notation. If A is preferred to B, we write $A \ominus B$. If the consumer is indifferent between A and B, we write $A \ominus B$. If the consumer either prefers A to B or at least is indifferent between A and B (i.e. does not prefer B to A), we write $A \ominus B$. We have put circles around the inequality and equality signs because these are preference statements, not simple inequalities and equalities as in algebra. The assumption of transitivity says that, if $A \ominus B$ and $B \ominus C$, then $A \ominus C$; and also, if $A \ominus B$ and $B \ominus C$, then $A \ominus C$.

The implication of this assumption is that *two indifference curves cannot intersect*. Figure 2-4 shows how we arrive at inconsistent conclusions if indifference

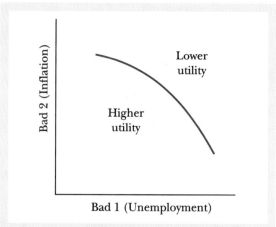

Figure 2-3   Indifference curve for two bads

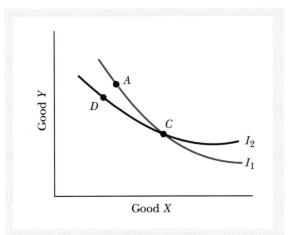

Figure 2-4 Intersecting indifference curves show that preferences are inconsistent

Table 2-2 Combination of pizzas and bottles of lager that give the same level of utility

Bundle	Pizzas	Bottles of lager
A	2	15
B	5	9
C	7	6
D	17	2

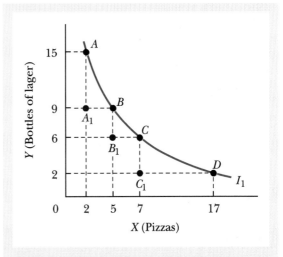

Figure 2-5 An indifference curve convex to the origin

curves intersect. From the diagram, we see that $A \ominus C$ and $C \ominus D$; so, by transitivity, $A \ominus D$. But this cannot be so, because A contains more of both goods and therefore $A \oslash D$. Thus, the preferences are intransitive or inconsistent.

It is not impossible for us to observe these inconsistencies in practice. However, such instances are very rare, and we cannot build a theory on such inconsistent behaviour. Hence in our analysis we assume that indifference curves do not intersect.

2-5 Marginal Rate of Substitution and Convexity of Indifference Curves*

Earlier we talked of marginal utility. Now we need to define another concept, the *marginal rate of substitution,* and examine its relationship to the slope of the indifference curve and to the ratio of marginal utilities.

Consider the hypothetical indifference curve shown in Figure 2-5. It gives the combination of pizzas and bottles of lager that the individual is indifferent between. The figure corresponds to the combinations of pizzas and lagers given in Table 2-2.

The slope of the indifference curve is negative, since the consumer is willing to give up some pizza to get more lager (and vice versa) and still have the same total utility or satisfaction.

We now consider the movement of the consumer from A to B. Suppose we ask how many bottles of lager

the consumer is willing to give up to get 3 more pizzas. The answer is clearly 6. The ratio of 6 to 3 is called the marginal rate of substitution (*MRS*) of pizzas and lagers. (The consumer is substituting pizza for lager.) Of course, if we consider the reverse movement from B to A, the consumer is substituting bottles of lager for pizzas. So, instead of calling this a substitution of pizza for lager or lager for pizza, we just call it the marginal rate of substitution in consumption.[5] If we are considering two goods X and Y, we define the marginal rate of substitution of X for Y as the quantity of Y that the consumer is willing to give up to gain a marginal unit of X. (This is also the quantity of Y that the consumer has to be given to compensate for a unit loss

---

*A mathematical treatment of some of this material is given in the Mathematical Appendix at the end of the book.

[5] This is the definition of J. R. Hicks in his famous book, *Value and Capital,* Clarendon Press, Oxford, 1939.

s, holding utility constant,

$$_Y = \frac{|\text{change in } Y|}{|\text{change in } X|}.$$

The fact that the indifference curve has a negative slope means that if one of these changes is positive the other is negative. It is customary to define the MRS as a positive number. Hence we take the absolute value of this ratio. Thus, if ΔY and ΔX denote the changes in Y and X respectively between two points on an indifference curve, holding utility constant, then

$$MRS_{X \text{ for } Y} = \left|\frac{\Delta Y}{\Delta X}\right|.$$

For very small changes in X and Y, this is nothing more than the absolute value of the slope of the indifference curve at the point under consideration.

In Figure 2-5, denoting pizzas by X and bottles of lager by Y, we have the marginal rates of substitution shown in Table 2-3. Thus, $MRS_{X \text{ for } Y}$ diminishes with increasing X. This is the principle of *diminishing marginal rate of substitution*. It makes intuitive sense, since the consumer is willing to give up more bottles of lager for another pizza when the consumer has more lagers (and fewer pizzas) as at A, than when the consumer has fewer lagers (and more pizzas) as at C. Clearly, this intuitive principle explains the fact that the indifference curve is convex to the origin, or bowed in towards the origin.[6] Look at Figure 2-6. The absolute

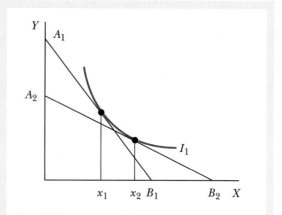

Figure 2-6 Diminishing marginal rate of substitution implies the convexity of the indifference curve

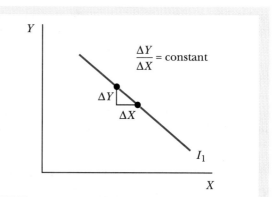

Figure 2-7 An indifference curve with a constant marginal rate of substitution

value of the slope of $A_2 B_2$ is lower than the absolute value of the slope $A_1 B_1$. Thus, the absolute value of the slope of the indifference curve diminishes as we increase the consumption of X. This is all that is required for convexity.

If the consumer is instead willing to give up the same number of bottles of lager for another pizza no matter how many lagers he has—that is, if the MRS is constant—then the indifference curve is a straight line as shown in Figure 2-7.

Relationship between the Marginal Rate of Substitution and Marginal Utilities

One important relationship to note is that the absolute value of the slope of the indifference curve is also equal

---

Table 2-3 Diminishing marginal rate of substitution

$MRS_{X \text{ for } Y}$	
Between A and B:	$\dfrac{AA_1}{A_1B} = \dfrac{6}{3} = 2.0$
Between B and C:	$\dfrac{BB_1}{B_1C} = \dfrac{3}{2} = 1.5$
Between C and D:	$\dfrac{CC_1}{C_1D} = \dfrac{4}{10} = 0.4$

---

[6] Some economists do not like this explanation. We see in the next section, after discussing the budget constraint, that there is an alternative explanation that does not rely on 'intuition'.

to the ratio of the marginal utility of X to the marginal utility of Y. Consider a small decrease in Y and a corresponding small increase in X which leaves the consumer on the same indifference curve. The decrease in utility arising from a decrease in the consumption of Y is $\Delta Y \cdot MU_Y$. The increase in utility arising from an increase in the consumption of X is $\Delta X \cdot MU_X$. Since the consumer is on the same indifference curve, the net change in utility must be zero. Hence, we have

$$|\Delta Y \cdot MU_Y| = |\Delta X \cdot MU_X|$$

or

$$\left| \frac{\Delta Y}{\Delta X} \right| = \frac{MU_X}{MU_Y}.$$

But for small values of ΔY and ΔX, $|\Delta Y / \Delta X|$ is the absolute value of the slope of the indifference curve. Thus, we have the important result:

$MRS_{X \text{ for } Y} =$ the absolute value of the slope of the indifference curve

$$= \frac{MU_X}{MU_Y}.$$

Earlier, we said that, as the consumption of X increases, $MRS_{X \text{ for } Y}$ decreases. This is only an alternative statement of the result that as the consumption of X increases MU_X / MU_Y falls. In the case where X and Y are both goods, it is easy to explain this by invoking the principle of diminishing marginal utility.[7] As the consumption of X rises, MU_X falls. But along an indifference curve, if the consumption of X rises, the consumption of Y falls, and hence MU_Y goes up. Thus, the ratio MU_X / MU_Y falls (the numerator goes down, the denominator goes up). As the consumption of X increases, eventually we might come to a point where $MU_X = 0$ but $MU_Y > 0$. At this point the slope of the indifference curve is zero and the indifference curve is parallel to the X axis. Similarly, as the consumption of X falls and that of Y rises, we might come to a point where $MU_Y = 0$ (but $MU_X \neq 0$). At this point, the slope of the indifference curve is infinity and the indifference curve is parallel to the Y-axis.

---

[7] As we argued earlier, the principle of diminishing marginal utility is also an intuitive principle. Some economists do not like to invoke intuitive principles such as diminishing marginal utility and diminishing *MRS*. See fn. 6 and the next section for an alternative explanation.

Curvature of Other Types of Indifference Curves

We have until now discussed the convexity of the indifference curves for two goods. The shape of the indifference curves between a good and a bad or between a bad and a bad that we have shown in Figures 2-2 and 2-3 can also be inferred from the rule that the absolute slope of the indifference curve = MU_X / MU_Y. Again, if we invoke the intuitive principle of diminishing marginal utility for a 'good' and increasing marginal disutility for a 'bad', then the slopes implied by the curvatures in Figures 2-2 and 2-3 result.

2-6   The Budget Constraint and the Equilibrium of the Consumer*

We have discussed the concepts of indifference curves and of the diminishing marginal rate of substitution. Now we discuss the consumer's choice of a bundle of commodities. For this we must describe the *budget line*. The budget line consists of all the possible combinations of the two commodities that the consumer can purchase with a given total expenditure (budget).

Suppose the price of pizza is £1 per pizza and the price of lager is £1.25 per bottle, and our consumer can spend £10. Then his budget is said to be £10. He can buy 10 pizzas or 8 lagers or some combinations of lagers and pizzas such as 5 pizzas and 4 lagers. The line

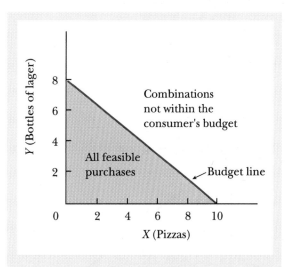

Figure 2-8   A budget line (slope of the budget line = $-P_X/P_Y$)

---

* A mathematical treatment of some of this material is given in the Mathematical Appendix at the end of the book.

joining these points is the budget line shown in Figure 2-8. The consumer can buy less and save money (be *within* his budget); but he cannot buy more. Thus, all the feasible purchases are *on* the budget line or *under* it, in the triangular area below it. The budget line is negatively sloped, and its absolute slope = 8/10 = price of pizza/price of lager.

More generally, if x and y are the quantities of good X and Y and if the prices are P_X and P_Y respectively, then the equation of the budget line is

$$(x \cdot P_X) + (y \cdot P_Y) = M,$$

where M is the consumer's total money income (all of which must be spent). Note that $x \cdot P_X$ is the amount of money spent on good X, while $y \cdot P_Y$ is the amount of money spent on good Y. They must sum to total expenditure.

Now, if the consumer buys only good X, he can just afford M/P_X units with his budget so that M/P_X is our horizontal intercept. Similarly, the vertical intercept is M/P_Y. In going from the vertical intercept to the horizontal intercept, $\Delta Y/\Delta X = (-M/P_Y)/(M/P_X) = -P_X/P_Y$, which is the slope of the budget line.

Shifts in the Budget Line

There are only two things that cause a budget line to shift:

1 Changes in the budget
2 Changes in the prices of the commodities

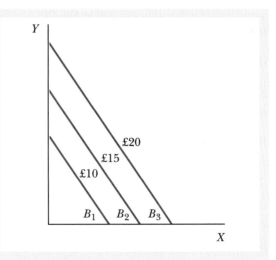

Figure 2-9 Shifts in the budget line with changes in the budget: prices remain unchanged

With a change in the budget but no changes in prices, we have parallel shifts in the budget line as shown in Figure 2-9. With an increase in the budget, for example, both intercepts increase, but the price ratio (the absolute value of the slope) is unaffected. The budget line also shifts in a parallel manner if both prices are changed proportionately, because the price ratio, and hence the slope, is unaffected.

If both prices change in the same direction but by different amounts, then both the intercepts and the slope are altered. This is demonstrated in Figure 2-10(a). If the price of one commodity increases, then

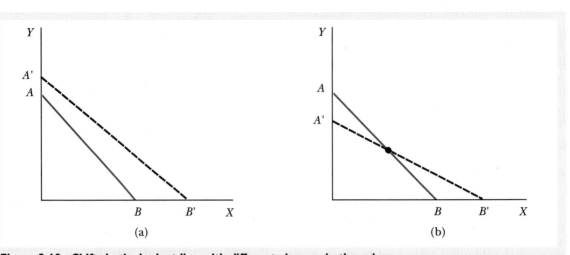

(a)   (b)

Figure 2-10 Shifts in the budget line with different changes in the prices

(a) P_X and P_Y both decline but P_X declines proportionately more than P_Y
(b) P_X declines and P_Y rises

the intercept (M/P) decreases. The opposite is true for a price reduction. Figure 2-10(b) shows the effect of an increase in one price with a decrease in the other. Of course, the slope declines in absolute terms. (Why?)

Different Shapes of the Budget Line

Until now we have assumed that the prices P_X and P_Y remain the same regardless of how much is purchased. This need not always be the case. If there are quantity discounts, then the per-unit price goes down as the quantity bought increases. In this case, returning to our example of pizzas and bottles of lager, the consumer is able to buy, say, 10 lagers or 12 pizzas, but if he tried to split his expenditure between lager and pizza he could not get 5 lagers and 6 pizzas—he might get just 3 bottles of lager and 4 pizzas. The budget line in this case is convex to the origin, as shown in Figure 2-11.

Another possible case is where the price gets lower after an initial volume of purchase, so that the price is, say, £10 per unit for the first 10 units but £5 per unit after that. There are several examples of such price changes. Cinemas and theatres, for instance, run discount schemes based on block bookings. Once a certain number of bookings have been taken (say 10), each ticket is sold at a discount. This is equivalent to a price reduction after the minimum quantity is reached. Thus, the budget line changes its slope after this minimum quantity. There is a kink, as shown in Figure 2-12; point B represents the minimum quantity purchase.

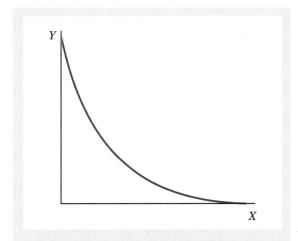

Figure 2-11   A budget line with discounts based on quantity purchased

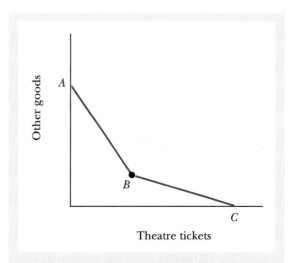

Figure 2-12   A kinked budget line: price discounts after a specific quantity is purchased

Equilibrium of the Consumer with Convex Indifference Curves

To find the consumer's equilibrium, we have to superimpose the budget line on the indifference map (family of indifference curves). The indifference map shows what is *desirable*. The budget line shows what is *feasible*. Now we have to match the feasible with the desirable. This is shown in Figure 2-13. I_1, I_2, I_3 are indifference curves; I_2 gives a higher utility than I_1; I_3 gives a higher utility than I_2; and so on. AB is the budget line: the consumer's feasible combinations of the goods X and Y are given by the points on the budget line AB or in the triangular area under AB. The consumer would like to get to the highest possible indifference curve representing the highest level of utility. This is shown as I_2 in Figure 2-13. The point of tangency C gives the optimal bundle of X and Y. Points on the curve I_3 are not within the reach of the consumer. As for I_1, the consumer can do better, since all points in the shaded area are still within the consumer's budget and yet yield more satisfaction.

Note that at point D the slope of the indifference curve is higher than the slope of the budget line (both in absolute values). Thus, $MRS_{X \text{ for } Y} > P_X/P_Y$. Substituting MU_X/MU_Y for the MRS and rearranging gives us $MU_X/P_X > MU_Y/P_Y$ at point D. Spending one less pound on Y reduces total utility by MU_Y/P_Y. But spending that same pound on X now increases utility by

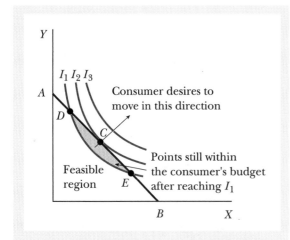

Figure 2-13 Equilibrium of the consumer with convex indifference curves

MU_X/P_X. The consumer can increase her total utility, without spending more, simply by purchasing additional units of X and fewer of Y, thus moving towards C. The opposite is true at a point such as E. And at the optimum, MU_X/P_X must be equal to MU_Y/P_Y, which is merely a restatement of the tangency condition. This is also the connection between utility and value presented by Jevons and discussed in Section 2-2.

Now it is possible that a consumer with convex indifference curves maximizes utility by consuming only one product. This situation is shown in Figure 2-14. Note that there is a tangency between the budget

line and an indifference curve. The first unit of product X is simply not worth its cost to the consumer. That is, MU_X/P_X for the first unit of X is less than MU_Y/P_Y for the last unit of Y that the consumer can afford. We argue shortly that this is not a typical case.

Equilibrium with Concave Indifference Curves

Now what happens if the indifference curves are concave to the origin rather than convex? In this case, the consumer always maximizes utility by consuming only one good. This is shown in Figure 2-15. Again I_1, I_2, I_3 are indifference curves; I_2 represents higher utility than I_1; I_3 represents higher utility than I_2; and so on. AB is the budget line. The highest indifference curve that the consumer can attain is I_2 and the optimal bundle is at point A, which means the consumer consumes only Y and not X. Point C is a point of tangency, but it is not optimal because the consumer can go to a higher indifference curve I_2.

This is the conclusion that some economists rely on to argue that indifference curves are convex to the origin. They argue that if indifference curves are concave to the origin individuals would consume only one good. However, in reality we observe individuals consuming several goods. So the argument that indifference curves are convex to the origin does not

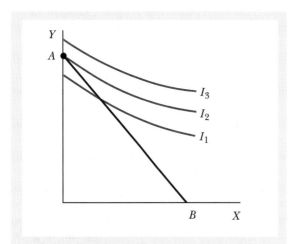

Figure 2-14 Specialization in consumption with convex indifference curves

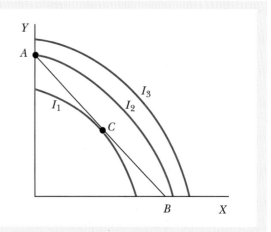

Figure 2-15 Equilibrium of the consumer with concave indifference curves

The consumer specializes in one good

have to rely on any intuitive principles such as diminishing marginal utility or diminishing marginal rate of substitution.[8] All that is needed is the empirical observation that consumers choose to consume several goods.

Equilibrium with Convex and Concave Segments

If indifference curves have both convex and concave segments, sometimes the consumer chooses points on the convex segment. This is shown in Figure 2-16, where the optimum point C lies on the convex portion of the indifference curve. However, in Figure 2-17 the optimum lies on the concave segment. C is a point of tangency on the convex segment, but this is on a lower indifference curve I_1. The consumer can do better by moving to I_2. Thus, B is the optimal point.

Synopsis

In summary, when working with two goods (not 'bads') and linear budget lines, we have the following

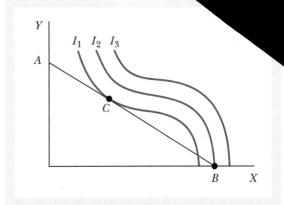

Figure 2-17   Indifference curves with convex and concave segments

The consumer's optimum is on the concave segment (at B)

results:

1   If both commodities are consumed, then either the entire indifference curves are convex to the origin or the indifference curves contain some convex portions.

2   Consumption of only one good can occur with either concave or convex indifference curves. Specialization can also occur where indifference curves have both concave and convex segments.

3   Because we do not generally observe specialization in consumption, we assume that indifference curves are convex to the origin. (This is equivalent to ignoring any concave portions that might exist.) We also assume that a tangency point between the budget line and an indifference curve exists.

2-7   The Composite Good Convention

Students frequently argue that the application of indifference curve analysis is extremely limited because we do not live in a two-commodity world. However, we can frequently extend the application by defining good Y to be all other goods except X.

We cannot, of course, measure a quantity of Y on the vertical axis. This would involve adding bottles of lager and pizza, which clearly makes no sense. Instead, we measure total expenditure for good Y on the vertical axis.

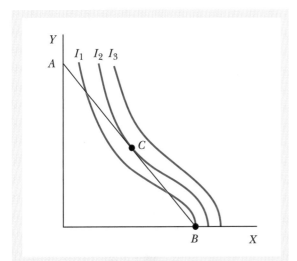

Figure 2-16   Indifference curves with convex and concave segments

The consumer's optimum is on the convex segment (at C)

---

[8] As one illustration of this assumption, see G. Becker, *Economic Theory*, A. A. Knopf, New York, 1977, p. 28. Becker goes on to argue (using a specific case) that the indifference curve can have both convex and concave segments, but in this case points on the concave segment are never optimal. They are never chosen. That this is not always true is illustrated in Figure 2-17.

ᵢ an indifference curve
. that the points $Y = 10$,
n the same indifference
erent between 2 units of X
ᵢds or 3 units of X with £8
. $MRS = 2$. This means the
: up £2 worth of other goods
ᵤnit of X. In other words, he is
willing ᵢor his third unit of X.

We must ᵢonsider the impact of the composite good convention on the budget line. The horizontal intercept (budget/P_X) is unaffected. But the vertical intercept is now equal to the amount of the budget. Why? Because, if we purchase no X, how much can we spend on other goods? The answer, of course, is the budget. The slope of the budget line was previously demonstrated to be $-P_X/P_Y$. But now we are measuring Y in terms of expenditure on other goods. Clearly, one more pound of other goods costs £1 so that P_Y is, by design, equal to 1. This means that the slope of the budget constraint becomes $-P_X$.

2-8 Application 1: Taxes and Subsidies

Taxes have come to be accepted as a 'necessary evil' under capitalism. Many a politician has promised to reduce taxes. In fact, most of us are convinced that lower taxes would improve our well-being. Although this may be true, it is not simply the overall tax bill that affects consumer welfare. Different types of taxes affect us differently even though they yield the same revenue to the government.

In this section we use indifference curve analysis to compare two different taxes. We demonstrate that the typical consumer is better off with an income tax than with a comparable excise tax on a single commodity. We then generalize our analysis to consider the relative benefits of a cash subsidy versus an in-kind subsidy (or a pay rise versus an increase in fringe benefits). Here our conclusion depends on whether the in-kind subsidies are taxable.

It should be noted that our analysis focuses on a single consumer (or possibly a small group). Some of our conclusions do not hold for society as a whole. We discuss this problem as we proceed.

Selective Excise Tax versus Income Tax

Consider the case of two goods, X and Y (Y stands for all goods other than X). The total income or budget of the consumer is M. By a selective excise tax, we mean an excise tax on X only. A proportional tax on both X and Y is the same as an income tax. In Figure 2-18 we compare the two situations. The budget line with no taxes is AB. With an excise tax on X, *assuming that the sellers can pass on the whole tax to the consumers*, the price of X rises by the amount of the tax. The budget line is now AB_1. The consumer's equilibrium before the tax is at point C, and after the tax the equilibrium is at point D. Thus, the consumer moves to a lower indifference curve and is, as expected, worse off.

Now with an income tax, or a proportional tax on both goods, the budget line shifts down and is parallel to AB. This is because both intercepts decline but the price ratio is unchanged. If the income tax gives the same revenue as the excise tax on A, this budget line has to pass through point D.[9] This is shown as the line

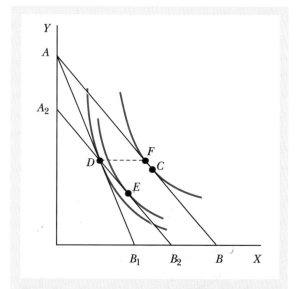

Figure 2-18 Selective excise tax versus an income tax

The consumer is better off with an income tax

---

[9] Consider the horizontal distance DF between the lines AB_1 and AB. At point D the consumer has the same quantity of Y but less of X than at F. This reduction is (the amount of tax)/ P_X. But this is also $B_2 B$. Hence the parallel line $A_2 B_2$ must pass through D.

$A_2 B_2$. But with this budget line the consumer's equilibrium is at point E on a higher indifference curve. Thus, the consumer is better off with an income tax than with a selective excise tax.[10] Note that the consumption of X is higher under the income tax than under the selective excise tax on X because the consumer has further opportunity to maximize in the region of the triangle $DB_1 B_2$.

The analysis of an income subsidy versus a selective price subsidy is analogous. The individual consumer is better off with an income subsidy rather than a selective price subsidy. An example of a price subsidy is government paying towards the cost of housing for low-income families. This is like a reduction in the price of housing. Another example is the subsidization of the costs of health care. Health care in the UK is funded by the state and, in the main, is offered free at the point of use. Patients do not incur user-charges, and their health care costs are therefore subsidized.

The above discussion is for a *price* subsidy. We now discuss a *quantity* subsidy.

Cash Subsidy versus Subsidy in Kind

Consider a cash subsidy of amount M that can be spent on either of two goods X and Y, and an equal subsidy tied to good X. The latter is what we mean by an *in-kind subsidy*. Examples of this in the UK were universal free school meals, whereby children of eligible low-income families received a free school meal every day, and free school milk, which was given to all children of primary school age.[11]

Education vouchers are another example of an in-kind subsidy.[12] There has been discussion for a number of years in the UK about the introduction of a voucher scheme in education. Around 90 per cent of children in the UK attend state schools. Education is provided free to the user and is financed from central and local government funds. A voucher scheme would replace the system of direct government financing, and would work in the following way. Vouchers would be allocated to families so that they could buy education for their children. Each voucher would entitle a child to a given amount of education and would be presented to a school as payment for the services provided. Schools would then redeem the vouchers from the government for cash. The vouchers would be non-tradable; otherwise they would be equivalent to a general cash subsidy.

We assume that the prices P_X and P_Y of X and Y respectively do not change and neither does the consumer's other income.[13] The shifts in the budget line and the equilibrium of the consumer are shown in Figure 2-19. The budget lines are shown in Figure 2-19(a). AB is the budget line without the subsidy. If the subsidy is tied to good X (say, the education voucher) and if AC is the amount of X that can be bought with the subsidy, then ACD is the new budget line. CD is parallel to AB, since the consumer has the same money income as before plus the extra quantity AC of X. Note that the consumer cannot purchase more units of good Y than before. With a cash subsidy the budget line would be ECD because the consumer would then be free to spend any part of the subsidy on either good X or good Y.

Now the consumer's equilibrium in the case of the in-kind subsidy is on the line ACD, and in the case of the cash subsidy it is on the line ECD. We show three cases in Figure 2-19(b)–(d). In all cases F is the equilibrium without any subsidy.

In Figure 2-19(b) the consumer's equilibrium with a subsidy is at G. This lies on both the lines ACD and ECD. Hence the consumer is indifferent between the two subsidies.

In Figure 2-19(c) the consumer's equilibrium with the subsidy is at point C. This is a corner point for the

---

[10] As mentioned earlier, this conclusion does not follow when we consider the economy as a whole, but this point is beyond the scope of our discussion. For a discussion of this aspect of the problem see M. Friedman, *Price Theory*, Aldine, Chicago, 1962, pp. 56–67.

[11] Some children of low-income families still qualify for free school meals. However, many of those who do qualify do not actually receive free meals, as many local education authorities no longer provide them. Free school milk was abolished by Margaret Thatcher when she was Education Secretary in the Heath government of 1970–74. The popular press at the time dubbed her 'Thatcher, the Milk Snatcher'.

[12] There are a number of different types of voucher scheme. These range from a flat-rate scheme where families receive a voucher for each child equal in value to the average cost of a year's schooling, to an income-related scheme where higher valued vouchers are given to lower-income groups. For more detail see J. Le Grand, C. Propper, and R. Robinson, *The Economics of Social Problems*, 3rd edn., Macmillan, London, 1992, pp. 79–83.

[13] Of course, if many individuals are given subsidies tied to X, the market price of X changes. In our analysis we are abstracting from this problem.

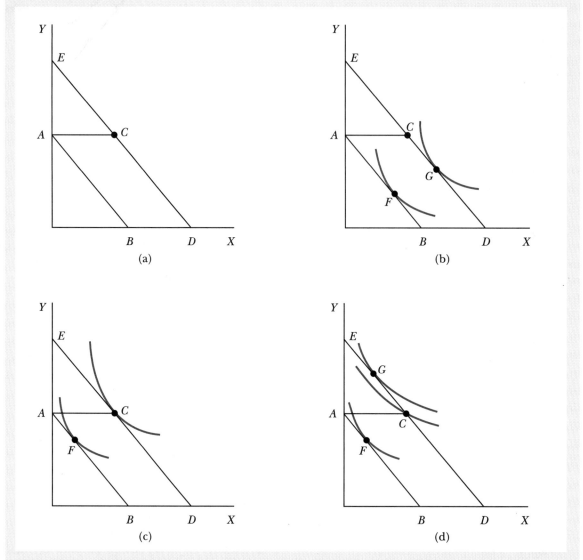

Figure 2-19 Shifts in the budget line and the equilibrium of the consumer under cash versus in-kind subsidies

(a) Shifts in the budget line: *ACD* is for in-kind subsidy and *ECD* is for cash subsidy
(b) The consumer is indifferent between the two subsidies: they give the same equilibrium *G*
(c) The consumer is indifferent between the two subsidies: they give the same equilibrium *C*
(d) Consumer prefers cash subsidy to in-kind subsidy: *G* is on a higher indifference curve than *C*

budget line *ACD* and a point of tangency for the budget line *ECD*. But this difference is irrelevant. The equilibrium point is the same. Hence the consumer is again indifferent between the two subsidies.

In Figure 2-19(d) the consumer's equilibrium occurs at the corner point *C* in the case of the in-kind subsidy. But in the case of the cash subsidy the consumer can get to a higher indifference curve, and thus the consumer prefers a cash subsidy to an in-kind subsidy.

In summary, the consumer is never worse off and is sometimes better off with a cash subsidy than an in-kind subsidy. This is because the budget set is larger with a cash subsidy and therefore gives the consumer a greater choice of points to select. Whether this conclusion carries over when we consider the economy as a whole is questionable, but we cannot answer this question with the tools of analysis we have studied so far. It is, of course, true that each consumer who takes the prices as given prefers a cash subsidy to an in-kind subsidy except in circumstances considered in the next example.

Taxes on Cash Subsidy

The preceding analysis shows that the consumer never prefers an in-kind subsidy to a cash subsidy. However, this conclusion changes if the cash subsidy is taxed but the in-kind subsidy is not. This is, for instance, the case with several fringe benefits that employees get.

With the in-kind subsidy the budget line is still ACD as shown in Figure 2-19. But with the cash subsidy the budget line, *net of tax*, is a parallel line to the left of ECD in that figure. This is shown as $E'C'D'$ in Figure 2-20. Now, it can be verified that the consumer may prefer the in-kind subsidy on good X to a cash subsidy, since he can attain a higher indifference curve. In this case neither budget set is wholly included in the other,

so no clear-cut conclusions can be made. This is shown in Figure 2-20(a). However, this is not always the case, as is shown in Figure 2-20(b). There are cases where a consumer would prefer a cash subsidy even if the cash subsidy is taxed. Clearly, these are cases where the consumer's preference for good X is very low.

Cash Subsidies Tied to a Particular Tax: The Case of Domestic Energy

We have until now discussed cash subsidies versus in-kind subsidies. Recent events in the UK allow us to link cash subsidies to a particular type of tax. In March 1993 the UK government announced that value-added tax (VAT) would be applied to sales of domestic energy, beginning at a rate of 8 per cent in April 1994 and rising to 17.5 per cent in April 1995. In November 1993 the government announced measures to compensate poorer households for the higher energy prices. As well as linking increases in benefits to the rate of inflation, the increase that VAT on energy adds to the inflation rate is being paid from April 1994, so that benefit increases take effect at the same time as the introduction of VAT. The government also introduced extra cash payments for all pensioners. Benefits have been increased above the inflation rate because indexation is

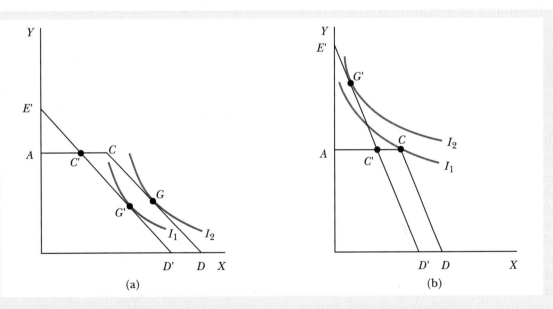

Figure 2-20   Equilibrium of the consumer when cash subsidy is taxed but in-kind subsidy is not

(a) Consumer prefers in-kind subsidy: G is on a higher indifference curve than G'
(b) Consumer prefers a cash subsidy even when it is taxed: G' is on a higher indifference curve than C

based on the pattern of spending of the *average* household, which underestimates the importance of energy in the spending of poor households. But even the extra payments may not maintain the standard of living of all poorer households.

According to the Institute for Fiscal Studies (IFS), the poorest 10 per cent of households in 1991 spent an average of £10.76 per week on domestic energy, which amounted to 17.4 per cent of their total spending on non-durable goods and services. This compares with figures for the richest 10 per cent of households of £14.86 and 5.9 per cent, respectively. The average figures for households were £12.25 and 9.9 per cent.[14] Thus, although the amount spent per week by richer households is higher than that spent by poorer households, it rises much less than proportionately with total spending.

The government cash subsidies help low-income groups, but this does not mean that all poorer households are as well off as they were before the VAT was introduced. This result can be illustrated with indifference curve analysis.

In Figure 2-21 the original budget line is *AB*. Taking the household unit to be a consumer, the low-income consumer is in equilibrium at point *P*. She is consuming Q_1 units of domestic energy. Imposing VAT on domestic energy raises the price of energy and so pivots the budget line to *AC*. The vertical distance between the lines *AC* and *AB* shows the amount of VAT paid for each quantity of energy consumed. If, after the VAT is imposed, the consumer's preferred point is *R*, where her consumption of domestic energy is Q_2, then her VAT bill is equal to the distance *RS*. Assuming that the government's cash payments total £*RS*, her new budget line must be parallel to *AC* and lie *RS* above it. This is shown by the line *DE*. Note that *DE* is parallel to *AC* because the cash payment does not affect the price ratio. Given budget line *DE*, the consumer's preferred consumption point is *W* and she consumes Q_3 units of energy.

The impact of the government's policy on our low-income consumer is as follows: (1) her consumption of domestic energy is reduced from Q_1 to Q_3,[15] but this is less than with the VAT alone; and (2) although the cash subsidy contributes to an increase in her level of

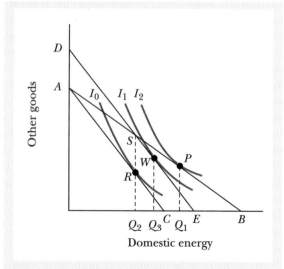

Figure 2-21 Effects of VAT and a cash subsidy on domestic energy consumption

welfare (she is on a higher indifference curve at *W* than at *R*), she is on a lower indifference curve at *W* than at *P*.

The intuition behind this is that the increase in her income from the cash subsidy induces her to consume more energy. Nevertheless, the VAT on energy raises the relative cost of energy in terms of other goods, so it is in her interest to consume less energy than initially, even after the cash subsidy. (She substitutes away from energy because it is relatively more expensive.) If the government's intention was to leave the consumer as well off after the VAT as she was before, then in *this* case it has failed because at *W* the size of the cash subsidy is lower than the amount of VAT paid.

Example 2-1 The Economics of Christmas Gifts

Analysis of cash versus in-kind subsidies suggests that individuals are better off with cash than in-kind gifts.

---

[14] See the IFS paper by I. Crawford, S. Smith, and S. Webb, 'VAT on Domestic Energy', Institute for Fiscal Studies, Commentary no. 39, London, 1993.

[15] The IFS estimate the effect on energy consumption of VAT imposed at the full rate of 17.5 per cent. Their results show that the poorest 20 per cent of households will cut their energy consumption by about 9 per cent compared with about 1 per cent for the richest 20 per cent. See Crawford *et al*, op. cit.

This raises the question: Why do people give gifts in a form other than money? Surely individuals would prefer to buy whatever they want with money instead of getting things that givers decide to buy. As far as the givers are concerned, it is much easier to send money than a gift. If both the givers and receivers are better off with money than with a gift, why do people buy so many gifts?

The answer is that giving money is considered by many as a thoughtless act. When you receive a Christmas gift, it is not just the item itself that you receive but the satisfaction of knowing that the sender has spent some time thinking about you. Thus, you have to add another 'good' to the value of the gift, a good you can label 'thoughtfulness', whose money value is difficult to assess.

Of course, with regard to some of the individuals who send you Christmas gifts, you might not care whether they have spent time thinking about you or not, and thus their thoughtfulness would not be a 'good' for you; but in that case you should not expect any money from them either.

With other people, who you know are thoughtful of you and show concern about you anyway (for instance your parents, grandparents, children), the thoughtfulness in the Christmas gift is again not so significant a 'good'. But here the reasons for giving a particular gift are different. Parents might feel they know your interests better and hence might send you things that they feel you would like to have. With presents from one's children, the good might be 'sharing'. They might want to share with you the things that interest them—a book they have read and liked, a new cooking gadget they have discovered, and so on. Or the good might be a feeling of 'remembrance'—they might want to show that they remember your interests. In each case, there is some 'good' involved other than the item given as the gift, and the money value of each such good is difficult to determine. Since it is a commodity that depends on personal relations, its money value can be determined only in those cases where personal relations are so close that explicit choices are offered.

2-9   Application 2: Price and Nonprice Rationing and Black Markets

If the consumption of any good is considered 'too high' in the interest of society as a whole, the government can reduce its consumption by *price rationing* (an excise tax) or *nonprice rationing* (controls on the quantity consumed).

Consider the rationing of petrol. Imposing an excise tax on the consumption of petrol is rationing by price; issuing petrol coupons is nonprice rationing.[16] The purpose of a coupon programme is to enable low-income families to obtain some petrol at affordable prices, which they could not do if rationing were done by price increases alone. With the coupon scheme, there develops a black market for coupons, and, in fact, this results in a better allocation of petrol than if such a black market did not exist. It is better for the government to encourage trading of the coupons. Those for whom the marginal utility of petrol is high buy the coupons from those for whom the marginal utility is low. Those who sell the coupons receive a money income. Thus, there is an income redistribution, hopefully, from rich to poor.

In the following sections, we analyse these problems step by step, first considering a single consumer, then two consumers with identical incomes but different tastes, and finally two consumers with different incomes. We then discuss the situation of black markets.

Price Rationing versus Quantity Allotments

Consider a consumer with the indifference map and budget constraint as shown in Figure 2-22. AB is the budget line and C the point of equilibrium; the quantity of petrol consumed is Q_0. With quantity allotments the price does not change, only the consumer is constrained to limit consumption to Q_1. The consumer is then at point D on the budget line, and, since it is to the left of the indifference curve passing through C, the consumer is worse off.

The same restriction in consumption can be achieved by imposing an excise tax.[17] With this the budget line pivots to AE, and the consumer's equilibrium is at F. The consumption of petrol is again reduced to Q_1, but the consumer is worse off

---

[16] Petrol coupons were distributed to all car owners in the UK in 1974 in response to the 1973–74 'Oil Crisis'. They were, though, never used. Interestingly enough, trading of the coupons was not to be permitted on the grounds that it would be unfair to low-income families.
[17] The magnitude of the excise tax is such that the consumer's optimum consumption of petrol after the tax is exactly Q_1.

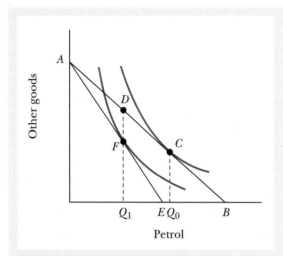

Figure 2-22 Proof that consumers are better off with quantity allotments than with price rationing when government revenues from taxes are wasted

than at D, since D is a point above the indifference curve passing through F and so corresponds to a higher level of utility. Thus, the consumer is better off with quantity allotments than with price rationing.

Of course, the conclusion is fairly obvious without even looking at Figure 2-22, which is used here for only pedagogical reasons. Under both scenarios, the quantity of petrol consumed is the same. But with quantity allotments consumers can spend the money that they would previously have spent on petrol on something else. With the excise tax, this same amount of money instead goes to the government as tax revenue. The government, of course, gets the tax revenue, but the question is: What does it do with it? It can waste the revenues on unproductive projects, in which case our analysis holds good. At the other extreme, it can give it back to consumers in the form of rebates (a cash subsidy), in which case, the equilibrium with excise tax and rebates is not at Q_1 anymore. This is the same idea as the case of a cash subsidy linked to VAT on domestic energy, which we discussed earlier.

Price Rationing versus Quantity Allotments: Consumers with Different Tastes but the Same Income

We now consider the case of two consumers who differ in tastes (two is enough to analyse differences in tastes)

and show that quantity allotments can make some consumers worse off as compared with price rationing. Actually, to analyse the problem completely, we need to know what the government does with the revenue from the excise tax. Such an analysis, however, gets too complicated for our purposes; hence we make the simplifying assumption (not unreasonable) that the government wastes the revenue on some unproductive projects. Hence the budget line of the consumers does not change.

Figure 2-23 shows the situation of two consumers with different tastes but both with the same budget line. AB is the budget line under quantity rationing. (We assume that market prices do not change.) With price rationing or an excise tax on commodity X, AE is the budget line. I_0 is the indifference curve of consumer 1; his equilibrium is at C with the consumption of X being x_1. J_0 is the indifference curve of consumer 2; her equilibrium is at D, and her consumption of X is x_2. Let the average of x_1 and x_2 be $\bar{x}$.

Now, let us say there is a quantity rationing scheme under which each of the consumers is allowed to purchase a quantity $\bar{x}$. The total consumption of good X under quantity rationing is then less than or equal to total consumption under the price rationing scheme. Quantity rationing allows the consumers to choose any bundle along AF. Consumer 1 is worse off with quantity

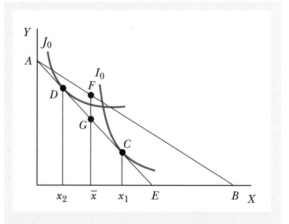

Figure 2-23 Price rationing versus quantity allotments: two consumers with different tastes

Consumer 1 is worse off at F than at C. Consumer 2 is better off at F than at D. Note that by making I_0 flatter so that F is to the right of I_0, we can show that consumer 1 is also better off

rationing, as all feasible bundles lie on indifference curves lower than I_0. But consumer 2 is better off under quantity rationing, because she can produce a commodity bundle on an indifference curve above J_0.

Of course, in our analysis we have not said anything about what the government does with the excise taxes it collects. We have assumed that the revenue is wasted.

Price Rationing versus Quantity Allotments: Differences in Tastes and Incomes among Consumers

We now extend the preceding analysis to the case of two individuals with different incomes. Since the prices of the commodities are the same for both, their budget lines are parallel. We also assume that in the case of price rationing we have a 100 per cent excise tax, and that this is completely passed on to the consumers. This is a high rate, but we can easily illustrate the results in a diagram without cluttering it up with too many lines.

The 100 per cent tax implies that after the tax the consumers can buy only half the quantity of X that they could before the tax. Figure 2-24 illustrates the situation: $A_1 B_1$ and $A_2 B_2$ are the budget lines of consumers 1 and 2, respectively, without any tax. $A_1 C_1$ and $A_2 C_2$ are the budget lines of the two consumers after the 100 per cent excise tax on X. With the excise tax the equilibrium of consumer 1 is at D_1, with his

consumption of X at x_1, and consumer 2's equilibrium is at D_2, with her consumption of X at x_2.

Let the average of x_1 and x_2 be $\bar{x}$. We assume, as before, that under quantity rationing each of the consumers is allotted a quantity $\bar{x}$. So the total consumption of X is at least as large under price rationing as under quantity rationing. This allotment puts both consumers on their original budget lines, but the portions of the budget lines below E_1 and E_2 are effectively eliminated.

As we have drawn the diagram, consumer 1 is definitely worse off; point E_1 is to the left of the indifference curve I_0 that he was on under price rationing.[18] As for consumer 2, she can reach indifference curve J_1 by consuming F_2. Her consumption of petrol is greater than under price rationing but still less than her allotment. Consumer 2 is clearly better off.

If the allotments are controlled through the issuing of coupons (as was the case in most European countries during the Second World War), consumer 2 might give her unused coupons to consumer 1. In this case, consumer 1 moves to point F_1, and his situation improves. In fact, consumer 2 is now better off with

---

[18] By making I_0 flatter, we can show that consumer 1 is better off with quantity rationing. However, we want to illustrate some consequences of trading in the black market.

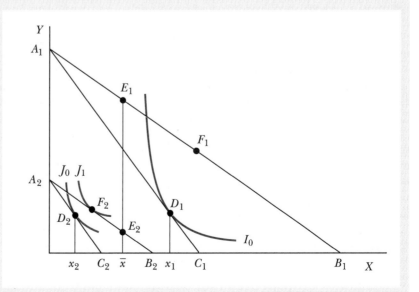

Figure 2-24 Quantity allotments with trading of coupons makes both consumers better off than under price rationing

Consumer 2 is better off even without trade, since she can move from E_2 to F_2 by buying less of X and more of Y. But consumer 1 is better off only after the trade

quantity allotments than with price rationing. She can sell the coupons that she does not need at some profit to consumer 1 and thus reach a higher indifference curve than J_1. In this case, not only is consumer 2 better off compared with her situation under price rationing, but she is better off even compared with her position before any quantity rationing was imposed. As for consumer 1, he is willing to pay a price for the coupons so long as he can improve his position over I_0.

This example illustrates how a market (black or grey) develops if something like a petrol coupon scheme is instituted.

Finally, note that all this discussion of quantity allotments versus price rationing does not account for the following factors:

1 Costs to the government of implementing the quantity allocations
2 Alternative uses for the government revenue from excise taxation in the case of price rationing

To discuss these is beyond our scope at this stage. Our purpose here has been to illustrate the use of indifference curve analysis in comparing different policies.

Quantity Allotments, Subsidies, and Black Markets

In the preceding example we showed how we get a black market with quantity allotments. As far as the individual consumer is concerned, if he gets an allotment of a good that is more than what he wants, he is better off trading the excess quantity in the black market and getting a higher price.

Consider, for instance, the case of education vouchers (an in-kind subsidy) illustrated in Figure 2-19. The budget line is ACD with education vouchers. If the consumer can freely trade any of the vouchers for cash, then the in-kind subsidy is equivalent to a cash subsidy, and the budget line is ECD. But if it is illegal to trade the vouchers, the individual can only trade in the black market, and because of the risks involved he might get less than the stated value. Thus, the budget line could be E_1CD where E_1 is a point between E and A in Figure 2-19. To show the equilibrium of the consumer with a black market, we expand the triangle ECA in Figure 2-19(d) and to that shown in Figure 2-25. In cases (b) and (c) in Figure 2-19, there is no incentive for the individual to go to the black market.

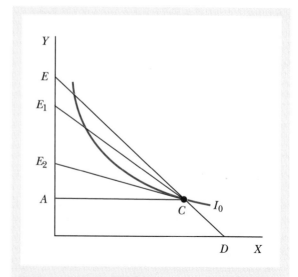

Figure 2-25 A black market in education vouchers

Consumers are better off if they can get to the budget line such as E_1C by trading in the black market if the low price received puts them on the line E_2C

As we said earlier, if consumers can freely exchange their education vouchers for cash, they move to line ECD. If they get a price below face value, they are still better off if they can get on the budget line E_1CD. But if consumers get a low price which puts them on the budget line E_2CD, they have no incentive to trade in the black market. There is no way they can get to a higher indifference curve.

In any case, the consumers have greater opportunities to improve their position by the existence of the black market. A black market can develop even with government-provided housing. The consumer can take the government-provided housing, rent it out, and live elsewhere. However, there may be a greater chance of being caught in this than in the case of trading education vouchers or petrol coupons.

The crucial issue in all these cases is whether the black market provides a desirable social function. In this respect a black market in housing or education vouchers is different from a black market in petrol coupons. To see this, we have to ask what the purpose of the programme is. For instance, the main purpose of education vouchers is to ensure that low-income families have the minimum amount of education. If trading in vouchers is allowed, it is equivalent to a cash subsidy. Then the question arises as to why the cash subsidy is not given instead of the vouchers. Presumably, the argument is that we do not want parents to spend the cash subsidy on food, holidays, clothing, etc. In other words, we are afraid that individual parents will make decisions about the consumption of education that are not in their children's long-term interest or in society's interest. In this case, it is not desirable to permit trading in education vouchers, and stiff penalties may be imposed for doing so. The case of a housing subsidy is similar. It is designed to ensure a minimum necessity and so a black market should be discouraged.

The case of petrol coupons is different. The main purpose of the coupons is to reduce the total consumption of petrol. If price rationing is used, it is argued that this produces undue hardship on low-income families. To alleviate this, income rebates may be given to low-income groups. We discussed earlier a similar idea using the example of a cash subsidy and VAT on domestic fuel. We have also discussed an alternative scheme, that of quantity allotments. Whatever the relative merits of these proposals, suppose that the quantity allotment method is chosen. Then it might be better to permit the trading of coupons than to ban it. The reason is that petrol is a consumer's commodity (luxury consumption like pleasure driving, and necessary consumption like driving to the supermarket) as well as a producer's commodity (business travel). It is a resource that should be allocated to the most productive use.

Of course, we saw in Figure 2-24 that allowing the trading of coupons might also increase overall consumption. So the benefits of improved allocative efficiency have to be weighed against the cost of a potential increase in consumption. In any event, the case for allowing the trading of petrol coupons is stronger than for allowing the trading of, say, education vouchers.[19]

2-10 Application 3: Consumption over Time

In this example we use indifference curves to show consumers' choices between current and future consumption. Consumers usually do not consume all their income during the period they receive it. They often save part of it for future periods. At other times they may borrow to increase current consumption and then pay off the debt from future income. In general, consumers try to maximize their utility or satisfaction over a number of time periods. In our example we consider only two time periods: current and future. This may not sound very realistic, but it captures many important aspects of intertemporal choice, or choice over time. These problems are discussed in greater detail in Chapter 17.

Consider a consumer with current income y_0 and future income y_1. We denote current consumption by c_0 and future consumption by c_1. If the consumer neither saves nor borrows, we have

$$c_0 = y_0 \text{ and } c_1 = y_1.$$

Suppose, for simplicity, that the consumer can borrow or save at an interest rate r, so that £1 today is the same as £$(1 + r)$ next period. Thus, borrowing on future income y_1 enables the consumer to get a maximum loan of $y_1/(1 + r)$ this period. So the consumer's total wealth in the current period, which we denote by w_0, is given by $w_0 = y_0 + y_1/(1 + r)$. This is the maximum amount of consumption the consumer can afford during the current period. Similarly, the consumer can save the entire income y_0 for the next period and get $y_0(1 + r)$. The consumer's maximum wealth in the next period is $w_1 = y_0(1 + r) + y_1$. This is the maximum amount of consumption that the consumer can afford during the next period. (Note that $w_1 = (1 + r)w_0$.)

There are, in essence, two goods we are considering: current consumption and future consumption. Since we know the maximum amounts of these two goods that the consumer can afford, we can draw the budget line. This is shown in Figure 2-26. The slope of the budget line is $-(1 + r)$. We can also interpret this in terms of the 'prices' of current and future consumption. If the prices of current and future consumption are denoted respectively by p_0 and p_1, then, from our discussion (in Section 2-6), we have

$$\frac{p_0}{p_1} = -(1 + r).$$

This relationship is just an alternative statement of the result that £1 saved today gives us £$(1 + r)$ the next period.

---

[19] We are not, however, justifying either of these programmes. All we are discussing is whether, given the existence of the programme, trading should be allowed.

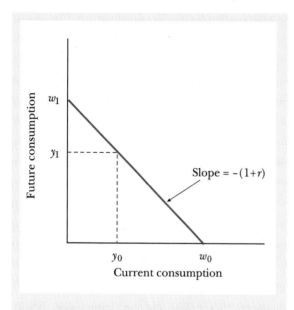

Figure 2-26 Budget line for current and future consumption

To derive the consumer's equilibrium, we have to consider the point of tangency between the consumer's indifference curves and the budget line. This determines whether the consumer is a lender (saver) or a borrower. The two cases are shown in Figure 2-27(a) and (b). Without any borrowing or lending, the consumer's equilibrium is at A. In Figure 2-27(a) the shape of the indifference curves is such that the tangency point is at C, which gives $c_1 > y_1$ and $c_0 < y_0$. Thus, the consumer is saving current income to increase future consumption. In Figure 2-27(b) the shape of the indifference curves is such that the point of tangency indicates that $c_0 > y_0$ and $c_1 < y_1$. This consumer is borrowing to increase current consumption over current income.

One can also show a case where the point of tangency is at point A, in which case the consumer is neither borrowing nor saving. We saw earlier in Section 2-6 that, at the point of tangency, the slope of the indifference curve (in absolute value) is equal to the ratio of the marginal utilities of c_0 and c_1. Hence we have the relationship, in equilibrium,

$$\frac{\text{Marginal utility of } c_0}{\text{Marginal utility of } c_1} = -(1 + r).$$

We have illustrated the use of indifference curves in deriving the consumer's choice between current and future consumption. Further analysis of this problem can be found in Chapter 17.

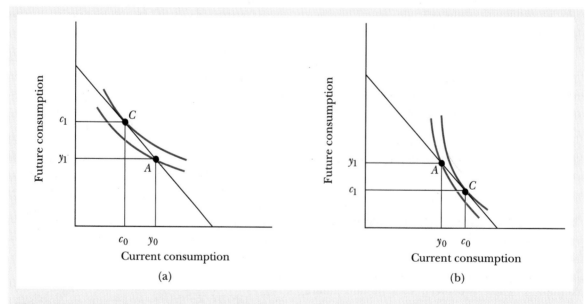

Figure 2-27 Consumer's choice of current and future consumption

(a) Consumer a lender
(b) Consumer a borrower

2-11   Summary

The satisfaction that a consumer derives from the consumption of commodities is called utility. The extra satisfaction derived from an additional unit of a commodity is the marginal utility of that unit. Cardinal utility theory says that utility is measurable; the units of measurement are utils. Ordinal utility theory says that the utility of different commodities (or commodity bundles) can be ranked or ordered but not measured. The law of diminishing marginal utility asserts that each additional unit consumed of a commodity yields less marginal utility than previous units.

An indifference curve consists of all the combinations of two commodities which provide equal utility to the consumer. When both commodities are valued by the consumer, indifference curves must be negatively sloped, with indifference curves farther from the origin denoting greater levels of utility. If preferences are transitive, then indifference curves cannot intersect.

The marginal rate of substitution is the rate at which one commodity can be substituted for the other, holding total utility constant. Mathematically, the marginal rate of substitution equals MU_X/MU_Y for commodities X and Y. Graphically, it is equal to the absolute value of the slope of the indifference curve. If the marginal rate of substitution declines as more X and less Y is consumed, then indifference curves are convex to the origin. Convexity can also be implied by observing that consumers do not specialize in the consumption of a single commodity.

A budget line consists of all the combinations of two commodities that the consumer can just afford with a given budget and given commodity prices. The slope of the budget line is $-P_X/P_Y$ for commodities X and Y. With convex indifference curves and positive marginal utility for both commodities, consumers maximize their satisfaction by choosing the commodity bundle defined by the tangency between the budget line and an indifference curve. This tangency implies that the ratio of marginal utility to price is the same for all commodities.

A consumer is always better off with an income tax than with an excise tax on one commodity if the two taxes yield the same total tax payment. The consumer is also better off with a cash subsidy than with an in-kind subsidy except when the cash subsidy is taxable and the in-kind subsidy is not. A cash subsidy linked to VAT on domestic energy can leave the low-income consumer on a lower indifference curve, consuming less energy.

A consumer is better off with a quantity allotment than with an excise tax that yields an equal reduction in consumption. Finally, two consumers with different incomes and/or preferences are at least as well off with a quantity allotment scheme under which coupons can be transferred as with a price rationing scheme which yields the same total consumption.

Key Terms

(Terms marked with an asterisk appear in the Glossary at the end of the book.)

Additive utility*
Budget line
Cardinal theory of utility*
Completeness of preferences*
Indifference curve
In-kind subsidy*
Law of diminishing marginal utility*
Marginal rate of substitution*
Marginal utility*
Ordinal theory of utility*
Price rationing
Quantity allotment
Selective excise tax
Specialization in consumption*
Transitivity of preferences*
Utility*

Questions

1   Commodity bundle 1 contains 5 units of commodity X. Commodity bundle 2 contains 3 units of commodity Y. Suppose that a consumer derives 11 utils from bundle 1 and 6 utils from bundle 2; yet, when given both bundles, his total utility is only 14 utils. Is utility additive? How do goods X and Y appear to be related? Why?

2   Suppose that a consumer derives no utility or disutility from good X, whereas the marginal utility from good Y is strictly positive. Draw an indifference curve map with these two commodities. If the prices of both commodities are positive, what does the consumer purchase? Does this make sense?

3 We have said that if preferences are transitive then indifference curves cannot intersect. Is tangency of indifference curves also ruled out? Why or why not?

4 Why is the convexity assumption so important in indifference curve analysis? In particular, does a consumer equilibrium exist if indifference curves are concave? Explain.

5 Construct indifference curves for two goods which are: (a) perfect complements and (b) perfect substitutes.

6 A student is first and foremost interested in beer and is willing to forgo any quantity of milk for the smallest additional quantity of beer. However, if the beer consumption is given, the student prefers to have more milk rather than less. Draw an indifference curve to represent these preferences. If you are unable to draw such a curve, briefly explain why. Why do you believe that in this case an indifference curve does not exist? (These sort of preferences are known as lexicographic preferences.)

7 Suppose that we have constructed a budget line where the two commodities are kebabs and pasta. The slope of the budget line equals −(price of pasta/price of kebabs). Which commodity is measured on which axis? Why?

8 Graph the budget line for a consumer in a two-commodity world with an income of £100, $P_x = £5$, and $P_y = £10$ where the two commodities are X and Y. Label both intercepts and compute the slope. Now graph the consumer's budget line if she is given a non-transferable coupon redeemable for three units of commodity Y.

9 A consumer suddenly realizes that $MU_x/P_x < MU_y/P_y$ with his current commodity bundle. Is he maximizing his utility? If not, which commodity should he consume more of, to improve utility, without increasing total expenditure? What happens to the MU/P ratio for each good as he begins to adjust consumption? Why?

10 A child with additive utility is given 50 pence to spend at a sweet shop. She likes three kinds of sweets, and the utils associated with the quantities of each are listed in the accompanying table. The price of the sweets is 10 pence per item.

(a) What combination of sweets should the child purchase to maximize her utility? Is the indifference curve between

sherbet dabs and jelly babies concave to the origin? If not, how do you explain your answer?

(b) Today the shop is out of jelly babies. What should she now purchase? (Saving the money is out of the question.)

	Total utils		
Quantity	Gobstoppers	Jelly babies	Sherbet dabs
1	15	30	20
2	29	58	37
3	42	84	50
4	54	108	60
5	65	130	68

11 Consider the subsidized education programme in many underdeveloped countries. An eligible student can go abroad at government expense, but if he accepts this offer, the quantity of education is beyond his control. Most commonly, he must complete four years and then return home. Of course, he is not forced to participate: he can forgo higher education altogether. Or he can pay for it himself, in which case he can choose the quantity purchased.

Measuring education on one axis and other goods on the other axis, draw the budget lines for an eligible student who accepts the offer and for the student who rejects it. Using indifference curve analysis, demonstrate that it might be rational to purchase one's own education. Now demonstrate that such a programme might actually induce the student to acquire less education. Why? What is the difference between this programme and a programme of education vouchers?

12 Using indifference curve analysis and a two-period framework, demonstrate how a proportional tax on interest income affects the consumer's choice between current and future consumption.

13 'I can't understand people who pay as much as £10 to see a first-run film when they can see it for much less on video six months later, or even watch it for free on TV a few years later.' Explain this, using the theory of consumption over time.

3

Analysis of Consumer Demand

3-1 Introduction

In the previous chapter we studied consumer preferences and how they can be graphically depicted with indifference curves. We also examined the consumer's budget constraint, and we combined an indifference curve map with a budget constraint to determine the consumer's optimal consumption bundle.

In this chapter we are primarily concerned with what happens to the quantity of a good demanded when (1) the consumer's income changes and prices of the goods remain constant, and (2) the price of one good changes and the prices of other goods and the consumer's income remain constant. The answers to (1) and (2) enable us to study the concept of 'elasticity'. Even though many of you may have already met this material in your introductory course, elasticity is a key concept and you should make certain that you fully understand the main ideas. Moreover, elasticity is a convenient way of summarizing exercises in comparative statics.

We can separate the impact of a price change into two components. When the price of one good falls, holding other prices and money income constant, the consumer generally purchases more of the now cheaper item. This is for two reasons. First, the consumer will substitute the good for other products because it has become relatively cheaper. This response is the *substitution effect*. Second, when the price of one good falls, *ceteris paribus*, the consumer's purchasing power or real income increases. For a normal good, this increase in real income also induces the consumer to buy more. This response to a larger real income is the *income effect*. Substitution and income effects are discussed in Section 3-5.

We apply our analysis to several issues from the field of labour economics. We consider how the quantity of labour supplied responds to a change in the wage rate. As the wage rate goes up, the cost of an hour of leisure goes up. However, the individual receives a higher income from the hours worked, and this increases the demand for leisure. The net effect of an increase in the wage rate on hours worked is, therefore, not clear. Having studied the labour supply curve, we then examine the impact of different income taxes and welfare programmes on work effort. In one further application, we compare and contrast two cost-of-living indexes. The chapter concludes with a discussion of the characteristics approach to analysing consumer demand.

3-2 Income-consumption and Engel Curves

In this section, we examine the impact of a change in income on the quantity of good X demanded. We confine our attention to two commodities by adopting

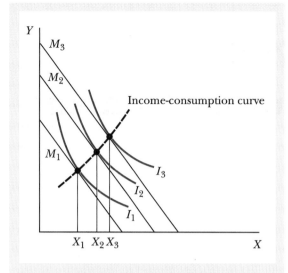

Figure 3-1 An income-consumption curve

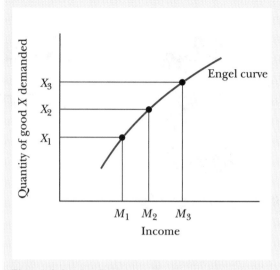

Figure 3-2 An Engle curve

the composite-good convention: Y represents all other goods. And, again, the quantity of the other goods is expressed in terms of expenditure on them.

If we hold all prices constant and increase the consumer's budget or money income, the budget line shifts outwards in a parallel manner as shown in Figure 3-1. The vertical intercept is now equal to the amount of the budget. So, M_1 is the income corresponding to the lowest budget line, M_2 is a higher income corresponding to the middle budget line, and so on.

For each budget line, we can locate the point of tangency with an indifference curve and thus observe the consumer's optimal consumption bundle. By connecting all these tangency points, we derive an *income-consumption curve*. From the points on the income-consumption curve, we can read off the quantities of X demanded at the different income levels (see Table 3-1).

Table 3-1 Changes in money income and quantity demanded

Income	Quantity of X demanded
M_1	X_1
M_2	X_2
M_3	X_3
$\vdots$	$\vdots$

These data can be plotted in a graph showing the quantity of X demanded for each income, M. This graph, shown in Figure 3-2, is called an *Engel curve* after the statistician Engel (1821–96), who first studied the relationship between family incomes and quantities demanded of different goods. There is also *Engel's law*, which states that, the lower a family's income, the greater is the proportion of it spent on food. Engel's conclusion was based on a budget study of 153 Belgian families and was later verified by a number of other statistical inquiries into consumer behaviour.[1]

The Engel curve is very often positively sloped, as in Figure 3-2, so that the quantity of the good demanded rises with income. In this case the good is a *normal good*. The Engel curve need not always be positively sloping, however. There are cases where it can be negatively sloped, so that an increase in income leads to a decrease in the quantity demanded. In this case the good is an *inferior good*. Figure 3-3 shows a set of indifference curves for which the consumption of good X falls as income rises. In this case the Engel curve is downward-sloping.

---

[1] Among Engel's other contributions was his examination of the relationship between the size of the Prussian rye harvest and the average price of rye over a number of years prior to 1860. This was perhaps the first empirical study of a supply function.

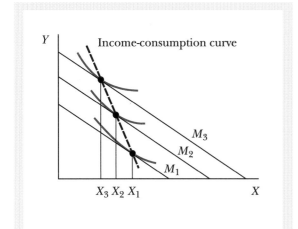

Figure 3-3 Income-consumption curve for an inferior good

The general form of the Engel curve is shown in Figure 3-4. We see that the Engel curve reaches a maximum at point B, corresponding to an income of M_2. To the left of B income and quantity demanded vary directly, indicating that X is a normal good for income levels below M_2. To the right of B income and quantity demanded vary inversely, indicating that X is an inferior good for income levels above M_2. The elasticity of the Engel curve is the income elasticity of demand. In Section 3-4 we further analyse this diagram with regard to income elasticity.

3-3 Price-consumption and Demand Curves*

In the previous section we derived the income-consumption curve as the curve that joins the points of tangency of successive budget lines (given by different levels of income) with the indifference curves. Since the prices of goods X and Y were fixed, changes in income gave us a set of parallel budget lines.

Suppose, instead, that we hold money income and the price of good Y (or all other goods) constant and vary the price of X. We again generate a set of budget lines. The curve joining the points of tangency of these budget lines with the indifference curves is called the *price-consumption curve* and is shown in Figure 3-5. Since the price of good Y and income are both fixed, maximum expenditure on Y is fixed at A. However, since the price of X changes, the amount of good X that can be bought changes. If M is the money income, and $P_1, P_2, P_3, \ldots$ are the successive prices of good X, then the amounts of good X that can be bought are $OB_1 = M/P_1$, $OB_2 = M/P_2$, $OB_3 = M/P_3$, etc. The budget lines are thus, AB_1, AB_2, AB_3, etc., where $OA = M$, the money income. The points of tangency

---

*A mathematical treatment of some of this material is given in the Mathematical Appendix at the end of the book.

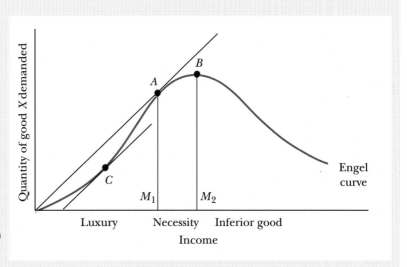

Figure 3-4 An Engel curve in its most general form

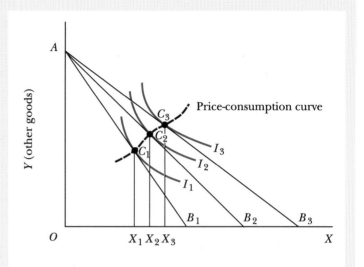

Figure 3-5 A price-consumption curve

with the indifference curves are C_1, C_2, C_3, etc. The curve $C_1 C_2 C_3 \ldots$ is the price-consumption curve. Also, from the points C_1, C_2, C_3, etc. we can read off the amounts of the good X that are demanded. As we can see in Figure 3-5, as the price of X falls, the quantity demanded of X rises. We thus get a downward-sloping demand curve.

However, there may be cases where the quantity demanded of a good falls as the price falls. If this happens the good is called a 'Giffen good' (see Section 3.6) and the demand curve is positively sloped.

3-4 Elasticity*

Demand curves and Engel curves are useful tools for illustrating how consumer behaviour changes in response to changes in the economic environment. Even so, it is helpful to have a numerical means of quantifying these changes. The concept of elasticity provides a means of measuring the effect of price and income changes.

Price Elasticity of Demand

We define the *price elasticity of demand* as the absolute value of the ratio of percentage change in the quantity demanded to the percentage change in price, *ceteris paribus*. Note that this is the same as the ratio of *relative* changes or *proportionate* changes. We use the Greek

letter η (eta) for price elasticity of demand. Thus, price elasticity can be written as

$$\eta = \frac{\text{percentage change in } Q}{\text{percentage change in } P} = \left| \frac{\Delta Q/Q}{\Delta P/P} \right| = \left| \frac{\Delta Q}{\Delta P} \cdot \frac{P}{Q} \right|.$$

The vertical lines denote that we take the absolute value of the ratio, and ΔQ and ΔP denote the changes in quantity and price.[2] (Δ is the Greek letter capital delta.)

Now we are ready to consider why we work with proportionate or percentage changes rather than simple magnitudes of changes. Why don't we just calculate $|\Delta Q/\Delta P|$ and use this to measure responsiveness of quantity demanded to a change in price? Graphically, this number is the inverse of the slope of the demand curve expressed in absolute terms.

This is because $|\Delta Q/\Delta P|$ depends on the units of measurement for both P and Q and, hence, is somewhat difficult to interpret. Suppose, for instance, that we are told that $|\Delta Q/\Delta P|$ for eggs is 7.3. How responsive is the quantity demanded of eggs to a change in price? What if P is measured in pence and Q is in millions of boxes? A 1 penny increase in the price of eggs causes a decrease in the quantity demanded of eggs of 7.3 million boxes. But suppose instead that P is measured in pounds and Q is in boxes; the picture changes dramatically.

---

*A mathematical treatment of some of this material is given in the Mathematical Appendix at the end of the book.

[2] In terms of derivatives, we have $\eta = |dQ/dP \cdot P/Q|$ or $|(d\log Q)/(d\log P)|$.

Elasticities, however, are pure numbers and are thus much less cumbersome to interpret. If the price elasticity of demand for eggs is 4.1, a 1 per cent increase in the price of eggs leads to a 4.1 per cent reduction in quantity demanded, holding other things constant. The units of measurement for P and Q are immaterial.

Arc and Point Elasticities

We defined the price elasticity of demand as

$$\eta = \left| \frac{\Delta Q/Q}{\Delta P/P} \right|.$$

The quantities ΔQ and ΔP are easy to define. But the question arises as to what value of Q and P we use. Are we supposed to take beginning values or final values, or some average? For example, suppose the price per unit of a watch goes up from £10 to £11, and the number of watches demanded falls from 100 to 95. Clearly, $\Delta P = £1$ and $\Delta Q = -5$. If we take the initial values, then $(\Delta Q)/Q = -5/100 = -1/20$ and $(\Delta P)/P = 1/10$ and $\eta = 0.5$. It seems reasonable to consider the starting values for both P and Q. However, economists more frequently calculate the *arc elasticity*, which uses the average of the initial and final values. Thus, if P_1 and Q_1 are the initial price and quantity respectively, and P_2 and Q_2 are the final price and quantity respectively, then $\Delta Q = Q_2 - Q_1$ and $\Delta P = P_2 - P_1$. For the divisors we use the average quantity and average price, which are $(Q_1 + Q_2)/2$ and $(P_1 + P_2)/2$.

Thus, the arc elasticity is (cancelling the factor 2 in both the denominator and numerator)

$$\eta = \left| \frac{\Delta Q/\Delta P}{(Q_1 + Q_2)/(P_1 + P_2)} \right| = \left| \frac{\Delta Q}{\Delta P} \cdot \frac{P_1 + P_2}{Q_1 + Q_2} \right|.$$

And in the example from the preceding paragraph,

$$\eta = \left| \frac{-5}{1} \cdot \frac{21}{195} \right| = 0.54.$$

We all know that the slope of a straight line is constant and that the slope between any two points is given by the change in y divided by the change in x. Thus, with a linear demand curve $\Delta Q/\Delta P$ is constant. However, since Q/P is not constant, the demand elasticity is different at different points on the demand curve. There is, however, a simple rule for finding the *point elasticity* of demand. This rule, for a linear demand

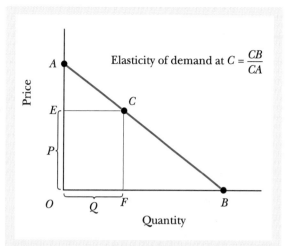

Figure 3-6   Geometric representation of elasticity for a linear demand curve

function, is

Point elasticity of demand =

$$\frac{\text{distance of the point from the } Q\text{-axis}}{\text{distance of the point from the } P\text{-axis}},$$

with both distances *measured along the demand curve.* Figure 3-6 illustrates this.

This result can be proven as follows. $\Delta Q/\Delta P = EC/AE$, and at point C we have $Q/P = OF/OE$. Hence, $\eta = (EC/AE)/(OF/OE) = OE/AE$, since $EC = OF$. Since CF and OA are parallel lines, $\eta = OE/AE = CB/CA$. As a consequence, we get the result in Figure 3-7 that $\eta = 1$ at the midpoint M of AB, $\eta > 1$

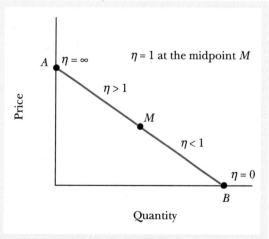

Figure 3-7   Elasticity of demand at different points on a linear demand curve

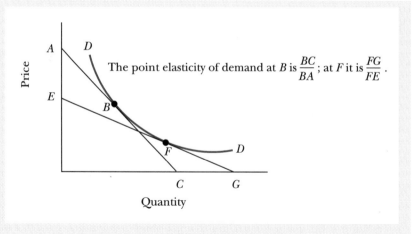

The point elasticity of demand at B is $\dfrac{BC}{BA}$; at F it is $\dfrac{FG}{FE}$.

Figure 3-8 Price elasticity of a curvilinear demand curve

for points on the demand curve between A and M, and $\eta < 1$ for points on the demand curve between M and B. (Why?)

For a nonlinear demand curve the same rule for calculating elasticity applies, except that we have to consider the tangent to the demand curve in place of the linear demand curve we considered earlier. (Note that the slope at a point on a curve is the slope of the tangent to that curve at that point.) This is shown in Figure 3-8. All we have to do is draw a tangent to the demand curve at the point we are considering and then use the rule for the elasticity at a point on a linear demand curve given earlier.

Finally, in Figure 3-9 we show a demand curve with elasticity equal to 1 at all points on the curve. This is a

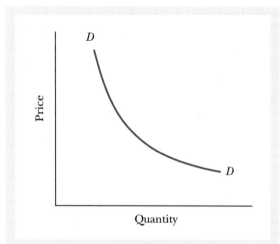

Figure 3-9 A demand curve with elasticity equal to 1 at all points: a rectangular hyperbola

curve for which $P \cdot Q$ is constant and is called a rectangular hyperbola.[3]

Price Elasticity and Total Expenditure

The numerical value of the price elasticity of demand determines how total expenditure on a good is affected by price changes. *Total expenditure* is defined as price times quantity, or $P \cdot Q$. If P rises then Q falls because the demand curve is downward-sloping. The effect on total expenditure is ambiguous without knowledge of the responsiveness of demand to the price increase, i.e. without knowing the value of η.

Suppose that the elasticity of demand is less than one ($\eta < 1$). This means that Q falls by a smaller percentage than P rises and so $P \cdot Q$ must increase. Therefore, when $\eta < 1$ we say that the demand curve is *inelastic* at that price. Intuitively, we are saying that quantity demanded is relatively unresponsive to a price change. In this case a price increase raises total expenditure. If $\eta > 1$, the demand curve is *elastic* at that price. Here the percentage change in Q is greater than the percentage change in P, implying that quantity demanded is highly responsive to a price change. In this case a price increase reduces total expenditure. Finally, if $\eta = 1$, demand is *unit-elastic* and the percentage changes in Q and P are equal. As the percentage increase in P is exactly matched by the percentage fall in Q, $P \cdot Q$ does not change. When

---

[3] Mathematically, the equation $Q = AP^{\alpha}$ is a curve with constant elasticity α, since $(d\log Q)/(d\log P) = \alpha$. For demand curves α is negative.

price rises and the demand curve is unit-elastic, total expenditure is constant.

Thus, if we know the price elasticity of demand we can calculate the effect on total expenditure of any price change, *ceteris paribus*. When demand is inelastic ($\eta < 1$) price and total spending move in the same direction; when demand is elastic ($\eta > 1$) price and total expenditure move in the opposite direction; and when demand is unit-elastic ($\eta = 1$) a change in price leaves total spending unaffected.

Short-run and Long-run Price Elasticities

When the price of a product changes, it takes some time for consumers to respond fully. For instance, the effect of a rise in the price of heating oil results in consumers switching to alternative fuels only after some time. Consumers initially try to economize on oil usage with existing appliances, but eventually they switch to alternative fuels. With a rise in the price of petrol, consumers try to economize on the use of petrol with their petrol burning cars, but eventually they get rid of these cars and buy fuel-efficient ones.

Figure 3-10 illustrates some typical demand curves in the short run, intermediate run, and long run. $A_1 B_1$ is the short-run demand curve, $A_2 B_2$ is the intermediate-run demand curve, and $A_3 B_3$ is the long-run demand curve. If the price of the product increases from P_1 to P_2, quantity demanded immediately falls only from Q_1 to Q_2. But as consumers have time to adjust to the higher price, quantity falls to Q_3 and eventually to Q_4 in the long run. Clearly, the long-run demand curve is more elastic than the short-run or intermediate-run curves.

How long is the long run? Its length depends on the goods being considered. Clearly, it is relatively long when durable goods and appliances are involved, as in the case of petrol or heating oil. It is also relatively long when it comes to longstanding habits. Suppose the price of cider falls. Although theoretically it is easy to switch from (say) lager to cider (there are no appliances involved as in the switching from natural gas to heating oil), we do not observe many people making such a switch immediately. For many individuals drinking cider is not the same as drinking lager. It takes time for them to change their drinking habits.[4]

---

[4] This does, however, depend on the definition of the good. If the price of one brand of cider falls, other cider drinkers may switch quickly.

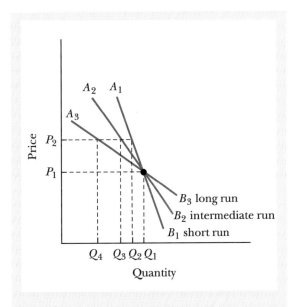

Figure 3-10 Short-run and long-run demand curves

In practice, there is no such thing as complete adjustment. Suppose the price of petrol goes up 10 per cent and stays there. Then, *ceteris paribus*, we can ask by what percentage the quantity demanded of petrol goes down. Suppose the initial quantity demanded is 100 (million litres per year). Then we observe the demand in successive years until the decline peters off. Table 3-2 records the decline over the first 10 years. The figures are, of course, hypothetical because in practice it is not possible to maintain the *ceteris paribus* assumption; nor is it possible to maintain the price of petrol at the 10 per cent increased level. To compute the elasticities in practice we have to use a statistical technique known as multiple-regression analysis to control for the other factors and estimate appropriate dynamic demand functions to disentangle the short-run and long-run effects. We have chosen a hypothetical example to illustrate the difference between short-run and long-run elasticities.

In Table 3-2 we have stopped at 10 years because the decline in quantity demanded seems to have almost petered out in 10 years. If we went another 10 years we would observe a little more decline, but for all practical purposes 10 years is enough. If we treat 1 year as short-run, 5 years as intermediate-run and 10 years as long-run, we have the respective elasticities as 0.2, 0.43, and 0.5.

Table 3-2 Effect of a price increase on the quantity of petrol demanded[a]

Year	Quantity demanded	Cumulative decline	Price elasticity	
1	98.0	2.00	0.200	Short run
2	97.0	3.00	0.300	
3	96.5	3.50	0.350	
4	96.0	4.00	0.400	
5	95.7	4.30	0.430	Intermediate run
6	95.4	4.60	0.460	
7	95.2	4.80	0.480	
8	95.05	4.95	0.495	
9	95.01	4.99	0.499	
10	95.00	5.00	0.500	Long run

[a] Initial quantity was 100 million litres, and increase in price was 10 per cent.

Note that the definition of what constitutes short run and intermediate run is somewhat arbitrary. For the definition of long run we have used the idea that it is the time taken for the decline in quantity to peter out (almost). In any case, it is important to note that the short-run elasticity is less than the intermediate-run elasticity, which, in turn, is less than the long-run elasticity.

Other Elasticity Concepts

Elasticities can be defined with respect to any two variables. We now examine the income elasticity of demand and the cross-price elasticity of demand.[5]

Income Elasticity

Income elasticity tells us how responsive quantity demanded is to a change in income. The *income elasticity of demand*, μ, is defined as

$$\mu = \frac{\Delta Q/Q}{\Delta M/M} = \frac{\Delta Q}{\Delta M} \cdot \frac{M}{Q},$$

where M stands for income and Q denotes quantity demanded. Again, the assumption of *ceteris paribus*

---

[5] It is customary for introductory (and intermediate)-level textbooks to say that, if we relax the assumption of *ceteris paribus* and allow consumer income or the prices of other goods to change, this causes a parallel shift of the demand curve. But when we apply the income elasticity and cross-price elasticity formulas to real data, we always get a rotation of the demand curve, *not* a parallel shift.

applies. But this time we are assuming that everything except consumer incomes remains the same. In particular, the price of the given good and also the prices of all related goods are assumed to remain constant. If the income elasticity of demand equals 2.3, then a 1 per cent increase in income leads to a 2.3 per cent increase in quantity demanded, *ceteris paribus*.

Notice that when we defined the income elasticity of demand we did not take the absolute value. That is because the sign is of interest. For most goods, when income increases the quantity demanded of the good also increases. In this case the income elasticity of demand is positive, and the good is a normal good at the level of income considered. However, if the quantity demanded of the good falls when income increases, the good is an inferior good at the income level considered, and in this case the income elasticity of demand is negative. Remember that no good is inferior at all income levels. Almost all goods are normal at sufficiently low levels of income and are inferior at sufficiently high levels of income. For example, at lower levels of income the demand for poultry increases as the income level rises, but at sufficiently high levels of income quality cuts of beef are substituted for poultry, causing the quantity demanded for poultry to decrease. Thus, poultry is a normal good at lower levels of income and an inferior good at higher levels of income.

Normal goods are further classified as necessities and luxuries. A good is called a *necessity* if its income elasticity of demand is positive and less than 1. Thus, when income rises, demand for the product increases, but less than proportionately.[6] Similarly, if income elasticity of demand exceeds 1, the good is called a *luxury*. A good can be a necessity at high levels of income and a luxury at low levels of income.

These ideas can be illustrated in relation to the Engel curve in Figure 3-4. Using our definition of point elasticity, we can draw a few tangent lines to the curve and further break down income elasticity. A line through the origin is tangent to the Engel curve at point A. This means that income elasticity of demand is 1 at an income level of M_1. To the left of M_1, at a point such as C, the tangent line has a negative vertical intercept, indicating that elasticity exceeds 1. So good X is a luxury for income levels less than M_1. Finally, you can verify that, for income levels between M_1 and M_2, the income elasticity of demand for X is positive but less than 1. This, of course, implies that X is a necessity for income levels between M_1 and M_2. In empirical studies, however, economists generally either assume a constant elasticity or report the elasticity at the mean (or median) level of income.

As with price elasticities, we can talk of short-run and long-run income elasticities. Because consumers can make the necessary adjustments in the long run, we expect long-run income elasticities to be higher than short-run income elasticities in absolute value.

Are there any cases where the short-run elasticity is higher than the long-run elasticity? Yes, for certain commodities when consumers experience a decrease in income. Eventually, the effect of a decrease in income is felt on all commodities. However, in the short run consumers overadjust (cut down drastically) their expenditures on commodities whose purchase they can easily postpone; these are usually items such as houses, cars, clothes, holidays, entertainment, and so on. These adjustments produce an effect that is higher in the short run than in the long run. This is an argument for why the demand for cars (or other durables, or owner-occupied housing) may be more income-elastic in the short run than in the long run.

Cross-price Elasticities

Another useful concept is the *cross-price elasticity of demand*. (Price elasticity of demand as discussed earlier is sometimes referred to as *own price elasticity*.) The elasticity of demand for good Y with respect to the price of good X measures the responsiveness of the demand for Y to a change in the price of X and is defined (with obvious notation) by

$$\eta_{Y,P_X} = \frac{\Delta Q_Y / Q_Y}{\Delta P_X / P_X} = \frac{\Delta Q_Y}{\Delta P_X} \cdot \frac{P_X}{Q_Y}.$$

Again, the assumption of *ceteris paribus* applies, and this time we assume that everything remains the same except the price of X.

A cross-price elasticity of -1.4 means that a 1 per cent increase in the price of good X leads to a 1.4 per cent reduction in the demand for good Y. Again, the sign of the elasticity is important. A positive cross-price elasticity means that an increase in P_X leads to an increase in Q_Y which happens if the two goods are substitutes. Fuel oil and natural gas are examples of substitutes for heating. However, a negative cross-price elasticity implies that an increase in P_X causes a reduction in Q_Y so that goods X and Y are complements. Petrol and tyres are complements. If the price of petrol rises, the quantity demanded of petrol falls but so does the demand for tyres. If the cross-price elasticity is zero, the goods are independent or unrelated.

With respect to two goods X and Y, there are two cross-price elasticities:

η_{Y,P_X} = elasticity of demand for Y with respect to the price of X

and

η_{X,P_Y} = elasticity of demand for X with respect to the price of Y.

These two elasticities are not in general equal.[7]

Note that cross-price elasticities frequently tell us something about the magnitude of the own price elasticity of demand. Why? Because an important determinant of own price elasticity is the availability and closeness of substitutes. Consider the demand for

---

[6] According to the Institute for Fiscal Studies, this is the case with domestic energy consumption in the UK. Domestic energy is found to be a necessity at all levels of income but more so for poorer households than for richer households. See I. Crawford, S. Smith, and S. Webb, 'VAT On Domestic Energy', Institute for Fiscal Studies, Commentary no. 39, London, 1993. The effect of imposing VAT on domestic energy was discussed in Section 2-8.

---

[7] In Section 3-7 we discuss what is known as an income-compensated demand curve. For such demand curves these two elasticities are equal.

Pepsi. If the price of Pepsi increases, many consumers quickly switch to Coke or similar cola products. What does this tell us about the cross-price elasticity of demand for these products? It should be positive and fairly large, indicating that these two goods are close substitutes. In turn, what does the high cross-price elasticity imply about the own price elasticity of demand for Pepsi? Demand should be fairly elastic. So, in general, when close substitutes are available, own price elasticity is large.

3-5 Income and Substitution Effects of a Price Change*

Earlier we said that, if money income and the price of good Y stay the same but the price of good X rises, the consumer is worse off, and if the price of good X falls the consumer is better off. This observation has led economists to try to separate the impact of a price change on quantity demanded into two components:

1 The substitution effect, which involves the substitution of good X for good Y or vice versa as the result of a change in the relative prices of the two goods
2 The income effect, which results from an increase or decrease in the consumer's real income or purchasing power as a result of the price change

The sum of these two effects is often called the total effect of a price change, or just the *price effect*. The decomposition of the price effect into the substitution and income effect components can be done in several ways, depending on what we wish to hold constant. There are two main methods suggested in the literature: (1) the Hicks method,[8] and (2) the Slutsky method.[9] We first illustrate the two methods in figures using indifference curve analysis and then discuss the relative merits of the two approaches.

---

*A mathematical treatment of some of this material is given in the Mathematical Appendix at the end of the book.
[8] This method is attributed to J. R. Hicks (1904–89) and is described in his book, *Value and Capital: An Inquiry into Some Fundamental Principles of Economic Theory*, Oxford University Press, 1946 (2nd edn.), pp. 29–33.
[9] This is the method suggested by E. Slutsky (1880–1948) in his paper, 'On the Theory of the Budget of the Consumer', reprinted in K. E. Boulding and G. J. Stigler (eds.), *Readings in Price Theory*, Irwin, Homewood, Ill., 1952, pp. 27–56.

The Hicks Method

Consider Figure 3-11. Initially, the optimal bundle is E_1 on indifference curve I_1. A fall in the price of good X pivots the budget line from AB_1 to AB_2 (income and the prices of other goods remain constant), and the new consumer optimum is E_2 on indifference curve I_2. Thus, the total effect of the price change is the movement from E_1 to E_2, or an increase in the quantity demanded of X from X_1 to X_2.

Now we can ask the question: 'What is the consumer's optimal bundle if she faces the new lower price for X but experiences no change in real income?' The answer is E_3 with X_3 units of good X demanded. To see this, we must realize that holding the consumer's real income constant amounts to *keeping her on the same indifference curve*. And with the new price ratio, the new optimum on I_1 is at E_3, where a line with the slope of the new budget line (or parallel to the new budget line) is tangent.

Thus, we argue that the movement from E_1 to E_3, or the increase in quantity demanded from X_1 to X_3, is solely in response to a change in relative prices. This is the substitution effect.

The remainder of the total effect is due to a change in real income. The movement from E_3 to E_2,

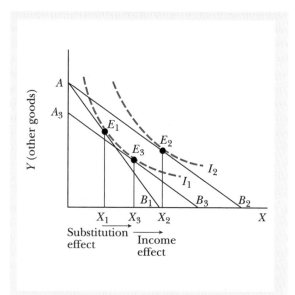

Figure 3-11 Substitution and income effects of a price change: the Hicks method

or the increase in quantity demanded from X_3 to X_2 is thus the income effect. The increase in real income is shown by the consumer's movement from I_1 to a higher indifference curve I_2.

The Slutsky Method

The Slutsky method is illustrated in Figure 3-12. The initial budget line is again AB_1. A fall in the price of good X pivots the budget line to AB_2. The consumer moves from position E_1 on indifference curve I_1 to position E_2 on indifference curve I_2.

In an attempt to isolate the substitution effect, Slutsky suggests that, as we change the price of X, we adjust the consumer's money income so that she can just afford her original consumption bundle. Doing so leads to the budget line $A_3 B_3$, which passes through E_1 but is parallel to AB_2, thus reflecting the new price of X. Slutsky then argues that the movement along this budget line from E_1 to E_3 is due to the change in the price of X or constitutes the substitution effect. Note that with the Slutsky method the substitution effect involves *a movement to a higher indifference curve*.

This leaves the movement from E_3 to E_2, or the increase in consumption of good X from X_3 to X_2, as the income effect. And again, the substitution effect plus the income effect equals the total effect.

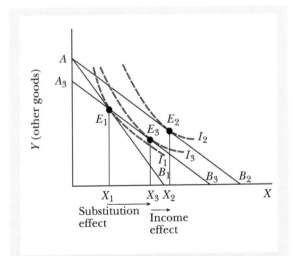

Figure 3-12   Substitution and income effects of a price change: the Slutsky method

The Difference between the Hicks Method and the Slutsky Method

The Hicks method is theoretically correct, because with this method the substitution effect measures the effect of movement along an indifference curve arising from a change in relative prices, whereas the income effect measures the effect of a movement between indifference curves at unchanged relative prices. However, the problem with this method is that it is *non-operational* in the sense that point E_3 in Figure 3-11 cannot be observed in practice.

However, the Slutsky method is operational in the sense that we can do something to observe point E_3 in Figure 3-12. What we do is adjust money income for the consumer to allow her to just afford the bundle of goods X and Y given by point E_1. Then we observe what she chooses, which is point E_3.

As an example, suppose that initially the prices of goods X and Y are $P_X = £10$ and $P_Y = £10$. The consumer's income is £150. Suppose the consumer buys 7 units of X and 8 units of Y. Now P_X falls to £5. Then in the Slutsky method we take away £35 of the consumer's income. With the income of £115 the consumer can still buy 7 units of X and 8 units of Y as before. Actually, the consumer chooses another bundle, and this is what we observe (as E_3 in Figure 3-12). Note that a similar experiment cannot be performed under the Hicks method, although one can talk theoretically about an income adjustment that keeps the consumer on the same indifference curve.

Although operational, the Slutsky method is not theoretically defensible, because the movement from E_1 to E_3 involves a movement between indifference curves and this is not really a substitution effect. The method, in general, overestimates the substitution effect and underestimates the income effect. (This is true in the case of Figures 3-11 and 3-12 the way we have drawn them.)

In the following sections and in subsequent chapters, whenever we decompose the effect of a price change into substitution and income effects, we use the Hicks approach. This is the correct approach for deriving theoretical conclusions.

Effects of a Price Increase

We have, so far, discussed the substitution and income effects of a decline in the price of X. The analysis of an increase in the price of X is similar. In this case the substitution effect results in a decrease in the consumption of X and so does the income effect, in the case of a normal good. In the Slutsky method we now have to compensate the consumer with an income subsidy that enables the consumer to buy the old combination of goods X and Y at the new prices. In the Hicks method, we again can think of an income compensation (although it is difficult to implement) that enables the consumer to stay on the same indifference curve as before the price rise. Since the analysis is symmetrical, we do not present it here but leave it as an exercise.

Example 3-1   Shipping the Good Apples Out

Suppose that a good apple costs 20 pence and a poor apple costs 10 pence locally in Kent. Then to eat two good apples costs the same as eating four poor apples. Suppose that it costs 10 pence per apple to ship apples to Yorkshire. The cost of a good apple there is 30 pence and the cost of a poor apple is 20 pence. Now eating two good apples costs the same as eating three poor apples (not four). Although the prices of apples are higher, good apples are *relatively* cheaper (relative to poor apples), and a higher percentage of good apples are consumed in Yorkshire than in Kent. The good apples from Kent are shipped to Yorkshire.

The proposition that, if the same fixed cost (for example a transport cost) is added to the prices of similar goods, the effect is to raise the relative consumption of the higher-quality or premium good first appeared in a textbook by Alchian and Allen in 1964.[10] Since then it has also appeared in other texts, such as those by Stigler and Hirschleifer.[11]

We can use similar reasoning to explain why fine tailoring is done on expensive fabric rather than on inexpensive fabric. (Tailoring is *relatively* cheaper on expensive fabric because it constitutes a smaller

proportion of total cost.) Similarly, houses situated on land with a high site value tend to be smarter than those situated in places with a low site value (because site value is relatively cheaper for expensive houses); and most top-grade beef is sold to restaurants (because the cost of restaurant services is relatively cheaper for high-grade beef).

There has been some controversy over whether the Alchian–Allen proposition can be derived solely by using the law of demand, although there is no question of its empirical validity. Also, although we quoted all the other examples as being similar to that of apples, it should be acknowledged that transport costs are different from tailoring services, land values, or restaurant services. However, the Alchian–Allen proposition holds even in these cases, although the reasoning may be different. (We shall not go into the details here because this involves the use of consumer surplus, which we discuss in Chapter 7.)

3-6   Giffen Goods and Inferior Goods

The distinction between Giffen goods and inferior goods can be made clearer by considering substitution and income effects. In Figure 3-11, note that the substitution effect and income effect both lead to an increase in the consumption of X when the price of X falls. This is not always the case. The substitution effect always produces a change in quantity demanded that is opposite to the change in price; that is, a fall in the price of X leads to a substitution of X for Y so that the quantity demanded of X increases. However, the income effect can work either way.[12] If the good is normal, an increase in real income (a fall in the price of X) leads to an increase in the quantity demanded (the income effect is positive). But if the good is inferior, the increase in income leads to a decrease in the quantity demanded (the income effect is negative). Thus, if the good is inferior and its price falls, the income and substitution effects work in opposite directions. If the (negative) income effect outweighs the substitution effect, the quantity demanded falls as price falls. This is the case with Giffen goods. Thus, Giffen goods are inferior goods, *but* not all inferior

---

[10] A. A. Alchian and W. R. Allen, *University Economics*, Wadsworth, Belmont, Cal., 1964, pp. 74–5.
[11] G. J. Stigler, *The Theory of Price*, 3rd edn., Macmillan, New York, 1966, p. 103, and J. Hirshleifer, *Price Theory and Applications*, Prentice-Hall, Englewood Cliffs, NJ, 1976, p. 321.

[12] In fact, we see this happening in the case of labour supply. This point is discussed in Section 3-8.

Table 3-3   Substitution and income effects of a price fall on quantity demanded

Type of good	Substitution effect	Income effect	Total effect
Normal	Increase	Increase	Increase
Inferior (but not Giffen)	Increase	Decrease	Increase
Giffen	Increase	Decrease	Decrease

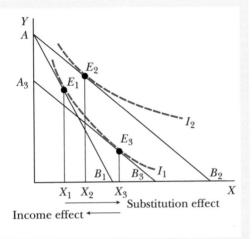

Figure 3-13   Income and substitution effects for an inferior good (not a Giffen good)

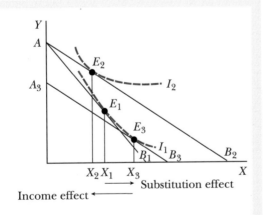

Figure 3-14   Income and substitution effects for a Giffen good

Negative income effect dominates the substitution effect

goods are Giffen goods. This point is set out in Table 3-3 and illustrated in Figures 3-13 and 3-14.

3-7   Ordinary versus Compensated Demand Functions

The separation of the effect of price changes into substitution and income effects has also led to the definition of two types of demand curves: (1) the *ordinary demand curve* (OD), which includes the substitution and income effects, and (2) the *compensated demand curve* (CD), which includes the substitution effect only. The compensated demand curve is so called because the consumer is compensated for any decline in real income arising from an increase in the price of a good, or is taxed (given negative compensation) for any increase in real income arising from a fall in the price of a good.

Since there are two ways of compensating the consumer, the Hicks method and the Slutsky method, we have two definitions of compensated demand curves. Recall that in the Hicks method consumers are compensated (or taxed) to keep them on the initial indifference curve. In the Slutsky method consumers are compensated (or taxed) to enable them to buy the original bundle of the goods X and Y.

The main differences between the ordinary demand curve and the compensated demand curve is that the ordinary demand curve can have a positive slope (as in the case of Giffen goods) but the compensated demand curve is always negatively sloped (as there is no income effect). Furthermore, for a normal good the compensated demand curve is steeper than the ordinary demand curve, as shown in Figure 3-15.

The reasoning is as follows. We start with an initial price P_0 and quantity demanded X_0. The price of X now falls to P_1. The change in quantity demanded from the OD curve is shown as $X_1 - X_0$ and from the CD curve as $X_2 - X_0$. Thus the increase in quantity demanded is higher if we consider both the income and substitution effects (OD curve) than if we consider the substitution effect alone (CD curve). The CD curve lies below the OD curve. Conversely, for an increase in price (P_0 to P_2), the decrease in quantity demanded is higher if we consider both the substitution and income effects ($X_0 - X_3$) than when we consider the substitution effect alone ($X_0 - X_4$). Thus, the CD curve lies

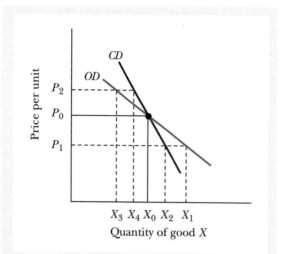

Figure 3-15   Ordinary demand curve (OD) and compensated demand curve (CD) for a normal good

above the OD curve. The CD curve is, therefore, steeper than the OD curve.

For an inferior good, the substitution and income effects work in opposite directions. Hence we get the CD and OD curves as shown in Figure 3-16(a). Figure 3-16(b) shows the CD and OD curves for a Giffen good. Since the reasoning is clear from Table 3-3, we do not elaborate on it here.

3-8   Application 1: Labour Supply Choices

The decomposition of the effects of a change in price into income and substitution effects has interesting applications in the theory of labour supply and in the analysis of different government policies on work effort. We now consider these applications.

Labour–Leisure Choice and Backward-bending Supply

There are some people with philanthropic motives who work for pleasure and not money. However, workers usually work for money and prefer to have leisure too. Thus, both income and leisure are 'goods'. As with any two goods, we can draw indifference curves between income and leisure. These are shown in Figure 3-17.

To find the equilibrium for the worker, we have to draw the budget line. The budget line depends on the wage rate. If the wage rate is £3 per hour, the maximum income per day is £72; if the wage rate is £4 per hour, the maximum income per day is £96; and so on. Figure 3-18 shows the amount of leisure per day demanded at different wage rates. Subtracting from 24, we get the number of hours of labour supplied per day at different wage rates. The supply curve is shown in Figure 3-19. Note that it is upward-sloping for a while and then bends backward after 12 hours of work.

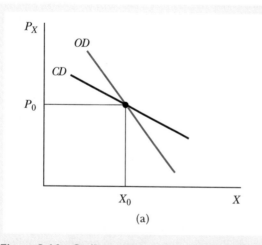

(a)

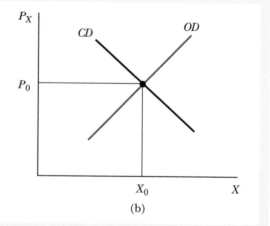

(b)

Figure 3-16   Ordinary and compensated demand curves

(a) (non-Giffen) inferior goods
(b) Giffen goods

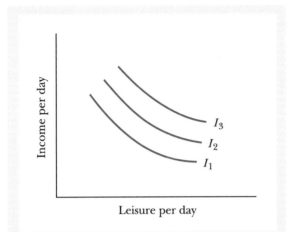

Figure 3-17   Indifference curves for income and leisure

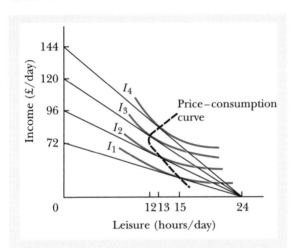

Figure 3-18   Determination of hours of leisure at different wage rates

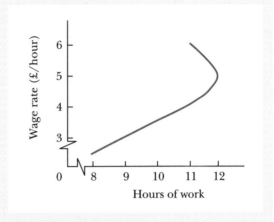

Figure 3-19   Supply curve of labour

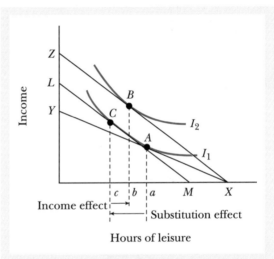

Figure 3-20   Income and substitution effects of a change in wage rates

We can separate the effect of a change in the wage rate on the demand for leisure into a substitution effect and an income effect. Figure 3-20 shows this. The worker is initially in equilibrium at point A on indifference curve I_1. The increase in the wage rate pivots the budget line from XY to XZ and the worker moves to point B on indifference curve I_2. The number of hours of leisure fall from a to b. The move from A to B can be broken down into a substitution effect and an income effect. To show the substitution effect, the worker is restored to his original level of utility at the new wage rate. This is shown by point C on

indifference curve I_1. (The worker's extra income is taken away in a (lump-sum) tax, hence the budget line LM.) So, as the wage rate rises, the price of leisure increases and the worker reduces his hours of leisure, thus increasing the number of hours worked. This is the substitution effect and is shown as the move around I_1 from A to C. However, once we give the worker his extra income (the budget line shifts from LM to ZX) he demands more hours of leisure (from c to b), since leisure is a normal good. This is the income effect, or the move from C to B. Thus, the income effect and the substitution effect work in opposite directions. At low wage rates the substitution effect dominates the income effect, so that we get an upward-sloping supply curve for labour. But at high wage rates the income effect outweighs the substitution effect resulting in a supply curve that bends backward (as in Figure 3-19).

The backward-bending supply curve is not necessarily observed all the time, but there is a good deal of empirical evidence in its favour. A number of studies carried out in the UK since the mid-1970s show that, for male workers, above a certain real wage the income effect dominates the substitution effect, producing a fall in hours worked with an increase in the real wage.[13] There is also some evidence that suggests the same pattern for female workers, although the findings are not as conclusive.

The phenomenon of the backward-bending supply curve for labour has also been verified in experiments with rats and pigeons.[14] The animals were required to push levers a certain number of times to get a unit of food. The wage rate was changed by changing the number of times the lever had to be pushed. As this number was decreased, beyond a point the animals reduced the quantity of labour supplied.

---

[13] For a summary of the main results see R. F. Elliot, *Labor Economics: A Comparative Text*, McGraw-Hill, London, 1991, Ch. 4.

[14] T. Alexander, 'Economics According to the Rats', *Fortune*, 1 (December 1980): 127–32.

Effects of Social Security Benefits and Negative Income Tax on Work Effort

Many social security benefits in the UK such as income support, housing benefit, family credit, and the social fund are intended to assist low-income groups in the population. However, many benefits are reduced pound for pound (and sometimes even more) with an increase in income, and/or they cease altogether as soon as an individual enters work. For instance, if a family member takes a part-time job which involves working more than 24 hours per week, housing benefit is reduced. Thus, social security payments may have a negative effect on work effort since any increase in earnings is lost through a reduction in benefits.[15]

Concern about the negative effect of the social security system on work effort has prompted radical proposals for reform. A proposal that has often been discussed is the negative income tax (NIT). The idea behind the NIT scheme is this. If an individual has an income level below that at which tax is paid, she receives a certain proportion of the difference between her income and the taxable income level in the form of a 'negative tax' payment. Several types of NIT scheme have been proposed, although they all involve (1) the provision of a guaranteed minimum-income level,

---

[15] See J. Le Grand, C. Propper, and R. Robinson, *The Economics of Social Problems*, 3rd edn., Macmillan, London, 1992, Ch. 9.

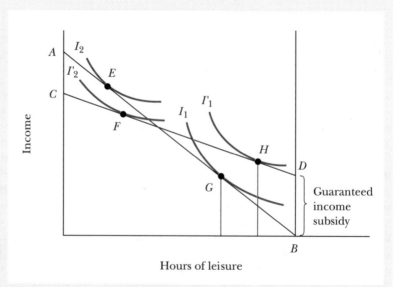

Figure 3-21 Effects of negative income tax on work effort

(2) the taxing of any income above this level at a particular rate, and (3) the imposition of ordinary tax at some income level.

We can analyse the effects of NIT on work effort in a figure similar to Figure 3-18 except that the budget line under the NIT programme is different. The analysis presented refers to Figure 3-21. AB is the budget line if the individual is not in the NIT programme. If she is in the NIT programme, she receives a guaranteed income of BD but her earned income is taxed at a specific rate. The budget line is, therefore, CD, which has a lower slope than AB. (Income earned by those not in the NIT scheme is also taxed, but at a lower rate than in the NIT programme.)

Now consider two individuals with indifference curves given by I_1 and I_2.[16] Individual 2 does not find it worth while to participate in the NIT scheme because he is worse off. (Point F is on a lower indifference curve, I'_2, than point E). Individual 1 is better off under the NIT programme (moving from point G to point H on a higher indifference curve, I'_1). As to what happens to work effort, individual 1 works fewer hours with the NIT scheme (her amount of leisure increases) compared with what she works in the absence of any income assistance programme.

However, with the NIT programme the individual has a work incentive, and hours worked are not zero, as in the case of the current social security payments. Under the social security system, since payments go down pound for pound (in effect, a 100 per cent tax rate on earned income), the budget line is essentially horizontal, and the optimal solution is at the corner point D.

We can easily demonstrate that with a sufficiently high wage rate even individual 1 finds it worth while to leave the NIT scheme. We can show this by drawing the budget line AB steeper. We leave this as an exercise.

---

[16] These are only portions of the two individuals' indifference curves. Completeness of preferences requires that every commodity combination for each individual lie on some indifference curve; for example, point E lies on some indifference curve for individual 1. The difference in preferences can be seen in the shapes of the two sets of curves. For a given commodity bundle, the ratio of marginal utility of leisure to marginal utility of income is higher for individual 1 than for individual 2. Portions of the indifference curves have been omitted merely for simplicity, since they are not needed for this analysis. Only the regions where tangencies occur are illustrated.

Effects of Progressive Income Tax on Work Effort

In almost every country, the income tax is progressive. In other words, as income rises, a greater proportion of it is taken away in tax. It is easy to see that this discourages work effort because the worker gets a reduced share of the additional income earned at higher levels of work effort.

We could argue that if we want to improve work effort then *all* income taxes should be eliminated. However, we address a different question: 'What is the effect of a proportional income tax on work effort compared with that of a progressive income tax?' The answer to this question is not clear. In Figure 3-22 we show indifference curves for two types of workers: worker 1, who consumes a lot of leisure (indifference curves I_1 and I'_1), and worker 2, who works lots of hours (indifference curves I_2 and I'_2).[17] The straight line $A_1 B$ is the budget line with a proportional income tax (everyone pays the same rate). The curved line $A_2 B$ is the budget line with a progressive income tax. They are drawn to cross each other because we are assuming that the government wants to collect the same tax revenue in both cases. Thus, the tax rate is

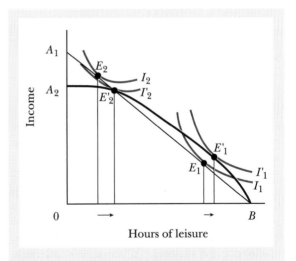

Figure 3-22 Comparative effect of a progressive income tax and proportional income tax on work effort

---

[17] Again, we have only illustrated the relevant portion of the indifference curves.

higher (and, hence, income received is lower) at lower incomes with a proportional tax rate.

With a proportional tax rate, worker 1 is at point E_1 on indifference curve I_1, and worker 2 is at point E_2 on indifference curve I_2. When the tax is changed to a progressive income tax, worker 1 moves to point E'_1 on a higher indifference curve I'_1, and consumption of leisure goes up so that work effort goes down. Worker 2 moves to point E'_2 on a lower indifference curve I'_2, but this worker also increases consumption of leisure and so reduces work effort. Thus, both workers reduce work effort except that worker 1 is better off and worker 2 is worse off with the progressive income tax.

It is possible to draw a set of indifference curves between the points E_1 and E_2 in Figure 3-22 where a worker moves to a higher indifference curve and thus is better off under a progressive income tax but also reduces consumption of leisure, and thus increases hours of work. We leave this as an exercise.

The impact on the economy-wide work effort of a switch from a progressive to a proportional income tax is unclear. First, we do not know what flat rate would provide the government with the same amount of revenue. Furthermore, we do not know what fraction of workers would increase or decrease hours worked.

3-9 Application 2: Cost-of-living Indexes

We now consider the use of cost-of-living indexes to measure changes in welfare. Here, we do not consider substitution and income effects. We simply apply the basic principles of indifference curve analysis.

One important use of indifference curve analysis is in the inferences we can make regarding cost-of-living indexes. We first explain the reasoning behind the construction of two different cost-of-living indexes— the Laspeyres index and the Paasche index—and then we illustrate the reasoning in terms of indifference curves.

Index numbers are used to measure how much something has changed from one time to another. Suppose the price of petrol in 1991 was £1.15 a litre and in 1990 it had been £1.10 a litre. Then the price index of petrol in 1991 relative to the base year 1990 is $(1.15)/(1.10) \times 100 = 104.5$. This means that the price of petrol has risen by 4.5 per cent. Note that the index

is always for a certain year relative to the corresponding value for a *base year*. By taking the base year as a year of very low prices, we can show how prices have risen, and by taking the base year as one of high prices, we can show how prices have fallen.

We can compute such price indexes for a great many commodities. But if we are considering an overall index, such as the UK retail price index (RPI), we have to find a way of weighting each of these component commodities. The RPI is constructed by the Central Statistical Office, and measures the change in the cost of a representative 'basket' of many consumption items including food, clothing and footwear, housing, alcohol, household goods, tobacco, fuel and lighting, and motoring costs. We can see the idea of the RPI by calculating the change in the cost of living from 1987 (the base year) to 1993 for someone consuming only four items: food, alcohol, clothing and footwear, and fuel and lighting. Between these years, food costs went up by 30.9 per cent, the cost of alcohol went up by 56.5 per cent, clothing and footwear costs went up by 22.2 per cent, and fuel and lighting costs went up by 25.7 per cent.

Given these price increases, how do we compute the percentage change in living costs? We could just calculate the average change, which gives an increase of 33.8 per cent. This is not correct, however, because the proportion of income spent on these four items is different. The procedure used in calculating the RPI is to compute a *weighted average*, the weights being the share of each item in total consumer expenditure. In 1987 the weights for these four items were: food = 0.167, alcohol = 0.076, clothing and footwear = 0.074 and fuel and lighting = 0.061. This says that the weight for food in the index was 16.7 per cent, for alcohol it was 7.6 per cent, and so on. To calculate the change in the cost of living, we take each weight and multiply it by the price increase for each good. Thus, we have $0.167(30.9) + 0.076(56.5) + 0.074(22.2) + 0.061(25.7)$, which gives an increase of 12.6 per cent. An index that uses base-year weights is a *Laspeyres index*.

Data on the shares of the different items in total expenditure come from the annual Family Expenditure Survey, so that each year's weight is based on expenditure during the previous period. This means that the weights set in 1987 were based on expenditure in 1986. The weights used in the RPI are changed every year. For our four commodities, the weights set in 1993 (based on 1992 expenditures) were food = 0.144, alcohol = 0.078, clothing and footwear = 0.058, and fuel and lighting = 0.046. Using these weights, we get an increase in the cost of living of 11.3 per cent. An index that uses final-year weights is a *Paasche index*. Thus, our answer to how much living costs changed between 1987 and 1993 depends on whether we use a Laspeyres or a Paasche index. In practice, the RPI (and almost all other cost-of-living indexes) is computed using base-period weights (a Laspeyres formula).

We now look in some detail at the way the Laspeyres and the Paasche price indexes are constructed. We do this with reference to two commodities, X and Y. The extension to the case of several commodities is straightforward, and since we want to discuss the meaning of the indexes in terms of indifference curves, we have to consider only two commodities.

Suppose we consider two years: year 1 (say 1987) and year 2 (say 1993). For these two years Table 3-4 lists these data for a representative family.

Total expenditure $E_1 = X_1 P_{X1} + Y_1 P_{Y1}$.

Share of X in year $1 = S_{X1} = \dfrac{X_1 P_{X1}}{E_1}$.

The other quantities are defined similarly. We first consider the price changes for X and Y separately:

$I_X = \dfrac{P_{X2}}{P_{X1}}$ measures the change in the price of X.

$I_Y = \dfrac{P_{Y2}}{P_{Y1}}$ measures the change in the price of Y.

These are called *price relatives* for X and Y.

To construct an overall index, we have to weight these price relatives. The Laspeyres index L, as we said earlier, uses base-period shares:

$L = S_{X1} I_X + S_{Y1} I_Y$.

The Paasche index P uses final-period shares as weights:

$P = S_{X2} I_X + S_{Y2} I_Y$.

These formulas are usually written differently:

$L = S_{X1} I_X + S_{Y2} I_Y$.

$$= \frac{X_1 P_{X1}}{E_1} \cdot \frac{P_{X2}}{P_{X1}} + \frac{Y_1 P_{Y1}}{E_1} \cdot \frac{P_{Y2}}{P_{Y1}}$$

$$= \frac{X_1 P_{X2} + Y_1 P_{Y2}}{E_1}$$

But

$E_1 = X_1 P_{X1} + Y_1 P_{Y1}$.

Thus,

$$L = \frac{X_1 P_{X2} + Y_1 P_{Y2}}{X_1 P_{X1} + Y_1 P_{Y1}}.$$

Similarly, we can show that

$$P = \frac{X_2 P_{X2} + Y_2 P_{Y2}}{X_2 P_{X1} + Y_2 P_{Y1}}.$$

Thus, in the construction of the Laspeyres index we take base-period quantities and use these as weights for the respective *prices* (not price relatives). In the Paasche index we use final-period quantities as weights. For example, consider the situation set out in Table 3-5. The Laspeyres price index is

$$L = \frac{(50)(9) + (100)(4)}{(50)(10) + (100)(3)} = \frac{850}{800} = 1.0625.$$

The Paasche price index is

$$P = \frac{(55)(9) + (95)(4)}{(55)(10) + (95)(3)} = \frac{875}{835} = 1.0479.$$

The Laspeyres index L compares the costs of obtaining the year 1 bundle of goods in the two years. The Paasche index P compares the costs of obtaining the year 2 bundle of goods in the two years. Suppose that

$$X_1 P_{X2} + Y_1 P_{Y2} < E_2. \qquad (1)$$

This means that the cost of the year 1 (1987) bundle at year 2 (1993) prices is less than year 2 expenditures. In other words, in year 2 the family could have bought the same bundle as in year 1 but chose not to do so. Thus,

Table 3-4 Data for constructing a price index

Year	Quantities	Prices	Total expenditures	Shares of X and Y in total expenditures
1	X_1, Y_1	P_{X1}, P_{Y1}	E_1	S_{X1}, S_{Y1}
2	X_2, Y_2	P_{X2}, P_{Y2}	E_2	S_{X2}, S_{Y2}

Table 3-5   Constructing a Laspeyres and Paasche price index

Year	Quantities		Prices		Expenditure
	X	Y	P_X	P_Y	E
1	50	100	£10	£3	£800
2	55	95	£9	£4	£876

the family must be better off in year 2 than in year 1. Dividing both sides of equation (1) by E_1, we get

$$L < \frac{E_2}{E_1}. \tag{2}$$

If this condition is satisfied, the family is better off. In our example we have $L = 1.0625$ and $E_2/E_1 = 1.094$. Thus, this condition is satisfied.

Consider another case:

$$X_2 P_{X1} + Y_2 P_{Y1} < E_1. \tag{3}$$

This means that the cost of the year 2 (1993) bundle at year 1 (1987) prices is less than year 1 expenditures. Thus, the family could have bought year 2 bundle in year 1 but did not. Thus, the family was better off in

year 1 than in year 2. Alternatively, the family is worse off in year 2 than in year 1.

Dividing both sides of equation (3) by E_2, we get

$$\frac{1}{P} < \frac{E_1}{E_2}$$

or

$$P > \frac{E_2}{E_1}. \tag{4}$$

Thus, if the Paasche index is greater than E_2/E_1, the family is worse off in year 2 than in year 1. In our example this condition is not satisfied. Thus, condition (2) shows that the family is better off in year 2 than in year 1, and condition (4) shows that the family is not worse off in year 2 than in year 1. The two conditions give the same conclusion.

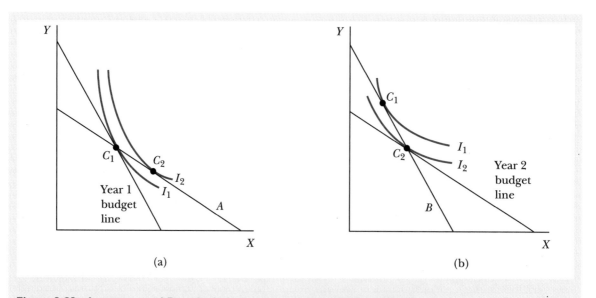

(a)   (b)

Figure 3-23   Laspeyres and Paasche indexes in terms of indifference curves

(a) Budget line A enables the family to buy year 1 bundle at year 2 prices. Family is better off in year 2
(b) Budget line B enables the family to buy year 2 bundle at year 1 prices. Family is better off in year 1

These points can be illustrated graphically in terms of indifference curves. This is done in Figures 3-23(a) and (b). In Figure 3.23(a) the family is initially at point C_1 on indifference curve I_1. If the family is given just enough income to buy the year 1 bundle at the year 2 prices, the budget line is line A shown in Figure 3-23(a). This clearly enables the family to attain a higher indifference curve I_2. The situation $L < E_2/E_1$ or $E_2 > L \cdot E_1$ corresponds to a budget line higher than (and parallel to) line A. Thus, the family is definitely better off in year 2 than in year 1.

In Figure 3-23(b) we show another configuration of indifference curves. The year 2 budget line puts the family on indifference curve I_2 at point C_2. If the family is given just enough income to buy the year 2 bundle at the year 1 prices, the budget line is line B shown in Figure 3-23(b). This clearly enables the family to attain a higher indifference curve I_1. The situation $P > E_2/E_1$ or $E_1 > E_2/P$ corresponds to a budget line higher than (and parallel to) line B. Thus, the family is definitely better off in year 1 than in year 2.

In practice, however, the RPI (and most other price indexes) is constructed using the Laspeyres formula. We are rarely given both the Laspeyres and Paasche indexes. Thus, we are often unable to make any welfare comparisons. However, note that when some prices go up the Laspeyres index overstates the rise in the cost of living (i.e. the cost of maintaining a given level of utility), because it ignores the possibility of substitution effects.

There are also problems with the weights used in the RPI. They do not reflect the spending patterns of all households. The very wealthy at one extreme and poorer pensioners at the other are excluded when the RPI is constructed. The effect of this is that items that pensioners consume relatively more of, such as fuel, are given too low a weight. Also, the RPI has been labelled an 'undemocratic' index because the weighting is done in relation to the amount a household spends. The more a household spends, the greater is the effect of its spending on the index. Thus, the expenditure pattern of a high spending, wealthy household carries more weight than that of a poorer household. Some people have argued that the UK should follow the lead of some other European countries and calculate a price index for different income groups. All we have in the UK is a separate index for pensioners, but it excludes housing costs.

3-10   A New Approach to Consumer Theory: The Demand for Characteristics

Throughout the preceding discussion, we have considered two goods, X and Y. An alternative approach to the theory of consumer demand was pioneered by Lancaster; it argues that goods are demanded because of their characteristics and it is these characteristics that give utility.[18] Thus, we may consider three different goods: sugar, honey, and saccharine. But there may be only two characteristics: sweetness and calories. If a new sweetener is produced we analyse it not as a new good, but as one more good that has the same characteristics. Thus, compared with the traditional analysis, the new approach has two advantages: (1) we can study the introduction of new goods; and (2) we can study the effects of changes in quality.

In the traditional theory, the consumer's indifference curves are given in terms of the original set of goods, and if a new good is introduced then we have to redefine a whole new set of indifference curves or surfaces. All the information on the preferences about the old set of goods is discarded.

Many so-called new goods are actually the same as the old goods with the characteristics in different proportions. A new car is not exactly the same as an old model but it does not differ fundamentally from the old one either. Similar is the case of refrigerators and many other goods. Thus, if we consider the preferences in terms of characteristics, we can analyse the introduction of new goods very easily. We do not have to discard any of the old set of preferences.

Of course, there are always some new goods with new characteristics. For example, when colour televisions, video recorders, and compact disc players were first introduced, we had products with new characteristics. In this case we have to introduce a new set of preferences.

A major advantage of the characteristics approach is that it permits the analysis of many goods. Often the number of goods is considerably higher than the

---

[18] This theory is discussed in K. J. Lancaster, 'Change and Innovation in the Technology of Consumption', *American Economic Review*, 56 (1966): 14–23, and 'A New Approach to Consumer Theory', *Journal of Political Economy*, 74 (1966): 132–57. The former paper is non-technical.

number of characteristics. Furthermore, once we start thinking in terms of characteristics, we have to consider a substitution effect that is different from the substitution effect we considered earlier.

For instance, suppose the consumer is interested in two characteristics: nutrition and warmth. Suppose that there are goods X_1, X_2, X_3, etc., that provide nutrition. The consumer chooses the one with the lowest price per unit of nutrition. Suppose this is X_1. If the prices of these goods change and X_2 is now the one with the lowest price, an efficient consumer substitutes X_2 for X_1. Lancaster calls this the *efficiency substitution* effect. This substitution does not have anything to do with indifference curves. Similarly, if Y_1, Y_2, Y_3, etc., are goods that provide warmth, the consumer chooses the one with the lowest price per unit and substitutes some other good with the lowest price if the prices change.

The substitution and income effects we discussed still apply for a choice between good X and good Y. But the intra-group substitution does not depend on any indifference curve.

In the above example X_1, X_2, X_3, etc., provide nutrition only and Y_1, Y_2, Y_3, etc., provide warmth only. Very often this is not the case. The same characteristic may be present in all the goods considered but in different proportions. To illustrate the analysis in this case we take the following example. There are two characteristics: carbohydrate, denoted by C, and protein, denoted by P. Consider two foods with the characteristics listed in Table 3-6.

The budget line for a consumer with a budget of £8 is shown by the line AB in Figure 3-24. If the consumer spends all the money on food A, he gets 16 units of C and 2 units of P. If he spends all his income on food B, he gets 2 units of C and 16 units of P. By superimposing the consumer's indifference curves, we can find his equilibrium and the amounts of the two foods A and B that he buys.

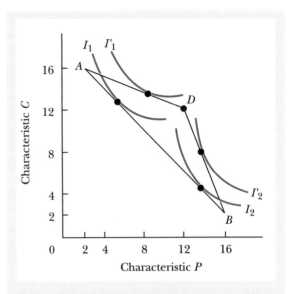

Figure 3-24 Analysis of consumer demand in terms of characteristics of goods

Suppose there is a new food D that comes on the market. It gives 3 units of C and 3 units of P per kilo and costs £2 per kilo. If the consumer spends all his income on the new food, he gets 12 units of C and 12 units of P. This is represented by point D in Figure 3-24. The new budget line is now ADB. A consumer with indifference curves I_1, I'_1 now consumes foods A and D only; a consumer with indifference curves I_2, I'_2 consumes only foods B and D. Note the following points:

1 Every consumer consumes at most two foods.
2 If there is sufficient dispersion in the preference of the consumers, we find that all three foods are consumed.
3 The consumers of both type 1 and type 2 are better off by the availability of food D.
4 No new good can be marketed unless it pushes the budget line of the consumer to the right.
5 The introduction of new goods with the same characteristics can be analysed by simply changing the budget line.

The important thing to note is that it is the budget line, not the indifference map, that changes with the introduction of new goods with a different proportion of given characteristics.

Table 3-6 Goods with known characteristics	
	Price
Food A: 2 units of C	£1/kilo
0.25 units of P	
Food B: 0.25 units of C	£1/kilo
2 units of P	

Example 3-2 The Demand for Breakfast Cereals

One interesting application of the theory that goods are demanded because of their attributes is in the case of a nondurable good—breakfast cereal.[19] Stanley and Tschirhart use the *hedonic pricing method* to estimate implicit prices of breakfast cereal characteristics.[20] These prices are then used to gain insights into the nature of consumer preferences in relation to the particular characteristics of the good.

They suggest that consumers derive utility from particular cereal services, such as the taste and nutrition of the cereal, with the services being provided by the characteristics of the cereal. They estimate marginal implicit prices of cereal characteristics from a hedonic price function. From utility maximization theory, this gives a measure of the value to the consumer of an additional unit of the characteristic relative to an additional pound's worth of other goods. If the implicit price is positive, this says that maximizing consumers are willing to pay more for that particular characteristic. It simply tells us which particular attribute of the cereal consumers prefer.

Data on prices and characteristics were collected for all cereals at a number of stores in the Portland area of the United States. In the analysis, the variable to be explained was price per serving, and the independent (or explanatory) variables were the cereal characteristics. These include the amount of fibre and sucrose per serving, the amount of vitamins in the box, the number of servings per box, whether the cereal contained fruit and preservatives, whether the cereal texture was flakey or puffed, whether the cereal was natural, and whether the grain was corn, rice, or oats.

Their results show that consumers expressed a strong preference for cereals that contained vitamins, fruit, and sucrose. They also preferred those cereals where the grain was oats and where the texture was puffed. (All of these characteristics are taken to have positive effects on the nutrition and taste services.)

Normally, economists use the hedonic pricing approach to study the demand for the characteristics of durable goods such as cars, houses, and refrigerators. This example shows that it can also be used to generate implicit prices in the case of a non-durable good, breakfast cereal. In Example 3-3 we show how non-market goods (characteristics) can also be valued using survey methods.

Example 3-3 Valuing Countryside Benefits

The question of the environmental quality of rural areas is often discussed by policy-makers without there being any quantitative information available on the benefits of promoting recreational activities in the countryside. The problem in quantifying benefits is to place a value on the non-market services (or characteristics) supplied by the countryside. One way of placing a figure on the benefits (fishing, hunting, scenic quality, and so on) of the countryside is by directly questioning a sample of consumers in order to obtain their willingness to pay to have such services. This method of valuing non-market goods is called the *contingent valuation* approach.

By directly asking people about their preferences, we can get a measure of the contingent willingness of consumers to give up income for a small change in the quality of the countryside. The contingent valuation approach was used by Hanley to value the non-market characteristics supplied by the Queen Elizabeth Forest Park in Central Scotland.[21] The Forest Park covers 17 000 hectares and extends from Loch Lomond in the West to the Trossach hills in the East. The survey took place in the summer of 1987, and 1148 questionnaires were completed.

[19] See L. R. Stanley and J. Tschirhart, 'Hedonic Prices for a Nondurable Good: The Case of Breakfast Cereals', *Review of Economics and Statistics*, 73 (1991): 537–41.

[20] Hedonic pricing is a popular method of valuing 'non-market goods'. Breakfast cereals are market goods and they have a market value (price). But the particular characteristics of the cereals are non-market goods which have an implicit market value. The implicit price of the characteristics is embedded in the observed prices and consumption levels of the cereals. Hedonic pricing allows the implicit prices to be computed.

[21] N. D. Hanley, 'Valuing Rural Recreation Benefits: An Empirical Comparison of Two Approaches', *Journal of Agricultural Economics*, 40 (1989): 361–74.

People were asked to place a monetary value on the benefits from certain aspects of the Forest Park. Those characteristics thought to be important were the wildlife, the landscape, and the recreational facilities. The questions framed are quite long, so we do not quote them in full. For the *wildlife* service, people were asked how much they would be willing to pay if they could watch the wildlife at closer quarters; for the *landscape* service, people were asked how much they would be willing to pay to save the trees in one part of the Park from being felled; and for the *recreational facility*, people were asked how much they would be willing to pay to prevent parts of the forest drive being fenced off. Hanley also asked how much people would be willing to pay to keep the Forest Park open. The average values (in 1987 prices) placed on each of these services were £0.80, £0.84, £1.58, and £1.25, respectively.

The total number of visitor-days per annum at the time of the study was 145 000, except for the forest drive (24 500 visitor days). From this we get aggregate bids for each of the Park's services of £121 800, £116 000, £11 025, and £181 250, respectively.

As there are problems with the contingent valuation approach, these estimates may be biased downwards.[22] Even so, it serves as a useful way of valuing non-market characteristics, and may be preferred to hedonic pricing when the good (the environment) confers indirect benefits.

3-11 Summary

An income-consumption curve is the locus of tangencies between indifference curves and a series of parallel budget lines. An Engel curve can be derived from an income-consumption curve. It shows the quantities of a good demanded at various income levels, holding prices constant. For a normal good the slope of the Engel curve is positive, whereas for an inferior good the slope is negative.

By holding the price of one good and money income constant while varying the price of another good, we can generate a set of budget lines. The locus

of the tangencies between indifference curves and these budget lines is the price-consumption curve. From the price-consumption curve we can derive a demand curve.

Elasticity measures the responsiveness of quantity to changes in some other variable. Price elasticity of demand is defined as the ratio of percentage change in quantity demanded to percentage change in price. Point elasticity measures the elasticity at a given point on the demand curve or, equivalently, at a given price. Arc elasticity is an approximate average of the elasticity at two points on the demand curve.

For a linear demand curve the slope is constant, and since P/Q falls as we move down the demand curve, price elasticity declines as we move down the demand curve. The numerical value of the price elasticity of demand determines how total expenditure on a good is affected by price changes. When $\eta < 1$, price and total expenditure move in the same direction; when $\eta > 1$, price and total spending move in opposite directions; and when $\eta = 1$, a price change leaves total expenditure unaffected.

Income elasticity of demand is defined as the proportionate change in quantity demanded divided by the proportionate change in income, with prices and tastes held constant. A normal good is one for which the income elasticity of demand is positive. An inferior good has a negative income elasticity of demand.

Cross-price elasticity of demand is defined as the proportionate change in quantity demanded divided by the proportionate change in the price of a related good. A substitute good is one for which the cross-price elasticity is positive. A complementary good is one for which the cross-price elasticity is negative.

The impact of a price change on quantity demanded can be separated into a substitution effect and an income effect. The substitution effect is the response to the change in relative prices. The income effect is the response to the change in real income.

There are two primary methods of decomposing the effect of a price change into an income effect and a substitution effect. The Hicks method isolates the substitution effect by adjusting the consumer's money income to leave her on the same indifference curve. The Slutsky method isolates the substitution effect by adjusting the consumer's money income so that she can just afford her original consumption bundle. The Slutsky method is operational, but the Hicks method is

---

[22] For a discussion of the problems with the contingent valuation approach, see T. Young and P. G. Allen, 'Methods for Valuing Countryside Amenity: An Overview', *Journal of Agricultural Economics*, 37 (1986): 349–64.

not. The latter, however, is the theoretically correct method.

All Giffen goods are inferior, but not all inferior goods are Giffen goods. For a Giffen good the income effect must outweigh the substitution effect. The uncompensated (or ordinary) demand curve for a Giffen good has a positive slope.

An ordinary demand curve reflects both the substitution effect and the income effect. A compensated demand curve reflects only the substitution effect.

A labour-supply curve can be derived from a price-consumption curve for leisure. The labour-supply curve is positively sloped as long as the substitution effect dominates the income effect. When the income effect becomes stronger than the substitution effect, the labour-supply curve bends backwards.

For an individual who opts to participate in a NIT programme, work effort is less than it is in the absence of any income assistance. But work effort is greater than it is with the current social security system.

A worker may be better off or worse off with a progressive income tax compared with a proportional income tax. Work effort could also be greater or smaller with a progressive income tax compared with a proportional income tax.

The Laspeyres index and the Paasche index both measure changes in the cost of living. The Laspeyres index uses base-period shares of total expenditure for weighting the price changes of the various commodities. The Paasche index uses the current shares of total expenditure as weights for the various price changes. If we are given both these indexes and data on total expenditures in two years, we can make welfare comparisons and sometimes decide whether the consumer is better off or worse off in year 2 compared with year 1.

The traditional theory of consumer behaviour in terms of choices between goods has been extended by Lancaster to choices between characteristics. This theory enables us to study the effects of the introduction of new goods as well as the effects of changes in quality. Non-market characteristics can be valued using the hedonic pricing method or by asking consumers to state their preferences.

Key Terms

Arc elasticity
Characteristics approach*
Cross-price elasticity of demand
Engel curve*
Giffen good*
Hicks method*
Income-compensated demand curve*
Income-consumption curve*
Income effect*
Income elasticity of demand
Inferior good*
Laspeyres index*
Long-run elasticity*
Luxury good*
Necessity*
Negative income tax
Normal good*
Ordinary demand curve*
Paasche index*
Point elasticity
Price-consumption curve*
Price effect*
Real income*
Short-run elasticity*
Slutsky method*
Substitution effect*

Questions

1   Explain the derivation of an Engel curve from an income-consumption curve. What does an Engel curve for an inferior good look like? Explain in words and graphically why both goods in a two-commodity world cannot be inferior.

2   Can a good be inferior at all income levels? How does a dramatic reduction in income affect the demand for a Giffen good?

3   If the demand for a product is perfectly inelastic, what does the corresponding price-consumption curve look like?

4   The price elasticity of demand for table salt is very small. Why is this the case? Could this explain why table salt is seldom advertised at a 'special price' by grocers?

5 A diabetic individual must take a prescribed amount of insulin per time period to avoid severe health risks. Draw the individual's demand curve for insulin. What is the price elasticity of demand?

6 The price elasticity of demand for a given commodity is alleged to be greater:

(a) the more numerous and closer the substitutes.

(b) in the long run as opposed to the short run.

(c) at high prices rather than low prices.

Give supporting arguments in each case.

7 Underdeveloped countries frequently argue that, unless they industrialize, they will remain for ever poor relative to the rest of the world. Does this argument make sense in light of the small (but positive) income elasticities for the agricultural commodities typically produced by many of these countries? Explain.

8 Market analysts often use cross-price elasticities to determine a measure of the 'competitiveness' of a particular good in a market. How might cross-price elasticities be used in this manner? What do you expect the cross-price elasticity coefficient to be if the market for a good is highly competitive? Why?

9 Suppose that, when the price of pork chops in a certain town was £2.20 per kilo, the quantity of chicken sold was 1200 kilos per week. But when the price of pork chops rose to £2.75 per kilo, the quantity of chicken sold increased to 1800 kilos per week. Nothing changed over this period except the price of the pork chops. Calculate and interpret the cross-price elasticity of demand. How are these two products related?

10 An airline is considering introducing an advance purchase fare to supplement its existing economy fare. It conducts a study to assess the likely patronage of such a fare. The accompanying table summarizes the projected weekly sales for various advance purchase sales. The economy class fare is £200.

(a) What is the own-price elasticity of advance purchase tickets when the fare rises from £100 to £180?

(b) What is the cross-price elasticity of economy tickets in response to advance purchase fares when the advance fare increases from £50 to £150?

Advance purchase fare (£)	No. of advance purchase tickets	No. of economy tickets
50	2000	200
100	1200	400
120	900	500
150	600	600
180	200	1000

(c) Would you expect (for the same price change) the cross-price elasticity of advance purchase tickets to economy fares to be lower or higher than your answer to question (b)?

11 Graphically decompose the impact of a price increase into the substitution effect and the income effect using both the Hicks and the Slutsky methods. Assume that the affected good is a normal good.

12 Repeat question 11 for an inferior good.

13 Explain the primary differences between the Hicks and Slutsky methods of decomposing the substitution effect and the income effect.

14 Graphically derive a price-consumption curve. Plot the corresponding compensated and ordinary demand curves. Use the Hicks method in determining the compensated curve. How do these two demand curves compare? Why?

15 Using indifference curve analysis, examine the impact of a higher overtime wage rage on work effort. Consider the case of the worker who typically works overtime without the higher wage rate as well as the worker who does not. Do your conclusions differ? Why? (Assume that leisure is a normal good.)

16 'A main argument against the income tax is the way it affects incentives to work. Just what those effects are is controversial, because raising taxes may encourage people to work more rather than less to maintain their living standards. At some point, however, high taxes become demoralizing; people emigrate, or try to dodge their taxes, or decide that extra work is simply not worth the effort.' Justify this statement.

17 Suppose that the Van Basten family faced the prices given in the accompanying table and purchased the corresponding quantities of the various goods listed in 1987 and 1993.

Good	Price 1987	Quantity 1987	Price 1993	Quantity 1993
A	£ 2	20	£ 5	15
B	5	50	5	60
C	10	30	8	25
D	20	10	30	0
E	100	5	150	10

Assuming that these were the only items purchased, and with 1987 as the base year, compute both the Laspeyres index and the Paasche index for 1993. Is the family better or worse off in 1993 compared with 1987? Why?

18 Consider the following two housing schemes to help poor families obtain better housing: (i) a cash-grant scheme and (ii) a rent-subsidy programme in which recipients locate and choose their own housing in the commercial market and the government pays 50 per cent of the rental price. Draw indifference curves and budget lines with income measured on the vertical axis and quantity of housing measured on the horizontal axis.

(a) What is the economic interpretation of the slope of the budget line?

(b) Show on the diagram the effect of a 50 per cent rent subsidy. If the new quantity of housing purchased is H, how much does it cost the individual to purchase H amount of housing without the rent subsidy? What is the amount of rent subsidy being paid for H?

(c) Show on the diagram how much cash the government has to give a recipient if he or she is to be made as well off as under the rent subsidy.

(d) What is the amount of cash that the government has to provide to the recipient to enable her or him to buy a quantity of housing H at market prices?

(e) Using the results from (a) to (d), compare the cost of providing H amount of housing under the two schemes. Present the results in a table as follows:

	Rent subsidy	Cash grant
Government cost		
Recipient cost		
Total cost		

(f) Prepare a similar table for the case where the recipient is on the same indifference curve under both schemes (question (c)). Note that in this case the amount of housing purchased is different under the two schemes.

19 Suppose that the government introduces a 10 pence per litre petrol tax. Would this tend to increase or decrease the equilibrium quality of petrol?

4 Theory of Production

4-1 Introduction

In the previous two chapters we presented the theory of consumer behaviour. This theory underlies the derivation of demand curves. In this and the following two chapters, we turn our attention to the supply side.

On the supply side things are a little more complicated. We must consider several factors:

1 *Theory of production*: how factors of production are combined to produce outputs or commodities
2 *Cost of production*: how the cost of production is determined
3 *Theory of the firm*: how production is organized

The supply of different goods and services depends on all these factors.

In this chapter we discuss the theory of production, and in Chapter 5 we discuss the cost of production. Actually, the two are closely interrelated and are really like two sides of the same coin. We deal with them in separate chapters only because a single chapter would be very lengthy. Finally, in Chapter 6 we discuss alternative models of the firm or how production is organized.

In the last chapter we assumed that the consumer had no control over the prices of the various commodities. Similarly, we now assume that the firm has no control over the price of its output or the prices of its inputs.

These assumptions are only a matter of convenience. We simply want to proceed step by step. The problem of the pricing of output is covered later in Chapters 8–12, and the problem of the pricing of inputs is dealt with in Chapters 13–15.

4-2 Technological Relationship between Outputs and Inputs

Suppose we want to produce computer games. We need land, buildings, micro-chips, other raw materials, workers, and some machinery. These are called *inputs* or *factors of production*. The output is computer games.

In general, a given output can be produced with many different combinations of inputs. A *production function* is a statement of the functional relationship between inputs and outputs. It shows the maximum output that can be produced from given inputs. It is a *technological relationship*, and summarizes the technology for producing the output.

In abstract terms it is written as

$$Q = f(x_1, x_2, \ldots, x_n),$$

where Q is the maximum quantity of output and $x_1, x_2, \ldots, x_n$ are the quantities of the various inputs. If there are only two inputs, labour L and capital K, we write

$$Q = f(L, K).$$

Not all firms produce the maximum output Q that is possible from given inputs L and K at any point in time. There are two main reasons for this:

1 Some firms may be inefficient. We discuss the problem of efficiency later in Chapter 7 (Section 7-3).
2 Different firms have machines and equipment of different vintages. Not everyone utilizes the latest technology.

Thus, the more efficient firms and those using the latest technology produce more output than other firms, even for the same levels of measured inputs.

In view of these problems, we cannot talk of a single production function for all firms. However, we need not worry about this complication here. We assume that we are considering a typical firm and we want to study the relationship between its output and inputs. Also, we are talking of a *given state of technology*.

To fix these ideas, we first consider a production process with a single variable input and then consider two inputs and substitution between inputs.

4-3 Production with a Single Variable Input: Total, Marginal, and Average Products

Let us say that in the example of production of computer games we have land, buildings, micro-chips, machinery, etc., all fixed at certain quantities. The only input we can adjust is the number of workers (labour). Thus, labour is our only variable input. If the labour input (measured in, say, worker-days) is zero, the output of computer games is, of course, zero. As we increase the labour input, we increase the output of computer games. But there comes a point where increasing labour does not increase the output of the games at all and, in fact, might even decrease it. For example, in a very small factory where 10 workers can produce the entire output, if we employ 100 workers they crowd the factory, get in each other's way, and might spend all their time playing the games!

As we did in the case of the individual consumer where we prepared a table of total utility and marginal utility (Table 2-1 above), we can prepare a hypothetical table of input and output for the production of computer games. There is, however, one major difference. Output or product is measurable in

absolute terms, whereas utility is measurable only on an ordinal scale.

Total, Marginal, and Average Products

Consider the data in Table 4-1, which gives the total output of computer games for different quantities of labour. Total output is usually called 'total product' by economists and is denoted by TP. From these data we can derive the marginal product MP, which is the increase in total product due to a one-unit increase in labour, or $\Delta TP/\Delta L$. We can also calculate average product, which is simply output per unit of labour, or TP/L.

Looking at the MP values, we see that initially MP is increasing. The second and third workers each add more to output than the worker before them. This is intuitively plausible. With only one unit of labour, that worker must do everything; with more workers, they can divide the work and specialize, thus increasing the productivity of each worker.

Eventually, though, MP begins to decline. This is what is known as the *law of diminishing marginal productivity*. It is also sometimes called the *law of diminishing returns*. Formally, the law of diminishing returns states: holding technology and the quantities of all other inputs constant as equal increments of the variable input are employed, a point is eventually

Table 4-1 Total product, marginal product and average product for different levels of input (labour)

Units of input (L)	Total product (TP)	Marginal product (MP)	Average product (AP)
1	100	100	100
2	220	120	110
3	360	140	120
4	460	100	115
5	530	70	106
6	570	40	95
7	595	25	85
8	600	5	75
9	594	−6	66
10	560	−34	56

reached where the increments to output begin to decline.

In the example in Table 4-1 there are increasing returns to labour for the first three units of labour employed. The law of diminishing returns sets in with the fourth worker. (In some cases we might have *constant* returns to labour in between.) The law of diminishing returns is also intuitively reasonable. Remember that capital, land, and so on are fixed. Eventually, additional workers do not have a machine to use or a place to work. Hence they add less to output than earlier workers who had access to ample quantities of the other inputs.

Returning to our example, we see that MP becomes negative with the addition of the ninth worker. This point should not be confused with the point of diminishing returns. As we see later, it is unlikely that firms would ever hire a unit of labour with a negative MP.

We now examine some relationships between total product (TP), average product (AP), and marginal product (MP).

Relationship between the MP and TP Curves

MP is equal to $\Delta TP/\Delta L$. So graphically it is the slope of the TP curve.

1 If $MP > 0$, TP rises as L increases. (The additional labour adds something to output.)

2 If $MP = 0$, TP is constant as L increases. (The additional labour does not affect output.)
3 If $MP < 0$, TP falls as L increases. (The additional labour actually reduces output.)

The law of diminishing returns refers to the decrease of MP—not to its sign. It says that MP may rise or stay constant for a time, but, as we keep increasing the units of the variable input, MP should start falling. It can keep falling and turn negative, or it can stay positive all the time.

Figure 4-1 shows TP curves where the slope is positive, so that $MP > 0$. In the first case the slope is increasing, whereas in the second it is decreasing. In both cases TP is increasing with an increase in the labour input. But in Figure 4-1(a) TP is increasing at an increasing rate (the slope at B is higher than the slope at A), and in Figure 4-1(b) TP is increasing at a decreasing rate (the slope at B is lower than the slope at A). So, although in both cases $MP > 0$, MP is increasing in Figure 4-1(a) but decreasing in Figure 4-1(b).

The total product curve reaches a maximum when $MP = 0$ and then starts declining when $MP < 0$. In Figure 4-2 we show a typical curve that exhibits all these characteristics:

1 $MP > 0$ and increasing (from O to A).
2 $MP > 0$ but decreasing (from A to C).

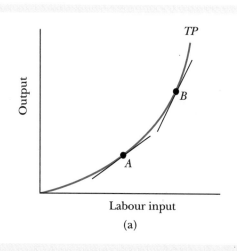
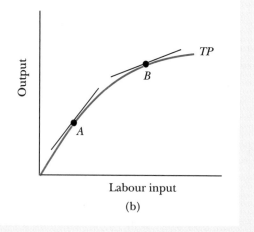

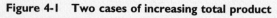

Figure 4-1   Two cases of increasing total product

(a) Increasing *MP*
(b) Decreasing *MP*

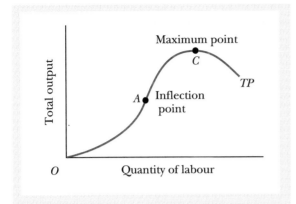

Figure 4-2   A typical total product curve

3 $MP = 0$ at point C.
4 $MP < 0$ after point C.

Point A, where MP stops increasing and starts decreasing, is called an *inflection point* because the curvature of the TP curve changes at this point. It is here that diminishing returns set in.

The *AP* Curve and its Relationship to the *MP* and *TP* Curves

The average product at each point on the TP curve is given by the slope of the line joining this point to the origin. This is illustrated in Figure 4-3(a). Consider point A on the TP curve. Average product is output/labour input $= AB/OB =$ slope of the line OA.

We can graphically examine what happens to AP as we alter the labour input. This is illustrated in Figure 4-3(b). As we increase labour from zero units to J units to K units and to M units, we see that lines from the origin to the corresponding points on the TP curve become steeper; that is, AP is increasing. For points on the TP curve beyond G, lines from the origin become successively flatter. So beyond M units of labour, AP is decreasing. Now if AP is increasing to the left of G and decreasing to the right of G, AP must reach its maximum at M units of labour corresponding to point G on the TP curve. G is the point where a line from the origin is just tangent to the TP curve. So AP is maximized at a quantity corresponding to the point of tangency between the TP curve and a line from the origin.

We also know that $MP = AP$ at the quantity of labour where AP is maximized. So in Figure 4-3(b), $AP = MP$ at M units of labour. How do we know this? MP is the slope of the TP curve, which, at a point, is the same as the slope of the tangent to the TP curve. At point G the tangent line is also the line from the origin. So the slope of the tangent line (or MP) equals the slope of the line from the origin (or AP).

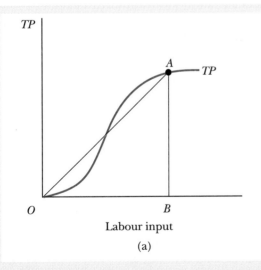

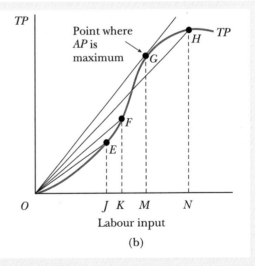

Figure 4-3   Relationship between average, marginal, and total product
(a) Average product at point A on the TP curve is the slope of the line OA (O is the origin)
(b) Average product equals marginal product at M units of labour

This result is also easy to see noting that if, and only if, $MP > AP$, AP rises as L increases, and if, and only if, $MP < AP$, AP falls as L increases.[1] Thus, $MP = AP$ when AP is at a maximum.[2]

The Three Stages of Production

Based on the behaviour of MP and AP, economists have classified production into three stages:

- Stage I: $MP > 0$, AP is rising. Thus, $MP > AP$.
- Stage II: $MP > 0$, but AP is falling. $MP < AP$ but TP is increasing (because $MP > 0$).
- Stage III: $MP < 0$. In this case TP is falling.

No profit-maximizing producer operates in stages I or III. In stage I, by adding one more unit of labour, the producer can increase the average productivity of all the units. Thus, it is unwise to stop production in this stage. As for stage III, it does not pay the producer to be in this region because by reducing the labour input she can increase total output and save the cost of a unit of labour.

Thus, the economically meaningful range is that given by stage II. All these results are shown in Figure 4-4. At the point of inflection A, we saw above that MP is maximized. At point B, since AP is maximized, we have $AP = MP$. At point C total product reaches a maximum. Thus, $MP = 0$ at this point. You should note that the relationships we have discussed do not hold exactly for the illustrative example in Table 4-1. For instance, TP is a maximum when the labour input is 8 units. However, at this point MP is not zero; it is 5. Similarly, AP is maximized for 3 units of labour. But at this point $AP \neq MP$.

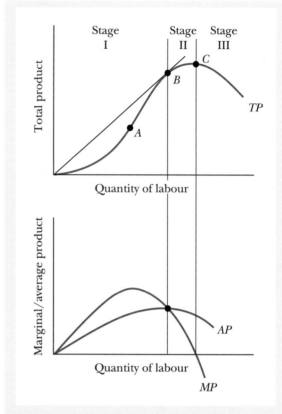

Figure 4-4   Relationship between TP, MP, and AP curves and the three stages of production

These discrepancies result because the input increments are discrete, but the curves we have drawn are continuous. If we can vary the labour input in finer intervals (instead of worker-days, say, worker-hours or worker-minutes) and observe output in finer intervals, then the relationships we have talked about hold true. As it stands, the TP, MP, and AP curves for the data in Table 4-1 are like steps rather than continuous curves. Note, however, that even with discrete data, when AP is rising $MP > AP$, and when AP is falling $MP < AP$.

Another useful relationship is that TP is the area under the MP curve.[3] This is shown in Figure 4-5. If we take a small change ΔL in the labour input, then $MP \cdot \Delta L$ is the shaded area of the thin rectangle. But $MP = \Delta TP / \Delta L$, and, multiplying both sides by ΔL, we see that this area is also TP or the change in output.

---

[1] These relationships hold for all averages and marginals and are intuitively plausible. Suppose that the average height of students in a classroom is 1.75 metres. Another student enters. If the average height increases, what do we know about the height of the marginal student? Clearly, it is higher than the average. Mathematically, $MP = \Delta TP / \Delta L$. But $TP = AP \cdot L$, and substituting yields $MP = \Delta(AP \cdot L) / \Delta L = \Delta L(AP / \Delta L + L)(\Delta AP / \Delta L) = (AP + L)(\Delta AP / \Delta L)$. Since AP and L are always positive, $MP > AP$ if and only if $\Delta AP / \Delta L > 0$. But the condition $\Delta AP / \Delta L > 0$ is merely a restatement of the requirement that AP increases with increases in L. Similarly, $MP < AP$ if and only if $\Delta AP / \Delta L < 0$.

[2] At maximum AP, the AP switches from increasing with increases in L to decreasing with increases in L. Thus, the MP must switch from being greater than AP to being less than AP. So at the point of maximum AP, the two must be equal. Mathematically, at maximum AP, $\Delta AP / \Delta L = 0$. Thus, from fn. 1 we know that $MP = AP$.

[3] $MP = dTP / dL$, so TP is the integral of MP.

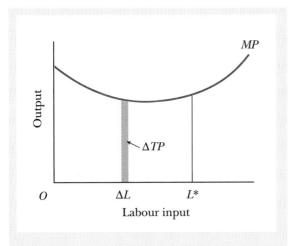

Figure 4-5   Total product is the area under the MP curve

Adding all these rectangular areas, we get the area under the MP curve. But this is equivalent to adding the small changes in total output. This addition gives us the total product.

To find the total product when using an amount of labour input equal to L^*, we just take the whole area under the MP curve from the origin up to point $L = L^*$.

Example 4-1   The Nobel Prize in Economics in 1979

In 1979 the Nobel Prize in economics was shared by Professors Schultz and Lewis. The interesting fact about these two economists is that Professor Lewis is famous for his theory of surplus labour, which essentially argues that the marginal product of labour in the agricultural sector in the less developed countries (LDCs) is zero or even negative,[4] and Professor Schultz held exactly the opposite view—that the marginal product of labour in the agricultural sector of the LDCs is positive.[5]

The theory of surplus labour argues that workers can be removed from the agricultural sector without decreasing agricultural output (because their marginal product is zero or even negative), and these workers can be transferred to the industrial sector at very low

wages and thus aid industrialization at very low cost. The emphasis in the economic development of the LDCs should, therefore, be on rapid industrialization, ignoring the agricultural sector (or even taking away resources from it). This improves the incomes of the people in the LDCs. This idea is also known as *industrial fundamentalism*.[6] The opposite view, that of *agricultural fundamentalism*, argues that the marginal product of labour in agriculture is positive, that transferring labour from there to the industrial sector reduces agricultural output, and that development of the industrial sector has not been hindered by a lack of workers—in fact, the major problem is finding employment for all the urban unemployed. According to this view, increased agricultural production is a prerequisite for increased income and industrialization.

There is also the question of what is meant by saying that the marginal product of labour is zero. Sen distinguishes between the marginal product of a labourer in agriculture and the marginal product of a worker-hour.[7] He defines household labour L as the product of the number of working members N and the hours of work H contributed by each member. Thus $L = NH$. For output to decrease, the quantity of household labour L has to decrease after a decrease in the number of workers N. But this may not necessarily happen because the remaining workers can contribute more hours of work. Thus, it can happen that the marginal product of L (a worker-hour) is positive, but the marginal product of N (a worker) is zero.

[4] W. A. Lewis, 'Economic Development with Unlimited Supplies of Labour', *Manchester School of Economic and Social Studies*, 24 (1954): 139–91; also W. A. Lewis, *The Theory of Economic Growth*, Allen & Unwin, London, 1955. This theory has also been propounded by R. Nurkse, *Problems of Capital Formation in Underdeveloped Countries*, Oxford University Press, New York, 1953. Nurkse talks of a 'painless' or 'up by the boot straps' process of development. A more elaborate treatment of the surplus labour theory is in J. C. H. Fei and G. Ranis, *Development of the Labour Surplus Economy: Theory and Policy*, Irwin, Homewood, Ill., 1964.
[5] Schultz's views are expressed in T. W. Schultz, *Transforming Traditional Agriculture*, Yale University Press, New Haven, Conn., 1964.
[6] This view was also propounded by the Marxist economist Baran: see P. H. Baran, 'On the Political Economy of Backwardness', *Manchester School of Economic and Social Studies*, 22 (1952): 66–84.
[7] A. K. Sen, 'Peasants and Dualism: With or Without Surplus Labour', *Journal of Political Economy*, 74 (1966): 425–50.

Further discussion of Sen's paper and the implications of the surplus labour theory is beyond the scope of this example. The empirical evidence that has been gathered, however, shows that there is not much support for the theory. Furthermore, the workers transferred from agriculture to the industrial sector are usually so unskilled that their marginal product there might also be zero until they are given enough training.

4-4 Profit Maximization and Input Choice

Earlier, in our discussion on consumer behaviour, we said that consumers maximize their utility. Here, we assume that producers maximize their profit. If the input is free, then producers increase the input until its marginal product is zero. (If TP is at a maximum, $MP = 0$.) In the case of the data with discrete jumps presented in Table 4-1, this maximum output occurs at 8 units of the labour input (just before MP turns negative).

But inputs are not usually free. In this case the input we are considering is labour, and the producer has to pay a price. Suppose the producer pays a price of £50 per unit of labour (working day). The producer hires labour, produces computer games, and sells them at a price. Let us assume that the price of a unit of output is £1. In this case the producer keeps hiring units of labour as long as

Price of a unit of output × marginal product > price of a unit of labour.

The left-hand side is the increase in revenue and the right-hand side is the increase in cost from adding one more unit of labour. As long as the increment to revenues exceeds the increment to costs, the producer's profit increases. As we increase the units of labour, we see that MP diminishes. We assume that the price of output and the price of labour input do not change. In this case, as MP declines revenues start to fall, and there comes a point when the increase in revenue equals the increase in cost. At this point the producer stops adding any more units of input. With further addition, since MP is declining, the additional revenue is less than the added costs, and the producer's profit declines.

Thus, profit maximization implies that a producer with no control over prices increases the use of an input until

Value of MP = price of a unit of input.

But there are two complications to this rule. First, the optimal level of input usage assumes that some of the input is employed. If the producer does not cover costs at this input usage, then the producer may produce nothing and, of course, will hire no variable inputs. We consider this possibility in future chapters.

Second, it is likely that the value of MP equals the price of a unit of input at two levels of input usage. This should be clear by considering the shape of the typical MP curve. But one of these levels of input usage corresponds to stage I. And in this region, we said that it pays the producer to extend input usage since $MP > AP$ and so AP is rising.

In summary, then, if the employer hires any of an input, he hires until the price of the input equals the value of MP. Also, AP must exceed MP at optimal usage.

Let us consider some examples based on the data in Table 4-1. Since the price of a unit of output is £1, what is shown as MP in the table is also the value of MP. If the price of a unit of labour is £50, only 5 units of labour are hired, because for the sixth unit the value of MP is £40 but the labour cost is £50, and thus the firm's profit falls by £10 if the sixth unit of labour is hired.

Suppose that the price of a unit of labour is £100; then the producer hires 4 units of labour (not 1 unit). As we said in the previous section, the usage up to 3 units of labour input corresponds to stage I of production. This is the usage where $MP > AP$, and it pays the producer to extend the usage of inputs.

4-5 Production with Two Variable Inputs

We have until now analysed a single variable factor of production: labour. Consider now the case of two variable factors of production: labour and capital. The question 'what is capital?' is difficult to answer. (In our example it includes buildings as well as machinery.) We discuss this in Chapter 15. For the present, capital is just another factor of production.

First, as an extension of the results for one factor of production derived in Section 4-3, we have the following results. (1) Output is at a maximum when marginal products of both labour and capital are zero. Denoting these by MP_L and MP_K, respectively, we have $MP_L = MP_K = 0$. Note that the definition of the MP of an input is essentially unchanged. MP_K is the increase in TP due to a one-unit increase in K, holding labour constant. (2) Profit maximization implies that: price of labour = value of MP_L, and price of capital = value of MP_K.

Both factors are increased to the point where the values of their marginal products are equal to their respective prices. Again, we are assuming that the producer has no control over output or input prices. As before, the law of diminishing marginal productivity applies to both labour and capital after a certain point.

There are four new things that we have to add when we consider the two factors:

1 The production isoquants
2 The law of diminishing marginal rate of substitution in production
3 The concept of returns to scale
4 The effects of changes in input prices on input choice and output

These items are discussed in order.

The Production Isoquants

The word 'iso' is of Greek origin and means 'equal' or 'same'. An isoquant is a curve along which quantity is the same. In this case, 'quantity' refers to the quantity of output or total product. With two inputs, labour and capital, the isoquant gives the different combinations of labour and capital that produce the same maximum total output.

Figure 4-6 shows two isoquants corresponding to two quantities of output, Q_1 and Q_2. Q_2 corresponds to a higher level of output than Q_1. (We explain in the next section why, like indifference curves, they are convex to the origin.) The primary difference between isoquants and indifference curves is that in the case of indifference curves all we can talk about is higher or lower levels of utility; in the case of isoquants we can say *by how much* Q_2 exceeds Q_1 in Figure 4-6.

We saw in the case of indifference curves that, as more and more of a good is consumed, the good may become a 'bad' and the indifference curve turns

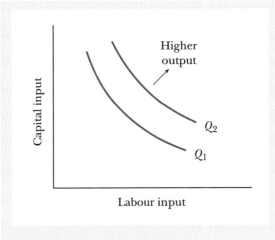

Figure 4-6   Production isoquants

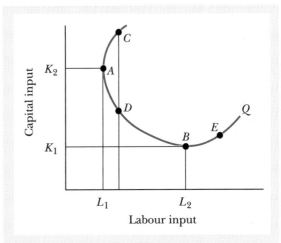

Figure 4-7   Upward and backward-bending isoquants

backward and upward. A similar thing happens in production. As more and more units of an input are used, after a certain point the successive units contribute negatively to production, and, hence, more of the other input is needed to compensate for this and maintain output. Figure 4-7 shows a production isoquant that is backward-bending and upward-sloping after a while. With more than K_2 units of capital, MP_K is negative. If we use more than K_2 units of capital, additional units of labour must also be hired to maintain constant output. Similarly, beyond L_2 units of labour, MP_L is negative.

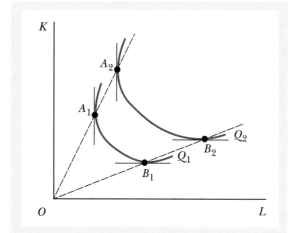

Figure 4-8 Ridge lines and the economic region of production

We have said that it makes little sense to hire a unit of input whose MP is negative. The isoquant in Figure 4-7 should reinforce this idea. Both input bundle C and input bundle A produce the same total output. But input bundle C contains more capital and more labour; this bundle must therefore be more expensive and would not be chosen. The same argument can be made to rule out input bundle E or any other bundle lying on a portion of the isoquant where the slope is positive. Only the negatively sloped segment of the isoquant (AB) is economically feasible.

The economic region of production

In Figure 4-7 we saw that the segment AB is the economically feasible portion of the isoquant for Q. If we consider such feasible portions of all the isoquants, then the region comprised of these portions is called the *economic region of production*. This is the region in which a producer operates. It is illustrated in Figure 4-8. The lines OA_1A_2 and OB_1B_2 are called *ridge lines*. They give the boundary of the economic region of production. We have drawn them as straight lines, but they need not always be.[8] The region between the lines OA_1A_2 and OB_1B_2 is the economic region of production.

---

[8] They are straight lines if the isoquants are radial blowups of a single isoquant.

Example 4-2 The Production of Health Care Services

The production of health services has a number of inputs, including doctors' and nurses' time, hospital buildings, medical equipment, and so on. Thus, we can show the production of health services by a production isoquant. One of the major objectives of the health service reforms in the UK is to introduce elements of competition and financial control. Many hospitals have become self-governing and have established contracts with health authorities to provide services. In effect, the government has created an internal market in health care. It is hoped that the greater competition and accountability will improve the productive efficiency of the health service.

This may, however, prove difficult to achieve. Even though hospital managers may wish to alter the mix of inputs used (for instance, substitute capital for labour or increase the hours of nurses and reduce the hours of doctors) in order to achieve more efficient production, this may not be possible immediately. There are rules and regulations in health care which may prevent a change in the input mix. Some of the rules are needed to ensure a safe service, while others relate to restrictive labour practices preventing a change in the mix of staff. Thus, it may take considerable time for the move from A to B in Figure 4-9 to take place. The consequence of this, as Normand

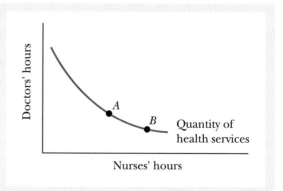

Figure 4-9 An isoquant for the production of health services

points out,[9] is that it is difficult to estimate production functions for health care services since we do not observe many of the technically feasible combinations of factors.

Marginal Rate of Technical Substitution and Elasticity of Substitution*

In the preceding section we depicted the isoquants as convex to the origin. We now explain the reasoning behind this. As with the case of indifference curves, we can define a marginal rate of substitution. In this case it is called the *marginal rate of technical substitution* (MRTS), since it is based on the technology of production. It is formally defined in the case of two inputs, labour and capital, as the amount of capital that can be replaced by an extra unit of labour, without affecting total output:

$$MRTS_{L \text{ for } K} = \left| \frac{\Delta K}{\Delta L} \right|,$$

holding Q constant, where Q = output, ΔK is the change in the capital input, and ΔL is the change in the labour input. This is shown in Figure 4-10. Since $\Delta K / \Delta L$ is the slope of the isoquant, the MRTS is given by the absolute slope of the isoquant.

There is a simple relationship between $MRTS_{L \text{ for } K}$ and the marginal products MP_L and MP_K of labour and capital, respectively. Since along an isoquant the level of output remains the same, if ΔL units of L are substituted for ΔK units of K, the increase in output due to ΔL units of L (namely, $\Delta L \cdot MP_L$) should match the decrease in output due to a decrease of ΔK units of K (namely, $\Delta K \cdot MP_K$). In other words, along an isoquant,

$$|\Delta L \cdot MP_L| = |\Delta K \cdot MP_K|,$$

which is equivalent to

$$\left| \frac{\Delta K}{\Delta L} \right| = \frac{MP_L}{MP_K}.$$

However, $|\Delta K / \Delta L|$ is equal to the $MRTS_{L \text{ for } K}$, and hence we get the following expression for the marginal rate of technical substitution of L for K as the ratio of

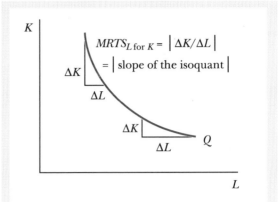

Figure 4-10   Isoquant and the marginal rate of technical substitution

the corresponding marginal products:

$$MRTS_{L \text{ for } K} = \frac{MP_L}{MP_K}.$$

As in consumer theory, we also have in the theory of the producer the *law of diminishing marginal rate of substitution.* As we move down the isoquant, the producer has fewer units of capital and more units of labour. So the MP_L is decreasing while the MP_K is increasing. This, of course, implies that the slope of the isoquant, in absolute terms, is declining, or that the isoquant is convex to the origin. An alternative explanation is similar to the one we gave earlier for the convexity of indifference curves at the end of Section 2-5. If isoquants are not convex but concave to the origin, then we would observe, after drawing in the firm's cost line, the producer using only one input—labour or capital—but not both. But this is contrary to our empirical observation. Since the argument is similar, we leave this as an exercise.

Earlier we said that profit maximization implies: P_L = value of MP_L and P_K = value of MP_K, where P_L and P_K are the prices of a unit of labour and capital, respectively. Thus,

$$\frac{P_L}{P_K} = \frac{MP_L}{MP_K} = MRTS_{L \text{ for } K}$$

at the point of maximum profit, which is a condition similar to the one we derived in the theory of the consumer.

An alternative way of deriving this same condition is to look at the objective of the producer as one of *cost*

---

[9] C. E. M. Normand, 'The Reform of the UK National Health Service', *European Economic Review*, 34 (1990): 625–31.
*A mathematical treatment of some of this material is given in the Mathematical Appendix at the end of the book.

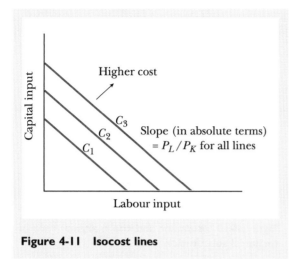

Figure 4-11   Isocost lines

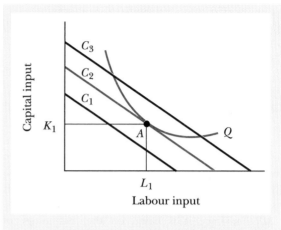

Figure 4-12   Input use under cost minimization

minimization. Clearly, minimizing the cost of the chosen output level is necessary if profit is to be maximized.[10]

Given the prices P_L and P_K of the inputs labour and capital, we can draw an *isocost line* like the budget line in consumer theory. The isocost line gives the combinations of L and K for which the total cost C is the same. The line's equation is given by

$$C = P_L \cdot L + P_K \cdot K,$$

where L and K are the numbers of units of labour and capital, respectively.

The slope of this line is $-(P_L/P_K)$ or, if we consider it in absolute terms, P_L/P_K. A series of isocost lines is presented in Figure 4-11.

Suppose the producer wants to produce an output Q. Then by imposing the isoquant for Q on the isocost lines, we see that the minimum cost corresponds to the level of cost for which an isocost line is tangent to the isoquant, as shown in Figure 4-12. Thus, at point A in Figure 4-12, we have

$$\frac{P_L}{P_K} = \text{slope of the isoquant} = \frac{MP_L}{MP_K} = MRTS_{L \text{ for } K},$$

as derived earlier. Corresponding to A, L_1 gives the amount of labour input used and K_1 the amount of capital input used.

---

[10] Note that cost minimization refers to minimizing the cost of a chosen output. This is a constrained minimization. An unconstrained cost minimization leads to the elimination of all variable inputs and hence to an output of zero.

The elasticity of substitution

As the price ratio P_L/P_K of inputs changes, the slope of the isocost line changes, and we get a new point of tangency and a new level of input usage for labour and capital. Thus, the L/K ratio changes. If P_L/P_K rises, the isocost line is steeper and the L/K ratio falls. There is a measure of responsiveness of L/K to a change in P_L/P_K. This is called the *elasticity of substitution*. It is usually denoted by the Greek letter σ (sigma) and is expressed in absolute terms. It is defined as follows:

$$\sigma = \left| \frac{\text{percentage change in } L/K}{\text{percentage change in } P_L/P_K} \right|,$$

holding Q constant. This concept is useful in deriving elasticities of input demand, which are discussed in Chapter 13.

Note that we define σ holding Q constant, so we observe the changes in L/K as we change P_L/P_K for the same isoquant. That is, we observe points of tangency on a single isoquant. One can define elasticities of substitution holding different things constant, but these elasticities are of limited use.

The elasticity of substitution gives us an idea of how the shares of labour and capital in total cost behave, if input prices change. If $\sigma = 1$, the share of labour in total cost is constant. (Labour's share is simply $(P_L \cdot L)/(P_L \cdot L + P_K \cdot K)$.) If $\sigma > 1$ as P_L/P_K increases, L/K declines by a greater percentage, and hence labour's share falls. If $\sigma < 1$ as P_L/P_K increases, labour's share increases.

A special case is that of $\sigma = 0$, or zero elasticity of substitution. In this case, whatever the change in the

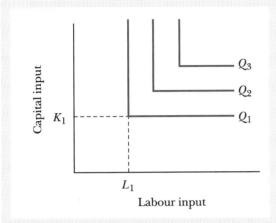

Figure 4-13 Isoquants with zero elasticity of substitution

price ratio P_L/P_K, the input ratio L/K does not respond. This is what is known as *the case of fixed proportions*. In this case the production isoquants look like those in Figure 4-13. For instance, for producing output Q_1, the minimum quantities of the labour input and capital input needed are L_1 and K_1, respectively, but any additions of only one input, keeping the other input constant, does not increase the output at all. That is why the isoquants are right angles. For the outputs Q_2 and Q_3 the situation is similar.

Similarities between consumer and producer behaviour

Throughout this chapter, we have mentioned similarities between the theory of consumer behaviour and the theory of producer behaviour. A summary of these similarities is presented in Table 4-2.

The Expansion Path and Returns to Scale*

In Figure 4-12 we considered the optimal input combination and the minimum cost for producing an output Q. We can do this for various levels of output. The points of tangency then give us the minimum cost and the optimal input usage for successive levels of output. The line joining these points of tangency is called the *long-run expansion path*. This is the broken line in Figure 4-14. Note that we keep the input price ratio P_L/P_K constant. It is only the input that is increased. Thus, the slopes of the isocost lines are the same.

It is necessary at this time to distinguish between the *long run* and the *short run*. To economists, the long run is a period of time sufficient to alter the quantities of *all* inputs into the production process. Thus, in the short run some inputs are fixed in quantity; for example, the firm might be stuck with a particular

---

* A mathematical treatment of some of this material is given in the Mathematical Appendix at the end of the book.

Table 4-2   Comparison between the theories of the consumer and the producer

Theory of consumer behaviour	Theory of producer behaviour
1 Consumer	1 Producer
2 Goods X and Y	2 Inputs L and K
3 Tastes are represented by the utility function $U(X, Y)$	3 Technology is represented by the production function $f(L, K)$
4 MU_X and MU_Y	4 MP_L and MP_K
5 Indifference curve	5 Isoquant
6 MRS_X for Y	6 $MRTS_L$ for K
7 (Absolute value of the) slope of the indifference curve $= MRS_X$ for $Y = |\Delta Y/\Delta X| = MU_X/MU_Y$	7 (Absolute value of the) slope of the isoquant $= MRTS_L$ for $K = |\Delta K/\Delta L| = MP_L/MP_K$
8 Consumers are price-takers in the goods markets	8 Producers are price-takers in the input markets
9 Budget line: $(P_X X) + (P_Y Y) = M$	9 Isocost line: $(P_L L) + (P_K K) = C$
10 Consumer *maximizes* the utility from a given money income	10 Producer *minimizes* the cost of a given output
11 At equilibrium, MRS_X for $Y = P_X/P_Y = MU_X/MU_Y$	11 At equilibrium, $MRTS_L$ for $K = P_L/P_K = MP_L/MP_K$

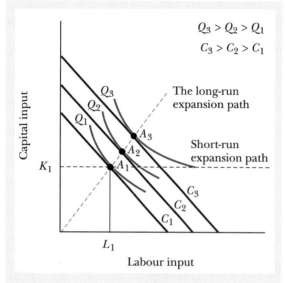

Figure 4-14 The long-run and short-run expansion paths

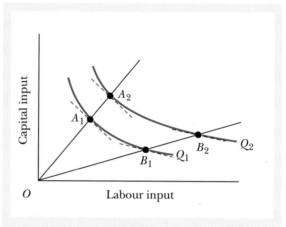

Figure 4-15 Homothetic production functions

capital stock or plant size. But these can be changed in the long run. The precise amount of time required for the adjustment of all input quantities obviously depends on the nature of the product and the state of technology, in particular the inputs that are being used.

When we draw the long-run expansion path, we assume that there is enough time to adjust the quantities of all (both) inputs to the optimal levels for the given outputs. This long-run expansion path tells us how optimal input usage changes in response to a change (or expansion) in output.

In Figure 4-14 the long-run expansion path looks like a straight line. It need not always be. This depends on the shape of the isoquants, which depends on the form of the production function.

In the short run, in the two-input case, we may treat capital as fixed. In this case only the labour input can be changed. If the producer expands output from the level Q_1, assuming that the capital input is fixed at K_1, the *short-run expansion path* is just a straight line with the capital input equal to K_1.

The long-run expansion path is a straight line if the production function is homothetic. A production function is *homothetic* if MP_L/MP_K does not change with any proportionate change in L and K. We explain the concept of a homothetic production function in

terms of two isoquants. The argument is shown in Figure 4-15.[11] Draw any lines OA_1A_2 and OB_1B_2 through the origin. Then the production function is said to be homothetic if

slope of Q_1 at A_1 = slope of Q_2 at A_2

and

slope of Q_1 at B_1 = slope of Q_2 at B_2.

Along OA_1A_2 or OB_1B_2, the ratio of L to K is constant, so that a movement along such a ray represents a proportionate change in L and K. If the slopes of the isoquants are equal along any ray, then MP_L/MP_K must not change with a proportionate change in L and K. But since the input price ratio is constant, all the isocost lines are parallel. Homotheticity now requires that all tangencies between the isocosts and isoquants lie along a single ray from the origin so that the long-run expansion path coincides with such a ray.

A special case of a homothetic production function is the *homogeneous production function*. With reference to Figure 4-15, the production function is homogeneous if, in addition, $OA_2/OA_1 = OB_2/OB_1$.

Returns to scale

Another concept used in the theory of production is that of *returns to scale*. Returns to scale refer to how

---

[11] The argument holds for any two isoquants.

output responds to an equiproportionate change in all inputs. In our case, suppose that labour and capital are both doubled. Then if output doubles we have *constant returns to scale*; if output less than doubles we have *decreasing returns to scale*; and if output more than doubles we have *increasing returns to scale*.

In the case of Figure 4-15, a proportionate change in inputs is a movement along a ray through the origin, such as a movement from OA_1 to OA_2 or from OB_1 to OB_2. The value of the proportion is OA_2/OA_1 or OB_2/OB_1. In other words, if $OA_2/OA_1 = 2$, then both inputs are doubled as we move from OA_1 to OA_2. For constant returns to scale, the change in output must be equal in proportion to the change in inputs. This requires that $Q_2/Q_1 = OA_2/OA_1$. For increasing returns, $Q_2/Q_1 > OA_2/OA_1$. For decreasing returns, $Q_2/Q_1 < OA_2/OA_1$.

Example 4-3   A Cobb–Douglas Function for the Production of Shakespearean Performances

One commonly used production function in applied economics work is the *Cobb–Douglas production function* suggested by Cobb and Douglas in 1928.[12] In its simplest form, with output Q and two inputs, labour L and capital K, it can be written as

$$Q = AL^\alpha K^\beta$$

(or taking logs, $\log Q = \log A + \alpha \log L + \beta \log K$). A is a constant that depends on the units of measurement of Q, L, and K. The coefficients α and β can be interpreted as the elasticities of output with respect to the labour and capital inputs, respectively. Also, $(\alpha + \beta)$ measures returns to scale. For instance, suppose we double L and K. Then the new output Q_1 is given by

$$Q_1 = A(2L)^\alpha (2K)^\beta = 2^{\alpha+\beta}(AL^\alpha K^\beta)$$

$$= 2^{\alpha+\beta} \text{ (old output)}.$$

Thus, if $\alpha + \beta = 1$, output is also doubled, and we have constant returns to scale. If $\alpha + \beta < 1$, output is less

than doubled, and we have decreasing returns to scale. If $\alpha + \beta > 1$, then output more than doubles, and we have increasing returns to scale.

In 1948, Douglas[13] estimated the Cobb–Douglas production function for US manufacturing industries, based on time-series as well as cross-section data, the former based on the period 1899–1922, and the latter based on a cross-section of industries (not firms) from the US Census of 1919. The estimates he obtained were:

	Time series	Cross-section
α	0.73	0.76
β	0.25	0.25

In both cases $\alpha + \beta \cong 1$, thus showing constant returns to scale. However, since the data referred to aggregates over industries or total manufacturing, it is questionable what 'constant returns to scale' means.

Since then, a large number of studies have estimated the Cobb–Douglas function based on time series-data and individual firm data in manufacturing, and based on individual farm data for agriculture.[14] However, during recent years other general functional forms have been used in empirical work.

Gapinski estimated a Cobb–Douglas production function for performances of Shakespeare by the Royal Shakespeare Company from 1965 to 1980.[15] He estimates, for the company's two theatres in Stratford-on-Avon and London, the elasticities α and β. He finds $\alpha = 0.62$ and $\beta = 0.33$. Thus, $\alpha + \beta = 0.95$, which is again close to 1. The measures of output and inputs were as follows:

$Q =$ output, measured as paid attendance
$L =$ labour input, including services of everyone involved: designers, directors, players, programme sellers, secretaries, and carpenters

---

[12] C. W. Cobb and P. H. Douglas, 'A Theory of Production', *American Economic Review*, 18 (1928): S139–165.

[13] P. H. Douglas, 'Are There Laws of Production?', *American Economic Review*, 38 (1948): 1–41.
[14] E. O. Heady and J. L. Dillon, *Agricultural Production Functions*, Iowa State University Press, Ames, Iowa, 1961; A. A. Walters, 'Production and Cost Functions: An Econometric Survey', *Econometrica*, 31 (1963): 1–66.
[15] J. H. Gapinski, 'The Economics of Performing Shakespeare', *American Economic Review*, 74 (1984): 458–66.

K= capital input, measured by depreciation, rental, utilities, etc.

Effects of Changes in Input Prices on Output

The analysis of the effects of changes in input prices on output proceeds along exactly the same lines as the analysis of effects of changes in the prices of goods in the theory of the consumer. If one of the prices, say P_L, falls while the other price and total cost (or production budget) remain constant, then we can separate the effect of the price change into two components: (1) a substitution effect—this is a movement along the original isoquant—and (2) a scale effect—this is a movement to a higher isoquant.

The impact of a fall in the price of labour is illustrated in Figure 4-16, which is essentially the same as Figure 3-11 with the following changes:

1 We are dealing with isoquants instead of indifference curves.
2 On the axes we are measuring inputs L and K instead of goods X and Y.
3 The movement to a higher curve is the scale effect instead of the income effect.

Suppose now that we want instead to analyse the impact of unequal changes in *both* input prices, holding

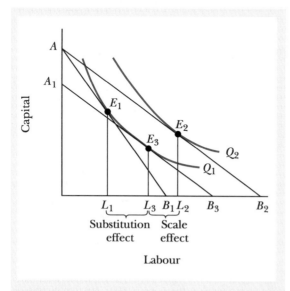

Figure 4-16 Impact of a fall in the price of labour on output

total cost constant. For example, suppose that P_L increases by 20 per cent and P_K increases by 50 per cent. Thus, the new ratio of $P_L/P_K = 1.20/1.50$ times the old ratio, and we can analyse the effect in two steps:

1 Both P_L and P_K rise by 50 per cent.
2 P_L *falls* by 20 per cent, P_K remaining constant. (Note that $1.20 = (0.80)(1.50)$.)

Step 1 can be analysed by drawing a parallel but *lower* isocost line. This is a pure scale effect (E_2 to E_3). Step 2 can be analysed as a decline in the price P_L, holding P_K constant. This involves a substitution effect and a scale effect (E_1 to E_3 to E_2).

For labour, the scale effect is a decrease from step 1 (E_2 to E_3), but the substitution and scale effects are both increases from step 2 (E_1 to E_3 to E_2). Thus, it is not clear whether the quantity of labour input used goes up or down.

For capital, the scale effect from step 1 is a decrease (E_2 to E_3). The substitution effect from step 2 is also a decrease (E_1 to E_3). But the scale effect from step 2 is an increase (E_3 to E_2). The net effect in general is negative, because with both input prices going up it is virtually impossible for the usage of both inputs to go up.

In consumer theory we mentioned that the income effect for a good is sometimes a decrease in quantity as income increases. In that case the good under consideration is called an inferior good. Similarly, in the theory of production, the scale effect for an input can be a reduction in usage as output increases. In this case the input is called an *inferior input* or *regressive input*. In the above analysis we assumed that neither input was regressive.

4-6 Multiple Products: The Production Possibilities Curve

In the previous sections we discussed the case of only one output. In practice, the same resources can be used to produce different products, and the producer has to choose between different product combinations. As with the production function, we discuss the technological possibilities first. Again, we consider only two outputs, X and Y (say, satellite receivers and camcorders). The curve that shows the different combinations of X and Y that the producer can

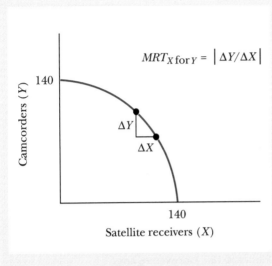

$$MRT_X \text{ for } Y = \left| \Delta Y / \Delta X \right|$$

Figure 4-17   A production possibilities curve

produce with the given resources is called the *production possibilities curve.*

As we did before, we present a table of hypothetical outputs. Table 4-3 gives different combinations of satellite receivers and camcorders the producer can produce with given resources. Figure 4-17 shows the production possibilities curve.

Just as we considered the concepts of *MRS* (marginal rate of substitution) in the theory of the consumer and *MRTS* (marginal rate of technical substitution) earlier, we consider the *marginal rate of transformation (MRT)* in production. If we have two products X and Y, then we define the *MRT* as follows. The marginal rate of transformation of product X for product Y is equal to the reduction in the output of

product Y necessary to increase the production of product X by 1 unit, holding resources constant. It is denoted by MRT_X for Y and is equal to $\left| \Delta Y / \Delta X \right|$, since we consider absolute values of the changes. We show MRT_X for Y in Figure 4-17. To determine the shape of the production possibilities curve, we have to think of what $\left| \Delta Y / \Delta X \right|$ is as we move down the curve. We show that, as we move down the curve (so that we reduce the output of Y and increase the output of X), $\left| \Delta Y / \Delta X \right|$ increases (see the last column in Table 4-3), and hence the production possibilities curve has a concave shape as shown in Figure 4-17.

Intuitively, the reasoning behind this is: when the output of camcorders is high and that of satellite receivers low, the marginal productivity of resources is low in the production of camcorders and high in the production of satellite receivers. Thus, if the producer reduces the production of camcorders by a small amount, the resources released produce a lot of satellite receivers. So, (reduction in output of camcorders)/(increase in output of satellite receivers) is low when camcorder output is higher and progressively rises as camcorder output is reduced and satellite receiver output is increased.

The formal relationship between the *MRT* and the marginal productivities of resources in the production of the two products can be derived as follows. Suppose we consider the labour input. Define

MP_{LX} = marginal product of labour in the production of $X = \Delta X / \Delta L$

MP_{LY} = marginal product of labour in the production of $Y = \Delta Y / \Delta L$.

When we reduce output of Y by ΔY, some labour is released, and this is $\Delta L = \Delta Y / MP_{LY}$. Now we can use this labour to produce X. The increase in the output of

Table 4-3   Outputs of satellite receivers and camcorders that can be produced with given resources

Combination	No. of satellite receivers X	No. of camcorders Y	$MRT_{XY} = \left\| \Delta Y / \Delta X \right\|$
1	0	140	—
2	30	135	5/30
3	60	120	15/30
4	90	105	15/30
5	120	65	40/30
6	140	0	65/20

X is

$$\Delta X = \Delta L \cdot MP_{LX}$$

$$= \frac{\Delta Y}{MP_{LY}} \cdot MP_{LX}.$$

Hence we get

$$MRT_{X \text{ for } Y} = \left| \frac{\Delta Y}{\Delta X} \right| = \frac{MP_{LY}}{MP_{LX}}.$$

At high rates of output of Y and low rates of output of X, MP_{LY} is low and MP_{LX} is high. Hence, $\Delta Y / \Delta X$ is small. As we reduce the output of Y, MP_{LY} goes up, MP_{LX} goes down, and, thus, $\Delta Y / \Delta X$ goes up. This explains the concave shape of the production possibilities curve. By a similar reasoning for capital, we can show that

$$MRT_{X \text{ for } Y} = \frac{MP_{KY}}{MP_{KX}}$$

where

MP_{KX} = marginal product of capital in the production of X

MP_{KY} = marginal product of capital in the production of Y.

These relationships are useful in judging the economic efficiency of production, a topic which we discuss in detail in Chapter 7. For the present, we show how the optimal levels of outputs of X and Y are determined.

Suppose that the prices of products X and Y are P_X and P_Y, respectively. Then the producer's total revenue is

$$R = XP_X + YP_Y,$$

where X and Y are the quantities produced of products X and Y, respectively. We can plot *isorevenue lines* for different values of R as shown in Figure 4-18. For instance, to get revenue of R_1, if the producer produces output X only, the required output is $X_1 = R_1 / P_X$. If the producer produces output Y only, the required output is $Y_1 = R_1 / P_Y$. The producer can produce other combinations in between. The slope of the isorevenue line is (in absolute terms) $\Delta Y_1 / \Delta X_1 = P_X / P_Y$.

Superimposing the isorevenue lines on the production possibilities curve, we get the outputs of X and Y that give the highest revenue (we try to achieve the highest line possible). These outputs are given as X_0 and Y_0 in Figure 4-19. R_1, R_2, and R_3 are three typical isorevenue lines. R_3 cannot be attained. R_1 can

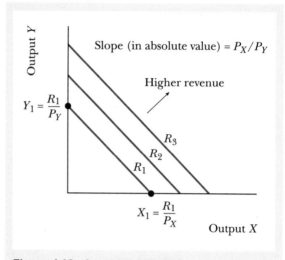

Figure 4-18 Isorevenue lines

be improved upon. The maximum revenue is R_2. The isorevenue line corresponding to R_2 is tangent to the production possibilities curve at point A. The output combination at A gives the maximum revenue. At this point the slopes of the possibilities curve and the isorevenue line are equal.

Thus, revenue maximization implies $MRT_{X \text{ for } Y}$ $= \Delta Y / \Delta X = MP_{LY} / MP_{LX} = MP_{KY} / MP_{KX} = P_X / P_Y$. Note that $MP_{LY} / MP_{LX} = P_X / P_Y$ can be rewritten as

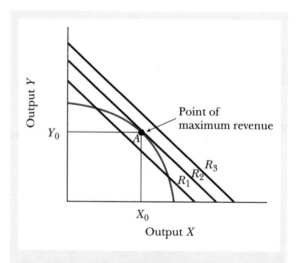

Figure 4-19 Optimal production of two outputs under revenue maximization

$MP_{LX} \cdot P_X = MP_{LY} \cdot P_Y$. What does this mean? The left-hand side is the value of the marginal product of labour in the production of X. The right-hand side is the value of the marginal product of labour in the production of Y. Thus, the producer keeps shifting labour between the production of the two products X and Y until the value of the marginal product is the same in the production of X and Y. The producer does the same with the capital input. Hence, we have

$$MP_{KX} \cdot P_X = MP_{KY} \cdot P_Y$$

for revenue maximization.

We have talked of revenue maximization; in this rather special (very short run) case it is equivalent to profit maximization, because we have assumed that producers have given resources at their command. This means that the costs of inputs are given and fixed.

4-7 An Application: Price Controls on Jointly Produced Goods

Suppose that two goods X and Y are jointly produced. Examples are beef and leather, oil and natural gas. We make the assumption that the outputs are produced in a fixed proportion, and we measure them in units such that 1 unit of the composite good is equal to 1 unit of X and 1 unit of Y. For instance, in the case of beef and leather the composite good is cattle, and we are measuring beef and leather in units such that one cow produces 1 unit of beef and 1 unit of leather. Similarly, 1 unit of petroleum product is equivalent to 1 unit of oil and 1 unit of natural gas.

There is, in this case, a single supply curve (supply of cattle, supply of petroleum products, and so on) but two demand curves—demand for leather and demand for beef, if we are considering cattle. By a vertical summation of the two demand curves, we get the demand curve for cattle. In Figure 4-20, SS is the supply curve of cattle, $D_1 D_1$ is the demand curve for leather, and DD is the summation of two demand curves: demand for leather and demand for beef. (We do not show the demand curve for beef separately.) For $D_1 D_1$ the vertical axis measures the price of leather, and for DD the vertical axis measures the price of a cow, which is equal to the price of a unit of leather plus the price of a unit of beef. (Note that we have defined the units so that one cow produces 1 unit of leather and 1 unit of beef.) The intersection of the demand and supply curves determines the output of cattle. In Figure 4-20

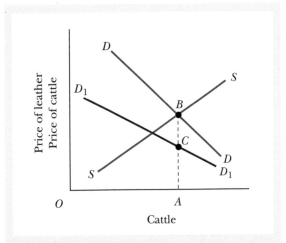

Figure 4-20 Price and output determination with joint products

the output is OA. The price of a unit of leather is AC, and the price of a unit of beef is BC.

In some cases, we find governments imposing price controls on one of the jointly produced products. Oil and natural gas are jointly produced; hence, the analysis of the effects of price controls on natural gas can be analysed within the framework of price determination of joint products discussed above. The result, however, depends on whether X and Y are substitutes in consumption or are independent. In the case of cattle, it is reasonable to assume that leather and beef are not substitutes in consumption. In the case of natural gas and oil, there is some substitution in consumption. However, we begin the analysis by assuming that there is no substitution in consumption.

Suppose there is a price control on one commodity. This produces a kinked demand curve as shown in Figure 4-21: if the price is controlled at the level OA, the demand curve becomes ABD (shown as the black line in the figure).

Returning to the case of the joint products natural gas and oil, a price control on natural gas produces a kink in the demand curve for natural gas. Adding to this the demand curve for oil, we get the demand curve for petroleum products. This is shown in Figure 4-22. $D_1 D_1$ is the demand curve for natural gas. With the price of natural gas controlled at the level OA, the demand curve becomes ABD_1. To this we have to add (a vertical addition) the demand curve for oil. This is done by measuring the vertical distance from each

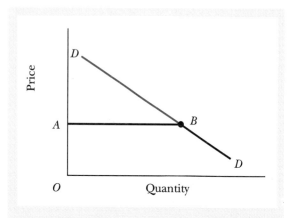

Figure 4-21   Demand curve under price control

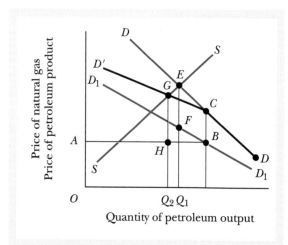

Figure 4-22   Effect of natural gas price control on the price of oil

point on AB, the distance between $D_1 D_1$ and DD (DD is the demand for petroleum products without price controls). Note that the portion CD remains unaffected. Thus, we get $D'CD$ (shown by the black line in Figure 4-22) as the demand curve for total petroleum products.

Without any price controls, the demand curve DD intersects the supply curve SS at point E. Output is OQ_1. The price of natural gas is FQ_1 and the price of oil is EF. With the price of natural gas controlled at the level OA, the demand curve for petroleum output is $D'CD$. This intersects the supply curve at point G. The output declines from OQ_1 to OQ_2. The price of natural gas is at the controlled level HQ_2. But the

price of oil rises from EF to GH. Thus, the result is a fall in output and a rise in the price of oil.

We have until now assumed that the demand for oil and demand for natural gas are independent. However, this is not appropriate, since there is some substitution among the fuels. At the controlled price OA, there is an excess demand for natural gas. This excess demand spills over into the oil market and pushes the demand curve for oil to the right. The net result is a tilt upward (or clockwise) of the curve CD'. This pushes output back towards Q_1 and raises the price of oil further. In fact, it is possible that the output level remains unchanged at the level Q_1. Then the effect is seen completely in the rise in the price of oil.

4-8   Summary

A production function specifies the maximum output that can be produced with a given set of inputs. 'Total product' is another term for total output. The average product of labour is equal to total product divided by the quantity of labour employed. The marginal product of labour is equal to the change in total product divided by the corresponding change in labour, holding all other inputs constant. Average product and marginal product can be similarly defined for any input into the production process.

The law of diminishing marginal productivity states that, as equal increments of a variable input are added to fixed quantities of other inputs, a point is eventually reached where the corresponding increments to output begin to decline. If $MP > 0$, then TP is rising. If $MP < 0$, then TP is falling. If $MP > AP$, then AP is rising. If $MP < AP$, then AP is falling. MP is the slope of the TP curve or the slope of a tangent to the TP curve. AP is the slope of a line from the origin to a point on the TP curve. TP reaches its maximum where $MP = 0$. AP reaches its maximum where $AP = MP$. MP reaches its maximum at the inflection point on the TP curve.

There are three stages of production. Stage I is characterized by $MP > 0$ and $MP > AP$. Stage II is characterized by $MP > 0$ and $MP < AP$. Stage III is characterized by $MP < 0$. The economically meaningful range is stage II.

If the producer employs any of an input, she maximizes profit by hiring to the point where the value of the marginal product equals the price of the input.

(We assume that the producer has no control over output price or input prices.)

A production isoquant consists of all the combinations of two inputs that yield the same maximum output. An upward-sloping isoquant implies that the MP of one input is less than zero. The economic region of production consists of the negatively sloped portions of all isoquants. The marginal rate of technical substitution is the absolute value of the ratio of ΔK to ΔL, holding output constant. Graphically, it is the absolute value of the slope of the isoquant. The law of diminishing marginal rate of substitution implies that isoquants are convex to the origin.

An isocost line consists of all combinations of two inputs that have the same total cost. The absolute slope of the isocost line is the input price ratio.

The elasticity of substitution measures the responsiveness of the input ratio to a change in the input price ratio and is the absolute value of the percentage change in the input ratio divided by the percentage change in the input price ratio, holding output constant. The long-run expansion path demonstrates how the input ratio changes as output expands, holding input prices constant. The path consists of the tangency points between the isoquants and a series of parallel isocost lines. The long run is a period of time sufficient to alter the quantities of all inputs in the production process.

A production function is homothetic if the MP ratio remains the same as long as the input ratio remains constant. If doubling all inputs just doubles output, then the production process is characterized by constant returns to scale. If doubling all inputs more than doubles output, we have increasing returns to scale. If doubling all inputs less than doubles output, we have decreasing returns to scale.

The impact of a change in input price on input usage can be separated into a substitution effect and a scale effect.

The production possibilities curve consists of all combinations of two outputs that can be produced from a given set of inputs. The marginal rate of transformation is the reduction in the output of one product required to increase the output of another product by one unit, holding inputs constant. The MRT is the absolute slope of the production possibilities curve. To maximize profit, the value of the marginal product of each input must be identical in the production of each output.

Key Terms

Average product*
Cobb–Douglas production function*
Constant returns to scale*
Decreasing returns to scale*
Economic region of production*
Elasticity of substitution*
Fixed proportions production process*
Homogeneous production function*
Homothetic production function*
Increasing returns to scale*
Inflection point*
Isocost line*
Isoquant*
Isorevenue line*
Law of diminishing marginal productivity*
Law of diminishing marginal rate of substitution in production*
Long run
Long-run expansion path*
Marginal product*
Marginal rate of technical substitution*
Marginal rate of transformation*
Production function*
Production possibilities curve*
Regressive or inferior input*
Ridge line*
Scale effect*
Short run
Stages of production*
Substitution effect
Total product*

Questions

1 Suppose the production function for compact disc players is

$$Q = 100L^{0.6} K^{0.4},$$

where Q is total output, L is the quantity of labour employed, and K is the quantity of capital in place.

(a) Calculate TP, AP, and MP for the sixth, seventh and eighth units of labour employed if capital is fixed at 240 units.

(b) To which stage of production do these quantities of labour correspond? Why?

2   E. Merckx & Co. produce bicycles using only two variable inputs—bicycle frames and wheels. Draw the isoquants for 100 and 200 units of output. Why do they look like this?

3   Consider the production function $Q = 150L$, where Q is total output and L is the quantity of labour employed. What does the total product curve look like? Describe the corresponding AP and MP curves. Why is it unlikely that a true production function has this form?

4   Consider the production function

$$Q = 5L + 10K,$$

where Q is total output, L is the quantity of labour employed, and K is the quantity of capital employed. Find two input bundles on the isoquant for $Q = 100$. What is the slope of this isoquant? What does the isoquant look like graphically? What law does it violate?

5   Explain why a profit-maximizing firm (using only one variable input) produces in stage II.

6   Best and Marsh Ltd produce a football game called 'The Entertainers'. The company has just completed a study of its production process and it has determined that one more unit of labour could increase its output of the game by 200. However, an additional unit of capital could increase its output by only 150. What are the marginal products for capital and labour? If the current price of capital is £10 and the current price of labour is £25, is the firm employing the optimal input bundle for its current output? Why or why not? If not, which input's usage should be increased?

7   What does the long-run expansion path look like if one input is regressive? Can both inputs be regressive? Why?

8   Explain why an AP curve and the corresponding MP curve must intersect at the maximum point on the AP curve.

9   Is the production process in question 4 characterized by constant, increasing, or decreasing returns to scale? Why?

10   Explain why profit maximization for a two-product firm requires that the marginal rate of transformation is equal to the product price ratio.

11   Suppose that the price of capital doubles while the price of labour triples. If the firm's total expenditure remains constant, can you ascertain whether capital usage increases or decreases? Why? Does your answer change if capital is regressive? Why?

12   Suppose that you wake up tomorrow to discover that you have 12 hours of study time in which to prepare for three exams. For each hour of study you can expect your marks to be as given in the accompanying table. You want to allocate your time to maximize your total numerical score on all three exams. (Each is weighted equally in your final result.)

Hour	Exam A	Exam B	Exam C
1	40	60	39
2	65	90	46
3	80	100	60
4	90	100	72
5	95	90	82
6	99	75	90
7	100	55	96
8	100	33	100
9	99	8	100
10	95	0	100

(a) Calculate the marginal product (score) of each hour of study for each exam.

(b) State briefly the meaning of negative marginal product in this example.

(c) State a general rule for dividing your time to maximize the total score on all three exams. How many hours should be devoted to the preparation of exams A, B, and C?

5 Costs of Production

5-1 Introduction*

In the previous chapter we outlined the theory of production and concentrated more on the production side than on the cost side. As we said, the problem of output maximization given a total cost and the problem of cost minimization given a total output are two sides of the same coin. In this chapter, therefore, we discuss the other side of the coin. We did talk a little about isocost lines in Section 4-6 above (see Figures 4-11, 4-12, and 4-14), but here we pursue the cost side in greater detail.

The relationship between output maximization and cost minimization is outlined in Table 5-1.

In the last chapter we saw that:

1 The production function gives information necessary to trace the isoquants.

2 The input prices determine the budget lines or isocost lines.

3 Production occurs at that combination of inputs for which $MRTS$ = ratio of input prices. Each position of tangency determines a level of output and the associated total cost.

The similarity between output maximization given the budget or total cost and cost minimization given the total output is shown in Figure 5-1. In part (a) of

---

*A mathematical treatment of some of this material is given in the Mathematical Appendix at the end of the book.

Table 5-1 Maximizing output and minimizing cost

Output maximization	Cost minimization
Given (1) input prices (2) a budget or total cost	Given (1) input prices (2) total output to be produced
Find: Maximum output	Find: Minimum cost

the figure we show output maximization given total cost. This procedure amounts to drawing the total cost line and moving to the highest isoquant we can reach. In part (b) we show cost minimization given total output. This procedure amounts to drawing the isoquant for the given output and moving to the lowest isocost line.

Note that both procedures lead to the same level of input use, and hence the same levels of total cost and output, because the cost lines have the same slope and the isoquants the same shape in the two figures.

5-2 Different Concepts of Costs

We have frequently used the word 'cost' without explaining exactly what it means, because the word is in common usage. If we pay £5 per hour to a worker

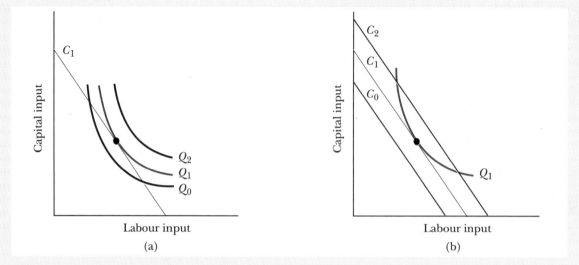

Figure 5-1 Output maximization versus cost minimization

(a) Output maximization given total cost
(b) Cost minimization given total output

whom we employ for 20 hours, then our cost is clearly £100. This is the common usage of cost, which in economics is called *accounting cost* (so called because accountants use this cost concept.) The concept of cost in economics is somewhat different. *Opportunity cost* is the cost concept most relevant to economic decisions.

Opportunity cost is defined as the value of a resource in its next best use. Suppose that Mr Gower quits his job making £50 000 per year and instead opens his own business. Although the accounting cost of Mr Gower's labour to his business is zero, the opportunity cost is £50 000 per year—the earnings he forgoes by working for his own firm. Is this opportunity cost meaningful? We see later that it is very important. If Mr Gower cannot cover this cost, then he may return to his old job.

Opportunity cost can similarly be defined for the other factors of production. For example, the opportunity cost of using a piece of machinery (or building or land) is the value of the product generated in its next-best use. If the machine is owned by the firm, this value could be realized by renting or selling the machine to someone else. The price at which the machine would rent is the opportunity cost of the machine to the producer. This opportunity cost could be less than or greater than the accounting cost, which is likely to reflect only some estimated depreciation and not the market rental value at all.

Several other cost concepts are used in economics: sunk costs, user costs, shadow costs, private costs, social costs, and so on. We define some of these concepts here and some others in later sections and chapters.

Sunk costs are costs only in the accounting sense. These are costs that the producer cannot recover by renting or selling the productive resource. Suppose that a firm purchases a custom-designed piece of specialized machinery with no alternative use. Once purchased, the price of the machine is a sunk cost. The concept of sunk cost is generally related to equipment (or even some labour) that is already in place and that has no alternative use. The opportunity cost of such resources is zero, and hence sunk costs are not relevant to economic decisions.

User cost is a concept that applies to capital equipment; we explain it in Chapter 15 (Section 15-4) when we discuss the pricing of capital services taking into account depreciation, obsolescence, and capital gains.

Shadow cost is the scarcity value of a resource. This is a concept that arises in the evaluation of scarce resources (scarce foreign exchange, scarce skilled labour, and so forth). We discuss this in the next chapter when we consider the linear programming model of production.

In making production decisions, the producer generally calculates only his own costs or the *private costs* of production. These are the opportunity costs of the resources employed in the course of production. But sometimes the producer imposes other costs on society that he does not consider. An example that is often used is that of a paper mill polluting a nearby river. The private costs of production combined with the cost of the pollution make up the full *social costs* of production. If the producer is benevolent, he may take account of the costs of cleaning up the pollution in making any production decisions. Otherwise, some measures may have to be taken to solve this problem of discrepancy between the private cost and social cost. This problem is covered in greater detail in Chapter 16.

In the following sections we ignore this discrepancy between private and social costs. We assume that the costs that are relevant are private costs and that they are opportunity costs.

alternative use value of their time is to estimate their lost earnings. This value can be interpreted as the opportunity cost of students' time. There is a good deal of evidence showing that a degree is worth getting, in the sense that future higher earnings outweigh the earnings that are lost in the short run.

The opportunity costs of education may be private costs to the individual or costs to society as a whole. The cost to the individual student (say, in lost earnings) is not the same as the cost to society. For the student who decides on full-time education rather than joining the labour force, the costs are his or her lost earnings. But the social costs of these lost earnings represent the value of output forgone by society as a whole (assuming he/she is not unemployed). Actually, we should also include unpaid taxes if we want to measure the true cost of lost output.

Example 5-1   The Opportunity Costs of Education

The concept of opportunity cost is central to an understanding of the cost of education. In measuring education costs, we need to distinguish between the money that is spent on education and the opportunity cost of the resources that are used in the education process. The real resources used in education include: teachers, students, equipment, buildings, books, and materials. All these resources have alternative uses. For instance, if teachers were not used to teach they could be used to produce output in some other economic activity; the buildings used for a new university could instead be used for a new technical school. So, all of these resources have an opportunity cost (the value of the resources in their next-best use).

The cost of education is not, then, simply a money cost. Some of the real resources used are purchased (for example, teachers are paid a salary) and we can measure the value of teachers' time in money terms. But not all resources are bought. Students' time has alternative uses and has, therefore, an opportunity cost, even though this is not measured in expenditure (they are not paid a salary). However, the opportunity cost of students' time needs to be included when resources are being valued. The conventional way of measuring the

5-3   Total, Marginal, and Average Costs

In the last chapter (Section 4-5) we considered the long-run expansion path for a producer. As we move the isocost line to higher cost levels, we can produce greater and greater quantities of output. The line joining the successive points of tangency, as shown in Figure 4-14, is the long-run expansion path. All points on the expansion path correspond to the choice of an optimal combination of inputs, so that $MRTS =$ input price ratio. Thus, from the expansion path we obtain the minimum total cost at which various quantities of output are produced.

We can then construct a table showing total cost TC, marginal cost MC, and average cost AC. Table 5-2 presents such a (hypothetical) table. Marginal cost is the cost of the additional unit of output. Mathematically, it is equal to $\Delta TC/\Delta Q$. Graphically, it is the slope of the total cost curve. Looking at the values for MC, we see that it is first decreasing and then increasing. We argue that this pattern is typical.

Average cost is simply cost per unit of output. Mathematically, it is equal to TC/Q. Graphically, it is the slope of a line from the origin to a point on the total cost curve. Looking at the values for AC, we see that it, too, initially decreases and later increases. Again, we argue that this is a typical pattern.

Table 5-2 Total, marginal, and average costs

Units of output	Total cost (TC)	Marginal cost (MC)	Average cost (AC)
0	0		
1	50	50	50
2	90	40	45
3	120	30	40
4	140	20	35
5	150	10	30
6	156	6	26
7	175	19	25
8	208	33	26
9	270	62	30
10	350	80	35

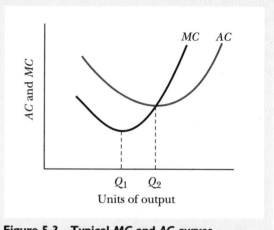

Figure 5-3 Typical MC and AC curves

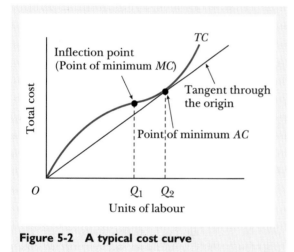

Figure 5-2 A typical cost curve

A typical total cost curve, not drawn to scale for the data in Table 5-2, is shown in Figure 5-2. At the point of minimum marginal cost, the total cost curve has an inflection point (change in curvature). Also, the point of minimum AC is found by drawing a tangent to the total cost curve from the origin (compare Figure 4-3). Note that Q_1 and Q_2 in Figure 5-2 correspond to Q_1 and Q_2 in Figure 5-3 (discussed below).

The same relationships that we considered between AP and MP in the previous chapter (Section 4-3) hold true for MC and AC:

1 If $MC < AC$, then AC falls as output increases.
2 If $MC > AC$, then AC rises as output increases.
3 At the point of minimum AC, we have $AC = MC$.

Typical MC and AC curves satisfying these relationships are shown in Figure 5-3.

Note that the first two conditions are clearly satisfied in the case of the numbers in Table 5-2. As for the third condition, we do not see it because of the discrete steps in the data. The minimum average cost occurs somewhere between 7 and 8 units of output. If output and costs were measured in finer units, this relationship would be satisfied. As it stands, the minimum AC listed is 25 and occurs for 7 units of output, but $MC = 19$ for this level of output. Thus, it looks as if $AC \neq MC$ at the minimum point on the AC curve. The problem is similar to the one we mentioned in the previous chapter with reference to the data in Table 4-1.

Example 5-2 Marginal Costs in Higher Education

At a time of expansion in higher education, it seems reasonable to suppose that policy-makers would like to achieve the expansion at minimum cost. Questions that need to be addressed include: Does the expansion require new departments, or can it be spread across existing departments? Does extra teaching come cheaper in those departments that specialize in teaching than in those specializing in research, or does it not matter? To answer such questions, it would help policy-makers to have information on marginal and average costs.

Estimating such costs in education is not an easy task. While there are problems in estimating the value of the inputs (we discussed this in Example 5-1), it is in the measurement of university output that the fundamental problem lies. It is not clear that we can treat higher education as equivalent to a firm, and if we do it may be misleading. What is the output of a university? Is it the transmission of knowledge via teaching, or is it the extension of knowledge via research? Or is it both?

Despite these problems, Verry and Davies carried out a major analysis of costs and outputs in UK universities.[1] The scope of their study is well beyond our purposes, so we limit our discussion to their findings on average and marginal costs. Verry and Davies estimated cost functions, using 1968–69 data, for both undergraduates and postgraduates across a number of subject areas. They found that postgraduate costs were a good deal higher than undergraduate costs and that they varied significantly across subject groups. Undergraduate marginal costs ranged from £310 in arts and social sciences to £680 in engineering. Postgraduate marginal costs varied from £710 in arts to £2100 in the physical sciences (in 1974 prices). The figures for undergraduates and postgraduates in each subject area were (postgraduate figures in brackets): arts £310 (£710), social sciences £310 (£860), mathematics £350 (£1470), physical sciences £480 (£2100), biological sciences £550 (£1580), engineering £680 (£1610). The research also showed that average costs were invariably higher than marginal costs, suggesting that universities were operating to the left of Q_2 in Figure 5-3.

5-4 Fixed Costs and Variable Costs: Short- and Long-Run

In the previous chapter we distinguished between the short run and the long run. We said that the short run is a period insufficient to alter the quantities of all inputs. So some factors are fixed in the short run. The costs of these fixed factors are called *fixed costs*. Since the quantities of the fixed inputs cannot be changed as output varies, fixed costs do not change with the level of output. Common examples of fixed costs are the costs of land, factory buildings, or even labour under long-term contracts.

The quantities of some other inputs can be altered even in the short run. These inputs are called variable inputs, and their costs are called variable costs. Since the usage of these inputs varies with the level of output, variable costs also vary with the level of output. It is often customary to consider the costs of labour input, materials and energy inputs, and so on as *variable costs*; that is, their amount can be changed depending on the level of production.

What is fixed and what is variable depends on the time horizon. For instance, a factory owner can, over the course of five or ten years, either sell her factory building and equipment or expand it by enlarging it and adding more equipment. Thus, what we considered as fixed becomes variable if the time horizon we consider is long enough. So for long time horizons, or in the long run, all costs are variable and nothing is fixed.

We now formally define the terms:

- *Fixed costs*: costs that do not change with output
- *Variable costs*: costs that change with changes in output
- *Short run*: a period over which the quantities of some inputs (fixed inputs) cannot be changed as output is changed
- *Long run*: a period long enough for all inputs to be changed with changes in output

How short is the short run and how long is the long run? This depends on the industry and production techniques used. Period length varies from firm to firm. If there are no transactions costs and no specialized inputs, then all inputs can be quickly and cheaply adjusted, and the long run is not very long. Also, although one can talk of intermediate runs, for our analysis a classification into two categories is enough.

Corresponding to the above discussion, we can define the total, marginal, and average costs for the short run:

TFC = total fixed costs
TVC = total variable costs
TC = total cost = $TFC + TVC$
AFC = average fixed costs = TFC/Q where
$\quad\quad\quad Q$ = output
AVC = average variable costs = TVC/Q

---

[1] D. Verry and B. Davies, *University Costs and Outputs*, Elsevier, Amsterdam, 1976.

$$ATC = \text{average total costs} = AFC + AVC = TC/Q$$
$$MC = \text{marginal cost} = \Delta TC/\Delta Q = \Delta TVC/\Delta Q$$

Note that marginal cost can be expressed either as the ratio of change in total cost to a change in output, or as the ratio of change in total variable cost to a change in output. This is because fixed costs do not vary with output, so that any change in the total cost must result from a change in the cost of the variable inputs.

Consider the data in Table 5-2. We see that the total costs when nothing is produced are zero. Since fixed costs would remain constant even for this level of output, we can deduce that there are no fixed costs. These data must, therefore, correspond to the long-run situation. We know this is true because the data were derived from the long-run expansion path. This is also the reason why a single column for average cost is presented.

The data presented in Table 5-3 correspond to the short run. This is evident from the presence of fixed costs. Figure 5-4 illustrates the various total cost curves. Since total fixed costs are constant, the *TFC* curve is simply a horizontal line at 200. And because total cost is the sum of total variable costs and total fixed costs, the *TC* curve has the same shape as the *TVC* curve but lies above it by a vertical distance of 200.

Before presenting the *AFC*, *AVC*, *ATC* and *MC* curves graphically, we examine the relationships between them (Table 5-3). We see that the *AFC* curve steadily declines. Recall that $AFC = TFC/Q$. As Q increases, *TFC* remains constant so that *AFC* clearly falls.

Table 5-3 Total, marginal, and average costs in the short run

Output Q	TFC	TVC	TC	MC	AFC	AVC	ATC
0	200	0	200				
1	200	50	250	50	200.0	50	250.0
2	200	90	290	40	100.0	45	145.0
3	200	120	320	30	66.7	40	106.7
4	200	140	340	20	50.0	35	85.0
5	200	150	350	10	40.0	30	70.0
6	200	156	356	6	33.3	26	59.3
7	200	175	375	19	28.6	25	53.6
8	200	208	408	33	25.0	26	51.0
9	200	270	470	62	22.2	30	52.2
10	200	350	550	80	20.0	35	55.0

We also know that *ATC* always exceeds *AVC*. This is because *ATC* is the sum of *AVC* and *AFC*. Furthermore, since *AFC* falls as output increases, *AVC* and *ATC* get closer as output rises.

Our now familiar relationships between marginals and averages hold for both *ATC* and *AVC*. That is, if $MC < ATC$, then *ATC* is falling; if $MC > ATC$, then *ATC* is rising. And if $MC < AVC$, then *AVC* is falling, whereas if $MC > AVC$, then *AVC* is rising.[2] This implies that *MC* must intersect *ATC* at its minimum point and that *MC* must also intersect *AVC* at its minimum point.[3] Looking at our data, we see that the lowest *ATC* listed occurs at 8 units of output. But at this output, $ATC \neq MC$ as one might think it should do. However, the minimum *ATC* actually occurs between 8 and 9 units of output, and we would find $MC = ATC$ at the

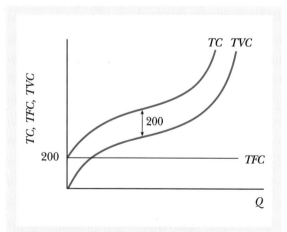

Figure 5-4 The *TFC*, *TVC*, and *TC* curves

[2] $MC = \Delta TC/\Delta Q$. But $TC = ATC \cdot Q$. Substitution yields $MC = \Delta(ATC \cdot Q)/\Delta Q = [(\Delta ATC/\Delta Q) \cdot Q] + [ATC \cdot (\Delta Q/\Delta Q)]$. Since *ATC* and Q are non-negative, $MC > ATC$ if and only if $\Delta ATC/\Delta Q > 0$, which means that *ATC* increases as Q increases. Also, $MC < ATC$ if and only if $\Delta ATC/\Delta Q < 0$, which means that *ATC* decreases as Q increases.

Since $TC = TVC + TFC$ and $\Delta TFC/\Delta Q = 0$, *MC* is also equal to $\Delta TVC/\Delta Q$. But $TVC = AVC \cdot Q$. We can follow the procedure above to get $MC = [(\Delta AVC/\Delta Q) \cdot Q] + AVC$, which indicates that $MC > AVC$ if and only if $\Delta AVC/\Delta Q > 0$, and $MC < AVC$ if and only if $\Delta AVC/\Delta Q < 0$.

[3] At minimum *ATC*, the *ATC* curve switches from falling to rising. Thus, the *MC* curve must switch from lying below the *ATC* curve to lying above it. This means that *ATC* and *MC* must intersect at minimum *ATC*. We can similarly argue that *AVC* and *MC* must intersect at minimum *AVC*.

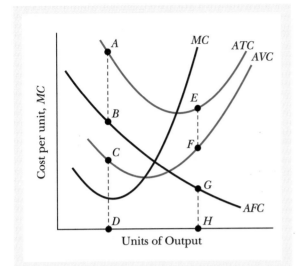

Figure 5-5   The AFC, AVC, ATC, and MC curves

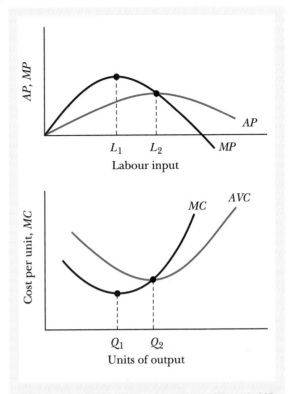

Figure 5-6   Relationship between AP and MP, and AVC and MC

minimum ATC if we could observe our data in finer intervals. The same thing is true with respect to MC and AVC.

Note also that ATC reaches its minimum at an output larger than that at which AVC reaches its minimum. This is because $ATC = AVC + AFC$; and even though AVC has begun to rise, AFC is still declining, pulling ATC down. Eventually, the increase in AVC offsets the decrease in AFC and ATC, too, begins to increase.[4]

The relationship between the various average and marginal curves are illustrated in Figure 5-5. The figure shows typical AFC, AVC, ATC, and MC curves but is not drawn to scale for the data in Table 5-3. Note that the distance between points A and B is equal to the distance between C and D. The same relationship applies between points E and F and G and H. (Why?)

There is also an important relationship between MC and TVC. Since MC is the change in TVC for a unit change in output, TVC is the area under the MC curve. This, of course, means that TC is the area under the MC curve plus TFC.

Factor Productivity and Output Costs

There is a straightforward relationship between factor productivity and output costs. To see this, let us

consider a single variable factor, labour. All other inputs are fixed. AP and MP denote the average and marginal products of labour, respectively. If W is the wage rate and L is the quantity of labour, then

$$TVC = W \cdot L.$$

Hence, if Q is the output,

$$AVC = \frac{TVC}{Q} = W \cdot \left(\frac{L}{Q}\right).$$

But $Q/L = AP$. Hence, $AVC = W/AP$. Also, $TVC = W \cdot \Delta L$. (W does not change. It is assumed given.) Differentiating with respect to Q we get

$$MC = \frac{\Delta TVC}{\Delta Q} = W \cdot \frac{\Delta L}{\Delta Q}.$$

But $\Delta Q/\Delta L$ = marginal product, MP.

Hence, we have $MC = W/MP$. The relationships $AVC = W/AP$ and $MC = W/MP$ show that MC is at a minimum when MP is at a maximum, and AVC is at a minimum when AP is at a maximum. Also, when AP is

---

[4] Mathematically, $ATC = AVC + AFC$. $\Delta ATC/\Delta Q = (\Delta AVC/\Delta Q) + \Delta AFC/\Delta Q$. ΔAFC equals zero.

at a maximum, $AP = MP$. Hence, when AVC is at a minimum, $AVC = MC$. These relationships are illustrated in Figure 5-6, where labour inputs L_1 and L_2 correspond to output levels Q_1 and Q_2.

5-5 Long-run and Short-run Average Cost Curves

In the long run all factors are variable. Thus, the producer has an opportunity of minimizing the costs of the chosen output with respect to *all* factors. This accounts for the fact that the short-run average total cost curve (which we denote by $SRAC$) cannot be below the long-run average total cost curve (which we denote by $LRAC$). In the short run there are more constraints than in the long run (capacity constraint and constraints imposed by other fixed factors), and the constrained minimum is never less than the unconstrained minimum.

Another thing to note is that the $SRAC$ curve and the $LRAC$ curve touch each other, as illustrated in Figure 5-7. The point of tangency corresponds to an output of Q_S. The producer is unable to reduce the cost of this output even in the long run, when fixed inputs can be varied. This implies that the quantities of the fixed factors are optimal for this output.

To understand why the point of tangency is at Q_S and not generally at the lowest point of the $SRAC$ curve, we have to digress a little to discuss what is commonly known as *plant capacity*.

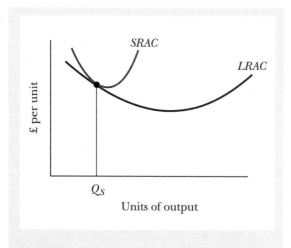

Figure 5-7 Long-run and short-run average cost curves

We have frequently talked of some factors of production being fixed in the short run. One such important factor is plant capacity. When we talk of capital being fixed in the short run, we often mean the stock of capital equipment or plant.

When a producer is building a factory or plant, within some limits, different levels of output can be produced by varying the quantities of the variable input, which we call labour. The producer can operate the plant for 4 hours per day, 8 hours per day, even 24 hours per day. But the machines may break down if operated continuously. Thus, the marginal costs of increasing output beyond a certain level can be enormous.

What is the 'capacity of the plant'? Economists and business people often use this term when referring to the output that corresponds to the minimum average total cost. Capacity is *not* the maximum possible output. Instead, by this definition it is the largest output that can be produced without encountering rising average or per-unit costs.

A producer producing an output smaller than that given by the minimum average total cost is operating with *excess capacity*. A producer may also produce an output greater than that corresponding to the minimum average total cost. In this case the producer is operating *above capacity*.

Why would a producer operate with excess capacity? One reason is that there are alternative ways of producing a given output. The producer can build a smaller plant and operate it at capacity (that is, at the point of minimum average total cost). Alternatively, he can build a larger plant and operate it below capacity. He will choose whichever is cheaper. If the long-run average cost curve is downward-sloping, building a larger plant is cheaper because the short-run average costs are decreasing with increases in capacity. This point is illustrated in Figure 5-8.

The producer wants to produce output Q_S. He can build the plant sizes so that Q_S is the output at which $SRAC$ is minimized. The $SRAC$ curve for this plant size is shown as $SRAC_1$ in Figure 5-8. Alternatively, the producer can build a bigger plant, the $SRAC$ curve which is shown $SRAC_2$ in Figure 5-8, and operate it below capacity. Clearly, the larger plant results in lower average costs and is therefore chosen.

Note that operating a given plant at the minimum point on the average cost curve and producing a given output at minimum average cost are two different

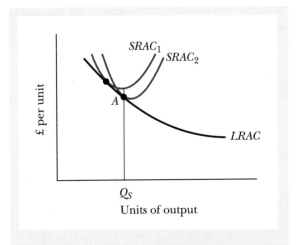

Figure 5-8 Short-run average cost curves for increasing plant sizes when long-run average cost is decreasing

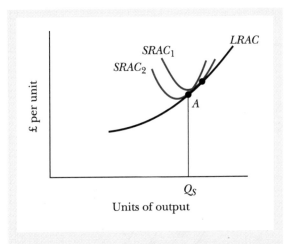

Figure 5-9 Short-run average cost curves for increasing plant sizes when long-run average cost is increasing

things. A profit-maximizing producer is interested in the latter. The two objectives are the same at only one point on the $LRAC$ curve. This is the minimum point of the $LRAC$ curve.

The reverse case—the producer operating above capacity—occurs if the $LRAC$ is increasing with increases in plant size or output. This is shown in Figure 5-9. In this case, to produce output Q_S the producer can operate at the point of minimum average cost on the bigger plant, whose $SRAC$ is given by $SRAC_1$, or can operate above capacity with a smaller plant, whose $SRAC$ curve is given by $SRAC_2$. Clearly, the latter method leads to lower average costs for producing output Q_S.

Some economists find all this puzzling and would like to redefine the phrase 'capacity output'.[5] Instead of defining it as the output for which average costs are minimum, they would rather define it as a rate of output at which the producer has no incentive to change the plant capacity. For instance, to produce output Q_S, in Figure 5-8, if the producer is operating with a plant size that has the $SRAC$ curve given by $SRAC_1$, then the producer has an incentive to change the plant capacity and operate with $SRAC_2$. However,

the producer operating at point A on $SRAC_2$ has no incentive to change the plant size. Under this definition, the capacity output for plant size given by $SRAC_2$ is Q_S, not the minimum point of the $SRAC_2$ curve; that is, *capacity output is that output at which SRAC = LRAC.*

We must also consider the overall relationship between the $SRAC$ curves and the $LRAC$ curve as well as the shapes of these curves. The $LRAC$ curve is an envelope of the $SRAC$ curves, since it touches a series of $SRAC$ curves in such a way that the $SRAC$ curves lie above the $LRAC$ curve. This is shown in Figure 5-10(a), where the $LRAC$ curve is saucer-shaped, and in Figure 5-10(b), where the $LRAC$ curve is a straight line.

In the case where the $LRAC$ curve is a straight line, the $LRAC$ curve consists of the minimum points of the $SRAC$ curves. This is not so in the case where the $LRAC$ curve is downward-sloping, upward-sloping, or saucer-shaped. The $LRAC$ curve includes the minimum point of only one $SRAC$ curve: the $SRAC$ curve whose minimum point coincides with the minimum point of the $LRAC$ curve itself. Otherwise, as shown in Figures 5-8 and 5-9, the minimum point of the $SRAC$ curve is above the $LRAC$ curve. The $SRAC$ curve touches the $LRAC$ curve at a point other than its minimum point for the reason (explained earlier) that the minimum average cost attainable with a given plant is not the same thing as minimum average cost of producing a given output.

---

[5] For example, Friedman. The references are given in Chapter 11 when we discuss the problem of 'excess capacity' in monopolistic competition.

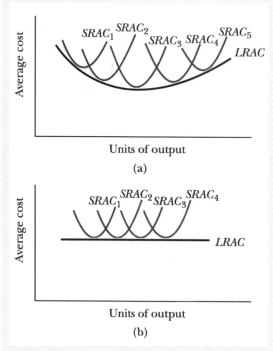

Figure 5-10   The long-run average cost curve is an envelope of short-run average cost curves

(a) A saucer-shaped *LRAC* curve
(b) A straight-line *LRAC* curve

The relationship between long-run and short-run cost curves was introduced by Viner (1892–1970) in a famous article in 1931.[6] Viner was confused between minimum short-run average cost for a given plant, as given by the minimum of $SRAC_1$ in Figures 5-8 and 5-9, and minimum long-run average cost of producing a given output (such as point *A*). He therefore instructed his draftsman to draw a smooth curve of *LRAC* as in Figure 5-10(a). The curve was to pass through the minimum points of all the *SRAC* curves and still be below all of them. The draftsman, who was a mathematician, said that this could not be done. However, Professor Viner insisted, and the result was an impossible figure. Later when the article was reprinted in 1952, Professor Viner refused the

---

[6]J. Viner, 'Cost Curves and Supply Curves', American Economic Association, *Readings in Price Theory*, Irwin, Chicago, 1952, Ch. 10. A reprint of the article of 1931 with a supplementary note in 1950.

opportunity to revise it, saying that he did not want to deprive future teachers and students of the pleasure of discovering the error.

5-6   Long-run and Short-run Marginal Cost Curves

In the previous section we discussed the long-run and short-run average cost curves. We now talk of the corresponding marginal cost curves. We denote the long-run and short-run marginal cost curves respectively by *LRMC* and *SRMC*. We need to study the relationships between (1) *LRMC* and *LRAC*, (2) *SRMC* and *SRAC*, and (3) *LRMC* and *SRMC*. (Note that the relationship between *LRAC* and *SRAC* has been discussed in the previous section.)

In Section 5-3, we discussed the relationship between *AC* and *MC*. Those relationships hold good separately both for *LRAC* and *LRMC* and for *SRAC* and *SRMC*. These relationships, as we recall, are: (1) if $MC < AC$, *AC* falls; (2) if $MC > AC$, *AC* rises; (3) at the point of minimum *AC*, we have $AC = MC$. Figure 5-3 thus holds good for both the long-run and short-run cost curves.

The more important relationship is between *LRMC* and *SRMC*. For this we have the relationship

$$SRMC = LRMC \text{ when } SRAC = LRAC.$$

Thus, at the rate of output Q_S given in Figures 5-8 and 5-9 we have $SRMC_2 = LRMC$. Note that there is only one *LRMC* curve. But, corresponding to each of the *SRAC* curves (or to each plant size), there is a *SRMC* curve.

It is not difficult to see that $LRMC = SRMC$ at the point where $LRAC = SRAC$. Consider the firm operating where $LRAC = SRAC$ or at Q_S in Figure 5-7. Currently, its fixed inputs (as well as its variable inputs) are at the optimal levels. What does it cost to produce one more unit of output? It costs more in the short run because the quantities of the fixed inputs cannot be adjusted. Thus, for outputs greater than Q_S, *SRMC* must exceed *LRMC*. But how much can be saved if output is reduced to one unit less than Q_S? More can be saved in the long run because we can get rid of some fixed units. And since our saving is simply the *MC* of the unit not produced, we conclude that $LRMC > SRMC$ for outputs less than Q_S. Now, combining these two

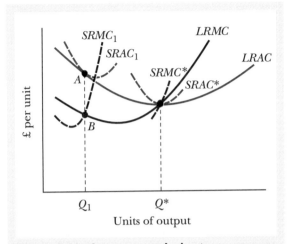

Figure 5-11 Long-run and short-run average cost and marginal cost curves

pieces of information, we know that at Q_s the $SRMC$ curve must switch from lying below the $LRMC$ curve to lying above it. And this, of course, implies that $SRMC = LRMC$ where $SRAC = LRAC$.

This is illustrated in Figure 5-11. The $LRMC$ curve intersects the $LRAC$ curve at its minimum point. Similarly, each $SRMC$ curve intersects the corresponding $SRAC$ curve at its minimum point. For the output Q_1, the tangent $SRAC$ curve is $SRAC_1$ and the corresponding marginal cost curve is $SRMC_1$. Since, as we have shown at the output level Q_1, $SRMC_1 = LRMC$, the intersection of these curves is shown at point B.

Another point we show in Figure 5-11 is the output $Q*$ at which the $LRAC$ is minimum. $SRAC*$ and $SRMC*$ are the corresponding short-run average and marginal cost curves. As we mentioned earlier, at this point the $SRAC*$ curve also has its minimum, and hence at $Q*$ we have $SRAC* = SRMC*$. Thus, at this point

$$LRAC = LRMC = SRAC* = SRMC*.$$

This relationship is used later in Chapter 8 when we discuss long-run equilibrium in a competitive industry.

Note that at output levels less than $Q*$ the intersection points of the $LRMC$ curve with the $SRMC$ curves lie below the $LRAC$ curve. For output levels greater than $Q*$, the intersection points lie above the $LRAC$ curve. You may find it instructive to draw them.

Example 5-3   Why Are Health Care Costs So High?

Outside the government itself, the largest public industry in many countries is the health care industry. There is concern in a number of European countries that the public system of health care provision and insurance is unnecessarily costly. As a result, many countries are considering ways of improving the efficiency of their health care system. In the UK competition in the public provision system has been introduced. In Sweden there have also been moves in this direction. In France, the Netherlands, and Germany there has been recent discussion about introducing a more competitive system of public health insurance.

One of the main reasons for high medical costs is the system of third-party payments in which neither the physicians nor the patients have any incentive to cut costs. Although all of us collectively do bear the costs, there is no incentive for any individual to cut costs.[7] If a test is needed, doctors put patients into hospital overnight because they know that insurance pays the bill. They order a number of tests, again because the insurance pays for them. Their attitude is: 'when in doubt, order'.

The absence of cost consciousness among physicians and patients has been a particular feature of the German national health insurance system.[8] The German system provides mandatory health insurance for persons with an income below a certain level. According to the law, only people with an income above this level may join a private health insurance plan. The public system is financed by a payroll tax, split equally between employees and employers, and the money is put into a sickness fund. Sickness vouchers are issued to insured people when they need treatment and these vouchers are given to the physician when a person is treated. The provider makes a note of the service provided on the voucher,

---

[7] This problem is known as 'moral hazard' and is discussed in greater detail in Chapter 18.

[8] K. Henke, 'What Can Americans Learn From Europeans? A Response', *Health Care Financing Review*, Annual Supplement (1990): 93–6.

which is not signed by the patient. The patient does not receive an invoice for the medical treatment.

Henke suggests that it is the institutional setting and the fact that there are relatively few user charges that lead to the lack of cost consciousness. Patients may insist on over-treatment, and since they have health insurance they do not object to what the physicians order because they are not paying the expenses (except for prescriptions). Doctors have an incentive to treat as many people as possible since they operate in a fee-for-service system. Moreover, they have no incentives to cut costs because they get reimbursed by the various statutory health insurance funds.

Suppose we all took out insurance for our lunch—the cost of whatever we eat is reimbursed by the insurance company. Then each of us would buy the best food, and a number of top-quality restaurants would spring up. The insurance company would charge each of us a 'premium' equal to the average price of a lunch. If the premium is £25 per day, many of us would not want to buy this insurance. But suppose our employer pays the insurance. Then we do not know the hidden costs. The employer deducts the insurance as a business expense for tax purposes and might also reduce our salaries by an amount equal to the after-tax cost of the insurance. Since none of us have any incentive to cut the cost of the lunch, the price of lunch keeps going up and so do the premiums we pay for lunch. The only way to stop this 'lunch inflation' is to abolish the third-party payment.

In the case of health care, the situation is not that simple because there will always be people who suffer serious illness and who, in the German system, need health insurance. One way of improving cost awareness in Germany according to Henke, is to move from a system of benefits in kind to a system of cost reimbursement, in which the patient pays the bill first and is then reimbursed by the sickness fund. Then, costs can be cut by letting individuals bear part of the cost through deductibility and co-insurance. To face the equity issue, every individual can be given a ceiling on out-of-pocket expenses, the ceiling being dependent on income. Doctors, knowing that the patient has to bear the costs in the first instance, would not be as irresponsible as before and would be more cost-conscious in prescribing treatment.

5-7 Returns to Scale, Economies of Scale, and Cost Curves

What determines the shape of the $LRAC$ curve? And why do we argue that it is typically saucer-shaped? We now consider these questions. First, we must define a couple of terms. If $LRAC$ declines as output increases, then we say that the cost structure is characterized by *economies of scale*. If, instead, the $LRAC$ increases as output increases, then we have *diseconomies of scale*. Finally, if $LRAC$ is constant, we have neither economies nor diseconomies of scale.

A firm's costs are determined by its production function, which dictates the quantities of the various inputs that can be used to produce a chosen output, and by the prices of those inputs. Both factors must be considered in analysing costs.

In the last chapter we defined constant, increasing, and decreasing returns to scale. These terms deal with how output responds to a proportionate change in all inputs. Returns to scale in production tell us something about the shape of the $LRAC$ curve, but the link is not as straightforward as you may first believe. For example, constant returns to scale in production do not necessarily imply that the $LRAC$ curve is horizontal. Why? First, firms do not usually vary their inputs in fixed proportions.[9] In fact, a firm producing a large output may employ inputs that the small producer does not find profitable to use. Second, even if the firm did opt to expand all inputs proportionately, it is quite possible that the prices of those inputs would vary (for instance, quantity discounts). So constant or even decreasing returns to scale in production could be associated with economies of scale in costs. What about increasing returns to scale in production? (To double output, inputs must be less than doubled.) Are scale economies present? This time we can answer 'yes' only if input prices do not rise significantly as the firm expands their usage.

Economies of scale might result from increasing returns to scale in production, access to more efficient capital equipment, quantity discounts for inputs, or other factors. Diseconomies of scale could result from decreasing returns to scale in production, increases in input prices resulting from increases in usage by the firm, or managerial limitations.

---

[9] An exception occurs in the case of a homothetic production function with constant input prices.

In this section we have considered the idea of economies of scale. The scale economies that we have discussed are sometimes called *internal economies* and *internal diseconomies of scale*, because the changes in long-run average costs result solely from the individual firm's adjustment of its output.

Economists generally argue that economies of scale are present over smaller outputs but that eventually diseconomies of scale set in. We consider some empirical evidence in Section 5-9.

5-8   Shifts in Cost Curves

Cost curves shift if there are changes in the firm's input supply curves or changes in technology:

1   A decrease in the supply of inputs to the firm causes the family of short-run and long-run cost curves to shift upward. An increase in the supply of inputs to the firm causes these cost curves to shift downward.

2   An improvement in technology or technological progress shifts the family of short-run and long-run cost curves downward because, with the same level of inputs (and hence total cost), we get more output.

As with demand functions, we have to be careful in distinguishing between movements along a given cost function and shifts in the cost function. In Figure 5-12 we show the $LRAC$ shifting down from $LRAC_1$ to $LRAC_2$ either because of technological change or as a result of an increase in factor supply. If a producer operating at point A switches to the output level corresponding to point B, then the observations A and

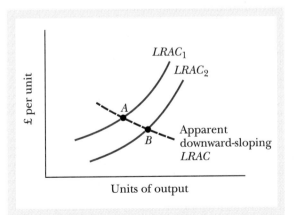

Figure 5-12   Shifts in cost curves and the apparent downward-sloping *LRAC*

B give the mistaken impression that the long-run average cost curve is downward-sloping. Actually, each $LRAC$ curve is upward-sloping, but there has been a downward shift in the $LRAC$ curve. This is an example of a general problem that can occur.

Changes in Input Supply

A change in the firm's input supply can result from a change in the market supply for the input. Such a shift in the market supply curve for the input may be the result of any of the factors we discussed in Chapter 1.

But a change in the firm's input supply may also result from an adjustment in output by several firms in the industry. For example, even if a single firm has no control over input price (the firm's input supply curve is horizontal), as all firms increase output, thereby increasing market demand, the input price increases. The individual firm's input supply decreases, and its average cost curves shift upward.

A change in a firm's average cost curves resulting from an overall increase or decrease in output by several firms is sometimes said to be the result of *external economies* or *external diseconomies* of scale. An external economy of scale occurs when a general expansion of output results in a downward shift of each firm's average cost curves—an economy because the curves shift downward, and external because the individual firm has no control over it. External diseconomies of scale cause each firm's average cost curves to shift upward as all firms expand their output.

External economies and diseconomies do not occur solely as the result of shifts in firms' input supply curves. An overall expansion of output could cause congestion in the transport of output, or extensive pollution that must be cleaned up (external diseconomies). However, new transport terminals or improved roads might come into existence as overall output is expanded (external economy). The important thing to remember is that internal economies and diseconomies determine the shape of a single firm's $LRAC$ curve, whereas external economies and diseconomies cause each firm's average cost curves to shift as several or all firms expand or contract output.

Types of Technological Change

Technological change consists of discovering better and improved methods of producing old products, of introducing better techniques of marketing, organization, and management, and of developing new products. From a purely business point of view, all forms of technological change enable the producer to produce more output with the same inputs as before, and thereby to reduce costs. However, economists like to classify technological change into three categories: (1) labour-saving, (2) capital-saving, and (3) neutral.

Technological change can be depicted as a shift in the production function and, thus, the production isoquants. The type of shift, however, is different for the three categories.

If the production isoquants shift so that the optimal K/L ratio remains unchanged at the same factor–price ratio and the same output, then we have *neutral* technological change. If the isoquants shift in such a way that the optimal K/L rises or the L/K ratio falls, at unchanged factor prices, then we have *labour-saving* technological change. Since the decline in L/K is the same as a rise in K/L, it can also be called *capital-using*. If the isoquants shift in such a way that optimal K/L declines at unchanged factor prices, technological change is called *capital-saving* (or *labour-using*). These three cases are shown in Figure 5-13.

To see whether technological change is labour-saving, capital-saving or neutral, we find the point of tangency A of the isocost lines to the old isoquant Q,

and the point of tangency B of the isocost lines to the new isoquant Q'. If O is the origin, then the slope of OA gives the old K/L ratio and the slope of OB gives the new K/L ratio. The isocost lines are all parallel because the factor–price ratio is unchanged. Assuming that K is on the vertical axis, technological change is

1 neutral if the slope of $OB =$ slope of OA;
2 labour-saving if the slope of $OB >$ slope of OA;
3 capital-saving if the slope of $OB <$ slope of OA.

Note that with a decline in the L/K ratio, we can have a decline in the capital input or even an increase. It is the ratio we are referring to. But in any case, total costs are lower. We are on a lower isocost line.

One important thing to note is that technological change can be labour-saving at one factor–price ratio and capital-saving at another factor–price ratio. Consider the isoquants Q and Q' in Figure 5-14, both corresponding to the same levels of output. Q is the old isoquant, and Q' is the new isoquant after technological change. Consider a factor–price ratio that gives A as the point of tangency for Q. Drawing a parallel tangent to Q', we get the point of tangency A'. The slope OA' is higher than the slope of OA, and thus the technological change is labour-saving. Suppose the price of labour falls relative to the price of capital. The slope of the isocost line (in absolute value) is now

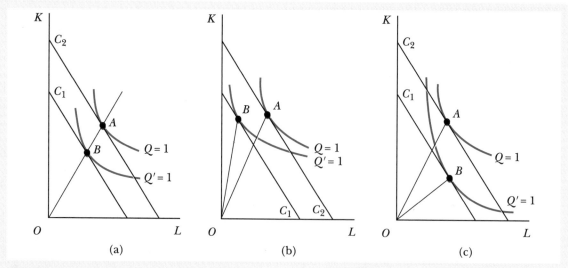

Figure 5-13   Types of technological change

(a) **Neutral**
(b) **Labour-saving**
(c) **Capital-saving**

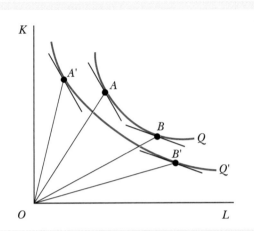

Figure 5-14 Technological change that is labour-saving and capital-saving at different factor-price ratios

lower. The point of tangency to Q is now at B, and drawing a parallel tangent to Q' we find the point of tangency B'. The slope of OB' is lower than the slope OB, and thus the technological change is capital-saving.

Thus, at a high P_L/P_K ratio the technological change is labour-saving, and at a low P_L/P_K ratio technological change is capital-saving. Of course, this need not be always the case. We can come to the reverse conclusion by drawing the isoquant Q rather flat and Q' with a lot of curvature. The important point to note, however, is that whether technological change is labour-saving or capital-saving depends on the factor–price ratio we consider. Of course, we can define a technological change as labour-saving if the L/K ratio declines for all factor–price ratios, with similar definitions for capital-saving and neutral technological change.

Technological Change and Change in Technique

One other point to note is that we should be careful to distinguish between *technological change* and *change in technique*. The former brings in new methods of production which were previously unavailable, while the latter occurs between existing alternative methods that are available. When factor prices change, the producer changes the capital–labour ratio (unless production takes place under fixed proportions). This

is a change in technique. For example, the producer might use a mechanical reaper instead of hand-harvesting if labour costs rise.

Is the shift to a mechanical reaper a change in technique or a technological change? The answer depends on whether the mechanical reaper was available when the producer was hand-harvesting. If it was available but the producer switched to it only when labour costs went up, then it is just a change in technique. This is a movement along a given isoquant. The isoquant that gives the different combinations of capital and labour to produce the same output has as its points the mechanical reaper with small labour input or hand-harvesting with large labour input.

However, if the mechanical reaper became available at the same time that labour costs went up, we have to view this as a combination of both technological change and change in technique. The availability of the mechanical reaper has shifted the isoquants.

Usually, technological change is accompanied by a change in technique. But this need not always be the case. For instance, in the case of the mechanical reaper, the availability of the reaper is technological change, and thus shifts the production isoquant. However, the factor–price ratio might be such that producers do not make any switch and do not change their technique of production. This is shown in Figure 5-15. The isocost line is tangent to Q and Q' at the same point A. At higher prices of labour we move on to Q' and see that the technological change is labour-saving.

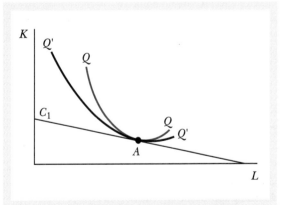

Figure 5-15 Technological change that does not result in a change in technique of production

Technological Change and Cost Functions

Except in the odd cases shown in Figure 5-15, technological change results in a downward shift in the cost functions. With neutral technological change, both labour costs and capital costs go down. With labour-saving technological change, labour costs go down but capital costs may go down, stay the same, or even go up. As we explained earlier, the L/K ratio goes down but the capital input may even go up in absolute terms. The important thing is that total costs go down. (We are on a lower isocost line.) Similarly, with capital-saving technological change, capital costs go down although labour costs may go down, stay the same, or even rise. In all cases, total costs do, of course, go down.

The impact of a change in factor prices on the position of the cost curves is somewhat different. A fall in the price of labour P_L, with the price of capital P_K unchanged, results in a reduction in total costs. As to whether labour costs go down, stay the same, or go up, this depends on the elasticity of demand for labour, which we may define as the percentage change in the quantity of labour demanded divided by the percentage change in the price of labour. (This is discussed in detail in Chapter 13.) If this elasticity is greater than 1 (in absolute value), the decline in P_L results in a more-than-proportionate increase in the labour input, and, thus, labour costs actually go up. If this elasticity is 1, labour costs remain unchanged, and if this elasticity is less than 1, labour costs go down. As for capital costs, they go down in any case.[10] Thus, a reduction in the price of labour when the price of capital remains unchanged is similar in its effects to capital-saving technological change. Similarly, a reduction in the price of capital when the price of labour remains unchanged is similar in its effect to a labour-saving technological change.

5-9   Application 1: Empirical Cost Curves

Economists have for many years examined ways of identifying the costs of real firms. We consider three different approaches to measuring costs.

Are Average Cost Curves U-shaped?

In our discussion of cost curves, we have drawn the average cost curves as U-shaped or at least saucer-shaped (in the case of long-run cost curves). One question that some economists examining empirical evidence have raised is whether curves are really so shaped. One way of finding out about the cost curves of firms is to ask businessmen. This is the approach adopted by Reid in a study of the cost curves of small entrepreneurial firms in Scotland.[11] Reid interviewed the representatives (normally the owner-managers) of 73 small firms in 1985. Each person was shown pictures on sheets of paper (known as 'show cards') of total cost curves and was asked to indicate which picture approximated his or her own firm's cost pattern. Explanations were also provided beneath each picture.

The results showed that 15 per cent of businessmen selected the picture depicting U-shaped average variable, average total and marginal cost curves; 14 per cent selected the picture showing average variable and marginal cost curves that were constant over a wide range of output and then rose sharply once plant capacity was reached; but the clear favourite with 55 per cent of firms was the picture showing falling average variable cost curves at all output levels.

This does not necessarily mean that we should abandon the idea of U-shaped cost curves. They may well be U-shaped, but turn upwards only well beyond normal levels of output.

Frontier Cost Functions

To understand the idea of frontier cost functions, we have to begin with Farrell's classification of the components of inefficiency.[12] In Chapter 4 (Section 4-2) we wrote the production function as $Q = f(x_1, x_2, \ldots, x_n)$. This describes the technically efficient combination of inputs for producing a given output. But some firms may be technically inefficient in that they use more inputs to produce the same output. Thus, the technical relationship between inputs and actual output (Q_A) is more appropriately described by $Q_A \leq f(x_1, x_2, \ldots, x_n)$. $Q = f(x_1, x_2, \ldots, x_n)$ is then

---

[10] Unless the scale effect dominates the substitution effect.

[11] G. Reid, 'Scale Economies in Small Entrepreneurial Firms', *Scottish Journal of Political Economy*, 39 (1992): 39–51.
[12] M. J. Farrell, 'The Measurement of Productive Efficiency', *Journal of the Royal Statistical Society*, A, 120 (1957): 11–28.

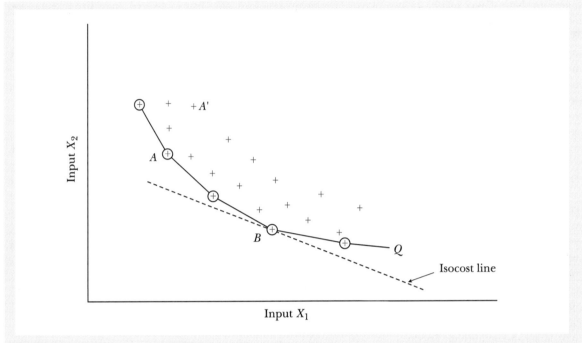

Figure 5-16   A frontier production function

the production frontier in that it shows the various minimum input bundles required to produce given levels of output. We see this in Figure 5-16.

The input bundles are shown by the + signs. Farrell's argument is that only the encircled + signs describe technical efficiency because these are the frontier points for the output Q. Joining the frontier points for each rate of output gives us the firm's isoquant. If a firm is technically efficient, it uses only the input bundles on the isoquant. All the points not on the isoquant are technically inefficient. One method used to estimate technical efficiency in this framework is to eliminate all data points not on the isoquant. The problem with this is that the estimations are prone to measurement error, and so the points identified as efficient may not actually describe the best-practice technology. To deal with this problem, economists, when specifying the production function, incorporate the possibility of random error terms. This allows for both measurement errors and deviations from best practice in the statistical estimations.

In order to arrive at a frontier cost function, we have to recognize that a firm may be technically efficient (i.e. on the isoquant) but not economically

efficient, in that the particular combination of inputs that it is using is not the least-cost combination. In terms of Figure 5-16, the firm at point A is technically efficient but it is not economically efficient. Economic efficiency requires the firm to produce at the least-cost point B (which is tangent to the isocost line), where the $MRTS$ = ratio of input prices. (We saw this result in Figure 5-1.) It may be the case that a typical firm is at a point such as A', where it is neither technically efficient nor operating at least cost.

In a study of the electricity generating industry in England and Wales in the interwar period, Hammond uses a frontier cost function to derive estimates of technical efficiency for individual generating plants.[13] He measures efficiency using an inefficiency index. This is the ratio of the observed unit cost to the technically attainable minimum cost at a given scale of operation. When judged against best-practice techniques, there was found to be substantial inefficiency and unexploited scale economies. Cost savings could

[13] C. J. Hammond, 'Privatisation and the Efficiency of Decentralised Electricity Generation: Some Evidence from Inter-War Britain', *Economic Journal*, 102 (1992): 538–53.

therefore have been made in two ways: (1) by increasing the rate of output (beyond normal levels, as suggested earlier), and (2) reducing the number of inputs. The case of the electricity generating industry is interesting because it has recently been privatized and may return to a less centralized structure similar to that operated in the late interwar period. An insight into the efficiency of the earlier system may be useful in designing efficient structures in the modern privatized system.

The Survivor Principle

The determination of the shape of average cost curves from actual data is a very difficult task. There are several problems of measurement of output and inputs, but the most important problem is measurement of cost.[14] The costs that are usually measured are accounting costs, which do not account for the opportunity costs of managerial skills. Further, different producers are at different stages of adjustment to their long-run equilibrium. Friedman, in fact, argued that one cannot infer anything about the nature of cost curves in an industry by observing different firms at a single point in time.[15]

To avoid these problems of measurement, Stigler suggested an indirect method called the 'survivorship method'.[16] His idea is that competition among different sizes of firms in an industry allows, in the long run, only the most technically efficient firms to survive. Thus, the nature of the industry's long-run cost function is revealed by the characteristics of the surviving firms.

According to Stigler, if firms of many different sizes in the industry survive in the long run, then we can assume that there are no economies or diseconomies of scale. If only large firms survive, we can say that there are economies of scale. If only small firms survive, we can say that there are diseconomies of scale.

One example Stigler studied is that of US firms making steel ingots by the open hearth process. Stigler classified the firms involved into size classes and observed the trends in the number of firms as well as in their total market shares. Stigler concluded that there appear to be economies of scale (falling average costs) up to a size of about 2.5 per cent of industry capacity. Then, there are neither economies nor diseconomies of scale (constant average costs) up to about 25 per cent of industry capacity. The decline in the market share in the largest class indicates diseconomies of scale (rising average costs) thereafter.

The survivor technique has been criticized on both theoretical and empirical grounds.[17] One of the few applications of the survivor method in the UK is by Rees.[18] He used the technique to estimate optimal plant (rather than firm) sizes in 71 UK manufacturing sectors. In only 30 of the sectors was there a clear pattern of an optimal size range. In this case the survivor method does not produce the required results. This conclusion also emerges from most of the survivor studies in the United States.

5-10   Application 2: Plant Closing and Concentration of Output in the Short Run

This is an example of the use of opportunity costs that we discussed earlier (Section 5-2). Consider a producer who owns two identical plants. Because of a decline in available raw materials, the producer has to cut the output by half. Should the producer operate both plants and produce equal output from each, or produce the entire output with a single plant? The problem is illustrated in Figure 5-17.

The total output is OD. Let OB be one-half the distance OD. If the entire output is produced in a single plant, the total cost is $CD \times OD$. However, if half the output is produced in each of the two plants the total costs are twice $AB \times OB$, or $AB \times OD$. Since

---

[14] Several of these problems with a critical review of early studies of cost functions are discussed in J. Johnston, *Statistical Cost Analysis*, McGraw-Hill, New York, 1960.

[15] M. Friedman, 'Comment' on a paper by C. Smith in *Business Concentration and Price Policy*, NBER, Princeton University Press, Princeton, NJ, 1955, pp. 230–8.

[16] G. J. Stigler, 'The Economies of Scale', *Journal of Law and Economics*, 1 (1958): 54–71.

[17] For a discussion of the main points, see D. Hay and D. Morris, *Industrial Economics and Organization: Theory and Evidence* (2nd edn.), Oxford University Press, 1991, pp. 54–7; also W. G. Shepherd, 'What Does the Survivor Technique Show about Economies of Scale?' *Southern Economic Journal*, 34 (1967): 113–22.

[18] R. Rees, 'Optimum Plant Size in United Kingdom Industries: Some Survivor Estimates', *Economica*, 40 (1973): 394–401.

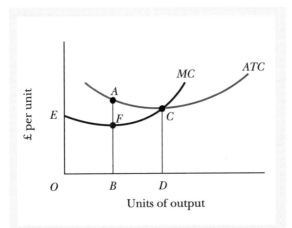

Figure 5-17 Production from a single plant versus production from two plants

Thus, the total variable costs of producing the entire output in a single plant is $OECD$. The total variable cost of producing half the output in each plant is twice the area $OEFB$. If area $OEFB$ is less than area $BFCD$, then it is better to produce half the output in each plant, which is the case in Figure 5-17. If area $OEFB$ is greater than $BFCD$, then it is better to produce the entire output in a single plant. This would be the case if the MC curve intersected the y-axis at a point much higher than point E in Figure 5-17, that is, if marginal costs are very high at low levels of output.[19]

In the preceding analysis we assumed that the marginal costs for the two plants are identical. If they are not, the proper allocation of output between the two plants requires that we equate the marginal costs of the two plants, as shown in Figure 5-18(a), if both the plants are used. We measure the output of plant 1 from

$AB > CD$, it appears that the total costs are lower if all the output is produced in a single plant.

But this reasoning is incorrect. In the short run, producers cannot do anything else with the equipment they have. Thus, the fixed costs are incurred whether or not the plant is under production. Thus, all that is relevant is total variable costs.

We noted earlier (in Section 5-4) that the area under the MC curve measures total variable costs.

---

[19] G. J. Stigler, in his book *The Theory of Price*, Macmillan, New York, 1952, p. 126, gives an example of this problem. During the Second World War the British government embarked upon a programme called 'concentration of production'. Because of shortage of raw materials, the British fabricating industries were operating at low rates of output. The Board of Trade argued that it was inefficient for all plants to operate at half the output and that it would be better if half the plants operated at full output, thus concentrating production. Clearly, this argument is not always correct.

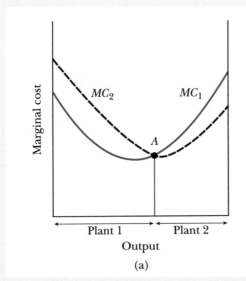

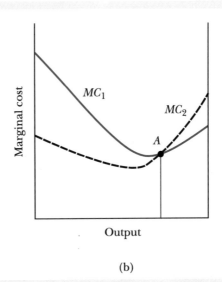

Figure 5-18 Choice between one and two plants and distribution of output between two plants in the short run

(a) Use both plants for production
(b) Choose only one plant

left to right and the output of plant 2 from right to left. Thus, the *MC* curve for the second plant has to be plotted as a mirror image of what it is when drawn normally (with output measured from left to right).

Since the total variable cost is the area under the marginal cost curve, the minimum total variable cost occurs at the point of intersection *A* of the marginal cost curves MC_1 and MC_2 of the two plants. This point gives the division of output between the two plants as shown in Figure 5-18(a).

However, note that the point of intersection of the marginal cost curves is not always the optimal point. This is illustrated in Figure 5-18(b), where the *MC* curve is steep for low levels of output. In this case note that the total variable costs are maximum, not minimum, at the point of intersection *A* of MC_1 and MC_2. (Note that total variable cost is the area under the *MC* curve.) In this case it is optimal to produce the total output from only one plant. Whether plant 1 or plant 2 is chosen depends on whether the area under MC_1 is less or greater than the area under MC_2. The way we have drawn the graph, it is the second plant that is operated.

This example illustrates the problem of how best to distribute a given output between two plants in the short run and when it is optimal to close down one of the plants.

5-11 Application 3: Variable Capital and Fixed Labour in the Short Run

We have frequently referred to capital as the fixed factor and labour as the variable factor. In practice this distinction is not quite so rigid. In fact, one can cite many instances where firms get rid of their capital equipment or acquire some from another firm at short notice. An example of this was the merger between Leyland UK and the Dutch truck company Daf in 1987. Daf took control of the manufacture of trucks. In early 1993 Daf was put into the hands of the receiver, and there are now (at the time of writing) plans for the management at the Leyland plant to buy out the truck division, thereby returning most of the manufacturing to Leyland. Many big corporations buy up small companies when they want to acquire capital equipment in a short time. All this suggests that in some cases capital may not be fixed even in the short run, as we have said frequently.

The case of labour is similar. It too is not as variable a factor as we have often said. There are many 'sunk costs' associated with labour, particularly at the higher end of the skill level. These sunk costs are search, hiring, and training costs. In this case the producer or firm is unlikely to dismiss the employee whenever there is a reduction in output. In the short run, all these employment costs have to be treated as fixed costs. It is only the costs of unskilled workers, who can be hired or fired at short notice, that can be treated as variable costs. The consequences of treating labour as a quasi-fixed factor are discussed in greater detail in Chapter 13.

Another point to note is that in the process of expansion of a producer's output, capital (and other 'fixed' factors) may appear as constraints in the short run but indeed may not be. The producer buys more equipment and hires and trains more skilled labour only if the expansion in output is seen as permanent. For goods that are fads (such as Mutant Ninja Turtles) the producer realizes that the high demand is relatively short-lived and so operates within the constraints of the existing capital equipment and skilled labour and does not expand these factors, especially in the long run.

5-12 Application 4: Cost Curves for Multi-product Firms

In the previous sections we assumed that the producer produces only one product. This assumption was made for the sake of convenience, so as to understand the basic principles. In practice, we encounter many cases where the producer produces several products. In this case we have to allocate the total costs to the different products to use the cost data for pricing purposes.

The case of multiple products can be classified into three categories: (1) joint products, (2) independent products, and (3) products whose proportions can be varied. For simplicity, we consider the case of two products. The theory is similar when we have more than two products.

In the case of *joint products*, the increase or decrease in the production of one of the products results in an automatic proportionate increase or decrease in the production of the other product. The producer has no choice in this case. Examples of joint products are: meat and leather from cows, and cottonseed and lint. In the case of joint products, since the different products are produced in the same proportion, we can just as well consider one product. Thus, the total costs, variable costs, marginal costs, and so on can be calculated using one of the products. There are no additional problems here.

In the case of *independent products* the costs of the different products are independent and, hence, again there are no problems. We just consider each product separately.

In the third case, calculation of costs is problematic. Now the marginal costs of each output depend on the level of output of the other product. Consider the example of fuel oil and petrol. The oil companies have a choice of changing the mix of production of these two petroleum products. Suppose the total cost of the production of petrol and fuel oil for different combinations of these outputs is given by the data in Table 5.4. Then we can easily calculate the marginal costs for the production of one of the outputs at any given level of the other output; for example, when production of fuel oil is at 400 litres, the *MC* of production of petrol when petrol output is 440 litres is

$$\frac{£84 - 70}{40} = \frac{£14}{40} = £0.35.$$

We can calculate such marginal costs for different levels of petrol output (see Table 5-5). Of course, we can plot these data as a series of *MC* curves. If we want to plot the total cost curve from the data in Table 5-4, we need a three-dimensional diagram with the two outputs measured on two axes and total cost measured on the third. Thus, we get a cost mountain. It is to avoid these three-dimensional diagrams that we avoid the discussion of multiple products.

Table 5-4   Total costs of producing two petroleum products

Output of fuel oil (litres)	Ouput of petrol (litres)				
	400	440	480	520	560
	£	£	£	£	£
320	48	60	74	90	108
360	58	71	86	103	122
400	70	84	100	118	138
440	84	99	116	135	156
480	100	116	134	154	176

Table 5-5   Marginal cost of producing petrol at given levels of fuel oil output

MC of petrol when output of petrol is:	Output of fuel oil		
	320	400	480
	£	£	£
440	0.30	0.35	0.40
480	0.35	0.40	0.45
520	0.40	0.45	0.50
560	0.45	0.50	0.55

5-13   Summary

Minimizing cost for a given output yields the same optimal input bundle as maximizing output for the given total cost. The concept of opportunity cost is the cost concept most relevant to economic decisions. It is defined as the value of a resource in its next-best use.

Long-run average cost equals long-run total cost divided by output. Long-run marginal cost equals the change in total cost divided by the corresponding change in output. Marginal cost reaches a minimum at an output corresponding to the inflection point on the total cost curve. Average cost reaches a minimum at an output corresponding to the point of tangency between the total cost curve and a ray from the origin.

In the short run the quantities of some inputs are fixed. The cost of these fixed inputs is called fixed cost. In the short run total cost equals total variable cost plus total fixed cost. And average total cost equals average fixed cost plus average variable cost. Each average cost is equal to the corresponding total cost divided by output.

When *MC* is greater than *ATC*, *ATC* rises, and when *MC* is less than *ATC*, *ATC* falls. Similarly, when *MC* is greater than *AVC*, *AVC* rises, and when *MC* is less than *AVC*, *AVC* falls. Thus, *MC* must intersect both of these average curves at their minimum points. Total variable cost is the area under the *MC* curve.

In the case of a single variable input, if average product is rising then *AVC* falls. And if marginal product is rising, *MC* falls.

The long-run average cost curve is the envelope of the short-run average total cost curves. Short-run average total cost is always greater than or equal to long-run average cost.

Plant capacity is defined as the output corresponding to the minimum point on the short-run average total cost curve. At the point of tangency between a short-run average total cost curve and the long-run average cost curve, short-run marginal cost equals long-run marginal cost. Economies of scale cause the *LRAC* curve to slope downward, whereas diseconomies of scale cause the *LRAC* curve to slope upward. External economies of scale cause the *LRAC* curve to shift downward, and external diseconomies cause it to shift upward.

Holding the input–price ratio and output constant, technological change is classified as labour-saving if the optimal capital–labour ratio increases. It is capital-saving if the capital–labour ratio falls. And the technological change is neutral if the optimal capital–labour ratio is unaffected. All forms of technological change cause a downward shift in the cost functions.

Firms operating at the frontier of efficient production are technically efficient. But a technically efficient firm may not be operating with the least-cost combination of inputs. According to the survivor principle, we can infer the shape of the *LRAC* curve from changes in the size distribution of firms over time.

In the short run, the proper allocation of output between plants requires that we equate the marginal cost of the two plants if both plants are used. We frequently refer to capital as a fixed input and labour as a variable input. In the real world, this is frequently not the case.

If two or more products are produced in fixed proportion, the cost curves can be constructed with reference to a single product. In the case of independent products, each product can be considered separately. In the case of multiple products with variable proportions, two-dimensional cost curves are infeasible.

Key Terms

Accounting cost*
Average cost
Capital-saving technological change*
Change in technique
Economies of scale (external)*
Economies of scale (internal)*

Excess capacity*
Fixed costs
Frontier cost functions*
Independent products*
Joint products*
Labour-saving technological change*
Long run
Marginal cost
Neutral technological change*
Opportunity cost*
Plant capacity*
Private cost*
Short run
Social cost*
Sunk cost*
Survivor principle*
Technical efficiency
Technological change*
Variable costs

Questions

1   What are the accounting costs of your university education? What are the economic costs? How do they compare?

2   Explain why short-run *MC* is equal to the slope of both the *TC* and the *TVC* curves.

3   How is the law of diminishing marginal returns related to the shape of the short-run marginal cost curve?

4   Draw the relationship between the long-run and short-run average and marginal cost curves when the *LRAC* is rising.

5   How does the change in an input's price affect the various short-run cost curves? Consider the case of both a fixed input's price and a variable input's price.

6   According to the survivorship principle, what might the plight of the family farm tell us about returns to scale in agriculture? What are some of the problems with this analysis?

7   How do external economies and diseconomies of scale affect the firm's long-run marginal cost curve? Why?

8   Using an isoquant map and a given input–price ratio, explain how we can derive the long-run and short-run total cost curves.

9 Weakbeer and Co. produces bottled lager. The company faces the following total cost function:

$$TC = 300 + 3Q + 0.02Q^2,$$

where TC is total cost in pounds sterling and Q is the number of bottles of lager produced. What is the corresponding TFC function? The AFC function? The TVC function? The AVC function? Plot these curves as well as the MC curve for the first six bottles produced.

10 If the long-run total cost curve is linear, what do the corresponding average and marginal cost curves look like?

11 Why is a typical short-run average total cost curve more U-shaped than the long-run total cost curve?

12 Examine whether the following statements are true or false. Explain your answer:

(a) Short-run average total cost is never less than long-run average total cost.

(b) Short-run marginal cost is never less than long-run marginal cost.

(c) If the production function exhibits increasing returns to scale everywhere, a firm's long-run average cost curve must be declining.

13 The following are hypothetical costs for an airline for a single flight from London to Stockholm on a Boeing 707 with 180 seats:

- Maintenance and depreciation £2400

- Fuel £5200

- Salary for crew £7200

- Administrative salaries £4200

- Cost of sales and publicity £2200

- Office rent £5600

- Interest on debt £7060

(a) What are the total fixed costs of the flight? What are the total variable costs of the flight?

(b) If the fare is set at a level that covers total costs at 50 per cent of the capacity, what is the fare? What then is the marginal cost to the airline of carrying the ninety-first passenger?

(c) Should the airline agree to supply a charter flight for a group that offers to guarantee the sale of 150 tickets at a price of £225 per ticket? Explain your reasoning. Assume that the charter uses the same equipment with the same costs of operation as the scheduled service.

(d) Now the airline buys a new wide-bodied 747 that holds 400 passengers and operates with essentially the same costs as the 707 except that the fuel costs and salary for crew double. If the airline follows the same pricing policy as before, by how much does the London–Stockholm fare décline for a traveller on a regularly scheduled flight?

14 The following is a production function for a firm that employs two inputs, capital K and labour L, to produce output X. Assume that $X = 0$ if $K = L = 0$. Assume that the wage rate is £10 per unit of labour and the rental price is £15 per unit of capital. Sketch the $LRTC$, $LRAC$, and $LRMC$ curves on the basis of the corresponding short-run curves for $K = 1, 2, 3,$ and 4.

Labour L	Capital K			
	1	2	3	4
1	50	60	70	75
2	60	100	115	135
3	70	115	150	160
4	75	135	160	200

6 Theory of the Firm and Production: Some Alternative Approaches

6-1   Introduction

In the previous two chapters we considered the technology of production. In practice, production is organized within a firm. The term 'firm' is an analytical label for an organization that transforms inputs into goods and services. A firm can consist of a sole proprietor or several thousands of employees (IBM, ICI, and so on). The common feature of all firms is that inputs are purchased and transformed into outputs of goods and services.

The *theory of the firm* is an important topic in microeconomics and is concerned with explaining and predicting the behaviour of firms particularly with respect to pricing and output decisions. Traditional theories of the firm are based on the assumption of profit maximization. This is the assumption we made in the previous two chapters. In order for firms to calculate appropriate prices and outputs, they need information on costs and revenues. We discussed the theory of costs in the last chapter. In Section 6-2 we introduce some key revenue concepts since these ideas are useful not only for the material in this chapter but also for many of the remaining topics in the book.

The theory of the firm also includes the study of the choice of production processes, promotion of sales through advertising, introduction of new products (product innovation), investment decisions, and dividend policy. Modern theories of the firm emphasize the separation of ownership and control.

The managers of the firm control the operations, and the ownership is dispersed among a large number of shareholders. Since output and pricing decisions are made by the managers rather than the owners, the new theories are called *managerial theories of the firm*. We consider three such models: those based on sales maximization, growth maximization, and utility maximization. Another set of theories is the *behavioural theories of the firm*, where the assumption that something is maximized is replaced with an assumption of satisficing behaviour. Principal proponents of this approach are Simon, Cyert and March.[1] A significant contribution of their work has been to focus attention on the internal organization of the firm. We do not discuss the behavioural theories because they depend on ideas from psychology and organizational theory.

Why do Firms Exist?

In a classic paper, Coase raised the question: 'How can economists explain the existence of firms?'[2] In principle, firms are not really necessary. One can imagine separate contracts for each function of a firm.

---

[1] See H. A. Simon, 'A Behavioural Model of Rational Choice', *Quarterly Journal of Economics*, 69 (1955): 99–118; also, R. Cyert and J. March, *Behavioural Theory of the Firm*, Prentice-Hall, Englewood Cliffs, NJ, 1963.
[2] R. H. Coase, 'The Nature of the Firm', *Economica*, 4 (1937): 386–405.

For instance, consider car assembly. One individual could manufacture part of a car and then sell it to another individual, who would add another part and sell it to a third individual, who would add another part, and so on. The assembly line is replaced by a series of individual contracts. The activities of car production are done individually and co-ordinated through prices.

There are two reasons why production is organized through firms rather than through a series of individual contracts: transactions costs, and higher productivity under teamwork.

Transactions and exchange are not costless. Firms economize on transactions. In the absence of firms, we would need multilateral contracts. Each individual would have to negotiate a contract with each person supplying materials and with each person buying the goods. In the example of car assembly, every individual in the chain would have to enter into at least two contracts. Such a complex set of contracts is costly to negotiate. Firms reduce these costs through their use of bilateral contracts. Each individual deals with the firm on a bilateral basis rather than with other individuals on a multilateral basis.

In many activities a larger output can be obtained from a team than from the separate individuals working independently.[3] Group production yields the benefits of specialization. However, group production has some costs. Problems arise because of shirking and 'free-riding'. Under group production, it is often difficult to assess the separate contribution of each individual. The costs of an individual's preferences for on-the-job leisure are shifted to the group. By contrast, under independent production the individual bears all the costs of leisure. This free-riding problem can be solved by hiring a monitor to discipline the team. This implies that the costs of monitoring have to be weighed against the benefits of the greater productivity arising from group production.

Agency Theory of the Firm

An alternative to the managerial and behavioural theories we have mentioned is the agency theory,

suggested by Jensen and Meckling.[4] This is also a managerial theory but with a different emphasis. Economists have long been concerned with the incentive problems that arise when decision-making in the firm is in the hands of managers who do not own a major share of the firm. The managerial and behavioural theories that were suggested in the 1960s (which we discuss below) reject the classical model of an entrepreneur who single-mindedly operates the firm to maximize profits, in favour of different motivations for the managers (sales maximization, growth maximization, utility maximization, satisficing, and so on). The agency theory also rejects the classical model of the firm (an entrepreneur maximizing profits) but assumes classical forms of economic behaviour on the part of agents of the firm. Alchian and Demsetz, and Jensen and Meckling, view the firm as a set of contracts among factors of production. In effect, the firm is viewed as a team, and its members act in self-interest because their survival depends on how best they compete with the other teams. The agency theory has attracted quite a lot of attention in the past 20 years.[5]

In Sections 6-3 to 6-6 we discuss the different managerial theories of the firm that were proposed in the 1960s (the sales maximization, growth maximization, and utility maximization models). They have been superseded by new theories since the 1970s, but, since they form the basis of the new theories, we discuss them here.

In Sections 6-7 and 6-8 we consider the special theory of production when inputs are combined in fixed proportions. This approach gives rise to the concepts of shadow prices and shadow costs, which are often used in planning models. Actually, we could have discussed this approach in Chapter 4, but we include it

---

[3] The advantages of group production are discussed in A. Alchian and H. Demsetz, 'Production, Information Costs and Economic Organisation', *American Economic Review*, 62 (1972): 777–95.

[4] M. C. Jensen and W. J. Meckling, 'Theory of the Firm: Managerial Behaviour, Agency Costs and Ownership Structure', *Journal of Financial Economics*, 3 (1976): 305–60; see also Alchian and Demsetz, op. cit.

[5] Interested readers can refer to the papers in the June 1983 issue of the *Journal of Law and Economics*: E. F. Fama and M.C. Jensen, 'Separation of Ownership and Control', pp. 301–25 and 'Agency Problems and Residential Claims', pp. 327–49; O. E. Williamson, 'Organisational Form, Residual Claimants and Corporate Control', pp. 351–66; B. Klein, 'Contracting Costs and Residual Claims: The Separation of Ownership and Control', pp. 367–74; and H. Demsetz, 'The Structure of Ownership and the Theory of the Firm', pp. 375–90.

in this chapter because it is ideally suited for solving managerial problems.

Example 6-1 How Separate Are Ownership and Control?

The UK evidence on the separation of ownership and control in large companies suggests that, while it is not universal, it is a significant feature.[6] However, one of the problems in measuring this effect is determining the percentage shareholding necessary for effective control. Many previous studies have used an arbitrary figure to indicate owner-controlled companies (say, 10 per cent of shares held by salaried managers). The choice of control threshold is subjective and can lead to different interpretations as to the extent of the separation of ownership and control depending on which figure is used.

This has been shown recently in research by Leech and Leahy. They show that if a 'fixed' rule is used the classification of firms as owner-controlled is very sensitive to the control value used.[7] Using data drawn from a sample of 470 large UK companies in 1983–85, they classified firms according to whether the largest shareholding is set at 5 per cent or more, 10 per cent or more, or 20 per cent or more. If the threshold for the dominant threshold is set at 5 per cent, then 91 per cent of their firms are classified as owner-controlled. But if the threshold is 20 per cent, only 34 per cent of firms are owner-controlled.

Leech and Leahy also show that the extent of ownership control is significantly less pronounced if one uses a 'variable' classification rule instead of applying a 'fixed' shareholding rule. The idea of a variable rule follows that of Cubbin and Leech,[8] in which control is defined in terms of the likelihood of the main shareholder securing a simple majority in a

shareholder vote. The amount of control a bloc of large shareholdings has is the probability of it attracting majority support in a contested vote (assuming that all shareholders vote).[9] Leech and Leahy define the degree of control in terms of whether the largest shareholding has a 90 per cent, 95 per cent, or 99 per cent chance of winning a vote. They use this as a proxy for practical control. They find that 29 per cent of firms are owner-controlled using the 90 per cent definition and only 14 per cent are owner-controlled using the 99 per cent definition.

The Leech–Leahy study is interesting since it shows that the extent of ownership and control depends on whether we use a variable- or fixed-rule definition of control. The variable-rule method reveals a pattern where a relatively small proportion of firms are owner-controlled on the basis of the largest shareholding. The fixed-rule method gives a different pattern depending on the percentage shareholding used.

6-2 Total Revenue, Average Revenue, and Marginal Revenue*

In Chapter 1 we said that a demand curve gives the *hypothetical* quantities that a consumer buys at different prices. From the sellers' point of view, the demand curve tells what price the sale of a number of units will fetch. Note that we are not talking of selling one unit of the commodity at a time. We are asking a hypothetical question as to what price sellers get if they *block-auctioned* different quantities.

If a seller offers 10 units of a commodity for sale and gets £100, then £100 is called the *total revenue* (*TR*). *Average revenue* (*AR*) or per-unit revenue is total revenue divided by the number of units sold, in this case £10. This is actually the *bid price* when 10 units are offered for sale. Table 6-1 shows a demand curve from the sellers' point of view. Note that the average revenue curve is the demand curve. For the data in the table we can compute total and average revenue. Also listed in

---

[6] For a summary of this evidence see D. Hay and D. Morris, *Industrial Economics and Organization: Theory and Evidence* (2nd edn.), Oxford University Press, 1991, pp. 276–81.

[7] D. Leech and J. Leahy, 'Ownership Structure, Control Type Classifications and the Performance of Large British Companies', *Economic Journal*, 101 (1991): 1418–37.

[8] J. Cubbin and D. Leech, 'The Effect of Shareholding Dispersion on the Degree of Control in British Companies: Theory and Management', *Economic Journal*, 93 (1983): 351–69.

---

[9] The principle and assumptions underlying the probabilistic voting model can be found in the paper by Cubbin and Leech, op. cit.

* A mathematical treatment of some of this material is given in the Mathematical Appendix at the end of the book.

Table 6-1   A demand curve from the sellers' point of view

Price	Quantity demanded	Total revenue	Average revenue	Marginal revenue
12	1	12	12	$12 - 0 = 12$
10	2	20	10	$20 - 12 = 8$
8	3	24	8	$24 - 20 = 4$
6	4	24	6	$24 - 24 = 0$
4	5	20	4	$20 - 24 = -4$

the table is marginal revenue (MR). *Marginal revenue* of the nth unit is the *extra* revenue that a seller gets by offering n units instead of $(n-1)$ units for sale. Since marginal revenue is the increase in total revenue for a one-unit increase in the quantity Q offered for sale, we can write[10]

$$MR = \frac{\text{change in } TR}{\text{change in } Q} = \frac{\Delta TR}{\Delta Q}.$$

Graphically, the MR at a point on the TR curve is the slope of the TR curve at that point.

Note that the demand curve (which is also the sellers' AR curve), like the TR and MR curves, is hypothetical. Transactions do not take place at all the points. Examining Table 6-1, we see that AR declines at a rate of 2 per unit, whereas MR declines at the rate of 4 per unit, and MR is equal to zero when TR is a maximum.

Figure 6-1 shows typical AR and MR curves when the demand curve is linear and downward-sloping. Note that OC is half the distance OB. Since the MR curve and the demand curve have the same vertical intercept, this means that the MR curve is twice as steep as the corresponding linear demand curve.[11]

Figure 6-2 shows a typical TR curve for a downward-sloping demand curve. MR is strictly diminishing as Q increases, and since MR at any point on the TR curve is the slope of the TR curve at that point, diminishing MR means that the slope of the TR curve is diminishing. This implies a hump-shaped TR curve. In

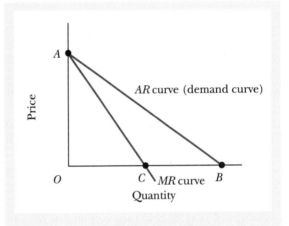

Figure 6-1   Linear AR and MR curves

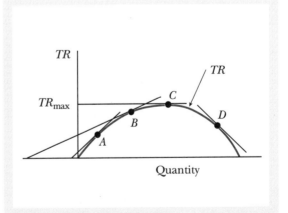

Figure 6-2   A typical TR curve for a downward-sloping demand curve

Diminishing MR implies that the slope of the TR curve diminishes as quantity sold increases

---

[10] For an arbitrarily small change in Q, $MR = d(TR)/dQ$.
[11] Mathematically, we can derive this as follows: $P = a - bQ$ is a linear demand curve. $TR = PQ = aQ - bQ^2$. Hence $MR = d(TR)/(dQ) = a - 2bQ$. Thus, the MR curve is linear. The intercept on the quantity axis (obtained by setting $P = 0$) is $-a/b$ for the demand curve. For the MR curve (at $MR = 0$) it is $-a/2b$. Therefore, OC is one-half of OB in Figure 6-1.

Figure 6-2, the slope diminishes as we go from A to B to C. At point C, or at maximum TR, the slope is zero. After that, the slope is negative as at point D, and continues to diminish or become increasingly negative.

6-3 The Sales Maximization Model

The sales maximization model developed by Baumol is a managerial theory of the firm.[12] It suggests that firms maximize sales revenue subject to a minimum profit constraint. Larger sales give managers satisfaction from greater firm size and the associated prestige. Their salaries and benefits may also be related to sales performance rather than profits. The profit constraint is specified as the minimum level necessary to secure shareholder acquiescence. Baumol suggested that this model is typical of oligopoly behaviour. (We discuss oligopoly in Chapter 11.)

If this constrained maximization problem is solved by the choice of output level, we can show that output is higher under the sales maximization model than under the profit maximization model. This is shown in Figures 6-3 and 6-4. In Figure 6-3 we show the derivation of the profit curve π from the TR (total revenue) and TC (total cost) curves. Profit $\pi = TR - TC$ is a maximum at the output level Q^*, where the slopes

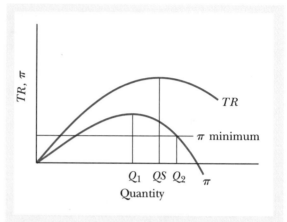

Figure 6-4 Output determination under sales revenue maximization

of the TR and TC curves are equal or where $MR = MC$). It is given by the vertical distance between the TR and TC curves.

In Figure 6-4 we show the constrained maximization. Q_1 is the level of output at which profit is a maximum. Q_2 is the maximum level of output that satisfies the profit constraint. The sales-maximizing firm chooses the output level in the range Q_1 to Q_2 that maximizes total revenue TR. This is the output level QS in Figure 6-4. Note that, at the profit-maximizing output level Q_1, TR cannot reach a maximum since at this point $MR = MC$ and, since MC must always be positive, MR has to be positive; hence TR is increasing.

We have assumed that the output level is the only choice variable. Suppose that we also include advertising as a choice variable. Then it can be shown that either the advertising *or* the output level must be higher than the profit-maximizing levels, but not necessarily both.[13]

6-4 The Growth Maximization Model

The growth maximization model is another managerial theory of the firm and was suggested by Penrose and Marris.[14] This theory is considered appropriate to a

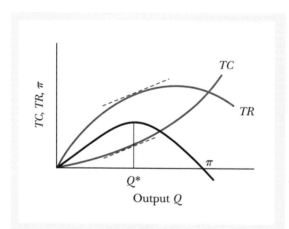

Figure 6-3 Total cost (TC), total revenue (TR), and profit (π) curves

[12] W. J. Baumol, *Business Behaviour, Value and Growth*, Macmillan, New York, 1959; review by F. M. Fisher in *Journal of Political Economy*, 68 (1960): 314–15.

[13] This can be proved algebraically but we omit the proof. A geometric illustration is cumbersome.
[14] E. T. Penrose, *The Theory of the Growth of the Firm*, Basil Blackwell, Oxford, 1959; and R. L. Marris, *The Economic Theory of Managerial Capitalism*, Macmillan, London, 1964.

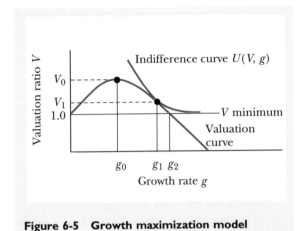

Figure 6-5   Growth maximization model

corporate economy and is concerned with the time path of expansion of the firm. Managers are assumed to satisfy instincts of power, dominance, and prestige (and possibly higher salary) by pursuing growth as an objective. They also take account of the valuation ratio, which is the ratio of the stock market value of the firm to its accounting or book value.

The relationship between the valuation ratio and the growth rate is described by the *valuation curve*, shown in Figure 6-5. The valuation curve takes into account the relationship between growth and profitability and the present value of shareholders' dividends and capital gains. After a point the valuation ratio declines, perhaps because shareholders consider too rapid a growth as unsustainable. If it is below 1, then the firm is threatened by a takeover because a low market value is attractive to potential buyers. The managers' preferences for valuation and growth can be depicted by indifference curves, as shown in Figure 6-5. The maximum satisfaction obtained by the managers occurs at the growth rate g_1 with the corresponding valuation ratio V_1.[15] The growth rate that maximizes shareholders' equity (which is also the profit-maximizing point) is at the growth rate g_0 with the corresponding valuation ratio V_0. The growth maximization model results in a higher growth rate and lower valuation ratio than the profit maximization model. Note that the maximum growth rate the managers can pursue is g_2, corresponding to a

valuation ratio of 1. Any higher growth rate results in a threat of the firm being taken over.

6-5   The Utility Maximization Model

A more general model in the managerial theory of the firm is the utility maximization model by Williamson.[16] In this model the utility function of the managers depends on expenditures on staff, managerial emoluments, and so on. Managers obtain satisfaction and prestige from the number of staff under their control and from the luxury offices, company cars, expense accounts, and bonuses they get. Managers maximize their utility subject to a minimum profit constraint. There are several variations of this model, but we illustrate a few simple ones. Suppose that the utility function of the managers depends on their firms' profit and the size of the staffs under their control. The indifference curves are shown in Figure 6-6. Profits increase for a while as the number of staff increases, but after a point they decline. The profit-maximizing model gives S_0 as the optimum level of staff. The utility-maximizing model results in a staff of S_1.[17] If the minimum profit constraint is as shown in Figure 6-6, the utility-maximizing model results in a staff of S_2.

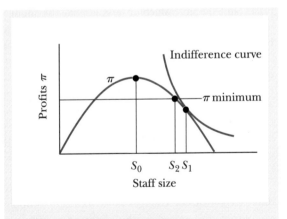

Figure 6-6   Utility maximization model

Utility is a function of profits and staff size

---

[16] O. Williamson, *The Economics of Discretionary Behavior: Management Objectives in a Theory of the Firm*, Prentice-Hall, Englewood Cliffs, NJ, 1964.
[17] Note that the value of S_1 depends on the shape of the indifference curve. S_1 may, in fact, coincide with S_0.

---

[15] Note that the position of g_1 depends on the shape of the indifference curve; g_1 may, in fact, coincide with g_0.

The final solution is a higher level of staff and lower total profits than under the profit-maximizing model. A similar conclusion holds when we consider other objectives in the utility function.

6-6 Effects of Profit Taxes in the Alternative Models of Firm Behaviour

We have presented three alternatives to the profit maximization model. There is, however, a fundamental debate over whether we choose between the alternative models on the basis of realism of assumptions or their predictive accuracy. Friedman argued that it is not meaningful to talk of realism of assumptions on which a theory is based, because theories, being abstractions, cannot exhibit complete realism, and the question of whether a theory is realistic enough can be settled only by seeing whether it yields predictions that are good enough for the purpose at hand or are better than predictions from alternative theories.[18] Thus, the assumption of profit maximization can be tested only by the theory's predictions, and not by any measure of the 'realism' of the 'profit-maximizing firm'.

How are predictions tested? They are tested by studying the effects of different policies (taxes, subsidies) or changes in economic conditions on prices and outputs. Machlup argues that the models of the firm are not designed to explain and predict the behaviour of real firms. Instead, he believes that the models are designed to explain and predict changes in observed prices as effects of particular changes in conditions (wage rates, interest rates, import duties, excise taxes, and so on). 'In this causal connection, the firm is only a theoretical link, a mental construct helping to explain how one gets from the cause to the effect. This is altogether different from explaining the behaviour of a firm.'[19]

Instead of a detailed analysis of the impact of different policies or changes in economic conditions on output and prices in the different models, we consider one policy: that of a profit tax. First, consider a lump-sum profit tax. It is clear in Figure 6-4 that the profit curve shifts vertically downward with such a tax.

The profit-maximizing output Q_1 remains unaltered. But Q_2 is now closer to Q_1, and thus we conclude that, although output remains unchanged under profit maximization, output may decline under sales maximization.

What is the effect of a percentage tax on profits? Now the profit curve is flatter than before but it has its maximum at the same output level as before. Thus, the profit-maximizing output remains unchanged at Q_1. However, since the profit curve is flatter, output falls under sales maximization (with a binding profit constraint).

What about the utility maximization model? With a lump-sum tax, since the profit curve shifts downwards vertically in Figure 6-6, we can conclude that output falls. With a percentage tax (which makes the profit curve flatter) we cannot say whether output rises, falls, or remains unchanged. It depends on the shape of the indifference curves. (Drawing the appropriate diagrams is left as an exercise.)

The above cases illustrate how we can analyse the effects of different policies in the alternative models.

6-7 Linear Programming

Linear programming is a mathematical technique for solving maximization or minimization problems where the constraints and the functions to be maximized or minimized are linear and thus can be represented by straight lines. We discuss this technique here because it is an important development in the theory of the firm, and managers must often solve constrained optimization problems. There are now computer programs available to solve complex optimization problems.

Choice of Production Processes

Although linear programming can be used to solve a variety of managerial problems, it is used most frequently in production decisions. Often managers need to determine the least-cost input bundle that yields a specified output, or they might want to determine the maximum output obtainable from specified quantities of inputs.

We first examine these problems in a simple setting: we consider the firm that produces only one output but has several production processes available to it. The linear programming approach is based on

---

[18] M. Friedman, 'The Methodology of Positive Economics', in *Essays in Positive Economics*, University of Chicago Press, 1953.
[19] F. Machlup, 'Theories of the Firm: Marginalist, Behavioural, Managerial', *American Economic Review*, 57 (1967): 9.

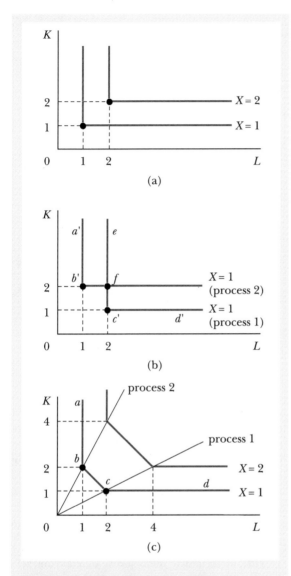

Figure 6-7 Isoquants when production takes place under fixed input proportions

(a) Single production process
(b) Isoquants for each production process
(c) Two production processes

the assumptions of (1) constant input and output prices, (2) constant returns to scale, and (3) the existence of several technologically fixed input proportions (called 'processes') with which to produce the single output. These assumptions imply that long-run average cost curves are horizontal. Assumption (3) implies that the isoquants are not smooth (as we

discussed in Chapter 4) but are made up of straight-line segments.

To see what the isoquants look like under fixed input proportions, let us consider two inputs: capital K and labour L. Suppose it requires 1 unit of L and 1 unit of K to produce 1 unit of output X. Then the isoquants are as in Figure 6-7(a). If we have 1 unit of L and 2 units of K, the extra unit of K is a waste. All we can produce is 1 unit of output. In this case K is called a *slack* variable.

In the preceding example the output X can be produced by a single production process. Consider now the case of two processes. (The case of more processes is similar.) Suppose that, to produce 1 unit of X, process 1 requires 2 units of L and 1 unit of K and process 2 requires 1 unit of L and 2 units of K. These isoquants are shown in Figure 6-7(b). If a firm can produce using process 1 or process 2 or both, then its isoquants are as shown in Figure 6-7(c). The portion ab of the isoquant for 1 unit of output X is the portion $a'b'$ of the isoquant for 1 unit of output using process 2. For these input bundles, process 2 yields a larger output. Similarly, the portion cd of the isoquant for 1 unit of output corresponds to the portion $c'd'$ of the isoquant for 1 unit of output using process 1. For the input bundles along cd, process 1 yields a larger output. The segment bc is a linear combination of the points b' and c' in part (b) of the figure. The input bundles along bc produce 1 unit of output only if both production processes are used. For example, one point on the segment bc represents the bundle $L = K = 1.5$. This bundle does not contain enough K to produce 1 unit of output with process 2 and does not contain enough L to produce 1 unit using process 1. But to produce 0.5 unit of output using process 1 requires $K = 0.5$ and $L = 1$, whereas producing 0.5 units using process 2 requires $K = 1$ and $L = 0.5$. Thus, 1 unit of output can be produced by combining the two processes.

Suppose now that we specify the amounts of L and K that the producer has at her disposal, and determine the maximum output the producer can produce and the production processes to be used. We can draw the isoquants and locate the highest isoquant feasible for the given input combination. This is shown in Figure 6-8. We get the results given in Table 6-2.

We can also determine the production process (or processes) that are chosen from input prices. This is shown in Figure 6-9: $abcd$ is our isoquant. Note that the

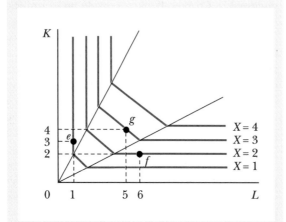

Figure 6-8   Maximum output obtainable from given input quantities

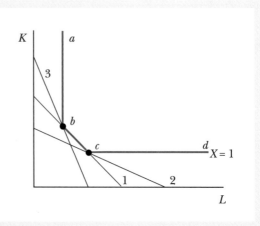

Figure 6-9   Choice of production process based on input prices
With isocost line 1, $P_L/P_K = 1$; with line 2, $P_L/P_K < 1$; with line 3, $P_L/P_K > 1$

Table 6-2   Choice of production process with a given amount of labour and capital

Input combination	Result
1 unit of L, 3 units of K (point e)	1 unit of X; process 2 used; 1 unit of K wasted
6 units of L, 2 units of K (point f)	2 units of X; process 1 used; 2 units of L wasted
5 units of L, 4 units of K (point g)	3 units of X; process 1 produces 2 units; process 2 produces 1 unit; no inputs wasted

slope of segment bc equals -1. Now as we know, for a given total cost the producer tries to reach the highest possible isoquant. If $P_L = P_K$, then the isocost lines are parallel to segment bc (labelled 1 in Figure 6-9), and both production processes are used. If $P_L > P_K$, then the process labelled 3, which uses less of L and more of K, is used. And if $P_L < P_K$, then the process labelled 2, which uses more of L and less of K is used.

Until now we have illustrated the nature of isoquants when production is carried under fixed input combinations and the determination of the output level and choice of production processes when (1) input prices are given or (2) input quantities are given. In both cases we simplified the analysis by considering a single-product firm. We are now ready to apply linear programming to the production problems of a multi-product firm.

Profit-maximizing Output Mix

Suppose that a firm produces two commodities X and Y and has at its disposal 8 units of labour L, 5 units of capital K, and 3 units of raw materials R. Suppose that each unit of output X requires 1 L, 1 K, and 1 R, and each unit of output Y requires 2 L, 1 K, and no R. The firm earns £15 on each unit of X it sells and £10 on each unit of Y it sells. Since input quantities are given, we take the maximizing of total revenue as equivalent to maximizing total profit.

We want to know how many units of X and Y are produced. We follow the following steps:

1   First, we formulate the objective function and state the constraints. The objective function is (assuming no fixed costs)

Total profit $\pi = 15X + 10Y$.

The input constraints are

L: $1X + 2Y \leq 8$
K: $1X + 1Y \leq 5$
R: $1X \leq 3$

The non-negativity constraints are

$X \geq 0, \; Y \geq 0$.

The last constraints merely state that outputs cannot be negative.

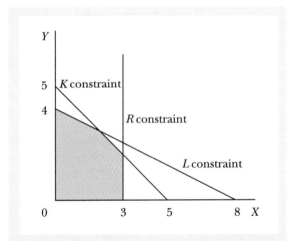

Figure 6-10   Feasible region implied by the input constraints

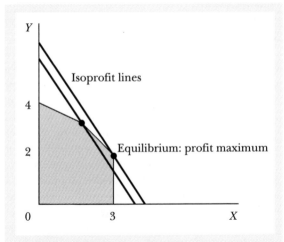

Figure 6-11   Determination of the optimal production levels

2 The second step is to plot the *feasible* region of production. We plot a line corresponding to each constraint, and the feasible region is shown in Figure 6-10 as the shaded area.

3 The third step is to superimpose the isoprofit lines and see the maximum level of profit that can be reached. This is shown in Figure 6-11. We see that the maximum profit occurs when $X = 3$ and $Y = 2$; profit $\pi = £65$. Also, for this level of production both K and R are completely utilized, but an extra unit of L is left over. In the next section, when we discuss shadow

prices, we see that the shadow prices are £0 for L, £10 for K, and £5 for R. Note that the total value of the resources of the firm is £65, which is exactly equal to the maximum profit. This is indeed the way shadow prices should be.

Cost Minimization

Linear programming can also be used to determine the cost-minimizing input mix when products are produced in fixed proportions and output requirements are given. For example, consider Gotcha Ltd, a firm in the commercial fishing business. The firm has a deep-water and a shallow-water fleet. The cost of one day of deep-water fishing is £3000, whereas the cost of a day's shallow-water fishing is only £2000. The firm has a contract to supply a packing plant with three qualities of fish: X, Y, and Z. A day of deep-water fishing produces 1 tonne of X-quality fish, 1 tonne of Y-quality fish, and 2 tonnes of Z-quality fish. A day of shallow water fishing yields 1 tonne of X-quality fish, 2 tonnes of Y-quality fish, and 1 tonne of Z-quality fish. The firm's contract calls for 28 tonnes of X-quality fish, 36 tonnes of Y-quality fish, and 36 tonnes of Z-quality fish per month.

The question we ask is: How many tonnes of X, Y, and Z fish does the firm produce and at what cost? To solve this problem, again, we go through the following steps:

1 First, we formulate the objective function and state the constraints. (Define D to be the number of days of deep-water fishing and S the number of days of shallow-water fishing.) The objective function is

Costs $C = 3000D + 2000S$.

The output constraints are

X: $1D + 1S \geq 28$
Y: $1D + 2S \geq 36$
Z: $2D + 1S \geq 36$.

The non-negativity constraints are

$D, S \geq 0$.

2 The second step is to plot the feasible region of production. We plot a line corresponding to each constraint and the feasible region is shown as the shaded area in Figure 6-12.

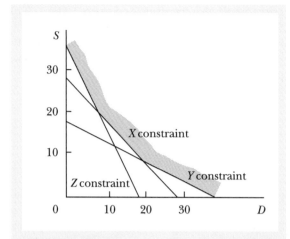

Figure 6-12 Feasible region implied by the output constraints

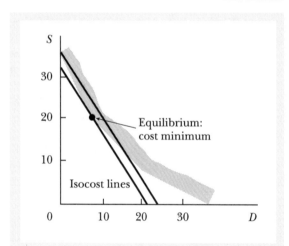

Figure 6-13 Determination of the optimum input usage

3 The third step is to superimpose the isocost lines and see the minimum level of cost reached. This is shown in Figure 6-13. We see that the minimum cost occurs when $D = 8$ and $S = 20$, so that $C = £64\,000$. For these inputs the outputs are $X = 28$, $Y = 48$, and $Z = 36$. The firm produces the minimum required amounts of X and Z but overproduces 12 units of Y. In the next section, when we discuss shadow prices, we see that, since there is surplus output of Y, its shadow price is zero. The shadow prices of X and Z are each £1000. The shadow price of total output is thus £64 000, which is exactly the minimum cost of production.

Applications of Linear Programming

We have given very simple illustrations of two types of linear programming problems: profit maximization and cost minimization. There are several applications of the linear programming methods. One prominent example is that of the petroleum industry, of which there were many studies in the 1950s.[20]

For profit maximization problems we are interested in determining the optimum product mix given the input constraints. In the case of the petroleum industry we can consider the product mix as consisting of petrol (leaded or unleaded), heating oil, diesel fuel, kerosene, and lubricants. The input constraints are limited crude supplies and refining capacity. Another example is that of forest products. The product mix consists of lumber, plywood, and paper. The input constraints are the given supply of logs and fixed milling capacity.

For cost minimization problems we are interested in determining the amounts of inputs used subject to the minimum requirements of the different outputs. One prominent example of this is the computation of a minimum-cost diet. The inputs here are different foods: milk, bread, eggs, meats, vegetables, and so on. The output constraints are minimum levels of carbohydrate, protein, minerals, and so forth. Another application of linear programming techniques is for the determination of least-cost transport systems. If we have a number of warehouses with given supplies and a number of consumption centres with specified demands, then the task is to devise a scheme of shipments that can be made with minimum cost. The procedures are useful in numerous cases where deliveries of products have to be made at different retailing centres and production is carried out at some other centres.

Computational Problems

The examples we have given above are very simplified versions, and we are able to obtain the solutions graphically because there are only two choice variables.

[20] See e.g. A. Charnes, W. Cooper, and B. Mellon, 'A Model for Programming and Sensitivity Analysis in an Integrated Oil Company', *Econometrica*, 22 (1954): 193–217; and A. Manne, *Scheduling of Petroleum Refinery Operations*, Harvard University Press, Cambridge, Mass., 1956.

With more choice variables, we have to use an algebraic method. The commonly suggested method is the simplex method.[21] We do not, however, discuss it because it involves quite a lot of algebraic detail. Many computer packages are available which solve such problems quickly and easily.

6-8 Shadow Prices

One of the most important economic applications of the linear programming method is the derivation of shadow prices.[22] In the profit maximization problem discussed in the last section, we specified output prices, and the firm had given quantities of inputs at its disposal. The firm was not purchasing the inputs. Based on the constraints the firm faces, it can assign some imputed prices to the inputs (based on their scarcity value). These imputed prices are called 'shadow prices' of the inputs. Similarly, in the cost minimization problem, we are given input prices but not output prices. Again, the firm can assign some imputed prices to the outputs. These prices are called 'shadow prices' of outputs. The term 'shadow price' is used in other contexts as well, particularly in the planning of investment projects when market prices do not reflect social values. This is the case when a project uses inputs that are purchased in a distorted market where the distortion takes the form of a divergence between the demand price and marginal cost. The problems of private versus social costs are discussed in Chapter 16. For the present, we use the term 'shadow price' as it relates to linear programming models.

The shadow prices are derived by considering an alternative linear programming problem called the 'dual problem'. Every linear programming problem has a corresponding problem called its dual; the original problem is called the 'primal problem'. If the primal is a maximization problem, the dual is a minimization problem, and vice versa. In the profit maximization problem in the previous section, we considered the production of two outputs, X and Y,

given 8 units of L, 5 units of K, and 3 units of R. The dual for this problem is a cost minimization problem. Let P_{L1}, P_{K1}, P_{R1} be the (shadow) prices or imputed values of a unit of L, K, and R, respectively. Then total cost is

$$C = 8P_{L1} + 5P_{K1} + 3P_{R1}.$$

The imputed value of a unit of X is $P_{L1} + P_{K1} + P_{R1}$ and that of a unit of Y is $2P_{L1} + P_{K1}$. The given market prices are £15 for a unit of X and £10 for a unit of Y. Thus, we minimize C subject to the constraints

$$P_{L1} + P_{K1} + P_{R1} \geq 15$$

$$2P_{L1} + P_{K1} \geq 10.$$

This is the dual cost minimization problem to the profit maximization problem discussed in the previous section. We can solve this linear programming problem and get the shadow prices P_{L1}, P_{K1}, P_{R1}.

We first reduce the problem to one of two choice variables (otherwise, we cannot use the geometric method). There is an alternative way of looking at shadow prices. The shadow price of labour L is obtained by asking the question: 'How much would profit rise if we increase L by one unit?' The shadow prices of the other inputs are obtained by asking a similar question. We have already seen that there were surplus units of L. Thus, increasing L by one unit, keeping other input constraints constant, does not increase profits at all. The shadow price of L, which is P_{L1}, is therefore zero. So the cost minimization problem becomes

Minimize $C = 5P_{K1} + 3P_{R1}$
subject to $P_{K1} + P_{R1} \geq 15$
$$P_{K1} \geq 10$$
$$P_{K1}, P_{R1} \geq 0.$$

The solution is $P_{K1} = £10$, $P_{R1} = £5$, and minimum $C = £65$, which is the result we stated earlier. It can be checked (this is left as an exercise) that, if K is increased by 1 unit (other inputs remaining constant), total profit rises by £10, and if R is increased by 1 unit, total profit rises by £5.

Returning to the cost minimization problem considered in the previous section, the dual is a revenue maximization problem. P_{X1}, P_{Y1}, P_{Z1} are the imputed prices of the outputs of X, Y, and Z, respectively. Total revenue is

$$TR = 28P_{X1} + 36P_{Y1} + 36P_{Z1}.$$

[21] See G. Dantzig, *Linear Programming and Extensions*, Princeton University Press, Princeton, NJ, 1963. In 1984 N. Karmarkar of Bell Labs suggested an alternative algorithm which permits much faster solutions of linear programming problems.
[22] Many other economic applications are discussed in R. Dorfman, P. Samuelson, and R. Solow, *Linear Programming and Economic Analysis*, McGraw-Hill, New York, 1958.

We maximize this subject to the constraints

$$P_{X1} + P_{Y1} + 2P_{Z1} \leq 3000$$
$$P_{X1} + 2P_{Y1} + P_{Z1} \leq 2000.$$

Again, we can look at the shadow prices another way. We ask the question: 'How much would costs increase if we were required to produce an extra unit of X, other output constraints remaining the same?' This extra cost is the shadow price or imputed value of a unit of X. The shadow prices of the other outputs are obtained by asking similar questions. We saw that the firm, in trying to meet the minimum requirements for X and Z, already overproduced Y. Thus, increasing the requirement of Y by 1 unit does not increase costs. The shadow price of Y, which is P_{Y1}, is zero. Thus, the maximization problem reduces to

Maximize $TR = 28P_{X1} + 36P_{Z1}$
subject to $P_{X1} + 2P_{Z1} \leq 3000$
$\qquad\qquad P_{X1} + P_{Z1} \leq 2000.$

This gives $P_{X1} = £1000$, $P_{Z1} = £1000$, and $TR = £64\,000$, as we stated in the previous section.

Answering questions such as 'How much would costs rise if one output requirement is increased by 1 unit?' involves solving the linear programming problem with the new output constraint. In practice, linear programming problems involve several constraints. Instead of solving so many linear programming problems, we solve a single dual problem. This gives us the required shadow prices.

In summary, in a profit maximization problem with given quantities of inputs, the shadow price of each input is the increase in profit that results if an extra unit of this input is made available. Similarly, in a cost minimization problem with minimum output requirements, the shadow price of each output is the extra cost of production if the requirement for that output is increased by 1 unit. We can obtain these shadow prices by increasing each input or output constraint, one at a time, by 1 unit, and solving the resulting linear programming problem. However, an easier way of obtaining all the shadow prices simultaneously is to solve the dual problem.

6-9   Summary

Production is organised through firms, rather than through a series of individual contracts, in order to economize on transactions costs and to enjoy the benefits of specialization. Total revenue is the product of price and quantity demanded of the good at that price. Average revenue is total revenue divided by the quantity sold. Marginal revenue is the change in the total revenue divided by the change in the quantity sold. TR, MR, and AR are related as follows: (1) MR is the slope of the TR curve; (2) TR is increasing if $MR > 0$ and decreasing if $MR < 0$; (3) TR is a maximum when $MR = 0$.

The sales maximization model suggests that the goal of the firm is the maximization of sales revenue subject to a minimum profit constraint. This model predicts a larger output than under profit maximization.

The growth maximization model stresses the trade-off between the growth rate and the valuation ratio for the firm. According to this model, managers maximize their satisfaction by choosing a higher growth rate and lower valuation ratio compared with profit maximization.

The utility maximization model suggests that the manager's utility is a function of staff size and other similar considerations. The manager maximizes utility subject to a minimum profit constraint by employing a larger staff than is consistent with profit maximization.

A lump-sum profit tax does not affect output under profit maximization, but may reduce output under sales maximization. The same is true for a percentage profit tax. Output declines under utility maximization with a lump-sum tax, but the result is unclear with a percentage tax.

Linear programming is a technique for solving constrained optimization problems when the objective function and constraints are linear. There are two common types of problem: output or profit maximization, and cost minimization. Under the profit maximization problem, the firm solves for the profit-maximizing output mix given fixed quantities of inputs available. In the cost minimization problem, the firm solves for the cost-minimizing input bundle, given minimum output requirements.

Shadow prices tell us how the maximum (or minimum) value of the objective function responds to a unit change in a constraint. In the profit maximization problem, the shadow price of an input is the increase in maximum profit that results if 1 more unit of the input is made available. In the cost minimization problem, the shadow price of an output is the increase in minimum cost if 1 more unit of an output is required. Shadow prices can be found by solving the dual problem.

Key Terms

Average revenue
Behavioural theories of the firm
Dual problem*
Feasible region
Growth maximization model*
Linear programming*
Managerial theories of the firm*
Marginal revenue
Primal problem
Sales maximization model*
Shadow price*
Total revenue
Transaction costs*
Utility maximization model*
Valuation ratio*

Questions

1   Why is the profit maximization model more realistic when ownership is concentrated? Can well-informed owners force the managers to behave as profit-maximizers? What information do they need?

2   Suppose that producing one satellite dish requires 2 units of K and 3 units of L using process 1; process 2 requires 1 unit of K and 4 units of L. Draw the isoquant for one satellite dish if the firm can utilize either or both processes.

3   If the price of capital is £5 and the price of labour is £3, which production process does the satellite dish producer in problem 2 utilize? Support your answer graphically.

4   Suppose a firm has 10 units of labour, 20 units of materials, and 8 units of capital available in the short run. A unit of output X requires 2 units of labour, 4 units of materials, and 1 unit of capital. A unit of output Y requires 1 unit of labour, 5 units of materials, and 4 units of capital. Graph the feasible region of production. If the price of Y is £2 and the price of X is £3, what output combination maximizes profit?

5   If the shadow price of capital is £100 but capital can be purchased for £20 per unit in the long run, what can you recommend to the firm in question 4?

7 Economic Efficiency and Economic Surplus

7-1 Introduction

The purpose of an economic system is to allocate the scarce resources of the economy to the production of good and services for the use of individuals. This allocation should be done efficiently. We already have a general idea of what efficiency means. Suppose initially that 1000 cars and 1 million microwave ovens are being manufactured. If, by reshuffling the resources, we can produce 1001 cars and 1 million microwaves, then the original allocation of resources is inefficient.

In his *Manuel d'Economie Politique* (1906), Pareto laid down some marginal conditions that must be satisfied if economic inefficiency is to be avoided. The basic idea of Pareto's conditions is that, if, starting from the existing allocation of resources and goods, we can find a new allocation that makes someone better off without making anyone else worse off, then the original allocation is inefficient. We first give some definitions and then some examples.

A *Pareto optimum* is defined as a state of affairs such that no one can be made better off without at least one other person being made worse off. A change in the allocation of resources or goods is said to constitute a *Pareto improvement* if at least one person is made better off without anyone being made worse off. Thus, a Pareto optimum is a situation from which no Pareto improvement is possible. Also, according to Pareto, a policy is said to improve economic welfare only if it results in a Pareto improvement, that is, only if at least one person is made better off without anyone else being made worse off. A study of economic welfare based on Pareto's conditions is known as *Paretian welfare economics*.

Clearly, Pareto's conditions are very stringent and do not cover all the likely practical cases. Suppose an economic policy makes 1 million people better off and only 1 person worse off. According to Pareto, this policy is not considered to be an improvement! The reason for this argument is that it is hard to compare or weigh the utilities of two individuals. Suppose I buy a Rottweiler for protection against burglary. I am better off. But my neighbour cannot stand the dog's barking. My neighbour is worse off. How can we judge whether my neighbour is worse off by more than I am better off? This is the problem of *interpersonal comparison of utilities*. Pareto's method treats this problem as impossible to solve and tries to make judgements only in those situations where such comparisons are not needed.

One suggested solution to the problem of interpersonal utility comparisons is that we determine whether the person who is made better off can compensate the person who is made worse off and still be better off. If this is so, then the new situation is better than the old one. For instance, in the above example, suppose that having the Rottweiler is worth £700 to me. My neighbour feels that the barking damages him to the tune of £400. The value to me is greater than the cost to him. I could compensate him fully for damages and still be better off by £300. In this case my having the Rottweiler is justifiable. This method of compensating those who are made worse off and judging whether there is a net increase in welfare is known as the *compensation criterion*.

We first discuss Pareto's criteria of economic efficiency. We see in Chapters 8, 9, and 10 that under a competitive system Pareto's criteria are satisfied whereas under monopoly they are not. Thus, there is an inefficient allocation of resources under monopoly, and this results in a loss of social welfare.

Three basic conditions must be satisfied if Pareto efficiency is to be attained. The economy must achieve:

1 Efficiency in the use of outputs in consumption (Section 7-2)
2 Efficiency in the use of inputs in production (Section 7-3)
3 Efficiency in matching production to consumption (Section 7-4)

After discussing each of these, we briefly review criticisms of Pareto's conditions and discuss applied welfare economics based on the concepts of consumer surplus and producer surplus. The final part of the chapter presents some applications of these concepts.

7-2 Efficiency in Consumption

Efficiency in consumption requires that it is impossible to redistribute a given set of goods among consumers in a manner that improves one person's welfare at no one else's expense. In economic terms, this requirement says that if X and Y are two goods, then the marginal rate of substitution of X for Y ($MRS_{X \text{ for } Y}$) should be the same for all individuals consuming both of the goods. For example, suppose that X = pizza and Y = bottles of lager:

For individual A, $MRS_{X \text{ for } Y} = 2$
For individual B, $MRS_{X \text{ for } Y} = 1$.

This means that individual A is willing to exchange 2 bottles of lager for 1 pizza. Individual B is willing to exchange 1 bottle of lager for 1 pizza. We can now reallocate pizzas and lagers between them to make at least one of them better off, without making the other one worse off. We take 1 pizza from B and give it to A. He gives us 2 bottles of lager. Now we give one of these

to B. He is no worse off because he is willing to exchange 1 pizza for 1 lager. But we have 1 bottle of lager left. We can give it to A (or B) and thus make A (or B) better off without making the other person worse off. Thus, the initial allocation was not efficient.

We cannot make any such redistribution if (and only if) the $MRS_{X \text{ for } Y}$ is the same for all consumers. In that case, we make one person better off only by making another worse off. In other words, if the MRS_X for Y is the same for everybody, then there is no redistribution of goods that constitutes a Pareto improvement. We have efficiency in consumption.

7-3 Efficiency in Production

Production efficiency requires that it is impossible to redistribute inputs to produce more of one product without reducing the output of another product. If an increase in the output of one product makes someone better off at no one else's expense, then the old allocation of inputs was not efficient.

Given two inputs, labour L and capital K, production efficiency requires that the marginal rate of technical substitution of L for K ($MRTS_{L \text{ for } K}$) should be the same for (1) all products that a single firm produces using these two inputs and (2) all producers producing the same output.

The first condition is sometimes referred to as the requirement for *managerial efficiency*, because it deals with input allocation within a single firm. If this condition is not satisfied and two products have different $MRTS_{L \text{ for } K}$, then we can redistribute the inputs so that this firm can produce more of one good without reducing the production of the other good. Suppose that the two products are satellite receivers and camcorders, and suppose the $MRTS_{L \text{ for } K}$ is 2 for satellite receivers and 1 for camcorders. This means that we can substitute 1 unit of labour for 2 units of capital and keep the output of satellite receivers constant. Similarly, we can substitute 1 unit of labour for 1 unit of capital and keep the output of camcorders constant. So all we do is take 1 unit of labour out of the production of camcorders and switch it to the production of satellite receivers. This releases 2 units of capital from satellite receiver production, 1 unit of which is transferred to the production of camcorders. Now the output of satellite receivers and camcorders is unaltered, but we are left with an extra unit of capital.

We can allocate this to satellite receivers (or camcorders) and get more satellite receivers (or camcorders). Thus, one output is increased without reducing the other output.

The second condition deals with the efficient allocation of inputs between firms. If the condition is not satisfied, then a redistribution of inputs between firms produces an increase in at least one output with no reduction in the other.

As an example, consider two firms A and B both producing satellite receivers and camcorders. The two factors of production are labour and capital. Suppose the marginal products of the two factors are as listed in Table 7-1. For producer A, $MRTS_{L \text{ for } K}$ is 4 in both satellite receiver production and camcorder production. For producer B, the $MRTS_{L \text{ for } K}$ is $\frac{5}{6}$ for both outputs. Thus, the managerial efficiency condition is satisfied for both firms.

However, since $MRTS_{L \text{ for } K}$ is not the same for both firms, we can increase output by moving labour from firm A to firm B. Now for firm B the marginal product of labour falls (there are more units of labour per unit of capital), and the marginal product of capital rises (since there are fewer units of capital per unit of labour). For firm A the reverse happens: the marginal product of labour rises, and the marginal product of capital falls. We continue this transfer of labour until the marginal product of labour and capital are the same for both firms. We can do the same for each of the two outputs: satellite receivers and camcorders. Finally, after the transfer of labour from firm A to B, we might end up with a situation where the marginal products are as in Table 7-2. Now the $MRTS_L$ for K is 2 for both outputs as well as both firms.

Table 7-1 Marginal products of labour and capital before a redistribution of inputs

	Firm A		Firm B	
	Labour	Capital	Labour	Capital
Satellite receivers	160	40	100	120
Camcorders	360	90	150	180

Table 7-2 Marginal products of labour and capital after transferring labour from firm A to firm B

	Firm A		Firm B	
	Labour	Capital	Labour	Capital
Satellite receivers	140	70	140	70
Camcorders	280	140	280	140

7-4 Efficiency in Matching Production and Consumption

This efficiency concept requires that we produce the correct mix of outputs. The condition for efficiency in the matching of production and consumption is that it must be impossible to rearrange outputs in a manner that constitutes a Pareto improvement. This type of efficiency necessitates that for two goods X and Y the marginal rate of transformation (in production) of XY ($MRT_{X \text{ for } Y}$) is the same as the marginal rate of substitution (in consumption) of X for Y ($MRS_{X \text{ for } Y}$). That is,

$MRT_{X \text{ for } Y}$ for all producers $= MRS_{X \text{ for } Y}$ for all consumers.

Suppose this condition is not satisfied and for firm A we have $MRT_{X \text{ for } Y} = 2$ and for a consumer B we have $MRS_{X \text{ for } Y} = 1$. Suppose $X =$ satellite receivers and $Y =$ camcorders.

Then, since $MRT_{X \text{ for } Y} = 2$, the firm can decrease production of satellite receivers by 1 unit and increase production of camcorders by 2 units (with the same total inputs). Now the firm can give consumers 1 less satellite receiver and 1 extra camcorder. Since MRS_X for $Y = 1$ for consumers, they are neither better off nor worse off. But the firm is better off—it has 1 camcorder left. If the firm gives it away to the consumer, the consumer is better off and the firm is no worse off. Thus, at least one of the two can be made better off, without the other being made worse off, by the change. Thus, the original situation was not Pareto optimal.

One can state many other conditions for efficiency but they all come down to two basic principles: (1) any MRT must equal any corresponding MRS, and (2) any

MRT must equal anyone else's MRT, and any MRS must equal anyone else's MRS.

When all the conditions of economic efficiency are fulfilled simultaneously, a society is said to have achieved a *Pareto optimum*. As long as these conditions are not fulfilled and inequalities persist, a reallocation of resources or goods can be made that increases total economic welfare.

Pareto's conditions for efficiency are satisfied if profit-maximizing firms and utility-maximizing households determine the optimum quantities of goods and services that they wish to trade with the help of equilibrium prices established in perfectly competitive markets. In this case,

$$MRS_X \text{ for } Y = \frac{P_X}{P_Y} \text{ is the same for all consumers}$$

$$MRTS_L \text{ for } K = \frac{P_L}{P_K} \text{ is the same for all producers}$$

$$MRT_X \text{ for } Y = \frac{P_X}{P_Y} \text{ for all producers}$$

$$= \frac{P_X}{P_Y} \text{ for all consumers}$$

$$= MRS_X \text{ for } Y$$

Example 7-1   The Allocative Efficiency of Traditional Agriculture

It is frequently assumed that farmers in poor agricultural communities do not make the best use of their factors of production; that is, they do not allocate their resources efficiently. Schultz[1] disputes this claim arguing that the farmers are 'poor but efficient', and presents evidence to support his argument. In his discussion of empirical evidence, Schultz excluded poor agricultural communities in transition or those adjusting their production to outside circumstances, such as civil wars and the partitioning of a country, large changes in relative prices of agricultural commodities, and technical advances in agricultural production.

One of the studies Schultz cites is that by Tax[2] which covered Panajachel, a small community of 800 in Guatemala over the period 1936–41. This was a society that was 'capitalist' on a microscopic scale. There were no machines, no factories, and no co-ops or corporations. Each individual was his or her own 'firm' and worked alone. There was money, and there was trade. After a careful analysis of the way transactions took place in this small community, Tax concluded that the village economy could be characterized as a 'money economy organised in single households as both consumption and production units, with a strongly developed market which tends to be perfectly competitive'.

Research in India has also found that farmers allocated their resources efficiently.[3] This evidence, along with that in Schultz's book, suggests the farmers in developing countries do know how to allocate resources efficiently. Schultz concludes that, 'although schooling may increase greatly the productivity of the human agent, it is not a pre-requisite to an efficient allocation of the existing stock of factors. The notion that these poor agricultural communities do not have enough competent entrepreneurs is in all probability mistaken.'[4]

7-5   The Edgeworth Box Diagram

The Edgeworth box diagram is a graphic way of describing the efficiency conditions discussed in the previous sections and showing how the allocations of some goods and resources can be improved upon by exchange. The box diagram is named after the British economist Edgeworth. Although named after him, this box diagram does not appear in any of Edgeworth's writings and apparently was first used by Pareto in 1893.[5]

---

[2] S. Tax, *Penny Capitalism*, University of Chicago Press, 1963.
[3] See L. J. Lau and P. A. Yotopoulos, 'A Test of Relative Efficiency and Application to Indian Agriculture', *American Economic Review*, 61 (1971): 94–109. Also, S. S. Sidhu, 'Relative Efficiency in Wheat Production in the Indian Punjab', *American Economic Review*, 64 (1974): 742–51.
[4] Schultz, op cit., p. 49.
[5] See V. J. Tarascio, 'A Correction On the Genealogy of the So-Called Edgeworth–Bowley Diagram', *Western Economic Journal*, 10 (1972): 193–7. A more extensive discussion is in W. Jaffe, 'Edgeworth's Contract Curve', parts I and II, *History of Political Economy*, 6 (1974): 343–59 and 381–404.

---

[1] T. W. Schultz, *Transforming Traditional Agriculture*, Yale University Press, New Haven, Conn., 1964, Ch. 3.

To illustrate the use of the box diagram, consider the following:

1 There are two individuals, A and B, and two goods, X and Y.

2 Each individual has an initial stock of the goods (called *initial endowments*) but not in the proportion that gives the individual the greatest satisfaction.

3 There is no new production, but the individuals can exchange the goods between themselves.

The initial endowments of X and Y held by A and B are denoted by (X_A, Y_A) and (X_B, Y_B), respectively. Then,

$\overline{X} = X_A + X_B$ is the total quantity of X available for exchange.

$\overline{Y} = Y_A + Y_B$ is the total quantity of Y available for exchange.

The Edgeworth box is a rectangle where the horizontal side measures $\overline{X}$ and the vertical side measures $\overline{Y}$. This is shown in Figure 7-1. The lower left-hand corner is denoted O_A and the endowments of X and Y held by individual A are measured horizontally left to right and vertically from bottom to top. For individual B, however, the graph is inverted. The origin is O_B, and her endowment of X is measured horizontally but right to left, and her endowment of Y is measured vertically but from top to bottom. The initial endowments are therefore shown by point C in Figure 7-1.

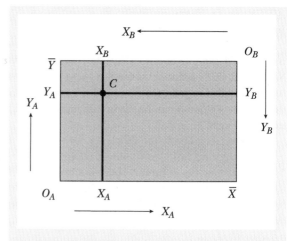

Figure 7-1   Initial endowments of *A* and *B* shown in a box diagram

Now consider the indifference curves for A and B. Note that the origin for B is the right top corner. (The graph for B is inverted.) The indifference curves for A and B are shown in Figure 7-2.

The next thing to consider is the curve consisting of the points of tangency of the indifference curves for A and B. This curve is called the *Edgeworth contract curve*. It is called a 'contract curve' because the points on the curve are equilibrium positions that A and B can reach

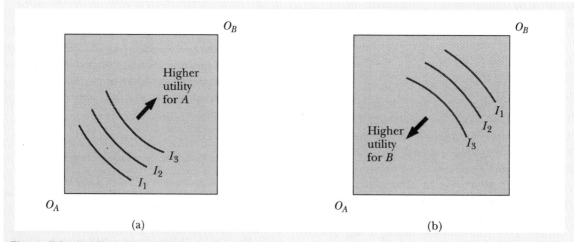

Figure 7-2   Indifference curves in the box diagram

(a) Indifference curves for A
(b) Indifference curves for B

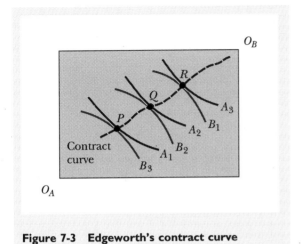

Figure 7-3   Edgeworth's contract curve

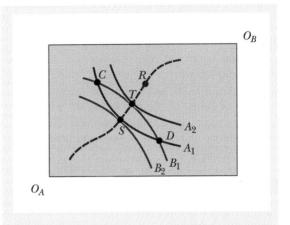

Figure 7-4   Movement from initial endowment to the contract curve through exchange

through exchange. This curve is shown in Figure 7-3. The indifference curves for A are denoted by $A_1, A_2, A_3, \ldots$, and the indifference curves for B are denoted by $B_1, B_2, B_3, \ldots$. Note that the indifference curves for B are convex to the origin O_B and higher utility means moving south-west, as shown in Figure 7-2(b).

Now consider points P, Q, and R on the contract curve. We first compare points P and Q. At P, A is on indifference curve A_1 and B is on indifference curve B_3; at Q, A is on indifference curve A_2 and B is on indifference curve B_2. Thus, a movement from P to Q makes A better off but B worse off. Similar is a movement from Q to R. Thus, no point on the contract curve is a Pareto improvement over another point. In other words, every point on the contract curve is Pareto optimal. At each point on the contract curve indifference curves are tangential, hence the MRS_X for $_Y$ is the same for both A and B.

Which of these points are reached by A and B? To answer this question we start with the initial endowment of A and B and their preferences. In Figure 7-4 C is the point that shows the initial endowments of both A and B. We now draw the indifference curves for A and B passing through point C. We label these A_1 and B_1. Next we consider the indifference curve A_2 that is tangent to B_1 and the indifference curve B_2 that is tangent to A_1. The points of tangency S and T are on the contract curve. Both A and B could move to S or T or to a point in between. At S, A is on indifference curve A_1, and B is on indifference curve B_2.

Thus, compared with point C, where A and B both started, B is better off (moving to a higher indifference curve) and A is no worse off. Thus, S is a Pareto improvement over C. Similarly, T is also a Pareto improvement over C, since A is made better off (moving to a higher indifference curve) and B is no worse off (staying on the same indifference curve). If A is very powerful in bargaining, he might be able to make B move to point T from point C. If B is very powerful in bargaining, she might be able to make A move to point S. More likely is it that both move to a point between T and S. In this case, they both move to a higher indifference curve than at C.

In summary, we note the following:

1 A and B can, by exchanging X and Y, reach any point in the box.
2 If the initial point is off the contract curve, they can both be made better off by moving to certain points on the contract curve.
3 Any points outside area $CTDS$ in Figure 7-4, even on the contract curve, are not attainable through voluntary exchange when starting from C. Take, for instance, point R: A is better off but B is worse off. B would not want to move to point R from point C. Thus, the only feasible final points are on the segment ST. In between S and T, both A and B are better off. Which point is reached depends on the bargaining power of A and B.
4 Any point on the contract curve is efficient with respect to consumption, or is Pareto optimal.

The Edgeworth Box for Production

The Edgeworth Box for examining efficiency in production is similar. We consider two factors of production, labour L and capital K. There are two outputs, X and Y. The total amount of labour available is $\overline{L}$ and of capital $\overline{K}$. L_X and K_X are the amounts of labour and capital used in the production of X, and L_Y and K_Y are the amounts of labour and capital used in the production of Y.

The analysis is the same as before. We begin with Figure 7-1. The length of the rectangle is now $\overline{L}$ and the height is $\overline{K}$. Point C now shows the initial allocation of inputs L and K to the production of X and Y. Since the analogy is direct, we do not present another diagram.

Next we consider Figure 7-2. Instead of indifference curves for A, we have production isoquants for output X. Similarly, instead of indifference curves for B, we have production isoquants for Y.

We now come to Figure 7-3. Label O_A as O_X, O_B as O_Y. Now A_1, A_2, A_3,..., are isoquants X_1, X_2, X_3,..., and B_1, B_2, B_3,..., are now isoquants Y_1, Y_2, Y_3,... The curve PQR is now the contract curve for production. Since the slope of a production isoquant is $MRTS_{L \text{ for } K}$, $MRTS_{L \text{ for } K}$ is the same in the production of X and Y at each point on the contract curve. As before, we can show that each point on the contract curve is Pareto optimal, or satisfies the conditions for efficiency in production.

Since the analysis is so similar, we have avoided the repetition of Figures 7-1 to 7-3. We do, however, replicate Figure 7-4. This is shown in Figure 7-5. O_X is the origin from which we measure production isoquants for X, increasing in the usual north-east direction, and O_Y is the origin from which we measure the production isoquants for Y (going south-west). C is the point of initial allocation. L_X units of labour and K_X units of capital are used in the production of X to produce output X_1. Similarly, L_Y units of labour and K_Y units of capital are used in the production of Y to produce output Y_1.

We now draw production isoquant Y_2 which is tangent to production isoquant X_1 (the point of tangency is P), and we also draw production isoquant X_2 which is tangent to production isoquant Y_1 (the point of tangency is Q).

Compared with C, point P is better because we have the same output X_1 of X but an output Y_2 for Y

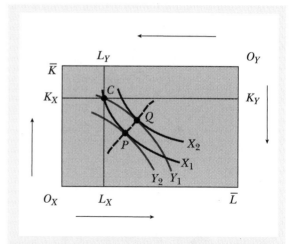

Figure 7-5 Movement from initial allocation to optimal allocation along a contract curve

that is higher than the earlier output Y_1. Thus, a reallocation of inputs produces more of the output of Y without reducing the output of X. Point Q is similar. We have more of X and the same output of Y compared with the situation at point C. As before, we can show that all points along PQ on the contract curve are better allocations of the given inputs than the initial allocation at C because they yield more of both X and Y. Which of these points is reached depends on the prices of X and Y.

The Production Possibilities Curve

From the Edgeworth box for given labour input $\overline{L}$ and capital input $\overline{K}$ and the production isoquants for X and Y, we get a contract curve that gives the combinations of the outputs of X and Y that result from an efficient allocation of the inputs. The curve showing these combinations is called the *production possibilities curve* and is illustrated in Figure 7-6.

The absolute value of the slope of the production possibilities curve is called the marginal rate of transformation of X for Y. (We examined this idea in some detail in Section 4-6 when we talked about the production of multiple products.) And efficiency in the matching of production and consumption requires that the MRT is equal to the $MRS_{X \text{ for } Y}$ in consumption. So for any output bundle on the production possibilities curve, we can determine the correspond-

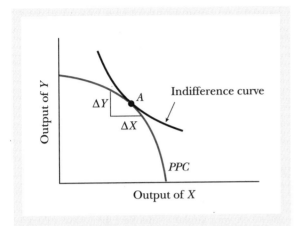

Figure 7-6   The production possibilities curve derived from the contract curve

Full economic efficiency occurs at point A

ing MRS_X for $_Y$ that results in full economic efficiency. This is shown in Figure 7-6. We have superimposed one individual's indifference curve on the production possibilities curve. Point A is the only point on the production possibilities curve that maximizes the individual's utility. At point A, the slope of the indifference curve (the MRS) and the slope of the production possibilities curve (the MRT) are equal. Thus, output is being produced efficiently at point A since the $MRS = MRT$ between the two goods.

7-6   Efficiency in Consumption and Production over Time

The conditions derived earlier in Sections 7-2 to 7-4 can be easily extended to consumption and production over time. In the case of consumption, instead of two goods X and Y we have C_p and C_f, which are present and future consumption, respectively. As we did in Section 2-10, we can draw indifference curves between current and future consumption for each of two individuals A and B. Now, instead of pizza and lager, we talk of C_p and C_f.

If we denote the marginal rate of substitution between C_p and C_f by MRS_{pf}, then we have

$$MRS_{pf} = \frac{\Delta C_f}{\Delta C_p},$$

where $\Delta C_f / \Delta C_p$ is the slope of the indifference curve at the point under consideration.

Again, if two individuals have different values of MRS_{pf}, then we can redistribute present and future goods between the two individuals so that no one is worse off and at least one is better off. The reasoning is exactly the same as in Section 7-2 except that instead of bottles of lager and pizza we have present and future goods.

Thus, the condition for efficiency in consumption over time is that MRS_{pf} is the same for all individuals. Note that we showed in Section 2-10 that

$$MRS_{pf} = \frac{\Delta C_f}{\Delta C_p} = -(1+r),$$

where r is the rate of interest. Thus, if the rate of interest is the same for all individuals, the efficiency condition is satisfied. However, if the borrowing and lending rates are different, then MRS_{pf} is different for borrowers and lenders, and thus the efficiency condition is not satisfied.

The situation with production over time is similar. Instead of satellite receivers and camcorders, we have present and future production. This could be interpreted as present consumption goods and investment goods or future consumption goods. Now we define MRT_{pf} as the marginal rate of transformation of present goods for future goods. Again, the equilibrium for any producer is attained when

$$MRT_{pf} = -(1+r),$$

where r is the rate of interest.

If MRT_{pf} is different for different producers, we can reallocate the inputs among the producers so that no one is worse off and at least some one is better off. The argument is exactly the same as in Section 7-3, with satellite receivers replaced by present production and camcorders by future production. Thus, the condition for efficiency is that MRT_{pf} is the same for all producers. If the rate of interest r is the same for all producers, this condition is satisfied.

The condition for overall efficiency is that MRS_{pf} is the same for all consumers, MRT_{pf} is the same for all producers, and

$$MRS_{pf} = MRT_{pf} = -(1+r).$$

7-7   X-inefficiency

In the previous sections we discussed the marginal conditions required for economic efficiency. How often are these conditions satisfied in reality? Some economists such as Leibenstein argue that these conditions are not usually satisfied in practice because people are not always fully motivated towards maximization or minimization (profit maximization, cost minimization, utility maximization, and so on). Leibenstein coined the phrase *X-inefficiency* to describe this inefficiency.[6]

If there are two firms with identical production conditions and identical measured inputs, the one with the lower X-factor has the lower output. What is this X-factor? The X-factor is the 'APQ bundle': activity type, pace, and quality.

Leibenstein distinguishes between what he calls *principals* (owners) and *agents* (those who work for others). Most people work for others in relatively large establishments. In the UK, firms with over 100 employees represent only 0.5 per cent of the total number of businesses, yet they account for over 50 per cent of all people employed.[7] In a small firm activities and the pace of work can be closely supervised, but in large organizations with several managers, many of whom have predetermined labour contracts, owners cannot supervise everything. (Moreover, the owners are generally a group of diffuse shareholders.) The managers have discretionary choices regarding (1) some of their activities, (2) the rate at which they carry out these activities, and (3) the quality of their efforts. This is the APQ bundle.

Leibenstein's theory is not well accepted by mainstream economists. For instance, Stigler argued that X-inefficiency is a result of ignorance, mistakes, or differences in production techniques.[8] Firms that are seemingly identical could be operating under different constraints. Business people, however, do not question the existence of X-inefficiency. In fact, organizational behaviour studies address the motivational factors that Leibenstein talks about.

Those supporting Leibenstein's theory argue that the results of academic research in a number of different areas may be interpreted as evidence that

managers do not minimize costs or maximize profits, or that productivity could be higher than it actually is, and so on. We report a few of these examples here.

1 One way to examine the managerialist idea of the firm (which we discussed in Chapter 6) is to compare the profitability of owner-controlled firms and manager-controlled firms operating in similar markets. Evidence from Europe suggests that owner-controlled firms have higher average profit rates than manager-controlled firms, although the findings are not conclusive.[9] An American study by Shelton compared manager-operated and owner-operated fast food restaurants. Menus, raw materials, accounting systems, and so on were similar or identical; but owner-operated units averaged a 9.5 per cent profit margin versus an average of 1.8 per cent profit margin for manager-operated units.[10]

2 For many years labour economists have researched the effect of trade unions on wages. Unions are seen as successful in increasing the wages of their members and so raising input costs for firms. Much less work has been done on the effect of unions on labour productivity. Even so, research in the United States has shown that unionized firms experience relatively fast productivity growth.[11] Recent research in the UK finds that during the late 1980s productivity growth was faster in unionized firms subject to increased foreign competition than in non-unionized firms subject to the same increased competition.[12] For Leibenstein and others, one way of explaining the positive link between unions and productivity is that the increase in the price of the input exerts pressure on managers to be more effective in their effort at cost minimization, and that the resulting decrease in X-inefficiency might actually compensate for the increase in the price of the input.

[6] H. Leibenstein, 'Allocative Efficiency vs. X-Efficiency', *American Economic Review*, 56 (1966): 392–415.
[7] G. Bannock and M. Daly, 'Size Distribution of UK Firms', *Employment Gazette*, May (1990): 255–8.
[8] See G. J. Stigler, 'The Xistence of X-Efficiency', *American Economic Review*, 66 (1976): 213–16. For a reply, see H. Leibenstein, 'X-Inefficiency Xists—Reply to an Xorcist', *American Economic Review*, 68 (1978): 203–11.

[9] See e.g. H. Radice, 'Control Type, Profitability and Growth in Large Firms', *Economic Journal*, 81 (1971): 547–62 and J. Bothwell, 'Profitability, Risk and the Separation of Ownership and Control', *Journal of Industrial Economics*, 28 (1980): 303–11. P. Thonet and O. Poensgen, 'Managerial Control and Economic Performance in Western Germany', *Journal of Industrial Economics*, 28 (1979): 23–38, find no difference in average profitability between owner-controlled and manager-controlled firms.
[10] J. Shelton, 'Allocative Efficiency vs "X-Efficiency": Comment', *American Economic Review*, 57 (1967): 1252–8.
[11] R. L. Freeman and J. L. Medoff, 'The Two Faces of Unionism', *Public Interest*, 57 (1979): 69–93.
[12] P. Gregg, S. Machin, and D. Metcalf, 'Signals and Cycles? Productivity Growth and Changes in Union Status in British Companies 1984–9', *Economic Journal*, 103 (1993): 894–907.

3 Primeux compared 49 US cities having two or more electricity companies with cities having only one. The former, he found, had costs of production that were, on average, 11 per cent less than the latter (after adjusting for economies of scale).[13] Note that this is not an inefficiency resulting from monopoly. According to theory, monopolies have as much incentive to minimize costs as do competitive firms. This example is used to argue that the X-inefficiency is a consequence of a firm's 'sheltering' from competition.

There are two questions one might raise: (1) How important is X-inefficiency for the economy as a whole? (2) What can we do about it? The answer to the second question is simple. Devote more attention to a study of how individuals and firms *do* behave rather than to how they *ought* to behave, as is done by many economists. This will help us to see how motivation can be increased.

Regarding the first question, no one has made a careful assessment. Leibenstein says that a 'back of the envelope' calculation suggests that the production sector in the United States is only 70 per cent as efficient as it could be.[14] But if households are also X-inefficient, then the whole US economy is only 60 per cent X-efficient—or 40 per cent inefficient!

Much of what Leibenstein calls X-inefficiency may, in fact, be consumption of leisure and relaxation, and these have a value too. Instead of constantly driving themselves and risking heart diseases or neuroses, individuals might simply choose to take things easy. This does not rule out the existence of X-inefficiency, but it would mean that Leibenstein's estimates are exaggerated.

The most important criticism of the X-inefficiency theory is that it does not provide a systematic framework for predicting when and how firms fail to minimize costs; that the theory is just a label given to ignorance regarding why firms and individuals behave in certain ways; and that giving different names for ignorance does not dispel ignorance. Some of the examples cited in support of the X-inefficiency theory can be explained by accounting for the institutional restrictions and transaction costs in addition to the usual constraints.[15]

7-8 Pareto's Conditions and Applied Welfare Economics

According to Pareto, total economic welfare is the sum of individuals' welfare. But one individual's welfare cannot be compared with another individual's welfare, so *interpersonal comparisons* are ruled out. Thus, only those policies that make at least one person better off without making anyone else worse off are seen as increasing total welfare. As mentioned earlier, even if a policy makes a million people substantially better off and one individual slightly worse off, the policy does not increase welfare by Pareto's definition.

Very few economists find Pareto's conditions satisfactory, so some modifications have been suggested. Even these modifications, however, do not help us in practical applications. All the modifications are theoretical exercises, and the best that can be said about this whole area is that it is practically impossible to study it without learning a lot of economics in the process.

One method that is widely used to evaluate economic policies is based on the concepts of *consumer surplus* and *producer surplus*. These concepts are defined in the next section. Using this approach, the problem of interpersonal comparison of utilities is essentially swept under the carpet, and benefits and costs are added without regard to whom they accrue to. This method of applied welfare economics does not appeal to some economists because it involves the simple addition of benefits and costs across all individuals. For instance, suppose a theft is committed, and the thief walks away with £1000 from Mr Fagen's house. The thief is better off by £1000; Mr Fagen is worse off by £1000. Adding up the total benefits and costs, the net effect is zero, and we might say there is no social cost. Of course, there are other social costs if Mr Fagen has to install a burglar alarm system for his house and

[13] W. Primeux, 'An Assessment of X-Efficiency Gained through Competition', *Review of Economics and Statistics*, 59 (1977): 105–9.

[14] H. Leibenstein, 'Microeconomics and X-Efficiency Theory: If There Is No Crisis, There Ought to Be', *Public Interest*, Special Issue (1980): 97–110.

[15] For a detailed discussion of this, see L. De Alessi, 'Property Rights, Transaction Costs, and X-Efficiency: An Essay in Economic Theory', *American Economic Review*, 73 (1983): 64–81. For a discussion of empirical evidence on property rights, see L. De Alessi, 'The Economics of Property Rights: A Review of the Evidence', *Research in Law and Economics*, 2 (1980): 1–47.

ԑԑ

less nights, and if his neighbours, too, feel ⸍install burglar alarm systems. There is also ⸍the police investigation of the crime. All this involᵥᵥₑ waste of otherwise productive resources. But if none of these other things happens, then all we have is the thief's benefit of £1000 and Mr Fagen's loss of £1000, and adding the two, we have a net cost of zero.

On the face of it, this procedure does not sound very reasonable. However, the method of consumer surplus and producer surplus does give us some means of evaluating the comparative merits of different economic policies. It is a method of great pedagogical value, and it gives us some insight into the factors that should be taken into account when analysing different economic proposals. Harberger was a strong advocate of the use of surpluses to evaluate the impact of various economic policies on social welfare. In fact, this method is sometimes called the Harberger triangle method, because it involves the measurement of various triangles.[16]

7-9 Consumer Surplus and Producer Surplus

Suppose you go into a shop and like the look and sound of a compact disc player so much that you are willing to pay £250 for it. If it actually costs only £200, you have a consumer surplus of £250 − £200 = £50.

The concept of consumer surplus was first formulated in 1844 by Dupuit, who was concerned with evaluating the worthiness of a subsidy towards the cost of constructing a bridge.[17] He was aware that a consumer might be willing to pay more for a good than he actually has to pay. The 'excess satisfaction' the consumer gets is the 'consumer surplus'.

The concept of consumer surplus gained prominence after Marshall's *Principles of Economics* was published in 1890. Marshall defined consumer's surplus as 'the excess of the price which the consumer

[16] A. C. Harberger, 'Three Basic Postulates for Applied Welfare Economics: An Interpretive Essay', *Journal of Economic Literature*, 3 (1971): 785–97.
[17] An English translation of Dupuit's famous article is: J. Dupuit, 'On the Measurement of the Utility of Public Works', in American Economic Association's *Readings in Welfare Economics*, Richard D. Irwin, Homewood, Ill., 1969, pp. 255–83.

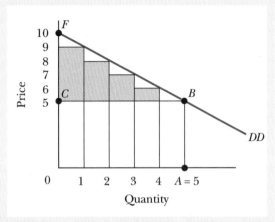

Figure 7-7   Consumer surplus

would be willing to pay rather than go without the thing over what the consumer does actually pay'.

The way Marshall measured consumer surplus is shown in Figure 7-7. *DD* is the demand curve. Suppose the individual buys 5 units and pays a price per unit of £5. If the consumer is given the choice of buying a certain quantity of the good or going without it, she might be willing to pay £9 for the first unit, £8 for the second unit, £7 for the third unit, £6 for the fourth unit, and £5 for the fifth unit. Thus, when the actual price is £5, the consumer surplus is £4 + £3 + £2 + £1 + £0 = £10. As an approximation to this, we take the area of the triangle *BCF*. The area under the demand curve *DD* up to the output level 0*A* measures the amount the consumer is *willing to pay*. This is the area 0*ABF*. The amount the consumer *actually pays* is given by the area 0*ABC*. Hence consumer surplus is given by the area of the triangle *BCF*, which is equal to 0*ABF* − 0*ABC*.

One can define a similar concept for producers. The analogous concept, called producer surplus, is the amount that the producer receives over and above what he is willing to sell for rather than forgo a sale. This is illustrated in Figure 7-8.

The producer sells *OA* units at a price *OC*. His revenue is given by the area *OABC*. However, the prices at which the producer is willing to sell each successive unit rather than go without selling the unit are given by the points on the supply curve. (The points on the supply curve give the producer's marginal cost of production and, hence, his reservation price—the

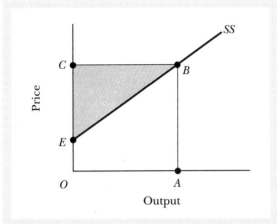

Figure 7-8   Measurement of producer surplus

minimum price at which he is willing to sell.) Thus, the area under the supply curve up to output OA (area $OABE$), measures the minimum amount at which the producer is willing to sell the output OA. The difference $OABC - OABE = CBE$ measures the producer surplus.

Figure 7-9 illustrates the concept of consumer surplus and producer surplus together. DD is the demand curve, and SS is the supply curve. The equilibrium price is OC, and the equilibrium quantity is OA. The area of the triangle BCF measures consumer surplus, and the area of the triangle BCE measures producer surplus.

Marshall popularized the notions of consumer surplus and producer surplus and had high hopes for their use as tools of public policy. However, the concepts were widely criticized. Consider, for instance, the case of consumer surplus. The effect of a fall in the market price of a good is shown in Figure 7-10. DD is the demand curve. Suppose the price is OC. Then the consumer surplus is given by the area of the triangle BCF. Now if the price falls to OC', the consumer surplus is given by the area of the triangle $B'C'F$. Thus, the increase in the consumer surplus is given by the shaded area $BB'C'C$.

However, a fall in the price of a good also has an income effect. This changes the answer to the question, 'What is the consumer willing to pay rather than go without?' Marshall realized this problem and, hence, confined his discussion to small changes in price and goods with negligible income effects. To take care of income effects, it is customary to say that the demand curve DD in Figure 7-10 is the *income-compensated demand curve*. (This concept was explained in Chapter 3.) In our discussions of consumer surplus, we assume that income effects are small or else that the demand curve we are considering is the income-compensated demand curve.

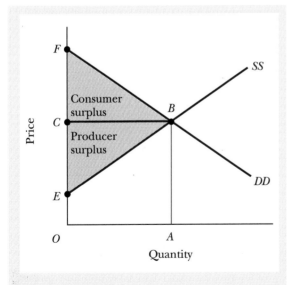

Figure 7-9   Measurement of consumer and producer surpluses

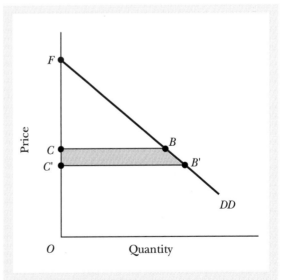

Figure 7-10   Effect of a fall in price on consumer surplus

There have also been criticisms concerning the usefulness of the concept of consumer surplus. Some economists have dismissed it as completely useless. For instance, Samuelson said, 'it is a tool which can be used only by one who can get along without its use and not by all such'. Little described it as a 'totally useless theoretical toy'. However, Lerner considered it of great use as a heuristic device for showing students of economics the social benefits or costs of policy decisions.[18] Many other economists have argued in its favour because, they say, there is no alternative computable measure of the welfare loss (or gain) from different economic policies.[19] For the purpose of this book, we use it as a pedagogical device to evaluate economic policies.

The concepts of consumer and producer surplus has been used in a number of practical problems to judge the desirability or undesirability of economic policies. In this analysis the change in the sum of consumer and producer surpluses and government's surplus (or deficit) is defined as the *deadweight loss* (or *gain*) to society. This is the amount by which the government's expenditures exceed the increase in consumer and producer surpluses, or by which the government's receipts fall short of the loss in producer and consumer surpluses. There are also cases (for example, tariffs) where consumer surplus declines, producers' surplus rises, and government's surplus also rises (the tax revenue that government receives). In this case the deadweight loss is the difference between the loss of consumer surplus and the gain to producers and the government.

Note that the measurement of welfare cost or deadweight loss does not take into account the other incidental costs involved, which can be substantial. These are costs of the governmental bureaucracy and the costs that individuals incur in 'seeking the surpluses'. The surplus we are talking about is for consumers as a group or producers as a group. But some consumers and producers waste resources in getting a bigger share of these total surpluses. We postpone a discussion of this, however, until Chapter 9, when we discuss the welfare cost of monopoly.[20]

Example 7-2   Pricing Admissions to EuroDisney

The concept of consumer surplus can be used to analyse the pricing of entrance to EuroDisney (or any other theme park). Individuals going to EuroDisney are interested in going on the different amusement rides. The question we are interested in is how much EuroDisney should charge for entrance and how much for each ride.

For simplicity, we assume initially that all customers are identical and that the demand curve is linear, as shown by *AD* in Figure 7-11. We also assume that the marginal cost (for EuroDisney) of offering a ride to any

---

[20] This phenomenon is called 'rent-seeking' and has been discussed by Tullock, Kreuger, Buchanan and others. See Section 9-8 below.

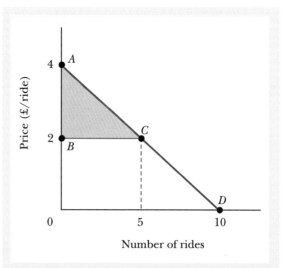

Figure 7-11   Pricing at EuroDisney: identical customers

---

[18] These and many other quotations, and some criticisms and applications of the consumer and producer surplus, can be found in: J. M. Currie, J. A. Murphy, and A. Schmitz, 'The Concept of Economic Surplus and its Use in Economic Analysis', *Economic Journal,* 81 (1971): 741–99. An opposing view, recalling earlier criticisms, can be found in E. R. Morey, 'Confuser Surplus', *American Economic Review,* 74 (1984): 163–73.

[19] G. W. McKenzie, *A New Approach to the Measurement of Welfare,* Cambridge University Press, 1983, suggests an alternative measure, which is free of the usual defects of measures of consumer surplus, is operational, and can be calculated from observable information. However, a discussion of this measure is beyond the scope of this book.

individual is zero. The demand curve shows that at no charge (£0) 10 rides are taken, whereas at a price of £4 no rides are taken. (This latter number is unrealistic, but is a consequence of the linear demand curve. However, for the purpose of illustration it is all right.)

Suppose that EuroDisney charges a price of £2 per ride. Since 5 rides are taken, it gets £10 in revenue from the rides. The consumer reaps a consumer surplus given by the shaded triangle ABC. Since this is the amount that the consumer is willing to pay rather than go without the rides, EuroDisney can charge an admission fee equal to the area of this triangle which in this case is £5. Thus, EuroDisney receives £10 on rides and £5 on entrance fees, which is a total of £15. However, if it did not charge for the rides it could do better. If the rides were free, the consumer would take 10 rides and reap a consumer surplus equal to the area of the larger triangle $A0D$. EuroDisney can extract this consumer surplus by charging an entrance fee equal to the area of the triangle—that is, £20. Thus, with identical customers EuroDisney does better by charging nothing for the rides and simply charging an entrance fee. This, in fact, is what EuroDisney does.

In the year from October 1992 to the end of September 1993, EuroDisney made a loss of £614 million. It responded to this loss by lowering the entrance fee to try to attract more visitors. We can see the logic behind this policy if we relax the assumption of identical customers. Suppose that we have two types

of customer whose demand curves are given by AD and $A'D'$ in Figure 7-12. Individual 1 takes 10 rides at a zero price and no rides at a price of £5. Individual 2 takes 15 rides at a zero price and no rides at a price of £6.

EuroDisney has to charge the same price for all customers. Suppose it tries to capture the consumer surplus of individual 2 and charges an entrance fee equal to the area $A'0D'$. This is an entrance fee of £45. But at this entrance fee individual 1 does not go to EuroDisney. (He is only prepared to pay £25.) EuroDisney gets a revenue of £45. Alternatively, it can try to capture the consumer surplus of individual 1, which is given by the area $A0D$. The entrance fee is then £25, and it gets a revenue of £50 from the two consumers. Thus, by lowering the entrance fee EuroDisney has raised its revenue. The lower entrance fee attracts people who were not prepared to pay the higher fee but are prepared to go to EuroDisney if the fee is lower.

The lowering of the entrance fee represents an increase in consumer surplus to individual 2. This is shown in Figure 7-13. The demand for visiting EuroDisney is shown by the (income-compensated) demand curve. Initially, EuroDisney charges an entrance fee equal to F_1. The number of visits taken by individual 2 is V_1 and the size of the consumer surplus is ABC. After the entrance fee is lowered to F_2, the number of visits increases to V_2 (individual 1 now

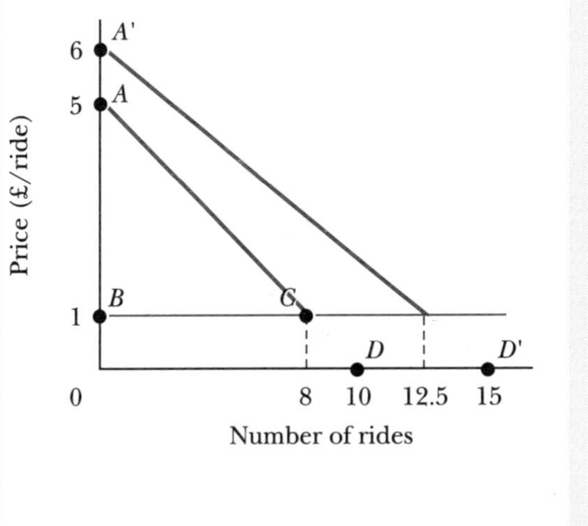

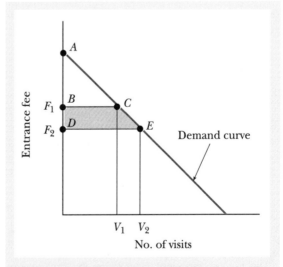

Figure 7-12   Pricing at EuroDisney: two types of customer

Figure 7-13   Increase in consumer surplus from a lower entrance fee at EuroDisney

goes to EuroDisney) and the surplus is now *ADE*. The increase in consumer surplus for individual 2 is the shaded area *BDEC*.

Is a zero price for the rides the best policy? Suppose EuroDisney charges £1 per ride. In Figure 7-12 the consumer surplus for individual 1 is given by the area of the triangle *ABC*. This is the entrance fee, and it is £16. At the price of £1 per ride, individual 1 takes 8 rides and individual 2 takes 12 rides (actually $12\frac{1}{2}$, but there is no half-ride). The revenue for EuroDisney is £52 (£32 from entrance fees and £20 from tickets) and is thus higher than with an entrance fee scheme only. Thus, with two types of customers EuroDisney can increase its revenue by charging an entrance fee plus tickets for rides. This procedure of charging an entrance fee to the park and tickets for rides is known as a *two-part tariff*.[21]

What is the price that maximizes revenue for EuroDisney? By considering similar triangles, we arrive at the following conclusion. If p is the price per ride, the entrance fee (area of triangle *ABC*) is $(5-p)^2$. The number of rides taken by individuals 1 and 2 are, respectively, $2(5-p)$ and $\frac{5}{2}(6-p)$. Total revenue is

$$2(5-p)^2 + 2p(5-p) + \tfrac{5}{2}\,p(6-p)$$

(entrance fees plus rides). The profit-maximizing price is £1 per ride, which is the price we considered.[22]

For comparison, at a price of £2 per ride, the entrance fee is £9. Individual 1 takes 6 rides and individual 2 takes 10 rides. Total revenue is $2(£9) + 16(£2) = £50$, which is the same as with an entrance fee of £25 with free rides.

7-10   Application 1: Price Controls

The first application we consider is that of price controls. We know from Chapter 1 that if price is set below the equilibrium level, output falls and a shortage

results. There may be a social cost associated with the reduction in output, and there may also be a social cost associated with the allocation of the product.

In Figure 7-14 we present an analysis of welfare costs of price controls. *DD* is the demand curve, and *SS* is the supply curve. The equilibrium price is *OB* with equilibrium quantity *OA*. In equilibrium, the sum of consumer and producer surpluses is the area of the triangle *NKC*. Now suppose that price is controlled at the level *OE*. The quantity supplied, and hence the quantity consumed, is *OF*. However, at the controlled price there is an excess demand of *FJ* or *GH*. The welfare cost of the price control depends on how this excess demand is handled and on which consumers along the segment *KH* of the demand curve receive the output. If the available quantity *OF* is allocated to those who obtain the highest satisfaction (how this could be done is a question that is discussed below), then the consumer satisfaction is measured by the area *OKLF*. The consumers pay *OEGF*, and hence the consumer surplus is *EKLG*. Producer surplus is the area of the triangle *EGN* under the price controls. Thus, the sum of the producer and consumer surpluses is *NKLG*. And the deadweight loss to society, or the reduction in the sum of the surpluses, is given by the triangle *LCG*. This deadweight loss is the excess of consumers' value over production costs for the units *FA* which are no longer produced owing to the price controls. Note that the rectangle *BRGE* was producer surplus before the price

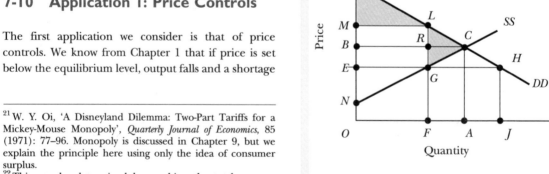

Figure 7-14   Welfare costs of price controls

controls were imposed but became consumer surplus with the controls. Thus, this area merely represents a transfer from producers to consumers. Such a transfer does not affect total social welfare.

Now let us consider the impact on social welfare when the same available output (OF) is allocated at random among consumers willing to pay the regulated price. One way this may work is illustrated in Figure 7-14. With random allocation, some consumers along the segment LH receive output. But these consumers value the output less than those along the segment KL. In fact, at the price OE, total consumer surplus for the consumers along LH is equal to the area of the triangle LGH which is $(LG \cdot GH)/2$. Average consumer surplus for this group is, thus, $(LG \cdot GH)/(2FJ)$. But $FJ = GH$, so this becomes $\frac{1}{2}LG$. Total consumer surplus for the consumers along KL is equal to the area of the triangle KLM plus the area of the rectangle $EMLG$. This sum is equal to $(KM \cdot ML)/2 + (EM \cdot EG)$. Average consumer surplus for this group is obtained by dividing by OF (which equals EG and ML). Thus, average consumer surplus for this group is $\frac{1}{2}KM + EM$.

The amount by which average consumer surplus for consumers along KL exceeds average consumer surplus for consumers along LH can now be expressed as $(KM/2) + EM - (LG/2)$. Since LG equals EM, this becomes $(KM + EM)/2$. This is the expected loss in consumer surplus for each unit of output that goes to a consumer along LH rather than to a consumer along KL. What fraction of output is expected to go to consumers along LH? With random allocation, this depends on the number of consumers along this region relative to the total number willing to purchase at a price OE, which is FJ/OJ. The corresponding number of units of output expected to go to the consumers along LH is, thus, $(FJ/OJ) \cdot OF$. And the total expected loss in consumer surplus due to random allocation is $(FJ/OJ) \cdot OF \cdot \frac{1}{2}(KM + EM)$. If FJ/OJ is $\frac{1}{2}$ (as drawn), then $KM = EM$ and the total expected loss due to random allocation becomes $\frac{1}{2} \cdot OF \cdot KM$, which in this particular case is the area of the triangle KML.

The area of the triangle KML, it should be noted, is only the expected loss in consumer surplus arising from the fact that the output is randomly allocated. The total loss in social welfare that is due to the price control coupled with random allocation is the sum of the triangles LCG and KML. Thus, triangle LCG can be thought of as the cost of the output reduction, and

triangle KML as the cost of the random allocation process in the case where $OF = FJ$ only.

Suppose the available output OF is distributed at random to the total number of customers OJ, but those who obtain any of the output can resell it to others who are willing to pay a higher price. Then the output is consumed by individuals on the demand curve in the segment KL, and the welfare cost is given by the area of the triangle LCG as we derived earlier. Thus, with price controls and a situation of excess demand, it is best to distribute the available output at random and permit a resale to others. If the resale is not permitted, the welfare cost is higher, as we have shown.

7-11 Application 2: The Economics of Health Care

There are many applications of microeconomics in the area of health services. Health expenditures have been steadily increasing over time in many countries, even after adjusting for changes in the general price level. By the late 1980s total health spending in the UK was 6 per cent of GNP and in the United States it was 11 per cent. In most Western European countries it was somewhere between these two figures. Furthermore, in some countries most of the expenditure on health care is made by the public sector. For instance, in the mid-1980s 83 per cent of all health care spending in Sweden and 73 per cent of health spending in the UK took place within the public sector. It is likely that the demand for health care will increase with a rise in per capita income and increased health consciousness. However, the large increases in health care costs cannot be explained by these factors alone.

A major contributory factor to the large increase in health care costs is the system of third-party payments (payments by either private insurance companies or government). We discussed this problem in Example 5-3. In countries such as Germany and France, health care is funded from social insurance contributions. Most citizens are covered by a compulsory system of national health insurance whereby the government pays for the health care of most people. Only a small proportion of the population have private health insurance. In other countries, such as the United States, third-party payments are made to a greater extent by private insurance companies. We first analyse the effect of private health insurance on the demand for health care. We then analyse the effect of social insurance schemes, such as those operated in Germany and France, on the demand for health care and on the price of health care. We also show that there is a net welfare cost resulting from such a scheme and that doctors are the beneficiaries.

Effect of Private Health Insurance

In Figure 7-15 SS' is the supply curve, $D_0 D_0'$ is the demand curve in the absence of insurance, and $D_1 D_0'$ is the demand curve if the insurance company pays half of total expenses. Q_0 and P_0 are the quantity and price without insurance; Q_1 and P_1 are the quantity and price with insurance.

The doctors' surplus is initially $P_0 AS$. With the insurance programme it is $P_1 BS$. Thus, doctors' profits increase by $P_1 BAP_0$. The consumer surplus initially is $D_0 AP_0$. With insurance it increases to $D_1 BP_1$. But we have not considered the insurance payments that consumers have to make. Thus, we cannot say whether they are better off or worse off. Of course, to analyse the effects on consumers, we also have to consider the risks that consumers are insuring against. A simple analysis such as this, in terms of consumer and producer surpluses, is not enough. However, this simple analysis does show that prices, numbers of visits, and doctors' profits all rise in the presence of health insurance.

Effect of Social Insurance

We now consider the effect of government-paid insurance. We begin by assuming that the government pays the costs of health care for everyone. The effects we are likely to observe are shown in Figure 7-16.

AB is the demand curve if there is no government insurance. HC is the supply curve of health services. Initially, the price is OD, the quantity of health care is OF, and total consumers' expenditures are $ODEF$. The consumer surplus is ADE, and the producer surplus (doctor and hospital) is DEH.

When the government pays the entire cost, the demand curve is completely inelastic, shown by the vertical line BC. The effects of this are as follows:

1 The price rises from OD to OG.
2 The quantity of health care consumed increases from OF to OB.
3 The total expenditures on health care increase from $ODEF$ to $OBCG$.
4 The producer surplus (doctors and hospitals) increases by the amount $DECG$.
5 The consumer surplus increases by $ODEB$.

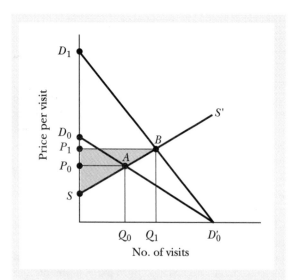

Figure 7-15   Effects of private health insurance

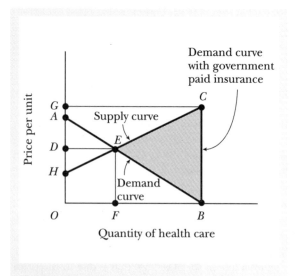

Figure 7-16   Effect of government-paid insurance for all

However, government expenditures, which are $OBCG$, are higher than the sum of the increase in producer and consumer surpluses ($DECG+OBED$). The difference is given by the area of the shaded triangle BCE. This represents the net welfare loss. Since the government revenue has to be financed by taxes that society has to bear, there is a net welfare loss to society.

Now we consider the situation where the government pays for the expenses of most (but not all) of the population. This is similar to the social insurance systems in Germany and France, where most people are part of the compulsory national insurance scheme. Only those on relatively high incomes (or those self-employed) are allowed to opt out of the system. These people may choose to take out private insurance or remain uncovered. We first derive the aggregate demand curve for health care from the demand curves of those covered under the government scheme and those that are not covered. This is shown in Figure 7-17. $D_1 D_1'$ is the demand curve of group 1—those not covered by social insurance—and $D_2 D_2'$ is the demand curve of group 2—those covered by social insurance. The two demand curves have different slopes and intercepts. For illustrative purposes, we have drawn $D_2 D_2'$ so that at high prices the quantity demanded by this group is larger than that demanded by the first group. (We assume for simplicity that group 2 consists of more sick people than group 1.)

We first derive the total demand curve, which can be obtained by adding the quantities demanded by the two groups at each price. Above the price OD_1 the demand by group 1 is zero. Hence the total demand curve is given by the portion $D_2 C$ of $D_2 D_2'$. After this, the total demand curve is obtained by a horizontal addition of $D_1 D_1'$ and $D_2 D_2'$. Since the demand curves are straight lines, this is easy to derive. From D_1' measure $D_1' D_3' = OD_2'$. Then OD_3' is the total demand at zero prices. Hence the total demand curve is given by $D_2 C D_3'$.

Now if the government pays the entire health expenses of group 2, the demand curve for this group is completely inelastic, as shown by the vertical dashed line $D_2' D_3$ in Figure 7-17. The aggregate demand curve is then given by the horizontal summation of the two demand curves and becomes the dashed line $D_3 C' D_3'$.

We can now analyse the effects of the social insurance programme. This is done in Figure 7-18. The demand curve for the non-covered group is $D_1 D_1'$. Without any social insurance, the aggregate demand curve is $D_2 C D_3'$. SS is the supply curve. OA is therefore the price, OK is the quantity consumed by the non-covered group, and KL is the quantity consumed by group 2 members before they were covered by the social insurance.

Now with the social insurance, the aggregate demand curve shifts to $D_3 C' D_3'$. This intersects the

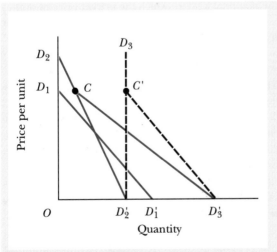

Figure 7-17 Derivation of aggregate demand curve for health care

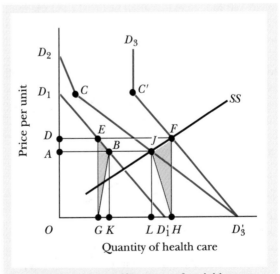

Figure 7-18 Net welfare cost of social insurance

supply curve SS at point F. We now observe the following changes:

1 The price rises from OA to OD, and the total consumption of health care rises from OL to OH.
2 Consumption for the non-covered group falls from OK to OG. There is a loss in consumer surplus for this group of area $ABED$.
3 Consumption for the covered group rises from KL to GH. Since GH is the same as $D'_1 D'_3$, and this group does not pay any expenses, the increase in consumer surplus is the area between the demand curves $BJD'_3 D'_1$. But since $D'_1 D'_3 = EF = HG$, this area is the same as $BJHG$. This is also the sum of rectangle $BJLK$ (previous health expenditure by the covered group) and triangles GBK and JHL (the value to the covered group of the additional units consumed).
4 The producer surplus of the medical profession increases by $AJFD$.
5 Finally, the government's expenditures on the social insurance are given by $EFHG$.

Thus, we have the following gains and losses:

1 The non-covered group loses—their loss in consumer surplus is $ABED$.
2 The medical profession gains—their gain is $AJFD$.
3 The covered group gains—the gain is $BJHG$.

The net gain so far is $BJHG + AJFD - ABED = BJHG + BJFE$. But this gain is less than the government expenditure on the programme, which is $EFHG$. Thus, we are left with a net loss given by the shaded triangles EBG and FJH. This measures the net welfare loss to society from the scheme.

The group that is not covered by the programme suffers most. There is a loss in consumer surplus as well as a tax burden arising from the programme. The medical profession is a beneficiary of the programme and so is the covered group, since their increase in consumer surplus $BJHG$ will more than likely be higher than their increased tax burden.

7-12 Application 3: Transport Improvements and Land Values

In the area of transport economics, one question that is often raised is whether an improvement in transport (say, a new motorway) benefits consumers or the landlords owning the land along the motorway. The

answer to this question tells us whether the consumers or the landowners should pay for the cost of the motorway. We discuss the effect of transport improvements on land values by using a simplified model.

Consider a city where all the activity is in the centre. Suppose that there is a road to the city which is used to transport food to the people living in the city. Land along this road is used to produce food. Assume that the costs of production are constant and the same for all land and that costs of transport vary in direct proportion to the distance from the city.

With these assumptions, the supply curve for food is SS_1 in Figure 7-19. The intercept gives the average cost of production, and the slope is the cost of transport per unit distance. If there is an improvement in the mode of transport (say a better road), so that the costs of transport fall, the supply curve shifts down to SS_2. Note that the average cost of production is the same. DD is the demand curve for food.

With the improvement in transport, output rises from OQ_1 to OQ_2, and price falls from OP_1 to OP_2. Since the land is of uniform quality and productivity, some land farther away from the city that was formerly unprofitable to cultivate can now be used to grow food, and hence to command a price. Before the improvement, land closest to the city commanded a rent of CP_1 (cost of production was OC and price OP_1; hence rent was CP_1).[23] After the transport improvement, the rent falls to CP_2. Thus, land values closer to the city fall. For land at Q_1, previously there was no rent; it was the marginal land for which the market price of output was equal to the cost of production plus the cost of transport. After the improvement in transport, the land at Q_2 is the marginal land. Thus, all land between Q_1 and Q_2, which earlier had no rent, now has some rent. Thus, the land values between Q_1 and Q_2 definitely increase.

To see who gains and who loses, we have to compare the vertical distance between $P_1 A$ and SS_1 (the rent before improvement) with the distance between $P_2 B$ and SS_2 (the rent after improvement). At some point Q_0, the land rents start to increase. For points between O and Q_0, the land rents fall. Thus, land values fall for land located between O and Q_0,

---

[23] We discuss the concept of rent in much greater detail in Chapter 15. For now it is sufficient to define rent as the return to a factor that is in short supply. In this case it is land at a particular location that is in short supply.

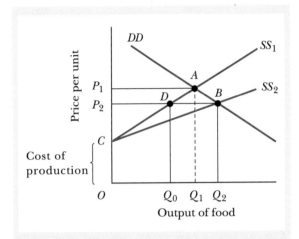

Figure 7-19   Effect of a transport improvement on land values

and land values rise for land located between Q_0 and Q_2. Therefore, landowners in the range O to Q_0 oppose the transport improvement; landowners in the range Q_0 to Q_2 support it.

The consumers in the city definitely benefit from the improvement in transport. The consumer surplus increases by the amount $P_1 ABP_2$. The total rent to landowners changes from $P_1 AC$ to $P_2 BC$. It is difficult to tell whether landowners as a whole gain. Since the common area is $P_2 DC$, the landowners gain as a whole if CDB is greater than $P_1 ADP_2$; if CDB is less than $P_2 DAP'$, they lose.

The net social benefit is the increase in consumer surplus plus the change in land rents. This is

$$P_1 ABP_2 + P_2 BC - P_1 AC = P_1 ABC - P_1 AC = ABC.$$

Whether the consumers' benefit is greater than or less than the net social benefit depends on whether land rents have decreased or increased. Note that increase in consumer surplus minus net social benefit

$$= P_1 ABP_2 - ABC$$
$$= P_1 ADP_2 - CDB,$$

which is the criterion for whether total land rents have decreased or increased.

7-13   Summary

A Pareto optimum is a state of affairs such that no one can be made better off without at least one person

being made worse off. A Pareto improvement is a change in the allocation of resources or goods which makes someone better off and nobody worse off. The designation of a change as a Pareto improvement does not require an interpersonal comparison of utilities. A suggested method for evaluating a change in the allocation of goods which makes one person better off at someone else's expense is the compensation criterion.

Efficiency in consumption requires that the marginal rate of substitution for any pair of goods is the same for all individuals consuming that pair of goods. Production efficiency requires that the marginal rate of technical substitution for any pair of inputs is the same for: (1) all products that a single firm produces using these two inputs, and (2) all producers producing the same output. Efficiency in the matching of production and consumption requires that the marginal rate of transformation in production equals the marginal rate of substitution in consumption.

The Edgeworth box diagram can be used to illustrate efficiency conditions or to examine when and how voluntary exchange can improve the allocation of goods. The contract curve consists of all Pareto-optimal allocations of goods or factors of production. The production possibilities curve consists of all combinations of two products that can be produced with an efficient allocation of inputs.

Efficiency in consumption over time requires that the marginal rate of substitution of present consumption for future consumption is the same for all consumers. Efficiency in production over time requires that the marginal rate of transformation of present goods for future goods is the same for all producers.

Consider two firms using the same technology and the same quantities of all inputs but producing different quantities of output. The X-factor accounts for the output difference. The X-factor encompasses activity type and rate and quality of effort.

Consumer surplus is the excess of the amount that consumers are willing to pay over the amount that they actually do pay. Producer surplus is the excess of the amount actually received by producers over the amount required to induce them to sell. Consumer surplus can be measured as the area below the demand curve and above the price line. But the demand curve must be income-compensated or the income effect must be negligible. Producer surplus can be measured as the area under the price line and above the supply curve.

Price ceilings reduce output and create a shortage. The welfare cost arising from the reduction in output is the amount by which society values the lost units over their production costs. The total cost of the price controls can exceed this amount if the product is not optimally allocated.

Health insurance increases the demand for health care. Hence both price and quantity consumed rise. Physicians' revenues and profits increase. For those people covered by social insurance, the quantity of health services consumed rises; the quantity of health care consumed by the non-covered group falls. Covered consumers gain and physicians gain; non-covered consumers lose. And since the cost of the programme exceeds the net gain (gain to covered consumers and physicians minus loss to non-covered consumers), there is a net social loss.

Improved transport increases the land values for more distant land and reduces the value of land closest to the market. Consumers benefit because transport costs fall, the supply curve shifts downward, and therefore prices fall.

Key Terms

Compensation criterion
Consumer surplus*
Consumption efficiency*
Contract curve*
Deadweight loss*
Edgeworth box*
Initial endowment*
Interpersonal utility comparison*
Pareto improvement*
Pareto optimum*
Producer surplus*
Production efficiency*
Production possibilities curve*
Welfare cost*
X-inefficiency*

Questions

1 Consider Woody and Mia who consume both pizzas P and lagers L. Currently, for Woody the MRS_P for L equals 3,

whereas for Mia the MRS_P for L equals 5. Explain numerically how Woody and Mia could trade these items so that both of them are better off.

2 Do government welfare programmes result in an allocation of resources that constitutes a Pareto improvement over the allocation that would prevail without such programmes? Why or why not?

3 If a reallocation of goods satisfies the compensation criterion and the necessary compensation actually occurs, does the resulting allocation constitute a Pareto improvement? Why or why not?

4 In the case of consumption, does every point on the Edgeworth contract curve represent a Pareto improvement over a point not on the curve? Why or why not?

5 In the case of consumption, does the Edgeworth contract curve go through O_A and O_B? Why or why not?

6 In the Edgeworth box diagram for consumption, what does a vertical movement involve? Can such a movement result from voluntary exchange? What about a horizontal movement?

7 Using an Edgeworth box diagram, demonstrate that an equal division of two goods between two people might not be Pareto optimal.

8 Consider two firms, A and Z, which are almost identical. But suppose that the output of firm Z is of a slightly higher quality. If efficiency is evaluated without considering this quality difference, which firm appears to have a higher X-factor? Suppose, instead, that the labour at A is a little better educated than at Z. If efficiency is again evaluated without considering the difference in labour quality, which firm now appears to have a higher X-factor? Why? What other measurement problems might X-factors pick up?

9 Is the welfare cost of a price control larger when the demand curve is flatter or steeper? Why? When is the loss associated with random allocation larger?

10 Does measuring consumer surplus with an uncompensated demand curve cause the true value to be overstated or understated? Why? Does it matter whether the good is normal or inferior?

11 Suppose that the demand for kebabs is given by $Q = 100 - 20P$. If the price of kebabs is £2, calculate consumer expenditure and consumer surplus. If the price of kebabs increases to £3, what is the reduction in consumer surplus? What is the total value of the associated quantity of kebabs to consumers?

12 Draw an Edgeworth box diagram reflecting preferences between yourself and a friend for pizza and bottles of lager. Suppose initially that you have all the lager and your friend has all the pizza. By constructing the relevant indifference curves, determine the maximum utility level that you can reach through exchange, and that your friend can reach through exchange. In practice, where is the final allocation of pizza and lager likely to be, and what determines this allocation? Suppose your friend who is allergic to fish discovers that the pizza has anchovies in it: how does this affect the analysis?

13 During most market periods anglers catch Q_1 fish and offer it for sale in the market-place. Suppose that in the current period the catch is unusually large, resulting in Q_2 fish offered for sale.

(a) What is the effect on anglers' incomes? Do they gain or lose? Do the anglers hold back some fish from the market?

(b) What is the effect on consumers?

(c) What is the net effect on society?

(d) If it pays anglers to destroy some fish, what measures can be taken to prevent this?

14 Consider the market for a good in which no consumer ever buys more than 1 unit over the market period (for example, football season tickets).

(a) What does an individual's demand curve look like?

(b) What does the market demand curve look like? Explain why the market quantity demanded increases as price falls.

(c) Show in a graph the consumer surplus that a consumer obtains if the consumer purchases the good. Show how it changes if the price falls.

(d) In such cases, is the law of diminishing marginal utility violated? Explain.

15 Explain how the loss in consumer surplus resulting from an increase in price can be broken down into:

(a) the loss in benefit on the units no longer consumed.

(b) increased expenditure on the units still consumed.

(c) decreased expenditure on the units not consumed.

16 'The individual's marginal benefit curve is the same as the individual's demand curve'. Explain the meaning of this statement.

8 Pricing in Product Markets: Competitive Markets

There is no 'invisible hand' in the market place; there are so many hands that most of them cannot be observed at any instant.

George Bernard Shaw

8-1 Introduction

In previous chapters we considered the theory of the consumer and the theory of the producer. We now explain how prices of output and inputs are determined. This chapter and the following three consider pricing in the product market. Chapters 13–15 consider pricing in markets for inputs. In Chapter 1 we said that the market price is determined by the intersection of the market demand and supply curves, but we did not go into detail about how market supply is determined. This is done here and in Chapters 9, 10, and 11. Furthermore, the pricing of output depends on how product markets are organized—that is, whether there are one, two, or many producers, whether the product is homogeneous, and so on. Thus, we have to begin with a classification of markets.

From the point of view of an individual, a market consists of those firms from which the individual can buy a well-defined product. From the point of view of a firm, a market consists of those buyers to whom it can sell a well-defined product. For example, for an individual buying yoghurt, the market for yoghurt consists of all firms from which the individual can buy yoghurt; and for the firm supplying yoghurt, the market consists of all buyers of yoghurt. How many of these buyers a particular firm can attract depends upon how many other firms are operating and how they price yoghurt relative to that firm. These factors fall under the title of *market structure* and are discussed in this and the following chapters.

A group of firms that sells a well-defined product or closely related set of products is said to constitute an *industry*; for example, a group of firms that sells yoghurt (and other related products such as milk, fromage frais, whipped cream, mousse, and so on) is called the dairy industry. The industry can sell its products in different markets (markets in Glasgow, Cardiff, Leicester, and so on). The branch of economics that deals with how an industry is organized is called the *economics of industrial organization*. In practice, an industry can be organized in a large number of forms depending on: (1) the number of firms in the industry, (2) whether the firms produce identical products or similar (but not identical) products, (3) whether entry into the industry is easy or difficult, (4) whether the markets are closely clustered or widely dispersed, (5) whether firms do a lot of advertising, and so on.

However, to make the analysis manageable, economists concentrate on a few models of industrial organization: (1) perfect competition, (2) monopoly, (3) monopolistic competition, and (4) oligopoly. Model 1 is discussed in this chapter, model 2 is

Table 8-1 Different models of industrial organization

Market type	No. of sellers	Entry barriers to sellers	Nature of product
Perfect competition	Many, small; independent	None	Homogeneous
Monopolistic competition	Many, small; virtually independent	None	Differentiated
Oligopoly	Few; interdependent	Substantial	Homogeneous or differentiated
Monopoly	One	Insurmountable	Homogeneous

discussed in Chapters 9 and 10, and models 3 and 4 are discussed in Chapter 11.

All of these are idealized models, and many industries fall in between. The reason we consider these idealized models is that they are manageable and enable us to study some basic principles in the pricing of output. Since many industries fall between the different models, some economists use terms such as 'workably competitive', 'effectively monopolistic', and so on. The question here is: Which of these different models does the dairy industry most closely approximate? Agriculture is often cited as closely approximating the model of perfect competition. Other examples of competitive industries are the service industries and commodity markets.

Although we shall discuss the different models in detail as we proceed, we first give a brief outline of the different characteristics of the four models. This is shown in Table 8-1. In this chapter we consider perfect competition.

8-2   The Profit Maximization Rule*

Before we begin analysing the different forms of industrial organization, we need to lay down some ground rules by which firms operate.

We assume that the goal of the firm is profit maximization. This assumption generally implies that output is expanded to the point where $MR = MC$ (marginal revenue equals marginal cost). Figure 8-1

---

* A mathematical treatment of some of this material is given in the Mathematical Appendix at the end of the book.

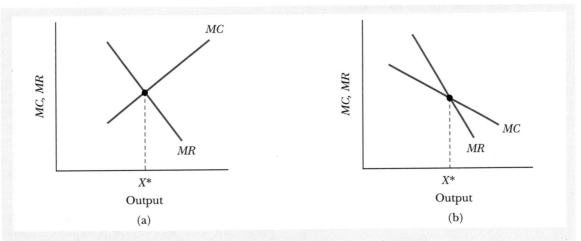

Figure 8-1   Determination of the optimum level of output

(a) Increasing MC
(b) Decreasing MC

demonstrates this implication for two cases: (a) increasing MC and (b) decreasing MC. (Recall that, as long as the demand curve is downward-sloping, the MR curve is also downward-sloping.)

Consider an output level less than X^*. For any such output, $MR > MC$. This means that if the firm expands output it adds more to its revenue than to its costs, thus increasing profit. But once the firm reaches X^*, it has no further incentive to increase output. This is because beyond X^*, $MR < MC$. Thus, by increasing output past X^*, the firm adds more to its costs than to its revenue, thus reducing profit. Hence the profit-maximizing output occurs at X^* where $MR = MC$.

But let us consider the case of declining MC in a little more detail. In order for there to be a determinate level of profit-maximizing output, the MR curve must be steeper than the MC curve as in Figure 8-1(b). The opposite case is illustrated in Figure 8-2, where the condition $MC = MR$ does not give the profit-maximizing output. In fact, in Figure 8-2 the firm can increase profit by increasing output beyond X^*, since $MR > MC$ for levels of output beyond X^*. Unless MC rises above MR, the profit of the firm keeps on increasing as output increases. If MC eventually does rise above MR, then the second point of intersection of these two curves gives the profit-maximizing output. This is shown in Figure 8-3. For both X_1^* and X_2^* we have $MR = MC$. But it is X_2^*, not X_1^*, that gives the profit-maximizing level of output.

Before continuing, it is worth mentioning that many economists argue that the assumption of profit

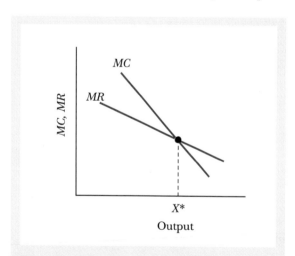

Figure 8-2   Optimum level of output unbounded

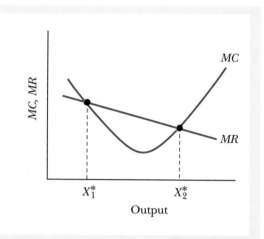

Figure 8-3   Multiple intersections of MR and MC curves

maximization as the goal of the firm is unrealistic. This might be particularly so in large corporations, where there is a split between ownership by shareholders and control by managers. In this case, the profit maximization approach represents only the interests of owners and is probably not applicable. We considered these alternative theories in Chapter 6 (Sections 6-1 and 6-3 to 6-5).

8-3   What is Perfect Competition?

'Perfect competition' is a phrase used often in everyday discussions, and many people have an intuitive and vague understanding of what it means. The concept of perfect competition is very old and was discussed in a casual way in the late eighteenth century by Smith in *The Wealth of Nations*. Edgeworth was the first to attempt (in *Mathematical Psychics*, 1881) a systematic and rigorous definition of perfect competition. The concept received its complete formulation in Knight's book, *Risk, Uncertainty and Profit* (1921).[1]

The concept of perfect competition is based on a large number of assumptions, but the following are the most important:

1   Every firm in the market is so small relative to the market that it cannot exert any perceptible influence on price. Thus, the firm is a *price-taker*.

[1] See G. J. Stigler, 'Perfect Competition Historically Contemplated', *Journal of Political Economy*, 65 (1957): 1–17.

2 The *product is homogeneous.* In the eyes of the consumer, the product of one seller is identical to that of another seller. This ensures that buyers are indifferent as to the firm from which they purchase. If a firm can differentiate its product from that of others, it has at least a partial control over price.

3 The industry is characterized by *freedom of entry and exit.* Any new firm is free to set up production if it so wishes, and any existing firm can stop production and leave the industry if it so wishes.

4 There is *free mobility of resources.* All resources are perfectly mobile. For instance, labour is mobile geographically and among jobs.

5 The participants in the market have *perfect knowledge.* Consumers know prices; producers know costs; workers know wage rates; and so on. In addition, everyone has complete knowledge of the future.

No industry, in practice, satisfies all these conditions. But the usefulness of any theory lies in the predictions it can generate. And the accuracy of such predictions depends in part on whether there are industries that come close to the theoretical model. An industry with 20 firms, none of which is dominant in the market, might be considered closer to competitiveness than another industry with only two or three firms. Thus, the car industry is not a perfectly competitive industry, but the financial services sector might be considered competitive. Whether an industry is perfectly competitive depends on the demand curve *facing the individual firms.* If the demand curve is downward-sloping, then the firm can change price by changing its output and the industry is not perfectly competitive. (The firm is not a price-taker.)

Sometimes a distinction is made between 'pure' and 'perfect' competition—'pure' being a shade less perfect than 'perfect'. Chamberlin defined *pure competition* as 'competition unalloyed with monopoly elements'.[2] The only conditions required for this are a large number of traders and a standardized commodity. Thus, of the five requirements for perfect competition, Chamberlin's concept of pure competition requires only the first two.

Stigler defines an alternative concept, *market competition,* which includes the fifth requirement but not the third and fourth. Thus, market competition

can exist even though resources or traders cannot enter or leave the market in question. The industry does not reach long-run equilibrium, but market competition can still operate.

Note that the assumption of perfect knowledge is not special to the concept of perfect competition. In fact, we can argue that full knowledge of prices is easier to achieve under monopoly than under a system with a larger number of firms.

The preceding discussion illustrates that there are weaker definitions of competition than perfect competition, and each definition is obtained by relaxing a few of the assumptions underlying the concept of perfect competition. We now discuss the problem of pricing.

8-4 Short-run Equilibrium in a Competitive Industry

We first discuss the determination of price and output in a competitive industry in the short run. By 'short run' we mean a length of time during which (1) no new firms enter the industry, (2) no existing firms leave the industry, and (3) the individual firms cannot make any adjustments to fixed inputs.

The price and output in a competitive industry in the short run are determined by the short-run supply and demand curves for the industry. We examined the demand side in earlier chapters. Now we have to consider where the short-run supply curve for the industry comes from. To do this we must derive the short-run supply curve of an individual firm and then aggregate the supply curves of all the firms to get the industry supply curve.

The Demand Curve Facing the Competitive Firm

Consider a relatively homogeneous product such as wheat. The price of the product is determined by the interaction of the total market demand for and supply of the product. But, as we discussed in Sections 8-1 and 8-3, the essential feature of a competitive industry is that there is a large number of firms selling the same homogeneous product. Since each individual firm produces such a small portion of the total, it has a very small or negligible effect on the price of the product. For simplicity, we say that the firm has a zero effect on the price. Alternatively, we say that the competitive firm is a *price-taker.* It takes the market price

---

[2] E. H. Chamberlin, *The Theory of Monopolistic Competition,* Harvard University Press, Cambridge, Mass., 1933, p. 6.

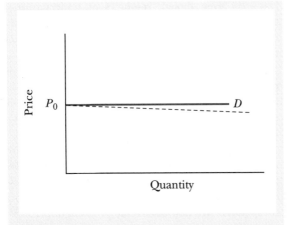

Figure 8-4   The demand curve facing a competitive firm

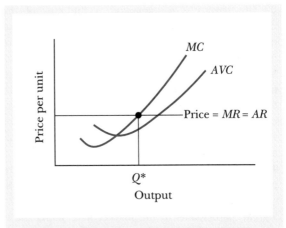

Figure 8-5   Equilibrium of a competitive firm

as given and can sell any amount it wants to at that price; it can sell nothing above that price, and has no reason to sell below it. Thus, the demand curve that a competitive firm faces for *its* output is depicted as a horizontal line D, as shown in Figure 8-4. The elasticity is, therefore, infinity. In reality, the elasticity is very high, and the demand curve is almost horizontal, as shown by the dashed line in Figure 8-4. (It has, in fact, a very small downward slope, but for convenience we take it as horizontal.)

Equilibrium of a Competitive Firm

Since the competitive firm is a price-taker, it calculates its revenue taking price as given. The firm's profit is $TR - TC$ (TR is total revenue and TC is total cost), and the firm produces that output which yields the maximum profit. In Section 8-2 we argued that the condition for profit maximization is $MC = MR$. But for the competitive firm the price is constant, and hence marginal revenue and average revenue are constant and equal to price. Thus, for the competitive firm that is maximizing profit we have

$$AR = P = MR = MC.$$

The equilibrium output is shown in Figure 8-5. Note that the firm does not necessarily produce at the point where its average variable cost AVC is a minimum.

The optimal level of output is Q^* where price $=$ MC. It is not necessarily true that the firm makes a profit at this level of output. Since $AR > AVC$, the

revenue of the firm more than covers the variable costs. Whether they cover total costs depends on the level of fixed costs. In the short run the firm continues to produce as long as revenue covers variable costs. But in the long run the firm's revenue has to cover fixed costs as well in order to enable the firm to stay in production. In the short run the firm must pay the fixed costs even if it chooses not to produce, but in the long run the fixed inputs, and hence the fixed costs, can be eliminated if the firm leaves the industry.

Figure 8-5 shows how much output the competitive firm produces at a given price. By varying the price, we get different levels of output, and this gives the short-run supply curve of the competitive firm. This is shown in Figure 8-6. The minimum output the firm produces is Q_0 where price P_0 is equal to the minimum point on the AVC curve. For any price below P_0 the firm's revenue does not even cover variable costs, and it does not pay for the firm to produce any output.

In Figure 8-6(a) we plot the MC and AVC curves. For different levels of price, we get different quantities supplied by equating price to MC. In Figure 8-6(b) we plot these prices and quantities to get the supply curve.

The supply curve we obtain is a firm's *short-run supply curve* because we assume that the minimum price P_0 is equal to the minimum AVC. That is, we assume that the revenue of the firm must cover variable costs. In the long run, unless revenue covers fixed costs as well, the firm cannot stay in business.

In summary, we have until now discussed the short-run supply curve for a competitive firm. We have

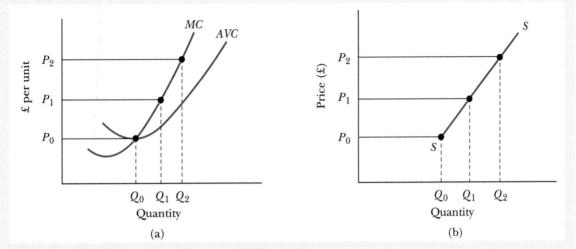

Figure 8-6   Short-run supply curve of a competitive firm

(a) MC and AVC curves
(b) Supply curve

said:

1   If price is less than minimum *AVC* the firm does not produce. Note that this does not mean the firm leaves the industry: it only means a temporary halt in production.

2   If price is equal to or greater than minimum *AVC*, then the firm produces in the short run. And it maximizes its profit by producing where $P = MC$.

3   The firm makes a profit only if price is greater than minimum *ATC*. In all of this discussion, the *MC*, *AVC*, and *ATC* we are considering are the short-run values. That is,

MC = short-run marginal cost
AVC = short-run average variable cost
ATC = short run average total cost

Industry Supply

We now consider the short-run market supply curve for the competitive industry. We obtain the *short-run industry supply curve* by adding the supplies of all the individual firms in the industry. This is based on the marginal costs of the individual firms. The minimum amount supplied by each firm is the level of output where its *AVC* reaches a minimum. Suppose, for the sake of illustration, that there are three firms in the industry. Table 8-2 shows the individual supply curves

and the total industry supply. Of course, in a competitive industry there are a large number of firms. But the industry supply curve is obtained in a similar fashion.

It is important to note that we make a simplifying assumption in deriving the short-run industry supply curve as the horizontal sum of the individual firms' short-run supply curves. We implicitly assume that all the firms move along their individual supply curves without affecting the cost structure of the other firms. In many cases this assumption is unrealistic. For

Table 8-2   The industry supply curve derived as the sum of the supply curves of individual firms: a simplified case

| | Output supplied by | | | |
Price	Firm 1	Firm 2	Firm 3	Total output supplied
10	100	90		190
15	120	105	100	325
20	130	120	120	370
25	140	135	140	415
30	150	150	160	460
Minimum AVC	10	10	15	

example, the expansion of output by all firms might drive up the price of a specialized input. If this happens, then as product price rises and firms attempt to move upward along their individual supply curves, their marginal cost curves (hence their supply curves) shift upward. Thus, firms do not increase output to the extent predicted by their original marginal cost curves.

What does all this mean? It means that the market or industry short-run supply curve is steeper than the sum of the individual firms' supply curves. Similarly, if the short-run expansion of output by all firms favourably affects the costs of the individual firms, then the short-run industry supply curve is flatter than the sum of the individual firms' short-run supply curves.

Industry Equilibrium

The short-run industry supply curve and the short-run market demand curve (derived by aggregating the demand curves of individual consumers) together determine the equilibrium market price. This is shown in Figure 8-7. Note that, although no firm can exert any influence on price, the *collective* action of suppliers and buyers determines the price.

At the price P^*, the industry output is Q^*. This is made up of all the outputs supplied by firms for which P^* exceeds minimum AVC. Firms for whom minimum $AVC > P^*$ do not produce anything. At the price P^*, some firms might be enjoying a short-run profit. These are the firms where P^* exceeds minimum ATC. Still

other firms might be suffering a short-run loss. These are the firms where P^* is less than minimum ATC. And finally, the market clears because quantity demanded equals quantity supplied. Hence, there is no upward or downward pressure on price.

8-5 Long-run Equilibrium in a Competitive Industry

We defined one of the characteristics of perfect competition as easy entry into and exit out of the industry. But such entry and exit can occur only in the long run. This is because potential firms cannot acquire the necessary fixed inputs in the short run, and existing firms cannot get rid of their fixed inputs in the short run.

Also, existing firms have the option of adjusting the quantities of their fixed inputs in the long run. Thus, in the long run we expect two things to happen: (1) existing firms make adjustments to their output and costs; (2) if, after these adjustments, a firm is still unable to cover its total costs, it leaves the industry (and if existing firms are earning profits, then new firms are lured into the industry).

We first consider existing firms. These firms adjust their output to maximize profit. They produce where $LRMC = P$. And each firm adjusts its plant size to minimize the cost of producing its chosen output. Thus, each firm moves to a point on the $LRAC$ curve.

Figure 8-8 illustrates the adjustment process for an existing firm. In the short run, the firm might be stuck with plant size 1 and short-run average and marginal cost curves $SRAC_1$ and $SRMC_1$, respectively. If the price of the product is P, firm 1 maximizes its short-run profit by producing Q_1 units of output so that $MR = SRMC_1$. The firm enjoys a profit equal to the area of the rectangle $abcd$, or $(P - SRAC_1)Q_1$.

But this firm can do better in the long run. If price remains at P, then the firm improves its profit by expanding output to Q_2, where $MR = LRMC$. It must also adjust its plant size to minimize the cost of its output. Thus, plant size is increased to plant size 2 with cost curves $SRAC_2$ and $SRMC_2$. Its profit is now equal to the area of rectangle $aefg$.

In the situation depicted in Figure 8-8, the firm is profitable in both the short run and the long run. In Figure 8-9, we consider a firm that may not operate in the short run but is profitable in the long run. In the short run the firm has plant size 1 with short-run

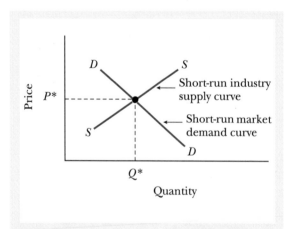

Figure 8-7 Determination of equilibrium price in a competitive market

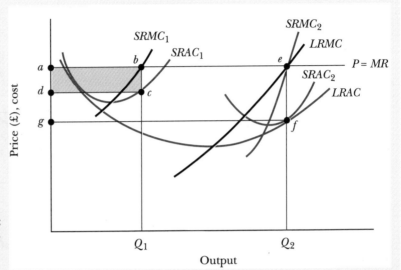

Figure 8-8 Increase in profit for a competitive firm by adjusting output and plant size

average total cost curve $SRAC_1$. If price is equal to P, the firm cannot cover its total costs. If P exceeds minimum average variable cost, then the firm continues to operate at a loss in the short run. But if P is less than minimum AVC, then the firm minimizes its losses by shutting down in the short run. In either case, the firm suffers a short-run loss.

If price remains at P, however, the firm can scale down its plant and operate at a profit in the long run. It produces Q_2, where $LRMC = MR$. And it must also reduce its plant size to minimize the cost of producing

Q_2. The plant size is reduced to plant size 2 with cost curves $SRAC_2$ and $SRMC_2$.

In the previous example, the firm was able to eliminate short-run losses by adjusting output and plant size. But if price is below the minimum point on the long-run average cost curve no such adjustment can eliminate losses, and the firm leaves the industry in the long run.

It is perhaps a good idea to summarize what we have said so far about the behaviour of existing firms as we move from the short run to the long run. (1) The

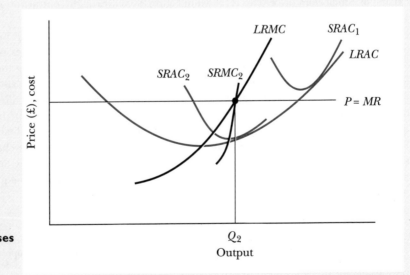

Figure 8-9 Short-run losses but long-run profits

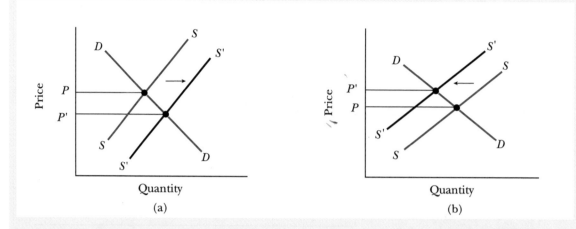

Figure 8-10   Effect of entry and exit of firms on the equilibrium price of a competitive industry

(a) Entry of new firms
(b) Exit of existing firms

firm adjusts output so that $LRMC = P$. (2) The firm adjusts plant size so as to operate along the $LRAC$ curve. (3) If (and only if) price is less than minimum $LRAC$, the firm leaves the industry.

We now examine the impact of entry and exit of firms on the competitive industry. Consider the firm in Figure 8-9. If price remains at P, then the firm enjoys a profit after adjusting output and plant size. But if this is a typical firm, then this profit lures new firms into the industry. The effect of this is to shift the short-run industry supply curve to the right with a consequent decline in equilibrium price. This is shown in Figure 8-10(a). Entry occurs until price falls sufficiently to eliminate all profit. This happens only when price falls to the minimum point on the $LRAC$ curve.

Similarly, if price is less than minimum $LRAC$, so that a typical firm cannot cover costs, the least profitable firms leave. This results in a leftward shift of the short-run industry supply curve and a consequent increase in equilibrium price. This is shown in Figure 8-10(b). Firms continue to leave the industry, shifting supply leftward until losses are eliminated for a typical firm or until price increases to minimum $LRAC$. At that price, the surviving firms cover their full opportunity costs.

We have said that entry or exit of firms occurs until price is equal to minimum $LRAC$ for the typical firm. But entry and exit of firms is not the only factor responsible for the adjustment in price.

In Figure 8-8, we assumed that the market price remains constant while the particular firm we are considering adjusts its output and plant size. But if several firms expand their plant size, then the short-run industry supply curve shifts rightward and price falls.[3] In fact, there might not even be an increase in profit as shown in Figure 8-8. The effect is similar to that of new firm entry into the industry. Thus, an increase in industry short-run supply can occur through expansion of plant size by existing firms or by the entry of new firms. Similarly, a decrease in industry supply can occur through contraction of plant size by existing firms or through exit.

In summary, in the long run a competitive industry undergoes two sorts of adjustment. Existing firms are adjusting their outputs so that $LRMC = P$ to maximize profit. Existing firms are also adjusting their plant sizes so that $SRAC = LRAC$, to minimize the cost of their output. At the same time, new firms may be entering or unprofitable firms may be leaving. All these adjustments cause changes in price which trigger still more adjustments. So when does the industry settle down or reach an equilibrium state?

---

[3] As the firm adjusts plant size, it faces a new $SRMC$ curve and hence a new firm supply curve. Thus, the short-run industry supply curve, which is derived from the individual firm supply curves, shifts.

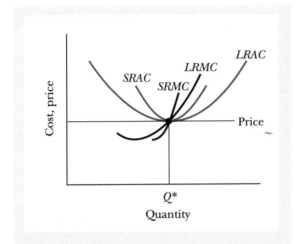

Figure 8-11   Competitive firm in long-run equilibrium

Long-run equilibrium in a competitive industry requires that all incentives for entry or exit be eliminated. This means that price must equal minimum *LRAC* for a typical firm. The typical firm must also be in equilibrium so that it has no incentive to adjust either output or plant size. This requires that $P = LRMC$ and $SRAC = LRAC$. Combining all of these conditions, we have

$$P = LRMC = LRAC = SRAC = SRMC$$

for a typical competitive firm in long-run equilibrium. This situation is illustrated in Figure 8-11.

8-6   The Meaning of Zero Profit in Long-run Competitive Equilibrium

In the previous section we argued that price must equal long-run average cost in equilibrium. Clearly, if price is equal to *LRAC* for each firm, then profit is zero for every firm. What does this zero profit mean? It means that firms are just covering their total costs. But these total costs are economic costs. (We discussed this idea in Section 5-2.) The zero profit is an *economic profit*, so that zero profit means that firms are just able to cover their full opportunity costs. This implies that all factors of production are earning what they could earn in their next best use.

A zero economic profit for all firms does not imply that *accounting profit* is zero or even equal for all firms.

To illustrate these points, consider the following example. Suppose there are two firms, A and B. For A, total revenue is £200 000, and its tangible costs (hired labour, materials bought, rent on equipment, and so on) are £140 000. The firm shows an accounting profit of £60 000. For firm B, total revenue is £200 000 and tangible costs are £100 000. Thus, the firm shows an accounting profit of £100 000. For these two firms accounting profits are positive and different. How can they coexist in a competitive industry over a period of time?

The so-called profit of £60 000 for firm A is the return to the specialized skills of the entrepreneurs operating firm A. (We are ignoring other intangibles such as goodwill.) The so-called profit of £100 000 for firm B is the return to the specialized skills of the entrepreneurs operating firm B. Both these profits are profits only in an accounting sense. In economic terms they are costs—opportunity costs that these entrepreneurs need to be paid for their specialized skills. In the short run these entrepreneurs might receive more or less than their opportunity costs. But in the long run, in a competitive industry the entrepreneurs receive their opportunity cost. Thus, what appear as profits for the different firms are actually opportunity costs for the specialized skills of the entrepreneurs of these firms. Such profits can exist even in the long run in a competitive industry. Since in economic terms they are not profits but opportunity costs, Friedman argues that in a competitive industry, in the long run, we should define total costs as identically equal to total revenue.[4] Here total costs are just the total explicit costs plus the total implicit costs (costs of goodwill and entrepreneurial skills).

The concept of long-run equilibrium is an idealized one. No industry is ever characterized by a situation where none of the firms makes a profit (economic profit) and all firms operate at the minimum point of their *LRAC* curves. In practice, there is continuous technological progress, and those firms using newer equipment and the latest technology have lower costs than others and so make a profit (economic profit). This, in turn, prompts new firms to enter, or existing firms to change their technology; and the profits disappear. Those with the old equipment

---

[4] M. Friedman, 'Comment' on a paper by C. Smith in *Business Concentration and Price Policy*, NBER, Princeton University Press, Princeton, NJ, 1955, pp. 230–8.

continue their operations so long as price covers AVC. If the equipment is so old that price does not cover even AVC, the equipment is replaced. Thus, there is a continuous process of entry and exit, and a continuous modernization of equipment taking place.

Some industries, however, are characterized by exit only. These are *declining industries* where, because of some new developments, the demand for the industry's product is in long-run decline. Examples of this in the UK are the textile, shipbuilding, and steel industries, which for a long time have been exposed to cheap competition from markets in the Far East. As demand declines, price falls, and firms that were previously covering ATC are no longer able to do so. But it takes time for the firms to leave. With declining demand the firms do not undertake any investment in new equipment, but they can continue to operate with existing equipment as long as the price covers AVC. Of course, firms with minimum AVC greater than price shut down immediately. Eventually the industry looks 'sick', with only antiquated equipment. But the antiquated equipment is a result of the industry's decline which is a result of declining demand. In such a situation it does not pay for new firms to enter or the old firms to modernize the equipment.

The manner by which entry of new firms drives down the profits of existing firms in a competitive industry can be seen clearly by looking at the recent experience of the minicomputer and microcomputer manufacturers, and of the manufacturers of electronic games. Initially some of these firms made huge profits, but this induced many new firms to enter the market, and soon the field became so crowded that many companies suffered losses and some were on the verge of bankruptcy. Eventually, this process results in an industry shake-up, and only the fittest survive, with the rest going out of business.

8-7 The Long-run Supply Curve in Constant-, Increasing-, and Decreasing-cost Industries

In Section 8-5 we discussed the response of individual firms in the long run. Each individual firm adjusts its plant size until it is producing at the minimum cost for its chosen output. Furthermore, new firms enter if existing firms are making a profit and existing firms

that are suffering losses leave. Figure 8-10 showed the effect of this entry and exit of firms on the short-run industry supply curve, and Figure 8-11 illustrated long-run equilibrium. One interesting question that we now ask is: What does the long-run supply curve of the competitive industry look like, and how is it obtained?

One important point to note is that the long-run supply curve is *not* obtained by the same procedure as the short-run supply curve. In Section 8-4 we obtained the short-run supply curve of a competitive firm as a portion of its short-run marginal cost curve (see Figure 8-6), and the short-run industry supply curve as an aggregation of the individual firms' supply curves (or short-run marginal cost curves). We *cannot* do this to obtain the long-run supply curve; that is, we cannot get the long-run industry supply curve by aggregating the individual firms' long-run marginal cost curves. This is because we have to account for exit from and entry into the industry.

To obtain the long-run industry supply curve, we make use of the fact that in long-run equilibrium all firms are operating at the minimum point of their long-run average cost curves and this minimum value is equal to the market price for every firm. Thus, to obtain the long-run industry supply curve, we have to ask what happens to the individual firms' average cost curves when the industry output expands. The answer depends on whether the industry is a constant-cost industry, an increasing-cost industry, or a decreasing-cost industry. Thus, we have to consider the following three cases:

1 *Constant-cost industries* These are industries where the individual firm's long-run average cost curve remains stable as the industry expands its output. An example of this is the restaurant industry, where, apart from chefs, the industry employs no specialized inputs.
2 *Increasing-cost industries* These are industries where the individual firm's long-run average cost curve shifts upward as the industry expands its output. This situation arises if some of the productive resources are in limited supply. For example, if there is a limited supply of specific skilled labour, then, as the industry expands its output, each individual firm has to pay a higher price for a unit of this skilled labour. There are several other sources of increasing costs. One such source is increased cost due to congestion in a manufacturing area or in a transport and distribution area. The result is a slowing down of traffic and

distribution. All these sources of increasing costs to the individual firms are called *external diseconomies of scale*. They are 'external' because the firm has no control over them. They are 'diseconomies' of scale because, as the scale or level of industry output rises, each firm's long-run average cost curve shifts up.

3 *Decreasing-cost industries* These are industries where the long-run average cost curve of the individual firm shifts downward as the industry expands its output. One source of decreasing costs is the growth of auxiliary facilities or services. As the industry grows, transport terminals might become available. Information-processing equipment tailored especially for the industry's needs could be provided. Firms supplying inputs to the industry might begin to specialize in serving only that industry, improving service and efficiency. None of this happens in response to a single firm's expansion of output, so we say the resulting decrease in the individual firm's long-run average cost curve is due to *external economies of scale*. Again, they are 'external' because the individual firm has no control over them, and they are 'economies' because, as the scale of industry output increases, each firm's long-run average cost curve shifts downward.

The Long-run Industry Supply Curve

We now consider what the long-run industry supply curve looks like in each of these cases. We really need

to remember only that, in long-run equilibrium, price is equal to minimum long-run average cost.

In the case of constant-cost industries, as the industry expands its output, the *LRAC* curve for each individual firm stays the same. Hence, price, which is the minimum point on the *LRAC* curve, does not change in the long run. The long-run industry supply curve is horizontal. This is shown in Figure 8-12(a).

In the case of increasing-cost industries, the *LRAC* curve of each firm shifts upward as the industry expands its output. Thus, the market price, which is the minimum point on the *LRAC* curve, has to rise in order for the industry to expand its output. The long-run industry supply curve is therefore upward-sloping, as shown in Figure 8-12(b).

Finally, in decreasing-cost industries the *LRAC* curve shifts downward as the industry expands its output. In this case the long-run industry supply curve is downward-sloping, as shown in Figure 8-12(c).

Effect of Changes in Demand

Now that we know the shape of the long-run supply curve of the competitive industry, we can study the effect of changes in demand on the output of the industry and the price level.

In Figure 8-13, SS is the long-run industry supply curve for the constant-cost case; ΣMC_1 is the initial sum of the marginal cost curves or the initial short-run industry supply curve; $D_1 D_1$ is the initial demand

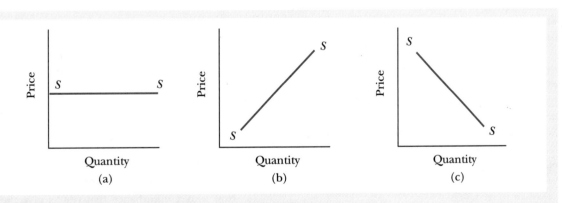

Figure 8-12 The long-run supply curve for a competitive industry

(a) Constant-cost industry
(b) Increasing-cost industry
(c) Decreasing-cost industry

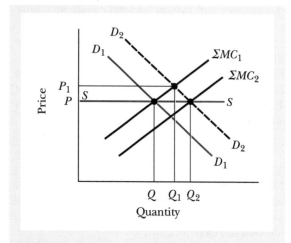

Figure 8-13 Effect of an increase in demand in a constant-cost industry

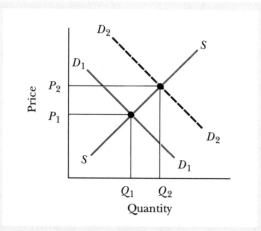

Figure 8-14 Effect of an increase in demand in an increasing-cost industry

curve. Now suppose that demand increases to $D_2 D_2$. Immediately, there is a shortage at the initial price of P. This causes price to rise to P_1. As price rises, existing firms expand their output along their short-run supply curves so that industry output increases from Q to Q_1. But at a price of P_1, firms can earn a pure economic profit as P_1 is greater than minimum $LRAC$. Thus, new firms are drawn into the industry. As new firms enter, the industry short-run supply curve shifts to the right, putting downward pressure on price. Price continues to fall until it again equals minimum $LRAC$, or until it returns to P. Thus, in the long run an increase in demand brings about an increase in industry output with no change in price. A decrease in demand has the opposite effect.

The situation with an increasing-cost industry is shown in Figure 8-14. Again, SS is the long-run industry supply curve, and $D_1 D_1$ is the initial demand curve. Now the demand curve shifts to $D_2 D_2$. It is clear that, once the industry settles back to a long-run equilibrium, the equilibrium quantity has increased to Q_2 and the equilibrium price has increased to P_2. The effect of a decrease in demand is the opposite. Both the long-run equilibrium price and quantity decline.

Decreasing-cost Industries

The case of decreasing-cost industries is a little more complicated. Now both the demand and long-run supply curves are downward-sloping. To analyse the

effects of changes in demand, we have to decide which of these two curves is the steeper. The two cases are shown in Figure 8-15. In part (a) the supply curve is steeper than the demand curve. P^* is the equilibrium price. Suppose the equilibrium is disturbed and the price rises temporarily to P_1. At this price the quantity supplied is greater than the quantity demanded, and the price has a tendency to fall. Thus, the market price falls back to the equilibrium level P^*. Similarly, with a temporary decline in price, quantity demanded is higher than quantity supplied and, therefore, price rises to the original equilibrium level. Thus, the equilibrium is said to be *stable*.

The reverse appears to be true in case (b). It appears in Figure 8-15(b) that, with a disturbance that raises the price to P_1, quantity demanded is greater than quantity supplied, and so price has a tendency to rise further and, thus, deviate more and more from the equilibrium level P^*. However, this is not so. Note that, even when the long-run industry supply curve is downward-sloping, at each point on this curve the short-run supply curve is upward-sloping. This is shown in Figure 8-16. The short-run supply curves are shown as broken lines. They are denoted by S_1, S_2, and so on.

Now with a disturbance that results in a rise in price from the equilibrium level P^* to P_1, each firm tries to increase its output, and so there is an increase in the quantity supplied and a consequent excess supply. This pushes the price down to the equilibrium level P^*. This is shown in Figure 8-17. The initial

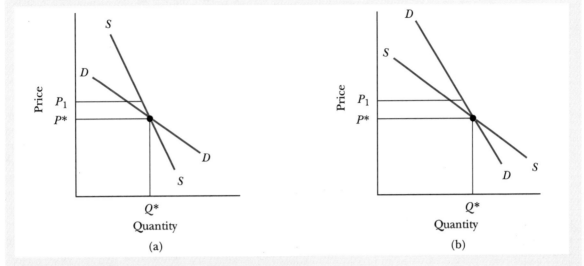

Figure 8-15   Equilibrium in a decreasing-cost industry

(a) Supply curve steeper than demand curve
(b) Demand curve steeper than supply curve

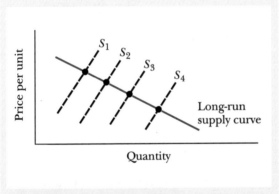

Figure 8-16   Short-run industry supply curves in a decreasing-cost industry

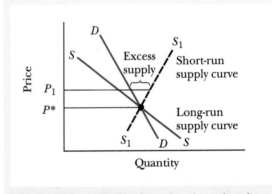

Figure 8-17   Effect of a rise in price in a decreasing-cost industry

equilibrium price is P^*, and the short-run supply curve is $S_1 S_1$. With the price rising to P_1 we see that there is an excess supply, and this pushes the price back to the equilibrium level P^*.

It is not easy to think of many examples of decreasing-cost industries, although we might suggest computers and electronics industries. In practice, however, as we see in the next section, it is hard to distinguish between decreasing-cost industries and industries with rapid technological progress.

Decreasing costs are likely to occur only after the industry has reached a certain scale of output, hence the long-run industry supply curve bends forwards at higher levels of output. This is shown in Figure 8-18. The industry is an increasing-cost industry until the output level reaches Q_1 and a decreasing-cost industry thereafter.

Since the supply curve is more likely to be only slightly forward-bending for a decreasing-cost industry, we use Figure 8-15(b) to analyse the effects

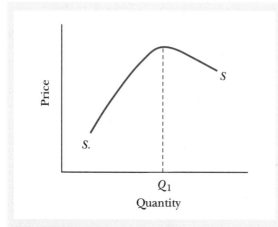

Figure 8-18   A forward-bending long-run industry supply curve

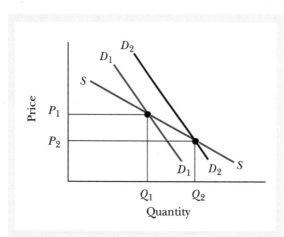

Figure 8-19   Effect of an increase in demand in a decreasing-cost industry

of changes in demand. In this case the demand curve is steeper than the long-run supply curve, and the effect of an increase in demand is that the long run equilibrium price declines and the equilibrium output rises. This is shown in Figure 8-19. SS is the long-run supply curve and $D_1 D_1$ the initial demand curve. The initial equilibrium price level is P_1 and output level is Q_1. With an increase in demand, the demand curve shifts to $D_2 D_2$. In the long run, the equilibrium price level falls to P_2 and the quantity rises to Q_2.

Decreasing-cost Industries and Government Intervention

With decreasing-cost industries, it is often argued that government should intervene to force firms to expand their output so that the benefits of external economies of scale are realized. It is argued that each firm has no incentive to expand its output because it does not know the benefits of the external economies of scale that would accrue to it from the expansion of the industry output. However, this argument is valid only if we assume that the entrepreneurs of the individual firms have no foresight at all. In the case of the US railway industry, economic historians have found that railway investment (before the Civil War) was based on optimistic expectations about the benefits that would come from an expansion of the industry output. Thus, there was no deficiency of private investment and no need for government coercion.[5]

8-8   Technological Change and the Long-run Industry Supply Curve

Suppose that over time we observe an industry where price per unit of output has declined while quantity produced has risen. This has been the case with personal computers, video recorders, pocket calculators, and so on. Then can we say, using the conclusions in Figure 8-19, that the industry is a decreasing-cost industry? Not necessarily. To see this, we have to consider the effects of technological change on the industry supply curves.

   The term *technological change* refers to all those commercially applicable scientific discoveries that enable us to produce more of a particular output from the same given sets of inputs. For example, more potent fertilizer enables us to produce more wheat on the same land with the same amount of labour as before; some hybrid seeds have been found to increase output several times; advances in computer technology enable us to perform calculations much faster than previously. The effect of technological change is to lower the long-run average cost curves of firms, and hence to shift the long-run supply curves to the right.

[5] See A. Fishlow, *American Railroads and the Transformation of the Ante-bellum Economy*, Harvard University Press, Cambridge, Mass., 1965.

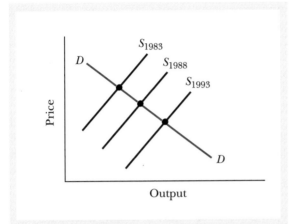

Figure 8-20   Shifts in supply curves produced by technological change

8-9   Application I: Rent Control

In many countries during and after the Second World War, price controls were imposed on rented accommodation with the purpose of protecting renters from avaricious landlords. These price controls, known as rent controls, persisted for many years after the war;[6] in Sweden, for instance, rent controls which were introduced in 1942 survived until 1975. (A new rent regulation system was then introduced in 1978.) In the UK rent control was first introduced as an emergency measure in 1915 but continued until 1957, when an element of decontrol was permitted. In 1965 rent controls were imposed again, but the 1988 Housing Act saw more moves towards deregulation, with all *new* tenancies subject to the market rent. Over all, however, rent controls have proved difficult to abolish; in fact, some of the rent controls in Europe can apparently be traced to the time of the Napoleonic Wars.

Thus, even with an unchanging demand and an increasing-cost industry (so that the supply curve is positively sloped), we can have falling prices and increasing output, as the supply curve shifts to the right in response to technological change. This is shown in Figure 8-20. As the supply curve shifts to the right, we note that the equilibrium price falls but the equilibrium quantity rises. Thus, the long-run behaviour of price and quantity is the same in the cases of both Figures 8-19 and 8-20; but the interpretation of the results is different. (1) Figure 8-19 refers to an industry with a downward-sloping supply curve and a shifting demand curve. (2) Figure 8-20 refers to a stable demand but an upward-sloping supply curve that is shifting over time.

Earlier we said that in decreasing-cost industries there are external economies of scale. These economies can be technological as well. In this case, in Figure 8-19 we have external technological economies of scale and in Figure 8-20 we have technological change. We have to distinguish between these two terms. For example, availability of better computers, availability of better production equipment, and so on constitute technological change. These result in shifts of the supply curve as shown in Figure 8-20. However, availability of computer services at a cheaper rate when the industry output expands comes under technological economies of scale. This causes the long-run industry supply curve to slope downward.

The consequences of rent controls can be easily demonstrated with a simple demand and supply analysis. (As we shall presently see, this analysis conceals a lot of complications and detail.) This simple analysis is shown in Figure 8-21. *DD* is the demand curve and *SS* the long-run supply curve. (The industry supplying rental housing is assumed to be an increasing-cost industry, and so we draw the supply

[6] The experience of a number of countries is analysed in M. Walker (ed.), *Rent Control: A Popular Paradox*, Fraser Institute, Vancouver, BC, 1975, and R. Albon and D. Stafford, *Rent Control*, Croom Helm, London, 1987.

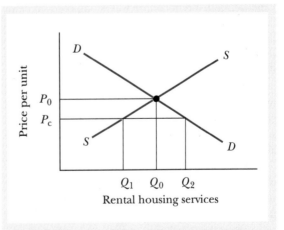

Figure 8-21   Consequences of rent control

curve as positively sloping.) P_0 is the initial equilibrium price, and Q_0 is the equilibrium quantity. If price is controlled at the level P_c, the quantity supplied falls to Q_1, the quantity demanded rises to Q_2, and a 'shortage' develops.

This simple analysis, however, leaves a number of questions unanswered:

1 How does the quantity of rental housing services decline from Q_0 to Q_1?
2 What happens to the excess demand $Q_2 - Q_1$?
3 Who benefits and who loses from the rent controls?
4 Why do rent controls persist if they are harmful?

We shall answer these questions in turn, but before we proceed, we have to realize that the simple demand and supply analysis shown in Figure 8-21 conceals several institutional arrangements involved in rent control legislation. We cannot go through all these in detail here, but for the sake of illustration we point out a few of the issues.

Does the landlord have the right to evict the tenant? Suppose he does but still can rent the housing unit only at the controlled price. Then, in order to increase his income from the property, the landlord can evict the existing tenant and do one of two things. He can either convert the rented property into two or more smaller dwellings to rent, or he can rent it again but only on condition that the incoming tenant buy some furniture at an exorbitant price.

Does the rent control apply only to existing units or to newly constructed units as well? If rent control applies only to existing units, it should not affect the construction of new rental housing. If there is an expectation that rent control will be imposed on newly constructed units as well (possibly at a future date), then the suppliers of new rented properties will take this into account when making their investment decisions and setting the current rental rates on the new units. Thus, even if there is no rent control on newly constructed properties, the expectation of rent control being imposed at a later date reduces the supply of new rental units below what it would be in the absence of rent control.

If rent control does not apply to newly constructed units, and if landlords can evict tenants for the purpose of reconstruction, then they might find it profitable to demolish buildings that are still in good shape and reconstruct the rental units to rent out at a higher rate. This seems to have happened in Hong Kong following rent control legislation in 1921; during the following five years there was a 'reconstruction craze'.[7]

These complications suggest that the quantity of rental housing supplied under rent control could be greater than the amount Q_1 shown in Figure 8-21. However, to analyse the exact nature of the supply of rental housing under rent control legislation we have to make a detailed analysis of the institutional arrangements that are permitted. Since this is quite beyond our scope, we confine our analysis to that given in the simplified diagram in Figure 8-21 and answer the four questions we raised earlier.[8]

How Does the Quantity of Rental Housing Services Decline?

If landlords are prevented from raising rents and they cannot evict the existing tenants, they simply let the rental units deteriorate in quality over time. They do not undertake any maintenance expenditures, and for this reason rent control can breed slums. Thus, the decline in the quantity of housing services shown as a decline from Q_0 to Q_1 in Figure 8-21 comes about through (1) a progressive deterioration in the quality of rented properties or (2) the conversion of rented properties into flats.

What Happens to the Excess Demand?

Figure 8-21 shows an excess demand at the controlled price of P_c. This excess demand results in a queue for rental units at the controlled price. But people have to find a place to live even while they are in the queue.

---

[7] This is described in an analysis of the effects of rent control in Hong Kong by S. N. S. Cheung; 'Rush or Delay? The Effects of Rent Control on Urban Renewal in Hong Kong', in R. Albon (ed.), *Rent Control: Costs and Consequences*, Centre for Independent Studies, St Leonards, Australia, 1980.

[8] Some readers might find it interesting to study this problem in detail with special reference to a particular country or locale. One example is that of the Los Angeles housing market. References on this can be found in G. Fallis and L. B. Smith, 'Uncontrolled Prices in a Controlled Market: The Case of Rent Controls', *American Economic Review*, 74 (1984): 193–200. Fallis and Smith analyse the problem that in many instances of rent control newly constructed units, vacated units, and high-priced units are exempt from rent controls. They show that the rents on the uncontrolled market are likely to be higher (if there are rent controls on some units) than if there were no rent controls at all. The paper also discusses some earlier papers on the effects of price control on a related market.

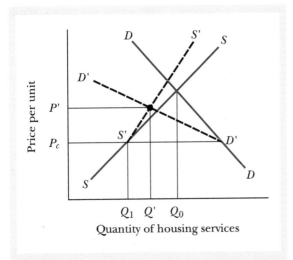

Figure 8-22 A black market in rental housing under rent control

Some of the people switch over to the owner-occupied housing market. Others may have their demand satisfied at higher effective rents (payment of 'key money', or agreeing to buy furniture at exorbitant prices set by the landlord in order to obtain the rental unit at the controlled price). The switch to owner-occupied housing implies that the demand curve shifts to the left, and the availability of some housing at the controlled price (but with the payment of key money or purchase of furniture) implies that there is a black market supply. These two factors result in a new equilibrium being established where the quantity of rental housing services supplied is greater than Q_1 (although still less than Q_0) and the equilibrium price is higher than the controlled price P_c. This is shown in Figure 8-22. $S'S'$ is the black market supply curve, and $D'D'$ is the new demand curve. The equilibrium quantity is now Q', which is greater than Q_1 although less than Q_0. The equilibrium price is P', which is higher than the controlled price P_c.

Who Benefits and Who Loses from Rent Control?

In the short run, immediately after the imposition of rent control, the owners of rental units are worse off. They find the return to their investment reduced by law. Over time, however, they are able to reduce their losses because they do not incur as many expenses for maintenance and repair.

As far as tenants are concerned, in the short run they are better off. In fact, the purpose of rent control is precisely to benefit tenants. However, in the long run tenants as a group are worse off because of the adverse effects rent control has on the long-run *quantity* supplied. Those tenants who cannot get rental units have to go to the owner-occupied housing market or pay a much higher effective rent in the black market (through the purchase of useless furniture or payment of key money).[9] Even those who are fortunate enough to obtain rental housing at the controlled price may find that the quality of their rental unit deteriorates over time and their neighbourhood turns into a slum area.

One of the primary arguments used in favour of rent control is that landlords are richer than tenants and so rent control has a desirable redistributive effect. There is, however, no empirical evidence supporting this claim. Many of the owners of rental housing have lower incomes than the tenants, and it is not necessarily true that it is the low-income tenants who benefit from rent control. Many of the families living in housing with controlled rents have been found to have higher incomes than families that are unable to find any rental housing. Rent control can produce a highly random redistribution of wealth.[10]

Finally, in the case of housing, the needs of families change over time with the increase or decrease in family size. But many families cannot make the necessary changes, because the costs of moving from a unit with controlled rent are very high. Thus, older couples whose children have left home continue to occupy large rental units and younger couples whose family size is increasing are stuck in small rental units.

Why Do Rent Controls Persist?

If, as we have argued, rent controls are harmful to tenants, one interesting question is: Why do rent controls persist? The answer is that, in the short run, rent control may be a rational choice of consumers. And, in fact, the likelihood of finding rent control in a

---

[9] Rent controls may be especially harmful to single mothers and members of minority groups because the excess demand creates a waiting list which allows landlords to discriminate at zero cost.

[10] See D. G. Johnson, 'Rent Control and the Distribution of Income', *American Economic Review*, 41 (1951): 31–41.

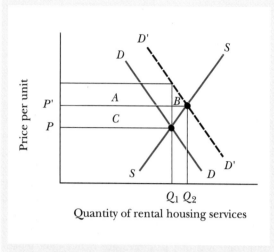

Figure 8-23 Consumers' preference for rent control under an exogenous increase in demand

particular locale increases with the size of the rental sector of the housing market.[11]

To see why consumers are likely to opt for rent control, we can use the analysis of consumer surplus (which we discussed in Chapter 7). Consider Figure 8-23. DD and SS are the initial demand and supply curves, respectively, with the equilibrium price P. Now a sudden change occurs which leads to an increase in equilibrium price. This could be a shift of the supply curve to the left or of the demand curve to the right. Examples of causes of a shift of the supply curve to the left are (1) the destruction of large portions of the housing stocks in several European cities during the Second World War and (2) the destruction of more than half the housing stock in San Francisco following the earthquake of 1906. Some causes of a shift of the demand curve to the right are (1) the influx of immigrants into Hong Kong in the 1920s and (2) the heavy immigration of refugees from the former Yugoslavia into Germany in the early 1990s. Since the analysis is similar, we have illustrated the latter case in Figure 8-23.

In all these cases, the result is a rise in the equilibrium price. Suppose the consumers have a choice between allowing the market price to rise to

the new equilibrium level or having rent controls. Which do they choose?

In Figure 8-23, $D'D'$ is the new demand curve and P' the new equilibrium price. If the price is controlled at the old price P, then consumer surplus is the area under $D'D'$, above P and up to Q_1. If, however, price is allowed to rise to P', then consumer surplus is the area under $D'D'$, above P' and up to Q_2. Thus, consumer surplus is larger with the price control if the area of rectangle C is larger than the area of triangle B. In many practical cases, therefore, particularly if the supply curve is steep, consumers gain, and they have an incentive to vote for price controls.

We have discussed the problem of rent control at length, since it has several fascinating aspects to it. We have seen that the simple analysis in Figure 8-21 is useful merely to give us a rough idea of the consequences of rent control. Unlike the case of the market for pizza and lager, the rental housing market involves different contractual arrangements between owners of the rental units and the tenants; and the consequences of rent control on the supply of and demand for rental housing depend on how rent control legislation affects these contractual arrangements. Thus, one needs a more detailed analysis than that in Figure 8-21.

8-10 Application 2: Price Control in Decreasing-cost Industries

In the preceding section we considered an example of price (rent) control in an industry that we said was an increasing-cost industry. (We drew the long-run industry supply curve as upward-sloping.) We also saw the adverse effects such price control has. Price controls have even more severe effects in decreasing-cost industries. In fact, the output can decline to zero.

The situation is illustrated in Figure 8-24. DD is the demand curve and SS the downward-sloping long-run supply curve. Suppose that price controls are initiated with the controlled price set below the equilibrium price. Then, price is P_c and the controlled quantity is Q_0. At Q_0, P_c is less than marginal cost, and so firms try to curtail output and move down their marginal cost curves (shown as ΣMC in Figure 8-24). However, as the industry output goes down, the marginal costs of each firm rise, and then each firm tries to curtail its output

[11] See D. Marks, 'Public Choice and Rent Control', *Atlantic Economic Journal*, 13 (1983): 63–9.

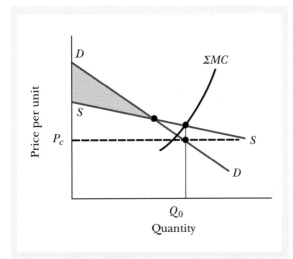

Figure 8-24 Effects of price control in a decreasing-cost industry

further. This process goes on until the output of the industry is reduced to zero. (If the decreasing costs start after a level of output Q_1, as in Figure 8-18, then the process continues until output contracts to Q_1.)

It is also easy to see this by noting that points under the SS curve (and above P_c) are not feasible (the suppliers suffer losses), and points above the DD curve are also not feasible (since the demand curve shows the *maximum* quantity demanded at each price). Thus, if we consider points above the supply curve and below the demand curve, the feasible region is given by the shaded portion in Figure 8-24, and the price level P_c is not in this region. However, we can easily see that a price *support* programme (where prices are supported at a level higher than the equilibrium price) is feasible even in a declining-cost industry. Thus, whereas price controls are harmful in an increasing-cost industry, they are potentially disastrous in a decreasing-cost industry.

8-11 Application 3: The Common Agricultural Policy

In the previous two sections we considered price controls, by which we mean situations where prices have ceilings or limits above which they are prevented from rising. These price ceilings are below the market equilibrium price. There is another form of price control—price floors or price supports. In this case prices are not allowed to fall below a certain level; that is, they are 'supported' at a level higher than the market equilibrium level.

Farmers in Europe are guaranteed a minimum price for many agricultural commodities through the European Union (EU) Common Agricultural Policy (CAP). The CAP aims both to stabilize prices and to support farm incomes at a level that gives a fair standard of living for the agricultural community. Incomes have been supported mainly by the high administered prices for agricultural products. In the CAP, the EU sets a minimum (or intervention) price above the market-clearing level, and it is this price that determines the floor in the domestic market. At this price the EU is obliged to purchase any excess supply that is on offer. A detailed analysis of the principles and method of the CAP are beyond the scope of this book, but we can, with the aid of a simple diagram, capture the essence of the policy and see the consequences of setting the minimum price.[12] This is shown in Figure 8-25. The analysis removes many of the complications (for instance, supply and demand outside the EU is ignored) in order to show the basic idea. The supply curve is the sum of all the producers' individual MC

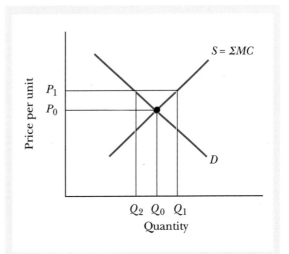

Figure 8-25 Effects of the Common Agricultural Policy

[12] For a comprehensive discussion of the principles and method of the CAP, see T. Hitiris, *European Community Economics* (2nd edn.), Harvester-Wheatsheaf, London, 1991, Ch. 7.

curves. The demand curve shows the total EU demand for the good (whether it be wine, cereals, butter, etc.). The closed economy equilibrium is P_0 with equilibrium quantity at Q_0. At the intervention price P_1 there is excess supply of $Q_1 - Q_2$. The question is: What happens to this excess supply? Since the EU guarantees a minimum price, it is obliged to purchase whatever output is not sold in the market. The surplus is either put into buffer stocks to prevent large fluctuations in the market price, or is sold at reduced prices either domestically or abroad at world prices as EU exports.

Who benefits and who loses from the CAP? On the whole, consumers may be said to lose. While they gain from price stability, they have to pay higher prices for agricultural products since EU prices are well above world prices. The farmers are supposed to benefit. The evidence, however, shows that, because the CAP has failed to concentrate on poor farmers, it is actually the richest farmers and the biggest agribusinesses who benefit most.

One aim of the CAP is to solve the income problem by setting high administered prices. Economic theory considers direct income payments (a lump-sum income transfer to farmers) as the more efficient way of solving the income problem. Manipulation of the market price introduces a divergence between MC and price, causing inefficiencies in the allocation of resources which do not occur with a simple income subsidy programme.

It is interesting to note the similarities and differences between the case of rent control we discussed earlier and the CAP. There is an income distribution aspect to both the problems. The presumed aim of rent control is to 'protect poor tenants from the exploitation of rich landlords'. There is some question as to whether tenants are poorer or richer than landlords and what 'exploitation' means, but we cannot question the fact that there are many poor tenants who do benefit from rent control. Furthermore, the income subsidy plan that we can devise for poor tenants is not very clear-cut (apart from a general negative income tax). We can think of a housing stamp programme for poor families, but the problems of such a programme are similar to those of education vouchers, which we discussed in Chapter 2.

In the case of the CAP, one of the aims is to protect the incomes of poor farmers from wide fluctuations. The income distribution consequences

here are more clear-cut than in the case of rent control. A major portion of the subsidies have gone to the richest farmers. The alternative solutions to price supports—lump-sum transfers—are also more easily implemented than in the rent control case.

There is one other important difference between the two cases. The sole aim of rent control is income redistribution. The purpose of the CAP is also to reduce the fluctuations in price that farmers receive. To the extent that farmers' supply decisions are based on expected prices and the price supports reduce the uncertainty about expected prices, price supports have some beneficial effect. The fact that there are other ways of reducing uncertainty about expected prices is another story. To analyse this aspect of uncertainty is beyond the scope of our analysis here, but this argument suggests that in Figure 8-25 the existence of price supports shifts the supply curve (through the effect on the supply decisions of farmers).

Thus, we see that Figure 8-25 gives a very simplified analysis of the CAP, although it is enough for the purpose of our discussion. In practice, the CAP is complicated by other problems—subsidies, uncertainty, and so on.

8-12 Application 4: Nonprice Competition in the US Airline Industry

In the previous section we discussed a situation where agricultural prices are supported at a level higher than the market equilibrium level. In this case the EU has to absorb the excess supply in some form or another. Suppose we have a situation where government regulates a price above the market equilibrium level and lets the firms take care of the excess supply. Then what can the firms do? Since they cannot compete with each other on price, they have to compete in other ways (by providing other accessory benefits). This continues to the point where the excess supply disappears. This type of competition is called *nonprice competition*, and the US airline industry is an example of it.

Before the Air Deregulation Act of 1978, the airline industry in the United States was regulated by the Civil Aeronautics Board (CAB). The CAB was established in 1938 under the Civic Aeronautics Act.

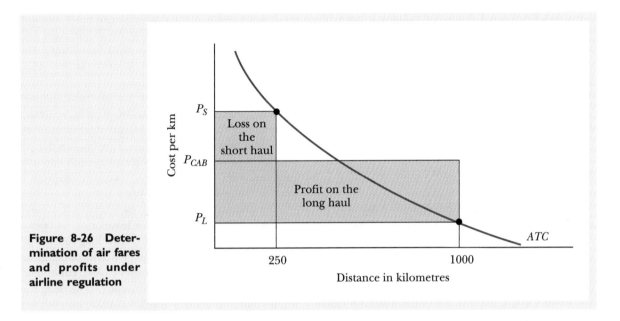

Figure 8-26 Determination of air fares and profits under airline regulation

The 1938 Act, amended later by another Act in 1958, gave the CAB absolute authority to set maximum as well as minimum fares. We cannot go through the details of all the objectives of the CAB and the means by which CAB intended to achieve them. We simply discuss the pricing scheme adopted by the CAB.

Broadly speaking, the fares that the CAB set were such that they subsidized short-distance traffic and taxed long-distance traffic. The purpose of the fare structure was to ensure the development of a comprehensive route network. (This was also the reason for the regulation of the Australian airline industry. It was deregulated in 1990.)

If price competition is allowed and there are no barriers to entry, price is equal to marginal cost in the short run and to average total cost in the long run. Thus, if we have two destinations, say one 250 kilometres away and another 1000 kilometres, and we equate price per kilometre to the average cost per kilometre, we have a higher price per kilometre for the short-distance destination than for the long-distance destination. This is because air transport involves a large amount of fixed costs (capital equipment, salaried personnel, cost of airport terminals, and so on), and the average variable costs (fuel costs) are fairly constant. This clearly implies that, since average fixed costs decline with distance, average total costs decline with distance. This is shown in Figure 8-26. ATC is the declining average total cost curve; P_S is the price

that is charged for the shorter distance, and P_L is the price that is charged for the longer distance under price competition. The CAB requires airlines to charge a uniform price shown as P_{CAB}. This amounts to a subsidy of $(P_S - P_{CAB})$ per kilometre for the short-haul traffic and a tax of $(P_{CAB} - P_L)$ per kilometre for the long-haul traffic.

At the prices P_S and P_L for the short-haul and long-haul traffic, respectively, the airline is not making a profit. At the CAB price, the airline is losing money on the short-haul traffic but making a profit on the long-haul traffic. The CAB fixed the price in such a way that the profit on the long haul was considerably greater than the loss on the short-haul traffic, as shown in Figure 8-26. This should have resulted in high profits for the airline industry. This did not, however, happen, for the following reason.

Since the CAB determined the fares, the airlines could not compete on price. Therefore, they began competing on service. This *nonprice* or *service competition* took several forms, such as greater frequency of flights, attractive flight attendants, free drinks, free movies, and so on. This service competition increased the average costs for the airlines to the point where they earned only normal profits. It is easy to see in Figure 8-26 that, as the ATC curve shifts upward, the profit on the long haul decreases (and the loss on the short haul might also increase), and the net profit disappears.

Thus, the effect of the price regulation by the CAB was that the airlines did not benefit and consumers had to pay higher average fares than they would have done without the regulation. They were provided with some frills that many perhaps did not need or care about. The only beneficiaries were the communities that would not have had air service without the subsidy provided by the CAB fare structure.

8-13 Summary

With an upward-sloping MC curve, profit maximization occurs where $MR = MC$. With a downward-sloping MC curve, the output where $MR = MC$ corresponds to a profit maximum if the MR curve is steeper than the MC curve but to a profit minimum if the MC curve is steeper than the MR curve.

Perfect competition involves many relatively small firms producing a homogeneous product in an industry characterized by freedom of entry and exit. Resources must be mobile, and all participants must have perfect knowledge of present and future market conditions. There are several weaker definitions of competition.

The market price, under competition, is determined by the intersection of the industry supply curve and the market demand curve. The demand curve facing the individual firm is horizontal at the market price. Equilibrium for the competitive firm requires $MC = MR = AR = P$. MC must equal MR for profit maximization. And $MR = AR = P$ because the firm is a price-taker. In the short run, the firm continues to produce as long as price exceeds minimum AVC. The firm's short-run supply curve is its MC curve above its AVC curve. The industry's short-run supply curve can be equal to, steeper than, or flatter than the horizontal sum of the individual firms' short-run supply curves.

In the long run, existing firms make adjustments to their outputs and costs. If, after these adjustments, a firm is still unable to cover its total costs, it leaves the industry. And if existing firms are earning a profit, new firms enter the industry. Long-run profit maximization requires that output is expanded to the point where $LRMC = P$. The firm must also be producing this output at the lowest possible cost, which requires that the firm operates on the $LRAC$ curve. If price is less than minimum $LRAC$, then the firm leaves the industry. If price exceeds minimum $LRAC$, then profits are made. Firms enter the industry, shifting the short-run industry supply curve to the right and pushing price down until $P = $ minimum $LRAC$. The opposite adjustment occurs if price is less than minimum $LRAC$.

Long-run equilibrium for a competitive industry requires that $P = LRAC = LRMC = SRAC = SRMC$. In long-run competitive equilibrium, a firm must be earning a zero economic profit. This implies that all factors of production are receiving their full opportunity cost. This does not imply that accounting profit is zero or that it is equal for all firms.

In a constant-cost industry, each firm's $LRAC$ curve remains stable as firms enter or leave or as the output of the existing firms expands. The long-run supply curve for a constant-cost industry is horizontal. In an increasing-cost industry, each firm's $LRAC$ curve shifts upward as firms enter the industry. The long-run supply curve for an increasing-cost industry is positively sloped. In a decreasing-cost industry, each firm's $LRAC$ curve shifts downward as firms enter the industry. The long-run supply curve for a decreasing-cost industry is negatively sloped.

Technological change shifts the firms' long-run average cost curves downward, and hence shifts the long-run industry supply curve to the right. Rent controls establish a price ceiling below the equilibrium price. In the long run, they result in a decrease in rental housing services and an excess demand for rental housing. It is still likely, however, that consumers would vote for rent control programmes.

The imposition of price ceilings (set below the equilibrium price) in decreasing-cost industries may reduce industry output to zero. The CAP results in an excess supply which is bought by the EU authorities. The excess supply is often sold at a discount to domestic consumers. The CAP serves to stabilize and supplement the incomes of some farmers, but at a high social cost. The imposition of a support price (or a price set above equilibrium) can result in nonprice competition. An example of this is the US airline industry prior to 1978. Such nonprice competition may cause an increase in costs until all economic profit is eliminated.

Key Terms

Accounting profit*
Constant-cost industry*

Declining industry*
Decreasing-cost industry*
Diseconomies of scale (external)*
Economic profit*
Economies of scale (external)*
Freedom of entry and exit
Free mobility of resources
Homogeneous product
Increasing-cost industry*
Industry
Long-run equilibrium
Market
Market competition
Market structure
Monopoly
Monopolistic competition
Nonprice competition*
Oligopoly*
Perfect competition
Perfect knowledge
Price control
Price-taker
Pure competition
Short-run equilibrium
Support price
Technological change*
Technological economies of scale

Questions

1   Graph the total revenue curve for a competitive firm with a price of £5. Demonstrate graphically and mathematically that $MR = AR = P$.

2   Graph a total revenue curve and a short-run total cost curve for a competitive firm. Identify the point of profit maximization. Now graph the corresponding MR, MC, $SRAVC$, and $SRATC$ curves. How do the two sets of curves correspond? What does the profit curve look like?

3   Can a perfectly competitive firm ever maximize profit by operating on the downward-sloping portion of its MC curve? Why?

4   Must short-run supply curves for competitive industries satisfy the law of supply? Why?

5   In a constant-cost industry, if demand increases must firms enter the industry to restore long-run equilibrium? Answer the same question for an increasing-cost industry.

6   Convenience shops typically charge a higher price for milk than do supermarkets. Does this mean that the retail milk market is not competitive? How do you explain this phenomenon?

7   In a constant-cost industry, the equilibrium number of firms can be determined if one knows only the position of the demand curve and the typical firm's $LRAC$ curve. Explain how. Can the number of firms be determined for an increasing-cost industry? Why?

8   Draw the firm's $LRAC$, $SRAC$, $LRMC$, and $SRMC$ curves which correspond to the adjustment process depicted in Figure 8-14, and explain what is happening at a price of P_1 and P_2.

9   Assuming that demand is stable, does technological change affect the equilibrium number of firms in a competitive constant-cost industry? Why? Does it affect the size of the typical firm? Why?

10   Give an example of technological change and an example of a technological economy of scale. How does each relate to the $LRAC$ curve?

11   What are the consequences of rent control? What are the arguments for deregulating the private rental housing sector?

12   The CAP is designed in part to stabilize farm prices and thereby to aid farmers. But stabilizing prices destabilizes both revenue and profit, and thus it is not clear that the farmer benefits. Evaluate this statement.

13   In a perfectly competitive industry, under what circumstances is a rise in demand for an industry's product met primarily by a short-run output response on the part of existing firms? By a long-run response on the part of existing firms? By entry of new firms?

14   In a perfectly competitive industry, if there are N identical firms and no 'external' effects on factor prices, is the industry supply curve more or less steep than the firm's supply curve? More or less elastic?

9 Pricing in Product Markets: Monopoly Markets

9-1 Introduction

In the previous chapter we discussed perfect competition, which is characterized by a large number of sellers each of whom is a *price-taker*. The other extreme type of market structure is *monopoly*, which is characterized by a single seller (or group of sellers) which acts as a *price-setter*. The word 'monopoly' comes from the Greek words *monos polein*, which mean 'alone to sell'. This single seller is called a *monopolist*. The term is also sometimes used for a single group of sellers that acts as a price-setter, although often such a group is called a *cartel*.

Monopolists are called price-setters because they select their own price and supply the entire quantity demanded. That is, they may set either price or quantity, but not both. In effect, they can choose a position on the demand curve. For a monopolist to have effective control over the pricing of a product, the monopolized product should have no close substitutes; otherwise, when a monopolist raises the product's price, consumers can switch to other products. The pricing policies of a profitable monopolist may be constrained by the threat of potential competition if market entry is at all possible. Thus, in order for such a monopoly to persist in an industry, there must be *barriers to entry*. As we see later, a monopolist need not always make a profit. All that monopoly implies is that a monopolist can make the best of the demand conditions.

We should also note that monopoly does not imply that there is a single producer, because monopolists need not produce their own product. There can be many producers supplying the product to a monopolist. The essence of monopoly is that there is a single *seller* (or group of sellers) that sets the price. The number of producers is not relevant. As an example we can cite OPEC (Organization of Petroleum Exporting Countries), which consists of 13 major producers which collectively set the price of oil.

A monopolist setting price may set a single price for all customers or may practise price discrimination, that is, set different prices for different customers. We discuss both these cases in Section 9-6.

The type of monopoly discussed so far is called *pure monopoly*. Just as the concept of perfect competition is an ideal one, so is that of monopoly. Ideally, the monopolist should be able to control 100 per cent of the market. In practice, that is not usually the case. Suppose a particular firm has 80 per cent of the market: is this a monopoly? To answer such questions, economists have devised measures of what is known as 'monopoly power'. We discuss these in Chapter 10. Some economists use a weaker definition of monopoly and monopolist. If a seller (or group of sellers) can change the price of a product by changing the quantity sold, then the seller is a monopolist.[1]

---

[1] See R. A. Posner, *Antitrust Law: An Economic Perspective*, University of Chicago Press, 1976.

In the following sections, unless stated otherwise, we talk about pure monopoly. Furthermore, since the pricing policies of a single seller (monopolist) and a single group of sellers (cartel) are similar, when we talk of monopoly our discussion applies to both a monopolist and a cartel.

We also discuss *natural monopoly*. A natural monopoly is a special type of monopoly that arises from economies of scale. Examples of this are a gas pipeline company, a telephone company, and an electricity utility. In these cases the average cost of production declines over a large range of output, and hence a single firm can supply the output at a lower price than two or more smaller firms. This monopoly is called 'natural' because it arises naturally from the type of product being sold. Here monopoly has advantages over competition. We discuss natural monopoly in Sections 10-5 and 10-6.

Examples of Monopolies and Cartels

1 *OPEC* One of the best-known cartels, OPEC was formed in 1960 by the governments of Iran, Iraq, Kuwait, Saudi Arabia, and Venezuela. By 1980 there were eight additional members. The cartel did not really wield any power until 1973. On 1 January 1973 the price of oil was around $2 a barrel; by the end of 1973, after the Yom Kippur War, OPEC, by restricting production, had raised the price to nearly $12 a barrel. In the mid-1980s prices reached close to $40 a barrel. Since then, because of internal dissension in the cartel and decline in world demand for oil, the oil price has been falling. The price was around $15 a barrel in mid-1993 with the cartel much weaker but still alive. Many economists (notably Friedman) predicted an early demise for OPEC.

2 *International Air Transport Association (IATA)* IATA has functioned as an effective cartel in civil aviation since it was established in 1945. One of the objectives of IATA was to set airline prices for each route. Until the late 1970s, all member-airlines in a particular region had to agree between themselves on a fares schedule, which then had to be ratified by each government before it could be introduced. This sort of pricing policy prompted collusive behaviour among the airlines, and fares were set to cover the costs of the most inefficient airline in the cartel. Since the late 1970s, however, the cartel has been weakened by price competition both from non-member airlines and

cartel members in response to a fall in the demand for air travel during years of economic recession. As with OPEC, IATA too is vulnerable to price-cutting among members when product demand falls.

3 *Taxis in New York* This is an example of a monopoly (not a pure monopoly) created by licensing. In New York (and many other cities) one cannot drive a taxi without a licence. In New York this licence is called a 'medallion'. Until 1937, any qualified taxi driver could get a medallion by paying a nominal licence fee. Since then, the city has put a limit on the number of medallions issued, thus effectively fixing the total supply of medallions. Current owners of medallions can sell them to others wanting to operate taxi services. Because of the limited supply and a growing demand over time, the price of medallions has increased substantially over the years. Some have sold for over $50 000—a 10 000-fold increase over the initial licence fee of $5.

4 *Input monopolies* These are monopolies that come into existence through ownership of a key resource. The Aluminum Company of America (ALCOA) once controlled most domestic bauxite deposits from which aluminium is made. The International Nickel Company once owned about 90 per cent of the world's nickel. Another company that has a virtual monopoly through its control of natural resources is DeBeers of South Africa, which handles about 80 per cent of the world's uncut diamonds. The company has run a worldwide cartel for more than a century.

Questions To Be Discussed

In this chapter we examine product pricing under monopoly. In the next chapter we consider the regulation of monopoly. There are many questions we need to ask regarding pricing under monopoly:

1 How does a monopolist determine the output to be produced and the price to be charged? (Section 9-2)

2 How do the output and price under monopoly compare with those under perfect competition? (Section 9-3)

3 What is markup pricing? (Section 9-4)

4 How do monopolists prevent others from entering the market? (Section 9-5)

5 Do monopolists charge different prices to different consumers, and, if so, how do monopolists determine these prices? (Sections 9-6 and 9-7)

6 What is the welfare cost of monopoly? (Section 9-8)
7 What are multi-plant and bilateral monopolies? (Sections 9-9 and 9-10)

After answering these basic questions, we consider an application of the theory.

9-2 A Monopolist Setting a Single Market Price*

The demand curve facing a monopolist is the market demand curve, which is downward-sloping. In Section 6-2 we examined the relationship between total revenue TR, average revenue AR, and marginal revenue MR for a downward-sloping demand curve. The average revenue curve coincides with the demand curve. Because the demand curve slopes downward, the MR curve must also slope downward. (Each unit of output adds less to revenue than the unit before it.) And because a monopolist charges a single price on all the units sold, MR is less than price. (In order to sell one more unit of output, the monopolist must reduce the price on all previous units.)

As the monopolist expands output, TR can increase or decrease. This depends on whether marginal revenue is positive or negative, which in turn depends on whether demand is price-elastic or price-inelastic.

To see these relationships, we start with an initial price of P and quantity Q on the demand curve. Then total revenue $TR = P \cdot Q$. Now we raise Q to $Q + \Delta Q$, where ΔQ is very small. With a downward-sloping demand curve, the price falls to $P - \Delta P$. (Note that we take the absolute values of ΔP.) Since ΔQ is very small, ΔP is also very small. TR is now $(Q + \Delta Q)(P - \Delta P) = PQ + P(\Delta Q) - Q(\Delta P)$. We have omitted the term $\Delta Q \cdot \Delta P$, since if ΔQ and ΔP are very small their product is negligible. Subtracting the initial total revenue of PQ, we get:
$$\Delta TR = P(\Delta Q) - Q(\Delta P);$$
hence

$$MR = \frac{\Delta TR}{\Delta Q} = P - Q \cdot \frac{\Delta P}{\Delta Q} = P\left(1 - \frac{Q}{P} \cdot \frac{\Delta P}{\Delta Q}\right).$$

But

$$\frac{\Delta Q}{\Delta P} \cdot \frac{P}{Q} \text{ is the price elasticity of demand } \eta.$$

So, finally, $MR = P[1 - (1/\eta)]$. *This is an important relationship, which occurs frequently in discussions of pricing in markets where the demand curve is downward-sloping.* Since P is the same as AR, we can also state that $MR = AR(1 - (1/\eta))$.

This establishes the relationship between AR and MR. We note the following results:

1 Since we have defined η as a positive number, $1 - (1/\eta)$ is less than 1, and so $MR \leq AR$.

2 As η keeps decreasing, $1/\eta$ keeps increasing, and MR keeps falling.

3 If $\eta > 1$, $[1 - (1/\eta)]$ is positive. Hence $MR > 0$, or TR increases as Q increases.

4 If $\eta < 1$, $[1 - (1/\eta)]$ is negative. Hence $MR < 0$, or TR decreases as Q increases.

5 If $\eta = 1$, $[1 - (1/\eta)] = 0$ and $MR = 0$. Thus, TR is constant.

6 If $\eta = \infty$, $[1 - (1/\eta)] = 1$, and so $MR = AR$.

We can show these relationships in relation to a monopolist's linear demand and MR curves and the TR curve. This is shown in Figure 9-1(a) and (b). When $MR > 0$, TR is increasing, and when $MR < 0$, TR is decreasing. At the maximum value for TR, MR is zero. Why?

The monopolist never produces in the inelastic region of the demand curve. If he does, TR falls. At the same time, the increased output causes total cost to rise. With revenue falling and costs rising, profit falls. We thus conclude that the monopolist always operates in the elastic region of the demand curve. This region is the coloured line in Figure 9-1(a).

We have considered the effect on TR of changes in output. To see whether TR increases or decreases as price changes, we need information on the price elasticity of demand. For a 1 per cent change in price, we have the results given in Table 9-1. Thus, if $\eta < 1$, the monopolist can increase revenue by raising price; if $\eta > 1$, the monopolist can increase revenue by cutting price. Note that this relationship does not hold for large price changes. This is because of the expression for TR. If P rises by ΔP, then Q falls by ΔQ. Hence the change in TR is given by

$$\Delta TR = (P + \Delta P)(Q - \Delta Q) - PQ$$
$$= Q\Delta P - P\Delta Q$$

---

*A mathematical treatment of some of this material is given in the Mathematical Appendix at the end of the book.

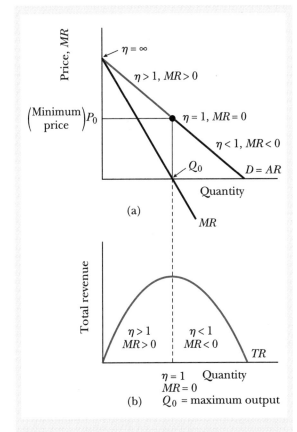

Figure 9-1   Elasticity of demand, MR, and TR for a monopolist's linear demand curve

(a) Elasticity of demand and MR
(b) Elasticity of demand and TR

Table 9-1   Price elasticity of demand and total revenue

	Price P	Quantity Q	Total revenue PQ
$\eta = 1$	Rises 1%	Falls 1%	No change
	Falls 1%	Rises 1%	No change
$\eta > 1$	Rises 1%	Falls > 1%	Falls
	Falls 1%	Rises > 1%	Rises
$\eta < 1$	Rises 1%	Falls < 1%	Rises
	Falls 1%	Rises < 1%	Falls

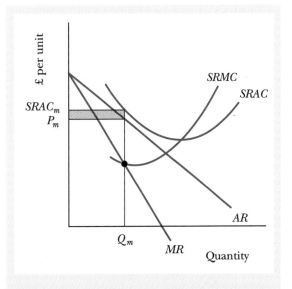

Figure 9-2   A monopolist suffering a short-run loss

if we ignore the term $\Delta P \cdot \Delta Q$. Thus,

$$\frac{\Delta TR}{\Delta P} = Q - P\frac{\Delta Q}{\Delta P}$$

$$= Q - Q\left(\frac{P}{Q} \cdot \frac{\Delta Q}{\Delta P}\right) = Q(1 - \eta).$$

Hence for a price increase, if $\eta < 1$ this expression is positive and ΔTR is positive, and if $\eta > 1$ this expression is negative and ΔTR is negative. However, this assumes that ΔP and ΔQ are small and that their product is therefore much smaller and can be ignored. If they are not small, the cross-product $\Delta P \cdot \Delta Q$ cannot be ignored.

In Section 8-2 above, we said that profit maximization requires setting output where $MR = MC$. Thus, a monopolist selects the output at the point where

$MR = MC$; he then charges the highest price that he can get for this output, according to the demand curve. Note that this does not imply that the monopolist can earn a profit. That depends on the cost structure of the firm.

A monopolist's profit-maximization point is illustrated in Figure 9-2. *SRMC* is the short-run marginal cost curve, and *SRAC* is the short-run average total cost curve. This monopolist equates *MR* to *SRMC* and produces output Q_m. He charges a per unit price of P_m. However, since *AR* (or price) is less than the average cost of this output, the monopolist suffers short-run losses, shown by the shaded area. Like the competitive firm, the monopolist continues to operate in the short run as long as variable costs are covered.

Whether the monopolist stays in business in the long run depends on the long-run average cost curve. A monopolist goes out of business in the long run if all costs are not covered. Long-run equilibrium for the monopolist requires that $LRMC = SRMC = MR$, so that profit is maximized, and $P \geq LRAC$, so that full opportunity cost is covered.

9-3 Competition versus Monopoly*

Before we can compare the output and prices under competition and monopoly, we must assume that market demand and costs do not change with the structure of the industry. Also, for simplicity, we consider a long-run equilibrium in a constant average cost. This means that $MC = AC$ and that the supply curve for the competitive industry is equal to both MC and AC. The competitive industry output is at the level where supply equals demand, and price (or average revenue) is equal to both MC and AC. In the case of monopoly, output is expanded only to the point where $MR = MC$. And MR is less than price for a monopolist.

The comparison is illustrated in Figure 9-3. P_c is the price and Q_c is the output for the competitive industry. P_m is the price and Q_m is the output for monopoly. Q_m is the level of output for which $MC = MR$, whereas Q_c is the level of output for which $MC = AR$. Thus, we conclude that *a monopolist produces a smaller output and sells at a higher price than the equivalent competitive industry.*

The monopolist's per-unit costs are P_c but the price he charges is P_m. The difference $P_m - P_c$ is called the monopolist's *markup*. The shaded area in Figure 9-3 gives the monopolist's profit.

There is another important difference between competition and monopoly that often goes unnoticed. Suppose there are some events that increase the monopolist's marginal costs. In the case of British Gas, this might be due to difficulties in extracting gas from a particular field in the North Sea. In this case the popular conception of a monopolist as an 'exploiter' suggests that the monopolist passes on all the increase in costs to the customers whereas a competitive industry does not. In fact, quite the opposite is the

---

*A mathematical treatment of some of this material is given in the Mathematical Appendix at the end of the book.

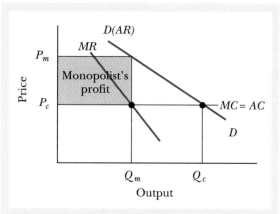

Figure 9-3 Comparison of output and price under perfect competition and under monopoly

case. To see this, note that the equilibrium condition under perfect competition is

$$P = MC.$$

Hence $\Delta P = \Delta MC$, where ΔP is change in price and ΔMC is change in marginal cost. Thus, the entire increase in marginal cost is passed on to the consumer. Under monopoly, the equilibrium condition is

$$MR = MC.$$

Thus, $\Delta MR = \Delta MC$, or change in marginal revenue equals change in marginal cost. But we know that

$$MR = \text{price}\left(1 - \frac{1}{\eta}\right),$$

where η is the elasticity of demand. As MR goes up, we move up the demand curve. With a linear curve as in Figure 9-1(a), as we move up the demand curve, the elasticity η increases. Thus, the factor $(1 - 1/\eta)$ increases. Hence the increase in price is less than the increase in marginal cost: the monopolist cannot pass on all of the increased costs to the consumer.

We can easily show this in a diagram, but it is left as an exercise at this stage. We shall see in Section 10-3 how we can use taxes to regulate the monopolist's profits. A lump-sum tax changes the monopolist's average cost without affecting marginal cost. A per-unit tax, however, increases the monopolist's marginal cost, which is what we have discussed here.

Is there a supply curve for the monopolist? In the case of the competitive firm, the supply curve gives the quantities of output that the firm is willing and able to provide at various prices. There is no comparable curve for a monopolist. The concept of supply is meaningless because a monopolist is a price-setter rather than a price-taker. The monopolist determines a single price and quantity based on the entire demand curve and the firm's cost structure.

9-4   Markup Pricing

Several studies on pricing in non-competitive markets have suggested that the manager of a firm typically arrives at a price by adding a *markup* over costs. The markup can be calculated as a difference between price and average cost, or as a percentage increase in price over average cost.

From our discussion in Section 9-3, the profit-maximizing price for a monopolist may be given by

$$\text{Price} = MC \cdot \frac{\eta}{\eta - 1},$$

where η is the elasticity of demand. This is the optimum markup formula for a monopolist; $\eta/(\eta - 1)$ is called the *markup factor*. For a price elasticity of 1.5, price is three times the marginal cost; for a price elasticity of 11, price is 10 per cent above marginal cost.

But markup pricing has been observed in other markets as well where the markup is based on average cost. In their 1939 article, Hall and Hitch report results from a survey they conducted.[2] They questioned 38 firms to discover what methods of price-setting were actually applied and what motivated firms to adjust prices. Their results reveal practices that appear to be at variance with widely accepted theories. Businesses typically set prices by calculating average costs of production and adding a markup for profit. Further, they did not habitually vary the markup with variations in demand. These findings were confirmed in other studies, such as the one by Andrews[3] in the UK and another by Kaplan, Dirlam and Lanzillotti in the United States.[4]

Theory suggests that price should be set by equating marginal revenue to marginal cost. The markup pricing adjustments conflict with this theory. Machlup suggests that the markup pricing adjustment can be interpreted as a rule of thumb by which profits might be maximized by trial and error.[5] Another explanation for the markup pricing method is given by Okun, who argues that the markets for most industrial products require that firms cultivate relations with their customers to encourage repeat sales.[6] Prices convey only limited information about the products. Okun calls these 'customer markets'. In these markets prices are determined largely by costs. The needs of producers to promote goodwill make them forgo any short-run advantage in raising prices when demand strengthens. Thus, customers are offered a stable price and prices are raised only when costs increase. The ideas of Okun are explored further by Carlton, who analyses a large amount of evidence on price rigidity in markets and concludes that price alone may not be clearing markets but that price, in conjunction with other mechanisms (such as sellers' knowledge of buyers' needs) does perform that function.[7]

Markup pricing implies that firms do not behave as short-run profit-maximizers, although they may have this objective among others over a long time horizon. The large amount of empirical evidence on markup pricing demonstrates that current microeconomic theory needs to be expanded to explain this behaviour. We discuss the issue of price rigidity again in Section 11-9.

9-5   Barriers to Entry and Long-run Monopoly

Earlier we saw that the condition $MR = MC$ does not necessarily imply that a monopolist enjoys a profit. But if the monopolist is making a profit, this profit provides an incentive for new firms to enter the industry. If entry occurs the equilibrium position changes, and since there are more firms than one, there is no longer a monopoly. Thus, for a profitable monopoly to survive,

[2] R. E. Hall and C. Hitch, 'Price Theory and Business Behaviour', *Oxford Economic Papers*, 1 (1939): 12–45.
[3] P. W. S. Andrews, *Manufacturing Business*, Macmillan, London, 1949.
[4] A. Kaplan, J. Dirlam, and R. F. Lanzillotti, *Pricing in Big Business*, Brookings Institution, Washington, DC, 1958.

[5] F. Machlup, 'Marginal Analysis and Empirical Research', *American Economic Review*, 36 (1946): 519–54.
[6] A. Okun, *Prices and Quantities*, Brookings Institution, Washington, DC, 1981.
[7] D. W. Carlton, 'The Theory and Facts of How Markets Clear', in R. Schmalensee and R. Willig (eds), *Handbook of Industrial Organisation*, North-Holland, Amsterdam, 1987.

we need *barriers to entry.*[8] Sometimes the barriers or impediments to entry are created at the time the monopoly is established; for example, the firm may be given the sole franchise or charter by law. In some other cases the barriers are created by the monopolist through threats and coercion. If a monopolist has a cost advantage over its rivals, then it can engaged in *preemptive price-cutting* to deter rivals from entering the market.

Whether a monopoly is sustainable or not (in the long run) depends on how the monopoly comes about. The following are some factors that give rise to monopolies:

1 *Control over raw materials needed for the production of the good* For instance, the Aluminum Company of America (ALCOA) once controlled most domestic bauxite deposits from which aluminium is made; DeBeers owns most of the South African diamond mines and controls the prices of diamonds by restricting production.

2 *Patents over new inventions* Patents are exclusive rights to the production of an innovative product. Patents are granted because they encourage inventions. Without patents, firms (and individuals) have little incentive to invest money and resources in research. However, if an important discovery is made, the owner of the patent has a monopoly over that product. Over time, other firms develop close substitutes and break this monopoly power, or the patent expires. For example, the instant camera was invented and patented by Polaroid in the late 1950s. In the mid-1970s the patent ran out and Kodak began selling instant cameras.

3 *Cost of establishing an efficient plant, especially in relation to the market* This is the case of natural monopoly mentioned earlier. Examples of this are electricity and gas utilities, telephone companies, and so on. It does not make economic sense to have two electricity, gas, or telephone companies in the same area (although this is perhaps less certain today). The problem is discussed in Section 10-5 below.

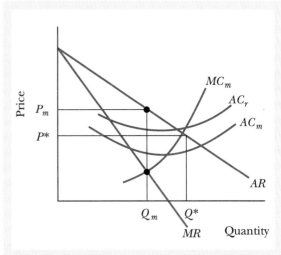

Figure 9-4 Preemptive price-cutting by a monopolist to restrict entry by a rival

4 *Market franchises* The government gives exclusive rights to a firm to sell a certain good or service in a certain area. In the UK the government invites tenders (or bids) from companies who wish to operate a particular public service, and the successful company is given the franchise. In recent years this has been done with refuse collection, regional independent television franchises, catering and cleaning in NHS hospitals, and so on. These franchises create monopoly profits for the holders of the franchises but they may be paid to the government as part of the franchising process.

Monopolists can create barriers to entry by pre-emptive price-cutting if they have a cost advantage over their rivals. This is shown in Figure 9-4. The average cost curve of the monopolist is denoted by AC_m, and the average cost curve of the rival is denoted by AC_r. To show that the monopolist has a cost advantage, we have drawn the AC_r curve above the AC_m curve.

In the absence of any potential rival, the monopolist produces output Q_m and charges a price P_m. However, when a rival with average costs given by AC_r threatens to enter, the monopolist lowers the price to P^* and produces the output Q^*. At the price P^* the rival cannot cover average cost and, hence, does not enter. This price cutting by the monopolist is called preemptive price cutting. As a consequence the output expands from Q_m to Q^*.

---

[8] We are talking loosely about barriers to entry as impediments to entry. For the exact definition of this term as given by Bain, Stigler and Ferguson and a criticism of these definitions, see H. Demsetz, 'Barriers to Entry', *American Economic Review*, 72 (1982): 47–57.

9-6 The Price-discriminating Monopolist

We have, until now, discussed the case of a monopolist setting a single price. We now discuss the case of a monopolist charging different prices to different customers, or a *price-discriminating monopolist*. Price discrimination is said to exist if a producer is selling the same good at different prices for reasons not associated with differences in cost.

For instance, if a producer has a manufacturing plant in Leicester and sells the commodity at £5 per unit in Leicester and £6 per unit in Plymouth, but transport costs are £1 per unit from Leicester to Plymouth, then the different prices charged are due to transport costs, and we cannot call this price discrimination. However, if the producer sells the product for £4 in Plymouth, then this is called price discrimination. Note that a customer cannot buy the product in Plymouth and profitably resell it in Leicester, because of the transport costs.

Price discrimination can occur between markets, and between individuals in the same market. *Perfect price discrimination* involves charging a different price (the maximum possible price) for each unit of output. This type of discrimination is difficult to achieve. But there are many cases of price discrimination in practice which are much simpler. Cinemas charge lower prices for students, children, and senior citizens. This is price discrimination. The costs to the cinema are the same whether the seat is filled by a student, a child, or a retired adult.

Why would a monopolist price-discriminate? Clearly, the incentive is to increase profit. But not all monopolists can profitably price-discriminate. We examine several conditions that must be met before a monopolist can successfully discriminate. One condition is the ability to prevent the resale of the product—otherwise, low-price buyers resell to high-price buyers, and the monopolist is unable to sell at the higher prices. In the case of cinema tickets, we can check that the person buying the ticket with a student identification card is the person that enters the cinema. When electricity companies charge lower rates to industrial users than to households, it is not possible for the industrial users to resell electricity to households. The main items that are not readily resaleable are personal services (admission to educational institutions, health services, cinemas) and utilities involving expensive connections (gas, water, electricity, telephone). But ordinary capital goods can also be made non-resalable. For instance, for a long time Rank Xerox did not sell its photocopying machines: it leased them.

9-7 Degrees of Price Discrimination*

In his book *The Economics of Welfare* (1920), Pigou presents what is perhaps still the most penetrating analysis of price discrimination. He identifies three degrees of discriminating power leading to three types of price discrimination.

First-degree price discrimination, or perfect price discrimination, occurs when the seller charges a different price for each unit of output. This involves charging different prices to different consumers as well as charging different prices for different units sold to the same consumer. The maximum price that someone is willing to pay for a unit of output is called the *reservation price*. The perfectly discriminating monopolist charges the reservation price for each unit of output. Thus, the *MR* curve for the monopolist becomes the demand curve. In this case, the equilibrium level of output, which is given by the intersection of the demand curve and the *MC* curve, is the same as the output under perfect competition. This is shown in Figure 9-5. The monopolist's output is *OC* and revenue

---

*A mathematical treatment of some of this material is given in the Mathematical Appendix at the end of the book.

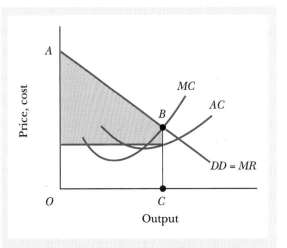

Figure 9-5   First-degree price discrimination

is given by the area *OABC*, since the monopolist charges a different price (the maximum possible price) for each unit. Subtracting from this the costs (which are *OC* multiplied by the average cost), we have the monopolist's profit, which is the shaded area in the figure.

Perfect discrimination is rather difficult to implement in practice. It can be used only for services for which no resale is possible, and even then a negotiation with each customer is costly.

Second-degree price discrimination occurs when the monopolist is able to charge several different prices for different ranges or groups of output. For example, in Figure 9-6, the first Q_1 units of output are each sold at a price of P_1; units between Q_1 and Q_2 are each sold at a price of P_2; and so on. Each additional unit sold from 1 up to Q_1 adds P_1 to revenue. Similarly, each additional unit sold between Q_1 and Q_2 adds P_2 to revenue. Thus, the *MR* curve is the step function shown by the thick coloured line in Figure 9-6. The output produced, Q_3, is given by the intersection of the *MC* and *MR* curves. Reading from the average cost for this output and multiplying by Q_3, we get total costs. Since the revenue is given by the total area under the *MR* curve up to output Q_3, the profit of the monopolist is given by the shaded area in Figure 9-6.

There are many examples of second-degree price discrimination. In the pricing of electricity, natural gas, or telephone calls, something called a *declining block price* is used. For instance, the first 200 kWh of electricity, or 1000 m^3 of natural gas, or 10 minutes of a long distance call, might cost a certain amount, but for subsequent units the price could be lower. Magazine subscriptions also frequently cost a certain amount for a one-year subscription but a lower average for a two-year subscription and a still lower average for a three-year subscription.

Third-degree price discrimination occurs when a monopolist partitions market demand into two or more groups of customers and then charges different prices to the different groups. (The price is uniform for members within a group.) The monopolist tries to exploit the different price elasticities of demand for the different groups. Third-degree discrimination is profitable only if the customer groups that can be separated have different elasticities of demand.

Consider the monopolist with two separable customer groups. For each group she computes total revenue and marginal revenue based on the group's demand curve. MR_1 is the marginal revenue for the first group and MR_2 is the marginal revenue for the second group. It can be shown that the monopolist allocates her output to the two markets so that

$$MR_1 = MR_2$$

and she chooses her total output so that

$$MR_1 = MR_2 = MC.$$

These conditions are intuitively plausible. MR_1 must equal MR_2, because otherwise the monopolist can improve her profit by shifting the output between the two groups. If $MR_1 > MR_2$, then revenue and profit increase as the monopolist shifts a unit of output from group 2 to group 1. If $MR_2 > MR_1$, then the monopolist increases profit by shifting output from group 1 to group 2. It is also clear that the common *MR* must equal *MC*. If $MR > MC$, then we saw in Chapter 8 that the firm has an incentive to expand output, and if $MR < MC$, the firm increases profit by reducing output.

We are now ready to compare the prices that are set for the two customer groups. We know that $MR = P(1 - 1/\eta)$, and, since $MR_1 = MR_2$, we have

$$P_1\left(1 - \frac{1}{\eta_1}\right) = P_2\left(1 - \frac{1}{\eta_2}\right),$$

where P_1 and P_2 are the prices for groups 1 and 2, respectively, and η_1, and η_2 are demand elasticities for the two groups. If $\eta_1 < \eta_2$, then $1/\eta_1 > 1/\eta_2$ and

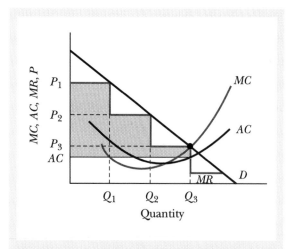

Figure 9-6   Second-degree price discrimination

$(1 - 1/\eta_1) < (1 - 1/\eta_2)$. Hence P_1 must exceed P_2. So we see that *a discriminating monopolist charges a higher price to the group with the less elastic demand*. Finally, if $\eta_1 = \eta_2$, the profit-maximizing price is the same for the two groups, and thus there is no price discrimination, since it is not profitable.

The separation of markets can take place on the basis of age and income, as in the case of cinema tickets (lower prices for children, students, and senior citizens). Very often the partitioning of markets is done on the basis of geographic location (domestic and foreign markets); sometimes products are sold at a higher price domestically than abroad. Many international corporations are accused of such *dumping* tactics. They are said to 'dump' their products in foreign markets (supposedly selling them at below cost). Of course, the firm is not selling below cost but can charge a lower price abroad than domestically if the elasticity of demand is higher abroad than domestically. Examples of this are Japanese companies selling televisions, camcorders, and video recorders at a lower price in Europe than in Japan.

How desirable is third-degree price discrimination from a social point of view? There are many who argue that price discrimination results in a more efficient allocation of resources. The general argument in several papers published in the 1950s and 1960s was that the objection to monopoly is not that some people make too much money, but that monopoly leads to a misallocation of society's resources through a restriction of output. Price discrimination very often results in more output and, thus, should lead to increased welfare. This argument was challenged by Yamey, who showed with a special example that a profitable increase in output associated with price discrimination *need not* increase economic welfare but *can* reduce it.[9] An increase in output is a necessary condition but not a sufficient condition. Schmalensee[10] and Varian[11] also show that a necessary condition for price discrimination to lead to an increase in welfare is that there be an

increase in output delivered. In all these discussions, social welfare is measured by the sum of consumer and producer surpluses.

9-8 Welfare Costs of Monopoly

We know that a monopolist restricts output and charges a price higher than that charged under perfect competition. This restriction of output results in a loss of consumer and producer surplus. By examining these losses, we can determine the net welfare cost to society from monopoly.

Consider Figure 9-7. *DD* is the demand curve; *SS* is the monopolist's *MC* curve, and the competitive short-run supply curve; *MR* is the monopolist's *MR* curve. The competitive price is *OB*, and the quantity supplied and consumed is *OA*. The monopoly price is *OE* and the monopolist's output is *OF*.

As we reduce output and increase price in moving from perfect competition to monopoly, the loss of consumer surplus is equal to the area *EGCB*. But the rectangle *EGJB* becomes part of revenue for the monopolist. Thus, this rectangle represents a transfer from consumers to the monopolist and not a net loss to society. Economists do not attempt to evaluate this transfer because such an evaluation is normative or based on principles of equity. The final area to account for is the triangle *JCH*, which represents the loss in producer surplus. The total net welfare loss to society is

[9] B. S. Yamey, 'Monopolistic Price Discrimination and Economic Welfare', *Journal of Law and Economics*, 17 (1974): 377–80. Yamey's paper contains references to several papers that argue in favour of price discrimination.
[10] R. Schmalensee, 'Output and Welfare Implications of Monopolistic Third-Degree Price Discrimination', *American Economic Review*, 71 (1981): 242–7.
[11] H. Varian, 'Price Discrimination and Social Welfare', *American Economic Review*, 75 (1985): 870–5.

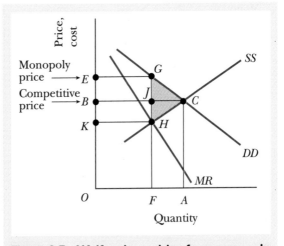

Figure 9-7 Welfare loss arising from monopoly

the sum of the triangles *GJC* and *JCH*, or the shaded area *GCH* in Figure 9-7. This area represents the excess of the value to society (as reflected in the demand curve) over the cost to society (as reflected in the supply curve) for the units of output lost because of monopolization.

Harberger used this theory to measure empirically the welfare costs of monopoly.[12] In doing so he made some simplifying assumptions. He assumed that the elasticity of demand is equal to 1, that producers do not engage in price discrimination, and that long-run average total cost is constant (and, therefore, equal to long-run marginal cost) for both firms and industries. The supply curve is, thus, horizontal, as shown in Figure 9-8. The welfare cost is given by the area of the shaded triangle *GCH*. This area is equal to $\frac{1}{2}(\Delta P)(\Delta Q)$. Harberger proceeded to measure this area by computing ΔQ and ΔP.

Harberger used data on US manufacturing industries for 1924–28. He used this period because he felt that it was reasonably close to a long-run equilibrium period with no violent shifts in demand or economic structure. Furthermore, data on industrial profits for this period were readily available. Harberger computed the average rate of profit on capital for each industry for 1924–28 and subtracted from it the average rate of profit on capital for the whole manufacturing sector. This difference he took as ΔP. Next, ΔQ was obtained from the assumption of unitary elasticity of demand (and values of *P* and *Q*). Note that $\eta = (\Delta Q / \Delta P) \cdot (P/Q)$. Using this procedure, Harberger estimated the total welfare loss to be about 0.1 per cent of US national income. Harberger's method for computing the welfare loss of monopoly was used by others to compute welfare loss of trade restrictions like tariffs and quotas, and the estimates were often surprisingly low. Harberger himself obtained estimates of 2.5 per cent of national income for the costs of trade restrictions in Chile and a number of Latin American countries.[13]

An important criticism of this method of evaluating the welfare losses due to monopoly is that the presence of monopoly profit induces others to waste resources in trying to capture part of this pie. Tullock[14] and Posner[15] pointed out that this wastage of resources is not captured in the Harberger method of computing welfare losses shown in Figures 9-7 and 9-8. For instance, Polaroid, by having a monopoly over instant photography, was earning monopoly profits, and Kodak spent a lot of resources trying to compete in the same area. From the social point of view, this is a waste. Similarly, if licences are issued for the importation of some products or for the monopolistic production of some products, many firms spend resources in hiring lawyers, lobbying members of government, and so on. These resources could be employed elsewhere more productively, and hence are a waste from the social point of view. These activities of trying to capture profits from monopolies, tariffs, quotas, and so on have been termed 'rent-seeking activities' by Kreuger[16] and 'DUP (directly unproductive profit-seeking) activities' by Bhagwati.[17]

How important are these activities, and what is their special social cost? Kreuger and Posner both

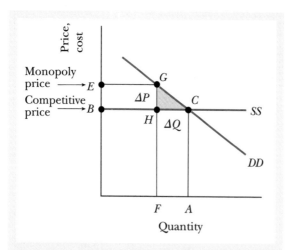

Price, cost

Monopoly price → *E*
Competitive price → *B*

G
ΔP
C
ΔQ
H
SS
DD

F   *A*

Quantity

Figure 9-8 Harberger's measurement of the welfare cost of monopoly

[12] A. C. Harberger, 'Monopoly and Resource Allocation', *American Economic Review*, 44 (1954): 77–87.

[13] A. C. Harberger, 'Using the Resources at Hand More Effectively', *American Economic Review*, 49 (1959): 134–46.
[14] G. Tullock, 'The Welfare Costs of Tariffs, Monopolies and Theft', *Western Economic Journal*, 5 (1967): 224–32.
[15] R. A. Posner, 'The Social Costs of Monopoly and Regulation', *Journal of Political Economy*, 83 (1975): 807–28.
[16] A. O. Kreuger, 'The Political Economy of the Rent-Seeking Society', *American Economic Review*, 64 (1974): 291–303.
[17] J. N. Bhagwati, 'Directly Unproductive Profit-Seeking (DUP) Activities', *Journal of Political Economy*, 90 (1982): 988–1002; and 'Lobbying, DUP Activities and Welfare: A Response to Tullock', *Journal of Public Economics*, 19 (1982): 395–401.

estimate these losses. Kreuger estimates a loss of 7.3 per cent of national income for India and 15 per cent of national income for Turkey from import licences. Posner estimates welfare losses in the United States from regulatory actions at 3 per cent of national income. The implicit assumption is that the welfare loss arising from these DUP activities is equal to the monopoly profit. Tullock, however, questions this assumption.[18]

Of course, unproductive activities are not confined to seeking monopoly profits or benefits from import licences alone. There are a host of activities that individuals engage in to seek special favours or privileges. Taking account of all these, Mishan[19] has estimated the losses from 'non-productive activities' in US society at 50 per cent of US national income. This merely shows that there is no end to all these estimates.

In Figure 9-8 the rectangle *EGHB* measures the monopoly profit. The mere fact that profit exists induces firms to invest resources in seeking and preserving monopoly power. This resource cost is likely to take up a major portion of the rectangle *EGHB*, and therefore the welfare cost of monopoly is likely to be much higher than that given by the area of the triangle *GCH*. An alternative way of looking at the problem is to argue that, because of the investments designed to secure and defend a monopoly position, the average costs for the monopolist are likely to be higher than for the competitive firm. (Harberger assumed them to be equal.)

Yet another argument as to why the monopolist's average costs are likely to be higher than for a competitive firm is given by Comanor and Leibenstein, who attribute it to X-inefficiency or the failure of the monopolist to minimize costs because of the absence of the 'competitive stick'.[20] The analysis of welfare cost of monopoly when the average costs of the monopolist are higher than under perfect competition is illustrated in Figure 9-9. *DD* is the demand curve, P_m the monopoly price, AC_1 the average cost of the

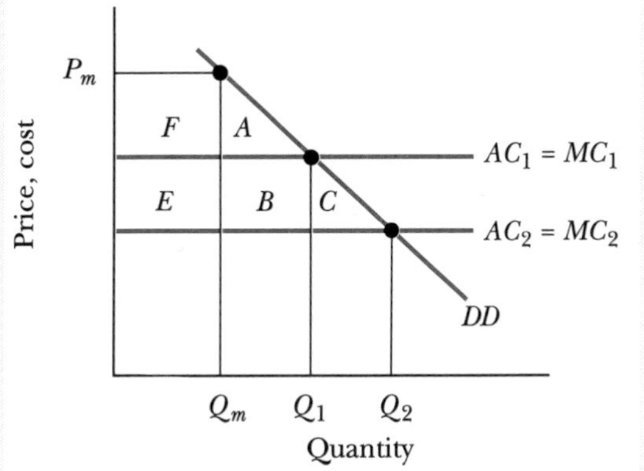

Figure 9-9   Welfare comparison between monopoly and competition

monopolist (we are assuming $AC = MC$), and AC_2 the average cost under competition. By assuming that AC_1 is also the average cost for the competitive firm, the output under competition is also expected to be Q_1, and the welfare cost of monopoly is estimated to be the area of the triangle A. However, if the true average cost under competition is AC_2, the output under competition is Q_2. The total loss in consumer surplus is $A + B + C + E + F$, and the monopolist's profit is F. Hence the net welfare cost is given by $A + B + C + E$, which is substantially larger than the area A.

Harberger's measure of the welfare costs of monopoly (which was about 0.1 per cent of US national income) has been criticized as being too low, and other investigators have corrected for various factors ignored by Harberger. In commenting on Harberger's study, Stigler wrote: 'if the estimate is correct, economists might serve a more useful purpose if they fought fires or termites instead of monopoly'.[21] Stigler, however, argued that Harberger's estimate might be low because of his method of estimating monopoly profit, his assumption of unitary elasticity of demand, and his neglect of rents to factors of production employed by the monopolist. Kamerschen estimated the welfare cost of monopoly to be as high as

---

[18] G. Tullock, 'The Welfare Costs of Tariffs, Monopolies, and Theft', in J. M. Buchanan, R. Tollison, and G. Tullock (eds.), *Toward a Theory of the Rent-Seeking Society*, Texas A & M University Press, College Station, Texas, 1980, pp 39–50.
[19] E. Mishan, *Economic Efficiency and Social Welfare*, Allen & Unwin, London, 1981.
[20] W. S. Comanor and H. Leibenstein, 'Allocative Efficiency, X-Efficiency and the Measurement of Welfare Losses', *Economica*, 36 (1969): 304–9.

---

[21] G. J. Stigler, 'The Statistics of Monopoly and Merger', *Journal of Political Economy*, 64 (1956): 34.

Table 9-2   Estimates of the welfare costs of monopoly

		USA (734 firms)	UK (102 firms)
(1)	Harberger's estimate	$448.2 million	£21.4 million
(2)	Harberger corrected	$4527.1 million	£385.8 million
(3)	(2) + advertising expenditure	$14005.4 million	£537.4 million
(4)	(3) + after-tax monopoly profit	$14997.6 million	£719.3 million
(5)	(4) as a percentage of the gross corporate product of *these* firms	13.1 per cent	7.2 per cent
(6)	(1) as a percentage of the gross corporate product	0.4 per cent	0.2 per cent

Source: K. Cowling and D. C. Mueller, 'The Social Costs of Monopoly Power', *Economic Journal*, 88 (1978): 740–2.

6 per cent of US national income, although his estimates were later criticized as being too high.[22]

Cowling and Mueller measured the social costs of the monopoly power of large firms in the USA and the UK and produced quite high estimates.[23] Their sample consisted of 734 firms from 1963 to 1966 in the USA and 102 firms during 1968 and 1969 in the UK. In addition to making corrections in Harberger's analysis based on the criticism mentioned earlier, they added two more items: (1) all advertising expenditure, which they view as a social waste, and (2) monopoly after-tax profits, which they argue are an indication of resources wasted in the process of gaining monopoly power. In effect, Cowling and Mueller estimated the welfare cost of monopoly as $A + B + C + E + F$ in Figure 9-9. The results obtained by Cowling and Mueller are shown in Table 9-2. These results show that Harberger's estimates are substantially low. Even without adding the after-tax monopoly profits, the percentages are 12.3 per cent (of gross corporate product for those firms) for the USA and 5.4 per cent for the UK.

Apart from these calculations, there are several papers arguing that the welfare costs of monopoly are quite substantial. Many studies have tried to refine the arguments. Posner's argument, for instance, was that firms contest for monopoly profits, that this 'rent-seeking' activity dissipates the monopoly profits, and hence that monopoly profits should be added to the welfare cost triangle. This argument implies two things:

1 *Rent dissipation*   The total expenditure by firms to obtain monopoly profit is equal to the level of this profit.
2 *Wastefulness*   This expenditure has no socially valuable byproducts.

Fisher discusses these two arguments and points out that, from the practical point of view, these arguments need to be qualified in several respects.[24] The monopoly profit need not be completely dissipated. The activity of rent-seeking cannot be considered competitive. Competition involves free entry, but monopolies are characterized by barriers to entry with incumbents enjoying advantages over potential entrants.[25] A firm that is farsighted enough to enter a monopolizable area early is able to monopolize at a cost lower than that which latecomers would have to expend to wrest monopoly power.

The Aluminum Corporation of America, for instance, was well placed to monopolize because of

[22] D. R. Kamerschen, 'An Estimation of "Welfare Losses" from Monopoly in the American Economy', *Western Economic Journal*, 4 (1966): 221–36.
[23] K. Cowling and D. C. Mueller, 'The Social Costs of Monopoly Power', *Economic Journal*, 88 (1978): 727–48.

[24] F. M. Fisher, 'The Social Costs of Monopoly and Regulation: Posner Reconsidered', *Journal of Political Economy*, 93 (1985): 410–16.
[25] D. Fudenberg and J. Tirole 'Understanding Rent Dissipation: On the Use of Game Theory in Industrial Organization', *American Economic Review*, 77 (1987): 176–83 show, using game theory (which we discuss in Chapter 11), that extreme incumbency advantages may allow established firms to blockade entry and appropriate the entire rent (monopoly profit).

the patents it had obtained; furthermore, it was in an industry requiring particular mineral resources and a cheap energy supply. It might have been drawn into patent research in aluminium by the possibility of monopoly profits, but once it was in, no further entry into the aluminium industry was possible without substantial cost.

Monopolies can also be obtained through luck rather than foresight, and luck can go either way. In some cases more is expended on the rent-seeking activity than the actual amount that the rents turn out to be. In many cases the expenditure on rent-seeking is much less than that given by the monopoly rent rectangle (*EGHB* in Figure 9-8). Jadlow argues that, in practice, the profit from the monopoly accrues over a period of time rather than during a single period, as we have been assuming (for simplicity, of course).[26] During this time period rent-seekers continue to compete for the valued monopoly prize, while consumers and regulators continue their efforts to eliminate the monopoly profit. Therefore, instead of a one-period prize, the rent-seeker has to calculate the present value of a stream of future monopoly profits, most of which are uncertain. This results in a significant reduction in rent-seeking activities, and the social costs are therefore not as high as was suggested by others.

However, Wenders argues that the social costs of monopoly are much higher than Posner suggests (maybe more than double), because we have to take into account not only rent-seeking costs but also *rent-defending costs*.[27] The monopolist also expends a lot of resources to *defend* the monopoly profit. We have been considering until now only the expenditures of others to capture a share of the pie. Since we have presented enough triangles and rectangles, we do not present the details of Wender's arguments here. The purpose of this discussion is to show that there are large (social) gains to be achieved by deregulating monopolies.

In summary, the welfare costs of monopoly may be substantial. In the next chapter we discuss policies followed by the UK government and the European Union to control the activities of monopolies. Whether they have succeeded in their purpose and at what cost is a different story.

9-9   Multi-plant Monopoly

The monopolist may operate more than one plant, and the cost conditions may differ from one plant to the other. As an illustration, we consider the case of two plants. In Table 9-3, MC_1 and MC_2 are the marginal costs of the first and second plant. The combined

---

[26] J. M. Jadlow, 'Monopoly Rent-Seeking Under Conditions of Uncertainty', *Public Choice*, 45 (1985): 73–87. See also G. Tullock, 'Back to the Bog', *Public Choice*, 46 (1985): 259–63.

[27] J. T. Wenders, 'On Perfect Rent Dissipation', *American Economic Review*, 77 (1987): 456–9.

Table 9-3   *MR* and *MC* of a two-plant monopolist

Units of output	Price	Total revenue	MR	MC_1	MC_2	MC	Produced from
1	6.00	6.00	6.00	2.30	2.45	2.30	Plant 1
2	5.50	11.00	5.00	2.40	2.55	2.40	Plant 1
3	5.10	15.30	4.30	2.50	2.65	2.45	Plant 2
4	4.80	19.20	3.90	2.60	2.75	2.50	Plant 1
5	4.56	22.80	3.60	2.70	2.85	2.55	Plant 2
6	4.35	26.10	3.30	2.80	2.95	2.60	Plant 1
7	4.17	29.19	3.09	2.90	3.05	2.65	Plant 2
8	4.01	32.08	2.89	3.00	3.15	2.70	Plant 1
9	3.87	34.83	2.75	3.10	3.25	2.75	Plant 2
10	3.73	37.30	2.47	3.20	3.35	2.80	Plant 1

marginal cost MC, shown in the next-to-last column of the table, is obtained as follows. The monopolist produces the first two units of output from plant 1 because the marginal costs are lower. Thus, MC for the first two units is 2.3 and 2.4, respectively. For the third unit of output, the MC is 2.5 in plant 1, but the monopolist can produce the unit with MC of 2.45 from plant 2. (It is the first unit for plant 2.) So the overall MC is 2.45 for the third unit. For each successive unit of output, the monopolist considers whether it can be produced at a lower marginal cost in plant 1 or plant 2 and chooses the plant with the lower MC. The overall MC and the plant from which the unit of output comes are shown in the last two columns of Table 9-3, respectively. Now we equate MC to MR and get 9 units of output as the optimal level. Of these 9 units, 5 are produced in plant 1 and 4 in plant 2.

This analysis applies to short-run equilibrium. We have considered only marginal costs but not average total costs for the two plants. If the fixed costs of plant 1 are very high, the monopolist could suffer losses in this plant. In the long run the monopolist closes down unprofitable plants.

In the long run, the monopolist with a single plant adjusts the plant size and produces output where $LRMC = MR$. Note that this position is not the minimum point of the $LRAC$ curve, as in the case of perfect competition. For perfect competition the long-run equilibrium is given by

$$LRAC = SRAC = LRMC = SRMC = MR = AR = P.$$

For monopoly, the long-run equilibrium is given by

$$LRMC = SRMC = MR \quad \text{and} \quad LRAC \leq \text{price}.$$

For the multi-plant monopolist, the long-run equilibrium condition is the same except that the multi-plant monopolist might adjust not only the plant size but also the number of plants. She might close down unprofitable plants and open new ones. The overall marginal costs and total costs are derived as for Table 9-3.

9-10 Bilateral Monopoly

A bilateral monopoly is said to exist when one producer has an output monopoly and there is only one buyer for the product. The following distinctions make things clear:

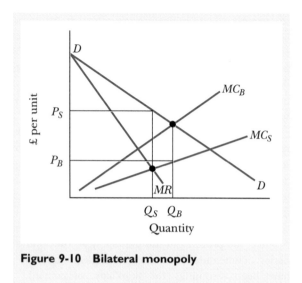

Figure 9-10 Bilateral monopoly

Perfect competition: many buyers, many sellers
Monopoly: many buyers, single seller
Bilateral monopoly: single buyer, single seller.

Since there is only one buyer and one seller in a bilateral monopoly situation, the price and quantity are determined by negotiation. However, we can find the upper and lower limits for prices and quantities, by considering alternately the single seller as all-powerful and the single buyer as all-powerful.

The situation is illustrated in Figure 9-10. DD is the demand curve, MR the marginal revenue curve, and MC_S the marginal cost curve of the single seller. If the monopolist is all-powerful, she makes the buyer behave as if there were many buyers. She equates her MC to MR, produces output Q_S, and charges a price P_S.

However, if the single *buyer* is all-powerful, he makes the monopolist behave like a perfect competitor. Thus, MC_S is the monopolist's supply curve. Corresponding to this supply curve, we can construct the MC_B curve, which shows the marginal cost of buying an additional unit. MC_B exceeds price because, in order to purchase an additional unit, the buyer must pay a higher price. And that higher price pertains to all units purchased. The buyer equates his marginal cost of buying an additional unit with the marginal value of an additional unit (as given by the demand curve) and purchases Q_B units. Since the seller behaves like a competitor with supply curve MC_S, she sells the Q_B units at a per-unit price of P_B.

Thus, if the seller has all the power, the quantity supplied Q_S is given by the intersection of the MR and MC_S curves with the corresponding price P_S read from the demand curve. If the buyer has all the power, the quantity demanded Q_B is given by the intersection of the DD and MC_B curves with the corresponding price P_B read off the MC_S curve.

The actual solution for the bilateral monopoly problem is indeterminate, depending on the respective bargaining powers of the buyer and the seller, but must lie between P_S and P_B and Q_S and Q_B.

9-11   An Application: Energy Conservation in Competition versus Monopoly

There are many resources that are considered 'non-renewable' or 'exhaustible'. The idea is that there is a limited amount of them, and if we do not use them carefully they will become exhausted, with none left for the future. This argument has been made with respect to oil and energy sources.

We do not debate the validity of this argument. We are simply interested in showing that more of the exhaustible resource is saved for the future under monopoly than under perfect competition. This result was first derived in a classic paper by Hotelling.[28] Thus, the monopolist and the conservationist are strange bedfellows.

To illustrate the point, we present a numerical example. This approach is more illuminating than discussion and diagrams. The market demand function is

$$P = 50 - Q. \tag{1}$$

The total fixed supply of the resource in question is $S = 56$. We consider two periods, and the total quantity is consumed in the two periods. Our question is: What are the quantity and price in the first period? If we know this, then we know the quantity in the second period, and from the demand function we get the price in the second period.

We assume that both the competitive firm and the monopolist discount the future profits at a discount rate equal to the market rate of interest. For example, if the profit next year is £110 and the interest rate is 10 per cent, then the firms consider next year's £110 profit as equivalent to £110/1.1 = £100 profit this year. We also assume that they try to maximize the present value of their total profits.[29] We have

$P_1 =$ price in the first period

$P_2 =$ price in the second period

$Q_1 =$ quantity sold in the first period

$Q_2 =$ quantity sold in the second period

We are given $Q_1 + Q_2$ as total supply, which equals 56.

The Competitive Solution

The competitive firm takes the market price as given. The total supply is in the hands of a large number of firms. The prices at which the competitive firm can sell are determined by the market demand function (1). Thus, we have

$$P_1 = 50 - Q_1$$
$$P_2 = 50 - Q_2.$$

Hence

$$P_1 + P_2 = 100 - (Q_1 + Q_2) = 100 - 56 = 44.$$

However, for each firm, a price P_2 received in the second period is the same as a price $P_1(1 + d)$ received in the first period, where d is the interest rate. Hence, in equilibrium we have

$$P_2 = P_1(1 + d).$$

Thus, we get

$$P_1 + P_2 = P_1 + P_1(1 + d) = P_1(2 + d),$$

or

$$P_1 = 44/(2 + d). \tag{2}$$

For different discount rates, we can now calculate the prices and outputs in the two periods. For $d = 0$, we get

$$P_1 = P_2 = 22$$

$$Q_1 = Q_2 = 28.$$

---

[28] H. Hotelling, 'The Economics of Exhaustible Resources', *Journal of Political Economy*, 39 (1931): 137–75.

[29] More discussion of discounting and present values is in Section 17-2 below.

For $d = 0.2$ (a 20 per cent rate of interest), we have

$$P_1 = \frac{44}{2.2} = 20; \qquad P_2 = P_1(1 + d) = 24.$$

Thus,

$$P_1 = 20, \qquad Q_1 = 30$$

$$P_2 = 24, \qquad Q_2 = 26.$$

As the discount rate goes up, the first-period output goes up. We now contrast this with the solution under monopoly.

Solution under Monopoly

The monopolist maximizes the present value of his profits. Since the total supply is given, this amounts to maximizing the present value of his revenue, which requires that $MR_1(1+d) = MR_2$. Substituting in the marginal revenue functions (remember that demand is linear) yields

$$(50 - 2Q_1)(1 + d) = 50 - 2Q_2.$$

But since $Q_2 = 56 - Q_1$, we can again substitute to get

$$(50 - 2Q_1)(1 + d) = 50 - 2(56 - Q_1).$$

Solving for Q_1 now yields

$$Q_1 = \frac{112 + 50d}{4 + 2d} = \frac{56 + 25d}{2 + d}. \qquad (3)$$

We can use this formula to get the prices and quantities for different rates of discount. But one interesting thing to note is that, for $d = 0$, we get

$$P_1 = 22, \qquad Q_1 = 28$$

$$P_2 = 22, \qquad Q_2 = 28.$$

which is the same as the competitive solution. For positive rates of discount, Q_1 is lower under monopoly than under competition. To see this, note that under perfect competition

$$Q_1 = 50 - P_1 = 50 - \frac{44}{2 + d} = \frac{56 + 50d}{2 + d},$$

whereas under monopoly,

$$Q_1 = \frac{56 + 25d}{2 + d}.$$

For $d > 0$, since $25d < 50d$, output under monopoly is always lower in the first period than in the second

period. As $d \to \infty$ note that $Q_1 \to 50$ under perfect competition and $Q_1 \to 25$ under monopoly.

The important result is that the restriction of current output under monopoly is a function of the interest rate or discount rate. With low interest rates, there is not much difference between the two.

The monopolist can claim that he is serving society by conserving scarce resources. In fact, when OPEC began raising oil prices, Sheikh Yamani of Saudi Arabia often argued that he was serving the interests of the industrialized world by conserving scarce resources for the future!

9-12   Summary

Pure monopoly is characterised by a single seller of a product with no close substitutes. The monopolist is a price-setter. The monopolist faces a downward-sloping market demand curve. Because the demand curve slopes downward, the MR curve also slopes downward. If the monopolist sets a single price, then to sell an additional unit she must reduce price on all units so that MR is less than price. Monopolists maximize profits by producing where $MR = MC$. They then sell this output for the highest possible price according to the demand curve.

A monopoly industry produces a smaller output and sells at a higher price than the equivalent competitive industry. Since monopolists are price-setters, it does not make sense to ask what output they produce at various prices. Hence the concept of a supply curve is meaningless for the monopolist.

For a profitable monopoly to survive in the long run, barriers to entry are required. These barriers can be in the form of control over essential inputs, legal protection, patents, or internal scale economies. The monopolist can also create barriers through pre-emptive price-cutting.

Price discrimination occurs when the monopolist sells different units of the same product at different prices with no cost justification. A requirement for successful discrimination is that profitable resale of the product can be prevented. First-degree discrimination means that the monopolist charges the reservation price for *each unit* of output; the MR curve becomes the demand curve and output is the same as under perfect competition. Second-degree discrimination means that the monopolist charges several different prices for different ranges of output; in this case, the MR curve becomes a step function and output occurs where $MR = MC$. Third-degree discrimination means that the monopolist separates customers into several groups or classes and charges different prices to the members of the different groups; the group with the least elastic demand is charged the highest price, and the group with the most elastic demand is charged the lowest price.

The traditional measure of the net welfare cost of monopoly is the excess of social value over cost for the units of output that are not produced because of the monopoly structure. This measure ignores the resources that are spent on securing and maintaining the monopoly position. It also ignores the possibility that X-inefficiency may occur as a result of the monopoly structure.

Multi-plant monopolists produce each successive unit of output in whichever plant has the lowest marginal cost. They produce to the point where overall marginal cost equals marginal revenue.

With bilateral monopoly, market price and output are indeterminate. If the buyer has total bargaining power, then output is expanded to the point where the marginal cost of buying another unit is equal to marginal value (as reflected in the demand curve). If the seller has total power, then output is expanded to the point where marginal cost of production equals marginal revenue.

With a positive discount rate, the monopolist conserves more of a fixed resource for the future than does a competitive industry.

Key Terms

Barriers to entry*
Bilateral monopoly*
Cartel*
Input monopoly*
Monopoly
Natural monopoly*
Perfect or first-degree price discrimination*
Preemptive price-cutting*
Price-setter
Rent-seeking*
Reservation price*
Second-degree price discrimination*
Third-degree price discrimination*

Questions

1 If the monopolist's demand curve is $P = 200 - 10Q$, and his marginal cost curve is $MC = 100 + 5Q$, what are his profit-maximizing price and output?

2 Graphically illustrate the impact of an increase in demand on price and quantity under a monopolistic market structure. Illustrate the impact of an increase in marginal cost.

3 In Figure 9-6, the MC curve crosses the MR curve at a corner point. If the MC curve crossed the MR curve in a horizontal segment, the monopolist might feel pressure to change her price. Why?

4 'If the average total cost curve dips below the demand curve at any point, then monopoly is profitable'. Is this statement true? Why?

5 Most small towns have only one bakery. Does such a bakery constitute a monopoly? Why or why not? What prevents more bakeries from opening in these towns?

6 What is consumer surplus with a perfectly discriminating monopoly? What is the net welfare cost to society of such a monopoly?

7 Explain why MC cannot intersect MR in the inelastic region of the monopolist's demand curve.

8 A regional basketball monopolist can separate his customers into two groups—tall customers and short customers. The demand curve for the tall customers is $P = 40 - 0.5Q$, and the demand curve for the short customers is $P = 18 - 0.25Q$. The monopolist's marginal costs are constant at £10. Calculate the profit-maximizing outputs and prices for the two groups if the monopolist practises third-degree discrimination. Compare the prices and demand elasticities for the two groups. Are they what we would expect? Why? Is it likely that this monopolist can successfully price-discriminate? Why?

9 The market demand curve for cricket balls is $P = 100 - 5Q$. The industry is currently monopolized, and the monopolist's total cost function is $TC = 300 + 20Q$. If the monopolist can practise first-degree discrimination, what is her output? How does this output compare with the output with no discrimination?

10 A monopolist operates plant 1 and plant 2. The marginal costs of the two plants are $MC_1 = 120 - 15Q + 3Q^2$ and $MC_2 = 90 - 26Q + 9Q^2$. Calculate the overall marginal cost for the first 10 units of output and indicate where each successive unit is produced.

11 A single buyer faces an upward-sloping supply curve given by $P = 40 + 10Q$. Graph the supply curve and the curve representing the marginal cost of buying an additional unit. How do the two curves compare? Why?

12 Can a perfectly discriminating monopolist maximize profit along the inelastic portion of the demand curve? Why or why not?

13 Price discrimination tends to be more common in the sale of services (for example, discrimination by age for air travel) than in the sale of manufactured goods. Explain.

14 In making efficiency comparisons between a monopolist and a competitive firm, the marginal cost function of the monopolist corresponds to the supply function of the competitive industry. Explain.

15 A multinational firm operates two plants in different countries. The marginal costs per additional unit of output and the prices for each output level are shown in the accompanying table.

(a) Construct the marginal cost schedule for the multinational as a whole.

(b) Determine the profit-maximizing output in each plant.

(c) Suppose the government in the country where plant 2 is located decides to levy a tax of £2 per unit. What are the new profit-maximizing outputs of the multinational?

Output	Plant 1 (MC_1)	Plant 2 (MC_2)	Price (£)
1	1.2	0.2	5.5
2	1.8	0.3	4.5
3	2.4	0.4	4.0
4	2.5	0.7	3.6
5	2.9	1.5	3.3
6	3.0	2.4	3.0
7	3.1	2.8	2.7
8	3.2	3.0	2.4
9	3.4	3.2	2.1
10	3.8	3.3	1.8

(d) Suppose the government in the country where plant 2 is located imposes a unitary tax on the worldwide profits of the firm. (The tax is a fixed percentage of the profits.) What is the likely response of the firm? Justify your answer.

16 (a) Imagine that health care is provided in a private market. Why does the market for doctors' services conform to the necessary conditions for third-degree price discrimination? Why might a doctor who discriminates in pricing not lose richer patients to other doctors—say, younger doctors who have just set up their practices?

(b) What justification is there for permitting price discrimination in health care? Is it any different from permitting discrimination in electricity utility rates?

(c) In a market system, would you expect doctors and hospitals to advertise and compete for patients? If they did, would this improve the quality of care and/or reduce its prices to the patient?

10 The Regulation of Monopoly

10-1 Introduction

In the last chapter we studied the behaviour of a monopolist. We saw that, if a monopolist is left alone to determine price and output, then, in general, too little is produced from a social point of view. In this chapter we look at the regulation of monopoly in theory and practice. What measures can, and should, be taken to alter the monopolist's behaviour in the desired direction?

Before tackling the question, 'How should we regulate?' we must answer the question, 'Whom should we regulate?' For the most part, we have discussed the extreme case of pure monopoly. But, in reality, most monopolies are of a weaker form. Economists generally argue that any firm with any control over the price of its product has some monopoly power. Does this imply that all such firms should be regulated? Clearly the answer is no, for we must realize that regulation itself is costly.

In order to determine which firms warrant regulation, we must be able to measure and compare the amount of monopoly power. A number of different approaches to the measurement of monopoly power are discussed in Section 10-2. Although none of these is officially used to determine regulation policy in the UK, they are used in the USA (notably, concentration ratios and the Herfindahl index).

After examining the measures of monopoly power, we focus our attention on policies that may be used to reduce the welfare loss of monopoly. These policies include price regulation, taxes, and competition policy. Price regulation is intended to induce the monopolist to produce a larger output by restricting the price it can charge. Taxes can be used to alter the monopolist's output or simply to redistribute income and alleviate the equity problems associated with monopoly. Competition policy is designed to prevent the acquisition of substantial market power. In this sense, competition policy is a preventive measure.

In Sections 10-5 and 10-6, we consider the regulation of a natural monopoly. We said that natural monopoly occurs as the result of economies of scale which result in an average cost function that is downward-sloping over the entire range of market demand. Society benefits from monopoly in this case, because a single firm can serve the entire market at a lower cost than can multiple firms. But measures must be taken to prevent the natural monopolist from exploiting the monopoly position.

In the final part of the chapter three applications are presented. The first one examines the use of an import fee to counter OPEC's monopoly price. The second looks at the impact of tariffs and quotas when the domestic industry is monopolized. The third deals with peak-load pricing where price discrimination may lead to increased efficiency.

10-2 Measures of Monopoly Power

In the last chapter we talked about the extreme case of pure monopoly. There are other degrees of monopoly. Economists generally consider that any firm that can alter its price, through an adjustment in its output, has some monopoly power. However, a very small amount of monopoly power may not warrant regulation or any other market intervention. (We see below that market share figures of 25 and 30 per cent have been used in the UK.) Clearly, before we can ascertain whether a problem exists and what, if anything, should be done about it, we must be able to measure the amount of monopoly power. This section discusses a variety of possible methods.

The Lerner Index

The ability to charge a price higher than MC is a characteristic of monopoly. Using this information, Lerner suggested an index to measure monopoly power.[1] This index, called the Lerner index, is defined as (price $- MC$)/price.

Since profit maximization implies that $MC = MR$, and price $= AR$, we can also write the Lerner index as $(AR - MR)/AR = 1 - (MR/AR)$. But $MR/AR = (1 - 1/\eta)$, where η is the price elasticity of demand. Thus, the Lerner index equals $1/\eta$, which makes intuitive sense. Note that, for a firm in a perfectly competitive industry, η is infinity, and hence $1/\eta$ is zero. The firm has no power to raise its price. If the demand elasticity is low, however, the firm has a high degree of monopoly power.

Unfortunately, the Lerner index is not as simple to calculate as it might first appear. Note that the demand elasticity we are referring to is the elasticity of the demand *facing the particular firm*. This is the same as the elasticity of demand for a product if there is only one firm producing the product. But if there are several firms, then we can only infer the elasticity of demand facing each firm from the number of firms and the elasticity of demand for the product.

We could also compute the Lerner index if we knew the firm's marginal cost, but even if the

monopolist knew his marginal cost, he would probably be reluctant to reveal it. So it is more than likely that we have to infer it from the monopolist's behaviour. To do so, there are two things we might look at:

1 We can sometimes examine other time periods when there was no monopoly in an industry. This is possible if an industry has periodic episodes of competition. Economic historians such as Temin and McCloskey have used this method to measure monopoly power in the iron and steel industry in the nineteenth century in the USA and the UK, respectively.

2 An alternative is to examine other markets where the monopolist acts like a competitor. This method works in those cases where, for instance, the monopolist has a monopoly domestically and acts like a competitor in the international market. Since a price-discriminating monopolist equates marginal revenue in the two markets, and in the international market $MR = AR =$ price $= MC$, we get a measure of the marginal cost of the monopolist from the price charged in the international market. This is illustrated in Figure 10-1, which also illustrates that there are some problems with this approach to measuring monopoly power.

In Figure 10-1 we show the marginal cost curve rising slowly and quite a high foreign price to illustrate the problems with this method of measuring monopoly power. First, we find the point of intersection of the MC curve with the foreign demand curve (which is horizontal at the foreign price, since the monopolist is a price-taker in the foreign market). This gives us point H. Since the monopolist equates marginal revenue in both markets, the marginal revenue in the domestic market is EG, and hence the point on the domestic demand curve that gives domestic quantity and domestic price is point D. We therefore have the domestic sales and export sales shown in Figure 10-1.

What is the measure of monopoly power? We can use the Lerner index and say that, since the marginal cost of the monopolist for the total output is $HL = EG$, and domestic price is DG, the Lerner index is equal to $(DG - EG)/DG = DE/DG$. But if there are no exports, the equilibrium of the monopolist is given by $MR = MC$, or point B, and the quantity and price are given by point A on the demand curve. The Lerner index is AB/AC, since price equals AC and marginal cost equals BC. Note that DE/DG is much lower than

[1] A. P. Lerner, 'The Concept of Monopoly and the Measurement of Monopoly Power', *Review of Economic Studies*, 1 (1934): 157–75.

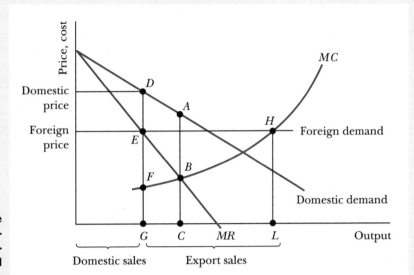

Figure 10-1 Measuring the monopoly power of a monopolist who acts as a competitor in the international market

AB/AC. (In our figure, DE/DG is about one-half of AB/AC.) Thus, the domestic price is higher, the domestic quantity is lower, the monopolist's profits are higher, and yet the measure of monopoly power is lower in the case where there is an international market!

The proper measure of domestic monopoly power is DF/DG, since FG is the marginal cost of domestic output. But there is no way of inferring FG from the price charged in the foreign market. What we can measure is the total monopoly power of the monopolist. This is approximately a weighted average of domestic monopoly power and foreign monopoly power (which is zero), weighted by the respective sales—domestic and export, respectively. Since the Lerner index,

$$\frac{\text{Domestic price} - \text{export price}}{\text{Domestic price}},$$

measures total monopoly power, domestic monopoly power equals

$$\frac{\text{Domestic price} - \text{export price}}{\text{Domestic price}}$$

$$\times \frac{\text{domestic sales} + \text{export sales}}{\text{domestic sales}}.$$

An alternative way of looking at this problem is to consider the relationship derived in Section 9-7

between the prices that a discriminating monopolist charges in two markets. There we showed that

$$P_1 (1 - 1/\eta_1) = P_2 (1 - 1/\eta_2)$$

or

$$\frac{P_2}{P_1} = \left(1 - \frac{1}{\eta_1}\right) / \left(1 - \frac{1}{\eta_2}\right),$$

where $P_1 = $ domestic price and $P_2 = $ foreign price. Then, since η_2, the price elasticity of foreign demand, is ∞, we have

$$\frac{P_2}{P_1} = 1 - \frac{1}{\eta_1} \qquad \text{or} \qquad \frac{1}{\eta_1} = 1 - \frac{P_2}{P_1} = \frac{P_1 - P_2}{P_1}.$$

And we saw earlier that the Lerner index is $1/\eta_1$. Thus, the Lerner index of monopoly power equals

$$\frac{\text{Domestic price} - \text{foreign price}}{\text{Domestic price}}.$$

Measures Based on Price Discrimination

The existence of price discrimination is evidence of monopoly power because price discrimination shows clearly that the monopolist has control over prices. Furthermore, if we know the elasticities of demand we can calculate a measure of monopoly power, as the preceding discussion shows. In fact, if there are two markets, then, since we know the market prices the monopolist charges, we need to know only one of the two elasticities of demand. In the previous example, we have $\eta_2 = \infty$. This enabled us to get an estimate of the monopoly power.

Suppose that η_2 is not known exactly. We can still get some estimates of monopoly power by making some assumptions about η_2. If, for example, the monopolist is charging three times the price in one market compared with the other one, we have $P_1 / P_2 = 3$. Thus,

$$\frac{P_2}{P_1} = \frac{1}{3} = \left(1 - \frac{1}{\eta_1}\right) \bigg/ \left(1 - \frac{1}{\eta_2}\right).$$

If $\eta_2 = 2$, then $1/\eta_1 = 5/6$.
If $\eta_2 = 4$, then $1/\eta_1 = 3/4$.
If $\eta_2 = \infty$, then $1/\eta_1 = 2/3$.

Thus, we can get some bounds on the amount of monopoly power by making some reasonable guesses about η_2.

Measures Based on Profit Rates

Frequently, the monopolist earns above-normal profits. We can, therefore, think of measuring monopoly power by comparing the accounting profit rate in an industry or a firm with the normal profit rate. There is, however, the question of what is 'normal'. How do we treat the return to special entrepreneurial talents? Furthermore, even the competitive firm can earn an economic profit in the short run until entry erodes it. These profits cannot be called monopoly profits.

Conversely, those who buy a right to a monopoly have to calculate the purchase price as a cost, and when this is done the profit rate appears normal. But this does not imply that there is no monopoly. For instance, a taxi driver in New York paying $45 000 for a 'medallion' (licence to operate a taxi) includes this in her investment cost, and we might say that she is just earning a 'normal' profit from her business. Suppose we can say this about every taxi driver. Then we have the paradox that everyone in this industry (or profession) is earning a normal rate of return, and yet we call the industry a monopoly.

This discussion demonstrates that there are serious problems with using profit rates to evaluate the extent of monopoly power. And one must use extreme care in interpreting the results of such an analysis.

Concentration Ratios as Measures of Monopoly Power

Concentration ratios measure the size of the largest firms' share in total industry employment (or sales or assets). For instance, using employment as our measure, an n-firm concentration ratio, denoted by CR_n, is the proportion of total industry employment accounted for by the n largest firms. It is customary to consider three-firm and five-firm concentration ratios denoted as CR_3 and CR_5, respectively, although we see below that this procedure has several drawbacks.

The idea behind concentration ratios is that in a competitive industry employment is more evenly distributed among firms, whereas in a monopolistic industry employment is concentrated in a few large firms. (In the extreme case of a pure monopoly, employment is concentrated in a single firm.)

Suppose there are five firms in an industry, and the employment shares of the firms arranged by decreasing size are as listed in Table 10.1. We can compute the cumulative shares for the n largest firms for $n = 1, 2, 3, 4, 5$. These cumulative shares are given in Table 10-2.

Table 10-1 Measuring concentration using employment share

Firm	Employment share
1	0.50
2	0.30
3	0.10
4	0.06
5	0.04

Table 10-2 Concentration ratios

Cumulative no. of firms	Cumulative employment share
1	0.50
2	0.80
3	0.90
4	0.96
5	1.00

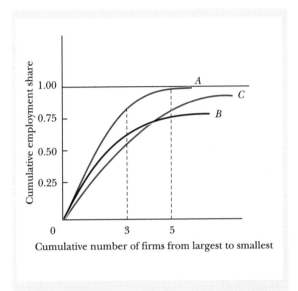

Figure 10-2   Concentration curves for three typical industries

Table 10-3   Five-firm concentration ratios for selected industries in 1989

Industry	Employment in the 5 largest firms (%)	Sales made by the 5 largest firms (%)
Tobacco	98	99
Asbestos goods	94	94
Cycles and motorcycles	63	74
Steel tubes	62	73
Soft drinks	52	54
Glass and glassware	46	54
Pharmaceutical goods	35	40
Toys and sports goods	21	18
Jewellery and coins	17	18
Leather goods	11	13

Source: CSO *Business Monitor* PA 1002, 1991.

Thus, $CR_2 = 0.8$, $CR_3 = 0.9$, and so on. We can plot the cumulative percentage of employment against the cumulative number of firms from largest to smallest. The curve we get is called a *concentration curve*. This is shown in Figure 10-2 for three typical industries. Industry A is more concentrated than industries B and C. But whether B or C is more concentrated depends on whether we use the three-firm concentration ratio (CR_3) or the five-firm concentration ratio (CR_5). If we use CR_3, B is more concentrated than C. If we use CR_5, then C is more concentrated than B. This is the basic defect of concentration ratios.

There are also other problems with concentration ratios. Do we consider employment, sales, or assets? Also, the concentration ratio does not take into account the number of firms. For instance, in our example of five firms, $CR_3 = 0.90$. In another industry with 100 firms, suppose $CR_3 = 0.92$. These two numbers are really not comparable.[2]

Table 10-3 presents a selection of five-firm concentration ratios for employment and sales. These figures are compiled by the UK government's Central Statistical Office from the Census of Production. The table shows that large firms are dominant in some industries, while in others employment and sales are less concentrated. In the tobacco and asbestos goods industries the five largest firms account for over 90 per cent of employment and sales, whereas in leather goods the five largest firms account for only 11 per cent of employment and 13 per cent of total sales. Although the figures in Table 10-3 are for only a sample of industries, they are sufficiently representative for us to say that UK industries tend to be dominated by a few large firms.[3]

---

[2] It is not clear which industry is more competitive. Another problem is that concentration ratios might be based only on the distribution of firms in the domestic industry. That is, they may ignore foreign competition, which could dramatically affect the behaviour of the domestic firms.

[3] An exhaustive survey of alternative measures of concentration and the effects of mergers on concentration ratios can be found in B. Curry and K. D. George, 'Industrial Concentration: A Survey', *Journal of Industrial Economics*, 31 (1983): 203–55.

The Herfindahl Index

To avoid some of the major problems involving the use of concentration ratios, Herfindahl suggested another index which takes account of the entire size distribution of firms.[4] This index, called the Herfindahl index and denoted by HI, is defined as follows:

$$HI = \sum_{i=1}^{n} s_i^2,$$

where n is the number of firms in the industry and s_i is the employment (or sales or output) share of the ith firm $(i = 1, 2, \ldots, n)$. This index reflects both the numbers of firms and their relative sizes.

For the example we considered earlier, we compute the Herfindahl index as

$$HI = (0.50)^2 + (0.30)^2 + (0.10)^2 + (0.06)^2 + (0.04)^2$$
$$= 0.3552.$$

If, instead, all firms have equal employment shares, then each share is 0.2 and the Herfindahl index is

$$HI = 5(0.2)^2 = \frac{1}{5}.$$

If there are n firms in an industry and all have equal shares, the share of each firm is $1/n$ and the Herfindahl index is $n(1/n)^2 = 1/n$, which is the reciprocal of the number of firms. If there is only one firm, its share is 1 and the Herfindahl index is 1. Thus, the Herfindahl index lies between 1 and $1/n$ where n is the number of firms.

You may know from elementary statistics that the variance (σ^2) of employment shares[5] is

$$\frac{1}{n}\left[\sum_{i=1}^{n} s_i^2 - n\left(\frac{1}{n}\right)^2\right].$$

So we have

$$HI = n\sigma^2 + \frac{1}{n}.$$

Thus, the Herfindahl index depends solely on the number of firms n in the industry and the variance of

the employment shares. A very small HI indicates that there are many firms of roughly equal size. A value close to 1 indicates a small number of firms and/or very unequal shares. Thus, a large HI is interpreted as indicating greater monopoly power.

10-3   Regulation of Monopoly

In the previous chapter we discussed the problem of welfare loss arising from monopoly. In principle, a number of policies may be used to regulate monopolies, with the objective of reducing the welfare loss. These policies fall into four basic categories: (1) price regulation, (2) lump-sum taxes, (3) per-unit taxes, and (4) competition policy.

Price Regulation

Suppose monopolists cannot charge a price higher than a ceiling price $\overline{P}$. In this situation, how does a monopolist choose her profit-maximizing output? To answer this question we have to determine the marginal revenue curve under a price ceiling, and then the profit-maximizing output is found by the intersection of the marginal revenue curve and the marginal cost curve.

Figure 10-3 shows the marginal revenue curve when the government imposes price ceiling $\overline{P}$. DD is

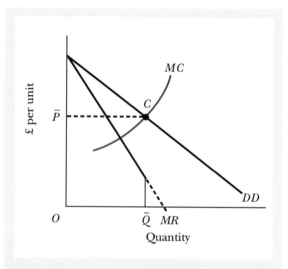

Figure 10-3   Price regulation of monopoly with price fixed at the competitive level

---

[4] O. C. Herfindahl, 'A General Evaluation of Competition in the Copper Industry', in *Copper Costs and Prices 1870–1957*, Johns Hopkins Press, Baltimore, Md, 1959, Ch. 7.

[5] This is simply a restatement of $\frac{1}{n}\left[\sum_{i=1}^{n}\left(s_i - \frac{1}{n}\right)^2\right]$. The average share is, of course, $1/n$.

the demand curve or the *AR* curve in the absence of the price ceiling. Over the range of output O to $\bar{Q}$, the price is constant, and hence $MR = $ price $= \bar{P}$. After that, price is given by the relevant portion of the demand curve, and marginal revenue is given by the corresponding portion of the downward-sloping *MR* curve. Thus, the marginal revenue curve under a price ceiling $\bar{P}$ is the dashed line in Figure 10-3. We can consider three situations depending on whether the price ceiling $\bar{P}$ is lower than, equal to, or higher than the price given by the intersection of the demand curve and the marginal cost curve. The case where $\bar{P}$ is at the level where the marginal cost curve intersects the demand curve is the most straightforward. It is shown in Figure 10-3. In this case the monopoly solution and the competitive solution coincide, and there is no welfare loss as a result of monopoly.

In Figure 10-4 we show the case where price is regulated below the competitive level. In this case the price charged by the monopolist is lower than the competitive price, but the quantity produced is also lower than the competitive output. The competitive equilibrium is at point *A*, and the monopolist's equilibrium is at point *B*. The welfare loss is given by the triangle *ABE*. (Note that we are using the traditional measure of welfare cost.) However, the welfare loss associated with an unregulated monopoly is equal to the triangle *ACD*. Thus, by imposing a price ceiling, the welfare cost of monopoly is reduced.

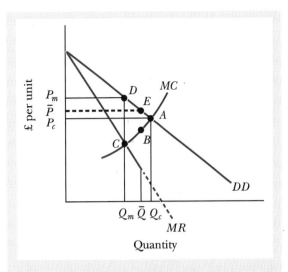

Figure 10-5   Price regulation of monopoly with price fixed above the competitive level

Note, however, that we obtained this result because $\bar{P}$ is above the level of point *C*, which is the point of intersection between the *MC* curve and the *MR* curve. If $\bar{P}$ is set below this point, then the output under price regulation is less than Q_m (the output under unregulated monopoly), and the welfare cost is higher than with an unregulated monopoly. Thus, it does not make sense to regulate the price at a level below that given by point *C* where $MR = MC$.

Finally, in Figure 10-5 we show the case where the regulated price is above the competitive level. With no price regulation, the quantity produced by the monopolist is Q_m and the price charged is P_m. With the price regulation, quantity produced is $\bar{Q}$ and price charged is $\bar{P}$. Thus, quantity is higher and price lower. However, $\bar{P}$ is higher than the competitive price P_c, and $\bar{Q}$ is lower than the competitive quantity Q_c. The welfare cost of unregulated monopoly is *ACD*, and the welfare cost of the price regulated monopoly is *ABE*, which is lower. The result is similar to the one in Figure 10-4. What then is the difference? The difference is merely that, in the case presented in Figure 10-4, price equals marginal cost, whereas in the case presented in Figure 10-5, price is higher than marginal cost and the monopolist therefore has higher profits (or lower losses, in case of a short-run loss). Thus, the basic difference between the two cases is in the profit the monopolist makes.

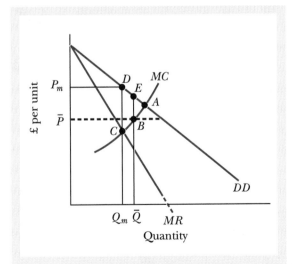

Figure 10-4   Price regulation of monopoly with price fixed below the competitive level

Lump-sum Taxes

The case of lump-sum taxes is easy to analyse. Since this type of tax is like a fixed cost, the MC curve for the monopolist does not change. Hence the output and price remain unchanged. (However, a sufficiently high tax can induce exit in the long run.) The only change is that the monopolist's profit falls. Thus, there is no change in the welfare cost, the way we have measured it: there is only a redistribution of income.

Per-unit Taxes

The case of a per-unit tax is different. This causes an upward shift in the MC curve by an amount equal to the tax. The effect is that the quantity produced falls and the price rises, although the increase in price is less than the amount of the per-unit tax. This is illustrated in Figure 10-6. For simplicity we assume that MC is constant, so that the MC curve is horizontal. MC_1 is the initial marginal cost curve, Q_1 is the initial output, and P_1 is the price. With the imposition of a per-unit tax, the MC curve shifts up to MC_2; Q_2 is the new quantity and P_2 the new price. Note that the increase in price is one-half of the per-unit tax.

Competition Policy

In the preceding chapter we discussed the welfare loss arising from monopoly. This took only the inefficiency aspects into account. There are many who also judge the income distribution consequences of monopoly as being detrimental to the ideal of equity. Thus, on the grounds of both efficiency and equity there may be legislation against monopolies. Here, we present a general outline of the principles guiding competition policy in the UK and the European Union (EU). A detailed discussion of the measures is beyond the scope of this book.

The purpose of competition policy is to promote competition and thereby ensure: (1) optimal allocation of society's resources across markets and the minimization of costs within each market; (2) maximization of dynamic efficiency by promoting a high rate of technical progress and by pressuring firms to innovate; and (3) promotion of equity by eliminating the income inequality generated by monopoly profits and restraints that limit economic opportunity. In addition, competition also helps in the attainment of other goals. Since economic power is not concentrated in a few hands, it cannot be used to manipulate the political process.

1   *Competition policy in the UK* has evolved in a fairly pragmatic (or rule-of-reason) manner. It dates back to the Monopolies and Restrictive Practices Act of 1948. The Act established a Monopolies and Restrictive Practices Commission which was empowered to examine the behaviour of any industry referred to it by the government on suspicion that the industry was operating against the public interest. The Act defined a monopoly as any firm with a market share of 30 per cent or more. The investigation of restrictive practices

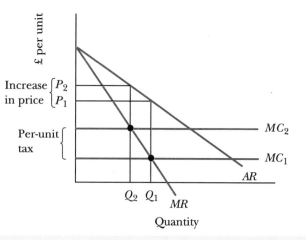

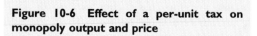

Figure 10-6 Effect of a per-unit tax on monopoly output and price

was removed from the Monopolies and Restrictive Practices Commission in 1956 with the passing of the Restrictive Trade Practices Act. This Act set up the Monopolies Commission, which continued to investigate monopoly behaviour until 1965 when, in the Monopolies and Mergers Act, its role was extended to include investigation of mergers. Any merger found by the Commission to be against the public interest could be blocked by the government. The Act also gave the Commission its present name, the Monopolies and Mergers Commission (MMC). In 1973 the Fair Trading Act altered the official definition of a monopoly to a firm with a market share of 25 per cent or more. The 1973 Act also set up the Office of Fair Trading. The final major piece of legislation came in 1980 with the Competition Act. This allowed referral to the MMC of anti-competitive practices (behaviour preventing competition mainly through the erection of entry barriers) and public-sector corporations.

Since its inception in 1965, the MMC has investigated a wide range of cases, from Kodak in 1966 to the brewing industry in 1989. In the case of Kodak, the MMC found Kodak's market share to be well over 25 per cent (Kodak in fact took over 75 per cent of all firm sales in the UK), and it argued that Kodak's profit margins were too high. Kodak subsequently acted to cut its prices. In the case of the UK brewing industry, by the mid-1980s there was concern over the number of public houses that were 'tied houses'. This means that any public house that is owned by one of the large brewing companies can only sell brands of beer made (directly or under licence) by that brewery. The MMC was concerned that this hindered consumer choice and prevented smaller independent 'free' houses from competing on equal terms. The MMC's original recommendations were not implemented by the government, partly because of extensive lobbying by the brewers. However, the government did say that no brewing company could own more than 2000 public houses, and that, eventually, all tied houses must provide at least one 'guest' beer.

Although the MMC has taken significant action in a number of areas over the years, some people have suggested that its performance is inadequate. Many cases take a long time to be resolved, and since 1965 only 3 per cent of all eligible mergers have been referred to the MMC with only 1 per cent ruled to be against the public interest. Even so, the legislation has

probably meant that the more blatant anti-competitive practices have not occurred.

Weir has investigated the extent to which public interest criteria influence the MMC's decisions as to whether or not to allow mergers to proceed.[6] Looking at merger reports from 1974 to 1990, he finds that very few public interest issues seem to have influenced the MMC. Interestingly, one issue that does not seem to be important to the MMC is large market share. A high market share seems to be seen as reflecting entrepreneurial flair rather than as an abuse of market power. However, the impact of the merger on competition has remained important for the MMC over the study period.

2   *Firms based in the EU* are subject not only to national government policy but also to the rules governing EU competition policy. In the EU competition policy aims to prevent firms from distorting trade by abusing their market power and allows for action where there exist anti-competitive practices that are incompatible with the common market. The Treaty of Rome includes the basic competition rules in Articles 85–94. The principal ones of interest to us are the following. Article 85 prohibits any agreements or practices (such as price-fixing) which affect trade between members and restrict or distort competition. Article 86 outlaws any dominant firms from abusing their market position to the detriment of consumers. Articles 92–94 cover national assistance to industry, preventing any subsidies that may distort competition.[7]

One of the problems with Article 86 is that it does not allow the EU to take any preventive action on mergers. By the late 1980s there was growing concern that the creation of the Single Market in 1992 would bring many more cross-border mergers. Action was taken on cross-border mergers late in 1989. It was decided that from September 1990 any cross-country mergers that produce a combined annual turnover of more than 5 billion ECUs would need to be approved by the Commission. With such a threshold it is unlikely that many mergers will come before the European

---

[6] C. Weir, 'Monopolies and Mergers Commission, Merger Reports and the Public Interest: a Probit Analysis', *Applied Economics*, 24 (1992): 27–34.

[7] For a comprehensive discussion of EU competition policy, see T. Hitiris, *European Community Economics* (2nd edn.), Harvester-Wheatsheaf, London, 1991, pp. 59–64.

Commission, although with a reduction in the threshold more mergers may come under EU control.[8]

3 *In the United States* there is a long tradition of competition (or antitrust) policy which is enforced by the Department of Justice and the Federal Trade Commission. Three laws, with their numerous amendments, constitute the basis of US antitrust policy. These are the Sherman Act (1890), the Clayton Act (1914), and the Federal Trade Commission Act (1914). How effective the antitrust legislation has been is open to question. Critics say that most of the cases take a long time to resolve (the US *v.* IBM suit settled in 1982 was initiated in 1969), and the penalties imposed are very small fines (usually no imprisonment).

10-4 Average Cost Pricing under Monopoly

Suppose that the government wishes to eliminate all (economic) profit for a monopolist and so sets price to equal the average cost of the unregulated monopolist's output. If monopolists are allowed to maximize their profit, the situation is as shown in Figures 10-4 or 10-5, and the conclusions derived there apply.

However, this is not what is meant by average cost pricing. Average cost pricing means that price equals average (total) cost, and both price and output correspond to the point where the average cost curve intersects the demand curve, as shown in Figure 10-7. The monopolist does not want to produce $\overline{Q}$ but is typically required to satisfy market demand at the regulated price $\overline{P}$. The output $\overline{Q}$ is higher than the competitive output Q_c. The price is also lower than the competitive price. There is a welfare loss shown by the shaded triangle in the figure. Note that this time the welfare loss is due to overproduction—the increase in consumer satisfaction is less than the increase in the cost of resources.

In the above example, the demand curve intersects the average cost curve along its upward-sloping portion. We now consider the case where the demand curve intersects the long-run *AC* curve (*LRAC*) to the left of its minimum point or in the region of economies of scale. Figure 10-8 depicts this scenario.

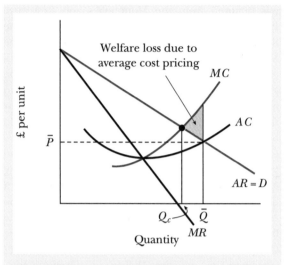

Figure 10-7 Effects of average cost pricing

We generally argue that the output, corresponding to the intersection of *LRMC* and the demand curve, is socially optimal, but in this case, since *LRAC* is declining at *A*, *LRMC* is less than *LRAC*. If the firm produces Q_c at a price of P_c, it suffers losses and leaves the industry. The lowest single price (and, hence, the largest output) at which this monopolist can cover costs is P_{ac}. Thus, in this sense average cost pricing is optimal.

10-5 Regulation of Natural Monopolies and the Theory of Marginal Cost Pricing

In the last chapter, we mentioned that there are many cases where monopolies arise naturally because of economies of scale. These monopolies, called *natural monopolies*, occur in those cases where the average cost of production declines over the entire range of market demand (as in Figure 10-8). This implies that one firm can produce the entire output more cheaply than can multiple firms. Often quoted examples are public utilities (gas, electricity, and water), telephone companies, and railways. The monopolistic firm, if left alone, does not produce a socially optimal level of output. But regulation can bring about the optimal output if the regulators are able and willing to make the necessary calculations.

---

[8] For a fuller discussion of EU policy regarding mergers, see P. R. Ferguson, G. J. Ferguson, and R. Rothschild, *Business Economics*, Macmillan, London, 1993, pp. 275–82.

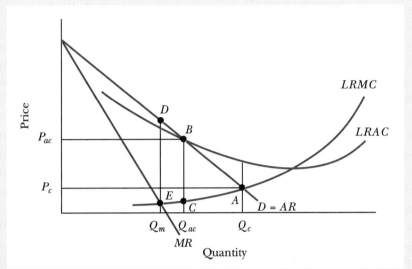

Figure 10-8 A case where average cost pricing for a monopoly is optimal

Our discussion of price regulation in Section 10-3 and of average cost pricing in Section 10-4 gives some clues about the nature of price regulation in the case of natural monopolies. There are three types of regulation: marginal cost pricing, average cost pricing, and price discrimination (or a two-part tariff).

Marginal Cost Pricing

Consider first the case of marginal cost pricing. Price is set at the level corresponding to the intersection of the demand and *MC* curves, and the monopolist is required to provide the entire quantity demanded at that price. Thus, the socially optimal output is produced.

A problem occurs, however, since by definition the natural monopolist's *LRAC* curve is downward-sloping over the entire range of demand. Thus, marginal cost is less than average cost at the optimal output (as in Figure 10-8), and marginal cost pricing results in losses for the monopolist. One solution to this problem is to subsidize the monopoly from general tax revenue for the losses it incurs, as has often been done with government-owned (or nationalized) industries.

It is easy to say that prices should be set equal to marginal cost, but it is very difficult to implement the rule in practice. This is particularly so with many of the natural monopolies that we find where investments are lumpy. (For example, building a new electricity generating plant involves a large amount of fixed investment.) There is a good deal of literature on marginal cost pricing in the case of public utilities.[9] It is not possible to review all this literature here, but we shall discuss a few aspects of the marginal cost pricing problem to clear some mistaken notions. The most important aspect is that 'marginal cost pricing' does not always imply that price equals marginal cost! Boiteux pointed this out in relation to publicly owned utilities, and the argument is as follows.[10]

Suppose that there is an electricity utility. It has a certain capacity and can supply a certain number of kilowatt-hours of electricity. Once it is built, sunk costs are sunk, and the proper pricing rule is to set price equal to marginal cost. By 'marginal cost' we mean marginal short-run operating costs. As demand increases, however, the electric utility cannot supply the total quantity demanded, and may have to increase the price to the point where quantity demanded falls to equal the existing capacity. Boiteux suggests the following rule. Set price equal to short-run marginal operating cost if quantity demanded is less than or equal to capacity at that price; if quantity demanded exceeds capacity at this price, then set price above

[9] For a detailed discussion, see J. Vickers and G. Yarrow, *Privatisation: An Economic Analysis*, MIT Press, London, 1988.
[10] M. Boiteux, 'Marginal Cost Pricing', in J. R. Nelson *et al.*, *Marginal Cost Pricing in Practice*, Prentice-Hall, Englewood Cliffs, NJ, 1964 (originally published in French in 1956).

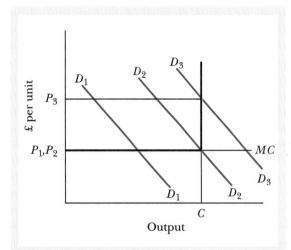

Figure 10-9 Marginal cost pricing with a fixed capacity and increasing demand

capacity is added. Boiteux suggests a rule for investment in new capacity, but since this involves inter-temporal decisions (treated later in Chapter 17) we shall not discuss it here. Anyway, there are two rules: a short-term pricing rule and a long-term investment rule. Once new capacity is added, then price falls again to the new level of marginal costs. This is shown in Figure 10-10. Initially, capacity is C_1, and demand is given by $D_1 D_1$. Price is $P_1 = MC_1$. When demand increases to $D_2 D_2$ price rises to P_2, but when the new capacity comes into existence so that capacity is C_2, price falls to $P_3 = MC_2$, the new marginal cost. When demand increases to $D_3 D_3$, price stays at P_3, but when demand increases to $D_4 D_4$ price increases to P_4. The price keeps on increasing until additional capacity comes on line, at which point price falls to the point of the new marginal cost.

Vickrey makes a similar argument with reference to the marginal cost pricing of water:[11]

> A more important consideration that is especially significant in the case of water supply is that new supplies come in very high lumps. What marginal cost pricing would require here is almost precisely the reverse of what often happens. When a new supply is brought in, this increases costs, and this is

short-run marginal cost at a level that equates quantity demanded to the available capacity.

This rule is illustrated in Figure 10-9. Suppose marginal operating costs are constant. The available capacity is C. By 'capacity' we mean the maximum possible output. When demand is given by $D_1 D_1$, we set price $P_1 = MC$. When the demand curve shifts to $D_2 D_2$, price P_2 is still equal to MC. Thereafter price keeps on increasing. When the demand curve is $D_3 D_3$, price is set at P_3. As the demand curve keeps shifting to the right, price keeps on rising. At some point, new

[11] W. S. Vickrey, 'Responsive Pricing of Public Utility Services', *Bell Journal of Economics*, 2 (1971): 337–46.

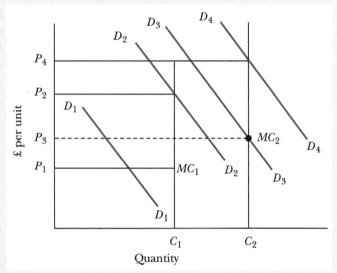

Figure 10-10 Marginal cost pricing with shifting capacity and increasing demand

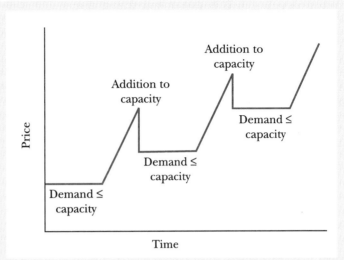

Figure 10-11 Pattern of prices over time under the marginal cost pricing rule with lumpy investments

very often used as a justification for an increase in the rates. The increase is even quite often postponed until the new supply becomes available, on the grounds that only those who benefit from using the new supply should be called upon to pay for it. What ought to be done, however, if demand grows gradually is to increase the water rates for a period before the new supply is available sufficiently to curtail demand to the capacity of the old supply.... Then when the new supply becomes available the rate should be dropped sharply to the point where the new supply is fully utilised, being subsequently raised as demand grows so as to keep the actual consumption within the capacity of the new supply.

Figure 10-11 shows what the marginal cost pricing rules suggested by Boiteux and Vickrey (and many others) imply for prices if investments are lumpy. In practice, it is politically not feasible to implement a price structure as shown in Figure 10-11. There are also many questions as to what is treated as fixed cost and what as variable cost in the computation of marginal cost.

Average Cost Pricing

Compared with the marginal cost pricing rule, it seems that the average cost pricing rule is easier to implement. All we have to do is check to see that the firm is earning a 'fair' rate of return on capital employed: if it is earning a higher-than-fair rate of return, then price is too high. But what is 'fair'? Ideally, the realized rate of return is the opportunity cost. But as we have seen, it is hard to account for such things as entrepreneurial talent, and therefore it is difficult to calculate actual rates of return as well as fair rates of return.

We have also seen (in Figure 10-7) that average cost pricing can involve a welfare cost, and in fact we can show (by drawing the curves in Figure 10-7 suitably) the welfare cost of average cost pricing to be higher than the welfare cost of monopoly pricing. But the case of natural monopoly, shown in Figure 10-8, is different. In this case, even if there is a welfare loss (equal to the area *ABC*), it is definitely less than the welfare loss due to monopoly (which is given by *ADE* in Figure 10-8). Thus, in this case we can say that average cost pricing is definitely preferred to monopoly pricing.

Both marginal cost pricing and average cost pricing are designed to induce the monopolist to expand output. As a monopoly's output approaches the optimal output (Q_c in Figure 10-8), the cost of the monopoly to society is reduced. A third tool used to induce the monopolist to increase output is a type of price discrimination.

Price Discrimination

Many natural monopolies are allowed to price-discriminate. In fact, most public utilities charge discriminatory prices. They employ a combination of second- and third-degree discrimination by charging different prices to residential, commercial, and industrial users and by charging different prices for different units of output to each customer. As we saw in Chapter 9, the output of the discriminating monopolist is, in general, larger than for the non-discriminating monopolist.[12]

Many utilities employ a declining block rate structure which we discussed as a form of second-degree discrimination. In Figure 9-6 we saw that, if the blocks are properly determined, then output occurs where MC equals D or at the competitive level. But we argued that the natural monopoly suffers a loss at that output. Our argument, however, assumes that a single price is being charged. Second-degree discrimination allows the monopolist to collect additional revenue on initial units sold so that it can cover costs while producing the socially optimal output. And in this case utility customers pay the full cost of production, thereby eliminating the need for subsidies from general tax revenue.

10-6   Regulation of Natural Monopolies in Practice

In the UK and most other European countries, nationalization (or government ownership) has been used as a form of regulation for many of the natural monopolies—the public utilities, railways, and so on. While such industries are likely to remain in public ownership in most European countries, in the UK only the Post Office will remain a public corporation in the medium term. All of the public utilities are now private companies, and the government has recently added British Rail to its list of privatizations. This does not mean that the private natural monopolies are unregulated. A number of regulatory bodies, such as OFTEL (telecommunications), OFWAT (water), and OFGAS (gas), exist to ensure that the monopoly runs as efficiently as possible.

In the previous sections we discussed the marginal cost pricing and average cost pricing approaches to the regulation of natural monopolies. In the UK, the

principle of setting price equal to marginal cost for the nationalized industries was first explicitly introduced in a 1967 White Paper.[13] In particular, the White Paper said that prices should be set to reflect long-run marginal costs, but could be adjusted in line with short-run marginal costs when capacity was clearly suboptimal. Such a pricing rule follows naturally from a desire to maximize allocative efficiency given the demand and cost conditions. One of the problems with this approach is that *there is no single number for marginal cost.* We have a marginal cost schedule (or *MC* curve) that gives marginal costs for various levels of output, and we cannot devise efficient prices without knowing the demand curve. The single number needed for marginal cost pricing is given by the intersection of the demand curve and the marginal cost curve.[14] Thus, to implement marginal cost pricing we need complete knowledge of the cost conditions as well as the demand conditions. A further problem with the 1967 measures was that there were no inbuilt incentive mechanisms to guarantee efficient manager performance, while ministers of state had the power to overrule pricing policies if they felt they conflicted with short-term political considerations. There was often a conflict between efficiency goals and political objectives.[15]

The 1978 White Paper on the nationalized industries relegated marginal cost pricing to a subordinate role.[16] Greater emphasis was placed on the idea of average cost pricing (in terms of the rate of return on invested capital), with investment programmes being required to achieve a real rate of return of 5 per cent. It was thought that this would make the assessment of investment performance easier.

One problem with this cost-plus approach is that managers have no incentive to hold down costs. If costs rise, the regulator allows a higher price to cover these costs. Since all variable costs are covered, managers have an incentive to increase costs by having expense accounts, payment of higher-than-necessary wages, and so on.

---

[12] Under third-degree discrimination, total output can be less than in the absence of discrimination.

[13] *Nationalised Industries: A Review of Economic and Financial Objectives*, HM Treasury, London, 1967.
[14] For further discussion, see Section 10-9 on peak-load pricing.
[15] For a detailed discussion see Vickers and Yarrow, op. cit.
[16] *The Nationalised Industries*, HM Treasury, London, 1978.

Also, with average cost pricing a firm may seek to increase its profits by increasing the size of its capital stock. This tendency is more pronounced if the allowed rate of return exceeds the actual cost at which the firm can borrow additional funds. This tendency for firms to 'overcapitalize' is called the *Averch–Johnson effect*.[17] As a consequence of this type of regulation, regulated firms are inclined to carry more reserve capacity than is needed and to invest in more capital-intensive methods of production.

At the same time, there is a tendency for the natural monopoly to suppress or slow down the introduction of technological innovations. This follows automatically from the fact that, as we observed, a natural monopoly regulated by the rate of return has few incentives to cut costs, and technological innovations do cut costs.

One way to overcome such problems, it is argued, is to use the $RPI - X$ style of regulation used in the UK to monitor the performance of the privatized (formerly public) monopolies. The idea is that prices increase by no more than the rate of general inflation minus X per cent annually. This means that prices must fall in real terms by X per cent per year. This formula was first applied to British Telecom with the X factor set at 3; by 1993 this X factor had risen to 6.25 per cent. This general pricing rule also applies in the case of gas, electricity, and water (although the X factors are different). With this approach it is not necessary to acquire cost data from the regulated firm (although it is necessary to obtain an estimate of the likely change in costs), and the firm has an incentive to operate efficiently since lower costs mean a higher profit.

10-7   Application I: An Import Fee on Oil

In this application we discuss the use of an import fee to counter the behaviour of a foreign monopoly (cartel), OPEC. This measure primarily attacks the

[17] This was pointed out in H. Averch and L. L. Johnson, 'Behaviour of the Firm under Regulatory Constraint', *American Economic Review*, 52 (1962): 1053–69. Since then there has been an extensive literature on the existence or non-existence of the Averch–Johnson effect and on measurement of its magnitude.

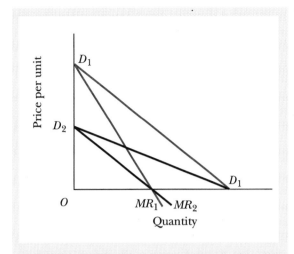

Figure 10-12   Effect of an import fee on the demand curve for imports

equity problem associated with monopoly, since output is only minimally affected.

On January 1 1973, the price of oil was about $2 a barrel. By the end of 1973, after the Arab oil embargo, the price was about $12 a barrel—a sixfold increase. By mid-1980, following the Iran–Iraq war, the price had risen to about $40 a barrel—a twentyfold increase in seven years. Since then the oil price has fallen, but the enormous increase in the price of oil since 1973 has resulted in large income transfers from the oil-consuming nations to OPEC.

We consider the effect of import fees imposed by oil-consuming nations on these income transfers. We assume that OPEC behaves like a monopolist, equating MC to MR. Figure 10-12 shows the effect of a 50 per cent import fee on the demand for imports. In the figure, $D_1 D_1$ is the demand curve for imports by the oil-consuming nations, and MR_1 is the corresponding marginal revenue curve for OPEC. With an import fee of 50 per cent, the demand curve swings to $D_2 D_1$, where D_2 is the midpoint of OD_1 on the vertical scale. The points on the demand curve $D_1 D_1$ show the prices that consumers are willing to pay for different quantities. The points on the demand curve $D_2 D_1$ show the prices that OPEC receives for different quantities. If the import fee is 25 per cent, OD_2 is three-quarters of OD_1 on the vertical scale, and if the import fee is 75 per cent, OD_2 is one-quarter of OD_1 on the vertical scale.

Marginal costs for oil production are very low. So in analysing the effects of the import fee on OPEC's output, we assume them to be zero. In this case the *MR* curves, with or without the import fee, both intersect the *MC* curves at the same point. Thus, output does not change. The only thing that changes is the price OPEC receives and the profit it makes. This is shown in Figure 10-13. Without import fees the profit OPEC makes is given by the shaded area D_2AFE plus the cross-hatched area *EFBC*. With the import fee these profits are reduced to the cross-hatched area *EFBC*. The governments of the oil-importing nations collect D_2AFE as revenue. In fact, in the case of zero marginal costs, by increasing the import fee to a high enough percentage, we can eliminate OPEC's profits. As the import fee is raised, the demand curve D_2D_1 swings toward the horizontal axis, and the price OPEC receives falls. Finally, when the demand curve D_2D_1 passes through point *B*, the price that OPEC receives is exactly equal to its average cost of production, and OPEC's profits are completely eliminated.

This analysis, of course, depends on the assumption of zero marginal costs of production. This may be an unreasonable assumption to make for most OPEC members, especially since the Gulf War. In this case the effect of the import fee is to curtail output.

Consider, for instance, the case where marginal costs are constant but not zero. In Figure 10-14 the

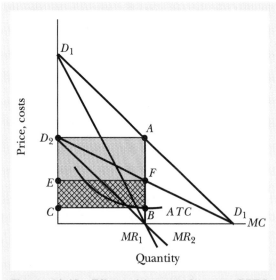

Figure 10-13 Effect of import fees on OPEC profits

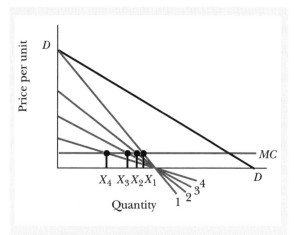

Figure 10-14 Effect of higher import fees on OPEC output

marginal revenue curve with no import fee is labelled 1 and the marginal revenue curves for higher and higher levels of import fees are labelled 2, 3, and 4, respectively. The corresponding quantities are X_1, X_2, X_3, X_4. Thus, the quantity imported decreases when the import fee is raised.

10-8 Application 2: Effects of Tariffs and Import Quotas under Competition and Monopoly

Here we examine the impact of trade restrictions on the behaviour of a domestic monopoly. It is worth noting, however, that it is now more difficult for member-states of the EU to impose trade restrictions. Member-states cannot impose tariffs, for instance, against other member-states, although the EU does impose a Common External Tariff (which was reduced in the 1993 GATT trade agreement) against non-member countries.

Under perfect competition, an import tariff or an import quota normally increases domestic production and thus employment. Here we show that this is not necessarily the case with monopoly, and that workers in a monopolized industry may therefore oppose tariffs and quotas.

First, we consider again the case of perfect competition. In Figure 10-15, *DD* is the domestic demand curve and *SS* the domestic supply curve. P_f is the foreign or world price at which world supply is perfectly elastic. Without any import tariffs, the domestic price is also equal to P_f. Hence, domestic quantity supplied is Q_1, but domestic quantity demanded is Q_4. The difference $Q_4 - Q_1$ is made up of imports. If a tariff T is imposed, the domestic price level rises to $P_f + T$, domestic quantity supplied rises to Q_2, and domestic quantity demanded falls to Q_3. Thus, imports decline to $Q_3 - Q_2$. Since domestic production rises to Q_2, domestic employment also rises, and workers benefit from the tariff.

The effect of import quotas is similar to that of tariffs under perfect competition. In Figure 10-15 the effect of an import quota of $Q_3 - Q_2$ on domestic production and domestic price is the same as that of an import tariff T. Imports are $Q_3 - Q_2$, domestic production is Q_2, and domestic price is $P_f + T$. The government has to issue import licences in the amount $Q_3 - Q_2$. If these are issued at random, the lucky importers who obtain the import licences reap the benefit $(Q_3 - Q_2)T$. However, if the government auctions the import licences, it gets a revenue of $(Q_3 - Q_2)T$, the same amount as with the imposition of the tariff. The welfare cost of import quotas is then the same as under tariffs. Also, as we increase the level of the tariff or decrease the size of the import quota, domestic production and employment increase.

Under monopoly the situation is different. The monopolist tries to equate marginal revenue with

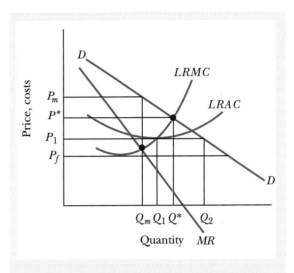

Figure 10-16   Effect of tariffs under monopoly

marginal cost. The situation is shown in Figure 10-16. DD is the domestic demand curve; MR is the corresponding marginal revenue curve. $LRMC$ is the marginal cost curve and $LRAC$ the long-run average cost curve. P_f is the foreign price; P_1 is the price corresponding to the minimum point of the average cost curve; P^* is the price where the $LRMC$ curve intersects the demand curve DD. Finally, Q_m is the output where $MR = LRMC$ and P_m is the corresponding price. This is the price the monopolist charges in the absence of any pressure from imports.

If the market price is less than P_1, the monopolist produces nothing. Thus, the minimum tariff level needed for domestic production is $P_1 - P_f$. If the tariff level is less than this, there is no domestic production. All the domestic demand is met by imports. With the tariff at $P_1 - P_f$, domestic price is P_1, domestic production is Q_1, domestic quantity demanded is Q_2, and imports are $Q_2 - Q_1$. Now as the tariff level rises the monopolist moves up the marginal cost curve, domestic production increases, domestic quantity demanded decreases, and imports fall. Finally, at the tariff level $P^* - P_f$, domestic production and domestic quantity demanded are both Q^* and there are no imports. If the tariff level is raised further, the monopolist takes advantage of this protection offered and cuts production. Finally, if the tariff reaches $P_m - P_f$ or higher, the monopolist charges the monopoly price P_m and produces output Q_m. Thus, in the case of

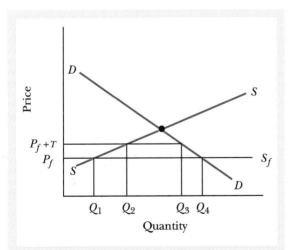

Figure 10-15   Effects of tariffs under perfect competition

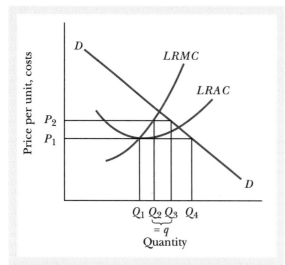

Figure 10-17 Effects of import quotas under monopoly

10-9 Application 3: Peak-load Pricing

Peak-load pricing is a form of price discrimination in which the firm charges a higher price for peak use than for off-peak use. British Telecom, for instance, has followed this practice for a long time. The charge during the day is higher than during the night or at weekends. Peak-load pricing can also be seen in the pricing of electricity.[19]

Actually, the idea of peak-load pricing need not be confined to the case of large public enterprises such as public utilities and telephones. The principles of peak-load pricing are, in fact, equally applicable to such private enterprises as hotels, restaurants, health clubs, airlines, cinemas and to some degree most retail establishments.[20] Thus, we observe cinemas charging a lower price before 6 pm, hotels charging low off-season rates, restaurants charging a lower price at lunch for basically the same meal as served in the evening, airlines offering off-season low rates, and so on.

In all these cases, the demand for the service fluctuates predictably during the peak and off-peak periods. The demands have different elasticities, and furthermore there are cost differences between the two periods. Any expansion in output during the peak period can be achieved only if the firm has sufficient capacity. A telephone company has to add more lines to accommodate higher peak demand; a hotel needs to have sufficient rooms to accommodate more residents at peak periods. During off-peak periods, however, the output can be expanded with no increase in capacity costs. The marginal costs the firm incurs are only operating costs. This leads to the frequently suggested rule that customers at peak periods should be charged a price equal to the marginal operating cost plus marginal capacity cost (since they are the ones responsible for increased capacity), and customers at off-peak times should be charged a price equal to just the marginal operating cost, since capacity is a 'free' good for them. In the UK, for instance, people who use the Economy 7 electricity system are charged a lower price when using electricity during the night. This off-

monopoly, an increase in the tariff rate can actually result in a decline in output (and employment).

The effects of import quotas under monopoly are also similar to those of tariffs. In Figure 10-16, the maximum number of imports that can be permitted is $Q_2 - Q_1$. For import levels higher than this, there is no domestic production. For any other levels of the import quota, the domestic price rises to the corresponding point between P_1 and P^*. To find the market price, all we have to do is measure a horizontal distance equal to the import quota between the *LRMC* curve and the demand curve. This is shown in Figure 10-17. The import quota is q. We then measure a horizontal distance equal to q between the marginal cost curve and the demand curve. This gives us the market price P_2. Q_2 is the domestic monopolist's output. $Q_3 - Q_2 = q$ which gives imports. Q_3 is the total quantity demanded. In the figure we also show again the price P_1 where $LRMC = LRAC$ (the minimum point on the *LRAC* curve). At this price the monopoly output is Q_1, domestic demand is Q_4, and imports are $Q_4 - Q_1$. This is the maximum level of quota one can set if any domestic production is to occur.[18]

---

[18] $Q_2 - Q_1$ in Figure 10-16 equals $Q_4 - Q_1$ in Figure 10-17.

[19] See the symposium on peak-load pricing in *Bell Journal of Economics*, 7 (1976): 197–206.
[20] See T. Nagle, 'Economic Foundations for Pricing', *Journal of Business*, 57 (1984): 5–20.

peak price is set on the basis of just the marginal operating costs of the electricity company. This pricing rule was suggested by Kahn for the pricing of electricity provided that there is only one type of capacity serving both the peak and off-peak users.[21] (We see in Example 10-1 that usually there are different kinds of plants.) With different types of capacity, the different capacity costs have to be allocated to the different customers. The proper pricing rule involves identifying which capacity is not a free good in equilibrium for which class of users, and allocating the capacity costs accordingly. For instance, with two plants, one operating at full capacity during both peak and off-peak periods and the second operating during peak periods only, the capacity costs of the first plant are borne by all the users, whereas the capacity costs of the second plant are borne by the peak-demand users only.

Example 10-1   Pricing of Electricity

An example of price discrimination in different forms is the pricing of electricity. Demand for electricity fluctuates seasonally, with heavy demand in midsummer if it is used for cooling (air-conditioning) and heavy demand in midwinter if it is used for heating. It also fluctuates between weekdays and weekends (many production facilities are closed at weekends) and even during different hours of the day (with a low around, say, 4 am and a peak during the day). Over twice as many kilowatts may be required at the daytime peak as at the nighttime trough. Such variation occurs in almost every country in the world.

Electricity is costly to store and therefore must usually be produced as it is used. To avoid blackouts, a power system must have enough capacity to satisfy the peak demand. However, different power plants have different cost structures. A large nuclear or coal-fired plant has low fuel costs but high capital costs; this plant is justified if it can operate most hours of the year. A small turbine plant has high fuel costs but low capital

costs; these are used only for a few hours at a time and for only a fraction of the year to satisfy peak demand.

Some utilities also have pumped storage plants. Water is pumped up to a reservoir during off-peak hours using low-cost electricity. It is then used during peak hours to run hydroelectric plants. Only about three-quarters of the electricity used in pumping the water up is recovered when the water flows down. However, this can be more economical than other methods of generating electricity during peak hours.

Yet another way of satisfying peak demand is by purchasing electricity from another utility. This may be expensive because the electricity must be transmitted over long distances.

Thus, supply of electric power comes from the following sources:

1 *Primary generators* These are large coal-fired and nuclear-powered steam generators. They spin constantly because they are too costly to stop and start. They can generate electricity at low marginal cost.
2 *Secondary generators* These are smaller steam generators or jet turbines (and hydro plants) that can be started and stopped at short notice. Their marginal costs are higher than for primary generators.
3 *Borrowed electricity* The marginal costs of borrowed electricity are generally higher than for secondary generators.

It can be seen that the marginal cost of producing electricity is much greater during peak periods than during off-peak periods. Unless demand for electricity is perfectly inelastic during both periods, gains in economic efficiency are possible by charging different prices for electricity during the peak and off-peak periods.

As noted above, peak-load pricing of electricity operates for some residential customers in the UK via the Economy 7 system. More common is second- and third-degree price discrimination in the form of *declining block pricing* and charging different rates to residential, commercial, and industrial customers. (See price discrimination in Section 10-5.)

In France, however, Electricité de France adopted peak-load pricing in 1958 for non-residential customers. The rates vary by season, day of the week, and hour of the day. There are three rates: base, shoulder, and peak. The shoulder rates are almost twice the base rates, and the peak rates are about 66 per cent above the shoulder rates. In addition, the high-voltage

---

[21] A. E. Kahn, *The Economics of Regulation*, vol. 1, John Wiley, New York, 1970, pp. 89–103. Kahn also suggested that if, at a price equal to the short-run marginal cost, the capacity is fully utilized during the off-peak period, then the off-peak users should also bear some of the marginal capacity costs, because the capacity is not a free good to them either.

customers have to pay a maximum demand charge which is over 14 times the charge for the base period. Thus the rate differences are high, and this creates powerful incentives to vary the use by time of day. French industry has responded by scheduling many production operations accordingly. Such vast differences in time-of-day rates require costly metering equipment, but with the current state of computer technology this is not a big problem: the whole operation can be scheduled by computer. It is for households that the metering costs are still high; moreover, it is difficult to vary household operations by time of day (although washing machines and storage radiators can run on Economy 7). Thus, peak-load pricing is probably less feasible for households.

10-10 Summary

The Lerner index of monopoly power is equal to $(P - MC)/P$ or $1/\eta$. A higher Lerner index indicates greater monopoly power. The ability to price-discriminate indicates monopoly power. Furthermore, if we know one elasticity and the price charged, we can determine the second elasticity.

Monopoly is frequently associated with above-normal profits. Thus, in theory, we can infer the amount of monopoly power by comparing a firm's actual profit rate with the average or normal profit rate in that industry. In practice, it is extremely difficult to determine the extent of monopoly from a comparison of accounting profit rates.

Concentration ratios measure the size of the largest firms' share in total industry employment, sales, or assets. The idea is that a large concentration ratio indicates the presence of firms that are large relative to the market and, hence, have some monopoly power. A concentration curve illustrates the entire size distribution of firms.

The Herfindahl index is equal to the sum of the squared employment (or sales or output) shares for all firms in the industry. If firms are equal in size, then $HI = 1/n$ where n is the number of firms. Otherwise, $HI > 1/n$. This index reflects both the sizes and number of firms. A larger HI is taken to be indicative of more monopoly power.

By imposing a price ceiling at the level where the MC curve intersects the demand curve, regulators can induce the monopolist to produce the competitive output.

Lump-sum taxes do not affect the position of the monopolist's MC curve, and hence do not affect her output. They merely redistribute income from the monopolist to the government. A per-unit tax shifts the monopolist's marginal cost curve upward, thus reducing output and increasing price.

Competition policy is used by national governments and by the EU to limit the acquisition of monopoly power and to restrict the behaviour of firms with monopoly power. Policy has largely been applied pragmatically rather than by using hard and fast rules.

Average cost pricing means that both price and quantity correspond to the point where the AC curve intersects the demand curve. If $MC > AC$ at this point, then the welfare cost of unregulated monopoly can be larger or smaller than the welfare cost from average cost pricing. But with natural monopoly, average cost pricing reduces welfare loss in comparison with unregulated monopoly. Under natural monopoly, marginal cost pricing results in losses to the firm. It is also difficult to implement marginal cost pricing, especially when investment is lumpy. Average cost pricing induces the natural monopolist to expand output, thereby reducing the social cost of monopoly.

By allowing natural monopolies to price-discriminate, we can induce them to expand output and reduce the welfare cost of monopoly. In practice, UK governments have used both the marginal and average cost pricing approaches for the nationalized industries. Almost all of these industries are now operating in the private sector. Most are regulated according to the $RPI - X$ formula.

When marginal costs are negligible, an import fee reduces the foreign monopolist's profit with little impact on output. The reduction in profit is transferred to the importing government. Increasing a per-unit tariff may induce the domestic monopolist to increase or decrease output and, hence, employment. Peak-load pricing is a type of price discrimination, and by charging different prices during peak and off-peak periods firms may make efficiency gains.

Key Terms

Average cost pricing*
Averch–Johnson effect*

Competition policy
Concentration curve*
Concentration ratio*
Herfindahl index*
Import fee
Lerner index*
Marginal cost pricing*
Peak-load pricing
Price discrimination*
Price regulation

Questions

1 Explain the advantages of the Herfindahl index over a three-firm or five-firm concentration ratio.

2 As a new firm enters the industry, what happens to the Herfindahl index? Can we make a general statement?

3 We said that a lump-sum tax does not affect the output of a monopolist (unless it is high enough to induce exit), and that the welfare cost of monopoly is therefore unchanged. How does the analysis differ if the monopoly engages in rent-seeking activities?

4 Can a concentration curve ever be downward-sloping? Can it ever be convex to the origin? Why?

5 Demonstrate graphically that the welfare cost of average cost pricing can exceed the welfare cost of monopoly pricing.

6 Over time a firm may lose its natural monopoly status. What factors may bring this about?

7 In Figure 10-16, choose a tariff between $P* - P_f$ and $P_m - P_f$. Indicate the monopolist's marginal revenue curve and the profit-maximizing output under this tariff.

8 What is the impact of an import fee on domestic output and price? Does your answer depend on the market structure of the domestic industry?

9 For a natural monopolist, which of the following applies?

(a) MC is less than MR.

(b) MC is less than AC.

(c) Price is constant.

(d) $MC = AR$.

10 What is the 'efficiency dilemma' when there is a natural monopoly?

Pricing in Product Markets: Monopolistic Competition and Oligopoly

11-1   Introduction

So far, we have examined in detail the two extreme market structures: monopoly and perfect competition. In reality, most industries lie in the grey area between these two extremes. In this chapter we look at two such intermediate industrial structures, monopolistic competition and oligopoly.

1 *Monopolistic competition* is characterized by a large number of firms, each of which has a little market power because it offers a differentiated product. Yet all the firms are in competition because their products are close substitutes. Examples include the retail clothing, hair styling, and restaurant industries.

2 *Oligopoly* consists of a few firms which dominate the industry and among whom there is frequently intense rivalry. Examples include car manufacturing and petrol refining.

In some sense it can be argued that monopolistic competition is closer to the extreme of perfect competition, whereas oligopoly is closer to monopoly.[1] There are no barriers to entry under monopolistic competition, and hence there are no economic profits in the long run. Also, monopolistically compe-

titive firms behave independently, with competition taking the impersonal form characteristic of perfect competition. Under oligopoly, however, there is intense personal rivalry. Also, barriers to entry are present which allow for long-run profit, as in the case of monopoly.

11-2   Pricing under Monopolistic Competition

In the early 1930s, economists began turning their attention to the middle ground between monopoly and perfect competition. In 1933, Chamberlin published his book *The Theory of Monopolistic Competition: A Re-Orientation of the Theory of Value*. It was received very enthusiastically, and many economists talked of the 'Chamberlinian revolution'. In the same year, Robinson published her book, *The Economics of Imperfect Competition*. Chamberlin spent a lot of time later differentiating his product from that of Robinson.[2] Although there are similarities in the books, there are major differences as well. For instance, Chamberlin

---

[1] An elaboration of the parallel between monopolistic and perfect competition can be found in H. Demsetz, 'Do Competition and Monopolistic Competition Differ?', *Journal of Political Economy*, 76 (1968): 146–8.

[2] E. H. Chamberlin, *The Theory of Monopolistic Competition: A Re-Orientation of the Theory of Value*, Harvard University Press, Cambridge, Mass., 1933. J. Robinson, *The Economics of Imperfect Competition*, Macmillan, London, 1933. Robinson is said to have remarked: 'I'm sorry I ruined his life'.

treated at length product differentiation and advertising, which were neglected by Robinson. She discussed problems such as price discrimination and monopolistic and monopsonistic exploitation, which were not covered by Chamberlin.

We start our discussion by defining monopolistic competition. Monopolistic competition is said to exist when there are many firms, as in perfect competition, but each firm produces a product that is slightly differentiated from that of others. Examples of this are numerous: retail clothing stores, pizza restaurants, hair salons, dry cleaners, and so on. There are several distinguishing characteristics of monopolistic competition:

1 *Product differentiation* Products are heterogeneous rather than homogeneous. However, products are only slightly differentiated. The output of one firm is a close (but not perfect) substitute for the outputs of other firms. Differentiation grants each firm some monopoly power, whereas the presence of close substitutes provides competition. There are many sources of differentiation, such as chemical composition, advertising, packaging, brand names, location, and design. The products do not have to be physically different: they must simply be perceived as somewhat different by consumers.

2 *Nonprice competition* Since the products are only slightly differentiated, the different firms try to play up the difference in their products in order to increase their demand. They do this primarily by advertising the differences.

3 *Large number of firms and freedom of entry and exit* In monopolistic competition there is a large number of firms and there is the same freedom of entry and exit as in perfect competition. When firms in an industry are making a profit, new firms enter the industry with slightly differentiated products and drive profits down. Thus, in the long run no firm is able to make an above-normal profit.

4 *Independent behaviour* The economic impact of one firm's decisions is spread sufficiently evenly across the entire group so that the effect on any single competitor goes unnoticed. This implies that conscious rivalry is missing or that competition is impersonal. Each firm behaves independently.

The word 'monopolistic' refers to the small monopoly power that firms have by virtue of their differentiated product. The word 'competition' implies that there is a large number of firms and there is freedom of entry and exit so that firms cannot make above-normal profits in the long run. Because of the monopolistic component, the demand curve facing each firm is downward-sloping. Each firm has some control over the price of its product.

The Firm's Demand Curve

The concept of an industry is somewhat nebulous when differentiated products are concerned, and we discuss this problem later. Chamberlin talked instead of a product group made up of all the products that are close substitutes. We can then talk of the total or product group demand curve. Such a demand curve is a typical downward-sloping curve. In Figure 11-1 the group demand curve is D_g.

The group demand must somehow be divided up among the members of the group. Chamberlin assumed that all firms in the group are roughly identical so that they face similar cost and demand conditions. Thus, if all firms charge the same price, they have identical market shares. In Figure 11-1, the curve D_p is the proportionate demand curve, or the demand curve facing a particular firm when all firms charge the same price. It is obtained by horizontally dividing the group demand curve by the number of firms. D_p is clearly a short-run curve, since we hold the number of firms constant when constructing it.

The firm, however, does not perceive D_p to be its demand curve. If the current price and quantity are $\overline{P}$ and $\overline{Q}$, then the firm perceives its demand curve to be D_f in Figure 11-1. D_f is more elastic than D_p. It is the

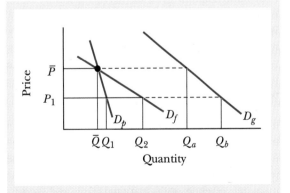

Figure 11-1 The group demand curve, proportionate demand curve, and perceived demand curve under monopolistic competition

demand curve facing the firm if all other firms continue to charge $\overline{P}$. The perceived demand curve is more elastic than the proportionate curve because, if only one firm reduces price, then that firm can capture sales and market share from other firms. Similarly, if only one firm increases price, it loses customers and market share to other firms. For example, in Figure 11-1, if one firm alone reduces price from $\overline{P}$ to P_1, then its sales increase from $\overline{Q}$ to Q_2; but if all firms reduce price to P_1, then each firm's sales increase only to Q_1. Why do sales increase at all when every firm reduces price? Because the group demand curve is downward-sloping. $Q_1 - \overline{Q}$ is simply $Q_b - Q_a$ divided by the number of firms. In other words, when all firms act together, market shares do not change.

Why does the individual firm perceive its demand curve to be D_f? Because under monopolistic competition there is a large enough number of firms for each firm to believe that its actions go unnoticed. Each monopolistically competitive firm behaves independently, so each believes that it can adjust price without other firms following its lead.

Short-run Equilibrium

Consider Figure 11-2, where D_p and D_f are as previously defined, MC is the firm's marginal cost curve, and MR_f is the marginal revenue curve corresponding to the firm's perceived demand curve. Suppose that momentarily all firms charge $\overline{P}$. The firm in Figure 11-2, believing its marginal revenue curve to be MR_f, has an incentive to expand output to Q^* and reduce price to P^*. But since all firms are identical, each firm attempts to increase output to Q^* and charge a price of P^*. Yet if all firms charge P^*, then each firm can sell only Q_1. With price equal to P^* and each firm producing Q^*, the market does not clear and there is a surplus.

As each firm realizes that it can sell only Q_1 at a price of P^*, its perceptions of demand change. The perceived demand curve shifts to intersect D_p at point A. The firm's new perceived demand curve is D_f' and indicates the quantities that the individual firm can sell at various prices if all other firms continue to charge P^*. Corresponding to D_f' is a new perceived marginal revenue curve. The firm equates the new perceived marginal revenue with marginal cost and adjusts output accordingly. But once again, all firms adjust output and price, each firm's perceptions change, and so on until an equilibrium point is reached.

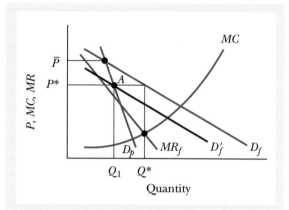

Figure 11-2   Short-run adjustment under monopolistic competition

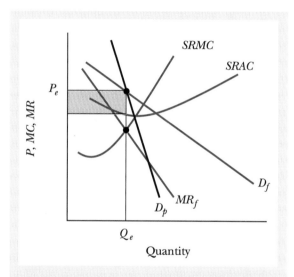

Figure 11-3   Short-run equilibrium under monopolistic competition

Short-run equilibrium for the monopolistically competitive firm is illustrated in Figure 11-3. In equilibrium, each firm produces Q_e and charges a price of P_e. Each firm perceives that it is maximizing profit because $MR_f = MC$. And finally, the market clears because the point (Q_e, P_e) lies on the firm's proportionate demand curve.

Long-run Equilibrium

Under monopolistic competition there are no barriers to entry or exit in the long run. In Figure 11-3, the

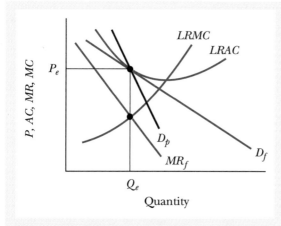

Figure 11-4   Long-run equilibrium under monopolistic competition

firms are earning an economic profit in short-run equilibrium. The amount of the individual firm's profit is the shaded rectangle. (We could have instead illustrated a short-run equilibrium with losses incurred.) The profit induces new firms to enter this product group. (Losses, of course, induce firms to leave.)

As new firms enter, each firm's proportionate demand curve shifts to the left and becomes steeper. This is because the overall product group demand must be divided among a larger number of firms. (Exit causes D_p to shift rightward for the remaining firms.) Firms now find they are unable to sell Q_e at a price of P_e. Firms continue to enter, causing all firms to adjust output and price until an equilibrium with no economic profits or losses is reached.

A long-run equilibrium situation is illustrated in Figure 11-4. Each firm perceives that it is maximizing its profit, so that there is no incentive to adjust output. But each firm is just covering its full economic cost, so that there is no incentive to enter or leave. And finally, because (Q_e, P_e) lies on the proportionate demand curve, the market clears.

The long-run equilibrium position has aspects of both monopoly and perfect competition. There are no economic profits, which is characteristic of perfect competition. But $MR < P$, which is characteristic of monopoly. We should also note that the firms maximize only their perceived profit. Actual profits are not maximized as this would require that $MR_p = MC$.

11-3   Excess Capacity under Monopolistic Competition

As shown in Figure 11-4, the long-run equilibrium for the firm under monopolistic competition is at the point where the perceived demand curve is tangent to the $LRAC$ curve. Since the demand curve is downward-sloping, the $LRAC$ curve must also be downward-sloping at this point. Thus, unlike perfect competition, the firm's equilibrium is never at the minimum point of the $LRAC$ curve. Hence, it is argued that the firm's output under monopolistic competition is not the ideal output and that, because of excess capacity, there is a wasteful use of society's resources. Production costs are higher than necessary.

Ideal output is that output which is associated with the minimum point of the $LRAC$ curve. *Excess capacity* is the difference between ideal output and the output actually attained by the firm in long-run equilibrium.

As argued by Cassels, the excess capacity under monopolistic competition can be divided into two parts.[3] This is shown in Figure 11-5: OQ_E is the long-run equilibrium output; OQ_I is the ideal output, the output corresponding to the minimum point of the $LRAC$ curve; $SRAC_1$ is the short-run average cost curve, corresponding to the optimal plant for output OQ_E; and $SRAC_2$ is the short-run average cost curve, corresponding to the optimal plant for output OQ_I.

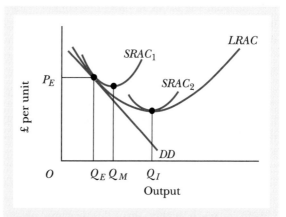

Figure 11-5   Excess capacity under monopolistic competition

---

[3] J. M. Cassels, 'Excess Capacity and Monopolistic Competition', *Quarterly Journal of Economics*, 51 (1937): 426–33.

OQ_M is the output corresponding to the minimum point of $SRAC_1$.

The excess capacity $Q_E Q_I$ can be broken down into two parts:

1 $Q_M Q_I$, the result of not building the technically optimal scale of plant (being on $SRAC_1$ instead of $SRAC_2$)

2 $Q_E Q_M$, which is due to not operating the plant at the point of minimum average cost.

Chamberlin, however, argues against treating the higher production cost arising from excess capacity as a social loss, contending that product differentiation is not worthless. People may be willing to pay for this differentiation and variety in the form of excess capacity. Thus, the ideal output is not necessarily the one given by the minimum point of the $LRAC$ curve. Of course, excessive proliferation of products of different quality is a waste of society's resources, but the cost of boredom produced by having uniform products has to be taken into account as well.

11-4 Monopolistic Competition and Advertising

An essential characteristic of monopolistic competition is product differentiation. In order that consumers are informed about what makes a product different, a firm needs to advertise its product. However, there is informative advertising and persuasive advertising. Advertising, particularly in newspapers, which also quote prices, has certain advantages. It saves consumers the costs of searching and shopping. However, much of television and radio advertising is geared to differentiating the product and developing brand loyalty.

Advertising expenditures in most European countries account for between 0.5 and 1.5 per cent of national income. Some economists believe that the benefit is much higher than this because of the increased information provided to consumers who are saved the cost of searching and shopping. Others, like Galbraith, argue that advertising promotes 'contrived obsolescence' and a wasteful use of resources. Often the firms, by their advertising, shape the tastes of consumers so that it is the firms that determine which

Table 11-1 Effects of advertising: Definition of variables

	Without advertising	With advertising
Average total cost	ATC_1	ATC_2
Demand curve	DD_1	DD_2
Equilibrium point	A_1	A_2
Price	P_1	P_2
Quantity	Q_1	Q_2

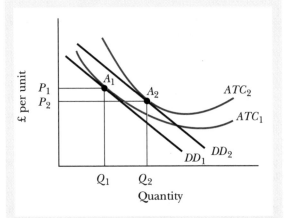

Figure 11-6 Effects of advertising on price and output: a decrease in price and an increase in quantity

products consumers buy. Thus, Galbraith attacks advertising as a violation of consumer sovereignty.[4]

What is the effect of advertising on prices charged to the consumer? Advertising increases costs, but it also shifts the demand curve. The net effect could be a fall or a rise in price, and since we are considering two different demand curves it could also mean a fall or rise in quantity. Figure 11-6 illustrates the case of a decrease in price and an increase in quantity. Figure 11-7 depicts the case of an increase in price and an increase in quantity.[5] For both figures, the definition of variables is given in Table 11-1.

---

[4] J. K. Galbraith, *The Affluent Society*, Houghton-Mifflin, Boston, 1958.
[5] We can draw another diagram to show an increase in price and a decrease in quantity.

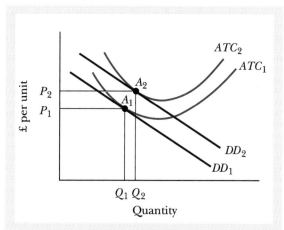

Figure 11-7 Effects of advertising on price and output: an increase in price and an increase in quantity

The preceding analysis, however, is very simplistic and ignores one important aspect of advertising in real life: namely, its role when consumers are uncertain about the quality of the product they are purchasing. Klein and Leffler argue that in practice advertising does increase the price, but consumers necessarily receive something when they pay a higher price for an advertised brand.[6] Firms making heavy expenditures on advertisements have to make sure that they maintain high-quality production. A sufficient investment in advertising implies that a firm does not engage in short-run quality deception, since the advertising expenditures produce a non-salvageable cost gap between price and production cost. Consumers are, therefore, assured of high quality even if they have to pay a higher price. This is the case with products whose quality is costly to determine before purchase. According to Klein and Leffler, it is not that it pays a firm with a 'best buy' to advertise more, but rather that advertising implies the supply of 'best buys' or, more correctly, the supply of promised high-quality products.[7]

---

[6] B. Klein and K. B. Leffler, 'The Role of Market Forces in Assuring Contractual Performance', *Journal of Political Economy*, 89 (1981): 615–41.
[7] Further discussion of the role of advertising in providing information can be found in Chapter 12.

11-5 Criticism of the Theory of Monopolistic Competition

As mentioned earlier, the model of monopolistic competition was received very enthusiastically in the 1930s. Yet, despite its almost instant success, it later generated a lot of criticism and controversy. The attacks on this model were numerous; we mention only a few of them here.

Problems with the Product Differentiation Assumption

The downward-sloping demand curves are derived from the assumption of product heterogeneity. This is inconsistent with the assumption that the cost curves or demand conditions are the same for all firms. If the outputs of two firms are genuinely different, then the costs per unit are not really comparable. Furthermore, the long-run equilibrium of a firm with only normal profit as shown in Figure 11-4 is also logically incorrect. If the firm is providing a unique product and making super-normal profits as a consequence, other firms can compete away these profits only by providing the same product.

Another problem created by the introduction of product heterogeneity is that it is difficult to define an industry or 'competing group'. For example, tea, coffee, soft drinks, beer, wine, and spirits could form a chain of competing products. Under perfect competition or monopoly, these are considered different homogeneous products; under monopolistic competition, it is not clear where we draw the line.

Finally, differentiated products are not necessarily produced by different firms. For instance, the fact that there are different brands of soaps and detergents—Sun, Persil, Comfort, Frish, Jif, Lifebuoy, Surf, Lenor, and Radion—does not mean that this market is one of monopolistic competition. All these (and many more) are produced by a single firm, Lever Brothers. What we have here is an oligopoly of multi-product firms. (Procter and Gamble is another large dominant firm in this area with many products of its own.)

The Predictive Content of the Theory

Another important criticism of the theory of monopolistic competition is that it is not useful for making any predictions. This criticism, made by Stigler, is based on the argument (discussed in Chapter 1 above) that the test of a theory is not whether it is descriptively accurate but whether it accurately predicts the effects of changes in the economic environment.[8] Unlike the theories of perfect competition and monopoly, the theory of monopolistic competition does not provide unambiguous predictions of the effect of changes in costs or demand on the price of the product, the size of the plant, or the number of firms in the industry.[9]

Consider, for instance, the question of the effect of an excise tax on output and price. We analysed this problem earlier under both perfect competition and monopoly and derived predictions about the effects of excise taxes on output and prices under some assumptions about the slopes of the demand and supply curves. No such predictions emerge from the monopolistic competition model, because we do not know whether few or many firms leave the industry when the share of the market for this taxed product falls. The existence of advertising further complicates the situation. We can, however, obtain some predictions by introducing restrictions on the way some of the variables affect each other.[10] Moreover, one prediction of the monopolistic competition model—that of long-run excess capacity and unexploited economies of scale (discussed in Section 11-3)—does not appear to be corroborated by empirical evidence.

All these reservations about the monopolistic competition model does not mean that it is useless. In fact, the enormous amount of literature criticizing it implies that it raises a lot of issues that are not considered in models of perfect competition and monopoly. For example, it has prompted economists to think of the problems of selling costs, advertising, nonprice competition, and so on.[11]

There are two other things that this controversy has highlighted:

1 We cannot judge theories on the basis of realism of assumptions: the theory has to be useful in deriving some observable predictions.
2 We have to be careful in defining costs, capacity, and so on in a manner consistent with the other assumptions of the model.

11-6 Oligopolistic Markets

We have now examined the two extreme market structures—monopoly and perfect competition—and we have also looked at a market structure that combines aspects of both monopoly and competition—monopolistic competition. In the remaining sections of this chapter we study another market structure which lies between monopoly and perfect competition: *oligopoly*.

Oligopoly is a market structure in which a small number of rival firms dominate the industry. The leading firms are well aware that their actions are interdependent. An extreme case of oligopoly is *duopoly*, where there are only two firms.

The term oligopoly means 'few sellers'. But the small number of sellers is important only in that it allows firms to recognize their interdependence. If there are two shops situated close together and selling similar goods to the same type of customers, and one of them cuts its prices, it has to guess how the other shop is going to react. Will it leave its prices unchanged, cut them by the same amount, cut them more, or even raise them? In oligopoly, although competition is lacking in the sense that we discussed for perfect competition and monopolistic competition, there is sometimes intensive rivalry or competition in the popular sense of the word.

[8] G. J. Stigler, 'Monopolistic Competition in Retrospect', in *Five Lectures on Economic Problems*, Macmillan, New York, 1950, pp. 12–24.
[9] Although the controversy on Chamberlin's theory and its criticism by the Chicago school is beyond the scope of our discussion here, it is interesting to mention that Archibald argued that Stigler and Friedman attacked Chamberlin's theory of monopolistic competition not on the grounds of poor predictive record, but on the grounds of consistency, simplicity, relevance, and so on—that is, on the basis of the theory's assumptions rather than its predictions. See G. C. Archibald, 'Chamberlin vs. Chicago', *Review of Economic Studies*, 29 (1961): 2–28; and his 'Reply to Chicago', *Review of Economic Studies*, 30 (1963): 68–71; also M. Friedman, 'More on Archibald vs. Chicago', *Review of Economic Studies*, 30 (1963): 65–67.
[10] See J. Hadar, 'On the Predictive Content of Models of Monopolist Competition', *Southern Economic Journal*, 36 (1969): 67–73.

[11] See R. L. Bishop, 'The Theory of Monopolistic Competition after Thirty Years: The Impact on General Theory', *American Economic Review*, 54 (1964): 33–43, for a positive view on Chamberlin's contribution.

There are several important differences between oligopoly and monopolistic competition:

1 In oligopoly, entry of new firms is difficult, and relatively few sellers dominate the industry. In monopolistic competition, entry of new firms is easy, and a large number of sellers compete with each other.
2 In oligopoly, the product can be homogeneous (cement, steel) or differentiated (cars, soaps). In monopolistic competition, the sellers offer differentiated products.
3 In oligopoly, the actions of the firms are interdependent. In monopolistic competition, to a large extent they are independent.
4 In oligopoly, prices are relatively rigid; they do not change frequently except when there are price wars. In monopolistic competition, prices can change frequently.

11-7 Price and Quantity Determination in Duopoly*

Since interfirm rivalry is a basic feature of oligopoly, we first have to study the effect of this rivalry. To do this we initially concentrate on the case of duopoly—two sellers. We discuss the following models: (1) the classical models of Cournot, Stackelberg, and Edgeworth, (2) Hotelling's spatial equilibrium model, and (3) the modern game theory model. There have been other models, but these are sufficient to illustrate the type of problems we encounter in the analysis of duopoly (or oligopoly).

The essential difference among duopoly and oligopoly models is in the formulation of the firm's expectations concerning rivals' reactions to a change in its price, output, location, and so on. Cournot's approach is based on the assumption that each duopolist believes that its opponent will not change the *quantity* supplied. Stackelberg's approach is based on the assumption that one of the duopolists is a 'leader' and the other a 'follower'; it is, therefore, a model of *asymmetric* duopoly. Edgeworth's contribution is based on the assumption that each of the duopolists

believes that its opponent will maintain the current *price*. The game theory approach is concerned with analysing strategic interaction among duopolists. We shall now explain these approaches in greater detail.

The models of Cournot and Edgeworth are based on naive conjectures about the reactions of opponents. They can, therefore, be considered as simplistic versions of a class of models called *conjectural variations* models, in which firms are assumed to conjecture that changes in their own decisions provoke reactions from others. A special class of such models is the *consistent conjecture model* presented by Bresnahan,[12] Perry,[13] and others (cited below). Perry explains the consistency condition for a duopoly, in which firms' decisions are output quantities, as follows:

> Each firm's first-order condition defines its profit maximising output as a reaction function on (1) the output of the other firm and (2) the conjectural variation about the other firm's response. Thus, a conjectural variation by one firm about the other firm's response is consistent, if it is equivalent to the derivative of the other firm's reaction function with respect to the first firm's output at equilibrium.

Further elaboration of the consistent conjecture duopoly model is too complex to warrant inclusion here.[14] The classical duopoly models can be explained diagrammatically and, although naive, give an idea of what can happen in duopoly with more complicated conjectural variations. Furthermore, even the consistent conjecture model has been criticized as inconsistent.[15]

---

[12] T. F. Bresnahan, 'Duopoly Models with Consistent Conjectures', *American Economic Review*, 71 (1981): 934–45.
[13] M. K. Perry, 'Oligopoly and Consistent Conjectural Variations', *Bell Journal of Economics*, 13 (1982): 197–205. The quote is on p. 197.
[14] The model is also called a 'rational conjecture model'. Some other papers are: D. Ulph, 'Rational Conjectures in the Theory of Oligopoly', *International Journal of Industrial Organisation*, 1 (1983): 131–54; and J. Laitner, 'Rational Duopoly Equilibrium', *Quarterly Journal of Economics*, 95 (1980): 641–62.
[15] L. Makowski, 'Rational Conjectures Aren't Rational, Reasonable Conjectures Aren't Reasonable', Economic Theory Discussion Paper no. 66, University of Cambridge, 1983.

---

*A mathematical treatment of some of this material is given in the Mathematical Appendix at the end of the book.

Cournot's Solution

Cournot published his theory of duopoly in 1838.[16] Although most of his models were crude and involved very unrealistic assumptions, his method of analysis has been very useful for subsequent theoretical development in the area of duopoly and oligopoly. Cournot assumes that (1) there are two profit-maximizing duopolists, say A and B; (2) each duopolist produces an identical product; (3) both duopolists sell at identical prices; (4) each duopolist fully knows the linear market demand curve; (5) both duopolists act independently without collusion; and (6) each duopolist acts under the assumption that its rival's output remains exactly where it is now.

The final assumption is very naive, because it implies that the duopolists do not learn from

---

[16] A. Cournot, *Research on the Mathematical Principles of the Theory of Wealth*, 1838. The book was translated into English by N. T. Bacon, with a bibliography of mathematics of economics by I. Fisher: Macmillan, New York, 1897. Cournot (1801–77) was the first mathematical economist.

experience, but this assumption gives a determinate solution to the problem.

Cournot's example is that of mineral water from two adjacent springs produced at zero marginal cost. The analysis is illustrated in Figure 11-8. DQ_c is the demand curve. Since MC is zero, the competitive output is OQ_c (the quantity demanded at zero price). MR_1 is the marginal revenue curve corresponding to the demand curve DQ_c. Equating MR_1 to MC_1, we get the monopoly output as OQ_1, monopoly price as OP_1 and monopoly profit as $OP_1 AQ_1$. This is the solution if the two duopolists collude. Cournot's solution to the duopoly problem proceeds as follows.

Suppose initially that A is the only seller. A behaves like a monopolist, produces output $OQ_1 = \frac{1}{2}OQ_c$, sells at a price OP_1, and makes a profit $OP_1 AQ_1$. Now B enters the market. Since Cournot assumes that each duopolist expects its rival never to change its output, B expects A always to market OQ_1. Thus, B cannot sell anything above a price of P_1. Below a price of P_1, B can sell the quantity demanded in excess of OQ_1. For example, at a price of P_3, B can sell $Q_1 Q_3$. (Remember that A drops his price to P_3.) The

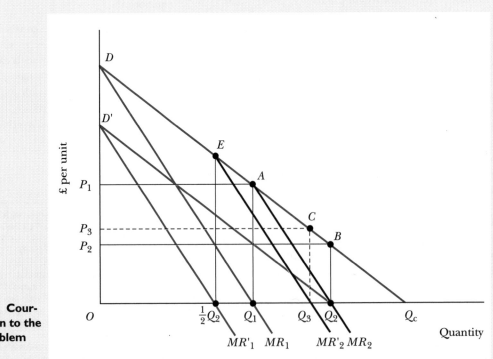

Figure 11-8 Cournot's solution to the duopoly problem

demand curve for duopolist B can be viewed as the portion of the market demand AQ_c where quantity is measured from the point Q_1. (Q_1 becomes B's origin.) Duopolist B's marginal revenue curve is now MR_2, where output again is measured from Q_1. MR_2 equals marginal cost at an output of $Q_1 Q_2$. So $Q_1 Q_2$ is duopolist B's initial profit-maximizing output. Total output has increased with B's entry, and therefore product price falls.

Now A realizes that B has entered the market and re-evaluates the situation. Duopolist A expects B always to sell $Q_1 Q_2 = Q_2 Q_c$. Duopolist A's new demand curve is $D' Q_2$ which is obtained by horizontally subtracting B's output from the market demand curve. The new marginal revenue curve for A is MR_1' which intersects the horizontal axis at $\frac{1}{2} OQ_2$. Hence A, in an attempt to maximize profit, reduces output to $\frac{1}{2} OQ_2$. The combined output now declines, and product price increases.

Now B re-evaluates the situation. B's new expectation is that A always sells $\frac{1}{2} OQ_2$. B's new demand curve is constructed as before and becomes EQ_c with $\frac{1}{2} OQ_2$ as the origin. B's new marginal revenue curve is MR_2' and crosses the horizontal axis at an output of $\frac{1}{2} OQ_c - \frac{1}{2} OQ_2$. Duopolist B thus maximizes profit by increasing output to $\frac{1}{2} OQ_c - \frac{1}{2} OQ_2$. Total output for the market has increased, and, thus, market price falls.

This process goes on, with A decreasing output and B increasing output, until both A and B produce the same output of $\frac{1}{3} OQ_c$. The total output produce by A and B together is $OQ_3 = \frac{2}{3} OQ_c$, and the price charged is $OP_3 = \frac{2}{3} OP_1$, shown in Figure 11-8. Thus, we have the following results: (1) the output under duopoly is less than the competitive output OQ_c but greater than the monopoly output OQ_1; (2) the price under duopoly is two-thirds of the price under monopoly; (3) total profits of the two duopolists are

$$OP_3 \, CQ_3 = \tfrac{2}{3} OP_1 \cdot \tfrac{2}{3} OQ_c = \tfrac{4}{9} \cdot OP_1 \cdot OQ_c.$$

Profits under monopoly are $OP_1 \cdot \frac{1}{2} OQ_c = \frac{1}{2} OP_1 \cdot OQ_c$. Thus, profits under duopoly are eight-ninths of profits under monopoly.

The equilibrium properties of the Cournot model can also be derived algebraically. This is done in the Mathematical Appendix at the end of the book. Instead of using diagrammatic reasoning to explain each firm's profit-maximizing output choice, we derive equations for firms A and B which show how $A(B)$

reacts to the quantity offered by $B(A)$. These equations are called *reaction functions*, and we can represent them diagrammatically, as shown in Figure 11-9. A's reaction function is labelled $Q_A^* = R_A(Q_B)$ and B's reaction function is labelled $Q_B^* = R_B(Q_A)$. B's reaction function, for example, shows that if A produces Q_A^o then B chooses output Q_B^o. The intersection of the two reaction functions gives the Cournot equilibrium. At this point the profit-maximizing output levels for A and B are shown as Q_A^e and Q_B^e. Why are these quantities the equilibrium levels? Suppose that A initially produced output Q_A^o. B responds by choosing output Q_B^o as determined by its reaction function. With B producing this amount, A responds by picking the corresponding point on its reaction function. B then responds to A's output on its reaction function; and so on. The path to equilibrium is shown by the direction of the arrows. Eventually the process ends in a stable equilibrium at the intersection of the two reaction functions with each firm maximizing profit and producing one-third of the total market demand. At this point A's (B's) belief about B's (A's) behaviour is confirmed by B's (A's) actual behaviour.

Cournot's analysis of duopoly can be generalized to the case of several firms and to the case of positive marginal cost. Let n be the number of oligopolists, Q_c the competitive output, P_c the competitive price, and P_m the monopoly price. Then total output in equilibrium under oligopoly is $nQ_c/(n+1)$. Each firm's output is $Q_c/(n+1)$. Price is $2P_m/(n+1) + nP_c/(n+1)$. In the duopoly case we considered, $n = 2$ and $P_c = 0$. As the number of firms tends to infinity, $n/(n+1)$ tends to 1. Hence the total output tends to Q_c and price to P_c, as we would expect.

Cournot's assumption that each firm believes that the rival firm will not change its output was criticized by French mathematician Bertrand in his review of Cournot's book in 1883. Bertrand argued that a more realistic assumption is that each firm believes that the rival firm will not change its *price*. Bertrand changes only this assumption, and he adds the assumption that each of the duopolists has sufficient capacity to satisfy the entire market. In this case A first starts with the monopolistic price; B then enters the market, reducing the price somewhat, and captures the whole market. A then lowers the price below B's price and captures the market; and so on. Finally, the price war ends when price $= MC = 0$, and the total output produced is equal to the competitive output.

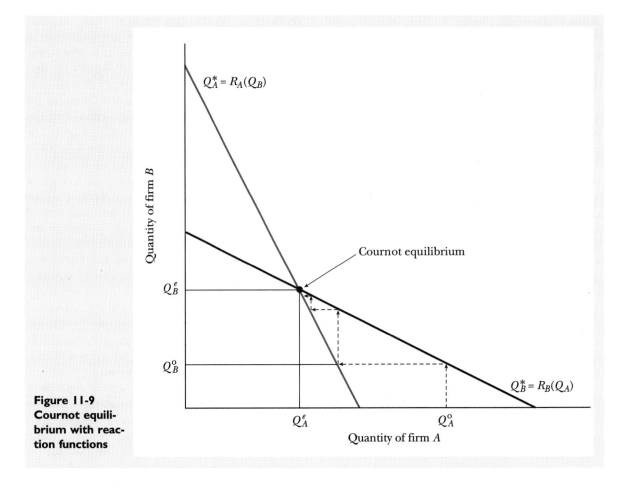

**Figure 11-9
Cournot equili-
brium with reac-
tion functions**

Chamberlin too changed Cournot's assumptions slightly. He replaced Cournot's assumption of a naive belief in fixed output with the assumption that firms recognize their interdependence. His argument runs as follows: A starts with output OQ_1 and price OP_1 in Figure 11-8, and B produces Q_1Q_2, as was the case with Cournot. A, however, then realizes that B will change its behaviour if A changes its output and that the maximum (joint) profit occurs at output level OQ_1. A, therefore, cuts output to $\frac{1}{2}OQ_1$, leaving B to produce $\frac{1}{2}OQ_1 = Q_1Q_2$. A stable solution is reached which is the monopoly solution. There is no explicit collusion. There is only some understanding of mutual benefit.

Stackelberg's Solution

Stackelberg's contribution to duopoly theory was to consider what happens if one firm knows that its rival

behaves as a naive Cournot follower and takes advantage of this.[17] That is, what is the equilibrium solution if we assume that one firm is a *leader* and the other a *follower?* The model is thus one of *asymmetric duopoly*. In Cournot's model, both firms are followers.

The Stackelberg model is often used to describe industries in which there is a leader, or a dominant firm. (See Section 11-11 for a discussion of the dominant firm.) For instance, IBM has often been taken to be a dominant firm in the computer industry. Smaller firms in this industry wait for IBM's announcements on new products and prices and then adjust their own products and prices accordingly.

---

[17] This was suggested by the German economist von Stackelberg (1905–46) in his thesis *Marktform und Gleichgewicht*, 1934.

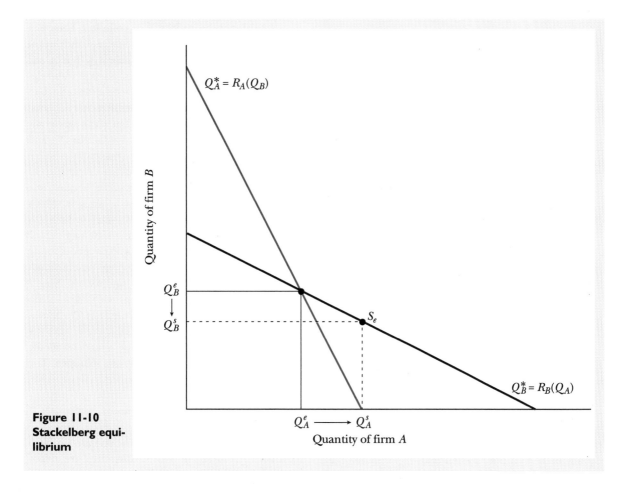

Figure 11-10
Stackelberg equilibrium

In the Stackelberg model, the leader firm (firm A) knows that its rival (firm B) behaves as a naive Cournot firm. In other words, it recognizes that its own choice of output influences firm B's choice of output via its reaction function. A is therefore in a position to make strategic use of its knowledge of B's reaction function. Thus, since A knows how B reacts to a change in its output, A uses this knowledge when calculating its own profit-maximizing output. The way in which this is done is shown in the Mathematical Appendix at the end of the book. The result is that the leader produces $\frac{1}{2}Q_c$ and the follower produces $\frac{1}{4}Q_c$; total output is three-quarters of the competitive output. The Stackelberg equilibrium is shown as point S_e in Figure 11-10. Note that the leader chooses an output on the follower's reaction function. As we would expect, A's output (Q_A^s) is higher compared with the Cournot solution, while B's output (Q_B^s) is lower. A also makes a

higher profit in Stackelberg equilibrium; in fact, it can be shown that the profit of the leader is twice that of the follower. We can, therefore, summarize the *industry outputs* under the different models as follows:

Competitive solution: Q_c (output of each firm $= \frac{1}{2}Q_c$)
Monopoly solution: $\frac{1}{2}Q_c$ (output of each firm $= \frac{1}{4}Q_c$)
Cournot's duopoly solution: $\frac{2}{3}Q_c$ (output of each firm $= \frac{1}{3}Q_c$)
Bertrand's duopoly solution: Q_c (output of each firm $= \frac{1}{2}Q_c$)
Stackelberg's duopoly solution: $\frac{3}{4}Q_c$ (output of the leader $= \frac{1}{2}Q_c$ and output of the follower $= \frac{1}{4}Q_c$)

Edgeworth's Solution

The model proposed by Edgeworth in 1897 is similar to Bertrand's in that each duopolist assumes that its rival does not change its price. The only difference is that

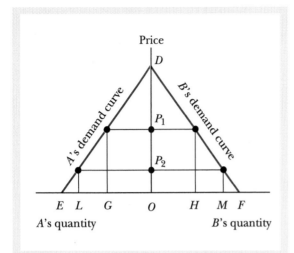

Figure 11-11 Edgeworth's solution to the duopoly problem

Edgeworth assumes that neither of the duopolists can produce an output as large as the competitive output. Figure 11-11 illustrates the situation. For the sake of simplicity, we assume that the two duopolists have zero marginal costs and that the maximum possible output is the same for both. The entire market is divided equally between A and B when both firms charge the same price. DE is the demand curve facing A, and DF is the demand curve facing B, assuming prices are equal. The total competitive output is EF. The maximum output A can produce is OL, and the maximum output B can produce is OM ($OL = OM$). If the duopolists collude, the total output produced is $\frac{1}{2}EF$, which is shown as GH. A produces OG, and B produces OH ($OG = OH = \frac{1}{2}GH$), and they charge the monopoly price OP_1.

Now suppose that there is no collusion. Then one of the duopolists, say A reduces the price slightly below OP_1. Then all of B's customers go to A. But A can provide only an amount OL. Thus, B is left with sales equal to EL (or MF). Rather than accept the reduction in revenue, B reduces the price slightly below A's price and captures all of A's customers; but B can serve only OM. This process goes on until price falls to OP_2 and each of the duopolists produces the maximum possible output. A sells OL, and B sells OM.

However, the price OP_2 is not stable, because one firm can raise its price and increase its revenue (which increases profit in this case since MC is zero). Thus, for instance, A tries to raise the price, assuming that B keeps the price of OP_2, and there is no danger of losing customers to B since B is producing its maximum output. A raises its price all the way to OP_1. Now B realizes that any price increase up to OP_1 loses it no sales, and so B raises prices almost up to OP_1. Now A responds by cutting price below B's price; and the process goes on all over again. There is no determinate solution in this case (unlike Cournot's solution). The prices fluctuate in the range $P_1 P_2$.

Hotelling's Spatial Equilibrium Model

Hotelling proposed a solution to the duopoly problem in which the products of the duopolists are differentiated in the eyes of the buyers by virtue of the location of the duopolists. Buyers are uniformly distributed (one per unit of distance) along a line KL, and the duopolists A and B locate themselves at X_A and X_B, respectively, on the line, as in Figure 11-12. Each buyer purchases a single unit from A or B and transports the purchase home. It is assumed that $LRMC = 0$ for each seller and that demand is completely inelastic. We also assume that the transport

Figure 11-12 Hotelling's duopoly model

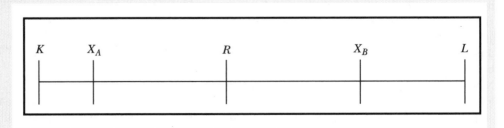

costs, paid by the customer, are cx where x is the distance of the customer from a sales point (X_A or X_B).

A and B have some leeway in setting prices, but A never sets its price so high that buyers along KX_A find it cheaper to buy from B than from A. (Doing so puts A out of business.) Similarly, B does not set its price so high that buyers along $X_B L$ find it cheaper to buy from A than from B. Thus, A has the sheltered market KX_A, and B has the sheltered market $X_B L$. They both compete for the market in between X_A and X_B.

Hotelling's solution says that there is a point in between X_A and X_B, say R, such that the delivered price from X_A and X_B is the same. If the distance of R from X_A is x and the distance of R from X_B is y, and P_A and P_B are the prices charged by A and B, respectively, then at R,

$$P_A + cx = P_B + cy.$$

A gets all the customers along KR, and B gets all the customers along RL. A's profit is $P_A \cdot KR$, and B's profit is $P_B \cdot RL$.

A has an incentive to move towards X_B and expand its sheltered market. Similarly, B has an incentive to move towards X_A and expand its sheltered market. Hence a stable solution is reached when both A and B locate themselves at the midpoint of KL.

Hotelling's solution is interesting because it shows how the sellers' location at the same point raises transport costs. If the duopolists colluded and split the market, with A and B locating at one-quarter and three-quarters of the distance from K to L, then the transport costs would be minimized. (They would be half of what they are under the assumption of competition among the duopolists.)

Hotelling's solution also explains the phenomenon that sellers tend to locate themselves in close proximity. Thus, it explains the concentration of business districts and firms in many cities. Since the firms are located close to each other, they have to compete with each other by advertising and by product differentiation, as well as by price.

11-8   Game Theory Approaches

Almost all the economic problems we have discussed so far involve maximizing or minimizing by economic agents (firms, consumers). In the case of duopoly (and oligopoly), as is clear from the models of Cournot,

Table 11-2   Payoff matrix for two duopolists*

		Firm A	
		Cut price 5%	No change
Firm B	Cut price 5%	−60, −80	−80, +60
	No change	+60, −100	0, 0

*Profits are denoted by +, losses by −, both in £'000.

Stackelberg, and Edgeworth, this problem becomes complicated because each agent's actions depend on other agents' actions as well. One firm's desire to maximize profits is opposed by other firms' desires to maximize profit. To solve this type of problem, von Neumann and Morgenstern suggested what is known as *game theory*.[18] This theory looks at any decision-making problem where a person's return (or *payoff*) depends on not only his or her own choice but on other people's choices as well, as a *game*. If there are only two people (or firms) involved, it is called a two-person game. Otherwise, it is called a multiple-person game. In the case of a two-person game, if one individual's profit is the other individual's loss and vice versa, it is called a *zero-sum two-person game*. However, many problems in economics are non-zero-sum games.

There are two concepts that are necessary for analysing any problem using the game theory approach: *strategy* and a *payoff matrix*. Strategies are alternative courses of action, and a payoff matrix is a table of numbers showing a person's returns (or payoffs) for various combinations of that person's and his or her rival's strategies. Consider the case of two competing duopolists A and B, where each has two strategies: to cut prices by 5 per cent, or to make no change. The possible outcomes for A and B are illustrated in a payoff matrix, shown in Table 11-2.

The payoffs are interpreted as follows. If both A and B cut price, A's loss is 60 and B's loss is 80. If A

---

[18] J. von Neumann and O. Morgenstern, *Theory of Games and Economic Behaviour*, Princeton University Press, Princeton, NJ. The book first appeared in 1944, but the revised edition of 1947 is the more standard reference. Von Neumann (1903–57), a Hungarian-born mathematical genius, was one of the three co-inventors of the hydrogen bomb. Morgenstern (1902–77) was a professor of economics at Princeton University.

makes a price cut and *B* does not, then *A* makes a profit of 60 and *B*'s loss is 100. The same reasoning applies for the other two possibilities. What is the outcome of this game?

We begin by asking, What strategy should each firm choose? First, consider firm *A*. Firm *A* should cut price since, no matter what *B* does, *A* does best by making a price cut. To see this notice that, if *B* cuts price, *A*'s loss is 60 if it cuts price and 80 if it does not. If *B* makes no change, *A*'s profit is 60 if it cuts price and zero if it does not. Thus, *A* should make the price cut. It is a *dominant strategy* for *A*. A dominant strategy is one that is best for a player (firm) *no matter what* the other does. The same is also true for firm *B*. No matter what *A* chooses, *B* does best by cutting price. Making the price cut is a dominant strategy for *B*. The outcome of the game is that both firms cut price. This solution is straightforward, since they both have a dominant strategy.

The outcome of the game is that both firms lose—total losses are 140. The best joint strategy is not to change the price. However, individually they choose strategies that harm them both. This problem is known as the *prisoners' dilemma*. The situation described is that of two prisoners locked up in two different rooms who are told that the following deal is being given to both of them:

1 If one prisoner confesses but his partner does not, the co-operating prisoner gets a 1-year sentence whereas the partner gets a sentence of 13 years. (The confession becomes Queen's evidence.)
2 If they both confess, each gets a sentence of 10 years. (The sentence for the crime is 13 years, but it gets reduced to 10 because of the confession.)
3 If both prisoners keep quiet, since the prosecution's evidence is weak, they each get charged with a smaller crime and get a 2-year sentence.

The question is: What does each prisoner do? The payoff matrix for two prisoners, Ronnie and Reggie, is shown in Table 11-3. Clearly, the best course of action for both prisoners is to keep quiet. Instead, however, each prisoner confesses, because confessing is a dominant strategy for both. First, consider Ronnie's strategy. If Reggie confesses, Ronnie gets 10 years if he confesses and 13 years if he does not; if Reggie keeps quiet, Ronnie gets 1 year if he confesses and 2 years if he does not. Thus, confessing is a dominant strategy for

Table 11-3 Payoff matrix for the prisoners' dilemma*

| | | Ronnie | |
		Confess	Keep quiet
Reggie	Confess	−10, −10	−13, −1
	Keep quiet	−1, −13	−2, −2

*The minus sign indicates that a stay in prison has disutility.

Ronnie. The same applies for Reggie. So they both end up confessing, and they are both worse off. Again, the solution is straightforward because they both have a dominant strategy.

The prisoners' dilemma arises from a lack of communication and from distrust among the prisoners. If Ronnie and Reggie could communicate with each other and trust each other, then they would arrive at a solution that is optimal for them both. Similar conclusions apply to all economic problems where the 'game' is comparable to the example in the prisoners' dilemma.

The above describes equilibrium in dominant strategies. However, in many games one or both players do not have a dominant strategy. In this situation we need a broader definition of equilibrium. This broader definition is known as a *Nash equilibrium*.[19] We can see this idea with reference to Table 11-2 by changing the payoff for firm *A* in the top left-hand corner from −60 to −90. Now *A* no longer has a dominant strategy. If *B* cuts price, *A*'s loss is 90 if it cuts price and 80 if it does not. If *B* makes no change, *A*'s profit is 60 if it cuts price and 0 if it makes no change. Clearly, *A*'s best strategy now depends upon what *B* does. If *B* cuts price, *A* makes no change. If *B* makes no change, *A* cuts price. A Nash equilibrium thus describes a situation where each firm is doing the best it can, *given* what its opponent is doing. The outcome of the game (the Nash equilibrium) is the top right-hand corner of Table 11-2. *A* knows that because *B* has a dominant strategy it will cut price. Given this, it is best for *A* to make no change.

As well as playing a game according to dominant strategies, we could also use another decision rule,

_____
[19] This is named after the American mathematician, J. F. Nash, who introduced the concept in 1951.

called the *maximin decision rule.* This rule states that one should choose the strategy that maximizes the minimum payoff. Though somewhat pessimistic, the rule is reasonable under oligopoly, where each firm might expect its rival to respond in a manner that ensures that the worst possible outcome is realized.

In Table 11-2, suppose A's strategy is to cut price. Assuming that B responds to cause A the maximum loss, A ends up with a loss of 60. But what if A's strategy is not to cut price? Assuming again that B reacts, causing A the maximum loss, A's loss is 80. Since A could be worse off with the second strategy, A chooses to cut its price.

Similarly, consider B's two strategies. If B cuts price and A responds to cause B the maximum loss, B's loss is 80. If B makes no change and A causes B the maximum loss, B's loss is 100. Thus, B is better off cutting the price by 5 per cent. Thus, by following maximum strategies, both end up cutting price. We arrive at the same result as we had with dominant strategies because dominant strategies are also maximin strategies. This means that in the prisoners' dilemma game confessing is a maximin strategy (and a Nash equilibrium).

11-9 Pricing under Oligopoly

The previous analysis of duopoly illustrates the problems arising from rivalry among firms. In an oligopolistic situation, any firm's lowering of price can be interpreted by other firms as an attempt to eliminate them by capturing their market. This kind of price reduction is called *predatory price-cutting.* The other firms respond by cutting their prices, and the round of price-cutting goes on. This chain of price cuts is called a *price war.* Such price wars have occurred in several industries: petrol retailing in the late 1970s and early 1980s, holiday companies in the mid-1980s, and grocery retailing in the late 1970s. These price wars reduce the profits of each firm, and those firms that reduce prices below their costs might even go out of business. If lowering price eliminates profits, so may raising prices. A firm that raises prices unilaterally in an oligopolistic industry loses customers to other firms.

The net conclusion of this discussion is that there is an incentive for firms in an oligopolistic industry either (1) not to change prices or (2) to collude with each other in changing prices. We discuss (1) now and (2) in Section 11-10.

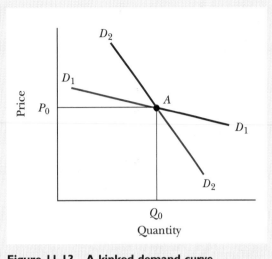

Figure 11-13   A kinked demand curve

Kinked Demand Curve

In 1939 two papers, one by Hall and Hitch and the other by Sweezy, argued that oligopolistic firms have 'sticky' prices.[20] One reason for this is that the oligopolistic firm faces a *kinked demand curve.* This is shown in Figure 11-13. All firms currently charge a price P_0. $D_1 D_1$ is the demand curve that a particular oligopolistic firm faces if the other firms *do not change* their prices. $D_2 D_2$ is the demand curve this firm faces if all firms charge the same price.

Suppose A is the current position of the firm, with price P_0 and quantity Q_0. The argument behind the kinked demand curve goes like this. If the firm raises price, the other firms do not, since they stand to gain by capturing the sales of this firm. However, if the firm reduces price, the other firms respond by matching the price reduction. Thus, the demand curve that this firm faces is given by the segment of $D_1 D_1$ to the left of A and the segment of $D_2 D_2$ to the right of A. The demand curve has a kink at A.

The marginal revenue curve corresponding to the kinked demand curve is shown in Figure 11-14. MR_1 is the marginal revenue curve corresponding to $D_1 D_1$,

[20] R. L. Hall and C. J. Hitch, 'Price Theory and Business Behaviour', *Oxford Economic Papers*, 1 (1939): 12–45, and P. M. Sweezy, 'Demand under Conditions of Oligopoly', *Journal of Political Economy*, 47 (1939): 563–73.

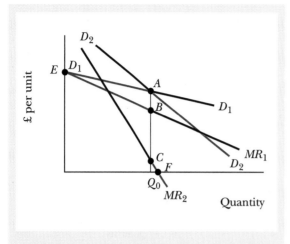

Figure 11-14 Marginal revenue curve corresponding to a kinked demand curve

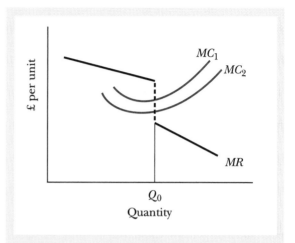

Figure 11-15 Price stickiness with a kinked demand curve

and MR_2 is the marginal revenue curve corresponding to D_2D_2. To the left of Q_0, the demand curve is given by the segment of D_1D_1, and the marginal revenue curve is therefore given by the corresponding segment of MR_1. To the right of Q_0, the demand curve is given by the segment of D_2D_2, and the marginal revenue curve is therefore given by the corresponding segment of MR_2. At the quantity Q_0, there is a sudden drop in marginal revenue—from point B to point C in Figure 11-14. The marginal revenue curve for the kinked demand curve in Figure 11-13 is, thus, given by EB, CF in Figure 11-14.

The consequence of this is that there is some range within which changes in the firm's marginal costs do not result in changes in price and quantity. This is shown in Figure 11-15. Note that for both MC_1 and MC_2 the price and quantity given by the equilibrium condition $MC = MR$ are the same.

The kinked demand curve is derived on the assumption that price increases by one of the oligopolistic firms are not followed by others but that price decreases are promptly followed. Stigler examined price histories of seven industries in the United States to see if this was indeed the case.[21] The seven industries were cigarettes, cars, anthracite coal, steel,

dynamite, petrol, and potash. He found that the vast majority of the recorded price episodes were not in keeping with the assumptions of the theory of the kinked demand curve. This was a test of the assumptions of the theory. Stigler also conducted other tests; these were tests of the implications of the theory that prices are less flexible under oligopoly than under monopoly or oligopoly with collusion. He studied a number of oligopolistic and non-oligopolistic industries over a complete business cycle from June 1929 to May 1937 and found the following results:

1 A comparison of 19 oligopolies with two monopolies showed that, even though the monopolies experienced greater output variation, they tended to have less flexible prices. This refutes the kinked demand theory.

2 A comparison of five oligopolies (rayon, copper, pineapple canning, typewriters, and midwestern oil) during, and outside, periods of collusion showed that prices tended to be less flexible during collusion. This again refutes the kinked demand theory.

3 A comparison of oligopolies subject to dominant firm price leadership with other oligopolies again showed that oligopolies with dominant firms have less flexible prices, and dominant firms would not have a kinked demand curve.

4 A comparison of six oligopolies producing heterogeneous goods (soap, tractors, grain binders, ploughs,

[21] G. J. Stigler, 'The Kinky Oligopoly Demand Curve and Rigid Prices', *Journal of Political Economy*, 55 (1947): 432–49.

tyres, and linoleum) with 13 oligopolies producing homogeneous goods showed that prices tended to be more flexible for industries producing homogeneous goods. This refutes the kinked demand curve, as greater homogeneity of the product tends to make the kink more pronounced.

Stigler's tests were criticized in detail by Efroymson. Primeaux and Bomball, and Primeaux and Smith, present additional evidence on the kinked demand curve.[22] We do not discuss the details of the criticism of Stigler's work here, but Stigler's own assessment of the criticism of his study is in his 1978 paper, where he complains that the kinked demand curve is 'a piece of scripture; it is to be taught and it is to be quoted in suitable contexts, but it is not to be tampered with'.[23] Reid, however, reviews the theory and evidence on the kinked demand curve and tries to show that it need not be buried as Stigler suggests.[24]

The Issue of Price Rigidity

The basic empirical observation that the kinked demand curve is supposed to explain is price rigidity. Stigler's argument is that this could as well be explained by transaction costs. If it is the kink that leads to inflexible prices, monopolists should have more flexible prices, since monopolists do not face a kinked demand curve. The empirical evidence is exactly the opposite: monopolists change prices less frequently than do oligopolists. Thus, any theory in which prices are rigid only because individual oligopolists fear 'upsetting the applecart' is suspect.

In a further, more detailed, study Stigler and Kindahl collected data from buyers on actual transaction prices paid for a number of products from 1 January 1957 to 31 December 1966.[25] These data were

Product group	No. of buyer–seller pairs	Average duration of spells of price rigidity (mos.)
Steel	348	13.0
Nonferrous metals	209	4.3
Petroleum	245	5.9
Rubber tyres	123	8.1
Paper	128	8.7
Chemicals	658	12.8
Cement	40	13.2
Glass	22	10.2
Truck motors	59	5.4
Plywood	46	4.7
Household appliances	14	3.6

Table 11-4   Price rigidity by product group

Source: D. W. Carlton, 'The Rigidity of Prices', *American Economic Review*, 76 (1986): 641.

further analysed by Carlton, who studied the relationship between the average length of a spell of price rigidity and the four-firm concentration ratio.[26] He found that the two were positively related: that is, the higher the concentration ratio, the greater the price rigidity, as measured by the average length of time over which prices do not change. A partial summary of a measure of price rigidity by product group is given in Table 11-4. A 'pairing' means a series of transactions over time for a good of constant specification.

All this evidence suggests that oligopolists tend to change prices more often than duopolists and duopolists more often than monopolists. 'Why?' is the obvious question. One possible reason is that there may be some fixed costs associated with price changes.[27] If so, then firms have to consider how these costs compare with the benefits from price changes. If we can show that the benefits from price changes vary across market structures, then we can explain why price rigidity varies by market structure.

Rotemberg and Saloner compare duopoly and monopoly and show that duopolists have a greater incentive than monopolists to change prices in

[22] C. W. Efroymson, 'The Kinked Demand Curve Reconsidered', *Quarterly Journal of Economics*, 69 (1955): 119–36; W. J. Primeaux and M. R. Bomball, 'A Re-examination of the Kinky Oligopoly Demand Curve', *Journal of Political Economy*, 82 (1974): 851–62; and W. J. Primeaux and M. C. Smith, 'Pricing Patterns and the Kinky Demand Curve', *Journal of Law and Economics*, 19 (1976): 189–99.
[23] G. J. Stigler, 'The Literature of Economics: The Case of the Kinked Oligopoly Demand Curve', *Economic Inquiry*, 16 (1978): 185–204.
[24] G. C. Reid, *The Kinked Demand Curve: Analysis of Oligopoly*, Edinburgh University Press, 1981.
[25] G. J. Stigler and J. Kindahl, *The Behaviour of Industrial Prices*, NBER General Series no. 90, Columbia University Press, New York, 1970.

[26] D. W. Carlton, 'The Rigidity of Prices', *American Economic Review*, 76 (1986): 637–58.
[27] This idea was first suggested by R. Barro, 'A Theory of Monopolistic Price Adjustment', *Review of Economic Studies*, 39 (1972): 17–26.

response to a change in costs.[28] However, the incentive to change prices in response to changes in demand is higher for monopolists than for duopolists. In practice, the cost effect dominates the demand effect, and hence the monopolist may adjust prices more sluggishly than duopolists. A detailed presentation of their arguments is too lengthy for our purpose, but the main points to note from our discussion on price rigidity are as follows:

1 The kinked demand curve is not an adequate explanation of price rigidity under oligopoly.
2 In fact, the empirical evidence suggests that prices are more rigid under monopoly than under duopoly, which, in turn, are more rigid than under oligopoly.
3 One explanation for this is a fixed cost of price adjustment.
4 Firms compare the costs and benefits of price adjustment, and the latter depend on market structure.
5 Comparing duopoly and monopoly, whether the benefits are higher under duopoly than under monopoly depends on whether cost changes or demand changes prompt the price adjustment. In practice, the cost effect dominates the demand effect.[29]

11-10 Cartels

The preceding discussion of pricing under oligopoly is based on the assumption that firms act independently even though they are interdependent in the market. Alternative methods of pricing are based on the assumption that firms, instead of competing with each other, enter into pricing agreements with each other. Interfirm agreements that restrain market competition, whether explicitly or implicitly, are referred to as *collusion*. Smith, in *The Wealth of Nations*, noted this tendency for firms to collude, saying: 'people of the same trade seldom meet together, even for merriment and diversion, but the conversation ends in a conspiracy against the public or in some contrivance to raise prices'. We now discuss the different forms of collusion. A cartel is one such form.

---

[28] J. Rotemberg and G. Saloner, 'The Relative Rigidity of Monopoly Pricing', *American Economic Review*, 77 (1987): 917–26.
[29] The issue of price rigidity has been an active area of research in industrial economics. We have presented only a few of the findings.

A *cartel* is a group of firms whose objective is to limit the scope of competitive forces in the market. One of the most famous cartels is OPEC. It was formed in 1960 but was not really an effective cartel until it raised the price of oil from about $2 a barrel on 1 January 1973 to over $11 a barrel by the end of 1973, following the Arab–Israeli Yom Kippur War. This unprecedented price increase eventually led to the predictable result—an entry of new firms. It led to the discovery of new oil fields and the development of existing high-cost oil fields in Alaska and the North Sea. This increased the supply and forced OPEC producers to further restrict production.

A cartel can be formed by producers within a country, in which case it is called a domestic cartel, or by producers (or governments) in different countries, in which case it is called an international cartel. OPEC is an example of the latter. As for domestic cartels, formal collusive agreements are outlawed in the UK and the European Union (EU), although in the UK the Cement Makers Federation (comprising three main companies) was allowed to fix prices until 1987. What we tend to find is tacit collusion. In the UK this has been seen in a number of markets, including the market for tea, the wholesale petrol market, and the market for white salt (see Example 11-2).

The major functions of a cartel are price-fixing and market division. Two problems must be faced before these two functions can be performed. First, the firms must be able to reach a collusive agreement. Second, once the agreement is reached, the firms must be able to enforce it over time.

Reaching agreement on a collusive price is not always easy. Different firms might have widely different cost conditions and different expectations about future demand. Thus, they have different perceptions of price should be. The type of product is also important in reaching a collusive agreement. If the good is homogeneous, the firms have only to agree on a single price. When the good is not homogeneous, it is necessary to set a whole array of prices for different qualities. In the case of OPEC, for instance, the cartel sets different prices for heavy and light crude oil and there has been some haggling about what this price difference should be. There are also substantial differences in costs of production between Saudi Arabia and the North Sea producers. Expectations about future demand also vary among the different members of OPEC.

Once the collusive agreement is reached, there is the question of how long it can last. This depends on whether any member of the cartel cheats by reducing its price, and thereby increasing its market share. Once widespread cheating starts, a price war can break out, and this can result in a breakup of the cartel. However, if the members of the cartel realize that this is in nobody's interest, they can take steps to come together even after some temporary bursts of cheating (this is what has happened with OPEC repeatedly), although how long this can go on is an open question. Very few international cartels have managed to last more than five years. OPEC has had a much longer life than expected.

The life expectancy of a cartel depends on several factors:

1 *The price elasticity of demand* If demand is fairly elastic, then a larger reduction in output is necessary to increase price. And, of course, a larger output reduction is more difficult to attain and maintain. One determinant of demand elasticity is the availability of substitutes. The copper cartel formed by Chile, Peru, Zaire, and Zambia was unsuccessful because of the availability of close substitutes which made the demand for copper quite elastic.

2 *The stability of demand* A stable demand is conducive to cartel survival because constant adjustment of output, and the associated negotiation, are unnecessary.

3 *The ability to control a substantial share of actual and potential output* It is especially important that the cartel control a substantial share when the elasticity of supply is large. For example, as OPEC raised the price of oil, the quantity supplied from new fields and from non-members increased dramatically. This increase undermined OPEC's power.

4 *The political climate, in the case of international cartels* The rivalry between Iran and Iraq has contributed to the instability of OPEC. In fact, many possible international cartels do not come into existence because of political rivalries among the producing nations. For instance, a tea cartel composed of India and Sri Lanka is possible but unlikely under the current political climate.

As mentioned earlier, a cartel has to perform two functions: (1) fixing of price and (2) allocation of output among members. The way these functions are performed depends on how the cartel is organized. We discuss two types of cartels: the perfect or centralized cartel, and the market-sharing cartel.

In the *perfect cartel*, the objective is to maximize the total profits of the member-firms. This implies that each firm produces output where marginal costs are the same for all firms and equal to the marginal cost and marginal revenue for the cartel as a whole. If there are n firms with marginal costs given by MC_i $(i = 1, 2, \ldots, n)$ and MC_T and MR_T are, respectively, the marginal cost and marginal revenue for the cartel as a whole, then we have

$$MC_1 = MC_2 = \ldots = MC_N = MC_T = MR_T.$$

The situation is exactly the same as in the case of a multi-plant monopolist discussed in Section 9-9. The MC curve of the cartel is constructed from the MC curves of the individual firms in the same way that the MC curve of the multi-plant monopolist is constructed from the MC curves of the individual plants. The allocation of total output between the different firms in the cartel is made the same way that a multi-plant monopolist allocates total output between the different plants. Further, in a centralized cartel, the inputs are all purchased at the same price by all member-firms, as in the case of a multi-plant monopoly.

The centralized cartel makes all the decisions regarding prices, output, output allocation, profit distribution, and so on. Herein lie the problems with this type of cartel. In a multi-plant monopoly, the monopolist may not produce any output from some of the plants. Similarly, in the centralized cartel some of the firms may get very little or perhaps no output allocation. If this is the case, the firm that gets no output allocation drops out of the cartel and goes it alone. By not producing any output for a length of time, the firm can lose its goodwill, experienced labour force, and established marketing channels, and might therefore decide that it is not worth while to stay in the cartel. The departure of some firms can undermine the cartel. This is what gives rise to a market-sharing cartel.

In a *market-sharing cartel* there is no centralized body making all the economic decisions regarding prices, output, and profits. The cartel merely allocates output among the different firms. There are two ways in which this is done: nonprice competition and quotas.

Nonprice competition is usually found in 'loose' cartels. The cartel sets a minimum price, and each firm is allowed to sell all it can at that price. The only requirement in this is that firms do not reduce prices below the cartel price. The sellers compete with each other, but *not* by price competition. The nonprice competition takes the form of advertising, customer credit policies, and product variation.

Under the *quota system* each firm is allocated a certain quota. The quota any firm gets depends on: (1) the bargaining ability and importance of the firm, (2) relative sales of the firm in a pre-cartel base period and the productive capacity of the firm, and (3) geographical location (for example, the agreement between Du Pont and ICI to divide the North American and European chemical markets).

The bargaining ability of a firm also depends on the costs of production of the firm relative to those of other firms. The firm with the lowest costs of production has the best chance of surviving in a price war. For instance, in the case of OPEC, Saudi Arabia has the best bargaining ability by virtue of its enormous productive capacity as well as low costs of production.

In both of the market-sharing methods, we need some penalizing and policing arrangements. In a quota system a penalty has to be imposed on those who exceed the quota by accident or design. Where minimum cartel prices are fixed, penalties must be imposed on price-cutters. Policing price agreements is usually more difficult than policing quotas. In the case of price agreements, one has to get data on 'transaction' prices, and these differ typically from 'posted' or 'list' prices. Since this information is usually difficult and costly to obtain, the method commonly followed is to observe buyer shifts—for example, is a firm picking up business it would not otherwise be doing? If this is the case, then one may suspect that the firm is cheating. In those transactions where the bidding is done by sealed bids and the bids are later publicly opened, giving the name of the individual firm and the price at which the product is offered, we can easily identify who is doing the price-cutting.

Example 11-1   The Collapse of the Tin Cartel

In 1986 the world watched the simultaneous collapse of two commodity cartels: oil and tin.[30] Although the economic impact of oil is much wider than that of tin,

both of them suggest that cartels do not work for too long. During the period of overpricing, new sources are developed, substitutes are invented, and economies of use are achieved by means of investment in research. For instance, in the case of the OPEC cartel, several new countries started producing oil, and several investments were made in energy conservation devices. Eventually, when the cartel collapses, many of these investments are entrenched and irreversible, either because of vested interests or because they embody the latest technological advances. Because of these factors, the producers in the cartel face an ever-declining demand and probably a lower price than the one that would have prevailed had the cartel never existed.

In the case of tin, because of the high price maintained by the cartel, tin lost its place as a container material for beverages and gave way to aluminium and plastics. The aluminium beer can is a lasting monument to the cartel's price actions.

Unlike OPEC, which consists of petroleum-producing countries, the tin cartel, which was called the International Tin Council (ITC), included 16 consumer countries among its 22 members. The consumer countries had joined the ITC after the Korean War when tin was occasionally scarce. Like OPEC, the ITC imposed quotas on its producers; but unlike OPEC, it tried to regulate supply and demand through the operation of a buffer stock. The buffer stock manager in London used the London Metals Exchange (LME) for purchasing and selling tin.

Malaysia, Indonesia, and Thailand are the three biggest producers of tin, and together they accounted for 45 per cent of total world production of 192 000 tonnes in 1984. However, tin is not a major export earner for them. Only for Bolivia (which produced 10 per cent of total world output in 1984) was it of serious concern, but Bolivia was not even a member of the ITC.

The actual collapse of the tin cartel during late 1985 and early 1986 came when the buffer stock manager, in an effort to keep the price above the ITC floor of $11 440 a tonne, bought tin not only in the open market but through forward contracts. When he

---

[30] W. D. Sharpe, 'Tin Cartel Joins OPEC on the Crash List', *Wall Street Journal*, (7 April 1986): 23; and R. M. Bleiberg, 'Tin in a Box: One of the World's Oldest Cartels Has Come to Grief', *Barron's* (18 November 1985): 11.

ran out of funds and the market price fell, he could not buy any more; he also was stuck with forward contracts which amounted to 60 000 tonnes (or about one-third of the world's yearly production). In a rescue operation the LME settled the contracts at a price of $8580 a tonne. The buffer stock operation was suspended, and the free market price soon fell below $6600 a tonne. The thing that had kept prices soaring was the purchase of huge amounts of tin by the buffer stock manager. The cartel members were well aware of these purchases and knew that the high price was attracting other supplies, but apparently did nothing about it.

Buffer stock operations also exist in other commodities (cocoa, and agricultural commodities in the EU Common Agricultural Policy). The rubber cartel, known as the International Natural Rubber Organization (INRO), which includes Malaysia, Indonesia, and Thailand, also operates with a buffer stock operation. But the INRO has never indulged in forward purchases. If the INRO were to keep rubber prices artificially high, it would encourage research into the use of synthetic rubber and so would face the same fate as the other cartels.

11-11   Informal, Tacit Collusion

A cartel is a formal collusive agreement. Oligopolists who cannot manage to form a cartel but recognize that their actions are interdependent sometimes operate informal collusive agreements. Such tacit collusion does not involve any explicit agreement but merely an unspoken acceptance by the firms that it is in their interest to avoid potentially damaging price competition. The primary form of informal tacit collusion is price leadership.

Price leadership arises when one (or a few) firms typically initiate price changes and the rest of the firms in the industry follow. Note that the price changes can be either up or down. This removes the kink in the demand curve that we discussed earlier. Although there are many varieties of price leadership, the most common one is the so-called *umbrella price leadership*, where the dominant firm, controlling a major portion of the industry's output, sets a price that maximizes its profit and then allows the smaller firms in the industry to sell all they want at this price. Examples of dominant firm price leadership include: cars (Ford), breakfast

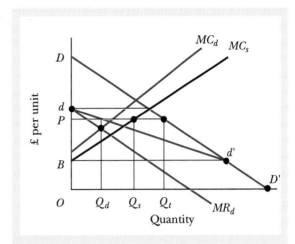

Figure 11-16   Price determination by a dominant firm

cereal (Kelloggs), computers (IBM), oil (Saudi Arabia), and tea (Brooke Bond). The informal arrangement to follow the dominant firm avoids any legal problems faced by the firms under explicit collusion. The smaller firms tend to follow the dominant firm either out of fear or as a matter of convenience.

The problem facing the dominant firm is to determine the price that maximizes its profits while allowing the small firms to sell all they wish at that price. The situation is illustrated in Figure 11-16. The small firms are price-takers, and the short-run supply curve is the horizontal sum of their marginal cost curves, above minimum average variable cost. This curve is labelled MC_s. The market demand curve is DD'. The dominant firm behaves like a monopolist and equates MR to its marginal cost, labelled MC_d. But before we can derive the dominant firm's MR curve, we need its demand curve.

We can first observe that at a price of Od, MC_s crosses DD'. This means that the small firms supply the full quantity demanded in the market at this price, leaving nothing for the dominant firm. So the quantity demanded from the dominant firm at a price of Od or higher is zero. We can also note that below the price OB, the small firms are not willing to produce anything. Hence, for prices below OB, the demand curve facing the dominant firm is the portion $d'D'$ of the market demand curve. Finally, for prices between OB and Od the quantity demanded from the dominant firm is the quantity demanded in the entire market minus the quantity supplied by the small firms. For example, the quantity demanded from the dominant firm at a price OP is Q_d, which equals $Q_t - Q_s$. The dominant firm's full demand curve is thus $dd'D'$.

MR_d is the marginal revenue curve corresponding to dd'. (Unless the dominant firm prices along the region dd', the model breaks down and we have monopoly.) The dominant firm equates MR_d with MC_d and sets price at OP. The dominant firm then produces Q_d while the small firms produce Q_s. And since, by construction, $Q_d + Q_s$ is the total quantity demanded at price OP, the market clears.

In practice, the analysis of price leadership is more complicated. There can be more than one dominant firm. There could be product differentiation, geographical difference among sellers, and so on. It is impossible to say anything concrete when all these complications are introduced. The analysis presented here merely captures the major important aspects of pricing in oligopoly under a dominant firm.

Example 11-2 Tacit Collusion in the UK Market for White Salt[31]

The UK market for white salt can be seen as a homogeneous duopoly in which the firms set prices subject to fixed capacities. The market was subject to an MMC inquiry in 1986 into the pricing behaviour of the two firms. The two producers in the market are British Salt, with about 55 per cent of the market, and ICI Weston Point, with 43 per cent (2 per cent is made up of imports). Both firms operate with a capacity constraint, although for much of the early 1980s this constraint was not binding. Much of the excess capacity seems to have resulted from a large unanticipated fall in demand.

The MMC investigation into the firms' price-setting revealed that there were 17 changes to list prices between 1974 and 1984. On each occasion the price increases were virtually identical. Prices were set in the following way. The leader notified the follower

(by letter) one month in advance of any planned price increases. The follower replied saying it would make an identical increase within a month. From 1974 to 1980 there were 13 price increases, with British Salt leading on eight occasions and Weston Point on five. From 1981 to 1984 Weston Point was the leader. The firms denied collusion, arguing that this practice prevailed because they bought salt from each other and they were simply notifying a buyer in advance of a proposed price increase. They also said that in a competitive market you expect to see identical price increases. Both firms understood the idea of tacit collusion, with one saying that if the price increases were not identical the firm with the lower price would take customers from the other and this would lead to long-term retaliation. The MMC judged that the firms had acted to restrain competition.

The behaviour of firms in this market can also be used to test the predictions of the sort of oligopoly models that we have covered in this chapter. For instance, according to the Edgeworth model (Section 11-7), if two firms are producing a homogeneous good and operating below capacity (as here), a non-cooperative equilibrium results in firms choosing mixed pricing policies. If the firms followed this model, we would not expect to see them choosing identical prices. But on 17 occasions price increases were identical. Thus, the behaviour of these firms does not support the Edgeworth model.

Most duopoly models that assume a homogeneous good and capacity constraints predict that non-cooperative price-setting is unlikely to lead to identical prices. This has clearly not been the case in the market for white salt.

11-12 Summary

Monopolistic competition is characterized by a large number of firms producing differentiated products. The firms behave independently, and nonprice competition is prevalent. There are no barriers to entry or exit.

Short-run equilibrium under monopolistic competition requires that each firm perceives that it is maximizing its profit and that the market clears. This requires that MC be equal to perceived MR at the output where the proportionate and perceived demand curves intersect.

[31] This example is based on the paper by R. Rees, 'Collusive Equilibrium in the Great Salt Duopoly', *Economic Journal*, 103 (1993): 833–48.

Since there are no barriers to entry, economic profits induce new firms to enter the monopolistically competitive market. Entry ceases when a new equilibrium with zero profit is attained. This requires that the *LRAC* curve is tangential to the firm's perceived demand curve at the output where *MC* equals perceived *MR*. (The opposite changes are prompted by short-run economic losses.)

Since in long-run equilibrium the monopolistically competitive firm operates on the downward-sloping portion of the *LRAC* curve, per-unit production costs are not minimized, or scale economies are not fully exploited. But one can view the higher (than under perfect competition) per-unit production costs as the cost of variety or product differentiation.

The impact of advertising on output and price is unclear because, although the average total cost curve shifts upward, the demand curve shifts to the right. The model of monopolistic competition has been criticized on the grounds that it contains conflicting assumptions, and has little predictive power.

Oligopoly is characterized by few sellers who are well aware of their interdependence. The product can be homogeneous or differentiated. Barriers to entry are present. Prices tend to be inflexible.

The Cournot model of duopoly is based on the assumption that each firm believes that its rival maintains its current output. The resulting output is smaller than under perfect competition and the resulting price is higher. But both quantity and price approach the competitive levels as the number of firms increases.

The Bertrand model is based on the assumption that each firm believes that its rival maintains its current price. Firms successively undercut each other's price until the competitive outcome is reached.

The Stackelberg duopoly model assumes that one firm is a leader and the other a follower. The leader knows the reaction function of the follower and exploits this knowledge to produce a higher output and makes a higher profit than in the Cournot case. Total output is less than the competitive level but higher than in the Cournot solution.

Edgeworth modifies Bertrand's model by assuming that neither firm can produce the full quantity demanded in the market at a zero price. There is no determinate solution in this model.

In the Hotelling model, products are differentiated by location. Each firm moves towards the other in order to shelter a larger market share. Eventually, both firms end up in the same location resulting in a waste of transport resources.

Game theory can be used to analyse strategic interaction among oligopolists. In some gaming situations both firms have a dominant strategy and the equilibrium outcome is easy to see. But in other games either or both firms may not have a dominant strategy. In these situations the outcome is called the Nash equilibrium. The maximin decision rule says that the firm chooses the strategy with the best of the worst outcomes.

If rival firms match price cuts but not price increases, then the firm faces a kinked demand curve. The corresponding *MR* curve has a gap. As long as *MC* stays within the gap, profit-maximizing output and price remain constant.

The purpose of a cartel is to limit the scope of competition. The major functions are price-fixing and market division. A cartel is most successful when (1) demand is inelastic and stable; (2) it can control a substantial share of actual and potential output, and (3) the political climate is conducive to co-operation.

Tacit collusion primarily takes the form of price leadership. Dominant firm price leadership involves price-setting by the dominant firm with smaller firms being allowed to produce all they want at that price.

Key Terms

Bertrand model
Cartel*
Collusion*
Cournot model*
Dominant strategy*
Duopoly*
Edgeworth model
Excess capacity*
Game theory
Hotelling model
Ideal output*
Kinked demand curve
Market-sharing cartel*
Maximin decision rule*
Monopolistic competition
Nash equilibrium*
Nonprice competition*
Oligopoly*

Payoff matrix*
Perfect cartel*
Predatory price cut*
Price leadership*
Price war*
Prisoners' dilemma
Product differentiation*
Product group
Reaction function*
Stackelberg model*
Strategy*
Zero-sum game*

Questions

1   Illustrate a monopolistically competitive firm in short-run equilibrium suffering a loss. Describe the process of adjustment to long-run equilibrium.

2   Explain the relationship between the perceived demand curve and the proportionate demand curve under monopolistic competition. Which curve determines the firm's choice of output and price? Why must the two intersect at the equilibrium point?

3   Explain why we cannot determine whether a monopolistically competitive 'industry' will have more or fewer firms than would be present under perfect competition.

4   Does the soft drink industry conform more closely to monopolistic competition or oligopoly? Support your answer.

5   In the Cournot model, explain why the two duopolists' marginal revenue curves are parallel. (Assume that the market demand curve is linear.)

6   In the Edgeworth model, does an increase in demand raise price? Why or why not?

7   In the Hotelling model, explain why a firm that sets price so high that it loses its sheltered market has no customers.

8   Two individuals are selling ice-cream on an isolated beach. Both ice-cream stands are easily movable.

(a) Assume that people do not mind the walk to the ice-cream stand. Where do the two individuals locate? Explain.

(b) As the sand heats up, customers become less willing to walk the distance and choose the nearest seller. As the day becomes hotter, what happens to the relative locations of the two individuals. Why?

9   In the kinked demand model of oligopoly, at what price does the kink occur? How useful is the model in explaining pricing under oligopoly?

10   Explain why the maximin decision rule is more appropriate under oligopoly than under perfect competition or monopolistic competition.

11   In a market-sharing cartel where price is set, is the agreement easier to police when the product is homogeneous or differentiated? Why?

12   When price is determined by a dominant firm, explain the impact of a reduction in market demand. Explain the impact of entry by a small firm.

13   'The higher the concentration in an industry, the higher the price rigidity.' Evaluate this statement.

14   How can oligopolists escape from the prisoners' dilemma?

12 Pricing in Product Markets: Some Extensions

12-1 Introduction

In the preceding four chapters we discussed four different forms of market organization: perfect competition, monopoly, monopolistic competition, and oligopoly. A study of these different forms of organization is a first step in the analysis of any industry. However, when we begin examining real-world markets, we have to take account of several complications. In real-world markets, buyers do not perceive all sellers' products as identical; and not all buyers are well informed, either about the price or about the quality of the product they buy.[1] In such markets, sellers have to undertake product selection and advertising. Although we discussed product differentiation and advertising in the previous chapter, we did not consider consumers' response to them, nor did we consider the interaction between product differentiation, advertising, and market structure. There is now an enormous literature on this subject, and some of these issues and findings are presented in Sections 12-2 and 12-3.[2]

We have also examined the sources and role of profits. An interesting debate centres on whether differences in the profit rates of firms are due primarily to differences in market structure or to differences in firm efficiency. We look at this question and at some of the empirical evidence in Section 12-4. Finally, in Section 12-5 we discuss a relatively new theory of market organization. This is the theory of 'contestable markets' suggested by Baumol and his co-authors.

The topics in this chapter are given somewhat limited coverage. A complete presentation is beyond the scope of this book but would be included in a course on industrial economics. The purpose in presenting a limited coverage of issues here is to give an idea of how the theories and the four basic models presented in the previous four chapters need to be extended when it comes to an analysis of real-world markets.

12-2 Product Differentiation, Advertising, and Monopoly Power

Product differentiation is one of the most important characteristics of modern markets. Sellers differentiate their products in a number of ways: selection of location, selection of type of service, physical differences in the product supplied, brand labelling, and so

---

[1] Work on the consequences of imperfect buyer information about price started with a paper by G. J. Stigler, 'The Economics of Information', *Journal of Political Economy*, 69 (1961): 213–25.
[2] For an excellent survey of this literature, see D. Hay and D. Morris, *Industrial Economics and Organization: Theory and Evidence* (2nd edn.), Oxford University Press, 1991, Ch. 5.

on. Customers prefer to avoid driving long distances or visiting places where there is only one shop. Thus, location of sales outlets is very important. Customers also prefer fast and courteous service. They do not like standing in long queues. Furthermore, they like attractive goods and will buy some brand names because of the assurance of quality. A large part of product differentiation is actually a consequence of consumers' demand for variety, because of differences in tastes. However, suppliers can, through aggressive advertising, create an image of differentiated products even when such differences are minor.

One question that is often asked is whether product differentiation leads to monopoly power. Of course, product differentiation can confer some power over price. But to confer any monopoly power, product differentiation must somehow lead to a deterrence of entry. There are examples of markets with considerable product differentiation and negligible barriers to entry, as in the case of restaurants. There are also examples of markets with product differentiation and substantial barriers to entry, as in the case of breakfast cereals.[3] So the question is, What produces entry deterrence? In his classic book *Barriers to New Competition*, Bain argues that product differentiation might, in some cases, impose barriers to entry if consumers prefer established brands to new brands.[4] In a world where there is some uncertainty about product quality and consumers incur some costs in the acquisition of information, it is rational on the part of consumers to stay with known brands and to shift to new brands only if there is considerable price advantage or expectation of higher quality. Marketing analysts have observed that, if a product is virtually identical to established competitive products, it has little chance of marketing success. If brand loyalty is important, then established firms' advantages might often depend heavily on buyers' uncertainty about the attributes of new brands; thus, a firm that is first in the market often has a considerable advantage.[5] Other firms entering the market with a 'me too' strategy will not be successful. This aspect of consumer behaviour gives monopoly power to a firm introducing a pioneering product. This conclusion is plausible given that consumers have a limited ability to receive, store, retrieve, and process information about different products. The marketing literature on consumer behaviour emphasizes this point.[6]

Along with product differentiation, advertising is another important characteristic of modern markets, and the two are intertwined. Does advertising create entry deterrence? Entry deterrence requires some asymmetries between established firms and new entrants because, if firms entering an industry face the same demand and cost conditions as the established firms, the established firms cannot prevent entry. One argument presented by Bain and others is that advertising provides established firms with advantages over potential entrants because it creates brand loyalty. New firms trying to enter the market have to overcome the preference consumers have for the established brands. This requires them to advertise more heavily, which increases their costs.

However, brand loyalty created by advertising does not necessarily prevent entry. Brand loyalty deters entry only if it gives sufficient power to established firms to drive an entrant's profit to zero while the established firms earn a positive profit. If incumbent firms cannot prevent entry by advertising, then we cannot say that advertising creates entry barriers.

Apart from the brand loyalty argument, established firms may have a strategic advantage over potential entrants even if they face the same demand and cost conditions. The advantage arises from the leadership position of the established firms; this enables them to take actions prior to entry that place the entrants at a strategic disadvantage. Salop calls this *pre-entry asymmetry*.[7] Strategic actions might involve overinvestment in productive capacity or overinvestment in advertising capital, but the effects of the two actions can be different. If an established firm overinvests in productive capacity, it can deter potential entrants because the capacity commitment makes the threat of a price war credible.

[3] See R. Schmalensee, 'Entry Deterrence in the Ready-to-Eat Breakfast Cereal Industry', *Bell Journal of Economics*, 9 (1978): 305–27.
[4] J. S. Bain, *Barriers to New Competition*, Harvard University Press, Cambridge, Mass., 1956, Ch. 4.
[5] See R. Schmalensee, 'Product Differentiation Advantages of Pioneering Brands', *American Economic Review*, 72 (1982): 349–65.

[6] See J. R. Bettman, *An Information Processing Theory of Consumer Choice*, Addison-Wesley, Reading, Mass., 1979.
[7] S. C. Salop, 'Strategic Entry Deterrence', *American Economic Review*, 69 (1979): 335–8.

In the case of advertising capital, however, an increased investment may be a handicap. When an established firm overinvests in advertising capital, it has a large group of loyal or captive customers who do not sample the new entrant's product. A large captive market reduces the established firm's incentive to respond aggressively to entry. It cannot reduce prices and raise advertising expenditures because it sacrifices the profit that it can earn from its captive market. (It has to charge the same price to all customers.) This inability of the established firm to cut prices and respond aggressively to entry is known as the 'fat-cat effect'. In fact, an established firm may find it optimal to underinvest in advertising if it chooses to deter entry, because by lowering its stock of goodwill it establishes a credible threat to cut prices in the event of entry. This is known as a choice to maintain a 'lean and hungry look'.

Two other strategies relating to investment in advertising are the 'top dog strategy', which is overinvestment to be tough, and the 'puppy-dog strategy', which is underinvestment in advertising that accommodates entry by turning the established firm into a small, friendly, non-aggressive puppy dog. Fudenberg and Tirole discuss the conditions under which these different strategies are optimal.[8] Their main conclusion is that overinvestment in advertising may not always deter entry, whereas underinvestment might sometimes deter entry.[9] Furthermore, established firms might choose to advertise to accommodate entry.

In summary, established firms have a first-mover advantage, and they can use advertising to deter entry; but the relationship between advertising expenditure and entry deterrence is complex. In some specific cases we may be able to say that advertising deters entry and thus reduces competition, but we cannot make a general statement to that effect.

12-3 Advertising and Market Structure

> Advertising is a subject about which the ratio of poetic opinion to systematic analytics approaches infinity. Like romance, advertising is an activity to which people have been exposed and about which little is known.
>
> Harold Demsetz[10]

The relationship between advertising and market structure is rather complex. Many questions are raised in this regard. Does advertising lead to monopoly? Is there more advertising under monopoly than under competition? To answer such questions we consider (1) the effect of market structure on advertising and (2) the effect of advertising on market structure.

The Effect of Market Structure on Advertising

Kaldor and Telser have suggested that monopoly can lead to a socially excessive level of advertising.[11] However, since monopolists appropriate only a part of the social gain from informative advertising, they may in some circumstances undersupply advertising.

Advertising can lead to two types of results: it can increase the overall demand for the product advertised, and it can increase the demand for the product of the advertising firm, at the expense of products supplied by other firms in the industry. In the former case, the benefits of advertising accrue to all the firms in the industry manufacturing the product. If the industry is monopolized, then advertising that increases the market demand for the product must also increase the monopolist's demand. Thus, the monopolist finds it profitable to undertake this type of advertising. For example, British Gas frequently advertises that using gas for cooking and heating is somehow better than using electricity.

---

[8] D. Fudenberg and J. Tirole, 'The Fat Cat Effect, the Puppy-Dog Ploy and the Lean and Hungry Look', *American Economic Review*, 74 (1984): 361–6.
[9] That firms might choose to underinvest in advertising to deter entry was suggested in R. Schmalensee, 'Advertising and Entry Deterrence: An Exploratory Model', *Journal of Political Economy*, 91 (1983): 636–53.

[10] H. Demsetz, *Journal of Industrial Economics*, 32 (1983): 229, in a paper by J. Arndt and J. L. Simon.
[11] N. Kaldor, 'Economic Aspects of Advertising', *Review of Economic Studies*, 18 (1950): 1–27. L. G. Telser, 'Advertising and Competition', *Journal of Political Economy*, 72 (1964): 537–62.

With a large number of firms in the industry, no single firm has much of an incentive to engage in advertising that increases overall market demand. In these cases, any such advertising is usually done by some association of producers. The Meat and Livestock Commission advertises that meat is good for you; the Dairy Trade Federation advertises the benefits of drinking milk. In a competitive industry, since an individual firm can sell as much as it pleases at the ruling market price, no individual firm has an incentive to advertise.

Where the benefits of advertising accrue to the firm, each individual firm has an incentive to advertise. But the perfectly competitive firm has nothing to advertise because its product is perfectly homogeneous.

In the case of oligopoly, the situation is different. Oligopolists advertise to capture a higher share of total sales, which expand with advertising. But even though advertising by oligopolists can increase the total product demand, a large proportion of the amount spent by each oligopolist can go to waste in cancelling the rivals' efforts. This has been shown by Metwally in a study into the effect of own- and rival-firm advertising on own-firm sales in the Australian washing powder market.[12] He found that, while own advertising boosted own-firm sales, advertising by the rival firm had an equally powerful effect on own-firm sales but in the opposite direction. Such wasteful advertising can be avoided if oligopolists co-ordinate their advertising policies with the purpose of joint profit maximization (i.e. if they tacitly collude). In practice, however, this does not seem to happen.

To summarize, in a competitive industry, no individual firm has an incentive to advertise because the benefits from advertising accrue to all firms in the industry while the advertising firm bears the costs. Under monopoly, the monopolist receives all the benefits, but in this case advertising is done only to increase the demand for the product, since there is no question of capturing rival firms' sales. Under oligopoly, advertising has two benefits—increasing the demand for the product, and capturing sales from rivals. However, in those cases when advertising does not increase total demand, all the advertising is somewhat wasteful as it cancels the efforts of all firms trying to capture a bigger share of a pie that is not increasing in size. Thus, incentives to advertise are higher under oligopoly than under perfect competition or monopoly. But so are the possibilities of wasteful advertising and high social cost.

The Effect of Advertising on Market Structure

Does advertising lead to monopoly power? It has been observed that the most important variable explaining differences in profitability between industries is the advertising–sales ratio; that is, the higher the advertising–sales ratio in an industry, the higher the profitability.[13] Based on this evidence, some economists have argued that advertising leads to brand loyalty, and this, in turn, leads to monopoly power. However, there is not much empirical support for this argument. Lambin examined 16 product classes in eight European countries and found that the relationship between brand loyalty and advertising expenditure was, on average, weak.[14] However, there were considerable differences between the different industries. Thus, we cannot depend on the connection between profitability and advertising expenditure via brand loyalty.

One other possible explanation for the observed correlation between advertising and profitability is that, through pioneering new brands or making important improvements in quality, some firms enjoy a favourable image in the minds of consumers and thus enjoy brand loyalty and earn above-normal profits. The firms do advertise, but this is for 'image reinforcement', that is, the advertising is designed to preserve the favourable image or brand loyalty. Thus, it is not the case that advertising expenditures are a causal factor in brand loyalty. Advertising is instead undertaken to preserve brand loyalty which itself is due to some other factors. Even some pioneering companies that stopped advertising their products later found that it was essential to advertise. For instance, the Hershey Company in the United States did not advertise its chocolates for a long time, but then it gave up this policy. IBM enjoyed a big

---

[12] M. M. Metwally, 'Advertising and Competitive Behaviour of Selected Australian Firms', *Review of Economics and Statistics*, 57 (1975): 417–27.

[13] A survey of this literature is in W. S. Comanor and T. A. Wilson, 'The Effect of Advertising on Competition: A Survey', *Journal of Economic Literature*, 17 (1979): 453–76.
[14] J. J. Lambin, *Advertising, Competition and Market Conduct in Oligopoly over Time*, North-Holland, Amsterdam, 1976.

market share and considerable price advantage over its competitors without much advertising.[15] Even so, when it introduced personal computers it spent a lot of money on advertising, because it was not a pioneer in that field. There is, however, another difference between mainframe and personal computers: in the former case the buyers are major corporations and educational institutions; in the latter case the buyers are mostly individuals. For the sale of mainframe computers, IBM maintained a large and efficient sales force. Thus, there was less advertising through the usual channels.

In those cases where one firm enjoys considerable price advantage because of brand loyalty arising from a pioneering brand, rival firms who wish to enter and capture some share of the market must undertake intensive advertising. Thus, it is not advertising that leads to brand loyalty, but the existence of brand loyalty that leads to high advertising expenditures. The established firms have to advertise less but the rivals have to advertise a lot to get in. By virtue of their large market share, the established firms might also reap economies of scale in advertising.

In summary, the observed association between profitability rates and advertising–sales ratios does not imply any causal link between the two. Both are simultaneously affected by other factors.[16]

Advertising as Information

Some economists believe that advertising not only fails to create monopoly power but that it is a bulwark of competition. This view is summarized by Brozen, who argues that advertising provides useful information about firms (their existence, size, location, and so on) and their products (their existence, prices, and qualities), and therefore reduces entry costs and makes demand curves more elastic than they would have been without advertising.[17]

An example that supports this view is the study of spectacles by Benham.[18] In some US states all advertising by prescription spectacle dispensers is prohibited; in other states there are no advertising restrictions. Benham argues that prohibition of advertising causes prices to rise by preventing firms from realizing significant economies arising from high sales volume. From a sample of 154 purchases, Benham found that prices were 25–30 per cent higher in states with total advertising bans than in states without restrictions or with only weak restrictions. In 1985 opticians in the UK began to advertise. One year later it was found that prices of spectacles had fallen by between 20 and 25 per cent.[19] However, the case of spectacles is perhaps not typical. Scherer gives a large number of US examples where nationally branded products sell at a substantially higher price than private-label products.[20]

There is, however, an element of truth in the argument that advertising provides useful information about firms and their products. At least, advertisements inform consumers about the existence of some products and induce consumers to try them. Nelson goes on to argue that firms advertise more if they are confident that their product is sufficiently good that it will be purchased repeatedly after an advertising-induced trial.[21] He, therefore, concludes that heavily advertised goods are the best buys.

Nelson distinguishes between two types of goods: those with 'search qualities' and those with 'experience qualities'. We might call these search goods and experience goods respectively. Examples of search goods are clothing, footwear, furniture, and jewellery. We can assess their quality merely by looking and comparing among different shops and brands. Examples of experience goods are durables such as cars, instruments, electronic equipment and appliances, and non-durables such as beer, wine, foods, medicines, and

---

[15] B. T. Ratchford and G. T. Ford, 'A Study of Prices and Market Shares in the Computer Mainframe Industry', *Journal of Business*, 49 (1976): 194–218.

[16] See I. Domowitz, G. Hubbard, and B. Petersen, 'The Intertemporal Stability of the Concentration-Margins Relationship', *Journal of Industrial Economics*, 35 (1986): 13–34.

[17] Y. Brozen, 'Entry Barriers, Advertising and Product Differentiation', in H. J. Goldschmid *et al.* (eds.), *Industrial Concentration: The New Learning*, Little Brown, Boston, 1974.

[18] L. Benham, 'The Effect of Advertising on the Price of Eye Glasses', *Journal of Law and Economics*, 15 (1972): 337–52.

[19] There may also have been an element of increased competition, not just advertising *per se*.

[20] F. M. Scherer, *Industrial Market Structure and Economic Performance* (2nd edn.), Houghton Mifflin, Boston, 1980, p. 389. For instance, Bayer aspirin was selling at a price twice that of the store-brand aspirin.

[21] P. Nelson, 'Advertising as Information', *Journal of Political Economy*, 82 (1974): 729–54, and 'The Economic Consequences of Advertising', *Journal of Business*, 48 (1975): 213–41.

perfumes: we can assess their quality only by trying them. In the case of search goods, there can be very little scope for misleading advertising, since customers can be fooled only to a limited degree. In the case of experience goods, there is a larger scope for misleading advertising, because at least first-time experimenters can be fooled. However, the consumer is not repeatedly fooled. Thus, the incentive for misleading advertising is less for lower-priced, frequently purchased items than for higher priced, infrequently purchased ones. Non-durable experience goods are typically cheaper and are bought more frequently than durable experience goods; hence there is less incentive for misleading advertising of non-durable experience goods.

In addition to search goods, whose qualities can be determined by inspection, and experience goods, whose qualities can be determined only after purchase, there is another category: 'credence goods', defined by Darby and Karni.[22] These are goods whose characteristics cannot be determined reliably even after use. An example is a preventative medicine. Now if consumers think that heavily advertised goods are the best buys, then firms producing low-quality goods have an incentive to undertake intensive advertising, particularly in the case of credence goods.

Another classification system for goods is that of 'convenience goods' and 'shopping goods' by Porter.[23] Convenience goods are goods that are usually purchased without consulting a retailer. Shopping goods are goods for which retailers serve as an important source of consumer information. Porter finds no association between advertising and profitability across markets in the case of shopping goods. He finds a strong positive association in a sample of convenience goods.

This discussion suggests that the response of consumers to advertising varies a lot with the nature of the goods under consideration. Questions like 'Does advertising increase profit?' or 'Does advertising give monopoly power?' are too simplistic and cannot be given any general answer. We need an analysis that takes into account the nature of the good under consideration, how consumers process information and react to advertising, how producers perceive consumers' response, and so on.[24]

If advertising conveys information, then consumers will demand it. Telser suggests a theory in which advertising supplies information to consumers in response to their demands.[25] He argues that the equilibrium between the supply and demand for advertising determines the total quantity provided. Most studies on advertising concentrate on the *effects* of advertising. By contrast, Ehrlich and Fisher study the *determinants* of advertising.[26]

An alternative approach to advertising as information is the view that advertising may indirectly signal quality; that is, the most heavily advertised goods are the 'best buys'. This is the view expressed in the papers by Klein and Leffler (see Section 11-4 for a discussion of their arguments) and Kihlstrom and Riordan.[27]

In summary, there is not much evidence to show that advertising, in general, promotes brand loyalty, deters entry of new firms into an industry, increases monopoly power, or increases profitability. In particular cases we might find some evidence for these claims, but as a general proposition there is no simple direct relationship between advertising and brand loyalty, entry deterrence, monopoly power, or increased profits. Perhaps the most important use of advertising is as a provider of information and as a signal of quality in markets where information about products or product quality is scarce.

Example 12-1 Advertising and the Consumption of Alcohol

The per capita consumption of alcohol (beer, wine, and spirits) in the UK has grown steadily over the past

---

[22] M. Darby and E. Karni, 'Free Competition and the Optimal Amount of Fraud', *Journal of Law and Economics*, 16 (1973): 67–88.

[23] M. Porter, 'Consumer Behaviour, Retailer Power, and Performance in Consumer Goods Industries', *Review of Economics and Statistics*, 56 (1974): 419–36.

[24] See G. R. Butters, 'A Survey of Advertising and Market Structure', *American Economic Review*, 66 (1976): 392–7.

[25] L. G. Telser, 'Towards a Theory of the Economics of Advertising', in D. G. Tuerck (ed.), *Issues in Advertising*, American Enterprise Institute, Washington, DC, 1978.

[26] L. Ehrlich and L. Fisher, 'The Derived Demand for Advertising: A Theoretical and Empirical Investigation', *American Economic Review*, 72 (1982): 366–88.

[27] R. Kihlstrom and M. H. Riordan, 'Advertising as a Signal', *Journal of Political Economy*, 92 (1984): 427–50.

30 years. This has prompted both politicians and doctors to express concern about the potentially harmful effects on public health and public safety of 'too much' alcohol consumption. It is suggested that one of the reasons for this growth in consumption is drink advertising. One way to counter this effect is to launch a concerted public awareness campaign warning of the dangers of 'excessive' alcohol consumption. If it can be shown that advertising alcohol has a strong effect on consumption, then this may justify controls on advertising and a publicity campaign.

One way to investigate whether there is a strong advertising effect is to carry out studies into the demand for alcohol. This sort of study identifies those factors that are important influences on alcohol consumption. An example of this approach can be found in the paper by Duffy for the period 1963–78.[28] He estimates separate demand equations for beer, wine, and spirits and includes in each one per capita advertising expenditure as an explanatory variable. (His other variables include per capita disposable income, the price of the good, and the price of all other goods.) His advertising variable is measured as per capita expenditure on television and press advertising. (Cinema, poster, and radio advertising was not included.) Duffy found that total advertising expenditure had a positive and significant effect on the aggregate demand for beer and spirits. No such effect was found for wine. Thus, advertising influences the demand for beer and spirits, but the estimated advertising elasticities are low; for instance, a 10 per cent increase in advertising expenditure raises beer consumption by only 1 per cent. This suggests that any compulsory reductions in advertising will have only a very small effect on demand. Furthermore, his results suggest that a public health campaign is unlikely to be successful.

The most important influences on the demand for alcohol were found to be income and price. All the income elasticities were above 1, while the price elasticities for beer and wine were about 0.7. The price elasticity for spirits was 1.25. This suggests that taxation may be the best way of restraining consumption.

Similar results regarding the effects of advertising have also been found in a study by Blake and Boyle into the demand for cider in the UK.[29] They found that, during the period 1952–86, advertising expenditure had a positive and significant effect on cider consumption but the effect was small: a 10 per cent increase in advertising expenditure raises cider consumption by only 0.3 per cent. As with the Duffy study, advertising has a weak effect on demand. Again, this suggests that any restriction on advertising is likely to be unsuccessful in reducing consumption. It is the standard economic variables (price and income) that exert the largest effect on demand. The demand for cider was found to be both price- and income-elastic.

Opponents of alcohol advertising object because of the harmful effects drink may have on public health and safety. Academic research suggests, however, that advertising alcohol has only a small effect on consumption. Those wishing to reduce alcohol consumption may be better advised to focus on taxation (which raises the price), since in the case of cider the price elasticity is greater than 1 and in the case of beer and wine it is close to 1.

12-4 Market Structure and Profitability Differences among Firms

In the previous section we talked of differences in advertising–sales ratios as being one of the potential explanations for profitability differences among firms. Another major question often raised concerns the effect of market structure on profitability. There are essentially three competing theories on this: the classical theory, the anti-classical revisionist theory, and the managerial theory.

1 *The classical theory* This theory follows Bain's work from the 1950s, and argues that profitability differences among firms are due mainly to differences among industries. Thus, it is the market structure of the industry that is important. Profitability of firms in an industry is determined primarily by the ability of the firms in that industry to limit rivalry among themselves and to impose barriers to entry. One of the important variables explaining differences in profitability is the

---

[28] M. Duffy, 'The Demand for Alcoholic Drink in the United Kingdom, 1963–78', *Applied Economics*, 15 (1983): 125–40.

[29] D. Blake and S. Boyle, 'The Demand for Cider in the United Kingdom', *Oxford Bulletin of Economics and Statistics*, 54 (1992): 73–86.

concentration ratio of the industry. Empirical evidence shows a positive association between profitability and the concentration ratio.[30]

2 *The anti-classical revisionist theory* This theory, advanced in the 1970s, holds that all markets are (at least approximately) competitive and that scale economies are negligible.[31] However, within at least some industries there are persistent efficiency differences among firms. More efficient firms tend to grow at the expense of their rivals and are more profitable. The greater the efficiency differences in an industry, the less equal are the market shares, and therefore the higher is the concentration ratio. Also, the higher profits of the larger firms lead to higher average industry profitability. We can observe a positive association between concentration ratios and profitability, but, according to the theory, this is due to the impact of efficiency differences on both the concentration ratio and average industry profitability, and not because concentration facilitates collusion.[32] Note that the argument is similar to the one that we discussed earlier regarding the relationship between profitability and the advertising–sales ratio: namely, there are some other variables that affect both. In fact, when efficiency measures are used (in addition to the concentration ratio) to explain the differences between firms in their profitability rates, the concentration ratio actually has a negative effect on profitability. Thus, the positive correlation between the concentration ratio and profitability may be a spurious one.

3 *The managerial theory* This theory is somewhat like the anti-classical theory. It stresses the importance of firm-level efficiency differences based largely on differences in organizational and managerial skills. Evidence for this hypothesis is presented in Mueller.[33]

Again, when measures of efficiency are used (in addition to the concentration ratio) to explain profitability, it is found that the concentration ratio has a negative effect on profitability.

In summary, the classical theory says that interfirm differences in profitability are due not to differences among firms but rather to differences in market structure among the different industries in which they operate. Thus, industry effects are important; firm effects are not. The opposite view holds that it is differences in the efficiency level among firms that are important, not the differences among industries, which are spurious and arise from interfirm differences in efficiency.

Schmalensee tested this simple hypothesis by using 1775 business units operated by 456 firms in 242 US manufacturing industries.[34] He decomposed the differences in profitability rates into different sources: differences between firms, between industries, and so forth. His findings are actually the opposite of the findings of those who tested the anti-classical theory. He finds that: (1) there are no firm effects, (2) industry effects are important and explain 75 per cent of the differences in profitability between firms; and (3) market share effects are negligible. He states, however, that these findings do not necessarily mean that the classical theory is correct, because the analysis is descriptive and the year (1975) chosen for the analysis may have been atypical owing to the severe US recession and energy price shocks.

12-5 Contestable Markets

In the preceding section we talked of the classical and anti-classical theories of market structure. We said that the anti-classical theory holds that all markets are (at least approximately) competitive. A relatively new theory of market structure has been advanced by Baumol and his coauthors.[35] This is the theory of *contestable markets*.

[30] This evidence is summarized in L. Weiss, 'The Concentration-Profits Relationship and Anti-Trust', in H. J. Goldschmid *et al.* (eds), op. cit.; and Scherer, op cit., Ch. 9.

[31] See H. Demsetz, 'Industry Structure, Market Rivalry and Public Policy', *Journal of Law and Economics*, 16 (1973): 1–10; and S. Peltzman, 'The Gains and Losses from Industrial Concentration', *Journal of Law and Economics*, 20 (1977): 229–63.

[32] Evidence in favour of this view is in S. Martin, *Market, Firm and Economic Performance*, NYU Graduate School of Business, New York, 1983, and D. J. Ravenscraft, 'Structure–Profit Relationships at the Line of Business and Industry Level', *Review of Economics and Statistics*, 65 (1983): 22–31.

[33] D. C. Mueller (ed.), *The Dynamics of Company Profits: An International Comparison*, Cambridge University Press, 1990.

[34] R. Schmalensee, 'Do Markets Differ Much?' *American Economic Review*, 75 (1985): 341–51.

[35] See W. J. Baumol, 'Contestable Markets: An Uprising in the Theory of Industry Structure', *American Economic Review*, 72 (1982): 1–15; and W. J. Baumol, J. C. Panzar, and R. D. Willig, *Contestable Markets and the Theory of Industry Structure*, Harcourt-Brace-Jovanovich, San Diego, Cal., 1982.

A contestable market has many of the characteristics of a competitive market. A contestable market is one into which entry is absolutely free and exit is absolutely costless. The entrant suffers no disadvantage in terms of production techniques or perceived product quality relative to the incumbent. The crucial feature of a contestable market is its vulnerability to 'hit-and-run entry'. The presence of shadow entrants forces competitive behaviour by the incumbents. The crucial assumption in perfect competition is price-taking behaviour; in the theory of contestable markets, this assumption is replaced with that of rapid entry and exit. The potential competitors have the same cost functions and can enter and leave *without loss of capital* before the incumbents change their prices. Sunk costs are thus assumed to be zero.

The use of the word 'contestable' has been criticized by Shepherd.[36] By dictionary definition, a *contest* is a struggle whose uncertain outcome depends on a series of actions and reactions. Thus, every market is at least partly contestable. However, the hit-and-run entry does not permit a contest. Also, according to Baumol, actual entry need not occur. The existing firm (or firms) in the industry can prevent entry by anticipatory price restraint. If actual entry does not occur, there can be no contest. Shepherd suggests the use of the term 'ultra-free entry' instead of 'contestable'. He also criticizes the assumption of ultra-free entry as inconsistent. If there are fixed costs, then entry cannot be at a small scale. The entering firm has to produce the same output as the incumbent firm, or it will have higher average total cost. Thus, the entry will be on a large scale, and it is implausible to assume that there will be no response by the incumbent.[37]

Many of the assumptions underlying the theory of contestable markets are open to question. The theory assumes that all producers have access to the same technology; that there are no sunk costs and exit is entirely costless; that incumbents cannot change prices instantly; and that consumers respond instantly to price differences. Under such circumstances, the entrant undercuts prices, serves all of the market, and leaves costlessly if price retaliation occurs. The entrant makes a profit if the incumbent is not minimizing costs or is making above-normal profits.

In practice, however, entry and exit are not costless. Production involves some sunk costs; entry and exit take some time; and it takes time to liquidate commitments. It is questionable whether consumers respond instantly to differences between the prices of the entrant and the incumbent. As we discussed earlier, in Sections 12-2 and 12-3, consumers take some time to assimilate new information. However, the incumbent can change prices much faster. The contestable market theory assumes long lags in the price behaviour of the incumbent firm and short lags in the behaviour of consumers and the entry and exit of the entering firm. Traditional theory of industrial organization assumes the opposite—that prices are adjusted faster than sunk capacity and that consumer response has significant delays. The empirical evidence supports the traditional view.

There is not much empirical evidence for the contestable markets theory. One industry—the airline industry—is presented by Baumol as an example of a contestable market. The argument is that a plane can be easily switched from one domestic route to another without incurring significant costs. The established airlines all act as potential entrants to each others' routes. Entry and exit can be costless, and there is no new capital equipment involved. But Shepherd disputes this argument as well.[38] There is the question of what the relevant market is, in the case of the airline industry. If we use Baumol's definition, and define the relevant market as the national market, then entry into the industry involves founding a new airline, and entry and exit are not costless. (In fact, they involve substantial costs.) However, even with the addition of routes, entry is not ultra-free. Existing carriers are not easily displaced and they can often respond effectively. It takes time to build ground facilities and lure customers from the previous airline. The success of the entrant also depends on the connections provided, but if we consider this we are expanding the scope of the relevant market. Shepherd argues that airline competition can be explained well by established concepts of market structure and entry rather than by the contestable markets theory.

---

[36] W. G. Shepherd, 'Contestability vs. Competition', *American Economic Review*, 74 (1984): 572–87.
[37] For other criticisms of the ultra-free assumption, see the paper by Shepherd, op. cit.

---

[38] Ibid.

Apart from airlines, Baumol offers three other possible cases where the contestable markets theory may be applicable: railways, road haulage, and telephone services. Shepherd discusses these examples and argues that they are not satisfactory.[39] The arguments are similar to those in the case of airlines: that the relevant market is not properly defined and that entry is not costless. However, there have been a number of empirical studies on this topic, and the debate of how relevant these studies are is likely to go on for a while. For instance, in a study of the international liner shipping industry, Davies argues that sunk costs are low, and entrants and incumbents are symmetrically placed.[40] The Canadian data show frequent entry and exit, hit-and-run entry, and large-scale entry. Davies claims that, rather than being a theory without facts, the contestability idea is extremely relevant in the economic analysis of the shipping industry.

In summary, questions have been raised about the usefulness of the contestable markets theory in modelling the behaviour of modern markets. Some have argued that the traditional theories can adequately explain the observed behaviour and that the new theory does not lead to any additional insights. In connection with their theory, Baumol and his co-authors develop an in-depth analysis of multi-product costs and prices, and even critics of the contestable markets theory agree that this is useful.

12-6 Summary

To confer any monopoly profit, product differentiation must somehow lead to deterrence of entry. If consumers prefer established brands, then firms introducing pioneering products might acquire some monopoly power.

Incentives to advertise are higher under oligopoly than under monopoly or perfect competition. Under oligopoly, advertising serves to increase overall market demand and also to reallocate market shares.

Higher advertising–sales ratios are associated with greater profitability, but there is little support for the argument that advertising leads to brand loyalty, which, in turn, increases profitability. In fact, it appears that the existence of brand loyalty leads to heavier advertising (by late entrants). Advertising may enhance competition by reducing entry costs and increasing the elasticity of the product demand curves. Advertising may also reduce price by allowing firms to realize scale economies, but there is limited empirical support for this argument.

There are three competing theories concerning the source of profitability differences among firms. The classical theory argues that profitability differences among firms are due to differences in market structure. The anti-classical revisionist theory argues that differences in profitability among firms are due to differences in efficiency. The managerial theory, again, argues that differences in profitability are due to differences in efficiency but stresses organizational and managerial aspects of efficiency.

In a contestable market, entry is absolutely free and exit is absolutely costless. This assumption replaces the one of price-taking behaviour in the model of perfect competition. Although it constitutes an important contribution, the theory of contestable markets has received extensive criticism.

Key Terms

Anti-classical revisionist theory*
Classical theory*
Contestable market*
Convenience goods*
Credence goods*
Experience goods*
Managerial theory*
Search goods*
Shopping goods*

Questions

1 Television advertising is considerably more expensive than other forms. Primarily what kinds of products are advertised on television? Does this support our observation that oligopolists have the greatest incentive to advertise?

[39] Baumol, op. cit. W. G. Shepherd, 'Illogic and Unreality: The Odd Case of Ultra-Free Entry and Inert Markets', in R. E. Grieson (ed.), *Antitrust and Regulation*, Lexington Books, New York, 1986, pp. 231–52.
[40] J. E. Davies, 'Competition, Contestability, and the Liner Shipping Industry', *Journal of Transport Economics and Policy*, 20 (1986): 299–312.

2 The managerial theory argues that differences in profitability among firms are due mainly to differences in managerial efficiency. If this is so, do the observed differences in profitability constitute differences in economic profit, or merely differences in accounting profit? Why?

3 Brozen argues that advertising serves to provide important information. Does information content vary with the form of advertising? If so, which forms appear to be most informative?

4 Is the division of goods into convenience goods and shopping goods independent of the division into search goods and experience goods, or does there appear to be a strong correlation between the groups?

13 Employment and Pricing of Inputs in Competitive Markets

13-1 Introduction

We began this book with an overview of supply and demand and the determination of price and output in the product market. We then examined the theory of consumer behaviour to understand the nature of the demand curve. We have also studied production theory and cost theory, as well as the structure of the product market, to understand the nature of supply. We are now ready to look at one more piece of the puzzle: namely, input markets. The correspondence of output to labour input shown in Table 13-1 gives us an idea of just where input markets fit in.

In this chapter and the following two, we discuss the pricing of inputs, or factors of production, in input markets, or what are commonly called *factor markets*. As with pricing in output markets, pricing in factor markets depends on the way sellers and buyers are organized. In this chapter we consider the pricing of inputs in competitive markets. In the next chapter we examine the pricing of inputs under imperfect competition.

Many of our discussions and applications in this chapter focus on a particular input—labour. (You may find it useful to review what we said about labour supply in Chapter 3.) Labour is a particularly important and interesting input, but the other factors are given more coverage in the subsequent chapters. We should point out that labour is not really a single input. There are all types of labour with different skills (or no skills), and these types are certainly not interchangeable. Yet in this chapter we talk about *the* wage rate and *the* quantity of labour employed. What we are really examining is the input market for a particular type of labour. We discuss wage differences for different types of labour in Chapter 15.

Table 13-1 Linking output and input markets

	Output	Labour input
Demand	Derived from preferences of consumers	Derived from production conditions
Supply	Derived from production conditions	Derived from preferences of workers

13-2 Profit Maximization in Relation to Factor (Input) Usage

In Chapter 8 we argued that if $MR > MC$, then another unit of output adds more to revenue than to costs, and, thus, expanding output increases profit. But, if $MR < MC$, then reducing output subtracts more from costs than from revenue, so that reducing output increases profit. Combining these observations, the firm clearly maximizes profit by expanding output to the point where $MR = MC$, but no further.

We can similarly argue that the firm maximizes profit by increasing its usage of input X until

$$(MRP)_X = (MFC)_X.$$

$(MRP)_X$ is the marginal revenue product of input X, which equals $\Delta TR/\Delta X$, where X is the quantity of input X employed. That is, $(MRP)_X$ tells us by how much total revenue increases if one more unit of X is employed and other inputs remain constant. $(MRP)_X$ can also be expressed as follows:

$$(MRP)_X = \frac{\Delta TR}{\Delta X} = \frac{\Delta Q}{\Delta X} \cdot \frac{\Delta TR}{\Delta Q} = (MP)_X \cdot MR,$$

where $(MP)_X$ is the marginal product of X and MR is marginal revenue. $(MFC)_X$ is the marginal factor cost of X, which equals $\Delta TC/\Delta X$. $(MFC)_X$ tells us by how much total cost increases if one more unit of X is employed and other inputs remain unchanged. Clearly, the firm should expand its use of X as long as $(MRP)_X > (MFC)_X$, because additional units add more to revenue than to costs. But the firm should expand its use of X only to the point where $(MRP)_X = (MFC)_X$. Once MFC exceeds MRP, additional input use reduces profit.

The values of MRP and MFC depend on the structure of the output and input markets. In this chapter we assume *perfect competition* in both the output and input markets.

Under perfect competition in the output market, the firm is a price-taker and $P = MR$. Hence

$$MRP = P_O \cdot MP = VMP,$$

where VMP is the value of the marginal product and P_O is the output price.

Also, if there is perfect competition in the input market, the firm can purchase all of the input that it wants at the market price. The input supply curve facing the firm is horizontal, and MFC equals input price.

Thus, with competition in both the output and input markets, profit maximization requires that

Output price × marginal product = input price.

And if we have several inputs, since output price is the same, we get

$$\frac{\text{Price of input 1}}{MP \text{ of input 1}} = \frac{\text{price of input 2}}{MP \text{ of input 2}}$$

$$= \frac{\text{price of input 3}}{MP \text{ of input 3}} = \dots \text{etc.} = P_O.$$

We illustrate this principle in the next section with a numerical example.

13-3 Demand Curve for a Single Variable Input

We first examine the case of a single variable input—labour. Consider a firm producing compact discs. The factory and machinery are assumed to be in fixed supply. The only input that varies is the number of workers, who are assumed to be homogeneous in ability.

Table 13-2 gives the changes in output, or marginal product of labour, as we increase the labour input. Assuming that each unit of output sells for £10, we compute the value of the marginal product (VMP). The wage rate per worker, or the price of labour, is £2000. The firm employs labour to the point where the $VMP =$ the wage rate. Increasing the labour input beyond this point results in a reduction in profit.

The number of workers employed from Table 13-2 is 8. If the wage rate is reduced to £1000 the number of workers employed rises to 9. If the wage rate is raised to £3000 the number of workers employed falls to 7.

The VMP curve rises at first and then falls, as shown in Figure 13-1. The VMP curve rises as long as the MP of labour is increasing. Once we reach the point of diminishing marginal return, the VMP curve declines. Some part of the declining portion of the VMP curve gives the demand for labour curve. This is shown in Figure 13-2.

Note that, if the wage rate is £5000 from Table 13-2, we might conclude that the firm employs five workers because this is where the VMP equals the wage rate. However, this firm could not even cover its variable costs. The labour cost is £25 000 (5 × £5000) and the value of output is £23 000. Hence the firm employs no workers and shuts down if the wage rate is £5000. The condition that input price equals marginal product × output price holds only as long as the firm

Table 13-2 Changes in output as labour input increases

No. of workers	Output	Marginal product	Value of marginal product (marginal product × £10) (£)	Wage rate (£)	Increase in profit (value of marginal product − wage rate) (£)
0				2000	
1	300	300	3000	2000	1000
2	700	400	4000	2000	2000
3	1200	500	5000	2000	3000
4	1800	600	6000	2000	4000
5	2300	500	5000	2000	3000
6	2700	400	4000	2000	2000
7	3000	300	3000	2000	1000
8	3200	200	2000	2000	0
9	3300	100	1000	2000	−1000
10	3300	0	0	2000	−2000

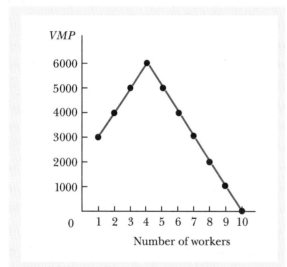

Figure 13-1 Value of marginal product (VMP) curve

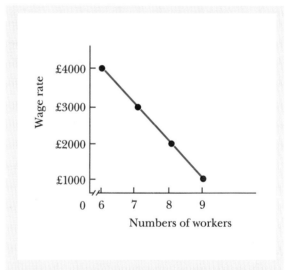

Figure 13-2 Demand for labour by an individual firm

opts to employ any of the input. And the firm employs the input in the short run as long as the revenue per unit of the input equals or exceeds the input price, which implies that variable costs are being covered.

Note that Figure 13-2 has been drawn on the assumption of a given output price $P_O = £10$. What

happens if the output price falls to, say, £8 per unit? The value of marginal product falls (the fourth column in Table 13-2), and the VMP curve shifts to the left. We can easily see that at a wage rate of £2000 the firm now employs 7 workers and not 8. Also, at a wage rate of £4000 we have VMP = wage rate when the number of workers employed is 3, but the firm employs no workers because the value of total output (or total revenue) for three workers is £8 × 1200 = £9600, whereas the wage bill is 3 × £4000 = £12 000. Thus, the firm cannot cover its variable costs.

In any case, it is easy to see that, with a decline in output price and the leftward shift in the *VMP* curve, the demand curve for labour in Figure 13-2 shifts to the left. With an increase in output price, it shifts to the right. This is an intuitive result. As product price rises, the firm expands output and hence needs more labour. The demand for the input is a *derived demand*. It is called a derived demand because it is derived from the demand for output. How much of the input a firm demands depends on the quantity of output the firm produces.

Figure 13-2 shows that, as the wage rate falls, the firm demands a larger number of workers. However, when each firm employs more workers, and produces more output, the industry output rises and the price of output falls. With this fall in the price of output, as we have seen, the input demand curve of each firm shifts to the left. Thus, in deriving the industry demand curve for an input, we have to account for the effect of a price fall on the individual firms' input demand curves.

Figure 13-3 illustrates this point. We can aggregate the individual firms' demand curves for labour by horizontal summation, i.e. by summing the individual quantities of labour demanded at each wage. We call this demand curve, obtained by simple summation, the *aggregate demand curve*. It gives the quantity of labour demanded at each wage rate for the industry as a whole, *holding output price constant*.

We can get such aggregate demand curves for each output price. In Figure 13-3, $D_1 D_1$ is an aggregate demand curve, and $D_2 D_2$ is another aggregate demand curve for a lower output price. Now when the wage rate falls from W_1 to W_2, more labour is employed; but this increases industry output, with a consequent decline in the output price. Thus, the aggregate demand curve for labour shifts to the left, and the amount of labour employed is given by point C_2 on $D_2 D_2$ (not by point A on $D_1 D_1$). The industry input demand curve is given by the dashed line $C_1 C_2$ in the figure. This demand curve takes account of the fall in output price due to an increase in industry output.[1]

Note that the industry demand curve $C_1 C_2$ is steeper than the aggregate demand curves $D_1 D_1$ and $D_2 D_2$. How much steeper it is depends on how much the aggregate demand curve shifts with the fall in output price. If the elasticity of demand for output is high, then the decline in price for a given increase in output is small. Thus, the shift in the aggregate demand curve is very small. So the difference in the elasticities between the industry demand curve and the sum of the individual firms' demand curves depends directly on the elasticity of demand for the output. In all cases, the industry demand curve is less elastic than the sum of the individual firms' demand curves.

13-4   The Case of Several Inputs

Consider the case of two variable inputs: labour and capital. The firm employs labour and capital to the point where the value of the marginal product of each factor is equal to the price of the factor. Thus,

$$(VMP)_L = (MP)_L \cdot P_O = P_L$$

and

$$(VMP)_K = (MP)_K \cdot P_O = P_K.$$

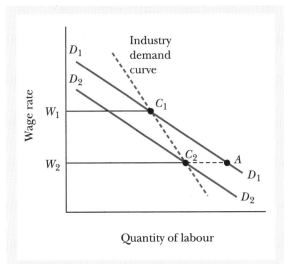

Figure 13-3 Demand curve for labour in a competitive industry

[1] Note that we are assuming that the demand curve $D_1 D_1$ is the aggregate demand curve for the industry output level corresponding to the wage rate W_1. Thus, C_1 is a point on the industry demand curve.

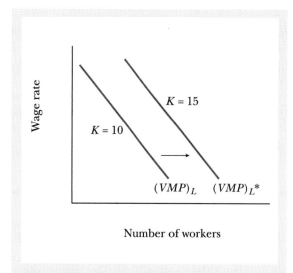

Figure 13-4 A shift in the demand curve for labour with an increased use of capital

But these relationships themselves do not enable us to derive the demand curves for the inputs. We now show how these curves are derived.

The demand curve in Figure 13-2 is derived on the assumption that the quantity of capital is fixed. What if we vary the quantity of capital? The impact on the demand for labour depends on the nature of the relationship between the inputs.

If the inputs are *independent inputs*, a change in the quantity of one input has no effect on the marginal product of the other, so that the marginal product of labour is independent of the amount of capital and vice versa. In this case the demand curves for each factor are derived separately, as in the previous section.

Normally, however, inputs are *complementary inputs*, so that the marginal product of one input increases with greater use of the other input. For example, if more tools and machinery are provided, each worker's marginal product rises. Thus, the marginal product of labour, for each unit of labour, increases with a larger quantity employed of the complementary input (capital in this case). This means that the VMP_L curve and the demand for labour curve shift to the right as the amount of capital is increased (from $K = 10$ to $K = 15$). This is shown in Figure 13-4.

Now consider the impact of a decline in the wage rate. The lower price of labour makes the firm hire more labour. But the lower wage rate also causes the marginal cost of output to fall so that the firm expands output. As the firm expands output, it may employ more capital. But as capital usage increases, the VMP curve and the demand-for-labour curve shift to the right, inducing a further increase in the quantity of labour employed.

The resulting demand curve for labour is shown in Figure 13-5 by the dashed line. It is flatter than the $(VMP)_L$ lines, which give the demand curves for labour

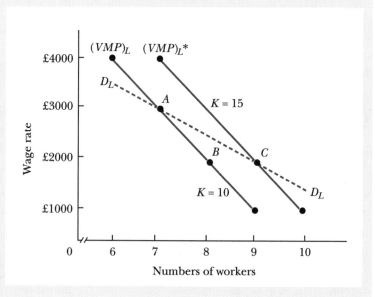

Figure 13-5 Demand for labour allowing for changes in the capital input

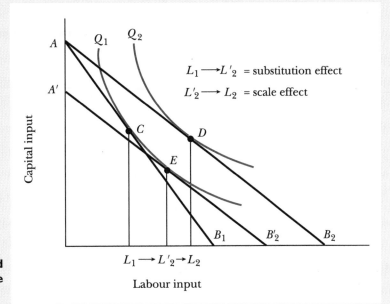

Figure 13-6 Substitution and scale effects of a decline in the price of labour

for *given* values of the capital input. The increase in the quantity of labour demanded can be broken down into two parts in much the same way as was done in the theory of the consumer in Chapter 3. There, the effect of a decline in the price of good X was broken down into a *substitution effect* and an *income effect.* Here we can do the same except that the income effect is called the *scale effect* or *output effect.* This is shown in Figure 13-6, which has the two inputs on the axes. Q_1 is the initial output level. The absolute slope of AB_1 is the ratio of the initial wage rate to the price of the capital input. Thus, bundle C represents the least-cost input bundle for producing Q_1 with the initial wage rate. Now suppose that when the wage rate falls the input price ratio is equal to the absolute slope of AB_2. If the firm expands output to Q_2, the optimal input bundle becomes D.

Now, as we did in Chapter 3 when we considered the substitution effect and income effect in consumption, we draw a line $A'B'_2$ parallel to AB_2 but tangent to the isoquant Q_1. The input bundle E represents the least-cost input bundle for the firm if it produces the initial output after the decline in the wage rate. Bundle E contains more labour and less capital than bundle C.

The movement from C to D can, thus, be decomposed into two components: a movement from C to E along the old isoquant—which is a pure

substitution effect—and a movement from E to D—which is a scale effect or output effect. Also, the total increase in labour input from L_1 to L_2 can be decomposed into two parts: (1) an increase from L_1 to L'_2 (the substitution effect), and (2) an increase from L'_2 to L_2 (the scale effect or output effect).

Note that we cannot show the substitution and output effects on the diagram in Figure 13-5 because the curves are for *given values of the capital input,* whereas what we want to consider is movement along an isoquant (substitution effect) and movement to a higher isoquant (output effect). The substitution effect involves a reduction in capital use. The output effect, in this example, involves an increase in the use of capital. So the quantity of capital used is not constant.

We can decompose the movement from 7 units to 9 units of labour (A to C) in Figure 13-5 into the following: 7 to 8 (A to B) is a movement along a demand curve and 8 to 9 (B to C) is a movement arising from a shift in the demand curve. But these do not represent substitution and output effects.

In the theory of the consumer, we mentioned that sometimes the income effect may be negative. In that case the good under consideration is called an 'inferior good'. Similarly, in the case of the theory of production, the scale effect or output effect for an input may be negative. In this case the input is called an *inferior input* or *regressive input*.

The derivation of the industry demand curve now proceeds along the lines we discussed in Section 13-3 (Figure 13-3). With two variable inputs, a decline in the price of labour has two effects: (1) the substitution and output effects, as described here, and (2) the effect of output price when the industry output expands. We have to take account of the first effect in deriving the individual firm's demand for labour. We have to take account of the second effect in deriving the industry demand curve for labour from the demand curves of the individual firms. Since we have explained this latter point earlier in Section 13-3 we do not go through it again.

13-5 Elasticity of the Input Demand Curve

In the previous two sections we discussed the demand curve for labour by the individual firm and by the industry. For policy purposes, it is important to know the elasticity of the input demand curve. In the case of the labour input, we would like to know the wage elasticity of demand for labour. The factors influencing the elasticity of industry demand for an input are summarized in four laws often called the Hicks–Marshall laws of derived demand, named after the two British economists.[2] These laws say that, other things being equal, the own price elasticity of demand for an input is higher:

1 when the price elasticity of demand for the product being produced is high;
2 when other factors of production can be easily substituted for the input;
3 when the supply curves of other factors of production are highly elastic;
4 when the cost of the input is a large share of the total costs of production.

The first three laws can be shown always to hold. There are conditions under which the last law may not hold. We now consider each in turn.

---

[2] J. R. Hicks, *The Theory of Wages*, St Martin's Press, New York, 1966, pp. 241–7; A. Marshall, *Principles of Economics* (8th edn.), Macmillan, London, 1923, pp. 518–38. Hicks's *Theory of Wages* was first published in 1932.

Elasticity of Demand for the Final Product

An increase in input price leads to an increase in output price, and the greater the price elasticity of demand for the final product, the larger is the decline in industry output for a given increase in price. The greater the decrease in output, the greater the decrease in input usage (other things being equal). Thus, the greater the elasticity of demand for the final product, the greater is the elasticity of demand for the input.

As we noted in Section 13-3, the individual firm's demand for an input is more elastic than the industry demand, although, as we also noted, the difference between these two elasticities is not large if the elasticity of demand for the output is high.

Finally, since the long-run elasticity of demand for output is higher than the short-run elasticity, we have a corresponding result that the long-run price elasticity of demand for an input is higher than the corresponding short-run elasticity.

Elasticity of Substitution

The ability to substitute one input for another is reflected in the *elasticity of substitution* between two inputs. A large elasticity indicates that the two inputs are close substitutes in production. Now if there is a close substitute available, then when the price of an input rises (other things remaining constant), the firm simply substitutes the other input. So, if labour and capital are close substitutes, then when the wage rate rises firms substitute capital for labour, and the fall in employment is greater. Hence the demand for an input is more elastic when close substitutes are available.

The elasticity of substitution is usually denoted by the Greek letter σ (sigma). The elasticity of substitution between labour and capital is defined as

$$\sigma = -\left[\frac{\Delta(K/L)}{K/L} \Big/ \frac{\Delta(P_K/P_L)}{P_K/P_L}\right]$$

with output constant. It shows the percentage change in the capital–labour ratio for a given percentage change in the input price ratio, holding the output level constant. If $\sigma = 1$, a 10 per cent fall in the P_K/P_L ratio results in a 10 per cent increase in the K/L ratio. Several studies have been conducted to estimate σ empirically. There is usually a great divergence in these estimates, depending on the type of data used, the time period considered, and so on. In fact, many economists are sceptical of these estimates because of this diversity. Harris estimated average values of σ for the manufacturing sector in each region of the UK.[3] He found that σ ranged from 0.23 in the South-West to 0.88 in Northern Ireland. Typically the values were low, being less than 0.5 in seven of the nine regions.

Elasticity of Supply of Other Inputs

The demand for an input is more elastic if the supply curves of the other inputs are more elastic. Suppose there is an increase in the price of labour. The individual firm would like to substitute capital for labour. However, if the supply of capital (machines) is inelastic, then the firm is limited in its ability to make a profitable substitution. This is because a small increase in demand for capital causes a large increase in its price. Thus, the decline in labour use is smaller, and demand for labour is less elastic.

Again, note that the substitution possibilities are higher in the long run than in the short run. In the long run, the producers of capital equipment expand their capacity and new producers enter the market. Thus, the long-run elasticity of supply of the other input is higher than the short-run elasticity. Consequently, the long-run elasticity of demand for an input is higher than the corresponding short-run elasticity.

The Share of the Input in Total Costs

Finally, the share of the input in total costs is also an important factor in determining the elasticity of demand for an input. If the share of labour costs is only 10 per cent, then a 10 per cent increase in the wage rate, other things being equal, raises total costs by only 1 per cent. However, if the initial share is 90 per cent, a 10 per cent increase in the wage rate increases total costs by 9 per cent. Since MC increases more in the latter case than in the former, price increases more in the latter case, and output, and hence employment, fall more in the latter case. Thus, the greater the share of labour in total costs, the higher is the wage elasticity of the demand for labour.

Although intuitively plausible, the law does not always hold. This argument suggests that the quantity of the input used per unit of output is independent of the price of the factor. In other words, the 'law' is necessarily true only in the case where inputs are combined in fixed proportions.

Empirical Evidence

What is the magnitude of the wage elasticity of demand for labour? Hamermesh surveyed over 20 empirical studies and concluded that the absolute value of the long-run wage elasticity of demand for labour in developed economies is around 0.15 to 0.50, holding output constant.[4] Although this range is wide, it does at least put some limits on the claims we can make for the ability of wage subsidies to increase employment by changing the relative labour intensity of production at a fixed rate of output. Estimates of wage elasticities when output is allowed to vary are somewhat higher than in the fixed-output case. Symons and Layard found that elasticities in six OECD countries ranged from 0.3 in France to 2.4 in Japan.[5]

A Word of Caution

In the previous discussion we referred constantly to the industry demand for labour. In practice, labour is mobile between industries, and the demand curve for labour summarizes the responses of a large number of industries. Thus, wage rates are determined not only by the demand of a particular industry. For example, an engineer or an electrician can move between different industries. There are some specialized labour skills that are not transferable between industries (air pilots, air traffic controllers, and so on); but these are more of an exception than a rule, and even in these cases (although the skills are industry-specific) the workers themselves can move to other industries at their own cost—their demonstrated ability in such a profession can be taken as an indication of their ability to acquire other skills.

---

[3] R. I. D. Harris, 'Estimates of Inter-Regional Differences in Production in the United Kingdom, 1968–78', *Oxford Bulletin of Economics and Statistics*, 44 (1982): 241–59.

[4] D. S. Hamermesh, 'The Demand for Labor in the Long Run', in O. Ashenfelter and R. Layard (eds.), *Handbook of Labor Economics*, vol. 1, North-Holland, Amsterdam, 1986, pp. 429–71.
[5] J. Symons and R. Layard, 'Neoclassical Demand for Labour Functions in Six OECD Countries', *Economic Journal*, 94 (1984): 788–99.

13-6 Some Comments on the Derived Demand for Labour

In our discussion we have talked of labour as homogeneous. This, however, is not the case, and we can consider at least two categories of labour: skilled and unskilled. We now have two wage rates—one for skilled labour and another for unskilled labour. When we talk of elasticity of demand, we mean the own-wage elasticity. Furthermore, we have to consider not only capital–labour substitution but also labour–labour substitution, or the substitution possibilities between skilled and unskilled labour. Also, like capital, skilled labour is in limited supply in the short run: it takes time to train it.

Empirical evidence on own-wage elasticities suggests that the own-wage elasticity is higher for unskilled production workers than for non-production and skilled production workers. This result appears to be a consequence of the fact that there is greater substitutability between capital and unskilled production workers than between capital and skilled production and non-production workers.[6]

Trade unions also limit the scope of substitution of labour for other inputs. Since the power of a union depends mainly on the elasticity of demand for labour (the higher the elasticity, the lower the union power), unions try to take measures that lower the elasticity of demand for labour. The elasticity of demand for the final product depends on the availability of substitutes. Frequently, this substitute product is an imported good. Unions try to seek quotas or tariffs on imports so that the competition from foreign goods is reduced.

As an example, we have the behaviour of the steel and car manufacturing unions during the 1970s in the UK. The elasticity of demand for these goods depends on (1) the number of non-unionized workers who are willing to work at wages below the wages of the unionized workers and (2) the supply of imported products that compete heavily with domestically produced steel and cars. The unions dealt with (1) by unionizing the entire industry or particular types of labour in the industry. With regard to (2), they pushed

for the imposition of tariffs and quotas on the imports of steel and cars from Europe and Japan. The first measure is an attempt to reduce the elasticity of supply of a substitute input, and the second is an attempt to reduce the elasticity of demand for output. According to the laws of derived demand in the previous section, both of these measures should decrease the elasticity of demand for domestic labour.

13-7 Input Supply

In discussing input supply, we differentiate among produced inputs (such as machinery or materials), labour, and natural inputs (such as land). We must also be careful to distinguish between the total or market supply of an input and the supply curve of the input facing an industry or a firm. Also, in this chapter we consider only input supply under competitive input market conditions.

We first discuss the market or total supply of produced inputs, such as materials, because this topic requires little additional attention. The market supply for materials is determined in the same manner as the market supply for any output; that is, the fact that a product is an intermediate product rather than a final or consumer product is irrelevant for purposes of supply. And we have already discussed the derivation of a market supply curve from the firms' cost curves, for a competitive industry, in Chapter 8.

We have also already considered several aspects of labour supply in Chapter 3. There, we examined (1) the backward-bending supply curve of labour, (2) the effects of social security and negative income tax on work effort, and (3) the effects of progressive income tax on labour supply. However, in Chapter 3 we focused our attention on the individual's decision regarding how much labour to supply at various wage rates. That is, we were concerned with the individual worker's supply curve of labour. The market supply curve of labour is derived by horizontally summing all of the individuals' labour supply curves.

There is a common objection to deriving a market supply curve of labour in this manner, and now is a good time to discuss it. In Chapter 3 we treated the number of hours of labour supplied as the choice of the individual. But casual observation tells us that it is the employer rather than the employees that determine the number of hours worked in most cases.

[6] D. S. Hamermesh and J. Grant, 'Econometric Studies of Labor–Labor Substitution and their Implications for Policy', *Journal of Human Resources*, 14 (1979): 518–42. More recent evidence is summarized in D. S. Hamermesh, 'The Demand for Labor in the Long Run', in Ashenfelter and Layard, op. cit.

Except for self-employed workers, the worker can adjust work hours only marginally, through overtime or perhaps extra sick leave. But if workers' preferences are similar, then a marginal adjustment is all that is needed when the standard working week is determined by the typical worker's preferences. So is the standard working week sensitive to worker preferences? Well, if most workers began looking for part-time work with only 30 hours per week, then in the long run the standard working week would undoubtedly respond. So at least in the long run the typical worker's preferences determine the number of hours worked.

We have one last input supply to discuss, and that is the supply of natural inputs such as land. The market supply curve for these inputs is vertical because the quantities available are fixed (although the productivity of the input can be changed with the use of complementary inputs, such as fertilizer). And the market supply curve tells us the quantities of the input available to all employers, at various input prices.

But does a vertical market supply curve imply that the supply curve of the input to one industry or one firm is also perfectly inelastic? Let us first consider the supply curve to the industry. If an input is employed in only one industry, then the supply curve facing the industry coincides with the market supply curve. This is only the case for very specialized inputs. More commonly, inputs are mobile across several industries. For example, unskilled labour is mobile across so many industries that the supply curve of unskilled labour facing an industry is close to horizontal at the market wage rate. Thus, in the case of unskilled labour, a single industry can generally employ all that it wants to, without affecting the wage rate. If an input is employed in only a few industries, then each industry faces an upward-sloping supply curve for the input. But in this case the supply curve facing each industry is more elastic than the market supply curve. This is because, if the input price in one industry increases, not only might new units of the input be drawn into the market, but existing units might relocate to take advantage of the higher input price. So in general, we can only say that the input supply curve to an industry is at least as elastic as the market supply curve.

In this chapter, the input supply curves facing the individual firms are perfectly elastic at the current market price. This is because we have assumed that markets are perfectly competitive. Even if the input is employed in only one industry, there are enough firms in the industry so that none of them has any control over input prices.

13-8 Determination of Equilibrium Input Price and Employment

In the previous sections we have frequently referred to the industry demand for an input. And the industry we have talked of is an output industry. For some specialized inputs that are not mobile between industries, the industry demand is the total or market demand. (Examples of specialized types of labour skills that are immobile between industries are heart surgeons, concert pianists, and astronauts.) In practice, most inputs are mobile between industries. (Examples of mobile labour are secretaries, salespersons, and general management executives.) In this case the market demand for the input is the horizontal sum of the industry demands for the input. (The market supply of an input was discussed in the previous section.)

The intersection of the market demand and supply curves determines the equilibrium input price and the total quantity of the input employed. This is shown in Figure 13-7 for the case of labour. W^* is the equilibrium wage rate, and L^* is the equilibrium employment. W^* and L^* are determined by the intersection of the market demand for labour DD

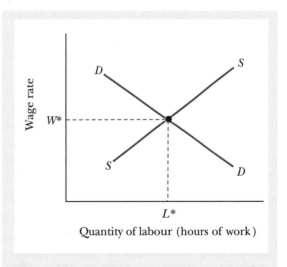

Figure 13-7 Equilibrium wage rate and employment

and the market supply of labour *SS*. If the wage is above *W** then there is an excess supply of labour, and if the wage rate is below *W** there is an excess demand for labour.

Note that in equilibrium the wage rate *W** must be equal across all the industries among which the input is mobile. If one industry pays a higher wage rate, then workers from other industries transfer until any wage discrepancy is eliminated.

As in the case of output markets, an increase in market demand for an input causes an increase in equilibrium price and employment for the input. An increase in market demand can be brought about by an increase in input demand by any of the employing industries. Of course, if the industry employs a large fraction of the total, then a change in that industry's demand has a larger impact on market demand and a larger impact on input price and total employment. A decrease in the market demand for an input clearly reduces equilibrium price and input employment.

An increase in market supply of an input causes a decrease in input price; and finally, a decrease in market supply of an input leads to an increase in input price.

13-9 Application 1: Effects of Minimum Wage Laws

A number of European countries have a statutory national minimum wage, including France, Luxembourg, the Netherlands, Portugal, and Spain. It is likely that as part of the European Union's Social Charter, a European-wide minimum wage will be recommended at perhaps two-thirds of each member-state's average manufacturing wage. Although the UK has never had a statutory national minimum wage, minimum wages have operated in some industries through the Wages Councils. These were set up in 1909 to set minimum wages for people in service occupations. Before they were abolished in 1993, they covered about 2.5 million workers.

If a minimum wage law is to be effective, then the minimum wage $\overline{W}$ must be set above the market equilibrium wage *W**. An effective minimum wage law produces unemployment. This is shown in Figure 13-8. Without the minimum wage law, employment is *Ob*. If the minimum wage rate is $\overline{W}$, then the wage rate is $\overline{W}$

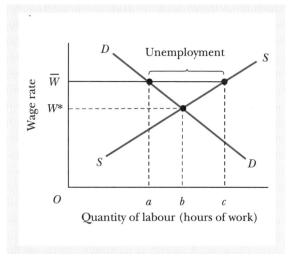

Figure 13-8 Effect of a minimum wage law

and employment is *Oa*. However, at the higher wage rate $\overline{W}$, the quantity of labour supplied is larger. More people enter the workforce, and those already working want to work more hours. Thus,

ab = decline in employment hours.
bc = increase in quantity of labour supplied,
and
ac = *ab*+ *bc* = unemployment in hours.

The observed unemployment *ac* is, thus, higher than the reduction in employment *ab* induced by the minimum wage law.

The enactment of minimum wage laws is often justified on grounds of equity. Whether such laws accomplish this purpose is open to question. It depends, in part, on the elasticity of the demand and supply curves. This is shown in Figure 13-9. In case (a) the decrease in employment *ab* is small, although the unemployment *ac* is high. Most of this unemployment comes from *bc*, the increase in quantity supplied. In this case the total wage bill rises, so in principle the original labour force could redistribute the wages so that all workers are better off. In case (b) the decrease in employment *ab* is large and accounts for most of the unemployment *ac*. In this case the wage bill falls and workers are definitely worse off. Which of these cases applies in practice is an empirical question, but clearly, the social cost of minimum wage legislation is greater in case (b).

The effect of a minimum wage law on employment as shown in Figure 13-8 applies only if *all* workers are

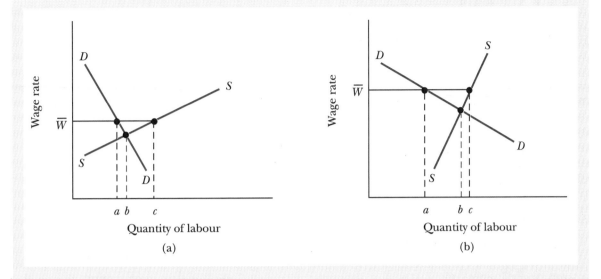

Figure 13-9   Effect of a minimum wage law on employment

(a) Decrease in employment *ab* is small
(b) Decrease in employment *ab* is large

covered by minimum wage laws. If there is only partial coverage, there may be no increase in unemployment. The unemployed workers in the covered sector switch over to the uncovered sector and seek employment there. This depresses the wage rate in the uncovered sector.

Thus, with effective minimum wage legislation, the wage rate in the covered sector goes up, and the wage rate in the uncovered sector goes down. The argument is easy to follow, but we illustrate it in Figure 13-10. Initially, the wage level is W_0 in both sectors. Employment is L_c in the covered sector and L_u in the

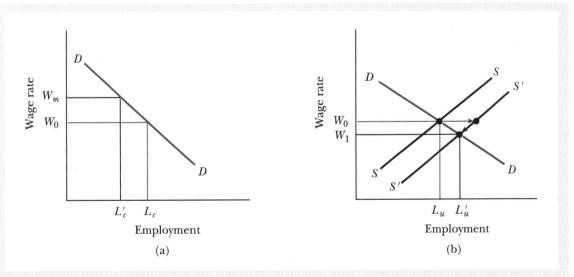

Figure 13-10   Effect of a minimum wage law on wage rates

(a) Covered sector
(b) Uncovered sector

uncovered sector. With a minimum wage W_m in the covered sector, employment falls to L'_c. The unemployed labour $(L_c - L'_c)$ attempts to find employment in the uncovered sector. This is shown by a shift in the supply curve from SS to $S'S'$ in part (b). The wage rate in the uncovered sector falls to the level W_1, so that the increase in employment $(L'_u - L_u)$ is less than $(L_c - L'_c)$ because some workers leave the market as the wage rate falls. Also, it is not true that the entire unemployed labour $(L_c - L'_c)$ can switch from the covered sector and find employment in the uncovered sector. Thus, there is a certain effect on unemployment. But the unemployment is less than with total coverage.[7]

Relatively little work has been done on the employment consequences of the UK Wages Councils. The work that has been done finds no evidence of any adverse employment effects.[8] (A fuller discussion of the role of the Wages Councils can be found in Section 14-7.) In the United States there has been a large number of studies on the effects of the minimum wage law on employment.[9] The empirical evidence is mixed, but one predominant conclusion that emerges is that the employment opportunities for teenagers have been reduced because of the minimum wage. Some found evidence of this reduction in the number employed, others in the number of hours worked (a switch from full-time to part-time employment). For adults, minimum wage laws seem to have a negligible effect, since most of them earn a wage rate higher than the minimum. Somewhat different results emerge from research into the effects of the minimum wage on youth employment in France. On balance, the research suggests that the minimum wage has not significantly

reduced youth employment.[10] As in the US case, little or no effect has been found on adult employment.

One of the major objectives of minimum wage laws is to promote a more equitable income distribution by raising the wages of low-wage-earners. However, as we showed in Figure 13-10, the wage rate in the covered sector rises and the wage rate in the uncovered sector falls, thereby promoting a greater wage disparity. The low-wage-earners in the uncovered sector are likely to get still lower wages because of increased pressure in this market coming from the unemployed in the covered sector. Thus, the income distribution consequences may be the opposite of what was intended. Some lucky workers get employment in the covered sector at a higher wage, but others are either unemployed or employed in the uncovered sector at a lower wage. Gramlich studied the impact of minimum wage laws on income distribution in the United States but found very little effect.[11] One reason could be that he examined the distribution of family income. And as mentioned earlier, in the United States it is frequently teenagers that suffer the effects of unemployment or reduced hours of work, and this does not have much impact on family income. Some of the teenagers might even come from middle- or high-income families.

13-10 Application 2: Overtime Pay

In Chapter 3 we derived the hours of work supplied by a worker and showed that the supply curve of labour can be backward-bending, so that as the wage rate increases, the hours of work supplied by a worker may actually decrease. Suppose that the wage rate is a fixed amount per hour for the standard hours of work (say, 40 hours per week) and is higher (say, one-and-a-half times) for any overtime hours. It is common practice among employers to let existing workers work overtime at a higher wage rate rather than hire additional

---

[7] Unemployed workers in the covered sector might decide to wait in the covered sector until an opening comes up. They could calculate the probabilities of attaining a higher wage in the covered sector taking account of periods of unemployment and compare it with the lower wage and certain employment in the uncovered sector.

[8] See C. Craig, J. Rubery, R. Tarling, and F. Wilkinson, *Labour Market Structure, Industrial Organisation and Low Pay*, Cambridge University Press, 1982. See also, S. Machin and A. Manning, 'Minimum Wages, Wage Dispersion and Employment: Evidence From the UK Wages Councils', Discussion Papers in Economics, no. 92-05, University College London, 1992.

[9] See F. Welch, *Minimum Wages: Issues and Evidence*, American Enterprise Institute, Washington, DC, 1978, and J. Mincer, 'Unemployment Effects of Minimum Wage Changes', *Journal of Political Economy*, 84 (1976): S87–104.

[10] For a detailed discussion of the employment effects of the minimum wage law in France, see S. Bazen and J. P. Martin, 'The Impact of the Minimum Wage on Earnings and Employment in France', *OECD Economic Studies*, 16 (1991): 199–221.

[11] E. Gramlich, 'Impact of Minimum Wages on Other Wages, Employment and Family Incomes', *Brookings Papers on Economic Activity*, part 2 (1976): 409–51.

workers when their demand for labour is temporarily higher than normal. The employers, thus, save any costs of hiring and training new workers. Also, employers' national insurance contributions are employee-related, not hours-related (except in the case of part-time workers), which gives employers a further incentive to let existing workers work overtime. We show that, unlike the case of paying a higher wage rate, such overtime pay does, in general, increase hours of work supplied. This is shown in Figure 13-11.

We consider the workers' indifference curves between income and leisure, and we measure hours of leisure on the horizontal axis. The maximum hours of leisure (measured on a daily basis) is 24. Thus, hours of work are measured from right to left in Figure 13-11.

At the initial wage rate, AB_1 is the 'budget line'. The worker is on indifference curve I_1 and supplies H_1 (standard) hours of work.[12] At a higher uniform wage rate, AB_2 is the budget line. The worker moves to a higher indifference curve, but the hours of work supplied fall from H_1 to H_2 since leisure is a normal good. (Remember that hours of work are measured from right to left.) With overtime pay, the budget line has a kink and tilts upward after the standard hours of work (assumed to be H_1 in Figure 13-11). The kinked budget line is shown as ACD. The worker is on a higher indifference curve I_3, and hours of work supplied increase to H_3.

Note that hours supplied of work need not always increase with overtime pay. Suppose the standard number of hours of work is greater than H_1. In this case the kink is at a point to the left of point C in Figure 13-11. Then it can be verified (we do not show it because it clutters up the diagram) that hours of work may not increase. In some cases it depends on how far left of C the kink occurs and how steep the new segment of the budget line is (how high the overtime pay rate is). And if the standard number of hours is less than H_1, so that the worker puts in overtime even without overtime pay, then the amount of overtime hours supplied might fall with the introduction of the overtime pay rate. But for any worker working only the standard number of hours, overtime pay always increases the hours of work supplied.

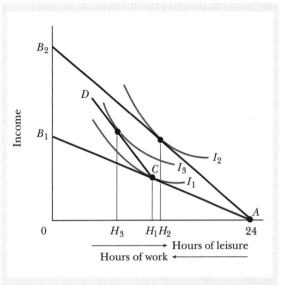

Figure 13-11   Effect of overtime pay on labour supply

It is important to realize that we have discussed only the supply side of the picture. To discuss the effect of overtime pay on actual hours worked, we have to consider the demand side as well. We do not, however, pursue this in detail. Instead, we make some casual observations.

As mentioned earlier, national insurance legislation is employee-related rather than hours-related. It increases the fixed costs of hiring new employees, thus providing an incentive for employers to use overtime hours. The pattern of overtime working has changed very little in the UK during the past 30 years. The average weekly overtime hours in manufacturing in the UK was about 8.5 hours per employee in 1965, 8 hours per employee in 1975, and 9 hours per employee in 1992. In 1965, 35 per cent of all employees in manufacturing worked overtime, compared with 31 per cent in 1975 and 35 per cent in 1992. Since the use of overtime hours reduces aggregate employment (in number of employees), there have been suggestions in some countries that, where overtime pay is one and a half times the standard rate, it should be increased to twice the pay rate for standard hours. The argument is that this increases the marginal cost of using overtime hours, so that employers will be more inclined to take on new employees instead.

---

[12] This assumes that point C is a tangency solution. We argued earlier in the book that hours of work supplied may not be, at least in the short run.

13-11 Application 3: Piece-rate Wages versus Time Wages

Throughout our analysis, we have assumed that workers are paid by the hour. This payment method is called time (or hourly) wages. This is the predominant method of wage payment in almost all countries. An alternative method of wage payment is that of piece-rate wages, where workers are paid by the work performed. Workers on piece rates usually earn more than those in comparable time-rate jobs. This is for two reasons: first, there is a compensating wage differential; second, the workers who opt for piece-rate jobs frequently work harder. We consider each of these reasons in turn.

Workers on piece rates find that their earnings fluctuate according to their day-to-day productivity. (Stomach upsets, hangovers, and so on can affect their productivity.) Such pay fluctuations do not exist for workers on time rates. If the average total wage income is the same under both payment methods, then workers will prefer the time rate because of the stability in earnings and, if possible, will switch into time-rate jobs. Therefore, if the employer wants to use the piece rate, he or she will have to pay a higher average total wage for piece-rate workers. There has to be some wage differential to compensate for the higher fluctuations in income. Under the time-rate scheme, employers bear the costs of fluctuations in worker productivity; under the piece-rate system, employees bear the costs of fluctuations in productivity. The employer may find it desirable to shift the costs of fluctuations even if it requires an increase in average total wages. In some cases the costs of fluctuations are shared by the employer and the employee, and time rates and piece rates are used in combination. This applies to salespersons who receive a fixed salary (usually a low one) and, in addition, a commission based on sales.

It is also argued that workers work harder on a piece-rate than on a time-rate system because they have an incentive to put in 100 per cent effort. This argument is not necessarily valid, because even with the time rate the employer can fire an employee who is lethargic and wastes time, but marginal reductions in effort are frequently difficult to detect. Furthermore, the less motivated worker does better on time-rate wages, and hence opts not to take a job paying piece rates.

Piece rates can be used only where the output of the worker is easily measurable. Examples of workers on piece rates are car repair mechanics, sales representatives, and people who work from home. Assembly-line workers, however, have to work in co-ordination with others, and hence cannot be paid on piece rates. Nor is it generally feasible to use piece rates with managers (although performance-related pay is similar).

Technological change, however, creates some problems even when the output can be clearly measured. For instance, if a new machine is invented and the same car repair job can be done in less time than before, then the employer has to renegotiate the piece rate with the workers. Such renegotiation can be difficult and expensive. Thus, piece rates are less likely to exist in an industry undergoing rapid technological progress.

13-12 Application 4: Occupational Health and Safety Regulations

For many workers the riskiness of a particular job is largely unknown. Because they do not have complete information about the extent of risk, they are protected by national government (and EU) legislation in the form of risk-reducing programmes. In the UK the responsibility for health and safety in the workplace lies with the Health and Safety Commission and the Health and Safety Executive. These bodies were established by the Health and Safety at Work [etc.] Act 1974. The Act did not spell out how much health and safety is to be provided by the employer, but it did lay down general guidelines to be followed. For instance, every employer must ensure the health and safety at work of employees; in particular, employers should provide plant and work systems that are safe, and they should provide and maintain a working environment that is safe and without risk to health. A new series of regulations were introduced in 1992 under the heading Workplace (Health, Safety, and Welfare) Regulations 1992. These apply to all new workplaces used for the first time after 31 December 1992 and to existing workplaces in 1996.

The purpose of these regulations is to reduce the exposure of workers to risks of loss of life or serious injury. If workers do understand the risks involved in the different jobs and there are compensating wage

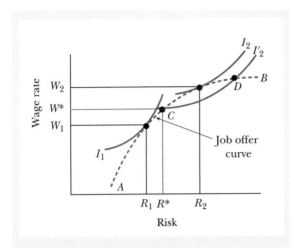

Figure 13-12   Effect of government regulation of risk on workers' utility

differentials for more risky jobs, then these regulations make some workers worse off.

This is shown in Figure 13-12. AB is the job offer curve. It gives the different jobs that the employers can offer with different wage and risk combinations. It is assumed that the wage rate increases with the riskiness of the job but does so at a decreasing rate.

The workers' indifference curves are upward-sloping with the slope increasing with increasing risk as shown in the figure. (Recall the indifference curves for a 'good' and a 'bad' discussed in Chapter 2.) Here wage is a good and risk is a bad. We are assuming that workers dislike risk; that is, they are *risk-averse*. (Those workers who like risk are described as *risk-loving*, and those workers who neither like nor dislike risk are called *risk-neutral*. We discuss these ideas more fully in Chapter 18.)

Worker 1 with indifference curve given by I_1 chooses a job with risk R_1 and wage W_1. Worker 2 is assumed to be less risk-averse and therefore has a less steep indifference curve, given by I_2. (She does not require as large an increase in wages as worker 1 for any extra risk incurred.) She chooses a job with risk R_2 and wage W_2. Now suppose that the government legislates that no jobs with risk levels greater than R^* can be offered to workers. The job offer curve is now the truncated curve AC. Worker 2 now gets a job with risk level R^* and wage rate W^*. However, this worker is now on a lower indifference curve I_2' and is, thus, worse off. Worker 1 is unaffected by the legislation.

This analysis assumes that (1) the worker has correct knowledge of the job risks involved, and (2) there are no external effects; that is, all potential hazards accrue to the worker making the decision. We now consider the implications of these assumptions.

If the first assumption is violated, then the solution is to inform workers of the job risks involved. Thus, the government, instead of legislating the maximum permissible level of risk, can legislate the distribution of information on the risks involved in the different types of job and let the workers choose. In the absence of such information, the legislation of maximum level of risk can, in some cases, make workers better off. For instance, in Figure 13-12 worker 2 might choose point D on the job offer curve, underestimating the risks involved and thinking that she is on a higher indifference curve I_2; however, she is actually on indifference curve I_2', and the government-mandated maximum risk R^* brings the worker to point C on the same indifference curve. Thus, she is actually not worse off, although she might mistakenly think so. This is, of course, a somewhat artificial example, but it illustrates the point that, when workers underestimate the risks involved in certain jobs, government-mandated maximum levels of risk can make workers better off, or at least no worse off.

The second problem of external effects (which we discuss in greater detail in Chapter 16) points to the fact that workers undertaking risky jobs may take into account only their own private costs; they may not consider the psychic costs for members of the family, close friends, and relatives. Also, the costs of medical treatment are borne by taxpayers, and some of the diseases can even be contagious. All of these external costs are not taken into account in the analysis in Figure 13-12, where only the indifference curves of the workers are considered. Thus, mandating maximum risk might make worker 2 worse off but make other affected individuals better off.

The violation of our assumptions does not allow us to conclude that the health and safety regulations are socially desirable. This discussion merely suggests that the simple analysis in Figure 13-12 needs to be modified to take account of these problems. In practice, one needs to evaluate the availability of information on risks involved in the different jobs and the magnitude of external effects in determining whether the regulations contribute positively to overall social welfare.

13-13 Application 5: Are Workers Paid their Marginal Products?

Throughout this chapter we have assumed that the wage rate for a worker is equal to the value of the worker's marginal product. If this is so, the relationship between the wage rates and the values of marginal product are given by the 45° line shown in Figure 13-13. In practice, however, the wage rates of workers within a firm vary much less than the workers' marginal productivities. The actual relationship between wages and marginal products is more like the flatter line AB in the figure.

Economists have advanced several explanations for this behaviour. One argument is that it is not possible to measure workers' marginal productivity accurately, and many firms follow strict pay formulas based on education, experience, length of tenure in the job, and other considerations, which are all supposed to influence the worker's marginal product. In other words, employers look for signals about the productivity of workers. They attempt to screen those people with higher productivity by identifying certain characteristics (such as education, race, sex, or residential location) associated with higher productivity. (These ideas are further discussed in Section 14-8, when we examine discrimination in employment.) In

this case, the relationship between the wage rate and the value of the marginal product is a line with a slope less than 1, such as the line AB in Figure 13-13. In statistical terminology, this is called a 'regression effect' (a regression towards the mean).

Another argument is that workers prefer employment contracts with more gently sloping earnings as a means of smoothing out their earnings over a lifetime. Such smoothing necessitates paying them more than the value of their marginal product in early years and less than the value of their marginal product in later years.[13] But this payment pattern is feasible only when labour contracts are binding over the long term. Otherwise, employees can change jobs when their pay falls below the value of the marginal product.

Yet another argument suggested by Frank is that workers care a great deal not only about the income they receive but also about the position they occupy in

---

[13] Note that this argument assumes that productivity increases with age. If it falls, elderly workers were paid less than their marginal product when young, but they now receive a wage above their marginal product. This gives employers an incentive to breach contracts for older workers. This argument has been used to explain mergers. After a merger, the new owners can scrap existing contracts. The old shareholders auction the firm and pocket the premium, which represents a transfer of income to shareholders from sackings or wage cuts. For a discussion of this idea, see 'Do Mergers Work?', *The Economist* (17 December 1988): 76–8.

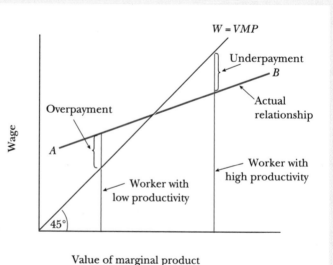

Figure 13-13 Theoretical and actual relationships between workers' wages and marginal products

Value of marginal product

the income hierarchies of the groups to which they belong.[14] The less productive workers normally do not want to associate themselves with the more productive workers, and therefore have to be paid a compensating wage differential to induce them to stay in the same pool as the more productive workers. This accounts for the wage being higher than the value of the marginal product for workers with low productivity and lower than the value of the marginal product for workers with high productivity (as shown in Figure 13-13).

13-14 Application 6: Labour as a Quasi-fixed Factor

In the theory of production discussed in Chapter 4, we considered capital as a fixed factor of production and labour as a variable factor of production. Although this is correct as a first approximation, in practice many of the costs associated with labour are also fixed costs.

With fluctuations in the demand for its products, a firm adjusts its variable factors of production to the point where the price paid for a factor is equal to the value of the marginal product of the factor. If there is a decrease in the demand for the firm's product, the firm lays off some of its unskilled labour, which it rehires when demand increases. However, the managers and the technical personnel cannot be as easily dispensed with. They are usually on longer-term contracts and, furthermore, are more difficult to replace if fired. There are search, hiring, and training costs associated with this kind of labour. Thus, in the short run the firm treats these costs as sunk costs. This is why labour is often called a *quasi-fixed factor*.

In Figure 13-14, we consider the impact of search, hiring, and training costs on the firm's hiring and firing decisions when demand fluctuates. We define

VMP_1 = initial value of the marginal product of labour
VMP_2 = value of marginal product of labour following a decrease in product demand
W = wage rate
S = per-unit search, hiring, and training costs.

[14] See R. H. Frank, 'Are Workers Paid their Marginal Products?' *American Economic Review*, 74 (1984): 549–71; also R. H. Frank, *Choosing the Right Pond: The Economics and Politics of the Quest for Status*, Oxford University Press, New York, 1985.

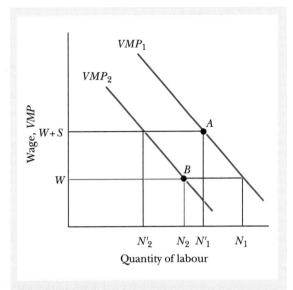

Figure 13-14 Response of firms treating labour as a quasi-fixed factor

In the absence of any search, hiring, or training costs, the firm initially employs N_1 units of labour. Following the decline in output demand, the firm reduces employment to N_2. In both cases, the firm equates VMP to the wage rate.

Now in the presence of search, hiring, or training costs, the cost of hiring an additional unit of labour is $W+S$. Thus, the firm initially employs labour until $W+S = VMP_1$, or it employs N'_1 units of labour. But once employed, the search, hiring, and training costs are sunk. The marginal cost of keeping an employee is only W. So when the output demand falls, the firm reduces labour usage only to N_2 (not N'_2).

The way Figure 13-14 is drawn, N_2 is less than N'_1. But with sufficiently high hiring, training, and search costs, N_2 may be greater than N'_1. This would mean that none of the employees are laid off as the result of the decline in demand. (But new employees are not employed, because the cost of a new unit of labour is $W+S$.)

If the decline in demand is permanent, then the number of units of labour is eventually reduced to N'_2. As existing employees retire or leave, they are not replaced unless VMP exceeds $W+S$ or unless the quantity of labour falls below N'_2.

13-15 Summary

The firm maximizes profit by increasing its usage of an input to the point where marginal revenue product is equal to marginal factor cost. Under perfect competition in the output market, marginal revenue product is equal to marginal product times output price or the value of the marginal product. And with competition in the input market, marginal factor cost equals input price.

The demand curve for a single variable input is a portion of the value of marginal product curve. The industry input demand curve is less elastic than the sum of the individual firms' input demand curves because it takes into account the change in output price which results from an expansion or contraction of industry output. With two variable inputs, the firm's input demand curve is no longer a portion of the *VMP* curve. This is because, when the price of one input changes, output and the quantity of the other input also change. As the quantity of the other input changes, the *VMP* curve shifts. With two variable inputs, the impact of a change in input price on the quantity demanded by the firm can be broken down into a substitution effect and a scale effect.

The elasticity of demand for an input is higher when: (1) the elasticity of demand for the output is high, (2) other factors can be easily substituted for the input, (3) the supply curves of other inputs are highly elastic, and (4) the cost of the input is a large share of total cost. There are exceptions to rule (4).

The market supply for produced inputs is determined in the same manner as the market supply for a final product. The market supply of labour is the horizontal sum of the individual workers' supply curves. Each worker's supply curve is derived from his or her preferences for leisure and income. The market supply of natural inputs is fixed. The input supply curve facing an industry is at least as elastic as the market supply curve. Under perfect competition, the input supply curve facing the firm is perfectly elastic. Equilibrium input price and employment are determined by the intersection of the market demand for the input and the market supply of the input.

An effective minimum wage law results in unemployment. Part of the unemployment results from a reduction in quantity demanded, while the rest results from an increase in quantity supplied.

When minimum wage laws cover only some employees, the result is a decline in the wage of workers who are not covered.

Higher overtime pay rates generally induce workers to supply additional hours. For workers currently working just the standard number of hours, overtime pay always increases the number of hours supplied.

Workers paid piece rates generally earn more on average than workers in comparable time-rate jobs. Part of the pay differential compensates the employee for bearing the cost of fluctuations in productivity. Also, workers paid piece rates may work harder.

Laws limiting risk exposure in employment may make less risk-averse workers worse off. This is because the extra pay may more than compensate them for the added risk. This argument does not hold, however, if the worker is poorly informed concerning the amount of risk or if there are external effects.

In reality, workers are not generally paid the precise value of their marginal product. This is because marginal product is frequently difficult to measure. Also, workers may prefer smoother earnings over time.

In the presence of search, hiring, and training costs, the firm employs workers only if *VMP* exceeds the wage rate plus the search, hiring, and training costs. But the firm retains existing workers as long as *VMP* exceeds (or equals) the wage rate.

Key Terms

Aggregate demand curve
Complementary inputs*
Derived demand
Elasticity of input demand*
Elasticity of substitution*
Factor markets
Health and Safety at Work etc. Act
Independent inputs*
Industry demand curve
Inferior or regressive input*
Marginal factor cost*
Marginal revenue product*
Market demand for an input
Market supply of an input
Minimum wage
Piece-rate wages*
Quasi-fixed factor
Scale effect*

Substitution effect*
Supply of an input to a firm
Supply of an input to an industry
Time wages*
Value of marginal product*

Questions

1   Explain why the upward-sloping portion of the *VMP* curve is not part of the firm's input demand curve.

2   An increase in the demand for laser discs does not increase the productivity of workers producing laser discs. So why does the demand for labour increase?

3   Using Figure 13-3, explain why the industry demand for a single variable input is more elastic when elasticity of demand for the output is high.

4   If a charitable organization donates shovels and other simple tools to landowners in underdeveloped countries, what is the impact on the demand for labour? On the wage rate? Explain.

5   Explain why trade unions are stronger when the demand for labour is less elastic.

6   Does the imposition of a minimum wage in the presence of search, hiring, and training costs cause more or less unemployment than in the absence of these costs? Why?

7   If a firm in equilibrium employs two variable inputs X and Y, and the marginal product of Y is twice that of X, what do we know about the relative input prices? Why?

8   Suppose a competitive firm's average and marginal product curves for labour are:

$AP = 100 - L$

$MP = 100 - 2L$

If the market price of the product is £5, determine the firm's demand curve for labour in the short run when other inputs are fixed.

9   Is the supply curve of engineers to the computer industry as a whole more or less elastic than the supply curve to IBM? Why?

10   Is the firm demand curve for labour more elastic when capital is variable or when capital is fixed? What does this tell us about the elasticity of demand for an input in the short run versus the long run?

11   Describe the effects on the markets for skilled and unskilled labour if a minimum wage scheme is abolished.

12   It has often been suggested that the impact of unionization on wage levels of organized workers is most noticeable during periods of recession. Why may this be?

13   Ignoring government legislation, why are trade unions less powerful today than they were, say, 20 years ago?

14   During the 1992 election campaign, the UK Labour Party said that, if elected, it would introduce a national minimum wage to help those people who it said earn 'poverty wages'. Imagine that the Labour Party won the election. It wants to introduce a minimum wage, but it is concerned about the cost of the policy and its effect on work effort. The government is considering the following two options:

(i) Pay a wage subsidy to employers who employ such workers at the minimum wage of £3 per hour. (The subsidy equals the difference between the minimum wage and the current wage paid.)

(ii) Pay a cash grant to the worker which gives the worker the same utility as option (i).

With income on the vertical axis and leisure on the horizontal axis, draw the indifference curves and the budget line. What is the economic interpretation of the slope of the budget line? Using this diagram, answer the following questions:

(a) Which of the two options gives the greater incentive to work?

(b) Which of the two options has the lower cost to the government?

15   'Minimum wages benefit most those who would otherwise earn wages below but close to the minimum, and least those whose wages are the lowest.' Critically appraise this statement.

14 Inputs under Imperfect Competition

14-1 Introduction

In the preceding chapter we discussed the pricing of inputs under the assumption of perfect competition in both the product and input markets. The individual firm has no control over the price of its output or the price of its inputs.

In this chapter we relax the assumption of perfect competition in the product market by considering monopoly. We relax the assumption of perfect competition in the factor market by considering *monopsony* (a single buyer of an input). These are the other extremes from perfect competition, and, as we said in Chapter 11, there is a large grey area in between. However, considering these extremes helps us understand the major differences in the pricing of inputs and the determination of input employment.

We shall see later that the effects of minimum wage laws, of trade unions on wages, and so on all depend crucially on whether we assume perfect competition in the product and factor markets. Thus, it should be noted that the discussion of the effects of different government and other policies in the previous chapter needs to be modified if the market organization in the product and/or factor markets is different. This is made clear in Section 14-5 below.

14-2 Input Demand under Monopoly

In Chapter 13 we saw that the firm maximizes profit by increasing its use of input X to the point

where

$$(MRP)_X = (MFC)_X.$$

We also said that $(MRP)_X = \Delta TR/\Delta X = (MP)_X \cdot MR$, and $(MFC)_X = \Delta TC/\Delta X$, holding other inputs constant.

But in the last chapter we assumed that the output market was perfectly competitive, which means that $MR = P_O$ where P_O is output price. $(MRP)_X$ for the competitive firm is thus equal to $(MP)_X \cdot P_O$, or the value of the marginal product of X, which we denote by VMP_X.

In this section we consider the demand for a single variable input by a firm that has a monopoly in the output market. As we know, the monopolist faces a downward-sloping demand curve for its product, so MR is not equal to output price. This, in turn, means that under monopoly $(MRP)_X$ is not equal to $(VMP)_X$. We assume that input markets are competitive so that MFC = input price.

Table 14-1 presents the calculations of MRP for a single variable input: labour. The first two columns summarize the short-run production function, and the third and fourth columns summarize the firm's demand curve for its output. $(MRP)_L = \Delta TR/\Delta L$ where L is the number of workers and TR is total revenue.

From the table we see that at a wage rate of £13 000 the monopolist employs five workers; at a wage

Table 14-1   Computation of marginal revenue product for a monopolist

No. of workers	Output	Price per unit of output (£)	Total revenue from product (£)	Marginal revenue product (£)
0	0		0	
1	300	44.0	13 200	13 200
2	700	42.0	29 400	16 200
3	1200	40.0	48 000	18 600
4	1800	37.5	67 500	19 500
5	2300	35.0	80 500	13 000
6	2700	33.5	90 450	9 950
7	3000	32.0	96 000	5 550
8	3200	31.0	99 200	3 200
9	3300	30.5	100 650	1 450
10	3300	30.5	100 650	0

rate greater than £5550 but less than or equal to £9950 he employs six workers; and so on. How many workers are employed at a wage rate of £16 200? The answer is none. Although $MRP = £16\,200$ with two workers, total revenue is not sufficient to pay them. That is, at this wage rate the firm cannot cover its variable costs, so it shuts down in the short run. (This also applies if the wage rate is £18 600 and £19 500.) So in summary, if the monopolist uses any labour, he employs to the point where $(MRP)_L$ equals the wage rate. And the firm employs labour as long as revenue per worker equals or exceeds the wage rate. Thus, the downward-sloping portion of the MRP curve is the input demand curve.

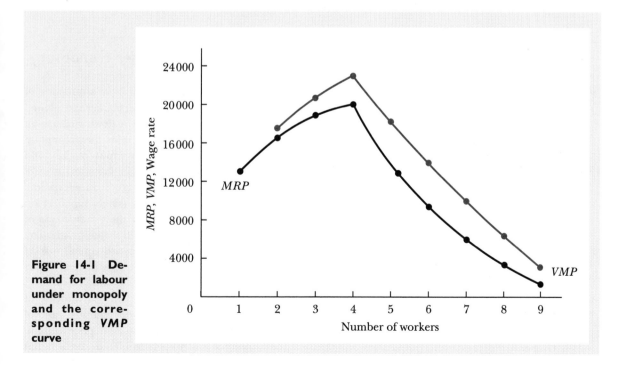

Figure 14-1 Demand for labour under monopoly and the corresponding VMP curve

The *MRP* and *VMP* curves described by the data in Table 14-1 are shown in Figure 14-1.[1] The *MRP* curve lies below the *VMP* curve. This is because $VMP = MP \cdot P_O$ while $MRP = MP \cdot MR$, and the monopolist's marginal revenue is less than product price. From the figure we see that, for a given wage rate, the monopolist employs less labour than a competitive firm. This is an intuitive result because the monopolist produces less output than is produced under competition. So fewer units of the input are used.

14-3 The Monopolist's Input Demand Curve with More Than One Variable Input

In the preceding section we derived the demand curve for a single input, labour, holding the level of other inputs constant. As we did in Section 13-4 of the last chapter, we can consider an example of the case of more than one variable input: labour and capital.

The monopolist employs labour and capital to the point where the marginal revenue product (*MRP*) of each factor is equal to the price of the factor. Thus, in equilibrium we have

$$(MRP)_L = (MP)_L \cdot MR = P_L$$

and

$$(MRP)_K = (MP)_K \cdot MR = P_K.$$

Thus, we get

$$\frac{P_L}{MP_L} = \frac{P_K}{MP_K} = MR$$

or

$$\frac{\text{Price of labour}}{\text{Marginal product of labour}}$$

$$= \frac{\text{price of capital}}{\text{marginal product of capital}} = \text{marginal revenue}.$$

---

[1] For ease of exposition, in all diagrams other than Figure 14-1, the *MRP* and *VMP* curves are drawn as straight lines. This is a special case. It assumes that *MP* is constant and that the demand curve for the product is linear. In the special case of linear *MRP* and *VMP* curves, note that the *MRP* curve is twice as steep as the *VMP* curve because the *MR* curve is twice as steep as the demand curve. (See Figure 6-1 and the proof in fn. 11 of Chapter 6.)

Note that the first equality is the same as in perfect competition. However, the difference is that this ratio is equal to output price under perfect competition but to marginal revenue under monopoly:

$$\frac{P_L}{MP_L} = \frac{P_K}{MP_K} = \begin{cases} P_o \text{ under perfect competition} \\ MR \text{ under monopoly} \end{cases}$$

These relationships do not, however, give us the demand function for labour when the capital input is variable. To get this we have to follow the procedure we used in Figures 13-4 and 13-5 of the last chapter. Since the procedure is exactly the same, we do not repeat the diagrams here. The only change required is that the *VMP* curves are replaced with the *MRP* curves.

One other point worth mentioning concerns the derivation of the industry demand curve. In the case of perfect competition, we argued in Section 13-3 that we cannot get the industry demand curve by simply adding up the individual firms' demand curves. This is because, with a fall in the input price, each firm expands employment, industry employment rises, industry output rises, and hence the product price falls and *VMP* changes. We have, therefore, to take account of this change in output price in deriving the industry demand curve. No such problem arises in the case of monopoly because the monopolist's demand curve for an input is the industry demand curve for that input.

14-4 Input Supply under Monopsony

In the previous sections we relaxed the assumption of perfect competition in the product market and allowed for the case that the firm faces a downward-sloping product demand curve. We now relax the assumption of perfect competition in the input market and consider the case where the firm faces an upward-sloping input supply curve. Just as we considered the extreme case of pure monopoly (single supplier) on the output side, we can consider the extreme case of pure monopsony (single buyer) on the input side. The monopsonist faces the entire upward-sloping market supply curve, and so has to pay a higher price to attract more units of the input.

In our earlier analysis, the *VMP* (in the case of perfect competition) or the *MRP* (in the case of monopoly) was compared with the input price to arrive at the quantity of the input demanded by the firm. But

Table 14-2 Average, total, and marginal factor costs

No. of units of factor	Input price or AFC	Total factor cost TFC	Marginal factor cost MFC
0		0	
1	15	15	15
2	16	32	17
3	17	51	19
4	18	72	21
5	19	95	23
6	20	120	25

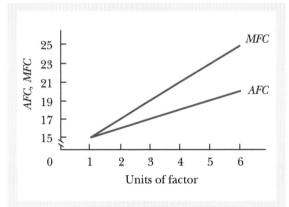

Figure 14-2 Average and marginal factor costs

now that the input price is not constant, the marginal factor cost is not equal to the input price. With an upward-sloping input supply curve, MFC exceeds input price because the firm has to pay a higher price to the extra input *and* the existing inputs. The firm maximizes profit by hiring to the point where $MFC = MRP$. (And, of course, $MRP = VMP$ in a competitive output market.)

Table 14-2 presents the calculation of MFC. The first two columns give the input supply curve. Note that average factor cost AFC is the same as input price. The MFC and AFC from Table 14-2 are illustrated in Figure 14-2.[2] The relationship between AFC and MFC for an input is given by

$$\frac{MFC}{AFC} = 1 + \frac{1}{e_F} \quad \text{or} \quad MFC = P_F \cdot \left(1 + \frac{1}{e_F}\right),$$

where P_F is input price and e_F is the elasticity of input supply.[3] With a competitive input market, the individual firm's e_F is infinite, and hence $MFC = AFC =$ input price. With imperfect factor markets, $0 < e_F < \infty$ and $MFC > AFC$ in most cases. The exception is the backward-bending supply curve of labour, and in this case $MFC < AFC$ because $e_F < 0$.

Earlier, we defined the input demand curve for a firm under perfect competition in the output market as part of the VMP curve and, under monopoly, as part of the MRP curve. When we have monopsony in the input market there is no demand curve for the input. In fact, the concept of an input demand curve is meaningless because the firm is not a price-taker. The firm determines the input price by the quantity that it employs. For a given input supply curve, the MFC curve is determined. The intersection of the MFC curve with the VMP curve (in the case of competition in the output market) or the MRP curve (in the case of monopoly) uniquely determines the quantity of the input employed. The price of the input is then determined from the input supply curve.

This is illustrated for the case of labour in Figure 14-3. SS is the input supply curve, MFC is the marginal factor cost curve, and VMP is the value of the marginal product of labour (assuming the output market is competitive). In Figure 14-3 the employment Q is determined by the intersection of the VMP and MFC curves. Once Q is determined, the wage rate W_m is obtained from the SS curve as the wage rate corresponding to employment Q. Note that, under perfect competition in the labour market, the wage rate W_c is equal to VMP; under monopsony, the wage rate is below the VMP. Robinson called this wage

[2] Note that the MFC curve is twice as steep as the AFC (supply) curve. Mathematically, we can show this as follows. The equation for the AFC curve may be written as $W = a + bL$ where W is the wage rate, L is the quantity of labour, and a and b are parameters to be estimated. Total factor cost $(TFC) = WL = aL + bL^2$. $MFC = d(TFC)/dL = a + 2bL$. Thus, the slope of the AFC curve is b and the slope of the MFC curve is $2b = 2 \cdot$ (slope of the AFC curve).

[3] Consider, for example, labour.

$TFC = W \cdot L$
$\Delta TFC = W \cdot \Delta L + L \cdot \Delta W / \Delta L$
$MFC = \Delta TFC / \Delta L = W + L \cdot \Delta W / \Delta L$
$\quad = W(1 + L/W \cdot \Delta W / \Delta L) = W(1 + 1/e_L).$
Since $W = AFC$, we have $MFC/AFC = 1 + 1/e_L$.

Table 14-3 Summary of results on demand for labour

Labour market	Product market	
	Perfect competition	Monopoly
Perfect competition	VMP curve is the demand curve for labour. W = VMP gives the level of employment.	MRP curve is the demand curve for labour. W = MRP gives the level of employment. Since MRP < VMP, we have W < VMP.
Monopsony	MFC = VMP gives the level of employment, and the corresponding point on the supply curve gives the wage rate. The demand curve is a single point. W < MFC.	MFC = MRP gives the level of employment and the corresponding point on the supply curve gives the wage rate. The demand curve is a single point. W < MFC, MFC = MRP, MRP < VMP.

difference the *monopsonistic exploitation of labour*.[4] We see in the next section how labour, by forming a trade union, can counter this monopsonistic exploitation.

We summarize the results on the demand for an input, such as labour, in Table 14-3. The results for monopsony in Table 14-3 are for a non-discriminating monopsonist. We now consider the case of wage discrimination by a monopsonist. Wage discrimination under monopsony is similar to the practice of price discrimination under monopoly (which we discussed in Chapter 9).

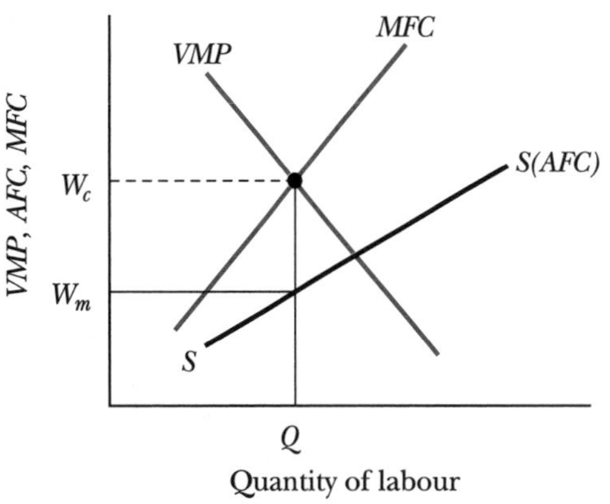

Suppose there are two labour markets with different supply elasticities, e_1 (for males) and e_2 (for females). The monopsonist equates marginal factor costs in both markets. This equality is clearly necessary for profit maximization. For, if *MFC* is lower in market 1 than in market 2, the monopsonist reduces his costs by increasing employment in market 1 and reducing employment in market 2. And, of course, if *MFC* is lower in market 2, then the opposite adjustment reduces costs. Hence we have

$$MFC_1 = MFC_2$$

or

$$W_1\left(1 + \frac{1}{e_1}\right) = W_2\left(1 + \frac{1}{e_2}\right).$$

If $e_1 < e_2$, we have

$$1 + \frac{1}{e_1} < 1 + \frac{1}{e_2}.$$

Hence, $W_1 > W_2$. That is, the monopsonist pays a higher wage rate in the market with the higher elasticity of supply.

In our discussion in Chapter 9 on monopoly, we also mentioned the case of perfect discrimination, where monopolists charge a different price to every customer; the monopolist charges customers their *reservation price*. Similarly, we can talk of perfect discrimination by a monopsonist. In this case the monopsonist pays workers their *reservation wage*.

The reservation wage for a worker is the minimum wage at which the worker is willing to work. Thus, the

Figure 14-3 Employment under monopsony

For monopoly, read *MRP* for *VMP*

[4] See J. Robinson, *The Economics of Imperfect Competition*, Macmillan, London, 1933.

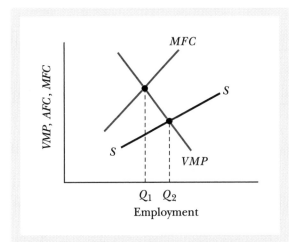

Figure 14-4   Increase in employment due to perfect discrimination by the monopsonist

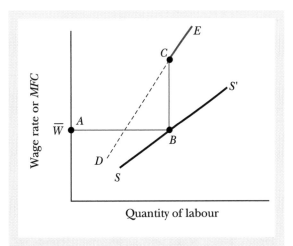

Figure 14-5   Effect of minimum wage law on the MFC curve

reservation wage for the first worker in Table 14-2 is £15, for the second worker it is £16, and so on. The monopsonist who is practising perfect discrimination pays the first worker £15, the second worker £16, and so on. In this case, the MFC curve is the supply curve of labour. And total employment is higher, since it is now given by the intersection of the VMP curve and the SS curve. This is shown in Figure 14-4. Employment increases from Q_1 to Q_2 if the monopsonist practises perfect discrimination.

14-5 Monopsony, Minimum Wage Laws, and Trade Unions

In Chapter 13 we argued that if the labour market is perfectly competitive a minimum wage law produces unemployment. However, under monopsony a minimum wage law can increase the wages of workers without any reduction in employment and can sometimes even increase employment.

To analyse the effects of minimum wages under monopsony, we have first to study the effect on the MFC curve, because it is the intersection of this curve with the VMP (or MRP) curve that determines employment. This effect is shown in Figure 14-5. Initially, the input supply curve is SS', and the MFC curve is DE. We now impose a minimum wage $\overline{W}$. Since no labour is supplied below $\overline{W}$, the supply curve of

labour is now ABS'. Since the wage rate is constant over the range AB, we have MFC equal to the wage rate over this range. After point B, the MFC is as it was before. Hence, the MFC curve is ABCE with the imposition of a minimum wage.

The important thing to note is that, with a minimum wage, the MFC curve is horizontal until it meets the supply curve; then it turns vertically up and joins the original MFC curve. Since employment is determined by the intersection of the MFC curve with the VMP curve, and wages are determined from the supply curve, all wage and employment combinations possible are bounded by the VMP and supply curves. This is shown in Figure 14-6. The wage and employment combinations possible are shown as the thick coloured lines. To demonstrate that minimum wages can increase employment, we consider setting the minimum wage $\overline{W}$ at a level higher than W_1, where W_1 is the wage prevailing under monopsony. This is shown in Figure 14-7. Initially, employment is Q_1 and the wage rate W_1. With the minimum wage fixed at $\overline{W}$, the MFC curve is ABCD. Taking the point of intersection of the MFC curve with the VMP curve, we see that employment rises to Q_2. The wage rate is $\overline{W}$, as given from the supply curve ABS'.

We now analyse the effects of different levels of the minimum wage $\overline{W}$. To do this we start with the initial position of wage and employment under monopsony and consider the extent of monopsonistic

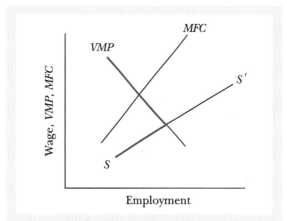

Figure 14-6 Wage and employment combinations produced by minimum wage laws (shown as thick lines)

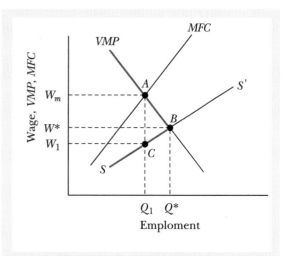

Figure 14-8 Increases in wages and employment with a minimum wage

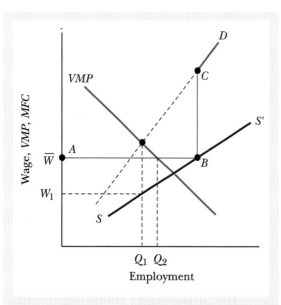

Figure 14-7 Effect of minimum wage law on employment

exploitation. This is shown in Figure 14-8 by the thick lines from Figure 14-6. Without minimum wage laws, Q_1 is employment and W_1 is the wage rate. The value of marginal product of labour at this level of employment is W_m. The degree of monopsonistic exploitation is $W_m - W_1$. If we fix the minimum wage at W_m, then

employment remains unchanged and the wage rate is W_m. Thus, with a minimum wage at W_m, all monopsonistic exploitation is removed.

The maximum employment that we can achieve by minimum wages is Q^*, the intersection of the VMP curve with the supply curve. This employment is achieved by setting the minimum wage at W^*. However, setting minimum wages anywhere between W_1 and W_m increases employment and wages above what would otherwise have prevailed under monopsony. Setting a minimum wage above W_m increases wages but reduces employment below Q_1. And, of course, setting a minimum wage below W_1 has no effect.

The elimination of monopsonistic exploitation of labour can be achieved without minimum wage laws. It can be achieved by trade union organization of labour. The wage that the trade union wants to negotiate depends on its objectives:

1 If the trade union wants maximum wages, with the current level of employment unchanged, it negotiates the wage rate at W_m in Figure 14-8.
2 If the trade union wants maximum employment, it negotiates the wage rate at W^* in Figure 14-8.
3 Intermediate levels between W^* and W_m correspond to various combinations of the objectives of raising wages and increasing employment. Note that, although negotiating wages in the range W_1 to W^*

raises employment and wages, the same increases in employment are achieved at a higher wage in the range W^* to W_m. Thus, the union is better off on the segment AB rather than on BC in Figure 14-8.

In summary, economic theory suggests that the effect of minimum wage laws in labour markets that are competitive is to reduce employment or increase unemployment. If labour markets are characterized by monopsony, the effect may be to increase employment. In the previous chapter we considered some of the empirical evidence available. Research into the effects of minimum wages in the UK and France suggests that minimum wages do not have significant adverse effects on employment. In the United States findings are mixed, although there is strong evidence that minimum wages increase unemployment for teenagers. But this may simply indicate that the segment of the labour market affected by minimum wage laws in the United States is competitive. Monopsony elements are likely to exist in the labour market, but at the higher end of the skill levels of the labour force, and workers at these levels are not affected by minimum wage laws.

14-6 Labour Exploitation under Monopoly and Monopsony

In the previous section we discussed how minimum wage laws or trade union bargaining can eliminate the 'exploitation' of labour by a monopsonist and how the wage rate can be brought into equality with the value of marginal product, *VMP*.

If the product market is characterized by monopoly, however, then instead of *VMP* we have to consider *MRP*, and we saw earlier that $MRP < VMP$. Thus, there is an additional exploitation of labour that cannot be eliminated by minimum wage laws.

Employment under monopoly and monopsony is illustrated in Figure 14-9. The intersection of the *MRP* curve with the *MFC* curve gives Q as employment, and from the supply curve we get W_1 as the wage rate. The value of *MRP* for this level of employment is W_2, and the value of *VMP* for this level of employment is W_3. Thus, we can break down labour exploitation as follows:

$W_2 - W_1$ = monopsonistic exploitation
$W_3 - W_2$ = monopolistic exploitation
$W_3 - W_1$ = total exploitation

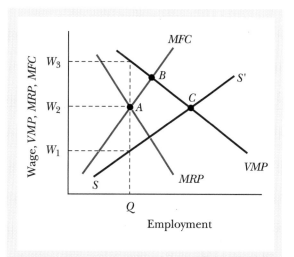

Figure 14-9 Exploitation produced by monopoly and monopsony

We saw earlier that $W_2 - W_1$ can be eliminated by minimum wage laws or trade union bargaining. But $W_3 - W_2$ cannot be eliminated by minimum wage laws. Raising the minimum wage to any point between W_2 and W_3 merely reduces employment, because the monopolist equates *MRP* to the wage rate in order to determine the number of workers to employ. How much of $W_3 - W_2$ can be eliminated depends on the bargaining strengths of the monopolist–monopsonist and the trade union. This is a case of *bilateral monopoly*, and, as we said in Chapter 9, there is no determinate solution to this problem.

Without a trade union or minimum wage laws, the monopolist equates *MRP* to *MFC* in Figure 14-9. She employs Q number of workers and pays a wage rate W_1. With a minimum wage set at W_2, employment remains at the same level Q. If the trade union is strong, it can force the monopolist to forgo monopoly profits and move the equilibrium to point *B*, where both employment and the wage rate rise relative to point *A*. At point *B* there is no monopoly exploitation and $VMP = MFC$. The ideal competitive solution is, of course, given by point *C*, but this point can be reached only in the following two cases:

1 If the trade union only negotiates increases in employment and lets the wage rate be given by the points on the supply curve SS', point *C* can be attained.

2 If the trade union negotiates increases in employment and also insists on the wage rate being determined by the points on the *MFC* curve, point *C* can be attained through perfect price discrimination by the monopsonist as illustrated earlier in Figure 14-4. Thus, what happens to wages and employment depends on the respective powers of the monopolist and trade union and on whether the union negotiates only increases in employment, or both increases in employment and increases in wages.

14-7 Application 1: Monopsony and Minimum Wages in the UK

The essential feature of pure monopsony is that there is only one firm that is the buyer of an input in a particular market. A typical example of pure monopsony is a town where employment is dominated by one large employer. But this is increasingly rare, since transport improvements have made it easier for workers to choose employment away from the town. A less extreme example is that of a firm that is a large employer, relative to the input market, and hence faces an upward-sloping input supply curve. An often quoted example of this is a town where there is only one hospital providing employment for nurses. In the UK context, Corby is an example of a town where employment was concentrated in one industry (steel). Despite these examples, there is an increasing feeling among economists that the traditional idea of monopsony is largely irrelevant for analysing modern labour markets.

Discontent with the traditional theory has led to new developments which make the model more relevant to a modern economy. In the modern approach the distinctive feature of the monopsony model remains—a positively sloped supply-of-labour curve. This occurs not because there is only one employer, but because employers paying higher wages experience less chance of their workers leaving (since these workers are less likely to find higher wages elsewhere) and find it easier to recruit new people. Underlying the modern approach is an assumption that workers are not fully informed about job opportunities. This means that firms paying wages below the market rate do not immediately lose their workforce, and it makes the model more applicable to labour markets dominated by small firms, where

information about jobs is harder to find than in markets controlled by a few large firms. Although the modern approach predicts a positive relationship between wages and labour supply, and that workers are paid below their marginal product, it does not say that minimum wages necessarily raise employment.

Further discussion of the theoretical arguments are beyond the scope of this book.[5] Instead, we examine the applicability of the model by considering evidence on the role of minimum wages in the UK Wages Councils (which we discussed briefly in Chapter 13).

Machin and Manning present evidence of the employment effects of the Wages Councils for the covered sectors during the 1980s.[6] Because economic theory predicts that employment may rise or fall as a result of minimum wages (as we have seen), Machin and Manning adopt an approach that can predict both increases and decreases in employment. Prior to the abolition of the Wages Councils in 1993, 2.5 million workers were covered by a minimum wage (about 6 per cent of the workforce). The largest sectors covered were catering, retailing, and clothing. From 1986, the Wages Councils were restricted to setting a single minimum wage for all types of workers over the age of 21. The government abolished the Wages Councils because, in its view, they had an adverse effect on employment.

As part of their study, Machin and Manning adopt a 'toughness' measure to describe the bite of the Wages Councils over the study period. They measure toughness by expressing the minimum wage as a proportion of average earnings: as the minimum wage rises, the measure of toughness increases. Their work shows that during the 1980s the bite of the Councils was reduced, largely as a result of the government's animosity towards the system. It is likely that this contributed to the observed increase in income inequality in the covered sectors.

Machin and Manning do not attempt to explain why employment is large in industries covered by some Wages Councils and small in others, but instead look at the link between changes in employment and changes

---

[5] For further discussion of the theory, see S. Machin and A. Manning, 'Minimum Wages, Wage Dispersion and Employment: Evidence From the UK Wages Councils', Discussion Papers in Economics, No. 92-05. University College London, 1992.
[6] Ibid.

in the toughness of the legislation. If a positive correlation is found, this supports the monopsony model. (The competitive model predicts a negative relationship.) The results do show a positive relationship between employment change and change in toughness. Machin and Manning also carried out tests to see if the employment effects differed across Wages Councils. A positive association between change in toughness and change in employment was found in clothing, retail, and catering; in hairdressing it was negative.

The results of this work suggest that the Wages Councils did not adversely affect employment in the 1980s (as the government suggested). In fact, it appears that they had a beneficial effect, especially in the catering sector. Given these results, the abolition of the Councils is likely to damage employment prospects and increase wage inequality.

14-8 Application 2: Discrimination in Employment

Question 7.

In all of the developed industrial countries, average female earnings are below those of males. The inequality in earnings is less marked in some countries, such as Sweden, where average female earnings in the late 1980s were about 90 per cent of average male earnings. In the UK the figure was about 70 per cent. The earnings differential tends to be larger in production occupations. For instance, according to UK figures for 1991, the gap between average male and female earnings was most marked for craft workers and plant and machine operatives (female earnings were 58 and 65 per cent of male, respectively) and least marked in clerical and secretarial jobs and in professional occupations (female earnings were 83 and 79 per cent of male, respectively).[7]

In all countries, the earnings gap has narrowed in the last 20 years. In the UK, although the relative pay of females has improved since the introduction of the 1970 Equal Pay Act and the Sex Discrimination (Equal Opportunities) Act in 1975, female earnings still lag behind male earnings. According to the Institute for Fiscal Studies, in the early 1990s the average hourly wage for males was £6.81, while for females it was £4.92. There is debate as to the effect of the anti-discrimination legislation on relative earnings, but it has been estimated that it improved the relative earnings of females by 19 per cent.[8] All workers in Europe are also covered by European Union directives on equal pay. The Treaty of Rome talks of 'equal pay for work of equal value', and this principle was confirmed in the Equal Pay Directive in 1975.

Not only are there differences in earnings by sex, but research in the UK and the USA suggests that there are also differences by race. McCormick's study of the relative earnings of white, West Indian, and Asian males in Birmingham suggests that in 1983 the average earnings of white workers were 12.6 per cent higher than Asian workers, who in turn earned 5.2 per cent more than West Indian workers.[9] In the United States the data suggest that the relative earnings of black workers has improved in recent years. In 1965 the median salary income for full-time black males was 64 per cent of the median salary for full-time white males; in the same year the median salary for black females was 71 per cent of the median salary for white females. By the early 1980s these figure were 73 and 93 per cent, respectively.

Given such figures, we may wish to conclude that discrimination is present. However, one must be careful not simply to attribute the entire salary disparity to discrimination, without more information. An operational definition of discrimination is 'the valuation in the labour market of personal characteristics of the worker that are unrelated to productivity'.[10] To isolate the impact of discrimination, we must first take account of many intervening factors such as education, job stability, job experience, and so on which might affect productivity and, hence, explain part of the salary disparity.

Many studies have tried to estimate how much of the difference in earnings is due to discrimination. In

---

[7] See S. W. Polachek and W. S. Siebert, *The Economics of Earnings*, Cambridge University Press, 1993, p. 139.

[8] A. Zabalza and P. Tzannatos, 'The Effects of Britain's Anti-Discriminatory Legislation on Relative Pay and Employment', *Economic Journal*, 95 (1985): 679–99.

[9] B. McCormick, 'Evidence about the Comparative Earnings of Asian and West Indian Workers in Britain', *Scottish Journal of Political Economy*, 33 (1986): 97–110.

[10] K. J. Arrow, 'The Theory of Discrimination', in O. Ashenfelter and A. Rees (eds.), *Discrimination in Labor Markets*, Princeton University Press, Princeton, NJ, 1973.

order to do this, most researchers adopt a variant of the *human capital theory* of earnings.[11] The essential idea behind human capital theory is an assumption that individuals make decisions to acquire personal characteristics which give them benefits in the future. The investments people make are assumed to be in education or job training. The benefits from acquiring human capital may be seen in terms of increased future income. In empirical studies of discrimination, we find differences in average earnings between the sexes/races explained by a number of human capital and productivity-enhancing measures such as years of schooling, educational attainment (in terms of qualifications), and years of work experience (whether full- or part-time). Allowing for these sort of factors, Wright and Ermisch, in a UK study of gender discrimination, produced results that suggest that about 80 per cent of the difference in the average earnings of males and females can be explained by the observed measurable characteristics.[12] This leaves 20 per cent of the disparity due to discrimination. Estimates of average earnings differences by race in the UK suggest that the amount due to discrimination was around 12 per cent in the early 1980s.[13]

However, there is circular reasoning involved. The factors mentioned here are true, but a question arises as to why women and minority groups tend to undertake less human capital investment. Socioeconomic and cultural factors may help to explain this behaviour, but of equal importance appears to be the role of expectations. Research in the USA suggests that differences in the amount of human capital investment can be explained in terms of the length of time women expect to be in the labour market and the degree to which minority groups expect to experience discrimination. In contrast to the USA, it has been found in the UK that years of schooling are greater for minority groups than for white males. This has prompted researchers to focus more on educational quality in explaining earnings differences.

Several theories concerning the sources of discrimination are based on (1) personal prejudice, (2) signalling, and (3) monopsony. The *personal prejudice* theory says that some employers are prejudiced against some particular groups, and hence underestimate their marginal product.[14] However, if a firm underestimates the marginal product of a certain class of labour, it employs less of this labour, and thus makes less profit, compared with a non-discriminating firm. Thus, the discriminating firm is at a competitive disadvantage, and we should find firms that practise discrimination going out of business. We should also find discrimination declining over time. However, we do not find much evidence of either of these things happening. This leads us to suspect that there must be substantial monopolistic and oligopolistic sectors in the economy, since it is firms in these sectors that can afford to discriminate.

It should be noted that discrimination arising from prejudice need not be confined to employers alone. It can be on the employees' side (some groups wanting to work only in segregated environments) or the consumers' side (some groups wanting to be served only by members of a certain group). Again, catering to these prejudices is inconsistent with profit maximization and can be done only under imperfectly competitive environments.

Signalling theory says that race and sex are used as 'signals' about the productivity of workers.[15] The employer cannot estimate correctly the marginal product of each potential employee, so she uses some screening method for selecting employees with higher productivity. The theory says that race and sex are used as screening devices if previous experience indicates that productivity is correlated with these characteristics; the use of race or sex as a screening device may look like prejudice, but really it is not. In essence, the employer is assigning some average group characteristics to each member of the group. If the employer finds that workers living in the north are more productive than those living in the south, then she may use residential location as a screening device. This is not considered prejudice.

This method of screening on the basis of group differences becomes very costly to firms if members in

[11] For a discussion of human capital theory, see R. F. Elliott, *Labor Economics: A Comparative Text*, McGraw-Hill, London, 1991, Ch. 6.
[12] R. E. Wright and J. F. Ermisch, 'Gender Discrimination in the British Labour Market: A Reassessment', *Economic Journal*, 101 (1991): 508–21.
[13] McCormick, op. cit.

[14] See G. S. Becker, *The Economics of Discrimination* (2nd edn.), University of Chicago Press, 1971.
[15] The signalling theory has been developed in A. M. Spence, 'Job Market Signalling', *Quarterly Journal of Economics*, 87 (1973): 355–74. We discuss the idea of signalling in some detail in Chapter 18.

a group are very dissimilar and the signals therefore are not very reliable. Also, the firm must reduce its use of a signal over time if there are structural changes in the characteristics of the groups. For example, if more women want regular employment, employers discriminating against women because they have traditionally spent less time in the labour market may make a costly error. After a while, employers, noting the structural change, will stop using sex as a screening device.

Finally, *monopsony* elements can be responsible for wage discrimination. In Section 14-4 we discussed how, under monopsony, there can be different wages paid to different groups based on their supply elasticities. Here is a case of discrimination that arises from the profit motive, not prejudice—it is profitable for the discriminators. The monopsonist might be able to segment the market into non-competing groups based on sex or race. Then it is profitable to practise discrimination.

Example 14-1 Employment Discrimination in Government

Through the Equal Employment Opportunity Commission in the United States the government is in charge of enforcing anti-discriminatory laws in civilian employment. However, many studies have found that the earnings of minority groups and women employed by the government are substantially lower than the earnings of 'similar' white males.[16]

Although discrimination is present in several government departments, there is considerable variation in the relative wages (relative to white males) of blacks and women employed by the different departments. Borjas tries to explain these differences through a political approach to government behaviour (that is, by assuming that the government's objective is to maximize its political support).[17] He finds that the relative wage of black males is higher in departments with heavy black constituencies and in departments

that make expenditures in enforcing positive action programmes in the private sector. Similarly, the relative wage of women in government departments also depends on the sexual composition of the constituency and on the department's output. He argues that these findings suggest that the characteristics of a firm and the markets it serves might offer clues to the sources of employment discrimination in the private sector as well.

14-9 Application 3: The Economics of Professional Sport

The most often quoted example of monopsony is in professional sport. This has been studied most frequently in US football, baseball, basketball, and ice hockey, but the arguments apply to all professional sporting leagues. The players are much less valuable in any employment other than in one particular sport. Sporting leagues have a virtual monopoly for that sport, and the individual teams operate like a cartel.

One of the most prominent features of labour markets in professional team sport is the controls to restrict competition for players. All leagues operate reserve rules so that players may represent only the club that holds their registration. A reserve rule system enables clubs unilaterally to renew players' registrations whether or not they are still under contract. That is, players may leave only with the consent of their current employer. Reserve rules first appeared in North American baseball in 1879, and by 1887 the 'reserve clause' had been inserted in all players' contracts. Clubs could annually renew the contracts of all players under contract to them. The reserve clause was changed in 1976, with players having the option of becoming 'free agents' once they had completed six years in the major league. A reserve rule system has also operated in English league football. By 1891 the 'retain and transfer' system was in place and this allowed clubs to renew players' contracts for an option period (normally one year) on top of the initial one-year contract. This meant that some players were tied to a club for life. The system was changed in 1978, mainly because of pressure from the Professional Footballers' Association (the footballers' trade union), enabling players to become free agents at the end of their contract period.

Another labour market restriction is 'the draft'. This is common in US sport and is a means by which

---

[16] The most exhaustive study is S. P. Smith, *Equal Pay in the Public Sector: Fact or Fantasy*, Princeton University Industrial Relations Section, Princeton, NJ, 1977. See also G. J. Borjas, 'Discrimination in HEW: Is the Doctor Sick or Are the Patients Healthy?' *Journal of Law and Economics*, 21 (1978): 97–110.

[17] G. J. Borjas, 'The Politics of Employment Discrimination in the Federal Bureaucracy', *Journal of Law and Economics*, 25 (1982): 271–98.

competition for new talent is restricted. This has increased the monopsony power of the major sporting leagues. It works in the following way. At the end of the official season, all teams are ranked on the basis of their won–lost record. The worst team in each league is given the first choice of players entering the profession; the next poorest team has the second choice, the third poorest has the third choice, and so on. No team can bargain with a player who has been drafted by another team. However, the reserve clause after 1976 permits a team to acquire the services of another team's player by purchasing the player's contract from the current owner. This switch does not increase the pay of the player, but the team that originally signed the player may sell the contract at a profit.

In essence, when players have signed with a team, they have sold the rights to their playing skills. For instance, in US football, if a player has signed for $40 000 with the LA Raiders and the Chicago Bears want to buy the player for $45 000, the player will receive the same salary as before but the LA Raiders get $5000. However, if the value of the marginal product of this player is more than $45 000 for the LA Raiders, then the team owners would not want to sell the contract to the Chicago Bears even at a profit of $5000. Note that (as shown in Figure 14-3), under monopsony, the wage rate paid to the players is below the value of the marginal product of each player, and so there is considerable leeway for the bargaining of contracts. One can thus talk of the 'exploitation' of players by the team owners.[18]

As we explained in Section 14-5, the gap between the player's wage and the value of the player's marginal product can be closed or reduced if the players form a trade union and use collective bargaining. However, in this case the correct analysis is the one in Section 14-6, because the teams have a monopoly over the sale of tickets and other rights for the sport. Thus, the situation is one of monopoly and monopsony.

In Section 14-6 we explained the nature of solutions that are feasible, depending on the power of the trade union and whether the union is interested in higher wages or higher employment. In the case of professional sport, if the existing players are members

<hr/>

[18] See G. W. Scully, 'Pay and Performance in Major League Baseball', *American Economic Review*, 64 (1974): 915–30. Scully estimates that in some cases the players were paid less than one-fifth of the value of their marginal product.

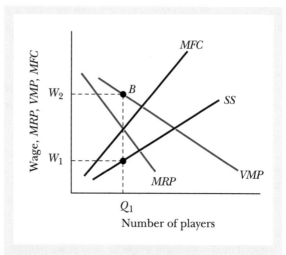

Figure 14-10 Collective bargaining in professional sport

of a trade union (such as the Professional Footballers' Association in English football), they are interested in getting a higher wage. Thus, the optimum point from the union's point of view is point B in Figure 14-10, with employment at Q_1 and the wage rate at W_2. Without any bargaining, equilibrium employment is Q_1 and the wage rate is W_1.

Now we consider the effect of the formation of a new league. In this case, the new league competes with the original league for players. Something like this has happened in English football with Premiership clubs competing for players with clubs in the Football League. It has also happened in a number of US sports, with the formation of the American Football League, the World Football League, the USFL (which went out of existence quickly), the American Basketball Association, and the World Hockey League. With a new league, the supply curve facing each league is more elastic, and the original league is no longer a pure monopsonist. The effect is a rise in employment and wages and not as much monopsonistic exploitation (which is given by the distance between the supply curve and the *MFC* curve).

This is shown in Figure 14-11. With the formation of a new league, the existing league faces the flatter supply curve S_2 with the corresponding marginal factor cost given by MFC_2. The original supply curve is S_1, and the original marginal factor cost curve is MFC_1. The initial equilibrium gives quantity Q_1 with a wage

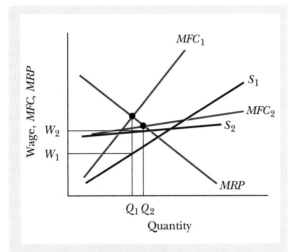

Figure 14-11   Effects of the formation of a new league on the wages of players

rate W_1; with the formation of the new league, the quantity increases to Q_2 and the wage to W_2. There is also less monopsonistic exploitation. However, the monopolistic exploitation still persists (given by the difference between MRP and VMP). This can be reduced by collective bargaining (or strikes).[19]

14-10   Application 4: The NCAA Cartel in College Sport

Until now we have discussed professional sport. The case of college sport in the United States is another, although less obvious, case of monopsony. The National Collegiate Athletic Association (NCAA) establishes athletic standards and official playing rules for college sports. It regulates the number of student athletes that universities can recruit, it controls the televising of college football games, it fixes the prices of sporting events, and it sets the 'wages' of student

athletes.[20] The NCAA strictly enforces its regulations by imposing penalties and sanctions for all violations of its rules.

The NCAA was founded in 1906. Its membership has grown from 13 schools to over 700 colleges and universities. The NCAA regulates the earnings of college athletes so that the richest universities cannot necessarily recruit the most promising athletes. The wages (scholarships) paid to some of the top college athletes are a long way below their marginal revenue product,[21] and it is not unusual for some universities to cheat on the NCAA rules by giving some athletes outside payments and gifts or employing their close relatives. However, if these violations of the NCAA rules are detected, the NCAA imposes stiff penalties in the form of reducing a college's number of athletic scholarships, preventing the college or university from appearing in Rose Bowl football games (the college equivalent of the Superbowl), preventing television broadcasting of the college's games (as happened with US football at the University of Florida in 1984), and so on.

Colleges and universities, however, do not protest against the penalties imposed by the NCAA and do not quit the cartel. Presumably, the cost of maintaining their athletic programmes would increase greatly if free competition were to be substituted.[22]

As for the college athletes, they are willing to accept lower wages while going to college because the colleges provide them with the necessary on-the-job training. Many of them are interested in maximizing their lifetime earnings rather than their approximate earnings while in education, although some athletes do turn professional before leaving college. The universities bear the cost of training prospective professional

---

[19] In the USA there were strikes by members of the Baseball Players' Association in 1981 and by those of the Football Players' Association in 1982 and 1987. In 1992 members of the Professional Footballers' Association in England and Wales voted for a strike over the amount of money paid to league clubs following the deal between television and the new Premier League (now Premiership). In the end, the players did not strike.

[20] The 'wages' are tuition, room, board, books, and some 'laundry money'. However, since tuition, room, and board are not the same at all universities, there is a permissible range of price competition in the market.
[21] The value of an athletic scholarship typically ranges from $5000 to $20 000. It has been estimated that the annual marginal revenue product of top college footballers is at least $500 000 and may be as high as $646 150. Over a four-year college career, a top player could therefore generate over $2 million in revenue for his college team. See R. W. Brown, 'An Estimate of the Rent Generated by a Premium College Football Player', *Economic Inquiry*, 31 (1993): 671–84.
[22] If competition were to be substituted, universities might have to sign student athletes on long-term contracts, and then professional leagues would have to purchase the contract of the student athlete from the university.

athletes and receive revenue in the form of gate receipts and donations.

Although the NCAA operates like a cartel, there are some essential elements of its structure that are potential sources of trouble; in fact, many of the characteristics of market structure that are most often associated with successful cartels are absent in the case of the NCAA (and many other sporting leagues).[23] Some of these characteristics are:

1 *The number of firms* A successful cartel does not have a large number of firms. The NCAA has around 700 members, and it is impossible to monitor all the actions of its members.

2 *Restrictions on entry* Successful cartels have restrictions on entry that the NCAA does not have. Any college or university that states that it will abide by the rules of the NCAA can join.

3 *Publication of violations* A cartel likes to be informed of all the violations by the members but does not like them to be known to the public. A cartel cannot function if its defects are discussed in public. The NCAA violations are publicized in the press and on television when they are known.

4 *Differences in costs and profits* A cartel's member firms cannot have wide discrepancies in costs because they all have the same pricing structure. The members of the NCAA, however, differ widely in the costs of their athletic programmes and their size. Some large universities have multi-million-dollar programmes; others have very small programmes. This problem is partly solved by having separate divisions of the NCAA.

In spite of all these differences, the NCAA does function like a cartel in collegiate sports. The colleges and universities are willing to stay within the NCAA, in spite of stiff regulations, for the reasons mentioned earlier.

14-11 Summary

For a monopolist, $MRP < VMP$, and the monopolist's input demand curve is a portion of the MRP curve. The monopolist's demand curve for an input thus lies below the corresponding VMP curve. When several inputs are variable, the monopolist maximizes profit where the

input price–marginal product ratio is the same for all inputs and is equal to marginal revenue.

A pure monopsonist faces an upward-sloping market supply curve of an input. This means that marginal factor cost exceeds input price. The monopsonist who is a competitor in the output market employs to the point where $VMP = MFC$. The monopsonist who is a monopolist in the output market employs to the point where $MRP = MFC$. In both cases, input price is determined by the corresponding point on the input supply curve. For the perfectly discriminating monopsonist, the MFC curve is the input supply curve, and employment is the same as for a competitive input market. For a monopsonist discriminating between several markets, the highest wage rate is paid in the market with the highest elasticity of input supply.

Under monopsony, a minimum wage law can increase the wage rate without reducing employment. In fact, employment may actually rise. This is because the minimum wage law flattens a portion of the MFC curve, so that MFC equals the wage rate over some region of employment.

When monopoly in the output market and monopsony in the input market are both present, employment occurs where $MRP = MFC$, and the wage rate is determined by the corresponding point on the labour supply curve. The difference between MFC and the wage rate is the monopsonistic exploitation of labour. The difference between VMP and MRP is the monopolistic exploitation. The monopolistic exploitation cannot be eliminated by minimum wage laws.

Monopsony theory has been extended to make it more relevant to modern labour markets. The theory suggests that employment may rise or fall with a minimum wage law. Evidence for the UK suggests that minimum wages have had a beneficial effect on employment. This supports the idea of monopsonistic elements in labour markets.

Discrimination in employment may be the result of prejudice, signalling, or monopsony power. We expect competitive forces to reduce discrimination, so that it is more likely to occur in monopolistic or oligopolistic sectors.

A prominent example of monopsony is in professional sport. If players are members of a trade union, wages can be increased. Also, the formation of new leagues tends to increase both players' wages and employment and to decrease monopsonistic exploita-

---

[23] See J. V. Koch, 'A Troubled Cartel: The NCAA', *Law and Contemporary Problems*, 38 (1973): 135–50.

tion of players. A less obvious example of monopsony is the NCAA in the United States. The member-colleges and universities function as a cartel.

Key Terms

Discrimination*
Human capital*
Marginal factor cost*
Marginal revenue product*
Monopolistic exploitation of labour*
Monopsonistic exploitation of labour*
Monopsony*
Reservation wage*
Signalling*

Questions

1 How can a firm be a monopolist in the output market and face a perfectly elastic input supply curve? Can you give an example of this?

2 Using the data in Table 14-1, demonstrate that $(MRP)_L$ is also equal to $MR \cdot (MP)_L$. Explain the logic of this relationship.

3 If there are two employers of an input, how does the elasticity of each one's input supply curve compare with that of the market input supply curve? Why?

4 Graphically demonstrate that the wage bill for a perfectly discriminating monopsonist is lower than for a non-discriminating monopsonist using the same quantity of labour.

5 Explain why trade unions support the 'Buy British' campaign. What is the impact on the wage rate and employment? Does it matter whether the labour market is competitive?

6 If labour is the only variable input, explain why a monopolist producing where $MR = MC$ must employ labour to the point where $W/(MP)_L$ equals marginal revenue.

7 Graphically illustrate the case where a minimum wage law reduces employment under monopsony.

8 Explain how the regulation of output price in a monopolistic industry reduces the exploitation of labour. How are the relevant curves affected?

9 Do you believe that male–female earnings disparities are due to monopsonistic profit maximization? Under this theory, which group do you expect to be paid more? Why?

10 In Application 3 (Section 14-9) we analysed the impact of a new sporting league on players' wages and employment. Explain how the analysis changes if the presence of a new league reduces demand for tickets, television rights, and so on for the original league.

15 Wages, Rent, Interest, and Profit

15-1 Introduction

In the previous two chapters we focused mainly on one factor of production: labour. We now discuss the other factors in greater detail.

Factors of production have traditionally been classified under the headings of *labour*, *land*, and *capital*. To this classification there corresponds three categories of factor returns: *wages* to labour, *rent* to land, and *interest* to capital. The distribution of total revenue into wages, rent, and interest is called the *functional distribution of income*. In the eighteenth and nineteenth centuries this functional distribution of income had major social significance. Land was owned by the aristocracy, capital (material assets other than land) was held by the bourgeoisie, and labour was confined to the working class. This classification lost its significance over time when it was discovered that it is not possible to classify the returns to the different factors into the 'functionally' distinct categories of wages, rent, and interest.

As for the term 'profit', we explained in Chapter 8 that we must distinguish between *accounting* profit and *economic* profit. When we use the term 'profit' in day-to-day use, we mean accounting profit. This also includes the returns to specialized factors of production (entrepreneurial skills and so forth). These are actually opportunity costs to the firm, and it is only the residual *after* taking account of these returns to

specialized factors that we call economic profit. In this sense, a major portion of accounting profit goes into the traditional returns to labour, land, and capital. For example, we might consider entrepreneurial skills as a specialized kind of labour. We discuss profit in greater detail in Section 15-5. For the present, we confine our attention to returns to the traditional factors: labour, land, and capital. Even here, however, the distinction is not totally clear.

15-2 The Distinction between Labour, Land, and Capital

The distinction between labour, land, and capital is rather blurred. Land is traditionally defined as 'natural and inexhaustible powers of the soil' and capital as 'produced means of production'. In other words, land is made by nature, capital by people. But this distinction loses its meaning when one takes into account all the human effort that goes into land development for agriculture or for other purposes. Thus, even in 'land' there can be a lot of human effort involved.

In today's society workers have a decision to make. Do they spend their time working in unskilled jobs (which involve raw labour) or training for jobs with higher skills? This training is part of what is called 'human capital' (which we discussed in the last chapter). Studies on human capital were motivated by the observation that the growth of physical capital, at least as conventionally measured, explains a relatively small part of the growth in income in many countries. The idea of human capital is, however, quite old. Marshall, in his *Principles of Economics*, said: 'the most valuable of all capital is that invested in human beings'.

There is, then, a labour element in land and a capital element in labour, and we see later that there is also a land element in labour and capital. Thus, all returns to these factors cannot really be classified into the strict categories of wages, rent, and interest.

A more important distinction is that between *capital* and *income* or between a *source of productive services* and the *productive services* themselves. The distinction is also between a *stock* and a *flow*. In this classification, under capital we have (1) land, (2) machines and buildings, and (3) human training and skills. The first two can be sold as a stock or their services can be 'hired' or 'rented'; for instance, a hectare of land can be sold or it can be rented for a year. A computer can be sold or rented for a year. Human training and skills, however can only be hired or rented: people cannot (in the absence of slavery) be sold as a stock.

15-3   Economic Rent and Quasi-Rent

In daily usage 'rent' is the price paid *per unit of time* (day, month, year) for the services of a durable good. We can rent buildings, carpet cleaners, satellite systems, typewriters, computers, cars, and so on instead of buying them.

In economics, however, the term has a specific meaning. *Economic rent* is the excess of total payments to a factor of production (land, labour or capital) over and above what is required to bring the particular factor into production. Suppose worker *A* is willing to work for £3 an hour but *B* is willing to work for £4 an hour. An employer needing two workers employs them both at £4 an hour. Then *A* has received an *economic rent*, or surplus payment, of £1 an hour. The classical economists applied the idea of rent to agricultural land only. In his book *The Principles of Political Economy and Taxation* (1817), Ricardo (1772–1823) argued that land was cultivated in descending order of fertility. Initially, the most fertile land was cultivated; then as the demand for corn grew, less fertile land was brought under cultivation. He assumed that labour costs and returns to capital were constant. The price of corn was equal to the cost of production (labour costs and returns to capital) on the marginal land. However, a surplus was earned on the superior land over the marginal land mainly because of differential fertility. This surplus is called *rent*.

Figure 15-1 illustrates this point. There are three farms *A*, *B*, and *C*, ordered by decreasing fertility or increasing marginal costs (which equal average costs). The marginal cost curve is shown as a thick line. When price is P_1, only farm *A* is cultivated. Since price equals average cost, there is no surplus or rent. When price rises to P_2, farm *B* is also brought under cultivation. For farm *A*, since price is greater than average cost, there is

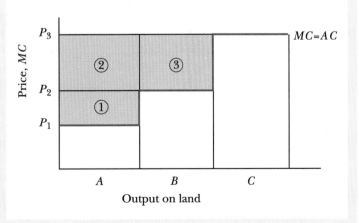

Figure 15-1 Increases in rent on fertile land with increases in the price of corn

a surplus given by the shaded rectangle 1. As for farm B, price equals average cost and there is no surplus. When price rises to P_3, farm C is also brought under cultivation. There is no surplus on this land, but there is a surplus on farm B given by the shaded rectangle 3; as for farm A, the surplus increases and is now given by the two rectangles 1 and 2.

At the time Ricardo was writing, the supply of corn in England was low because the Napoleonic Wars had reduced corn imports. The high price of corn was blamed on 'greedy' landlords who charged tenant farmers high rents. Ricardo's argument was that the rent was high because the price of corn was high, and not the other way around. He argued that, since the price of the corn was equal to the cost of production on the marginal land ('no-rent' land), rent did not enter the price; nor would taxing landlords have any effect on the price. The solution to the problem, according to Ricardo, was to allow free trade. With the importing of corn and the resulting fall in price, rents fall (and so does domestic production), because the land with inferior fertility is not brought under cultivation.

Note that the emergence of rent does not depend on the existence of inferior land. It arises from a scarcity of fertile land. In fact, the availability of inferior land acts as a dampening factor on the rents of land of superior fertility. This is illustrated in Figure 15-2. On the horizontal axis we measure output, and, assuming constant output per hectare, we can also denote hectares of land on the same axis.

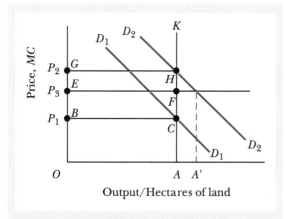

Figure 15-2 Changes in economic rent with the availability of inferior land

Suppose the amount of fertile land available is OA, and this is all of equal fertility. The marginal cost (which equals average cost of production) on this land is OB. The supply curve is BCK. When the demand curve is D_1D_1, all this fertile land is used for production, price $P_1 = MC$, and there is no rent. With the growth in population, the demand curve shifts to D_2D_2. The price rises to P_2, and, since the marginal cost of production is P_1, there is a rent or surplus which accrues to landlords. The amount of rent is given by the rectangle $BCHG$. This is what happens if there is no other land available.

Now suppose there is land of inferior fertility available. The marginal cost (average cost) of production on this land is OE. With an increase in demand to D_2D_2, price only rises to P_3 (which equals OE). Output rises from OA to OA', and the rent on the fertile land is given by the area of rectangle $BCFE$.

Thus, rent arises because of scarcity of fertile land. It exists whether or not there is inferior land. Note also in the above example that, when the demand curve lies to the left of D_1D_1, price is still P_1 (marginal cost OB), but not all the fertile land is used.

Ricardo also argued that, with the increase in price of corn, production was pushed up both *intensively* (by producing more on the existing land) and *extensively* (by bringing less fertile land under cultivation). We illustrate this point with the use of typically shaped marginal cost MC and average cost AC curves in Figure 15-3. We have two farms, A and B. Farm B is less fertile than farm A, and hence has higher average costs. Initially, when price is P_1, only farm A is cultivated with production at Q_1. There is no rent since price $= MC = AC$. When price rises to P_2, the production on farm A rises to Q_1'. This is the result of intensive cultivation of farm A. Also, farm B is brought into production with output Q_2. Farm B's output is called 'extensive' cultivation. Also, for farm B there is no rent since price $= MC = AC$. But for farm A there is rent given by the shaded area, which is price minus AC times the quantity produced.

The above analysis enables us to predict the effects of restrictions on the amount of land that can be cultivated. If the amount of land under production is controlled, existing landowners get higher and higher rents as the price of the produced grain rises. Often such policies are used to increase farm incomes. The result is an increase only in the income of landlords—not of farmworkers or tenant farmers.

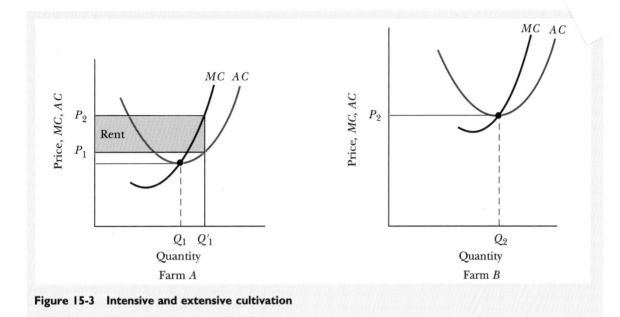

Figure 15-3   Intensive and extensive cultivation

Until now we have considered economic rent on land only. Marshall argued that the concept of economic rent need not apply just to land: it can apply to any factor of production that is in fixed supply for a short or longer period. He said: 'in a sense all rents are *scarcity rents*, and all rents are *differential rents*'. What is true of land or natural resources is true of certain types of machines, human-made capital resources, and special human skills. Thus, the incomes received by all factors may contain an element of rent above the price necessary to keep the factor in its current employment, and the division of the price between necessary price and surplus depends on the time horizon we are considering. The term 'quasi-rent' ('sort-of' rent) is commonly used to depict the surplus accruing to factors of production other than land.

We can illustrate the concept of quasi-rent with reference to labour. But before we do this, we define a few terms. Suppose an individual is offered a job at £4 an hour. If this individual has an opportunity to take a similar job elsewhere at £5 an hour, she rejects the first offer because the *opportunity cost* (the value of her labour in the alternative opportunity) is higher than the wage rate offered. Suppose the second job is a hazardous job and the individual is indifferent between the two jobs. Then the wage difference, £5 − £4 = £1, is called a *compensating wage differential* (a wage differential that compensates for the risk of injury or

death in a hazardous job). The difference is not economic rent. The bulk of the research into compensating wage differentials finds evidence of significant earnings premia for risky jobs. A UK study by Marin and Psacharopoulos found that the risk premium was between £600 and £700 (in 1975 prices) for an increase in the risk of death from zero to 1 in 1000.[1] This implies that 1000 people are willing to pay between £0.6 and £0.7 million for a 1-in-1000 reduction in the probability of dying. This sum is called the *statistical value* of a life. The findings in the UK have been backed up by research in the USA, and Sweden, where significant earnings premia for risky jobs have also been found.[2] The question of the value of a life is considered further in Example 15-1.

Not all wage differentials are compensating wage differentials. Some of the differences are pure rents created by scarcity—either natural or artificial. High salaries are paid to top-class athletes because their special skills are relatively scarce. As we saw earlier, restricting the supply increases the rents for the owner of that particular resource.

[1] A. Marin and G. Psacharopoulos, 'The Reward for Risk in the Labor Market: Evidence from the United Kingdom and a Reconciliation with Other Studies', *Journal of Political Economy*, 90 (1982): 827–53.
[2] See S. W. Polachek and W. S. Siebert, *The Economics of Earnings*, Cambridge University Press, 1993, Ch. 7.

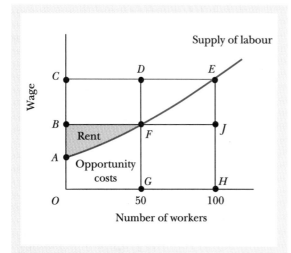

Figure 15-4 Opportunity costs and rents for labour

The above type of analysis was used by Oi to analyse the cost of the military draft versus an all-volunteer army in the United States.[3] We illustrate this idea in Figure 15-4. Suppose the government needs an army of 100 soldiers. If it recruits them on a voluntary basis it has to pay a wage rate *OC*. However, it could fix the wage at *OB* and 'draft' 100 soldiers. The impact of the draft policy is as follows:

1 The cost of the army goes down; taxpayers save *BCEJ*.
2 The rent to the first 50 soldiers falls by *BCDF*.
3 As for the remaining 50 soldiers, their opportunity costs are *GFEH*. But they get only *FJHG* in wages. Hence they lose *FEJ* in forgone opportunities. They also lose *DEF* in rent that they would have received under a volunteer army.

In summary, there is a redistribution of income between the soldiers and taxpayers. The loss to the first 50 soldiers is a loss in the economic rent they were receiving. The loss to the other 50 is not only a loss of economic rent but also a loss of forgone opportunities.

In our example we assumed that the number of volunteers forthcoming at the fixed wage rate for the draft was 50 (half the number desired). But this could be any number below 100. In Oi's example, the total number of new soldiers desired each year was 472 000. He estimated that the wage rate for an all-volunteer army would have been $5900. The draft army wage was $2500, and the estimated number of volunteers at this wage was 263 000. Thus, 209 000 were real 'draftees'. This gives the following figures: (1) Saving for taxpayers = ($5900 − $2500) × 472 000 = $1.6 billion (area *BCEJ* in Figure 15-4). (2) Loss in rent to the soldiers who would have voluntarily joined the army at the draft wage (similar to area *BCDF* in Figure 15-4) is ($5900 − $2500) × 263 000 = $894 million. (3) Opportunity loss to draftees is roughly the loss of rental income, which approximates ($5900 − $2500) × 209 000 = $355 million. (We have assumed that area *DEF* = area *EFJ* in Figure 15-4.)

Although there are other factors not taken into account in the above analysis, such as the costs of administering the draft and the costs of draft evasion (going into a draft-exempt occupation, studying in an overseas university, illegal activities), the above analysis

We now consider the idea of quasi-rent. In any labour market with a positively sloped supply curve and no discrimination, there is always some rent accruing to some workers. Differences in human capital are reflected in different skill levels. The higher earnings of skilled workers compared with unskilled workers in the same industry is (*ex post*) a quasi-rent which accrues to the specific skill. This is the same as saying that different workers have different opportunity costs (or *transfer earnings*), and therefore different reservation wages (the minimum wage at which they are willing to work).

This is illustrated in Figure 15-4: the first worker is willing to work at a wage *OA*, the fiftieth worker at a wage *OB*, the hundredth worker at a wage *OC*, and so on. If 50 workers are employed, everyone gets a wage of *OB*. The area under the supply curve is the summation of the opportunity costs or transfer earnings of all 50 workers. This is given by *OAFG*. The total wage bill is *OBFG*, and the area *ABF* represents the total rent accruing to the workers. Workers whose opportunity costs are low get higher rents.

If the number of workers employed goes up to 100, since the wage rate is *OC* and everyone gets paid the same, the first 50 workers get additional rent given by the rectangle *BCDF*. The total opportunity cost is *OAEH*, and the total rent accruing to labour is given by *ACE*.

[3] W. Y. Oi, 'The Economic Cost of the Draft', *American Economic Review*, 57 (1967): 39–62.

gives some idea of the magnitude of income transfers involved. The above example also illustrates how economic rent arises for labour and how methods to reduce this by force result in opportunity loss for others.

Example 15-1   How Much is a Life Worth?

Earlier we said that the statistical value of a life can be calculated from observed wage premia for risky jobs. Here, life is valued in relation to safety at work. The value of a life has also been calculated in relation to transport safety improvements (see Example 16-1 in the next chapter). Studies using the compensating wage differential approach typically use a statistical technique called multiple regression analysis to 'control' for those factors, other than risk, that may affect the equilibrium wage in a labour market.

An example of this approach is the study by Marin and Psacharopoulos.[4] They estimate an earnings equation where the change in earnings is 'explained' by a number of variables including number of years schooling and years of experience in the labour force (two human capital measures), the number of weeks worked in the year of the study, the proportion of workers in the industry covered by a collective agreement, and the degree of risk (measured as the number of fatal accidents minus the expected number of fatalities/the number of workers). The results show that the risk variable is a significant influence on earnings. That is, earnings do compensate for the disadvantage of a higher risk of death. In fact, their calculations show that each worker would have to be paid between £600 and £700 per year to accept a job with an extra 1-in-1000 chance of death per year. As we said earlier, the value of a life is estimated at between £0.6 and £0.7 million (in 1975 prices).

Jones-Lee summarizes the results of a number of compensating wage differential studies and notes that they have produced a wide range of estimates of the value of a statistical life.[5] This tends to reflect the empirical problems of carrying out research in this area. From these studies, he finds the average value of a life to be £1 900 000 in 1989 prices.

An alternative way of obtaining the value of a life is to calculate the present value of lifetime earnings. This approach is discussed in Application 2 in Chapter 17.

15-4   Capital, Interest, and the User Cost of Capital

We have discussed at length labour and land. We now turn to the third factor: capital. The term 'capital' is defined in the *Oxford English Dictionary* as 'wealth or property that is used or invested to produce more wealth; the money with which business is started'. In the finance literature, the term 'capital' is used in the latter sense (money invested). However, in economics 'capital' generally refers to the mass of long-lived and reproducible implements of production such as roads, bridges, factories, machines, and houses. These are also referred to as 'physical capital'. They provide services over a period of time. Earlier, we talked of 'human capital' in the sense that a worker also provides services over a period of time. However, the difference between physical capital and human capital is that the former can be bought and sold, but the latter cannot (unless there is slavery).

Since the production of physical capital takes up some of the current resources but returns flow only in the future, the choice of how much physical capital to produce involves decisions about current and future consumption. These decisions are called *intertemporal* decisions, and since a detailed discussion of this problem will take us too far away from our main discussion here, we shall take them up in Chapter 17. For the present, we make some convenient assumptions about these intertemporal decisions in order to derive the supply function of capital. (The demand function is derived in the same way that we derived the demand for labour or any other input.) The supply of labour was derived in Chapter 3 from the work–leisure choice of workers. Similarly, the supply of capital depends on choices between present and future consumption of individuals.

To illustrate these ideas, let us assume that Robinson Crusoe, alone on an island, catches 10 fish per day. If he devotes one-tenth of his time for 10 days,

---

[4] Marin and Psacharopoulos, op. cit.
[5] M. W. Jones-Lee, *The Economics of Safety and Physical Risk*, Basil Blackwell, Oxford, 1989.

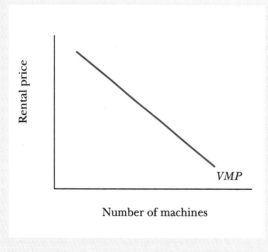

Figure 15-5 Demand curve for machines by a competitive firm

he can build a net, and with the net he can catch 12 fish a day (or take some time off for leisure). Thus, Crusoe faces two choices: (1) catch 10 fish per day every day, or (2) catch 9 fish per day for 10 days and catch 12 fish per day thereafter. The marginal product of the net is 2 fish per day. Now, assume that, if Crusoe builds another net, he can catch 13 fish per day. The marginal product of the second net is 1 fish per day. Next, suppose that one day a group of individuals land on this island. One of them has nets and rents them out in exchange for fish; the others just fish and are as productive as Crusoe. Now, if the rental price of a net is 2 fish per day, Crusoe rents one net; if the rental price of a net is 1 fish per day, Crusoe rents two nets. The number of nets rented is determined by equating the rental price to the marginal product (both expressed in terms of fish).

The building of machines, factories, roads, bridges, and so on all involve the same type of decisions that Crusoe faced in building a net. The decision is to use some labour and materials for the construction of capital equipment instead of producing goods for current consumption. Furthermore, the rental price of machines per hour (or day) is equal to the value of marginal product of the machines per hour (or day). The demand curve for machines is similar to the demand curve for labour shown in Figure 13-2 in Chapter 13. The demand curve for machines by

a competitive firm is shown in Figure 15-5. For a monopolistic firm, we have to change *VMP* (value of marginal product) to *MRP* (marginal revenue product).

We now have to derive the firm's supply curve. We assume that, as the rental price goes up, more machines are supplied. We do not formally derive this result here because, as we said earlier, this involves an analysis of intertemporal decisions by consumers. So we assume that the firm's supply curve is upward-sloping.

As we did with labour (in Chapter 13) we can also derive the market demand curve for machines and the market supply curve for machines; the intersection of the demand and supply curves gives us the equilibrium number of machines and the rental price. However, there are actually many different kinds of machines. Also, physical capital includes buildings, roads, and bridges in addition to equipment. Thus, we have a problem in constructing an aggregate measure of capital. The problem is not that simple with labour, either. We cannot just count heads to get a measure of the labour input: we have to take account of differences in skills and experience. However, the problems of getting an aggregate measure of capital are more serious, and there have been bitter controversies on this subject.[6]

Since we live in a monetary economy, it might seem best to convert the diverse types of capital equipment into monetary terms or market values. In this case, one might then think of taking the rental price of capital as the *rate of interest*, which is nothing but the rental price of money. If you have £10 000 and you lend it to someone at a 10 per cent rate of interest for one year, you are, in essence, renting your money for £1000, and you get back the rent and the principal at the end of the year (assuming that there is no default risk). A firm thinking of renting a machine or other capital equipment at a price of £10 000 compares the value of the marginal product of the capital equipment with the return earned from, say, a risk-free government bond.

However, it is not appropriate to take the rate of interest as a measure of the rental price of capital, for one main reason: when you lend (or rent) your money, at the end of the time period you get your money back.

---

[6] See G. C. Harcourt, *Some Cambridge Controversies in the Theory of Capital*, Cambridge University Press, 1972. This book has been translated into Italian, Polish, Spanish, and Japanese.

The money you get back may be worth less if there is inflation, but let us assume that there is no inflation. The same is not the case with machines. The machine is worth less because of depreciation and obsolescence. However, there may be some tax deduction the firm can get if capital loss due to depreciation and obsolescence is tax-deductible. Also, if during the time period the price of capital goods has gone up, then the capital equipment you have is worth more at the end of the period. Thus, the rental price of capital is not just the market rate of interest. You have to add (and subtract) the factors mentioned. Assuming no taxes and no inflation, the rental price of capital (also called the *user cost of capital*) is given by

$$c = q(i + \delta - g), \qquad (1)$$

where

$c =$ user cost of capital
$q =$ price of a unit of capital
$i =$ interest rate
$\delta =$ rate of depreciation (and obsolescence)
$g =$ growth rate of prices of capital goods

The firm compares c to the value of the marginal product of a unit of capital.[7] Note that

$qi =$ interest cost of borrowed funds
$q\delta =$ cost of depreciation and obsolescence = a capital loss
$qg =$ capital gain due to a rise in the price of capital goods

The finance literature replaces i with r, the cost of financing the capital expenditure. We can consider two sources of finance: (1) debt (or borrowing), with interest rate i, and (2) equity (or the selling of shares), with cost of equity ρ. Then if β is the marginal proportion of funds obtained from debt and $(1 - \beta)$ from equity, we have

$$r = \beta i + (1 - \beta)\rho. \qquad (2)$$

We now substitute r from equation (2) for i in equation (1).

The important thing to note is that money and physical capital (although we consider both in sterling terms) are not the same. Physical capital can

depreciate, or become obsolescent, or increase in value. (Consider the large rise in UK house prices during the late 1980s.) Assuming no general inflation or deflation, money cannot depreciate, or go out of fashion, or rise in value.

15-5   Profit

We now come to the last of the components of the functional distribution of income: profit. We have previously emphasized the difference between economic profit and accounting profit and said that in long-run equilibrium economic profit is zero in a competitive industry.

For firms to operate as production units they need labour, land, and capital; but they also need an organizer. The organizer of a firm is called an *entrepreneur*. Entrepreneurs devote their time to bringing potential investors together, choosing plant location, hiring labour or executives, and financing the operation of the firm.

There is, therefore, labour and financial capital involved on the part of the entrepreneur. The entrepreneur incurs costs today for returns in the future. The amount of money attributable to the entrepreneur's efforts is sometimes called *normal profit*. This includes wages for labour (wages are the amount the entrepreneur could earn elsewhere in the competitive industry) and interest for investment expenditure (interest is the return on investment that could be earned elsewhere). But these are really opportunity costs. The term 'profit' should, therefore, refer to any excess over this normal profit. This excess is called 'economic profit' or excess profit. It is the existence of this excess profit that lures new firms into an industry.

In a competitive industry, the excess profit disappears in the long run with the entry of new firms. This is not, however, the case with monopoly. Since entry is restricted, the excess profit may not disappear even in the long run. However, future excess profit can be capitalized and included in measuring the value of the firm. In this case, the excess profit is a return to this capitalized value. When the monopoly is sold, this is a cost to the new owner. Sometimes the excess profit earned by the monopolist is called 'monopoly rent'. The problem of monopoly profit is discussed in greater detail in Section 15-10 when we

---

[7] In Chapter 13 (Section 13-4) we wrote $P_K/MP_K =$ price of output. What we mean by P_K is the rental price of capital or the user cost of capital.

consider the question of how much a monopoly is worth.

In the short run, even in a competitive industry, there can be some excess profit. But this excess profit cannot be capitalized because it is transitory.[8] It serves the useful purpose of signalling to other firms to enter this market. With the entry of new firms, the excess profit disappears. The excess profit for a monopoly is capitalized (and reflected in the value of the firm) because it is permanent.

When there is uncertainty, the excess profit is not fully capitalized.[9] Since the excess profit is not certain, the value of the firm does not increase by the capitalized value of the future profit. There are some residual returns in each period. (These residual returns can be positive or negative.) If revenue and costs in the future are known with certainty, all net returns are capitalized, and then there are no residual returns or excess profits.

Residual returns or excess profits can occur in

1 a competitive industry in the short run, particularly to those who first enter the industry—these are the 'innovators';
2 a monopoly, although in this case the returns may be capitalized and then there are no residual returns;
3 conditions of uncertainty.

Schumpeter argued that profit results from the successful application of innovations (which are commercial applications of inventions).[10] Such successful innovations are made by the firms first entering a competitive industry, and these are the firms that make excess profit in the short run, before others enter the industry. Some of the innovative firms obtain a patent for the innovation and thereby form a monopoly. Thus, Schumpeter's innovative firms making a profit (economic profit) fall under cases 1 and 2 above.

Knight regarded profit as a return to taking risks.[11] His theory falls under category 3. Entrepreneurs who start a firm have to be rewarded not only for their labour input and investment, but also for the risks they take. There is always the chance that the business might fail and that the entrepreneur might lose all the investment and effort. Profit is a reward for this risk. It is the existence of this reward that prompts many individuals to innovate and produce new products or to produce old products by better production methods. It is the driving force behind all development. Thus, these rewards serve a socially useful and productive purpose.

The profit earned by monopoly, however, does not serve a social purpose and is indeed found to involve some social costs. The existence of monopoly profit results in a number of socially unproductive activities. The activities have been variously called 'rent-seeking activities' or DUP (directly unproductive profit-seeking) activities.[12] There is a variety of estimates of the directly unproductive profit-seeking activities because there is no end to their scope; from lobbying members of Parliament to wining and dining a prospective client, there is a host of unproductive profit-seeking activities that one can think of. We discussed the welfare cost of monopoly in some detail in Chapter 9.

15-6 Personal Distribution of Income

In the previous sections we examined the determination of wages, rent, interest, and profit. This distribution of income into wages, rent, interest and profit is called the *functional distribution of income*, and, as we said earlier, it had social significance for the classical economists. This is not so in modern societies.[13] What is important is the *personal distribution of income*. This is the distribution of income to individuals or to families. It is this distribution that forms the basis of most discussions about inequality. There are, of course, policies that try to change the personal distribution of income by manipulating wages, prices, and profits. But these have often been found to have negligible effects.

---

[8] In practice, this is not true. We often see some shares jump up in price, even with transitory excess profits.
[9] Actually, there is uncertainty as to whether the short-run excess profits of a competitive firm will continue in the future, because of the uncertainty of the speed of entry of other firms.
[10] J. A. Schumpeter, *The Theory of Economic Development: An Enquiry into Profits, Capital, Credit, Interest, and Business Cycles*, Harvard University Press, Cambridge, Mass., 1934.
[11] F. A. Knight, *Risk, Uncertainty and Profit*, Houghton Mifflin, Boston, 1921.

[12] See J. N. Bhagwati, 'Directly Unproductive Profit-Seeking (DUP) Activities', *Journal of Political Economy*, 90 (1982): 988–1002.
[13] However, something similar was of some significance in the UK in the 1970s. During the period of income restraint (dividends were also controlled), the returns to capital and labour were compared in an unusually explicit manner.

Table 15-1   Distribution of Net Equivalent Household Income in the UK, 1989

Income level of household	% of total income	Cumulative %
Bottom 20%	7.9	7.9
Next 20%	12.4	20.3
Middle 20%	17.0	37.3
Next 20%	22.7	60.0
Top 20%	40.0	100.0

Source: Figures adapted from *Social Trends*, Table 5.17, HMSO, 1993

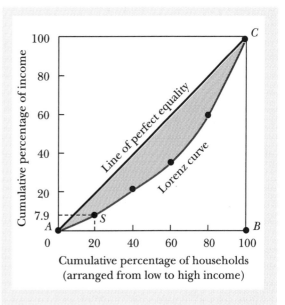

Figure 15-6   Lorenz curve and Gini coefficient

Table 15-1 shows the distribution of net equivalent household income in the UK in 1989.[14] A common measure of income inequality is the *Gini coefficient*, which is derived from the *Lorenz curve*. To construct a Lorenz curve, we plot the cumulative percentages of total income against the cumulative percentage of household income. This is done in Figure 15-6. Point *S* shows that the bottom 20 per cent of households in the income distribution get only 7.9 per cent of total income. The diagonal line is the *line of perfect equality* (20 per cent of households receive 20 per cent of income, 40 per cent of households receive 40 per cent of income, and so on). The closer the Lorenz curve is to the diagonal line, the more equal is the income distribution. Hence, a measure of equality measures how close the Lorenz curve is to the diagonal line. Such a measure is the Gini coefficient, which is defined as

Gini coefficient =

$$\frac{\text{area between the Lorenz curve and the line of equality}}{\text{total area under the line of equality}}.$$

In Figure 15-6 this is

$$\frac{\text{Shaded area}}{\text{Area of triangle } ABC}.$$

The Gini coefficient lies between 0 (perfect equality) and 1 (perfect inequality). The distribution of income in the UK, as measured by the Gini coefficient, is similar to that in Germany and the USA but more unequal than in Sweden.[15]

The important thing to note is that the term 'income distribution' refers to personal income, not the functional distribution of income, and the two need to be clearly distinguished. The functional distribution of income is more a resource allocation issue than an income distribution issue. It is more a question of efficiency than equity. Little useful purpose is served in meddling with the functional distribution of income (manipulating wage rates, for instance) to achieve a more equitable personal distribution of income.

15-7   Application 1: Land Use Restrictions in European Agriculture

In Chapter 8 (Section 8-11) we said that one of the aims of the Common Agricultural Policy (CAP) is to

---

[14] Equivalent income means that the figures have been adjusted to take account of household size and composition, so as to recognize different needs. That is, in order to achieve a comparable standard of living, a household with five individuals needs a higher income than a household with one individual. This should produce an income distribution where all households are on an equal footing regardless of size or composition.

[15] See J. Le Grand, C. Propper, and R. Robinson, *The Economics of Social Problems* (3rd edn.), Macmillan, London, 1992, Ch. 8.

support farm incomes through a programme of administered prices. The effect of this policy is to produce an agricultural surplus (as shown in Figure 8-25) which the European Commission is obliged to take care of. The surplus is either put into buffer stocks or is sold domestically or abroad (at prices below the support price) as European Union (EU) exports. The costs of disposing of the surplus are paid by taxpayers.

Another way of reducing the surplus is to restrict output. This may be done by reducing the amount of farming land under cultivation. In 1988 the EU introduced a programme called 'Set Aside', with the objective of controlling the supply of cereals. In order to qualify for price support, arable farmers were required to keep 20 per cent of their land fallow (but well maintained), for which compensation was paid. The Set Aside scheme was altered in 1992, and is now a key element in the EU's strategy of reducing the surplus. The 1992 CAP reforms weakened the price support mechanism for cereals so that, by the end of 1996, target prices should be 29 per cent lower than in 1992. Arable farmers in the EU may claim compensation for the lower prices, but only if they set aside 15 per cent of their land area.

The effect of this scheme on the industry supply curve depends on the number of farms setting aside land. The decision to set aside depends on the level of financial compensation relative to the forgone profit from setting land aside (which depends on the market price for cereals). Froud and Roberts argue that the number of farmers joining the scheme depends on the level of the market price of cereals in relation to the indifference price of farmers (the cereal price that makes each farmer indifferent about setting land aside).[16] Because not all farms are the same, different farmers have different indifference prices. If the market price is sufficiently high, no farmers join the scheme. But as the price falls, Set Aside becomes more attractive because the same profit can be made from farming 85 per cent of the land (plus compensation) as from farming 100 per cent of the land. Once the price falls below the indifference price of farmers, they join the scheme. We can see the effect of this on the industry supply curve in Figure 15-7.

[16] The discussion here is based on the analysis in J. Froud and D. Roberts, 'The Welfare Effects of the New CAP Cereals Regime: A Note', *Journal of Agricultural Economics*, 44 (1993): 496–501.

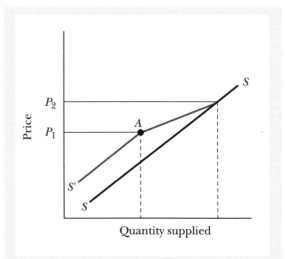

Figure 15-7   Supply curve under the Set Aside programme

(Source: J. Froud and D. Roberts, 'The Welfare Effects of the New CAP Cereals Regime: A Note', Journal of Agricultural Economics, 44 (1993): 498, Fig. 1.)

At prices above P_2 no farmer sets land aside, so the industry supply curve is the competitive supply curve SS. As the price falls below P_2, some farmers join the scheme and the supply curve rotates to the left as land is withdrawn. If the price falls below P_1, all farmers set aside land. The industry supply curve is now $S'AS$. It is estimated that, by the time the 29 per cent reduction in target prices is achieved, market prices will be below P_1, so that when all farmers have set aside land the industry supply curve is equal to $S'A$.

The effect of this on the agricultural surplus is shown in Figure 15-8. At the support price of P_s, the surplus (excess supply) is BC. After Set Aside is introduced, and assuming all farmers join the scheme, the supply curve shifts to the left, from SS to $S'A$. The surplus is reduced from BC to BE. Restrictions on the cultivation of land can be pushed to the point where the surplus is eliminated completely, but in practice there is a danger of 'overshooting the target' (producing a situation of excess demand) if this is attempted.

The Set Aside programme increases the rents to the land under cultivation. For instance, in Figure 15-1 above, if land areas B and C are removed from cultivation and the price of output increases above P_3, the rent to land A rises. Scarce resources always

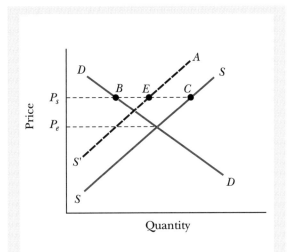

Figure 15-8   Effect of the Set Aside programme on the agricultural surplus

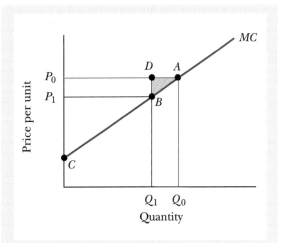

Figure 15-9   Royalty payments and rents on government-owned oil fields

command some rents. The restriction on land use artificially makes land a scarce resource.

A restriction on the amount of farm labour employed or fertilizer used would have the same effect. However, such policies are hard to implement. The Set Aside scheme is easier to monitor.

15-8   Application 2: The Exploration of North Sea Oil

In areas of the North Sea that have yet to be licensed for exploration and production, ownership of the oil is in the hands of the state. However, once a licence is granted, the ownership of the oil is transferred to the licensee. Therefore, the government should attempt to collect the maximum possible rents from the oil companies while seeing that the most efficient level of production is achieved.

The favoured method of successive UK governments for capturing economic rents from the oil companies is one that extracts rent only after the oil has been landed. This is done using (1) a 12.5 per cent royalty levied on the value of oil deliveries, (2) Petroleum Revenue Tax (PRT) charged at 75 per cent on the profit (net of royalties) from oil production under licence, and (3) corporation tax on profit (net of PRT and royalties).

In the United States, the preferred method of capturing rents is to combine royalty payments with a

tender for the licences. An auction is held where licences are awarded through competitive bidding. Through an auction, the government collects a rent (called a lease bonus) at the time of the lease. The oil company keeps all the revenue from production except for a royalty payment which goes to the government. The attraction of a *pure* lease bonus scheme is that it is possible to capture 100 per cent of the economic rent (assuming perfect foresight, many bidders, and no collusion among bidders) because companies bid an amount up to the net present value of any anticipated economic rent. The value of a licence, therefore, is the present discounted value of the economic rent.[17] The rent is the excess profit over and above that needed to attract a firm into oil exploration. The companies bid an amount that still leaves them an expected return equal to that available from alternative investment opportunities. Licences in the North Sea have been awarded mainly on a discretionary basis where applicants are judged on the basis of their experience and competence. However, on occasions a small proportion of the licences have been allocated by auction.

The effect of a combined lease bonus and royalty scheme is shown in Figure 15-9. MC is the marginal cost curve of the oil company and P_0 is the market price for oil. The output that we would like the firm to produce

---

[17] The concepts of discounting and present value are discussed in Chapter 17.

is therefore Q_0. The rent is $P_0 AC$, and this is the rent that the government captures in a pure lease bonus scheme. (Of course, we have to subtract the total fixed costs.) Now suppose that a royalty scheme is used as well. In this case, the price that the firm receives falls to P_1, and the difference $(P_0 - P_1)$ is the royalty payment. Output now falls to Q_1. The rent that the government captures is now $P_1 BC$. The royalty income that the government gets is $P_0 DBP_1$. The sum of these two incomes is less than $P_0 AC$. The difference is the shaded triangle ABD. This represents the loss to the government under a joint royalty–lease bonus scheme as compared with a pure lease bonus scheme. Thus, the government gets less revenue and the output is lower.

Although the above analysis shows that capturing rents with a combined royalty–lease bonus scheme (or the UK's financial regime) is inefficient, this practice is followed because of uncertainty in oil exploration. Before any drilling takes place, it is impossible to assess the exact magnitudes of the oil reserves under the sea. Sites that are highly promising might not turn out to be giant oil fields. Under a pure royalty scheme, the government assumes all the risk. Under a pure lease bonus scheme, the oil company assumes all the risk. In the combined royalty–lease bonus scheme, the government and the oil company share the risk.

There is, however, an alternative method of sharing risk besides the use of royalties. This is to share the lease bonus itself. This avoids the problem of restricting output below the socially optimal level, as happens with the royalty scheme. The lease bonus is shared in a two-part bonus scheme (or multipart lease bonus, if there are more instalments of payments). In the two-part lease bonus scheme there are no royalty payments. The government leases the oil field to the highest bidder, but the lease bonus is paid in two instalments. The first instalment is due immediately, and the second instalment is due before the commencement of commercial production. The oil company has the option of not paying the second instalment and cancelling the lease. The government can take the site and lease it again to the highest bidder.

15-9   Application 3: Taxing Oil Company Profits

During the 1970s, OPEC continuously raised the price of oil, leading to a tenfold increase in the (real) world price of crude oil by the end of the decade. Although production costs also rose, the higher prices raised the oil companies' expectation of profit and undoubtedly helped stimulate the speedy development of the North Sea reserves. The government also wanted to encourage development, partly to reduce oil imports, and so it provided a favourable tax regime at this time. If there are no domestic price controls on oil, the domestic price of oil rises to the level of the world price, and the domestic oil producers receive high economic rents (or 'windfall profits'). Controlling these profits by means of a ceiling on the domestic price of oil is not appropriate, because price controls discourage domestic production, boost domestic demand, and, thus, increase imports. The average price paid by consumers is a weighted average of domestic and foreign prices. We have

$P_0 =$ controlled domestic price
$P_1 =$ import price
$Q_0 =$ domestic production
$Q_1 =$ imports

Then the average price that consumers pay is

$$P_c = \frac{P_0 Q_0 + P_1 Q_1}{Q_0 + Q_1}.$$

Without price controls, the average price consumers pay is P_1 (because $P_0 = P_1$). Since with price controls $P_1 > P_0$, we have $P_c < P_1$. In other words, price controls stimulate domestic demand and result in an increase in imports. They also produce an income transfer to OPEC producers.

In the absence of price controls, the effects of the higher oil prices on the profits of OPEC and the domestic oil producers is shown in Figure 15-10. P_0 is the price before the OPEC price increases. P_1 is the higher world price. DD is the domestic demand curve, and SS is the domestic supply curve. At P_0, Q_1 is the domestic quantity supplied, Q_4 the domestic quantity demanded and $Q_4 - Q_1$ the amount imported. When the world price rises to P_1, domestic quantity supplied rises to Q_2, domestic quantity demanded falls to Q_3, and imports fall to $Q_3 - Q_2$. Assuming that the price P_0 measures the marginal cost of OPEC output, rectangle A gives the profit of OPEC producers. Rectangle B gives the increase in producer surplus (or economic rent or windfall profit) to the domestic producers before domestic supply has adjusted to the

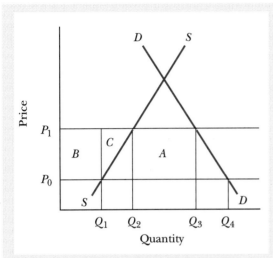

Figure 15-10   Effects of oil price increases

price increase. Area C shows the producer surplus arising from the new domestic production $(Q_2 - Q_1)$.

So, without any price controls high windfall profits accrue to the domestic oil companies. Price controls help to limit this profit, but they have the effect of raising imports and transferring wealth to OPEC. The best way, therefore, of controlling the profits is to levy a profit tax. Petroleum Revenue Tax (PRT) was introduced by the Labour government in 1975 and was charged at 45 per cent of the profits from offshore production. The figure was raised to its present level of 75 per cent in 1983. However, even with PRT it became clear that in some cases the expected returns on investment were far higher than were needed to make exploration worth while. Hence, royalty payments were introduced as well. However, companies have been able to claim exemption from the full rate of the PRT, and recently royalties have been abolished in some of the more costly fields to encourage exploration.

In the 1970s, rising world oil prices and the large economic rents accruing to the oil companies led to the introduction of a profit tax on oil. The PRT and the royalty scheme have been successful in extracting some of the rents. Also, governments have benefited from substantial amounts of revenue over the years. In the early 1980s North Sea revenues accounted for 9 per cent of total government tax revenue. The figure is now about 1 per cent. Oil exploration is a case where it is possible to get some idea of the level of rents. In

some situations, however, it is hard to determine what rents are. Further, land is not the only factor of production to which rents accrue. In Section 15-3, we discussed the concept of quasi-rent, which makes the point that rents can accrue to other factors as well.

15-10 Application 4: How Much Is a Monopoly Worth?

In Chapter 9 we discussed the theory of pricing under monopoly. There, we assumed the monopoly to exist and then asked: What is the profit-maximizing output? Here we ask the question: How much is a monopoly worth? In other words, suppose we start with a competitive industry. How much is the monopolist willing to pay for the right to purchase and monopolize the industry?

To answer this question, we have to consider not monopoly profits but the excess of rent under monopoly over rent under competition.[18] As explained earlier, in Figure 15-4 the area under the supply curve gives the opportunity cost or transfer earnings of the resources used; subtracting this from total revenue, we get the rent to these resources. We use this result in the following analysis.

We assume that the monopolist's marginal cost curve represents the supply curve of the industry if it were operating competitively. There are, thus, no cost advantages or disadvantages with either of these market structures. This assumption enables us to compare the rents with resources under competition and monopoly. The situation is described in Figure 15-11. P_c and P_m are prices under competition and monopoly, and Q_c and Q_m are outputs under competition and monopoly, respectively. Under monopoly we have:

Revenue $= OP_m A Q_m$
Cost of resources $= OCQ_m$
Rent $= OP_m AC$

---

[18] The following discussion is based on H. Demsetz, 'Purchasing Monopoly', in D. C. Colander (ed.), *Neo-Classical Political Economy*, Ballinger, Cambridge, Mass., 1984, Ch. 7. This paper gives a detailed discussion of this and other related issues such as the welfare cost of monopoly.

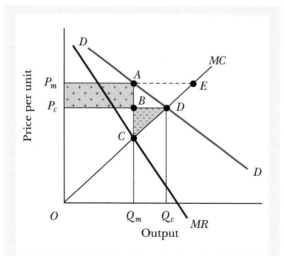

Figure 15-11 Profit from monopolizing a competitive industry

Under competition we have:

Revenue $= OP_c DQ_c$

Cost of resources $= ODQ_c$

Competitive rent to resources $= OP_c D$

If the monopolist purchases the competitive industry, he has to fully compensate all the productive resources. The factors producing $Q_c - Q_m$ are no longer employed in the monopolized industry. The monopolist could purchase them for $Q_m BDQ_c$ and resell them for $Q_m CDQ_c$ (their opportunity cost), or merely pay them CBD to leave the industry. Either way, the net cost to the monopolist is CBD. The resources producing Q_m continue to be employed in the monopolized industry and need to be paid $OP_c BQ_m$.

The profit from purchasing the monopoly is, thus, monopoly revenue $OP_m AQ_m$ minus the sum of CBD and $OP_c BQ_m$. But this is equal to the difference between monopoly rent $OP_m AC$ and competitive rent $OP_c D$. Taking away the common area $OP_c BD$ leaves us with the difference $P_m ABP_c - CBD$, or the area of plus signs minus the area of minus signs in Figure 15-11.[19]

What we can say about these two areas depends on the elasticities of the demand and supply curves. The

---

[19] Actually, at the higher price P_m more resources are forthcoming, and if these resources must also be compensated, the area to be subtracted can be as large as the triangle ACE in Figure 15-11.

more elastic the demand curve, the greater is the monopoly rent; the more elastic the supply curve, the smaller is the competitive rent. The important conclusion from this analysis is that the monopoly rent $OP_m AC$ does not measure the *profit from monopolization*. This latter profit is much smaller in value.

15-11 Summary

The distribution of revenue into wages, rent, and interest is called the functional distribution of income. The return to labour is wages, the return to capital is interest, and the return to land is rent. However, in practice it is not possible to classify the returns into functionally distinct categories.

Economic rent is the excess of total payments to a factor of production over and above what is required to bring the particular factor into production. The classical economists applied the idea of rent to land only. Economic rent accruing to other factors is therefore sometimes called quasi-rent. In any input market with an upward-sloping supply curve, as long as there is no discrimination, there is always some rent accruing to some units of the factor.

The rental price of capital is *not* the rate of interest. The interest rate must be adjusted for the rate of depreciation and the growth rate in the prices of capital goods.

Accounting profit includes the return to many specialized factors of production. Normal profit includes the opportunity cost of the entrepreneur's labour and financial capital. Economic profit is the excess profit—that is, profit over and above normal levels. Excess profit can occur in a competitive industry in the short run, in a monopoly, or under conditions of uncertainty.

The Lorenz curve graphically illustrates the cumulative personal distribution of income. The Gini coefficient measures inequality in the distribution—the coefficient is the area between the Lorenz curve and the line of perfect equality divided by the area under the line of equality.

The Set Aside programme is one way of reducing the agricultural surplus produced by the price support system in the CAP. Restrictions on land use increase the rents to land under cultivation. Licences for North Sea oil exploration have mainly been allocated using a discretionary system. Under this arrangement, government revenues are smaller and output is lower than under a pure lease bonus scheme.

A tax on existing rents, such as the PRT, does not affect supply but rather transfers rents from the producers to the government. The profit arising from purchasing and monopolizing a previously competitive industry is much less than monopoly rent.

Key Terms

Accounting profit*
Compensating wage differential*
Economic profit*
Economic rent*
Financial capital
Functional distribution of income*
Gini coefficient*
Interest
Lease bonus
Lorenz curve*
Nominal rate of interest
Normal profit*
Petroleum revenue tax
Physical capital*
Profit from monopolization
Quasi-rent*
Real rate of interest
Rent*
Royalty
Transfer earnings*
User cost of capital*
Wages

Questions

1   With the rapid increase in the demand for computers, the quasi-rents of computer engineers increased substantially. Explain what has happened to the supply curve of computer engineers over time and, consequently, what has happened to these rents.

2   Does the full difference between the wages of doctors and the average wage rate constitute a quasi-rent? Why or why not?

3   Oi implicitly assumes that those with the lowest opportunity cost (and not already enlisted) are drafted. If draftees are really randomly chosen, does Oi's analysis overstate or understate the full cost of the draft?

4   Based on Oi's analysis and your answer to question 3, can you make an economic case for allowing draftees to pay someone to replace them in the army?

5   We previously mentioned the licensing of taxis in New York through the issuing of 'medallions', which can be resold. Explain why medallions command such a high price when taxi drivers argue that their profits are negligible.

6   Can the Lorenz curve intersect the line of perfect equality? Why or why not?

7   How does the Lorenz curve for the distribution of after-tax (or net) income compare with the curve for pre-tax income? How do the Gini coefficients compare?

8   How does the Set Aside programme affect per-hectare usage of labour, fertilizer, capital, and so on? Can you determine the impact on total usage of these inputs? How are intensive and extensive cultivation affected?

9   If a monopolist can reduce the costs of production, what is the profit from purchasing and monopolizing a competitive industry?

10   'PRT does not affect the supply of domestic oil.' Is this true if producers fear that the tax will one day apply to fields that are not yet fully operational? Why? How does this expectation affect the ability to capitalize future rents?

16 Externalities, Public Goods, and Government Intervention

16-1 Introduction

In Chapter 1 we defined the economic problem as the determination of the efficient use of scarce resources to produce a maximum output, taking into account the production possibilities and consumers' preferences and tastes. In this chapter, we discuss the circumstances under which the market mechanism fails to achieve an efficient allocation of resources. This is often called *market failure*. The major sources of market failure are:

1 *Certain forms of market organization* Examples include monopoly and oligopoly.
2 *Externalities* The behaviour of some individuals or firms affects the welfare of others. For example, a chemical firm dumping waste in a river can increase production costs for fishermen.
3 *Existence of public goods* These are goods for which one individual's consumption need not exclude another individual's consumption. For example, if there is just one pizza and A eats it, then B cannot have a pizza. However, if there is a public park and A uses it, this does not exclude B's using it. The park is, thus, a public good, and a pizza is not.

We discussed monopoly and oligopoly in Chapters 9, 10, and 11. In this chapter we consider the problems of externalities and public goods.

Many economists argue that the mere existence of externalities and public goods does not by itself justify government intervention in markets. They argue that private markets exist for 'internalizing' externalities (we explain this term in Section 16-3) and for the private provision ('privatization') of public goods. We outline these arguments as we proceed, and we examine the case for government intervention in markets (see Section 16-10). We also discuss consumer protection and government regulation: two areas in which the government has acted as a 'big brother' in trying to protect consumers.

16-2 Externalities in Consumption and Production

In Chapter 7 we discussed the conditions for efficiency in consumption and production and overall economic efficiency. These conditions involved marginal rates of substitution (MRS) and marginal rates of transformation (MRT). The conditions were derived on the assumption that production costs are borne only by the producer of the product and that the utility derived from consumption is enjoyed only by the purchasers. This is not always so. Some products have *external effects* or *externalities* (which are also called *spillover effects* or *neighbourhood effects*). The externalities can be *negative externalities* (these involve external costs) or *positive externalities* (these involve external benefits). We first give examples of negative and positive externalities in production and consumption and then discuss how they change the conditions of efficiency discussed in Chapter 7.

1 *Negative externality in production* An often quoted example is that of a paper mill that produces paper and waste that is dumped into a river. The riverside residents and anglers are hurt by the waste.

2 *Positive externality in production* One example is the production of honey. Beekeepers try to put their beehives on farms because the nectar from the plants increases the production of honey. The farmers also receive advantages from the beehives because the bees aid pollination of the plants.

3 *Negative externality in consumption* Suppose a person plays 'heavy metal' music very loud. The person gets enjoyment from it. (Usually, the louder the music, the greater the enjoyment.) But for other people living nearby, the noise is a nuisance.

4 *Positive externality in consumption* An example of this is vaccinations. They help not only the person vaccinated but also the entire neighbourhood that the person lives in, by preventing the spread of contagious diseases.

We now analyse the consequences of these externalities. Pigou was the first person to deal with externalities in a systematic way. He argued that, in the presence of externalities, even if we have perfect competition we do not achieve a Pareto optimum. The social benefit or cost is a combination of private and external benefits or costs. We use the following notation to denote these costs and benefits:

MPC = marginal private cost
MEC = marginal external cost
MSC = *marginal social cost*

and

$MSC = MPC + MEC$.

Also,

MPB = marginal private benefit
MEB = marginal external benefit
MSB = marginal social benefit

and

$MSB = MPB + MEB$.

Overall economic efficiency requires that $MSC = MSB$ for each product. The reason is obvious. As long as

$MSB > MSC$, production should be expanded because additional benefit exceeds additional cost. Similarly, if $MSB < MSC$, then production should be decreased.[1] Consequently, we should have for each pair of products equality between the marginal social rate of transformation ($MSRT$) and the marginal social rate of substitution ($MSRS$). Thus, in the conditions derived in Chapter 7, we have to substitute the word 'social' in all the marginal rates MRT and MRS. If only the marginal private costs are considered, the economy does not reach efficiency. For economic efficiency, consumers and producers must weigh the full social benefits of consumption or production.

One way to get producers and consumers to weigh social benefits and costs is to impose taxes and subsidies which bring private benefits or costs into line with social benefits or costs. We now show how these taxes and subsidies work.

Negative Externality in Production

Figure 16-1 illustrates the case of a negative externality in production. Since we are assuming that there are no externalities in consumption, the demand curve DD shows the marginal private and social benefits ($MPB = MSB$). The competitive supply curve, however, reflects only the marginal private costs. The MSC curve lies above the competitive supply curve by an amount equal to the MEC. The optimal output is Q_0 with a price P_0. But the competitive market, if left alone, produces Q_1, with a price of P_1. Thus, there is a tendency to overproduce. At the optimal output Q_0, the price is P_0, but marginal private cost is C_0. Thus, the government could levy a per-unit tax of $(P_0 - C_0)$ on the firm, increase marginal private cost by $(P_0 - C_0)$, and reduce output from Q_1 to Q_0. Consumers then pay P_0, the full marginal social cost of production. The revenue from the tax can be used to pay for the external damage arising from the production of this product. (For example, in the case of the paper mill, the tax revenue could pay for the cleaning up of the river or for alternative ways of paying for the damage to those hurt by the waste dumped in the river.) Note, however, that the tax

---

[1] For simplicity, we assume that there is only one level of output for which $MSB = MSC$.

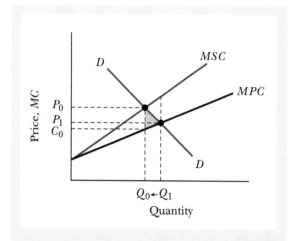

Figure 16-1 Negative externality in production

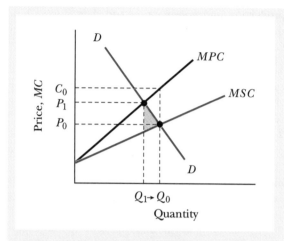

Figure 16-2 Positive externality in production

revenue may be more or less than the external cost. In Figure 16-1 the tax revenue equals $(P_0 - C_0) \times Q_0$, whereas the total external cost equals the area between MSC and MPC up to Q_0.

Finally, the net gain to society from the tax is given by the shaded area in Figure 16-1. This is the excess of costs over benefits for the units that are eliminated by the tax. It is the summation of $(MSC - MSB)$ over the output range Q_0 to Q_1.

Positive Externality in Production

This case is illustrated in Figure 16-2. Here, since there are external benefits to producers, the MSC curve lies below the MPC curve $(MSC < MPC)$. Since the demand curve gives the marginal social (private) benefit to consumers, the optimal level of output Q_0 is given by the intersection of the demand curve with the MSC curve. However, if left alone, the competitive market produces Q_1, where the demand curve intersects the MPC curve. Thus, too little is produced from the social point of view. At the output level Q_0, producers receive a price of P_0, but their marginal cost is C_0. Thus, output can be increased by providing the producers with a subsidy equal to $(C_0 - P_0)$. Consumers pay the marginal costs of production C_0 minus the external benefit $(C_0 - P_0)$, or a price P_0. In the previous case, we had a tax equal to the marginal external cost. In the present case, we have a subsidy equal to the external benefit. Where does the government get the money to pay the subsidy? It

could collect it from the people reaping the external benefit. But, again, the expenditures on the subsidy may not equal the total external benefit.

The net benefit to society from the subsidy is given by the shaded area in Figure 16-2. This is the excess of social benefit over social cost for the extra units produced as the result of the subsidy.

Negative Externality in Consumption

This is illustrated in Figure 16-3. Since there are no externalities in production, marginal social cost and

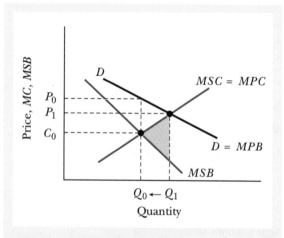

Figure 16-3 Negative externality in consumption

marginal private cost are equal, and the competitive supply curve reflects the common marginal cost. However, on the demand side, the demand curve reflects only the marginal private benefit *MPB*. And since the marginal social benefit is less than the marginal private benefit, the *MSB* curve lies below the *MPB* curve.

The optimal quantity is again Q_0 (the point where $MSB = MSC$). In the absence of any intervention, the quantity supplied and consumed is Q_1, and the price is P_1. Thus, there is an overproduction of the commodity as compared with the socially optimal level. To restrict output to Q_0, the price has to be raised to P_0. But the supply price for Q_0 is C_0. Therefore, a tax equal to $(P_0 - C_0)$ needs to be levied. The price the consumer pays is thus P_0, which equals the marginal private cost of production C_0 plus the cost of externality in consumption $(P_0 - C_0)$. Again, the revenue generated from the tax can be used to compensate those who are hurt by the external cost arising from the consumption of this product, and the area of the shaded triangle measures the net benefit of the tax to society.

Positive Externality in Consumption

This is illustrated in Figure 16-4. As before, the *MSC* (which equals *MPC*) curve is the supply curve. The demand curve *DD* is the *MPB* curve. Since there are external benefits to consumers, $MSB > MPB$, and the *MSB* curve lies above the demand curve by an amount equal to the *MEB*.

The socially optimal quantity is given by Q_0 where $MSB = MSC$. Without any intervention, the quantity produced is Q_1, and the price is P_1. Thus, there is underproduction as compared with the socially optimal level. If Q_0 is produced, the market price is P_0 but the marginal cost of production is C_0. Thus, the consumers need to be given a subsidy equal to $(C_0 - P_0)$.

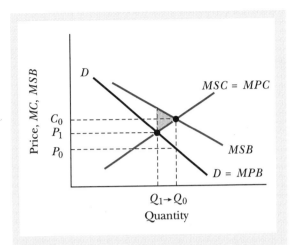

Figure 16-4   Positive externality in consumption

The producers receive C_0 but the consumers pay P_0. At least part of the cost of the subsidy $(C_0 - P_0) \times Q_0$ could possibly be collected from those reaping the external benefits arising from the consumption of this good.

As in Figure 16-2, the net benefit to society from the subsidy is measured by the area of the shaded triangle in Figure 16-4. It is the excess of social benefit over social cost for the output range Q_1 to Q_0.

Summary

We can summarize our results as follows. (1) In the presence of externalities, the socially optimal level of output Q_0 is given by the condition $MSB = MSC$. (2) The private production of output Q_1 is given by the condition $MPB = MPC$. (3) To bring about an output of Q_0 we can use the tax and subsidy programmes shown in Table 16-1. These correspond to the four cases we considered.

Table 16-1   Taxes and subsidies in the presence of externalities

Condition	Type of externality	Tax or subsidy	Amount of tax or subsidy*
$MSC > MPC$	−ve, production	Tax producers	$MSC - MPC$
$MSC < MPC$	+ve, production	Subsidize producers	$MPC - MSC$
$MSB < MPB$	−ve, consumption	Tax consumers	$MPB - MSB$
$MSB > MPB$	+ve, consumption	Subsidize consumers	$MSB - MPB$

*These amounts are measured at the socially optimal level.

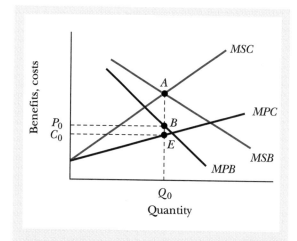

Figure 16-5 Externalities in consumption and production

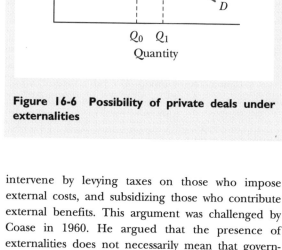

Figure 16-6 Possibility of private deals under externalities

We did not consider combinations of taxes and subsidies, but these combinations are possible if there . are externalities in both consumption and production. For example, there might be positive externalities in consumption and negative externalities in production. (Suppose, for the sake of argument, that this is the case with a vaccine.) We illustrate this case in Figure 16-5. The socially optimal output is Q_0. We can bring about this output if we subsidize consumers by AB and tax producers by AE. Alternatively, we can just tax producers by BE. The tax of BE on producers solves all the efficiency problems. Equity considerations might, however, require that both a subsidy and a tax be imposed.

Note that we could have the socially optimal output produced in the absence of intervention when there is an external benefit in consumption and an external cost in production. In Figure 16-5, this requires that the demand and supply curves (MPB and MPC) intersect at Q_0. In this case, taxes and subsidies are warranted only on the grounds of fairness. Furthermore, the subsidy has to equal the tax or the optimal output is no longer produced.

16-3 The Coase Theorem

The preceding analysis was based on the argument that in the presence of externalities the government should

intervene by levying taxes on those who impose external costs, and subsidizing those who contribute external benefits. This argument was challenged by Coase in 1960. He argued that the presence of externalities does not necessarily mean that government should intervene.[2] After all, the government intervention, or the administering of the subsidies and taxes, costs something. And, if these costs are higher than the social benefits from intervention (given by the areas of the triangles in Figures 16-1 to 16-4), then government intervention does not increase social welfare.

Coase argued, in addition, that there is a possibility of private deals that achieve the same result as government taxes and subsidies. Consider the case of a paper mill dumping waste in a river and thereby hurting anglers. In Figure 16-6, Q_0 is the socially optimal output but the competitive market produces Q_1. If the paper mill reduces its output from Q_1 to Q_0, the net loss in the producer and consumer surpluses is ACE, but the gain to the anglers is $ABCE$ (the excess of MSC over MPC for the output range Q_0 to Q_1). Since $ABCE$ is larger than ACE, so that the gain to the anglers is larger than the loss to the consumers and producers, it should be possible for the anglers to bribe the

---

[2] R. H. Coase, 'The Problem of Social Cost', *Journal of Law and Economics*, 3 (1960): 1–44.

producers and consumers to cut output to Q_0. Thus, the socially optimal level of output can be achieved without government taxing or subsidizing. Of course, if the number of people involved is large, the bargaining costs are very high.

Coase also argued that it makes no difference to the allocation of resources how the property rights to a contestable resource (here, the river) are assigned. If the property rights to the river are assigned to the anglers, then the paper mill has to pay the anglers compensation for dumping waste in the river. This compensation has to equal $MSC - MPC$ per unit in Figure 16-6, because that is the measure of harm done to the anglers. The paper mill has to take the costs of compensation into account when calculating its costs. Thus, its private marginal cost curve is no longer MPC but is now MSC in Figure 16-6. In this way, the *externality has been internalized*. The output of the paper mill is now the socially optimal level Q_0.

The same applies if the paper mill is assigned the property rights to the river and therefore has the right to dump waste in it. Anglers can then bribe the paper mill not to dump waste. The amount of the bribe is the difference $MSC - MPC$. When the paper mill calculates its costs, it has to add to MPC the amount of this bribe. (It is the cost of the bribe forgone by increasing output.) Thus, again the cost curve the firm faces is the MSC curve. The externality has again been internalized. Of course, to whom the property rights to the river are assigned (the paper mill or the anglers) does make a difference in income distribution, but Coase assumes small income effects.

The Coase theorem can be summarized as follows: under perfect competition, if income effects and transactions costs are ignored, voluntary agreements among the different parties concerned lead to a socially optimal output even in the presence of externalities, and the result is the same regardless of which party is assigned the property rights to the contestable resource.

The assumptions of the Coase theorem are that income effects are small and that transaction costs are negligible. The first assumption is unlikely to be valid in practice, while, in reality, transaction costs are an important problem. Suppose there is a large river into which several industrial plants are dumping waste; millions of people are using the river water for drinking purposes and recreational facilities. Obviously, it is impossible to assign property rights to

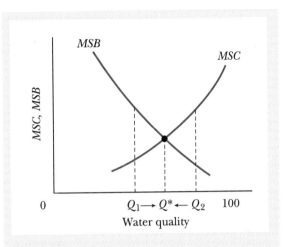

Figure 16-7   Determination of optimal level of pollution

anyone, and it is impossible for private parties to get together and reach an agreement. An example of this situation is the Ruhr basin in Germany, where many industries pollute the rivers in the area. What are the possible solutions?

First of all, it does not make sense to say that the industries should not pollute the rivers at all. There is a *socially optimal level of pollution*, and this is not, in general, zero pollution. Figure 16-7 shows the marginal social costs MSC and marginal social benefits MSB for improvements in water quality. We denote water quality as ranging from zero (useless dirty water) to 100 (pure water). The marginal cost of cleaning goes up as we reach higher and higher levels of purity, while the marginal benefits decline as we go to higher and higher levels of purity. For example, going from 95 per cent pure to 100 per cent pure may not make as much difference as going from 45 per cent pure to 50 per cent pure. (For almost all uses except drinking, perfect purity is not necessary.)

The optimal quantity of pollution is Q^*. If water quality is at Q_1 ($< Q^*$), then it pays to increase it since the extra benefit is greater than the extra cost. If the water quality is at Q_2 ($> Q^*$), then it pays to decrease it because benefits forgone are less than costs saved.

The diagram is, of course, of little practical value, because there are actually many insurmountable problems in measuring MSB and MSC. It does, however, illustrate the point that there is such a thing as the optimal level of pollution and that, in general, it is not zero pollution (100 per cent purity).

Example 16-1 The Optimal Level of Transport Safety

Loss of life in transport accidents serves to remind us that adequate levels of safety are essential on the major transport modes. In order to arrive at the optimal level of transport safety regulation, the costs and benefits should be carefully assessed. It is in the valuation of the benefits that the major problems arise, for two reasons: first, information is needed on the extent of accident prevention; second, a money valuation of the accidents prevented is required. This last point requires a value to be placed on human life and serious injury. This valuation is contentious, but the value selected determines the optimal level of safety regulation. If the value is high, regulations saving more lives are more desirable.

One way of calculating the value of a human life is to use the 'willingness to pay method'. (We discussed how the value of a life may be estimated using earnings equations in Example 15-1.) This involves asking a sample of people about their willingness to pay for (normally small) improvements in their own and others' safety. These amounts are then aggregated across all individuals so as to arrive at an overall value for the safety improvement concerned. The resultant figure is a clear reflection of what the safety improvement is worth to the particular group, relative to the other ways they could have spent their limited income.

Suppose that a transport safety improvement reduces the probability of death during some future period by 1 in 1000 for each member of a group of 1000 people. If each of 1000 people is willing to pay £y for this reduced probability, then aggregate willingness to pay is £y × 1000. With this approach, it turns out that an individual's willingness to pay, divided by the reduction in risk of death, is his or her marginal rate of substitution of wealth for risk. So the value of a 'statistical life' is the mean (over the affected group) of individual marginal rates of substitution of wealth for risk.

A study by Jones-Lee *et al.* in the UK used this approach to value transport safety.[3] The study used a sample of 1718 people from England, Scotland, and Wales. Among the questions the respondents were asked were how much extra a person would be willing to pay when buying a new car for an additional safety feature that would reduce passenger risks by various specified amounts. The value of a 'statistical life' based on the mean marginal rate of substitution was calculated to be £1 500 000 in 1982 prices.[4] Other questionnaire-type studies, by Persson in Sweden and Maier *et al.* in Austria, produced values of £1 500 000–1 800 000 (1989 prices) and £1 900 000 (1989 prices), respectively.[5]

Jones-Lee *et al.* also found that willingness to pay is significantly affected by age and income. The income elasticity value was 0.3, and individuals' valuations of safety peaked around 40 years of age.

16-4 Policies to Regulate Pollution

Given that there is a non-zero optimal level of pollution, what are the appropriate policies to achieve it? There are three types of policies: (1) pollution standards, (2) pollution taxes (or charges), and (3) pollution licences. The 'standards' policy is a method of direct control, whereas the other two are indirect methods. For the implementation of the 'standards' policy and the 'licensing' policy we need to know the optimal pollution quantity, whereas for the implementation of the tax policy we need to know $(MSC - MSB)$ at the optimal level of pollution.

---

[3] M. W. Jones-Lee, M. Hammerton, and P. R. Philips, 'The Value of Transport Safety: Results of a National Sample Survey', *Economic Journal*, 95 (1985): 49–72.
[4] The UK Department of Transport calculates the value of a life according to the cost of a fatal road accident. The cost is based on an assessment of the wider expenses of an accident, ranging from the actual physical damage to the time of police officers and ambulance crews involved. The Department of Transport calculates the cost of a fatal road accident (the value of a life) to be £715 330 in 1993 prices. This approach gives a much lower estimate than the willingness-to-pay method. For more detail on this, see the *Independent* (11 November 1993): 3.
[5] U. Persson, 'The Value of Risk Reduction: Results of a Swedish Sample Survey', mimeo, Swedish Institute of Health Economics, 1989; G. Maier, S. Gerking, and P. Weiss, 'The Economics of Traffic Accidents on Austrian Roads: Risk Lovers or Policy Deficit?' mimeo, Wirtschaftuniversitat, Vienna.

Pollution Standards

The way in which governments have traditionally aligned private and social costs is by setting pollution standards. Most countries monitor air pollution and water pollution and they regulate the amount of hazardous and toxic waste that is dumped into rivers and seas. The setting of pollution standards implies particular maximum levels of concentration for a pollutant, for example a given number of micrograms per cubic metre. In general, standards are set with reference to health criteria, in the sense that the pollutant must not exceed levels that would make water unsafe to drink or the air unsuitable to breathe. So, government may require companies to dilute waste by a prescribed amount before it is drained into the sea, or to build cars that meet targets on exhaust emissions. In short, a pollution standard is designed to achieve a predefined level of pollution at the lowest possible control cost.

Economists argue that standards are the least efficient method of pollution control. It is only by accident that we arrive at the optimal level of externality. In order for a government to work out the efficient amount of pollution, it needs to acquire information concerning all pollution-generating activities. This is an enormous task. In terms of Figure 16-7, the government needs to know the exact positions of at least part of the *MSB* and *MSC* curves; to find these, it needs to know water prices, the water firms' private costs, and the external costs to other users. Once we multiply this by the number of instances of pollution, it becomes clear that the information requirements are huge. So, in practice, regulations are usually set in a rather arbitrary manner.

A further weakness with standards is that all polluters are expected to meet the same target irrespective of the cost to different companies. Some firms may find it relatively cheap to convert machines to meet a specified standard on, say, carbon emissions, while others may find such conversions expensive, especially if they are using old and outdated equipment. It may be cheaper to use old and messy machines than convert to new ones. Thus, a law that is passed simply insisting on a change in a given time period would impose massive cost increases on some firms. Therefore, the monitoring agency that oversees polluters' activities generally has to compromise. Moreover, if it has no powers of punishment, the polluter is only likely to meet the standard out of a sense of social conscience. Recent pollution regulations in the UK are aimed at compromise. They include the concept of 'best available technology not entailing excessive cost' (BATNEEC). Both firms and inspectors are free to discuss what is meant by 'excessive cost' and 'best available technology'. This is an attempt to make firms cut their pollution in line with their own cost structure.[6]

Pollution Charges

An alternative way of achieving the socially optimum level of pollution is to impose a charge on the polluter based on the estimated damage done (or the external cost). The idea for such a charge was developed by Pigou in 1920. Essentially, his idea was to place a tax on the polluter to bring his cost function into line with what it would have been had he faced the true social costs of production. The tax should correspond to the marginal cost of cleaning up the waste at the optimal level of pollution. If the government imposes a tax of £5 per unit of waste, then firms can dump as much waste as they want at this price. Ideally, the charge is equal to the value of the *MEC* (in the notation we used to denote costs and benefits in Section 16-2). The polluter pays, and takes the costs of cleaning up into consideration when undertaking production. The pollution charge thus bridges the gap between private and social cost, and output is reduced to the socially optimal level. In short, the pollution charge is designed to produce an efficient outcome by forcing the polluter to compensate completely for all damage caused.

The key feature of the charge system is that the government only has to know the value of the damage done. To achieve the socially efficient level via standards, the government needs to know not only the value of the damage but also full details of firms' costs and revenues. Thus, a charge requires far less information. Furthermore, a charge allows a polluter to adjust in his own way to the quality standard. Polluters with high costs of abating pollution prefer to pay the charge, while those with low costs of abatement prefer to install abating equipment. The charge tends to cut down the total cost to firms and increases the flexibility of compliance.

[6] For a fuller discussion, see F. Cairncross, *Costing the Earth*, Business Books, London, 1991, Ch. 5.

A number of European countries have used the price mechanism as a means of altering individual behaviour. In the main, charges have been used to deal with water pollution rather than air pollution (which we consider in more detail in Example 16-2). France, Italy, Germany, and the Netherlands have all used effluent charges to control water pollution. In France and the Netherlands the charges were designed to raise revenue so as to fund activities specifically designed for improving water quality. In Germany, dischargers are required to meet minimum standards of waste water treatment for a number of defined pollutants. At the same time, a fee is levied on every unit of discharge depending on the quantity and noxiousness of the effluent. In Italy the system has been designed to encourage polluters to achieve provisional effluent standards in as short as time as possible. The charge was nine times higher for firms that did not meet the prescribed standards than for firms that did meet them.

Carbon taxes to deal with air pollution have been adopted in Finland, Sweden, and the Netherlands. In Sweden a tax on carbon dioxide (CO_2) emissions was introduced following the 1988 Toronto Agreement which called for a 20 per cent reduction of CO_2 emissions by the year 2005. In late 1988 the government announced that CO_2 emissions should be maintained at their 1988 levels. In 1991, however, the government ended the cap on CO_2 emissions alone and extended the emissions ceiling to all 'greenhouse gases'. The targets for CO_2 emissions were set at 1990 levels so as to be consistent with the proposed EU targets.

In Sweden, too, charges have been used to increase the rate at which consumers buy cars equipped with a catalytic converter. Cars not having a catalytic converter have been taxed, while new cars with a converter have been subsidized. This policy seemed to be successful in bringing low-polluting vehicles on to the road at a much faster pace than normal. It was not revenue-neutral, however, since subsidy payments were much higher than tax revenues.

Pollution Licensing

Many economists regard pollution licensing as the most efficient method of pollution control. The way it works is as follows. On the basis of cost–benefit analysis, the government determines the optimal level of pollution. (This can be done for each category of pollution, but we assume, for simplicity, that there is only one kind.) Suppose the government determines that, in a specified area, about 10 million units of waste per year can be dumped. It then auctions the pollution licences for this amount. The holder of the licence for X units has the right to dump X units of waste during the year in the specified area. The strictly limited supply of licences ensures that the pollution level does not exceed the limit set. The producers of goods take the costs of reducing waste versus the costs of obtaining the licences into account. The price of the licence is bid up by the firms with the highest pollution abatement costs. The purchasers of the licences are the polluters. If conservationists want to reduce the level of pollution below the level set by the government, they can buy the licences and not use them. Furthermore, a firm that buys a licence can later sell it to some other firm if the original purchaser finds ways of reducing waste. In this method, firms are able to make rational choices and calculations without government intervention, unlike in the case of standards.

The only experience of tradable permits to combat air pollution is that of the United States. There is debate as to whether this method has improved air quality. Even so, it seems that air quality has not deteriorated, so trading seems to have fared no worse in the United States than the system of direct controls (standards). There is nothing comparable as yet in Europe, although Germany, the Netherlands, and the Scandinavian countries have carried out limited experiments or studies of specific projects.

Example 16-2   A European Union Carbon Tax

The ideal pollution tax from an efficiency point of view is one that exactly reflects the costs of pollution at the margin. But it is usually impractical to tax on this basis, hence we have proxy solutions adopted in practice (as we saw above). One option considered by the EU is a tax on carbon emissions from power stations.

The basic idea of a carbon tax is to tax carbon-producing fuels on the basis of their approximate carbon pollution potential. This alters the polluting input price (and so makes the use of carbon-based energy more expensive) and encourages substitution towards fuels with lower pollution potential (gas for coal, for example) and towards non-fossil fuels, such as nuclear. The disadvantage of this is that it treats all polluters alike and, therefore, penalizes plants with higher efficiency, and so fails to deal with actual pollution.

In May 1992 the European Commission announced plans to introduce a carbon (or energy) tax. Although EU member-states produce only 13 per cent of the world's CO_2 emissions, the Commission believes that an energy tax is a necessary first step in stabilizing the output of CO_2, the main cause of global warming. It proposed that the tax should start at $3 on the equivalent of a barrel of oil and rise by $1 a year to reach $10 a barrel by the year 2000, by which time the EU is committed to stabilizing CO_2 emissions at 1990 levels. Half the tax would be levied on the fuel content of all non-renewable energy and half on the carbon content. At $10 per barrel, it is estimated that the tax would have the biggest impact on industry and power stations. They would have to pay 58 per cent more for hard coal, 45 per cent more for heavy fuel oil, and 34 per cent more for natural gas. The prices of petrol and diesel fuel would have to rise by 6 and 11 per cent, respectively. For households, the tax would be equivalent to a 16 per cent increase in light fuel oil prices while natural gas prices would rise by 14 per cent. The Commission estimates that by the year 2000 the tax would yield EU governments around 50 billion ECUs a year. The Commission is not convinced that voluntary reductions in the emission of greenhouse gases are enough. In the longer term, it wishes to see a tax system in place that yields reductions in CO_2 output rather than merely stabilizing current levels.

Although the EU has taken a firm stance, the tax will not be implemented unless both the United States and Japan agree to introduce a similar tax. Further, with the exception of some European countries outside the EU, few countries seem prepared to make the first move. Most member-states of the EU argue that, in raising the price of energy, the tax would make its more energy-intensive industries less competitive against Japan and the United States. As far as the UK is concerned, the government has said that it has no intention of unilaterally introducing a tax on carbon-based fuels.

The discussion of a carbo[n ...] good deal of research into the e[ffects] of carbon taxes.[7] Overall, these [...] possible to achieve significant [...] provided that the tax is relativ[e ...] has been supported by Agos[tini et al.] (OECD) Europe as a single country, they es[timate] the effects on CO_2 emissions of a uniform European carbon tax. They compute estimates with three different tax rates: $5, $50, and $100 per ton of carbon emitted by fuel. Their main finding is that, in order to maintain emissions from power plants at their 1988 levels, a $100 carbon tax would have to be imposed. They also suggest that policy should embrace other measures, such as tradable permits.

16-5 Public Goods

In the 1950s Samuelson laid down the theory of *pure public goods*. A pure public good is one that provides non-excludable and non-rival benefits to all people in a given society. *Non-excludability* means that it is technically impossible or extremely costly to exclude any individual from the benefits of a good. *Non-rivalry* means that there is no rivalry among the consumers because the enjoyment of the good by any one person does not reduce its availability for others. A classic example is that of a lighthouse: when the light is on, it is difficult to prevent any nearby ship from seeing it and taking advantage of it (non-excludability), and one ship's use does not affect other ships' ability to use it (non-rivalry).

In reality, there are no pure public goods. Even a lighthouse might send out a coded electronic transmission that could be unscrambled only by rented equipment: in this case, non-excludability would not apply. Also, if there were a dense concentration of ships, the ships with high masts could blot out the light

---

[7] See S. Barrett, 'Global Warming: Economics of a Carbon Tax', in D. Pearce (ed.), *Blueprint 2*, Earthscan Publications, London, 1991, Ch. 3.

[8] P. Agostini, M. Botteon, and C. Carraro, 'A Carbon Tax to Reduce CO_2 Emissions in Europe', *Energy Economics*, 14 (1992): 279–90.

other ships could not see it. In this case, umption is no longer non-rival.[9]

A model that shows that private markets under-produce public goods is well established in the economics literature.[10] The basic idea is that if no one can be excluded from consumption there is no way of charging a price for the good and, therefore, there is no incentive for private entrepreneurs to produce and sell it. Even if people could be selectively excluded from consuming it, the non-rivalry in consumption means that it is inefficient to exclude anyone. Since it costs nothing to provide the good to each additional customer after the first, social welfare is maximized by giving away the good free. The fact that, once a good is produced, the marginal cost of provision of the good to any individual is zero, leads to the *free-rider* problem. In other words, every individual wants to get a free ride, and does not want to pay for the provision of the good because it is possible to get it free once someone else pays for its provision.

The failure of the market to deal efficiently with the provision of public goods leads many economists to . suggest that the government should step in and produce them. There are, of course, some economists who argue that the costs of government bureaucracy and interference with liberty are so great that, except in the case of pure public goods such as national

defence, it is best to leave the production of many so-called public goods to the private sector. The argument is that private individuals come together and organize clubs to produce these goods efficiently. This is called *club theory*.[11] We consider the question of government intervention after outlining the main issues concerning the provision of public goods.

In our discussion we have to distinguish between two types of public goods: (1) pure public goods such as national defence, law and order, and basic research, and (2) goods that fall in between pure public goods and private goods. These include goods where partial exclusion is possible; examples are education, environmental quality, and transport. Also, there are three issues to be considered: (1) how much to produce, (2) how to cover costs, and (3) how to distribute the benefits.

16-6 Optimality Conditions for the Provision of Public Goods

We have consistently argued that the competitive market provides the optimal quantity of a private good because output is expanded just to the point where demand equals supply. At that point the demand curve represents the full social benefit of additional units MSB, and the supply curve reflects the marginal social cost of production MSC.

With public goods, too, output should be expanded to the point where $MSB = MSC$. But a market demand curve, which we derive by horizontally summing individual demand curves, no longer reflects MSB. This is because all individuals simultaneously benefit from each unit of the public good.

Figure 16-8 illustrates the derivation of a marginal social benefit curve for a public good from individuals' demand curves. For simplicity, we consider two individuals, A and B. MV_A represents the marginal value (or benefit) of the public good to A. This is individual A's demand curve for the good. MV_B is B's marginal value curve or demand curve for the good. In other words, the Xth unit of the good provides XD benefit to A and XE benefit to B. But both A and B

---

[9] Note, however the criticism of the lighthouse example in R. H. Coase, 'The Lighthouse in Economics', *Journal of Law and Economics*, 17 (1974): 357–76. Coase argues that the lighthouse example often cited as a public good is not a good illustration. He gives a sketch of the history and evolution of the British lighthouse system, which raises its revenues from the consumers of the service (ships calling on British ports). The service is operated by the Lights Advisory Committee representing Shipowners, Underwriters and Shippers, which is consulted on the budget. Thus, there is no need for government intervention in this case. Coase says: 'despite the extensive use of the lighthouse example in the literature, no economist, to my knowledge, has ever made a comprehensive study of lighthouse finance and administration. The lighthouse is simply plucked out of the air to serve as an illustration—economists should not use the lighthouse as an example of a service that could only be provided by the government.'

[10] See, for example, T. C. Bergstrom, L. Blume, and H. Varian, 'On the Private Provision of Public Goods', *Journal of Public Economics*, 29 (1986): 25–49, and R. Cornes and T. Sandler, *The Theory of Externalities, Public Goods, and Club Goods*, Cambridge University Press, 1986. For a non-technical approach, see M. Olson, *The Logic of Collective Action*, Harvard University Press, Cambridge, Mass., 1965.

---

[11] See J. M. Buchanan, 'An Economic Theory of Clubs', *Economica*, 32 (1965): 1–14.

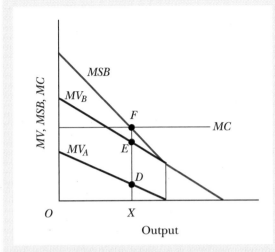

Figure 16-8   Optimal output of a public good

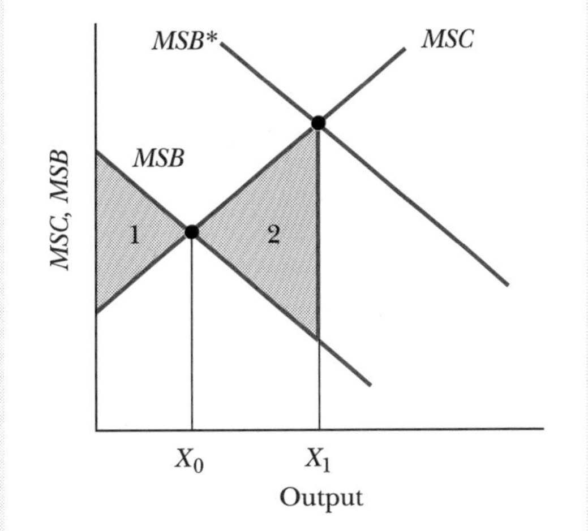

Figure 16-9   Net welfare loss due to overproduction of a public good

receive this benefit. So the *MSB* for the *X*th unit is $XD + XE$, which equals XF. Because of the non-rivalry in consumption with the public good, the *MSB* curve is derived by *vertically* summing the individuals' marginal value (or demand) curves. In Figure 16-8 the *MSB* curve is shown by the thick coloured line. The optimal output is now given by the intersection of the *MSB* curve with the marginal cost (both private and social) curve. The optimal output, therefore, is *OX* units of the public good. Note that at this output, $EF = XD$.

In practice, there is the problem of how to obtain the marginal benefits or valuations of individuals. With goods whose benefits accrue to a very large number of individuals, it is usually bureaucrats who estimate the social benefits and social costs. An underestimation of social costs and/or an overestimation of social benefits results in an overproduction of the public good. As a consequence, there can be a net social loss. This is illustrated in Figure 16-9.

The output corresponding to the intersection of the marginal social benefit *MSB* and the marginal social cost *MSC* curves is given by X_0. This is the optimal level of output. However, suppose the bureaucrats overestimate the *MSB* (in the interests of their own department). (The underestimation of costs can be similarly analysed.) The curve *MSB** shows the overestimated benefits. The actual production is X_1. The net social benefit when the output is X_0 is given by

the shaded area 1. However, if output is X_1, there is also a social loss given by the shaded area 2. If area 2 is larger than area 1 (as here), then society is better off without any of the good.

With the production of goods in government hands, it is often alleged that the costs of production invariably rise. The American economist Tullock[12] suggests a 'bureaucratic rule of two', which says that the transferring of any production activity from the private to the public sector results in a doubling of the unit costs of production. It is also customary to quote Parkinson's Law,[13] which says that employment in government agencies grows at a constant rate whether the work to be done rises, stays constant, or declines. Thus, many economists suggest that, except for pure public goods such as defence and law and order, the government should not enter into the area of direct production or provision of public goods. We now, therefore, discuss the methods for the private provision of public goods.

---

[12] G. Tullock, *The Politics of Bureaucracy*, Public Affairs Press, Washington, DC, 1965.
[13] C. N. Parkinson, *Parkinson's Law*, Houghton Mifflin, Boston, 1957.

16-7 Private Production of Public Goods

Examples of private production of public goods are hard to find, but increasingly in the UK we see the public sector subcontracting the provision of public goods to private producers. This is especially noticeable in local government (where local authorities are under increasing pressure to consider the financial implications of local public good provision) and in the National Health Service (NHS) following the introduction of compulsory competitive tendering. In view of this, it is interesting to consider the arguments concerning the private production of some public goods.

There have been papers that have attacked the classical proposition that free markets underproduce public goods.[14] These papers argue that, for an *excludable* public good, undersupply is not a problem since the competitive market can provide the good efficiently. Thompson, in fact, argues that an oversupply will result. His analysis, however, is based on the unrealistic assumption that producers have full knowledge of the demand curves of all consumers and can extract all the consumer surplus. He also assumes free entry. Hence, competition for the consumer surplus forces down the price and leads to oversupply.

Demsetz analyses the production of public goods the same way one analyses production with joint supply. As an example he cites the slaughtering of cattle, which provides goods to both leather users and meat consumers. The production of a public good similarly yields benefits that may be enjoyed by more than one person. Thus, Demsetz treats the same public good consumed by different individuals as different goods being supplied jointly. Since competitive markets can efficiently produce goods in joint supply, it follows that they can do so with public goods as well. However, his argument is flawed because the analogy with joint supply is not appropriate. In the case of joint supply (of beef and leather), a large number of consumers are competing for the goods jointly supplied. In the case of a public good, treated as

different goods for different consumers, there is only one consumer for each good.

One of the key assumptions made by both Thompson and Demsetz is that the preferences of individual consumers are completely known to sellers of the public good. Oakland shows that, once this key assumption is relaxed, the classical conclusion that if left to the private sector there is an underproduction of public goods still holds true, even for excludable public goods.[15]

16-8 Problems with Uniform Pricing of Public Goods

Suppose that there is a non-rival but excludable public good, and the government follows a socially optimal provision policy. In other words, it provides an amount for which $MSB = MSC$. If all users are charged the same price, and that price is set so that they are all willing to buy the full amount provided, then most users want to buy more units than they can, and no one wants to buy fewer units.

This is shown in Figure 16-10. Suppose that there are only two individuals, X and Y. Curves X and Y show

---

[14] Two papers that illustrate the arguments are E. A. Thompson, 'The Perfectly Competitive Production of Public Goods', *Review of Economics and Statistics*, 50 (1968): 1–12, and H. Demsetz, 'The Private Production of Public Goods', *Journal of Law and Economics*, 13 (1970): 292–306.

[15] W. H. Oakland, 'Public Goods, Perfect Competition, and Underproduction', *Journal of Political Economy*, 82 (1974): 927–39.

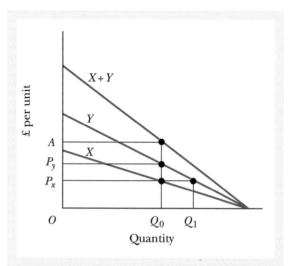

Figure 16-10 Problem with uniform pricing of a public good

the marginal values of each unit for the two individuals. Since each unit of the public good can be consumed by both X and Y, the total social value of a unit of the good is given by the curve $X+Y$, which is the vertical summation of the two curves X and Y.

Suppose the good is provided at a constant marginal cost OA. Then the marginal social benefit of the output is equal to the marginal social cost at the output level Q_0. To induce X to consume Q_0 units of the output, price must be P_x. But at price P_x individual Y wants to consume Q_1 units of output, which is greater than Q_0. Thus, with uniform pricing for the public good there are some individuals who want to consume more than is provided. If we can somehow charge price P_x for X and price P_y for Y, then both individuals freely choose to consume Q_0 units of the output and, furthermore, the production costs are completely covered because $P_x + P_y = OA$. Such a situation, where (1) the socially optimal amount of the public good is provided (where $MSB = MSC$), (2) each individual is charged a price equal to the marginal value for the individual, and (3) production costs are covered, is called a *Lindahl equilibrium*.

The system of charging different prices to different consumers is similar to the pricing of joint products considered by Marshall. The joint products are priced according to the demand for each product. In Figure 16-10, suppose that X and Y are two products jointly produced. The curves X and Y are the demand curves for these products. OA is the marginal cost of production. Then P_x and P_y are the prices charged for the two products.

How can we find the Lindahl equilibrium? Suppose sets of prices are proposed which just cover costs. Individuals are asked to record how much of the good they wish to consume at the various prices. When we find a set of prices for each individual at which all individuals want to consume the same amount of the good, we have found the Lindahl equilibrium. This mechanism, of course, assumes that individuals reveal their preferences truthfully. However, this may not be the case because of the free-rider problem we discussed earlier.

16-9   Revelation of Preferences for Public Goods

The problem of preference revelation is an important issue in the provision of public goods. All individuals try to under-report their own valuation, because once the good is produced they can get a free ride. The free-rider problem has long been regarded as insolvable in a world of imperfect information and self-interest. However, during the past 20 or so years economists have devised what is known as an *incentive-compatible mechanism*. This is the mechanism by which even self-interested individuals are induced to reveal their true preferences. The mechanism was first developed by Clarke and Groves around 1971 and since then has been extended in several directions. It is beyond our scope to discuss these later developments, but we shall outline the essentials of the original suggestions even though there are some problems that have been resolved in the subsequent literature. We follow the development in Tideman and Tullock.[16]

Consider the case of three voters and three options to choose from. All three voters are asked to state which option they prefer and the amount of money they are willing to pay to secure their preferred option. After the voters' responses are obtained, a Clarke–Groves tax is levied on each voter, which is actually a bizarre tax.

The voters' responses and their taxes are shown in Table 16-2. Voter A values options 1, 2, and 3 at £50, £20, and £10, respectively. Voter B values them at £10, £60, and £20, and voter C values them at £40, £10, and £55. On the basis of total value, option 1 is chosen.

Now consider voter A. Without A's vote, the total values are £50, £70, and £75 for options 1, 2, and 3, respectively. This is shown in the bottom part of Table 16-2. Thus, option 3 is chosen. Since A's vote changes the outcome from option 3 to option 1, the Clarke–Groves tax on voter A is £75 − £50 = £25. If option 3 is chosen, voter A gets a benefit of £10. By revealing her preferences, A sees that option 1 is chosen. A's increase in benefit is £40. The net benefit after tax is £40 − £25 = £15. This is shown in the last two columns of the top part of Table 16-2. Voter B's vote does not change the outcome, and B pays no tax.

Without C's vote, the total values are £60, £80, and £30 for options 1, 2, and 3, respectively. Thus, option 2

[16] T. N. Tideman and G. Tullock, 'A New and Superior Process for Making Social Decisions', *Journal of Political Economy*, 84 (1976): 1145–59. The paper by T. Groves and J. Ledyard, 'Optimal Allocation of Public Goods: A Solution to the Free Rider Problem', *Econometrica*, 45 (1977): 783–809, corrects some problems with earlier work.

Table 16-2   Clarke-Groves tax for public goods

Voter	Differential values of options (£)			Tax	Net benefit of voting after tax
	1	2	3		
A	50	20	10	25	15
B	10	60	20	0	0
C	40	10	55	20	10
Total	100	90	85		
Total without the individual's vote					
A: B + C	50	70	75		
B: A + C	90	30	65		
C: A + B	60	80	30		

is chosen. Since C's vote changes the outcome from option 2 to option 1, C's tax is £80 − £60 = £20. The benefit to C from voting is £40 − £10 = £30. The net benefit after tax is £30 − £20 = £10.

Note that, if voter A understated her preferences to avoid the tax (for example, if A stated that option 1 benefited her only £30), then with A's vote option 2 is chosen and without it option 3 is chosen. Thus, A's tax is reduced to £75 − £70 = £5. But the benefit for A from voting is £20 − £10 = £10 and the after-tax benefit is £10 − £5 = £5. Thus, A is made worse off. The tax we have obtained is very high, but this is because we have considered only three individuals. With a large number of individuals, the tax is minuscule.

The above example illustrates how, through a peculiar tax scheme, individuals can be made to reveal their preferences. There are, however, many practical difficulties in implementing the tax scheme. First, for the case of a large number of consumers, each of them has very little incentive to go to the trouble of giving a detailed value report, since each report has very little effect on the amount of the public good supplied. Also, the costs of administering the scheme for a large number of individuals are prohibitive. These costs can be reduced by requiring only a sample of the total population to report their marginal valuations. Only these individuals would then pay the Clarke–Groves tax, whereas all individuals pay a cost-share or a general tax.

The Tideman–Tullock process has been criticized in detail by Riker,[17] but we do not pursue this criticism

here because it is too lengthy for our purpose. The criticism suggests that there are many problems with preference-revealing mechanisms. Furthermore, there is not necessarily a large class of practical applications that correspond to the simple ones discussed here that can be solved as simply. Nevertheless, this literature does suggest that the free-rider problem can, in principle, be solved.

Example 16-3   Captain MacWhirr's Problem

The following example is similar to the demand-revealing process for determining preferences for public goods.[18] The similarity is that both are solutions to an information problem. The solution in each case is obtained by separating the information revealed by the individual from what the individual is entitled to.

In the novel *Typhoon*, Conrad poses a classic problem of information revelation. Two hundred Chinese workers are being transported home on a ship commanded by Captain MacWhirr, after working for seven years in various tropical colonies. Each

[17] W. H. Riker, 'Is a "New and Superior Process" Really Superior?', *Journal of Political Economy*, 87 (1979): 875–90.

[18] This interesting example is from G. E. Mumy, 'A Superior Solution to Captain MacWhirr's Problem: An Illustration of Information Problems and Entitlement Structures', *Journal of Political Economy*, 89 (1981): 1039–43.

worker's accumulated savings of silver coins are stored in his own wooden chest. However, the ship runs into a violent storm, all the wooden chests are smashed, and the silver coins are all scattered between decks. A riot ensues among the Chinese workers as they try to recover their silver coins. To stop the conflict, the captain sends the first mate and some men to pick up all the money with a plan to return it to the rightful owners. However, the captain has a big problem. How is he going to determine how much money each worker had? If he asks the workers, of course, each worker will overstate the amount. In the story, the captain imposes an arbitrary solution which he thinks is fair. He decides to assume that all men had the same amount of money, and he gives an equal share of the total to each worker.

This solution is not fair. Let us assume that only the captain knows the total amount of money and that each worker knows the amount he had but not the total amount or the amount that anybody else had. If the captain assumes that each worker is entitled to the amount he claims then each worker has an incentive to overstate this amount. The way to solve this problem is to cut the link between the claim each worker makes and the amount he is entitled to.

A straightforward way of doing this is as follows. Let the maximum amount to which an individual worker is entitled be the difference between the total amount of money and the total amount claimed by everyone else. If the individual claims less than this maximum entitlement, he gets what he claims. But if he claims more, he gets penalized (or taxed) and actually gets less than the maximum amount he is entitled to. Imposing a penalty for mis-revelation thus provides each worker with the incentive to tell the 'truth'. Telling the truth is, therefore, an optimal strategy, since it ensures that each worker receives the exact amount to which he is entitled. (A formal mathematical proof is given in the paper by Mumy.)

16-10 Government Intervention in Markets

Governments directly control a lot of economic activities in socialist countries. However, even in capitalist economies governments intervene in a large number of markets. The major role of the government in many countries is in the conduct of fiscal and monetary policies which are discussed in books on macroeconomics. In addition, governments intervene in the functioning of product and factor markets through a series of regulations. Some examples are:

1 Restrictive practices legislation aimed at preserving competition in the economy (discussed in Chapter 10)
2 Minimum wage laws (discussed in Chapters 13 and 14)
3 Agricultural price support programmes such as the EU's Common Agricultural Policy (discussed in Chapter 8)
4 Measures to control the amount of pollution generated by industry and car users (discussed earlier in this chapter)
5 A host of regulations on consumer protection (some of which are listed in the next section)

The list can be expanded to several pages. In view of the large role of government, we have to examine the purpose of government intervention and the way it comes about. There are two main goals of government intervention: (1) income redistribution and (2) a better allocation of resources. Regarding the first goal, research shows that the distribution of income in the UK was more unequal in the late 1980s than in the 1970s.[19]

Regarding the resource allocation objective, we discussed in the preceding sections two reasons for market failure: externalities and public goods. These two factors, along with monopoly and oligopoly (discussed in Chapters 9, 10, and 11), have formed the basis for government intervention in markets.

Broadly speaking, there are two theories of government intervention for the purpose of improving resource allocation: the public interest theory and the economic theory.

The Public Interest Theory

The public interest theory has a long tradition in economics. According to this theory, the market

---

[19] S. P. Jenkins, 'Income Inequality and Living Standards: Changes in the 1970s and 1980s', *Fiscal Studies*, 12 (1991): 1–28. For a discussion of the equity aspects of government policy, see e.g. R. Goodin and J. Le Grand, *Not Only the Poor: the Middle Classes and the Welfare State*, Allen & Unwin, London, 1987, and J. Hills (ed.), *The State of Welfare: the Welfare State in Britain since 1974*, Oxford University Press, 1990.

mechanism plays a major role in the optimal allocation of goods and services, but the public acts through the government to correct any failures in this allocation that might arise as a result of monopoly, externalities, or the existence of public goods. The theory rests on the assumptions that the government responds to a public demand for the correction of inefficient allocations and that the government can remove these inefficiencies at a lower cost than private organizations.

If this theory is correct, we should observe that government regulates monopolies, controls the output of public goods, and taxes or subsidizes externalities. In practice, however, we observe government tackling very few of these problems and instead intervening in other situations where there is little or no evidence of market failure. Restrictions by the EU on the importing (in the form of tariffs and quotas) of goods from outside the EU and government protection of inefficient industries and certain monopolies are examples of such actual behaviour.

A common explanation for these inefficient government activities is that there are certain special interest groups that lobby strongly for government intervention because they benefit from it. This idea is developed more adequately in the economic theory of regulation propounded by Stigler and others, who regard government intervention as another commodity whose equilibrium price and output are determined by demand and supply conditions.[20]

The Economic Theory

In the economic theory of regulation, introduced by Stigler and developed by Peltzman, regulation is treated like any other good. The equilibrium price and output are determined by the demand for and supply of regulation. Stigler argues that the behaviour of governments can be modelled as part of the market mechanism.

---

[20] G. J. Stigler, *The Citizen and the State*, University of Chicago Press, 1975, and S. Peltzman, 'Toward a More General Theory of Regulation', *Journal of Law and Economics*, 19 (1976): 211–40. A criticism of these theories can be found in R. Posner, 'Theories of Economic Regulation', *Bell Journal of Economics*, 5 (1974): 335–58 and J. Hirschleifer, 'Comment', *Journal of Law and Economics*, 19 (1976): 241–4.

Regulation confers benefits on some producers and groups by providing direct subsidies or controlling the entry of rivals. Examples of direct subsidies are those given to European farmers as part of the Common Agricultural Policy, and those given by many European governments to state-owned (or nationalized) industries, such as railways and public utilities. Prime examples of control of entry in the UK are the Civil Aviation Authority, which regulates the entry of airlines over different routes, and the Securities and Investment Board, which regulates the conduct of investment business, restricting entry to those who are authorized to practise. The regulations result in a transfer of wealth from one group to another. Thus, the commodity that is being transacted is the transfer of wealth by government intervention. The price of this commodity takes the form of open bribes, election campaign contributions, or more subtle forms of payment, such as lucrative jobs for relatives of politicians.

We first consider the demand side. The demanders are the firms or groups that benefit from the government subsidies or government controls over entry. There is, however, one problem on the demand side. Once a regulation comes into being, it benefits *all* the firms in the regulated industry, including those that did not contribute their time or money to politicians. This is the free-rider problem. Thus, regulation is more likely to occur in those cases where the beneficiaries form a small group. In this case it is easier to police the activities of individual members, and it is also easier to solicit lobby funds.

On the supply side, the political regulator wishes to maximize votes and thereby ensure security of tenure. (The price of wealth transfers is taken to be votes.) The number of votes the political regulator gets depends on such factors as the total transfers to the beneficiary group, the costs of forming the beneficiary group, the mitigation of opposition, lobbying, and the probability of opposition by the taxed group.

The economic theory of regulation gives some insights into the government regulatory process. It provides an explanation for why 'inefficient' regulations may come about. The political process introduces a regulation whenever the regulators and the beneficiary group can agree on a price. The economic theory has its critics as well. Posner argues that, although the economic theory is an important advance over competing theories, it does not enable us to predict specific industries in which regulation will be found.[21] The theory does not tell us the number of members in the beneficiary group that maximizes the likelihood of regulation. For instance, agriculture (with farm subsidies) is not a very concentrated industry, whereas the public utilities are and these are regulated. Posner argues that the economic theory is 'still so spongy that virtually any observation can be reconciled with the theory'. However, as Stigler argues, the main contribution of the economic theory is that it tells us to look, as precisely and carefully as we can, at who gains and who loses, and by how much, when we seek to explain a regulatory policy.[22]

16-11   Consumer Protection

Governments formulate several regulations to 'protect' consumers from exploitation by producers or special interest groups. Sometimes this exploitation occurs because consumers are not well informed, and in this case the government regulations serve a useful function. In other cases the government policies, although intended to 'protect' the consumer, might actually do more harm than good. This is particularly so where governments start tinkering with prices, as in the case of the Common Agricultural Policy.

The following is a partial list of different forms of consumer protection regulations:

1 *Requirements that the composition or possible effects of commodities be disclosed to consumers through labels or in advertising*   For instance, in the case of tobacco products, some advertisements in the UK have a footnote: 'SMOKING KILLS'.

2 *Requirements that commodities meet minimum standards prescribed by national governments and the EU as in the case of milk, meats, drugs, and drinking water*   We discussed the case of pollution standards in Section 16-4. The analysis of standards for different commodities is similar.

3 *Safety regulations in transport*   These include the compulsory wearing of seat belts in cars, limits on the speed of vehicles, maximum loads on lorries, and limits on the number of people carried on ferries and planes.

4 *Prohibition of the sale of various goods such as drugs and guns*   In the United States from 1920 to 1933 there was prohibition of the manufacture, sale, or transport of alcoholic drinks. This period, called the Prohibition Era, became famous for extreme violence and gangsterism. The widespread lawlessness gave the 1920s their nickname, 'Roaring Twenties'.

5 *Regulations aimed at controlling prices*   In the UK, many of the regulatory agencies of government are concerned with the regulation of prices. Those most often in the news are the regulators of the former nationalized industries, such as the Office of Telecommunications (OFTEL), the Office of Gas Supply (OFGAS), and the Office of Water Services (OFWAT). Each of these agencies passes to the relevant Minister of State its recommendations as to the appropriate level of prices to be charged to consumers. The industry may appeal against the decision of the regulator to the Monopolies and Mergers Commission. Thus far, the wishes of the regulatory agency have been complied with.

6 *Restrictions on persons permitted to supply certain commodities or services*   Examples are qualifications and registration requirements for lawyers, medical practitioners, and schoolteachers.

7 *Compulsory education for children*   One reason this restriction is imposed is because of the externalities arising from the consumption of education.

8 *'Citizens' Charter' (in the UK) which aims to protect the individual from poor-quality provision in the public services*   Consumers have the right to claim compensation for 'poor-quality services'; for example, if an Inter-City train arrives at its destination more than one hour late, passengers can claim a 25 per cent fare refund, and in the NHS individuals have the right to compensation if they have to wait more than two years for a hospital appointment.

There is no end to the list of consumer protection policies. The above discussion gives an idea of the different types of policies and their consequences to the consumer. We now look in more detail at a specific case of government intervention to protect the consumer: namely, regulation of health care.

16-12   Regulation of Health Care

In the UK, spending on health care accounts for around 6 per cent of national income. Most hospitals

---

[21] Posner, op. cit.: 347–8.
[22] A critical appraisal of various theories of regulation can be found in P. L. Joskow and R. G. Noll, 'Regulation in Theory and Practice: An Overview,' in G. Fromm (ed.), *Studies in Public Regulation*, MIT Press, Cambridge, Mass., 1983.

operate within the NHS, and the services within these hospitals are provided by salaried doctors and nurses employed by the Department of Health. Primary care is given by general practitioners who, although self-employed, work with NHS contracts and have the costs of most of their activities met by the public sector. Although there is a private health care sector, it is tiny in comparison with the NHS. In effect, the state is a monopoly provider. The system is, therefore, criticized on the grounds that a lack of competition allows inefficiencies to develop; as there is no competition, services are not produced at the lowest cost.[23]

The reform of the NHS has been designed to deal with such criticisms. Many hospitals now function as self-governing trusts, whereby they contract with area health authorities for the provision of services. In effect, an internal market for services has been created. This should ensure greater efficiency in the NHS as elements of competition and financial control are now in place. The service is still funded from general taxation, and most health care is still provided by the state. Although the reforms have introduced the discipline of the market into health care, we may ask why the government has not left the provision of health care to the unfettered operation of market forces.

Problems of resource allocation in health are as important as in other areas of life, and, as in other areas, government intervention is needed to deal with the failure of the market to allocate resources efficiently. In health, the market may 'fail' for a number of reasons:

1 *Imperfect information* There is an imbalance between the knowledge of the supplier of the treatment (the doctor) and that of the consumer (the patient). The supplier of medical care is also the supplier of information about the extent of any illness and the type of treatment and effectiveness of it. Consumers do not 'shop around', as they do not know (and cannot find out) the differences between good and bad treatment.
2 *Demand uncertainty* Generally, people cannot predict when they are likely to want health care treatment and so find it difficult to plan for expenditures that may be needed. Although private insurance is

available, the existence of *moral hazard* and *adverse selection* (discussed in Chapter 18) mean limitations in the operation of the insurance market.
3 *Externalities* Certain types of health care can create external benefits; for instance, vaccinations reduce the chances not only of those vaccinated catching a contagious disease but of others catching it as well. Thus, social benefits may not equal private benefits.
4 *Monopoly* The imbalance in information confers considerable monopoly power on the suppliers of medical services. Patients do not 'shop around', hence doctors and hospitals are not likely to compete with each other. Thus, each supplier can operate as a monopolist, raising prices without losing a lot of customers.

In view of these problems, we find governments intervening in the health care market in almost every country. One form of intervention, designed to deal with the imperfect information (and monopoly) problem, is regulation.

Much of the regulatory policy in the UK is designed to ensure that the quality of health care meets acceptable standards. Doctors need to complete a period of education and to gain acceptable qualifications before they can practise medicine, while nurses are required to complete specialist training and receive registration. The government itself is unlikely to have the specialist knowledge to carry out regulatory functions effectively, and so the responsibility for regulation is delegated to professional bodies within the health service. We have what is called *self-regulation*. In the UK such bodies are the British Medical Association, the Royal College of Surgeons, the Royal College of Nursing, and the Royal College of General Practitioners. All engage in different forms of regulation for their members.

As mentioned above, consumers do not have the level of medical information necessary to judge the competence of doctors. Acquiring such information is very costly, hence the system whereby providers assess other providers (self-regulation). One problem, though, is that these agencies may operate more to serve the interests of their own members than to protect the consumer. A particular criticism concerns the length of training, which may be seen as a means of restricting the supply (to raise incomes) rather than protecting against poor performance. In short, regulation often serves the interests of the regulated. Thus,

---

[23] The discussion here is based on Ch. 2 in J. Le Grand, C. Propper, and R. Robinson, *The Economics of Social Problems* (3rd edn.), Macmillan, London, 1992.

the intervention itself may create a system of incentives that lead to inefficiencies.

16-13 Application 1: Road Congestion and Optimal Pricing

The costs of car travel consist of: (1) costs of vehicle operation and (2) the time costs of travel. There are other unforeseeable costs, such as those of being involved in an accident. As additional cars join a congested road, this lowers the travel speed and raises the travel times of all car users. Thus, an additional car on the road, by increasing the overall cost of car travel, imposes a positive (though small) cost on *all* the vehicles on the road. Each motorist is assumed to take no account of the costs imposed on others via increased congestion. Motorists consider only the marginal private costs of a journey. We have, therefore, a divergence between the marginal private costs and the full social costs of a journey. This means that the amount of traffic using any road may be greater than the optimal flow.

This is illustrated in Figure 16-11. (Note that this diagram is the same as Figure 16-1.) *DD* is the demand curve for road travel and *MPC* and *MSC* are the marginal private and social costs of car travel, respectively. The *MSC* curve lies above the *MPC* curve by an amount equal to the *MEC*. The optimal level of road congestion is *OC* (where $MSC = D$). If no

account is taken of the external effects, *OF* is the level of congestion. We can arrive at the socially optimal level of congestion by charging motorists for the extra costs created. This payment may take the form of a tax levied on each motorist by the government. At the socially optimal level of congestion *OC*, we require a tax equal to *AB*. This raises the cost of car travel from *EF* to *AC*.

The best known, and oldest, example of road pricing is in Singapore. The concentration of population in a relatively small land area and rising car ownership have all led to major traffic congestion. Road pricing was first introduced in 1975 with the Area Licensing Scheme. This requires all cars entering or leaving the city centre in both the morning and evening peak periods to display an area licence. Private cars carrying four or more passengers are exempt, as are buses and commercial vehicles. In the first few months of the scheme, it is estimated that the amount of traffic entering the central zone was reduced by 40 per cent. The Area Licensing Scheme is a flat-rate price system, and so does not discriminate against drivers as much as the optimal pricing scheme shown in Figure 16-11. It is expected that by the mid-1990s an optimal road pricing scheme will be in place. Recently, as a complement to the pricing policy, controls on car ownership have also been introduced in Singapore. A quota system operates whereby any resident who wishes to buy a new car needs to have a 'certificate of entitlement'. These certificates are auctioned, and the first auction took place in April 1990. For the 14 000 certificates available there were 21 711 bids forthcoming.[24] It is unlikely that restricting car ownership by itself will have much effect on the level of congestion, although, if used in combination with road pricing and policies to support public transport, congestion may be eased.

16-14 Application 2: Public Transport

In most major European cities there is an underground transport system. The riders on the underground get some benefits, and by equating the marginal benefits and marginal costs, we get the price that users of the

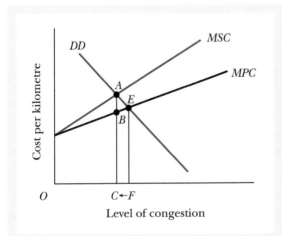

Figure 16-11 Congestion externality and road pricing

[24] For a fuller discussion of this, see P. Smith, 'Controlling Traffic Congestion by Regulating Car Ownership', *Journal of Transport Economics and Policy*, 26 (1992): 89–95.

underground system pay. This is shown in Figure 16-12. MB_u is the marginal benefit curve of underground users. MC is the marginal cost curve for underground use. The equilibrium quantity is OA, and the equilibrium price is AC.

However, the underground system confers benefits on car drivers through reduced congestion and travel time. In the calculation of total benefits to society, this needs to be taken into account. The benefit curve for car owners is shown as MB_c in Figure 16-12. However, the MC curve represents the full marginal social cost. Summing the two benefits MB_c and MB_u, we get the marginal social benefits as MSB.

The intersection of the MSB and MC curves gives OB as the optimal number of underground trips. However, since the demand curve for underground users is MB_u, to induce underground users to increase the number of trips to OB the price has to be reduced to BD. Thus, the optimal price is BD, and the optimal number of trips is OB. However, if the price is BD, the marginal costs are not fully covered (the shortfall is DE). But a shortfall in revenue can be met by taxing car users. Also, if the underground system increases property values, then we have to include another marginal benefit of property owners. Now the total MSB curve is obtained as a summation of the MB curves for car drivers, underground users, and property owners.

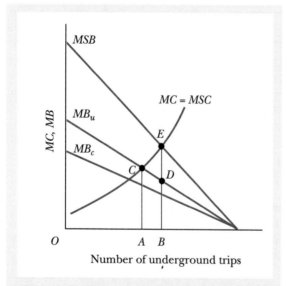

Figure 16-12 Optimal pricing of public transport

16-15 Summary

If production or consumption involves a negative externality, then the competitive output is greater than the socially optimal output. If production or consumption involves a positive externality, then the competitive output is less than the socially optimal output. The socially optimal output can be brought about by taxing the party imposing the external cost or subsidizing the party contributing the external benefit. The socially optimal output occurs where marginal social benefit equals marginal social cost.

Coase argued that the presence of externalities does not necessarily warrant government intervention because intervention is itself costly, and private deals could achieve the same result. Coase further argued that it makes no difference to the allocation of resources how the property rights to the contestable resource are assigned.

There are three types of policies designed to achieve the optimal level of pollution. Under the pollution standards scheme, the authority estimates the justifiable volume of discharge from each source and sets a quota at that amount. The permissible discharge must then be allocated among the various producers. The policy is inefficient because differences in pollution abatement costs are frequently ignored. Under the pollution charge method there is a tax charged per unit of waste dumped. Under pollution licensing, pollution permits are auctioned off and can then be resold. There are strict limits on the number of permits.

A pure public good is characterized by non-excludability and non-rivalry in consumption. Non-excludability means that individuals who do not contribute to the provision of the good cannot be excluded from the benefit once it is produced. Non-rivalry in consumption means that one person's consumption of the public good's benefits does not reduce the availability of benefits to others. It is economically inefficient to exclude anyone from the consumption of a public good, once it is produced. The provision of a public good should be expanded to the point where MSB equals MSC. The MSB curve is derived by vertically summing the individuals' marginal value or demand curves.

A Lindahl equilibrium occurs where $MSB = MSC$ for the public good, each individual pays a price equal to marginal value, and production costs are covered.

The Clarke–Groves tax is a method for providing individuals with the incentive to reveal correctly their preferences for a public good.

There are two theories of government intervention for the purpose of improving the allocation of resources. According to the public interest theory, government intervention is needed to correct market failures that arise because of monopoly, externalities, or the existence of public goods. According to the economic theory, regulation is an economic good. The amount of regulation is determined by the demand for and supply of intervention.

Governments formulate many regulations to protect consumers from exploitation by producers or other groups. Government regulation of health care is necessary because of problems of imperfect information and monopoly. The market is self-regulated in that the regulatory agencies of government consist of professionals monitoring the performance of fellow professionals on behalf of the consumer. One problem is that regulation may protect those regulated rather than the consumer.

When roads are congested, each additional car imposes an external cost on all other drivers. A tax can be used to bring about the optimal amount of road congestion. The marginal social benefit curve for public transport is the vertical sum of the marginal benefit to underground users and the marginal benefit to car drivers. To bring about the optimal quantity of ridership, the underground ticket price must be less than MC.

Key Terms

Coase theorem*
Economic theory of regulation*
External benefit*
External cost*
Free-rider problem*
Incentive-compatible mechanism*
Lindahl equilibrium*
Market failure*
Negative externality in consumption*
Negative externality in production*
Non-excludability*
Non-rivalry in consumption*
Pollution charges
Pollution licences
Pollution standards

Positive externality in consumption*
Positive externality in production*
Public interest theory of government regulation*
Pure public good*
Self-regulation
Social benefit*
Social cost*
Socially optimal output*

Questions

1   Give an example of a good or service whose production involves an external benefit or an external cost. Give an example of a good or service whose consumption involves an external cost or benefit.

2   What is the economic justification for government subsidization of education?

3   When the consumption of a good involves external benefits, can subsidizing the producers bring about the socially optimal output? Why or why not?

4   Explain why it is Pareto-inefficient to exclude anyone from consuming a pure public good once it is produced.

5   Is a radio broadcast a pure public good? How does the private sector manage to provide radio broadcasts? Do you think that the socially optimal quantity is provided? Why or why not?

6   Suppose that there are empty seats in your lecture theatre. Is your economics lecture then characterized by non-rivalry in consumption? Can an individual who does not pay tuition fees be excluded? Is it efficient to exclude those who do not pay? Does the situation change if the lecture theatre is crowded?

7   Give an example of a good that is characterized by non-excludability but not by non-rivalry in consumption. Give an example of a good that is characterized by non-rivalry in consumption but not by non-excludability. Which type of good do you think the private sector is more likely to provide? Why?

8   Why is the free-rider problem more likely to occur when a large number of people are involved?

9   Under Lindahl pricing, is it possible for an individual who benefits from a public good to be assigned a price of zero? Why?

10   With an external cost in production, is society clearly better off under perfect competition than with a monopoly in that industry? Why?

17 Intertemporal Choice

17-1 Introduction

In previous chapters we have ignored the time dimension, except to consider the distinction between the short run and the long run and the choice of present versus future consumption. We now examine problems that explicitly involve time.

Almost all problems in economics involve making choices that have consequences over a period of time. Consumers have to choose how much of their income to spend now and how much to save for the future. Producers have to decide how much to invest today in new equipment that generates output over a number of years. Students have to decide how many more years of study they are going to 'invest' in before entering the job market. All such choices involving time are called *intertemporal choices*.

In real life, decisions involving the future are even more complex because few aspects of the future are certain. Thus, intertemporal decision analysis must take account of uncertainty. However, we omit this problem and assume that future costs and returns are known. This is just a matter of simplifying our analysis and proceeding step by step.

Before we analyse the problem of intertemporal choice, we have to define two concepts that enable us to evaluate future costs and returns at the present time: *discounting* and *present values*.

17-2 Discounting and Present Values

We all know that £100 in the hand today is not the same as £100 paid in one year's time. We prefer to have the £100 today. But do we prefer the £100 today to £105 in one year's time? The answer depends on the rate we use to *discount* future payments. Suppose that we deposit the £100 today at 10 per cent interest. In one year's time we have £110, or $(1 + \text{interest rate}) \times (\pounds100)$. In this case, £100 today is equivalent to £110 in one year's time. Thus, we do not prefer the promise of £105 in one year's time to £100 today. We can, however, work backwards and calculate the present worth of £105 payable in one year's time. £105/1.10 equals approximately £95.45. That is, at an interest rate of 10 per cent, £95.45 could be invested today to yield £105 in one year's time. The £95.45 is called the 'present value' of the future £105. Thus, the *present value* (often abbreviated to *PV*) of a future payment is the amount received today that is equivalent in value to the future payment. The *discount rate* is the rate of interest we use in converting a future payment to its present value.

The above example considered a single payment, but sometimes payments are received over a period of time. Suppose the annual rate of interest is r, and it is constant over the entire period we are considering. We henceforth express r in decimal form so that a 10 per cent rate of interest means $r = 0.10$. Then £100 today is worth $£100(1+r)$ a year from now. This amount can be invested again at a rate of interest r to get $£100(1+r)(1+r) = £100(1+r)^2$ at the end of two years. At the end of three years we get $£100(1+r)^3$, and so on.

Conversely, if we are promised £100 now and £100 at the end of each of the next three years, the present values are calculated as follows:

£100 for the amount received now

$\dfrac{£100}{1+r}$ for the amount received one year from now

$\dfrac{£100}{(1+r)^2}$ for the amount received two years from now

$\dfrac{£100}{(1+r)^3}$ for the amount received three years from now

The total present value for this income stream is, therefore,

$$£100\left[1 + \frac{1}{1+r} + \frac{1}{(1+r)^2} + \frac{1}{(1+r)^3}\right]$$

For different values of r we can calculate the present value. For example, when $r = 0.05$ (or 5 per cent), the present value is

$$PV = (£100 + £95.24 + £90.70 + £86.38) = £372.32.$$

For $r = 0.10$, 0.15, and 0.20, the present values are as follows (you can easily check these with a calculator):

r	PV
0.10	£348.68
0.15	328.32
0.20	310.64

As the interest rate rises, the present value of the income stream falls.

Although many income streams are finite in time, sometimes it is convenient to talk of perpetual income streams. Suppose you buy a government bond from which you receive interest of £100 at the end of this year and £100 at the end of every year thereafter, for ever. This is called a *perpetual bond* or *perpetuity*. The

present value of this income stream is

$$PV = \frac{£100}{1+r} + \frac{£100}{(1+r)^2} + \frac{£100}{(1+r)^3} + \cdots$$

$$PV = £100\left[\frac{1}{1+r} + \frac{1}{(1+r)^2} + \frac{1}{(1+r)^3} + \cdots\right]$$

Now, you may know that the sum of the infinite series $x + x^2 + x^3 + \ldots$ is $x/(1-x)$, provided that x is less than 1 in absolute value. Since $1/(1+r) < 1$, we can define $x = 1/(1+r)$ and substitute to get

$$\frac{1}{1+r} + \frac{1}{(1+r)^2} + \frac{1}{(1+r)^3} + \cdots = \frac{\dfrac{1}{1+r}}{\left(1 - \dfrac{1}{1+r}\right)} = \frac{1}{r}.$$

Therefore, the present value of our perpetuity is $£100(1/r) = £100/r$. Suppose the rate of interest is $r = 0.05$. Then the present value (and hence the price) of the bond is £2000. If $r = 0.10$, the price of the bond falls to £1000. Thus, the higher the rate of interest, the lower the price of the bond. So, in the case of a perpetual bond, the bond price varies inversely with the rate of interest.

In practice, most bonds are not perpetuities. They have a fixed maturity. Most bonds pay interest every year and are redeemable at face value at the end of the maturity period. But the examples we have given show that bond prices fall when interest rates rise and rise when interest rates fall.

17-3 Choice of Investment Projects

One of the many important applications of the use of present values is in the choice of investment projects. Many investment projects, such as the building of factories, bridges, and power plants, involve costs at the beginning of the project and yield returns (revenues) only after a certain period of time. In these cases there are two questions to consider: (1) Should an investment project be undertaken? (2) Given that there are a number of investment projects worth undertaking, which is the best or how do we rank them?

There are a number of different methods available for answering these two questions. Textbooks on corporate finance discuss them at length. However, we limit our discussion to the following approaches: (1) the net present value rule, (2) the internal rate of return method, and (3) the profitability rate criterion (benefit–cost ratio). Each of these approaches has shortcomings, and, with suitable modifications, the *NPV* rule can be shown to be the most useful.

The Net Present Value (*NPV*) Rule

The *net present value (NPV)* rule says: rank projects according to their *NPV* and choose the project with the highest *NPV* first. The *NPV* is defined as

NPV = *PV* of returns (or revenues) − *PV* of costs.

Projects are worth while if the *NPV* > 0. If there are a number of projects with a positive *NPV*, then choose the project with the highest *NPV* first.

Where do these answers come from? When we begin talking about multi-period decisions, profits in various periods are no longer independent. Thus, the goal of profit maximization in each period is no longer reasonable for the firm. Instead, we treat the goal of the firm as the maximization of the present value of the entire stream of profits. Now, if *NPV* for a project is positive, then that project increases the present value of profits, and so should be undertaken. Similarly, projects with the highest *NPVs* add the most to the present value of profits, and so should be undertaken first. A few examples serve to illustrate this reasoning.

In Table 17-1 we present the stream of costs and returns for a hypothetical investment project over a number of years. Costs are assumed to be £200 for each of the first three years. The returns from the project begin only after the third year but then continue for ever at £100 per year. We assume that all the numbers in Table 17-1 are beginning-of-period numbers; that is, costs are due and returns are received at the beginning of the year. We can now compute present values of costs and returns.

$$PV \text{ of costs} = £200 + \frac{£200}{1+r} + \frac{£200}{(1+r)^2}$$

and

$$PV \text{ of returns} = £100 \left[\frac{1}{(1+r)^3} + \frac{1}{(1+r)^4} + \cdots \right]$$

The stream of returns is the same as a perpetuity of £100 with the first two payments missing. Thus, the *PV* of returns is equal to £100(1/r) − [£100/(1+r)] − [£100/(1+r)^2]. This is also equal to £100/[r(1+r)^2]. We can now calculate the *PV* of costs and returns for different values of r. These are shown in

Table 17-1 Stream of costs and returns for a hypothetical investment project

Year	Costs (£)	Returns (£)
1	200	0
2	200	0
3	200	0
4	0	100
5	0	100
6	0	100
7	0	100
8	0	100
9	0	100

Table 17-2 Present values of costs and returns at different interest rates

Interest rates r	PV of costs	PV of returns	NPV
0.05	571.88	1814.06	1242.18
0.10	547.11	826.45	279.34
0.15	525.14	504.10	−21.04
0.20	505.55	347.22	−158.33

Table 17-2. If the rate of interest is 5 per cent or 10 per cent, the *NPV* is positive and the project is worth undertaking; but it is not worth while if the rate of interest is 15 per cent or above.[1] Thus, projects with costs in the near future and returns in the more distant future are less and less attractive as the interest rate rises.

The *NPV* rule assumes that there is no uncertainty about the stream of costs and revenues and that there are no limits on the amount of funds the investor can borrow.

The Internal Rate of Return (*IRR*) Method

The *internal rate of return (IRR)* method says: rank projects by their *IRR* and choose the project with the

---

[1] In the case of more complex projects, the easiest way to calculate the *NPV* is to sum the combined revenues (R) and costs (C) accruing from year 1 (t = 1) and calculate $\sum_{i=1}^{n} [Y_t/(1+r)^t]$, where Y_t $R_t − C_t$ and may be positive or negative.

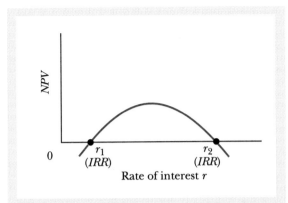

Figure 17-1 Multiple solutions to the internal rate of return

Table 17-3 Costs and returns of a mining project

Year	Costs*	Returns*	Explanation
1	4 000	0	Costs of opening the mine
2	0	25 000	Returns from the output
3	25 000	0	Costs of land reclamation and closing the mine

*All costs and returns accrue at the beginning of the year.

Table 17-4 Net present values from the operation of a coal mine

r	PV of costs	PV of returns	NPV
0.05	26 676	23 810	−2866
0.10	24 661	22 727	−1934
0.20	21 361	20 833	−528
0.25	20 000	20 000	0
0.50	15 111	16 667	1556
1.00	10 250	12 500	2250
2.00	6 778	8 333	1555
4.00	5 000	5 000	0

highest *IRR* first. The *IRR* is the rate of interest at which *PV* of returns = *PV* of costs. In other words, it is the rate of interest at which the *NPV* is zero. In the example in Table 17-2, this rate falls somewhere between 0.10 and 0.15. For $r = 0.14$ we have *PV* of costs = 529.33 and *PV* of returns = 549.62; hence $NPV = +20.29$. Since $NPV = -21.04$ at $r = 0.15$, the internal rate of return is roughly 0.145 or 14.5 per cent.

The internal rate of return method says: invest if $r < IRR$; otherwise, do not invest. If there are a number of projects where $r < IRR$, then choose the one with the highest *IRR* first. It might appear that this method gives the same answer to our question about investment as the *NPV* rule. This is true, however, only if the *NPV* is a smoothly declining function of the rate of interest r, as it is in Table 17-2. If, instead, there are multiple solutions to the internal rate of return, then the *IRR* method gives an implausible answer. For instance, in Figure 17-1, $NPV = 0$ for two values of r. Both r_1 and r_2 are internal rates of return. If the market rate of interest is less than r_1, then according to the *IRR* method we should invest. However, for values of $r < r_1$, *NPV* is negative, and so we lose money. Thus, we should not use the *IRR* method in these cases.

This example is not artificial. There are many real-world cases where investment projects have *terminal costs*. These are cases where there are large cleanup costs after a few years of operation. For example, in strip mining of coal there are returns during the mining process but there are large costs of land reclamation after the mining is over. Many chemical plants have large cleanup costs after a few years of

dumping waste. It is in cases such as these that problems with the use of the *IRR* arise.

Consider the case of a coal mine with three years of operation. The costs and returns are given in Table 17-3. The *NPV* for this mining project for different rates of interest is shown in Table 17-4. Note that $NPV = 0$ for $r = 0.25$ and $r = 4.00$. Thus, the internal rate of return has the values 25 and 400 per cent! However, at market rates of interest less than 25 per cent, *NPV* is negative. The *PV* of costs is higher than the *PV* of returns, and therefore the investment is not worth undertaking. The graph of *NPV* against r for this example is like the one shown in Figure 17-1.

The above example shows that investments with large terminal costs at a future date are not worth undertaking unless interest rates are high. Projects with returns in the near future and costs in the distant future are less and less attractive as the rate of interest *falls* (over some range). This is just the converse of the result we found in Table 17-2.

The Profitability Rate Criterion

The *profitability rate* criterion says: rank projects by the ratio of *PV* of returns to *PV* of costs and choose the project with the highest ratio. This is also known as the *benefit–cost ratio rule*. If this ratio is greater than 1, then the investment project is worth undertaking; otherwise, it is not. But if this ratio is greater than 1, then *NPV* > 0. Thus, the *NPV* rule and the profitability rate criterion always give the same answer to the questions of whether an investment is worth while. For example, the benefit–cost ratio for the project in Table 17-2 when $r = 0.10$ is 826.45/547.11 = 1.511, so the project is worth undertaking. This is in agreement with our earlier conclusion based on a *NPV* of +279.34.

Ranking Investment Projects

The ranking of different projects depends on which of the above approaches we use. This can be illustrated with an example. Consider the case of the project with costs and returns as in Table 17-1. We call this project *A*. Suppose a second project, project *B*, gives the same returns as project *A* (£100 each year after three years) but involves a cost of £550 in the first year and zero costs in the second and third years. Thus, *PV* of costs for project *B* = £550 at all rates of interest.

Consider, first, the *NPV* rule. If $r = 0.05$, then project *A* has a higher *PV* of costs than project *B*. Since both have the same *PV* of returns, *NPV* for project *A* < *NPV* for project *B*. Thus, project *B* is ranked higher than project *A*. The reverse is the case for $r = 0.10$: at this rate of interest project *A* is ranked higher than project *B*.

Consider next the *IRR* method. Let us assume that the multiple-solution problem we discussed earlier does not exist and that *NPV* is steadily declining as the rate of interest rises. This means that we can use the *IRR* method to decide whether or not an investment is worth undertaking. We saw earlier that the *IRR* for project *A* is 0.145. For project *B* we find the *IRR* by equating *PV* of returns to *PV* of costs, which is 550 at all rates of interest. Since we saw earlier that *PV* of returns is 549.62 for $r = 0.14$, the *IRR* for project *B* is close to 0.140. Thus, project *A* is ranked higher than project *B*, *at all rates of interest.*

Finally, the ranking by benefit–cost ratio or the ratio of *PV* of returns to *PV* of costs gives the same answer in this case as the ranking by *NPV*, because the

Table 17-5 The *NPV* rule and benefit-cost ratio give different rankings

	Project 1	Project 2
PV of returns	400	200
PV of costs	100	25
NPV	300	175
Ratio of PV of returns to PV of costs	4	8

PV of returns is the same for the two projects. However, one can easily construct examples where the two criteria give opposite answers. Consider the two projects outlined in Table 17-5. Using the *NPV* rule, project 1 is ranked higher than project 2. Using the profitability ratio criterion, we have the opposite ranking: project 2 is ranked higher than project 1.

The *NPV* rule is preferred to the other approaches because *NPV* is the net discounted total profit, and we wish to maximize total profit, not the profit rate. The profit rate argument applies to the *IRR* method. Implicitly, this approach assumes that funds can be reinvested at any time at the *IRR*, which is not the case. The *NPV* rule, by concentrating on the total net discounted profit, gives the correct answer, because this is the quantity we wish to maximize.

The applications in this chapter illustrate the use of the *NPV* concept in different contexts. But first we discuss the problems of intertemporal choices in consumption and production.

17-4 Intertemporal Consumption Decisions

In Chapter 2 (Section 2-10) we considered a consumer's choice between current and future consumption. The consumer, instead of choosing between different bundles of pizza and bottles of lager, chooses between a pizza today and a pizza in the future. This is what is known as a two-period model. In other words, we consider only two periods: present and future. There are, of course, more time periods over which decisions are made, but the two-period model gives us enough insights into the basic problems.

We first review the analysis in Chapter 2 and then extend it to cover different interest rates for borrowing and lending. We define the following:

y_0 = current income

y_1 = future income

c_0 = current consumption

c_1 = future consumption

r = rate of interest (for saving and borrowing)

We have to determine c_0 and c_1 given y_0, y_1, and r. We assume that the consumer's preferences can be represented by indifference curves that are convex, downward-sloping, and non-intersecting, as shown in Figure 17-2. We now need the budget line. Since the present discounted value of future income y_1 is $y_1 / (1+r)$, the maximum current consumption (or current wealth) is $w_0 = y_0 + y_1 / (1+r)$. Alternatively, consumers can save their entire present income, which is worth $y_0(1+r)$ in the future. Thus, maximum future consumption (or future wealth) is $w_1 = y_1 + y_0(1+r) = w_0(1+r)$. The slope of the budget line is, therefore, equal to $-(1+r)$.

In Figure 17-2 the consumer's equilibrium is at point A with current consumption c_0 and future consumption c_1. At point A the slope of indifference curve I_2 is equal to the slope of the budget line. We saw in Chapter 2 that the slope of the indifference curve (in absolute value) is equal to the ratio of the marginal utilities of c_0 and c_1. Thus, we have the relationship

$$\frac{\text{Marginal utility of } c_0}{\text{Marginal utility of } c_1} = -(1+r)$$

at point A.

We discussed in Chapter 2 how the consumer could borrow (or save) to increase (or decrease) current consumption c_0 over current income y_0. In Figure 17-2 the consumer is at point C on indifference curve I_1 if she is unable to borrow or save. (This point is called the consumer's endowment point.) But by saving some of the current income for the future, she can reach point A on the higher indifference curve I_2. One can also show the reverse case—that of the consumer borrowing against future income. Since we discussed this in Chapter 2, we do not go through it again.

We next consider the impact of a change in the rate of interest. Suppose there is a rise in the rate of interest r. What happens to current and future consumption? In particular, is the individual better off or worse off? This depends on whether the individual is a saver or a borrower. Figure 17-3 illustrates this point. BB is the initial budget line. With a rise in the interest rate, the budget line rotates to $B'B'$ through the endowment point (point C).

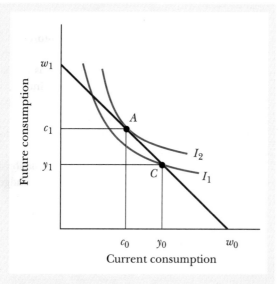

Figure 17-2   Choice between current and future consumption

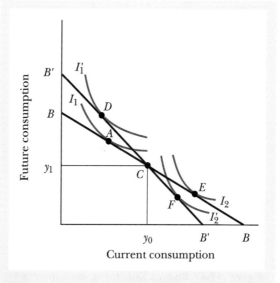

Figure 17-3   Effect of an increase in the interest rate on consumer behaviour

Now consider two individuals with indifference curves given by I_1, I_1' and I_2, I_2', respectively.[2] Individual 1 is initially at point A on indifference curve I_1. Note that individual 1 is a saver, since his current consumption is less than his current income (y_0). He moves to point D on a higher indifference curve I_1' when the interest rate rises. Individual 2 is initially at point E on indifference curve I_2. She is a borrower, since her current consumption is higher than her current income (y_0). When the interest rate rises, she moves to point F on a lower indifference curve I_2'. Thus, the result makes intuitive sense. A rise in the market rate makes savers better off and borrowers worse off.

We can now extend the analysis to consider the case where the consumer faces different interest rates for borrowing and saving. Suppose that the consumer gets an interest rate r_1 for saving and has to pay an interest rate r_2 for borrowing. We assume that $r_2 > r_1$. This is usually the case. The interest rate on a mortgage is often twice as high as the rate paid on instant-access savings accounts. What does the budget line look like under these circumstances? The budget line in this case is shown in Figure 17-4. The consumer can increase current consumption above current income y_0 by converting some or all of future income into current income at the rate of interest r_2. Similarly, the consumer can increase future consumption above y_1 by saving some or all of y_0 at the rate of interest r_1. Since $r_2 > r_1$, the budget line ($B_1 C B_0$) has a kink at point C, with the section $C B_0$ steeper than $B_1 C$. We can analyse the behaviour of the consumer by superimposing the indifference curves on the budget line. Since this analysis is straightforward, we do not pursue it further.[3] We can also study the effect of changes in borrowing and/or saving rates by the same procedure we used in Figure 17-3.

In the above analysis we implicitly assumed that prices are constant, and that the consumer is indifferent between various bundles of present and future goods and services. Thus, indifference curves must be expressed in real terms, and consumption must be expressed in real terms. If prices are not constant, then we must adjust for changes in the price level. Suppose that

$$P_1 = P_0(1+g),$$

so that g is the expected growth rate of prices (or inflation rate). The relationship between maximum real current consumption w_0 and maximum real future consumption w_1 is now

$$w_1 = \frac{w_0(1+r)}{1+g},$$

since w_0 invested now is $w_0(1+r)$ in the future but is worth only $[w_0(1+r)]/(1+g)$ in real terms. Thus, the slope of the budget line (in absolute terms) is $w_1/w_0 = (1+r)/(1+g)$. For example, if the rate of interest is 5 per cent and the inflation rate is also 5 per cent, the absolute slope of the budget line is $(1+0.05)/(1+0.05) = 1$: current goods can be substituted for future goods at the rate of 1 to 1.

The impact of a change in the rate of inflation is easily analysed by adjusting the slope of the budget line. It should be noted that the coordinates of point C in the previous diagrams are real incomes in each period.

---

[2] These are, of course, only portions of the indifference curves.

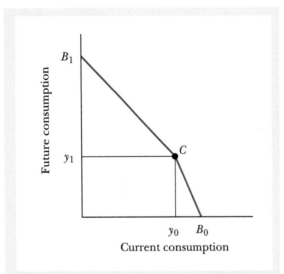

Figure 17-4 Budget line for a consumer who faces different interest rates for borrowing and lending

---

[3] It is worth noting that consumers tend to cluster at kinks such as point C, and so they do not respond to small changes in the interest rate (or the wage rate, in the case of labour supply decisions).

17-5   Intertemporal Production Decisions

In the preceding discussion we considered the equilibrium of a consumer with given current income y_0 and future income y_1. We can relax this assumption by considering the production side and the production possibilities. The resources an individual has at hand can be used to produce current goods (or current income y_0) or future goods (or future income y_1). For instance, the resources can be used to produce all consumption goods now, or some resources can be used for building better machines that increase the production of consumption goods in the future. Similarly, the individual can attend school now and increase future productivity, or she can work more now.

We can depict the production possibilities between current output and future output by a production possibilities curve. This curve is similar to the one we discussed in Section 4-6, except that instead of two goods we have current output y_0 and future output y_1. This is shown in Figure 17-5. By superimposing indifference curves on the production possibilities curve, we get the optimum for a producer–consumer who has no scope for exchanging current for future goods or vice versa. In other words, the individual's

consumption must equal production in each period. The optimal point is at P in Figure 17-5. The level of utility or satisfaction corresponds to indifference curve I_2.

Now, if there is a market for present and future goods, our producer–consumer can convert present goods into future goods and vice versa. This means that consumption no longer has to equal production in each period. The consumption possibilities are no longer directly constrained by the production possibilities curve.

Let us assume an interest rate of r. An individual producing at point R in Figure 17-6 produces y_0 in the current period and y_1 in the future. Maximum current consumption is w_0 where

$$w_0 = y_0 + \frac{y_1}{(1+r)},$$

and the individual's maximum future consumption is w_1 where

$$w_1 = y_1 + y_0(1+r).$$

In fact, the individual producing at R can consume anywhere along the line B_2, which is this person's 'budget constraint' or 'wealth line'. We saw earlier that the slope of the budget constraint is $-(1+r)$.

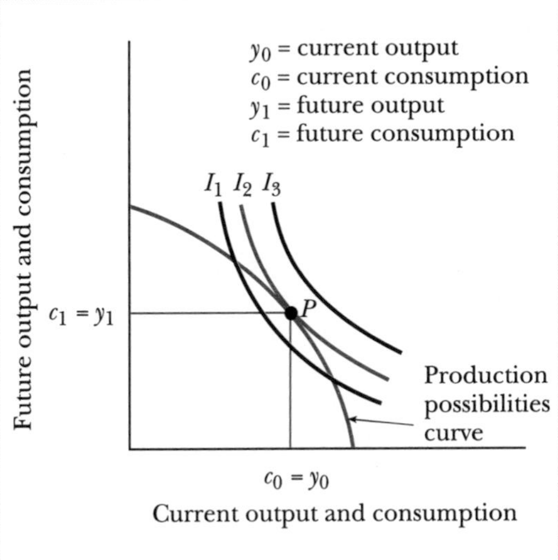

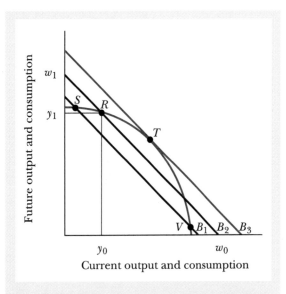

Figure 17-5   Equilibrium for the producer–consumer with no exchange

Figure 17-6   Budget lines when future goods can be exchanged for current goods and vice versa

We can construct a budget line corresponding to each point on the production possibilities curve. Since the interest rate is given as r, all the budget lines are parallel. For the individual producing at point T, the budget line is B_3. For the individual producing at S or V, the budget line is B_1.

The individual must now choose the production bundle (which determines the budget line) and the consumption bundle (given the budget line) to maximize satisfaction. Figure 17-7 illustrates the production and consumption equilibrium for a saver. Clearly, with a higher budget line, higher indifference curves are reached. Thus, the individual chooses the production bundle corresponding to the highest possible budget line. In Figure 17-7 this production bundle is T, where budget line B_3 is tangent to the production possibilities curve. Thus, the individual produces y_0 in the current period and y_1 in the future. Next, the consumer must choose the consumption bundle that maximizes satisfaction subject to budget line B_3. The optimal consumption bundle is Q in Figure 17-7, where I_2 is tangent to B_3. The individual consumes c_0 in the current period and c_1 in the future. Since $c_0 < y_0$, the individual is a saver. Note that the individual is better off because she can exchange

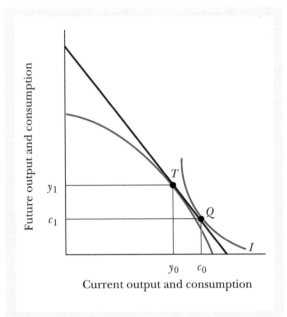

Figure 17-8   Production and consumption equilibrium for a borrower

current goods for future consumption. She can now reach I_2, whereas in the absence of intertemporal exchanges she could only reach I_1.

Figure 17-8 illustrates the choice of production and consumption for a borrower. In this case, $c_0 > y_0$ and $c_1 < y_1$. Again, the individual is better off with the ability to exchange future goods for current goods, since point Q lies on a higher indifference curve than point T.

One important point worth noting about Figures 17-7 and 17-8 is that the production optimum T is independent of the nature of the indifference curves. The indifference curves can alter position, but this merely changes the amount of borrowing and lending. The production optimum is determined solely by the production possibilities curve and the market rate of interest r. This result is commonly known as the *separation theorem* (separation of the production optimum from consumption choices).

Note, however, that this result is true only at the individual level. If the preferences of all individuals change, then this changes the aggregate level of borrowing and lending, which, in turn, changes the rate of interest r. This has an effect on the production optimum, and this in turn raises the question of how

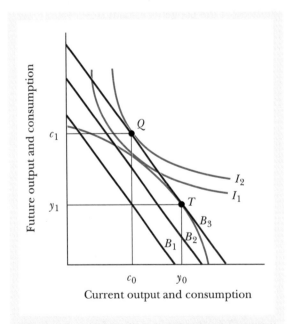

Figure 17-7   Production and consumption equilibrium for a saver

market interest rates are determined, which we discuss in the next section.

Example 17-1   Effects of Price Controls on the Supply of Natural Gas

In the case of non-storable products, price controls result in a decrease in the quantity supplied and an increase in the quantity demanded. However, the result is different for commodities whose supply can be changed over time. To illustrate this, we consider the supply of North Sea natural gas.

There are two effects of price controls that we have to consider: (1) the effect on North Sea gas exploration, and hence future supply, and (2) the effect on current supply from existing gas fields.

As far as future exploration is concerned, price controls, if they are effective, curtail exploration activity because the *NPV* of the future stream of earnings declines and some exploration activity that was marginally profitable before price controls is no longer undertaken. This affects the future supply of natural gas.

As far as existing gas fields are concerned, the decision that producers have to make is how much gas to supply now as opposed to supplying in future periods. Assuming for simplicity a two-period case, the producers adjust their current quantity supplied to the point where $P_1 = P_2 / (1 + r)$, where P_1 is the current gas price, P_2 is the next-period price, and r is the interest rate.

If both prices are controlled at $\overline{P}$ ($\overline{P} = P_1 = P_2$), a price $\overline{P}$ received next period is worth only $\overline{P}/(1+r)$ this period. Hence it pays producers to increase the quantity supplied this time period. They do this to the point where the current market price is equal to $\overline{P}/(1+r)$. Of course, there is an important geological constraint: namely, that the rapid pumping out of existing fields depletes the total supply. In any case, the immediate effect of price controls is to increase the current quantity supplied, and to create shortages in the future.

This seemingly perverse but natural reaction of producers, and the increase in the quantity supplied following price control, might delude politicians and customers into believing that the natural gas producers

were overcharging consumers. This would be detrimental to any rational policy-making.

17-6   How Are Interest Rates Determined?

In the previous section we saw that, given the production possibilities curve, the rate of interest determines the production optimum y_0, y_1 and the indifference curves determine the consumption optimum c_0, c_1. Based on this, we have some individuals who are savers (or lenders) and some individuals who are borrowers. We can aggregate the total amount of goods that are being lent and borrowed for each rate of interest. This gives the current demand for borrowed consumption goods and the current supply of loanable consumption goods at the different rates of interest.[4] The resulting demand and supply curves are shown in Figure 17-9. The intersection of these two curves determines the rate of interest.

Individual preferences might change, but as long as the aggregate demand and supply curves do not change, there is no change in the rate of interest. However, if there is a general shift of preferences for current over future consumption, the demand curve

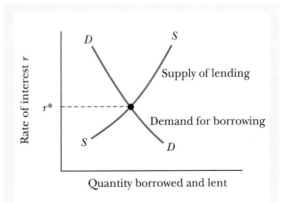

Figure 17-9   Determination of the market rate of interest

---

[4] In addition, we can consider the future period and draw the demand and supply curves for future goods. It does not make any difference.

for borrowing shifts to the right and the supply curve shifts to the left. These shifts occur because of increased borrowing by the previous borrowers, and an increase in the number of borrowers because some individuals who were lenders might become borrowers. This results in a rise in the rate of interest, and, as noted earlier, results in an optimum production level where y_0 is higher and y_1 is lower. The final equilibrium is reached where the quantity of goods supplied by lenders is equal to the quantity of goods demanded by the borrowers at an increased level of current production y_0.

17-7 Application 1: The Decision to Migrate

The decision to migrate (either from one country to another or from one region to another within the same country) is analogous to an investment decision. As with investment, individuals need to estimate the costs and returns to migration, and they need to consider that costs incurred today are in anticipation of returns in the future. Labour migration can, therefore, be considered as an investment in human capital.

Central to the migration decision is the identification of the costs and the returns from migration. The costs include the monetary expenses of the move and the forgone earnings during the move or while job searching. On top of this, we can add the psychic costs of leaving family and friends. The private monetary returns are the higher expected real wages, while the non-monetary returns may include a better climate, a more pleasant environment, better recreational facilities, and so on.

Because the costs and the returns are not (perfectly) synchronized in time (we incur costs now for returns in the future), the future returns need to be discounted to find their present value. By subtracting the initial costs from the discounted future returns, we have an estimate of the NPV of migration. It is customary to show the calculation in the following way:

$$NPV = \sum_{i=1}^{n} \frac{R_i}{(1+r)^i} - C$$

where R_i are the returns from migration that accrue from year 1, C is the initial cost of the move, and r is the discount (interest) rate. Thus, the NPV of migration is the sum of the discounted returns minus the cost. If the NPV is positive, migration is deemed worth while.

The human capital framework as presented here assumes that all the costs and returns from migration are known with certainty. In practice, migrants may not know all the pros and cons of a move, and so they may not act in the rational way that the model assumes (although their decision could still be rational, given the information they have). Because of this, refinements to the basic model have been made which allow for the risk and uncertainty that a migrant may face because of poor information about living and working conditions in other regions or countries.

17-8 Application 2: Are You Worth Your Weight in Gold?

Suppose that you start your career at the age of 25 and you earn an annual income of £25 000 for the next 40 years. Since 40 years is a long enough period to be considered a perpetuity, we can take the present value as £25 000/r where r is the rate of interest. At an annual rate of interest of 10 per cent, the present value of your income stream is £250 000.

We can now try to answer the question of whether you are worth your weight in gold.[5] This depends on the price of gold. The price of gold in November 1993 was $375.75 per troy ounce. Since there are approximately 14.6 troy ounces per pound, the price of gold was $5485.95 per pound. This is equivalent to a price per kilogram of $12 069.09. If we convert this to sterling (using the November 1993 exchange rate), the price of gold was £8154.79 per kilogram. So, with an income stream of £250 000, you are worth your weight in gold only if you weigh less than 30.6 kilograms.

However, your income is not going to remain at £25 000 for the next 40 years. Suppose your income grows at a nominal rate of 5 per cent per year. Then the present value is

$$\frac{25\,000}{1.1} + \frac{25\,000(1.05)}{(1.1)^2} + \frac{25\,000(1.05)^2}{(1.1)^3} \cdots$$

Since $1.05/1.1 \simeq 1/1.05$, this implies that the effective rate of interest is 5 per cent. In general, the rate of

---

[5] See H. G. Johnson, 'Are You Worth Your Weight in Gold?' *Journal of Political Economy*, 75 (1967): 205–7.

capitalization of the income stream is equal to the rate of interest minus the rate of growth of income.

At a 5 per cent rate of interest, the present value of your lifetime earnings is £500 000. Now you are worth your weight in gold if you weigh less than 61.3 kilograms. We can do the calculations with different values for the price of gold, starting income, growth rate of income, and rate of interest. If the price of gold was $500 per troy ounce, then with an income stream of £500 000 you need to weigh less than 46.1 kilograms to be worth your weight in gold. In this case, many people are not worth their weight in gold. Of course, with a higher inflation rate income grows at a higher rate, but the interest rate also rises. We assume that these two effects cancel out.[6]

Bennett *et al.* calculate present values of lifetime earnings in the UK using net earnings data for over 20 000 individuals drawn from the General Household Survey in 1985–88.[7] Their research focuses mainly on the effect that vocational qualifications have on expected lifetime earnings, but as a comparison they also calculate the effect of formal school (GCSE and A-level) and university (degree) qualifications on discounted lifetime earnings. The figures they calculate are for individuals who undertake a qualification on a full-time basis from the age of 16 (and 18) and complete it in the prescribed time. The only cost to individuals is the forgone earnings. (Tuition fees are paid.)

The results show that a decision at age 16 to pursue vocational qualifications or take A levels can be expected to produce significant additional lifetime earnings over and above that accruing with no qualifications. This is true for both males and females, and whether the discount rate is set at $r = 0.05$ or 0.10. For males, the present value of lifetime earnings for the no-qualification group was £138 500 (in 1992 prices) using a 5 per cent discount rate. This compares with a figure of £160 300 for males

with intermediate vocational qualifications. The figures for those with GCSE and A levels were £164 000 and £165 900, respectively. Females who joined the labour market at age 16 with no formal qualifications can expect lifetime earnings of £95 700 ($r = 0.05$) whereas those with intermediate qualifications can expect to earn £108 900. The figures for those with GCSE and A levels were £116 000 and £118 900, respectively.

The research also shows that it pays to have a degree as compared with high vocational qualifications, especially for females. Males with a degree have expected lifetime earnings of £190 200 ($r = 0.05$) compared with £187 600 for those with high vocational qualifications. In the case of females, the figures are £167 600 and £131 800, respectively.

The figures presented above assume that individuals are employed on a full-time basis throughout their lifetime and do not suffer any spells of unemployment. The effect of allowing for unemployment is to narrow the lifetime earnings differential between vocational and academic qualifications. This is because individuals with vocational qualifications are seen to experience fewer incidences of unemployment than those with equivalent academic qualifications.

These data on the present value of lifetime earnings show that investing in human capital pays. Whatever kind of vocational or academic qualification we consider, individuals can expect their lifetime earnings to be significantly higher than those individuals with no qualifications. Even so, Bennett *et al.* show that vocational training *per se* is not necessarily beneficial when compared with joining the labour market at age 16 with GCSEs. Expected lifetime earnings from lower vocational qualifications fall below those of school-leavers with only GCSEs. They suggest that, since employers seem not to have placed a high value on low-level vocational qualifications, young people have been acting rationally in not joining vocational training schemes in as large a number as in other European countries.

---

[6] As an anecdote, it is worth noting that the Ismaili community used to weigh the late Aga Khan III (1877–1957) every year on his birthday and present him with gold equal to his weight. It is doubtful whether this gave him any incentive to diet. But he had a long life anyway.

[7] R. Bennett, H. Glennerster, and D. Nevison, 'Investing in Skill: Expected Returns to Vocational Studies', Discussion Paper WSP/83, Centre for Economics and Related Disciplines, London School of Economics, November 1992; also by the same authors, 'Investing in Skill: To Stay On or Not to Stay On', *Oxford Review of Economic Policy*, 8 (1992): 130–45.

17-9 Application 3: Is the Channel Tunnel Worth While?

A case where the discounting of future returns is necessary is the Channel Tunnel project. The obvious feature of this investment project is its long time scale,

Table 17-6 NPV of the Channel Tunnel using different discount rates

Discount rate r	NPV (£ m)
0.00	21 034.00
0.03	5 878.84
0.05	1 725.71
0.06	431.73
0.08	−1 289.08
0.10	−2 328.20
0.12	−2 993.04
0.15	−3 609.65

Source: unpublished figures kindly supplied by Stephen Trotter.

so it seems appropriate to use the *NPV* method of investment appraisal.

On 18 November 1987, the Eurotunnel flotation prospectus was published in the *Financial Times*. The total costs of the project, in July 1987 prices, were estimated at £4874 million. (They are now significantly higher.) The real returns (measured in £ million in 1987 prices) were projected over a 54-year period from 1987 to 2041. The returns are zero for 1987–93 and positive from year 6. (In 1987 the tunnel was expected to open in 1993.) Given the initial cost figure and a future stream of returns, we can use the standard formula to calculate the *NPV* of the Channel Tunnel project.[8] The returns are 219, 317, and 339 (for years 6, 7, and 8) and 618 and 617 (for years 53 and 54). If we use a discount rate $r = 0.05$, our formula is

$$NPV = -4874 + \frac{219}{(1.05)^6} + \frac{317}{(1.05)^7} + \frac{339}{(1.05)^8} + \ldots +$$

$$\frac{618}{(1.05)^{53}} + \frac{617}{(1.05)^{54}}.$$

This gives a *NPV* of £1725.71 million (in 1987 prices). We can calculate the *NPV* using different discount rates. This is shown in Table 17-6.

We can see that if $r = 0.03$ the *NPV* is £5878.84 million, and if $r = 0.06$ the *NPV* is £431.73 million. If r is much above 6 per cent, the *NPV* turns negative and the project should not be undertaken. The *NPV*s are

also sensitive to a change in the initial costs. For example, if the initial cost increased by 36 per cent, this makes the *NPV* negative using $r = 0.05$.

17-10 Application 4: Forestry Expansion

Some economists have studied the returns to the economy and to society from investment in forestry.[9] As with any other type of investment, we can use standard investment appraisal methods to consider its worthiness. The question we can ask is: On the basis of the *NPV* rule, is investment in forestry (afforestation) worth while?

Before answering this question, we need to say something about the nature of this activity. Forestry is a multiple-output activity. The planting of forests produces a number of joint outputs and services which may generate benefits or costs depending on where the afforestation takes place. Pearce quotes numerous potential benefits from afforestation. These include: (1) the supply of timber (which can be sold in the market place), (2) recreational value, (3) reduced soil erosion compared with ploughing and road building, (4) reduced CO_2 emissions, so reducing the 'greenhouse effect', (5) increased security for the nation from reduced costs from interruptions to the supply of timber, (6) the creation of rural employment, and (7) a saving on imports (of timber). Apart from timber, it is difficult to value these benefits since they are not sold in the market place. When judged on commercial grounds, therefore, the returns to investment are low. But Pearce argues that a proper economic assessment of afforestation should take into account these other benefits. The costs of afforestation may be seen as land acquisition, planting costs, maintenance, felling, and so on. If the benefits outweigh the costs, afforestation is judged worth while.

The intertemporal dimension is important here because the benefits and costs accrue over time. It is necessary, therefore, to discount them in order to find their present value. Once this is done, afforestation becomes worth while if the discounted benefits

---

[8] I am indebted to Stephen Trotter for providing these figures.

[9] See e.g. D. Pearce, 'Assessing the Returns to the Economy and to Society from Investments in Forestry', Forestry Commission Paper no. 14, 1991.

outweigh the discounted costs. Pearce first of all calculates a series of *NPV*s for eight different types of forest (spruce in uplands, pine in lowlands, fir, spruce, broadleaves in lowlands, native broadleaves in lowlands, and so on) with the future returns calculated from the value of timber only. In this case all the *NPV*s are negative, ranging from −£458 per hectare for spruce in uplands to −£4283 per hectare for native broadleaves in lowlands. The discount rate is $r = 0.06$, and Pearce assumes a land value of 80 per cent of the market value. On this basis, then, investment in forestry should not be undertaken.

Pearce then calculates *NPV*s for each forest type with the returns adjusted so as to include values for recreation and carbon saving. It is not possible to get values for the other benefits. In this case the *NPV*s range from £20 per hectare for spruce in uplands to −£3490 per hectare for native broadleaves in lowlands. In all the cases where the *NPV*s remain negative, the figures are now lower. Even so, according to the *NPV* rule, afforestation is not worth while in seven out of the eight types of forest.

The *NPV* results suggest that afforestation is not justified on conventional grounds. Pearce argues, however, that the use of conventional investment appraisal methods is not really appropriate in the case of forestry investment because many of the benefits cannot be quantified, and so cannot be including in a *NPV* calculation. He argues that tax allowances and grants should be continued as they help make investment in forestry viable. Despite the arguments made for afforestation, the Forestry Commission continues to sell off forest land for private commercial use.

17-11 Application 5: The Market for Durable Goods

When purchasing a durable good like a car or a washing machine, the consumer is, in effect, purchasing a stream of services. The consumer purchases the good if the present value of the stream of services plus the discounted salvage value exceeds the purchase price. Alternatively, we can say that the maximum price a consumer is willing to pay is the present value of the services plus the discounted salvage value. The present value of this stream of services does, of course, vary across consumers. The salvage value is either the scrap

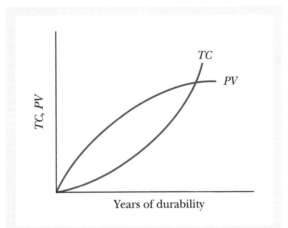

Figure 17-10   Impact of durability on present value and total cost

value at the end of the product's useful life or the price of the good in the second-hand market, depending on how long the consumer keeps the good.

In this section we examine two aspects of the durable goods market. The first aspect we consider is optimal durability. Here, we look at the impact of an increase in the discount rate on durability, and the impact of a change in durability on product price. The second aspect we consider is obsolescence. In particular, we examine obsolescence that is due to style changes.

First we analyse durability.[10] We assume, for simplicity, that the good provides a constant flow of services for a certain number of years (years of durability) and then breaks down. It is reasonable to assume that the marginal cost to the manufacturer of increasing the durability of the good is rising. However, in the computation of present values, the services in the distant future receive less and less weight. Hence the increment to present value is decreasing with increasing durability. The shapes of the total cost curve and the present value curve are, therefore, as shown in Figure 17-10. The corresponding increment to the *PV*

---

[10] The full analysis of optimal durability is more complicated than the simple analysis presented here. A more thorough analysis, and an argument that durability of consumption goods is the same under competition or monopoly, can be found in P. L. Swan, 'Durability of Consumption Goods', *American Economic Review*, 60 (1970): 884–94. Further discussion of this problem is in E. Sieper and P. L. Swan, 'Monopoly and Competition in the Market for Durable Goods', *Review of Economic Studies*, 40 (1973): 333–51.

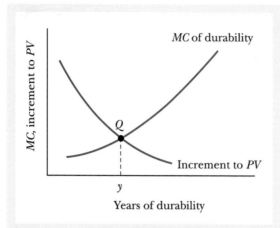

Figure 17-11 Determination of optimal durability for a consumption good

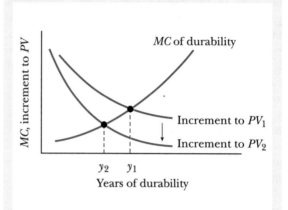

Figure 17-13 Impact of an increase in the interest rate on optimal durability

curve and the MC curve is shown in Figure 17-11. Since the increment to PV is the present value of the additional year's services, the increment to the PV curve can be viewed as the demand curve for durability. If all consumers are identical, the socially optimal durability is given by point Q with y years of durability.

We now consider the impact of a change in the discount rate on durability and the demand for durable goods. An increase in the rate of interest—that is, the rate at which future service flows are discounted—shifts the present value curve downwards, from PV_1 to PV_2 in Figure 17-12. The increment to PV for each unit of durability also falls, so that the increment to the PV curve shifts downwards as well. This is shown in Figure 17-13: optimal durability declines from y_1 to y_2.

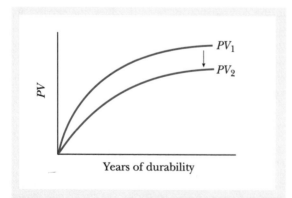

Figure 17-12 Impact of an increase in the discount rate on the PV curve

The increase in the discount rate thus causes the present value of a stream of services from a durable good to decline for two reasons. First of all, the PV of a fixed stream of services declines as the discount rate increases. Second, product durability declines, which reduces the length of the service stream. Since the price the consumer is willing to pay for a durable good is the present value of the service stream (which may vary among consumers) plus discounted salvage value, an increase in the discount rate reduces the demand for the durable good, and hence reduces price.

But what happens to salvage value? Suppose that the consumer plans to sell the good in the second-hand market. At any point in time, the price that someone is willing to pay for the used good is the present value (at that time) of the stream of services over the remaining life of the good. So a reduction in durability reduces the price of second-hand goods as well, reinforcing the reduction in the demand for new goods.

We can similarly examine the impact of style changes which produce obsolescence. Suppose, first of all, that style changes are anticipated, as in the case of cars. The services provided in later years have to be discounted more heavily because they do not provide as much satisfaction as before if new goods with newer styles are being introduced. This is equivalent to a rise in the interest rate. Hence both durability and price fall. If style changes are unanticipated, then they do not affect the price of the product when it is new. However, once the style change is announced, the present value of the remaining service stream declines, and the price of the used good falls.

We now discuss whether it is profitable to restrict resale. If the new goods and used goods compete with each other, some manufacturers who have a monopoly in the manufacture of the durable good can try to reduce this competition by various means, such as the introduction of new models (or new editions of a textbook) or the outright prohibition of resale. Consumers who typically purchase new goods take into account the reduced resale value, and this reduces their demand for the product. But the reduction in the availability of used goods induces some of the customers from the second-hand market to enter the new-goods market, thus increasing demand. What happens to the quantity sold and to the profits of the manufacturer depends on the degree of substitutability of the used good for the new good, the elasticity of demand, and the cost curves of the manufacturer.[11]

There are many problems associated with an analysis of durable goods. The purpose of our discussion here is to illustrate how present-value considerations enter in the determination of durability and the prices of new and used consumption goods.

17-12 Summary

The present value of a stream of future payments is the amount received today that is equivalent in value to the future payments. An increase in the discount rate reduces the *NPV*. The present value of a perpetuity is the amount of the annual payment divided by r, where r is the discount rate. The net present value rule says that only projects with a $NPV > 0$ should be undertaken and that projects should be ranked from highest to lowest according to their *NPV*s. The *NPV* rule leads to the maximization of the present value of the firm's profits.

Utility maximization requires that the marginal utility of current consumption/marginal utility of future consumption $= -(1+r)$. An increase in the interest rate makes savers better off and borrowers worse off. If borrowers and savers face different rates of interest, the budget constraint is kinked.

In analysing intertemporal consumption decisions, consumption and income must be expressed in real terms. A consumer–producer with no possibility of intertemporal exchange (consumption must equal production in each period) produces where the production possibilities curve is tangent to an indifference curve. When intertemporal exchange is possible, the individual produces where the slope of the production possibilities curve is $-(1+r)$ and consumes where the slope of an indifference curve is $-(1+r)$. All consumers are at least as well off with intertemporal exchange.

The intersection of the current demand for borrowed goods and the current supply of loanable goods gives the equilibrium interest rate in a simple two-period model.

You can discover whether you are worth your weight in gold by comparing the present value of your lifetime earnings with the price of gold. Individuals with vocational or academic qualifications can expect higher lifetime earnings than individuals with no qualifications. However, it does not pay to obtain low-level vocational qualifications at age 16 when the resulting lifetime earnings are compared with the expected lifetime earnings of school-leavers with GCSEs.

As the discount rate increases, other things being equal, optimal product durability declines, the demand for the durable good declines, and the price of the durable good falls.

Key Terms

Benefit–cost ratio rule*
Discounting*
Internal rate of return method*
Intertemporal choice*
Intertemporal exchange*
Net present value rule*
Perpetual bond or perpetuity*
Present value*
Profitability rate criterion*
Separation theorem*

---

[11] A more detailed analysis of the problem can be found in D. K. Benjamin and R. C. Kormendi, 'The Interrelationship between Markets for New and Used Durable Goods', *Journal of Law and Economics*, 17 (1974): 381–401.

Questions

1   Calculate the *NPV* for the investment project in Table 17-1 assuming that costs are due at the beginning of each year

but returns are received at the end of each year. Use a discount rate of 10 per cent.

2 In Figure 17-3, we examined the impact of a change in the interest rate on savers' and borrowers' well-being. Can you determine the impact of the increase in the interest rate on each group's current and future consumption? Assume that both current and future consumption are normal goods.

3 Use a diagram such as Figure 17-7 to examine the impact of an increase in the interest rate on production and consumption when intertemporal exchange is possible.

4 'If all members of society are equally productive and have the same preferences, there can be no intertemporal exchange'. Examine the validity of this statement in the context of our simple two-period model.

5 Tommy Waster is a consumer with a fixed income each period but a credit rating so bad that he is unable to borrow. What does his intertemporal budget constraint look like?

6 Assuming that the interest rate for borrowing exceeds the interest rate for lending, draw an intertemporal budget constraint for an individual with fixed income for both periods. What happens to this budget constraint if interest received on savings is taxed? What happens if interest paid on borrowing is tax-deductible?

7 Calculate the present value of £100 received at the end of one year, two years, and three years, when the interest rate is 5 per cent for the first year, 8 per cent for the second year, and 10 per cent for the third year.

8 In the analysis of durable goods, we argued that an increase in the discount rate reduces the demand for durable goods, *ceteris paribus*. One of the things held constant was prices. If the increase in the discount rate is due to a rise in the general level of prices, does this result hold?

18 Uncertainty and Imperfect Information

18-1 Introduction

The previous chapters in this book have ignored two major problems that are likely to be encountered in practice: *uncertainty* and *imperfect information*. We have assumed throughout that prices, costs, revenues, profits, and so on are all known with certainty. For instance, we have assumed that a firm making production decisions is certain about the prices it will pay for its inputs and the price it will receive from selling its output. Clearly, this is rarely the case. Both the demand for and supply of inputs and outputs fluctuate over time. This raises the question of how production and consumption decisions are made under uncertainty. The area of uncertainty in microeconomics is so vast that it is possible here to consider only a few of the most important and basic problems in a single-period context. The problem of multi-period decision-making under uncertainty is well beyond the scope of intermediate books in microeconomics.

The second problem to be covered in this chapter is that of imperfect information. This concept is related to uncertainty but deserves separate treatment. Throughout the book, we have assumed that consumers, producers, workers, and so on have complete information about the choices available to them. In practice, this is not so. Consumers have to search for a lower price. Workers have to search for information concerning alternative jobs. These problems form an

area called the 'economics of information'. Information is itself a commodity which economic agents can acquire only at some cost. Thus, there is a point at which each consumer stops searching for a lower price or each worker stops searching for an alternative job. This explains why the same product sells at different prices, or why workers with the same qualifications get different wages.

Before we consider these issues, we need to discuss a few basic results in probability theory. We explain the concepts of probability and expected values in Section 18-2, and in Section 18-3 we discuss the concept of risk.

18-2 Uncertainty, Probabilities, and Expected Values

The term 'probability' is used to give a quantitative measure to the uncertainty associated with uncertain events. There are two fundamental concepts in probability theory: *objective probability* and *subjective probability*. Objective probability is a concept based on long-run relative frequencies. Consider the case of a box containing three white balls and six red balls. The balls are identical, except for the colour. We shake the box and take out a ball (without looking at it). Is the ball drawn white or red? Of course, we are not sure about the outcome, but we can express our uncertainty by saying that the probability that a white ball is drawn is $\frac{1}{3}$ and the probability that a red ball is drawn is $\frac{2}{3}$. What this means is that, if we conduct the experiment of shaking the box well, drawing a ball without looking at it (and replacing it before the next draw), and we repeat this a large number of times, then in approximately one-third of cases the ball drawn will be white, and in the remaining two-thirds of cases it will be red.

In the above example, our interpretation of the probability of the outcome is an objective one because we can observe the frequency with which the outcome occurs. But if past observations of the frequency of an outcome are not possible, objective measures of probability cannot be deduced. In these cases we need a more subjective measure of probability. Subjective probability is the perception that an outcome will occur, where the perception is not necessarily based on the frequency with which an outcome has occurred in the past. When probabilities are subjective, different people may attach different probabilities to the same outcome and so make different choices.

Some early discussions of uncertainty in economics were couched in terms of objective probability. For instance, Knight drew a distinction between risk and uncertainty.[1] He described a situation as 'risky' if we can assign objective probabilities to the outcomes. A situation is described as 'uncertain' if the likelihood of the outcomes is unknown. Knight concluded that entrepreneurial decisions and profits are uncertain but not risky.

The problem with Knight's analysis is that he does not develop a theory of uncertainty. Following Knight, there developed a theory of probability based on subjective beliefs.[2] With this approach, the beliefs of consumers and producers can be given a probability interpretation. We therefore use the word 'uncertainty' to describe any situation where the probability of an outcome is not 0 or 1. The distinction made by Knight is no longer followed by writers in the area of uncertainty in economics.

Subjective beliefs can be translated into probabilities by using betting odds. For instance, suppose we consider a European Cup football match between AC Milan and Leicester City. If we say that

Probability that Milan wins $= \frac{1}{2}$

Probability that Leicester wins $= \frac{1}{4}$

Probability that the game is a draw $= \frac{1}{4}$

then we are prepared to bet 2 to 1 for Milan against Leicester and we are prepared to bet 1 to 1 for Leicester against a draw. Of course, consistency requires that we are also prepared to bet 2 to 1 for Milan against a draw. There are examples of some betting odds that do not result in a set of probabilities that are mutually consistent, but these do not concern us here.

A *random variable* is a variable whose value is uncertain but whose probability distribution is known. In the above example, the outcome of the match is a random variable. Suppose a firm cannot predict its actual profits but can describe its profits in probabilistic terms. Then the firm's profits are a random variable.[3]

If a random variable X takes on values x_1, $x_2, \ldots, x_n$ with probabilities p_1, p_2, $\ldots$, p_n (note $p_1 + p_2 + \ldots + p_n = 1$) then the *expected value* of the random variable, denoted by $E(X)$, is defined as

$$E(X) = p_1 \cdot x_1 + p_2 \cdot x_2 + \ldots + p_n \cdot x_n.$$

For instance, suppose a firm introduces an investment project but is not certain about its profits next year. However it believes that there is an even chance (probability) that they will be the same as this year, and that, if they do change, there is an equal chance (probability) that they will go up by £100 million or go down by £100 million. If this year's profits are £400 million, then we have the following probability distribution for next year's profits:

Probability that profits are £400 million $= \frac{1}{2}$

Probability that profits are £300 million $= \frac{1}{4}$

Probability that profits are £500 million $= \frac{1}{4}$

---

[1] See F. H. Knight, *Risk, Uncertainty and Profit*, Houghton Mifflin, New York, 1922.
[2] The pioneering essay is F. P. Ramsey, 'Truth and Probability', written in 1926. This, and other essays by Ramsey, can be found in D. H. Mellor (ed.), *Foundations: Essays in Philosophy, Logic, Mathematics and Economics*, Routledge, London, 1978, pp. 58–100. Ramsey was an English mathematician at Cambridge University who died in 1930 at the age of 26.

---

[3] A useful introduction to probability theory can be found in M. Barrow, *Statistics for Economics, Accounting and Business Studies*, Longman, London, 1988, Chs. 3–4.

Expected profits (π) are

$E(\pi) = \frac{1}{2}(400) + \frac{1}{4}(300) + \frac{1}{4}(500) = £400$ million.

Suppose the firm has an alternative investment in mind for which the probability distribution of profits is as follows:

Probability that profits are £400 million $= \frac{1}{2}$

Probability that profits are £0 $= \frac{1}{4}$

Probability that profits are £800 million $= \frac{1}{4}$

That is, if profits change, there is an even chance that they go up by £400 million or go down by £400 million. Again,

$E(\pi) = \frac{1}{2}(400) + \frac{1}{4}(0) + \frac{1}{4}(800) = £400$ million.

Thus, in both cases expected profits are £400 million, but the latter case seems riskier than the former. There is a chance of making much higher profits, but there is also a chance that all profits disappear. Thus, we need some measure of the risks involved. This is given by the variance of profits around the mean (average). If we denote the mean or expected profit by $\bar{x}$, then the variance $V(X)$ of the random variable X is given by

$$V(X) = p_1(x_1 - \bar{x})^2 + p_2(x_2 - \bar{x})^2 + \ldots + p_n(x_n - \bar{x})^2.$$

It is customary to denote the variance by using the notation σ^2. In the above example, in the first situation the variance of profits is

$$\sigma^2 = \frac{1}{2}(0)^2 + \frac{1}{4}(-100)^2 + \frac{1}{4}(100)^2 = \frac{(100)^2}{2} = £5000.$$

Usually, we take the square root of the variance, called the *standard deviation*, as our measure of risk. In this case the standard deviation $\sigma_1 = 100/\sqrt{2} = £70.7$.

In the second situation, the variance of profits is

$$\sigma^2 = \frac{1}{2}(0)^2 + \frac{1}{4}(-400)^2 + \frac{1}{4}(400)^2 = \frac{(400)^2}{2} = £80\,000.$$

The standard deviation $\sigma_2 = 400/\sqrt{2} = £282.8$. This confirms that the second situation is riskier than the first.

In our analysis of uncertainty, we use the expected values and variances of profits, prices, costs, and so on. Usually the firm can increase its expected profit only by making more risky investments, and this increases the variance of the profits. However, after a while even undertaking more risky investments does not help the

Figure 18-1   Profit opportunities for a firm

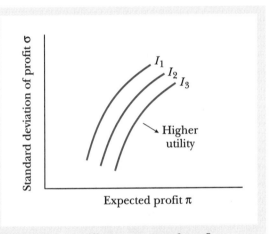

Figure 18-2   Indifference curves for a firm

firm to increase expected profits by much. This is depicted in the profit opportunities curve of the firm, which is shown in Figure 18-1. We see that at high levels of risk (a high standard deviation) there are relatively small increases in expected profit.

However, if the firm believes that high risk is bad, since high expected profits are good, then the indifference curves between a bad (risk) and a good (profit) are as shown in Figure 18-2.

In Figure 18-3 we show the equilibrium of the firm with respect to the optimal level of expected profits and risk (standard deviation of profits). AB is the profit opportunities curve. The highest indifference curve the firm can reach is I_1, with C as the point of

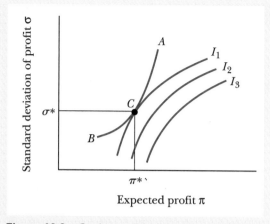

Figure 18-3   Optimum level of risk for a firm

tangency. Note that the greater (lesser) the risk aversion, the flatter (steeper) are the indifference curves; hence the firm chooses a point on the profit curve nearer to B (A).

18-3   Attitudes Towards Risk

In the preceding section we argued that a high variance of profit is bad. This need not always be the case. There are some individuals who love taking large risks. For them risk is not a 'bad': it is a 'good'. There are others who are indifferent. Finally, there are those who do not like taking risks at all. These individuals are said to be *risk-averse*. We now give a more formal definition of these terms.

Suppose that you toss a coin and you win £100 if it shows heads and you lose £100 if it shows tails. That is, you expect to win £100 with probability $\frac{1}{2}$ and you expect to lose £100 with probability $\frac{1}{2}$. Your expected return is

$$\tfrac{1}{2}(100) + \tfrac{1}{2}(-100) = 0.$$

This is called a *fair gamble*. A fair gamble is a gamble whose expected return is zero. Suppose you ask an individual how much he or she is prepared to pay to play this game (or gamble). A risk-loving person will pay a positive price to play this game. A risk-neutral individual will pay a zero price; that is, will play only if it is free. An individual afraid of taking risks will demand money to play this game. We now have the following

definitions:

Individuals are *risk-averse* if they are not prepared to undertake a fair gamble.
Individuals are *risk-neutral* if they are indifferent between accepting or rejecting a fair gamble.
Individuals are *risk-loving* if they are keen to undertake a fair gamble.

The utility function of wealth is different for these three groups of individuals. We explain these differences after explaining *expected utility theory*.

Suppose that an individual with a certain wealth of £800 is offered a fair gamble that gives an extra £100 with probability $\frac{1}{2}$ and takes away £100 with probability $\frac{1}{2}$. The initial utility for this individual is $U(£800)$. After the gamble the individual has a utility of $U(£900)$ with probability $\frac{1}{2}$ and $U(£700)$ with probability $\frac{1}{2}$. The expected utility (U^*) is therefore

$$U^* = \tfrac{1}{2}U(£900) + \tfrac{1}{2}U(£700).$$

It is a weighted average of the utilities of the different prospects, i.e. weighted by the respective probabilities. However, without the gamble the individual expects a utility of $U(£800)$, since this wealth is certain (has a probability of 1). Expected utility theory says that individuals behave as if to maximize expected utility. Hence in this case, if $U(£800)$ is greater than U^*, the individual does not gamble. This is the case for a risk-averse individual. If $U(£800)$ and U^* are the same, the individual is indifferent. This is the case of a risk-neutral individual. If $U(£800)$ is less than U^*, the individual is keen to gamble. This is the case of a risk-lover. The utility function of wealth for these three situations is shown in Figure 18-4. In each case, point A corresponds to $U(£700)$; point B corresponds to $U(£900)$; point C, which is the midpoint of AB, is half the sum of these and hence corresponds to the expected utility U^*; point D corresponds to $U(£800)$. For the risk-averse individual point D lies above point C. For the risk-neutral individual they are both the same. For the risk-loving person, point C lies above point D.

Expected utility theory was first formulated by Bernouilli over 250 years ago.[4] He observed that

---

[4] A translation of the original paper written in French in 1738 appears as D. Bernouilli, 'Exposition of a New Theory on the Measurement of Risk', trans. L. Sommer, *Econometrica*, 22 (1954): 23–6.

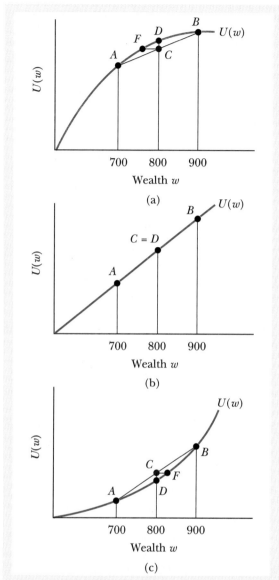

Figure 18-4 Utility functions for different attitudes towards risk

(a) Risk-averse individual
(b) Risk-neutral individual
(c) Risk-loving individual

ing because it can explain certain real-world phen. ena. For instance, insurance is typically an unfair gamble, that is, the expected money returned to the insured is less than the cost of the insurance. However, most individuals buy insurance because they are risk-averse.

Bernouilli's hypothesis about the behaviour of individuals facing uncertainty was later derived from more fundamental assumptions by Ramsey[5] and von Neumann and Morgenstern[6]. In a paper published in French in 1953, Allais presented a severe criticism of expected utility theory.[7] He presented examples to show the counter-intuitive character of some implications of expected utility theory. This problem has attracted the attention of several psychologists as well. For instance, Tversky and Kahneman found that very often the way a gamble is described, or 'framed', can have an important influence on individuals' choices;[8] according to expected utility theory, it should make no difference. To illustrate this point, they present the following two problems.

Problem 1 You are asked to make two decisions. You must choose between A, a certain gain of £240, and B, a 25 per cent chance of gaining £1000 and a 75 per cent chance of gaining nothing. In your second decision you must choose between C, a certain loss of £750, and D, a 75 per cent chance of losing £1000 and 25 per cent chance of losing nothing. When this problem was presented to 150 individuals, 84 per cent chose A over B, 87 per cent chose D over C, and 75 per cent chose the combination A and D. However, combination B and C dominates combination A and D, as is shown by problem 2.

[5] F. P. Ramsey, *The Foundations of Mathematics and Other Logical Essays*, Routledge, London, 1931, Ch. 7.
[6] J. von Neumann and O. Morgenstern, *Theory of Games and Economic Behavior*, Princeton University Press, Princeton, NJ, 1944.
[7] See M. Allais, 'Le comportement de l'homme rationnel devant le risque; critique des postulats et axiomes de l'école americaine'. *Econometrica*, 21 (1953): 503–46. This argument is known as the *Allais paradox*.
[8] A. Tversky and D. Kahneman, 'The Framing of Decisions and the Psychology of Choice', *Science*, no. 211 (1981): 453–8. These authors proposed an alternative descriptive model of economic behaviour called 'prospect theory' in their paper 'Prospect Theory: An Analysis of Decision under Risk', *Econometrica*, 47 (1979): 263–97.

different individuals responded differently to the same gambles. Thus, it is not the expected money value of the prizes but the expected utilities of the money values that matter. Bernouilli suggested that individuals behaved as if they maximized expected utility. The maximization-of-expected-utility hypothesis is interest-

between combination A and D—a
of winning £240 and a 75 per cent
£760—and combination B and C—a
ce of winning £250 and a 75 per cent
£750. All respondents to this problem
pre.... .bination B and C.

However, problems 1 and 2 are formally identical.

The answers to any problem should not differ depending on how the question is framed. In the above example, we could argue that individuals could not calculate things well. A more transparent case has been provided by McNeil *et al.*[9] Different groups of individuals, including a group of physicians, were presented with probabilities of survival during treatment for certain forms of cancer for one year and for five years, for each of two therapies: radiation and surgery. With these data, 84 per cent of the physicians preferred surgery and 16 per cent, radiation therapy. Then another group was presented with the same data but in a different way. They were shown probabilities of death, rather than probabilities of survival. But the probability of dying is just one minus the probability of survival. Also, the calculation is very trivial. However, the proportion of physicians choosing surgery over radiation therapy fell from 84 to 50 per cent!

We have presented a few examples which show that the way individuals actually respond to uncertain situations depends on how the uncertainty is presented.[10] This is contrary to the theory of expected utility. Although these results are important, we do not develop them here since this will take us off the main track we are following.[11] We bear them in mind, but continue to illustrate the idea of uncertainty using expected utility theory.[12]

[9] B. J. McNeil, S. G. Pauker, H. C. Sox, Jr, and A. Tversky, 'On the Elicitation of Preferences for Alternative Therapies', *New England Journal of Medicine*, 306 (1982): 1259–62.
[10] See the collection of papers in D. Kahneman, P. Slovic, and A. Tversky (eds.), *Judgment under Uncertainty: Heuristics and Biases*, Cambridge University Press, New York, 1982.
[11] For an application of the ideas of Tversky and Kahneman to the theory of consumer behaviour, see R. Thaler, 'Toward a Positive Theory of Consumer Choice', *Journal of Economic Behavior and Organisation*, 1 (1980): 39–60.
[12] For a discussion of expected utility theory and some alternatives, see M. J. Machina, 'Choice Under Uncertainty: Problems Solved and Unsolved', in J. D. Hey (ed.), *Current Issues in Microeconomics*, Macmillan, London, 1989, Ch. 2.

18-4 Insurance and Gambling

People who are risk-averse are prepared to pay to avoid risk. This is the basis of all insurance. Suppose my total wealth is £900, but I face the prospect of losing £200. I think there is a 50–50 chance of this happening. If I do not insure, my expected utility is given by point C in Figure 18-4(a). If we draw a horizontal line CF in part (a), we note that point F corresponds to the same level of utility as point C. Thus, if someone gave me a guaranteed wealth of £800 − CF, my utility is given by point F, and I am equally happy. So I am prepared to pay the insurance company a premium equal to

$$£900 - (£800 - CF) = £100 + CF,$$

provided the company guarantees that I get £900 even if I suffer a loss. *On average*, the insurance company pays me £100, and so its expected profits are equal to CF.

The wealth £800 − CF is the *certainty equivalent value* of the risky situation. It is that level of wealth offered with certainty that yields the same utility as the expected utility with the risk. The difference between the expected wealth (£800) and the certainty equivalent wealth is called the *cost of risk*. In our example the cost of risk is CF. The fraction of expected wealth an individual is willing to sacrifice for the sake of certainty (or to avoid taking a risk) is called the *risk premium*. In our example the risk premium is $CF/£800$. Note that the more risk-averse is the individual (the 'more curved' or more concave the utility function in Figure 18-4(a)), the greater is the cost of risk (and the risk premium).

This can be seen in Figure 18-5. The utility function for individual 1 is U_1, and for a second, more risk-averse, individual it is U_2. The cost of risk (the risk premium) for this person is ST. Person 2 is prepared to pay more than person 1 to avoid taking a risk.

The cost of gambling is the opposite of the case of insurance. Consider Figure 18-4(c). Suppose a gambler has a certain wealth of £800 with utility given by point D. Consider the uncertain prospect given by £900 with probability $\frac{1}{2}$ and £700 with probability $\frac{1}{2}$. The expected utility is given by point C, which gives a higher utility than point D, and the gambler is keen to take the gamble. How much is the gambler prepared to pay for this uncertain wealth? Draw a horizontal line CF. The certainty equivalent wealth is given by point F. This

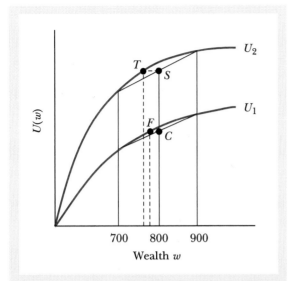

Figure 18-5   The cost of risk for two risk-averse individuals

U_2 is more risk averse than U_1

income is £800 + CF. The expected income is £800. Thus, the gambler is prepared to pay a price of up to CF to take the gamble. Note here that the more risk-loving is the individual (the 'more curved' or more convex is the utility function), the higher is the price he or she is prepared to pay to take a risk.

In practice, we observe the same individual buying insurance and gambling. How do we explain this? In a famous article, Friedman and Savage suggested that the utility function of a typical individual has both concave and convex segments (concave at low and high incomes and convex in between), as shown in Figure 18-6.[13] Suppose the individual has wealth w_0 and is at point B on the utility function $U(w)$. For a loss equal to L, the points that yield expected utility lie on the line segment AB (depending on the probability of loss). Since the utility function is above the line AB, the individual is better off buying insurance (as in Figure 18-4(a)).

Now consider gambles (lotteries) that pay a large sum M (with a small probability). The price of the lottery ticket is P. The individual is now at point $E(w_0 - P)$ on $U(w)$ in Figure 18-6. Point E lies close to point B if the price of the ticket is not high. If the probability of winning the lottery is 0.10, then the probability of winning M is 0.10 and the probability of losing P (the price of the ticket) is 0.90. In this case, the expected utility from the lottery is given by point F on the line CE. The distance between point F and point C

---

[13] M. Friedman and L. J. Savage, 'The Utility Analysis of Choices involving Risk', *Journal of Political Economy*, 56 (1948): 279–304.

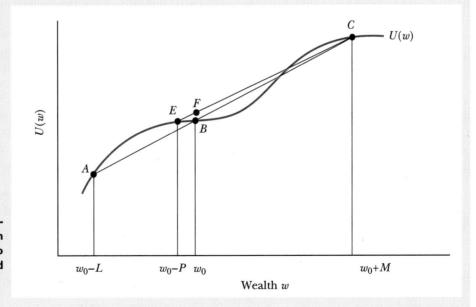

Figure 18-6   Utility function of an individual who buys insurance and gambles

is nine times the distance between F and E. As point F lies above $U(w)$, the individual buys the lottery ticket.

Note that a high probability of winning (say 0.50) and a high ticket price give an expected utility less than $U(w)$, and the individual does not buy the lottery ticket. The hypothesis is that there is only a small convex segment in the utility function and that this explains why individuals buy lottery tickets with a small price that promise to yield large payoffs (although with a very small probability).

18-5 Asymmetric Information: The Market for Lemons

In the preceding section we saw that a risk-averse individual is better off buying insurance against unforeseen circumstances (illness, fire, theft, and so on). We also saw that the insurance company can profit by providing the insurance. However, there is one major informational problem with the provision of insurance contracts. The problem arises from the fact that one party (the insurance company) has less information than the other party (the customer) about the risks involved. The customer has better knowledge than the insurance company about the probability of becoming ill. This is a case of *asymmetric information.*

An illustration of the problems created by asymmetric information is the market for lemons discussed by Akerlof.[14] The word 'lemon' is used to denote a defective product. Consider the market for used cars. We can, without any loss of generality, consider used cars that are identical except for quality differences. (That is, they are of the same age, size, and observable accessories.) Some of these cars are of good quality and others are lemons, which constantly break down and require many repairs. The owners of used cars know whether the car they own is a lemon. But all owners claim that they have a good car. Buyers, of course, cannot tell whether a car is a good one or a lemon until they have bought it. As a result, the market price of used cars depends on the average quality of the used cars available for sale. In this case, sellers of lemons get more than their cars are worth, and sellers

of good-quality cars get less than their cars are worth. Since buyers are not prepared to pay a price above what the average car is worth (indeed, if they are risk-averse they do not even pay the expected value), the owners of high-quality cars withdraw their cars from the market. This changes the distribution of used cars on the market, the average quality goes down, and so does the average price that buyers are prepared to pay. Again, cars with better-than-average quality are taken off the market, and the process goes on until no transactions take place. In effect, the 'lemons' drive out the good cars from the market. This phenomenon is also known as *adverse selection,* where only poor-quality products are left in the market and good-quality products are not offered for sale.

The problem here is that buyers and sellers are not able to communicate accurate information. However, in practice, numerous institutions exist that counteract the adverse effects of quality uncertainty suggested by the lemons model. In the case of used cars, one obvious institution is that of used car dealers who provide guarantees with the cars they sell. The more reputable dealers have their reputations at stake and the guarantee gives a certain assurance of quality. There are also service centres that can check the quality of used cars, and customers can get some information on quality from them, at a cost.

Some other institutions that counteract the effects of quality uncertainty are chain stores, named restaurant and hotel chains (Hilton, Holiday Inn, Post House, and so on), and licensed practices (doctors, lawyers). In all these cases, there is a certain assurance of quality. The consumer usually pays a higher price (a higher price for a burger at MacDonalds and a higher price for a pizza at Pizza Hut than a burger or pizza at a local restaurant), but there is an assurance of some standards of quality. In fact, we might argue that often customers interpret the higher price as an indication of higher quality (particularly in the case where sellers depend on repeat purchases). Scitovsky first wrote a note on the problem of inferring quality on the basis of price.[15] Stiglitz provides an exhaustive survey of the literature on the dependence of quality on price.[16]

---

[14] G. A. Akerlof, 'The Market for Lemons: Qualitative Uncertainty and the Market Mechanism', *Quarterly Journal of Economics*, 84 (1970): 488–500.

[15] T. Scitovsky, 'Some Consequences of the Habit of Judging Quality by Price', *Review of Economic Studies*, 12 (1945): 100–5.
[16] J. E. Stiglitz, 'The Causes and Consequences of the Dependence of Quality on Price', *Journal of Economic Literature*, 25 (1987): 1–48.

In the following sections we discuss alternative methods of dealing with the problems of asymmetric information and adverse selection.

18-6 The Insurance Market and Adverse Selection

As we said earlier, insurance markets are characterized by asymmetric information. The insurance company has less information about the risks (illness, accident proneness, and such) of the insured than the insured individuals themselves. We now illustrate the problem of adverse selection.

Suppose that there are two groups of individuals, a high-risk group (H of them) and a low-risk group (L of them). The probabilities of an illness (or accident) are Z_H and Z_L for the high and low groups respectively ($Z_H > Z_L$). Initially, both groups participate in the insurance programme, and if the company cannot distinguish them, a premium is set which reflects the weighted average level of risk for the whole group. This is

$$\overline{Z} = Z_H \cdot \frac{H}{H+L} + Z_L \cdot \frac{L}{H+L}.$$

Note that $Z_H > \overline{Z} > Z_L$. If the cost of illness (or accident) is C, the insurance premium I for full coverage is given by

$$I \geq C\overline{Z}.$$

If individuals know their own risks, since $\overline{Z} > Z_L$, individuals with low risk may not be prepared to buy insurance whereas high-risk individuals are anxious to accept it. If low-risk individuals drop out, the insurance company has to raise the premium, and then only high-risk individuals will buy insurance; low-risk individuals will have no insurance at all. Thus, if only high-risk individuals buy health insurance, we have adverse selection.

Low-risk people may be induced to reveal themselves if the government makes premiums tax-deductibile, or if the insurance company offers co-insurance. (The company pays a percentage of the premium.) This process is known as 'self-selection'. The insurance company can confront individuals with a structured set of choices with different rates of co-insurance, lengths of contract, and so on. From the choices made, the insurance company can infer the risk characteristics of individuals. However, the information problem is not completely solved. The information conveyed by the individual's choice of a particular contract depends on the set of contracts available to the individual.

With two groups of individuals with different probabilities of illness (or accident), it is possible to show that there cannot be a single insurance policy. If at all, there have to be two insurance policies, and it can be shown that high-risk individuals obtain complete insurance and low-risk individuals obtain insurance with a large deductible. Low-risk individuals obtain only partial insurance. Indeed, with a continuum of individuals with differing probabilities, it has been shown that there can be no equilibrium in the insurance market.[17]

How important is the problem of adverse selection in practice? Pauly maintains that, 'despite the outpouring of theoretical models of markets with adverse selection, there has as yet been no conclusive application of those models to the health insurance industry'.[18] He gives several reasons why adverse selection and the problems suggested in the theoretical literature have not been of great consequence in practice.[19]

18-7 The Problem of Moral Hazard

Another problem often mentioned in connection with insurance (although it occurs in almost every activity) is that of *moral hazard*. Moral hazard in the case of insurance arises whenever an individual's behaviour that affects the expected loss is altered by the quantity of insurance obtained. For instance, let C be the probability that an individual has a car accident. The problem of moral hazard is that this probability C is higher with insurance than without insurance. That is, individuals who buy insurance drive less carefully

---

[17] M. Rothschild and J. E. Stiglitz, 'Equilibrium in Competitive Insurance Markets: An Essay on the Economics of Imperfect Information', *Quarterly Journal of Economics*, 90 (1976): 630–49.
[18] M. V. Pauly, 'Taxation, Health Insurance, and Market Failure in the Medical Economy', *Journal of Economic Literature*, 24 (1986): 629–75, at p. 650.
[19] See also M. V. Pauly, 'What Is Adverse about Adverse Selection?' in R. S. Scheffler and L. F. Rossiter (eds.), *Advances in Health Economics and Health Services Research*, JAI Press, Greenwich, Conn., 1986, pp. 281–6.

because they are insured, and, therefore, the probability of their being involved in an accident is greater. Similarly, if an individual buys health insurance, there are two forms of moral hazard. First, individuals spend less on preventive health care, and so the probability of becoming ill rises. The incentive to adopt a healthier lifestyle is reduced. Second, because insurance reduces the price of health care at the point of use, it encourages a higher rate of use than would otherwise be the case. In fact, the probability of sickness or accident may be so much higher with insurance than without that a mutually beneficial insurance policy may fail to exist, or complete insurance may fail to exist. Countries with privately based insurance systems (such as the USA) tend to counter this problem by using copayments (user charges) at the point of treatment. In countries where health care is publicly financed (as in the UK) over-use of the system can be countered with non-price rationing, where individuals incur waiting costs for elective treatment.

The problem of moral hazard is pervasive and is not special to insurance markets. It occurs in all economic activities where economic agents do not bear the full consequences of their actions. In such instances the economic agents maximize their own utility to the detriment of others. The problem of moral hazard in the case of medical insurance was discussed by Arrow in 1963 and since then has attracted wide interest.[20]

Example 18-1   Doctors as Double Agents

We mentioned in Chapter 16 (Section 16-12) that one source of market failure in health care is imperfect information. Consumers are not well informed about the type or quality of health care that they need. It is the providers of health care (the doctors) that have this information. Doctors are assumed to act as agents for patients, serving their best interest by providing information and a service. Because consumers are not informed about health care provision, the relationship between doctors and patients is characterized by

asymmetric information. In this situation an efficient health care system requires that doctors act as perfect agents. By this we mean that doctors give all the information necessary for patients to make a decision and then they implement the decision once it is made. However, in both private and public health care systems doctors have a financial incentive to provide care over and above what would be provided if they negotiated with fully informed consumers. This is because doctors' fees are based on the amount of service they provide (in private systems) or because doctors are unaware of (or are not interested in) the cost of treatment (in public systems): it is the taxpayer who pays for the care. This problem may be dealt with by imposing cash limits on the size of doctors' budgets, as now happens in the NHS.

Even if doctors can be induced to act as perfect agents for patients, however, the health care system will not function efficiently unless it solves the 'double agency' problem.[21] Double agency results from a combination of asymmetric information and third-party financing (where the cost of health care is paid by a third party, such as a private insurance company). In this situation, patients are interested in doctors acting as perfect agents, and insurers are interested in doctors economizing on the use of health services, since this reduces the expected cost from claims. Thus, in an efficiently organized system doctors must act as double agents: efficiency requires that they take into account the interests of both patients and insurers. This means that there is information asymmetry not only between doctors and patients, but also between doctors and insurers. If doctors act as agents for the insurers, this conflicts with their acting as first-best agents for their patients.

Blomqvist shows that, unless the information asymmetry between doctors and insurers is resolved, efficiency cannot be achieved, even if doctors act as perfect agents for patients. His solution is for consumers to pay into an organization that employs its own medical staff to treat patients. An efficient system can then be achieved by using performance guarantees and liability rules to induce the organization to act as the patients' agent.

---

[20] K. J. Arrow, 'Uncertainty and the Welfare Economics of Medical Care', *American Economic Review*, 53 (1963): 941–73.

[21] A. Blomqvist, 'The Doctor as Double Agent: Information Asymmetry, Health Insurance, and Medical Care', *Journal of Health Economics*, 10 (1991): 411–32.

18-8 Signalling and Screening

In the previous sections we discussed the consequences of asymmetric information. The 'lemons' model showed the problem that sellers of high-quality products have when products of both high and low quality are marketed side by side and buyers have no knowledge of quality. Spence suggested a solution to this problem.[22] He argued that, if sellers of a high-quality product could find some activity that was less costly for them than for sellers of a lower-quality product, it might pay them to undertake this activity as a *signal* of higher quality. The buyers soon learn that the signal is associated with higher quality. One application of signalling, which we discussed earlier, is in insurance. An individual with low risk is more willing to co-insure than an individual with a high risk. Thus, the level of co-insurance is a potential signal of risk level.

Another application that Spence himself considered is in education. In human capital theory, education is an investment which increases individual productivity and so raises earnings relative to those who have not invested in education. A different view is that, rather than increasing productivity, education screens those individuals who would have enjoyed high relative earnings even without any education. According to the screening hypothesis, education does not make people more productive: it simply serves to distinguish different individuals' innate abilities. If individuals realize that employers are using education as a screening device, they will obtain qualifications in order to enhance their future earnings. It is years of schooling and qualifications that signal individuals' innate abilities to employers. The signal is strengthened if high-productivity people can acquire it at a lower cost than people with low productivity.

Consider two kinds of workers: workers with high productivity P_H (there are H of them) and workers with low productivity P_L (there are L of them); and $P_H > P_L$. The average productivity is

$$\overline{P} = P_H \cdot \frac{H}{H+L} + P_L \cdot \frac{L}{H+L},$$

where we measure productivity in terms of the value of goods produced. If employers cannot distinguish between workers, each worker is paid a wage $W = \overline{P}$. However, one way in which workers with higher productivity can distinguish themselves is by acquiring a *signal* such as education. If all high-productivity workers are educated and none of the low-productivity workers are, employers who can identify the two groups pay high-productivity workers a wage $W_H = P_H$ and low-productivity workers a wage $W_L = P_L$. There is thus an equilibrium, and it is sustainable. The question is: Under what conditions does this take place?

The model works in the following way. Suppose that the costs of education are C_H for high-productivity workers and C_L for low-productivity workers, and $C_H < C_L$. Furthermore, we should find that

$$C_L > P_H - P_L,$$

so that it is not worth while for low-productivity workers to invest in education. We should also find that

$$C_H < P_H - P_L,$$

so that it is worth while for high-productivity workers to invest in education. Note that if education is used as a signal, those with education get a wage $W_H = P_H$ and those with no education get a wage $W_L = P_L$. Thus, we should have the condition

$$C_H < (P_H - P_L) < C_L.$$

The above equilibrium is called a *separating equilibrium*, wherein the two groups of workers separate themselves by getting or not getting education.

However, other equilibria are also possible. Suppose that $C_L > P_H - P_L$ so that low-productivity workers do not find it worth while to invest in education. Since every worker gets a wage $\overline{P}$ if no one gets educated (and there is no separation), then if $C_H > P_H - \overline{P}$ it is not worth while for high-productivity workers to get educated either, and there is an equilibrium where no one invests in education. Thus, in the presence of differential information, multiple equilibria are possible.[23] Also note that in the above model, since education does not increase productivity,

[22] M. Spence, 'Job Market Signalling', *Quarterly Journal of Economics*, 87 (1973): 355–79, and *Market Signalling*, Harvard University Press, Cambridge, Mass., 1974.

[23] See J. E. Stiglitz, 'The Theory of "Screening", Education and the Distribution of Income', *American Economic Review*, 65 (1975): 283–300; also, J. E. Stiglitz and A. Weiss, 'Alternative Approaches to Analysing Markets with Asymmetric Information: Reply', *American Economic Review*, 73 (1983): 246–9.

it is a waste from the social point of view. Where education is used merely as a signal, there is a social cost; high-ability individuals consume more education than they would in the absence of low-ability individuals.

This view of education as a signal has serious implications for educational policy. In its extreme form (where education has no effect on productivity), the theory suggests that earnings differences associated with education reflect not improvement in individuals' productive capacity caused by education, but rather employers' use of education as a signal to identify pre-existing differences in productivity. The value of education is merely to place the right person in the right job.[24]

Before 1973 the prevalent view of education was that it increased individuals' productivity and hence could be regarded as an investment in human capital.[25] However, models of human capital do not explain how information about an individual's productivity gets transmitted to potential buyers of the individual's services. The signalling model suggests that it is the level of education that conveys such information. In its extreme form, the signalling hypothesis suggests that education has nothing to do with productivity, that its use is only as a signal. Furthermore, if some individuals have education, others who are more talented have to acquire even more education just to signal their superior talents. This leads to an overinvestment in education and a 'rat race', which is a waste from the social point of view because it does not lead to increased productivity.[26]

There have been many studies to test the signalling theory. Riley reviews the tests carried out before 1979 and argues that the studies were not well designed to test the signalling theory and hence do not constitute adequate tests.[27] He suggests an alternative method of testing the signalling model, based on the fact that some occupations need screening and others do not. The jobs where screening is used are those where employers cannot infer the individual's productivity by direct observation. In Riley's model individuals either accumulate minimum education for an unscreened job or continue in school and later accept a screened job. It follows that the discounted lifetime earnings of those individuals choosing screened jobs are, for any given educational level, less than the lifetime earnings of those in unscreened jobs. Riley claims that his results confirm this, and thus there is evidence in favour of the signalling hypothesis. The screenist interpretation of schooling as a provider of skills and information (signal) offers a more complete explanation than traditional human capital theory.

Liu and Wong also confirm the signalling hypothesis of education.[28] They find that firms offer higher initial wages to individuals with educational certificates in the absence of better information on productivity of new employees. They also find that, after the new employee has been with the firm for some time, employers no longer continue to pay individuals on the basis of educational certificates. In addition, they find evidence in favour of two conjectures: (1) the role of educational screening is more important for high-skilled jobs than for low-skilled jobs; (2) educational screening is performed by firms each time a new employee is hired, regardless of whether the employee has previously worked in the labour market.

Another study of the screening hypothesis, by Miller and Volcker, also claims support for it, and concludes that in the main screening is alive and well in Australia.[29] Using data on 1980 graduates in Australia, Miller and Volcker compare the salaries of graduates employed in areas where they might be expected to utilize skills acquired at the university, with salaries of graduates of equivalent background not so employed. If employers place little premium on skills acquired and use the awarding of degrees only as a filter, there should be no differences in the salaries of

---

[24] K. J. Arrow, in 'Higher Education as a Filter', *Journal of Public Economics*, 2 (1973): 193–216, presents and discusses the implications of a model where individual productive ability is completely unaffected by education and education is solely used as a signal.

[25] See G. S. Becker, *Human Capital*, NBER, New York, 1964, and J. Mincer, *Schooling, Experience and Earnings*, NBER, New York, 1974.

[26] G. A. Akerlof, 'The Economics of Caste, and of the Rat Race and Other Woeful Tales', *Quarterly Journal of Economics*, 90 (1976): 599–617.

[27] J. G. Riley, 'Testing the Educational Screening Hypothesis', *Journal of Political Economy*, 87 (1979): S227–52.

[28] P. W. Liu and Y. C. Wong, 'Educational Screening by Certificates: An Empirical Test', *Economic Inquiry*, 20 (1982): 72–83.

[29] P. W. Miller and P. A. Volcker, 'The Screening Hypothesis: An Application of the Wiles Test', *Economic Inquiry*, 22 (1984): 121–7.

the two groups. Miller and Volcker find this to be the case.

In summary, there is evidence to show that education is used by employers to screen prospective job applicants. Its role is not merely to improve the skills of individuals, but also to provide information on individuals' abilities.

18-9   Summary

Economic agents constantly face uncertainty. They are uncertain about prices, costs, market conditions, and so on. By uncertainty we mean those situations where the several possible outcomes can be described by a probability distribution. In economics the probabilities we use are often subjective probabilities. Given a probability distribution for the several possible outcomes, a firm can calculate the mean and variance for revenues, costs, and profits. Similarly, a consumer can calculate the mean and variance of utility.

Individuals can be classified as risk-averse, risk-neutral, and risk-loving, depending, respectively, on whether they are not willing to, indifferent to, or keen to undertake a fair gamble. A fair gamble is one whose expected return is zero.

Expected utility theory says that individuals behave as if they maximize expected utility. Although this theory has been criticized and shown to be at times contradictory to observed behaviour, we use it in our discussion because it is the simplest and most widely accepted theory. Based on expected utility theory, we explain why risk-averse individuals buy insurance and risk-loving individuals pay to gamble. We also explain why the same individual might buy insurance *and* gamble.

The provision of gambling does not involve many costs, but the provision of insurance has several problems. These are problems of adverse selection and moral hazard. The problem of adverse selection arises from the fact that the insurance company has less information than the insured about the risk involved.

Akerlof's model of the market for lemons (poor-quality used cars) highlights the problems created by asymmetric information. Where buyers are uncertain about the quality of used cars and offer to pay only a price for average quality, the better-quality cars disappear from the market because the sellers of these cars do not get a fair price. Similarly, if an insurance

company that is uncertain about the risk quality of the applicants offers an insurance premium appropriate for average risk, individuals with lower risk drop out (they consider the premium very high). Thus, only individuals with high risk buy insurance. This is the problem of adverse selection. However, economic institutions do arise to solve this problem. There are agencies providing information at a cost.

The problem of moral hazard arises because those who buy insurance have an incentive to take greater risks or consume more than they would normally do because the insurance company is paying for it. Moral hazard arises in all situations where individuals do not fully bear the consequences of their actions.

One way individuals can convey information about their productivity, degree of risk, or other attributes to the other party (employer, insurance company, and so on) is by acquiring a signal. There has been much controversy as to whether higher education serves to increase individuals' productivity or just acts as a signal. There is some evidence in favour of the signalling and screening hypothesis, that higher education does act as a signal and that wage differences resulting from such education are not solely due to increased productivity.

Key Terms

Adverse selection*
Asymmetric information
Certainty equivalent*
Cost of risk*
Expected utility theory*
Expected value*
Fair gamble*
Moral hazard*
Objective probability
Risk-averse*
Risk-loving*
Risk-neutral*
Risk premium*
Screening*
Signalling*
Subjective probability

Questions

1   Calculate the expected monetary value to you of the following games:

(a) I toss a coin. If it shows heads you pay me £20. If it shows tails I pay you £40.

(b) I toss a coin. If it shows heads you pay me £2000. If it shows tails I pay you £4000.

2   In the previous question suppose I charge you £9 to play game (a). Do you play it? If I charge you £999 to play game (b) do you play it? Give reasons for your answers.

3   Do risk-averse individuals gamble? Do risk-loving people purchase insurance? Give reasons and explain your answers with a graph.

4   A new hamburger bar opens across the road from Burger King. Local residents mostly eat at this new bar. Tourists eat at Burger King. Explain why this is so.

5   In the stock market, suppose share A has an equal chance of going up 20 per cent and going down 10 per cent. Share B has an equal chance of going up 30 per cent and going down 20 per cent during the same period. What is the expected return for the two shares? Which one does a risk-loving individual prefer?

6   Suppose the probability of your house catching fire is 1 in 10 000. If you estimate that the damage in the case of a fire is £1 million, what is the expected loss due to fire? If the insurance company asks for a premium of £150 will you pay it? Explain your answer with a diagram.

7   Imagine that Pizza Hut charges £5 for a pizza. A new pizza place charges £3 for the same kind of pizza. A friend says that the pizza from Pizza Hut must be better because it charges a higher price and that you should go there, and not to the new place. Explain the logic in this statement.

8   A monopolist faces the following demand function:

$$Q = 150 - CP.$$

The constant C is not known, but the monopolist believes that there is an equal chance that it is 10 or 15. What price does the monopolist charge to maximize expected revenue?

9   Suppose that your utility function is

$$U(Y) = 1000Y - 10Y^2.$$

You are asked to choose between two prospects:

(a) $Y = 30$ and $Y = 50$ each with probability $\frac{1}{2}$

(b) $Y = 40$ with probability 1 (certainty)

Which one do you choose? What is the certainty equivalent value for choice (a)? Define the cost of risk and the risk premium for prospect (a).

10   Explain the meaning of the following terms and their implications for economic policy: (a) adverse selection; (b) moral hazard; (c) signalling.

11   Suppose that there are 100 workers in a factory, half of them with productivity of £12 000 and the other half with productivity of £6000. The owner pays everyone a wage rate of £9000. Suppose that the workers with high productivity observe that in a similar neighbouring factory the owner pays £12 000 to its educated workers and £6000 to its uneducated workers. The high-productivity workers decide that they should get an education. If the costs of an education are £5000 for the workers with high productivity and £7000 for workers with low productivity, will the workers with high productivity get an education?

12   What is the moral hazard problem in the National Health Service? How do long queues at doctors' surgeries mitigate the problem of moral hazard?

Mathematical Appendix

In this appendix we first provide a brief review of some of the concepts that are used in deriving the more important mathematical results. The results are then presented according to the relevant chapters in the text.

Functions

A function is a rule that describes the relationship between variables. Often we say that some variable y depends on some other variable x, or that y is a function of x. We write this as

$$y = f(x)$$

y is the *dependent* variable and x the *independent* variable. Given different values of x, we can use this relationship (or function) to determine the values of y. If $f(x) = a + bx$, where a and b are given constants, then y is a linear function of x. The constant a gives the intercept and b the slope. If $f(x) = x^2$ or $2 - 3x + 4x^2$, or in general $a + bx + cx^2$, then we say that y is a *quadratic* function of x. This gives a curvilinear relationship. Another function to depict a curvilinear relationship is $y = c/x$, where c is a constant. In this case $xy = c$, a constant. If $c = 20$, then we have $xy = 20$. (Plot the graph.)

Derivatives

If $y = f(x)$, then the derivative of y with respect to x is

$$\lim_{\Delta x \to 0} \frac{\Delta y}{\Delta x} = \frac{dy}{dx},$$

where Δ means 'the change in'. So, the derivative is the limit of the rate of change of y with respect to x as the change in x goes to zero. The following are derivatives for some commonly used functions:

If $y = c$, a constant, then $\dfrac{dy}{dx} = 0$

If $y = x^n$, then $\dfrac{dy}{dx} = nx^{n-1}$

If $y = \log_e x$, then $\dfrac{dy}{dx} = \dfrac{1}{x}$

If $y = e^x$, then $\dfrac{dy}{dx} = e^x$

How do we interpret this? dy/dx at $x = c$ measures the slope of the function $y = f(x)$ at the point $x = c$. For a linear function $y = a + bx$, $dy/dx = b$, a constant, and hence the slope is constant.

Second derivatives

The second derivative of a function is the derivative of the derivative of that function. If $y = f(x)$, then the second derivative of $f(x)$ with respect to x is $d^2 f(x)/dx^2$. If $y = f(x) = 3x$, then $d(3x)/dx = 3$ and $d^2(3x)/dx^2 = d(3)/dx = 0$.

The second derivative measures the curvature of a function. If the second derivative of a function at a point is zero, then the function is flat near that point. If the second derivative of a function at a point is positive, then the function is convex near that point. If the second derivative of a function at a point is negative, then the function is concave near that point.

Partial derivatives

Suppose y is a function of two variables x and z so that $y = f(x, z)$. Then the derivative of y with respect to x, holding z constant, is called the partial derivative and is denoted by $\partial f / \partial x$. Similarly, the derivative of y with respect to z, holding x constant is denoted by $\partial f / \partial z$. With a linear function

$$y = a + bx + cz$$

we have $\partial y / \partial x = b$ and $\partial y / \partial z = c$ (both constants). If $y = f(x, z)$ and small increments dx in x, and dz in z produce an increment dy in y, then

$$dy = \frac{\partial f}{\partial x} dx + \frac{\partial f}{\partial z} dz \qquad (1)$$

dy is called the 'total differential' and dx and dz are called the 'partial differentials'.

Differentiation of a function of a function

If $y = f(z)$ and z is a function of x so that we write $z = g(x)$, then y is a function of a function and can be written $y = f[g(x)]$. We then have

$$\frac{dy}{dx} = \frac{dy}{dz} \cdot \frac{dz}{dx}.$$

For example, if $y = \log z$ and $z = a + bx$, then

$$\frac{dy}{dx} = \frac{dy}{dz} \cdot \frac{dz}{dx} = \frac{1}{z} b = \frac{b}{a + bx}.$$

Implicit functions

Suppose the relationship between x and z is not given explicitly but is specified by a relationship like

$$x^2 + 3xz + 4z^2 = c.$$

This is called an implicit function. We can write $y = f(x, z) = x^2 + 3xz + 4z^2$. Then

$$dy = \frac{\partial f}{dx} dx + \frac{\partial f}{dz} dz$$

$$= (2x + 3z)dx + (3x + 8z)dz.$$

But this is zero (since $y = c$, a constant, $dy = 0$). Hence we get

$$\frac{dz}{dx} = -\frac{2x + 3z}{3x + 8z}.$$

This method can be used to derive derivatives of implicit functions.

Criteria for maximum and minimum values

If $y = f(x)$, then at a maximum or minimum $dy/dx = 0$. At a maximum, dy/dx changes sign from positive to negative as x increases. At a minimum, dy/dx changes sign from negative to positive as x increases. These conditions can be checked by drawing a graph and noting that dy/dx at a point is the slope of the tangent at that point to the curve $y = f(x)$.

Chapter 1

Demand and supply functions
Quantity demanded (or supplied) is said to be a function of price. We write this as

$$q = f(p).$$

q is the dependent variable and p the independent variable. Given different values of p, we can use this function to determine the values of q. If $f(p) = a + bp$, then q is a linear function of p. Changes in the intercept a produce parallel shifts in the demand curve. For example, $q = 30 - 2p$ is a linear demand function. For $p = 0$, $q = 30$ and for $p = 15$, $q = 0$. (Plot the graph.) Changes in the intercept 30 produce parallel shifts in the curve. For a demand function, the slope coefficient b is (normally) negative. For a supply function it is (normally) positive. If $f(p) = a + bp + cp^2$, then we say that q is a quadratic function of p. This gives us a curvilinear relationship. If we have the curvilinear relationship $q = c/p$, expenditure on the commodity is constant.

Equilibrium
The equilibrium price and quantity are obtained by solving the two equations for demand and supply. For instance, suppose the demand and supply functions are:

demand: $q = -8 + 24p$
supply: $q = 40 - 24p$

Since in equilibrium quantity demanded and supplied are equal, we have

$$-8 + 24p = 40 - 24p \quad \text{or} \quad p = 1$$

and therefore $q = 16$

Ceteris paribus and shifts in demand and supply functions

Suppose quantity demanded depends on price p and income y. The demand function can be written as

$$q = f(p, y) = a + bp + cy$$

with a linear demand function. If y is held constant at level $\bar{y}$, then q is just a function of p. With a linear demand function, we can write this as

$$q = a + bp + c\bar{y} = a^* + bp$$

where $a^* = a + c\bar{y}$ is a constant. Changes in price p cause movements along this demand curve, with income y constant (*ceteris paribus*). Changes in y produce changes in the constant a^* and, thus, parallel shifts in the demand curve.

Chapters 2 and 3

Utility is assumed to be an increasing function of the quantities of goods consumed, but marginal utility is assumed to diminish as consumption is increased. For instance, our utility function may take the form $U(x_1, x_2) = \sqrt{x_1 x_2}$. This gives $MU_1 = \partial U / \partial x_1 = \sqrt{x_2/2x_1}$ and $MU_2 = \partial U / \partial x_2 = \sqrt{x_1/2x_2}$. This satisfies the law of diminishing marginal utility since MU_1 and MU_2 are decreasing functions of x_1 and x_2, respectively. This utility function also has another property; it is called *homogeneous of degree one*. This means that, if we increase the consumption of both x_1 and x_2 by some proportion, the utility increases by the same proportion; e.g., if you double x_1 and x_2, then U doubles.

However, if our utility function is of the form $U(x_1, x_2) = 20x_1 x_2$, then the law of diminishing marginal utility does not hold. Here, $MU_1 = 20x_2$ and $MU_2 = 20x_1$. Thus, MU_1 is constant across all levels of x_1 and it depends only on x_2.

A utility function that is commonly used in empirical work is the *Cobb-Douglas utility function*. This can be written as

$$U(x_1, x_2) = x_1^c x_2^{1-c} \qquad 0 < c < 1$$

This utility function generates the familiar shaped indifference curves shown in the text. We know that the slope of an indifference curve at any point is the *MRS* between the two goods. The *MRS* is equal to the ratio of the marginal utilities of the two goods. Thus,

$$MU_1 = \partial U / \partial x_1 = c\, x_1^{c-1} x_2^{1-c}$$

$$MU_2 = \partial U / \partial x_2 = (1 - c) x_1^c x_2^{-c}.$$

Then

$$MRS = \frac{MU_1}{MU_2} = \frac{\partial U / \partial x_1}{\partial U / \partial x_2} = \frac{c\, x_1^{c-1} x_2^{1-c}}{(1 - c) x_1^c x_2^{-c}}$$

$$= \frac{c}{(1 - c)} \cdot \frac{x_2}{x_1}.$$

The *MRS* depends on the ratio of x_2 to x_1, not on the absolute amounts of x_2 and x_1. These sort of preferences are called *homothetic preferences*.

Constrained maximization

To find the consumer's equilibrium, we have to maximize the utility function $U(x_1, x_2)$ subject to the budget constraint:

$$p_1 x_1 + p_2 x_2 = m \quad \text{or} \quad p_1 x_1 + p_2 x_2 - m = 0$$

where m is the money spent and p_1 and p_2 are the prices of x_1 and x_2, respectively. For this we use the *Lagrangian multiplier* method. This method starts by defining an auxiliary function called the *Lagrangian* (denoted by Z):

$$Z = U(x_1, x_2) - \lambda(p_1 x_1 + p_2 x_2 - m).$$

The new variable λ is called the Lagrangian multiplier. Then Lagrange's theorem says that the optimal choice must satisfy the three first-order conditions:

$$\frac{\partial Z}{\partial x_1} = \frac{\partial U}{\partial x_1} - \lambda p_1 = 0 \quad \text{or} \quad MU_1 = \lambda p_1$$

$$\frac{\partial Z}{\partial x_2} = \frac{\partial U}{\partial x_2} - \lambda p_2 = 0 \quad \text{or} \quad MU_2 = \lambda p_2$$

$$\frac{\partial Z}{\partial \lambda} = p_1 x_1 + p_2 x_2 - m = 0 \quad \text{the budget constraint}$$

The first two conditions give

$$\frac{MU_1}{MU_2} = \frac{p_1}{p_2}$$

which simply says that, in equilibrium, the *MRS* must equal the price ratio. (The optimal position for the consumer is a tangency point between an indifference curve and a budget constraint.)

Marginal utility of income

The Lagrangian multiplier λ has an economic interpretation. It measures the marginal utility of income. To see this, note that from the utility function we have (see equation (1) earlier)

$$dU = \frac{\partial U}{\partial x_1} dx_1 + \frac{\partial U}{\partial x_2} dx_2$$

$$= (MU_1) dx_1 + (MU_2) dx_2.$$

But $MU_1 = \lambda p_1$ and $MU_2 = \lambda p_2$. Hence we have

$$dU = \lambda(p_1 dx_1 + p_2 dx_2).$$

Also from the budget constraint we have

$$dm = p_1 dx_1 + p_2 dx_2.$$

Hence we get $dU/dm = \lambda$; in words, λ is the marginal utility of income. The Lagrangian multiplier is a *shadow price* of the constraint. Here the shadow price of the income constraint is the marginal utility of income.

Derivation of demand functions from utility functions

Consider again the Cobb–Douglas utility function. Maximizing utility is the same as maximizing the log of utility. Hence we can write the utility function as

$$U(x_1, x_2) = c \log x_1 + (1 - c) \log x_2.$$

We write the Lagrangian

$$Z = c \log x_1 + (1 - c) \log x_2 - \lambda(p_1 x_1 + p_2 x_2 - m).$$

We now differentiate with respect to x_1, x_2, and λ and set the partial deivatives equal to zero:

$$\partial Z/\partial x_1 = c/x_1 - \lambda p_1 = 0$$

$$\partial Z/\partial x_2 = (1 - c)/x_2 - \lambda p_2 = 0$$

$$\partial Z/\partial \lambda = p_1 x_1 + p_2 x_2 - m = 0$$

We now solve these equations for x_1 and x_2. The first two equations imply that

$$p_1 x_1 = c/\lambda \qquad (2)$$

$$p_2 x_2 = (1 - c)/\lambda \qquad (3)$$

If we combine these with the third equation (the budget constraint), we get

$$c/\lambda + (1 - c)/\lambda - m = 0, \qquad \text{or} \qquad \lambda = 1/m.$$

To get the demand functions, we substitute the expression for λ into (2) and (3). This gives

$$x_1 = (c/p_1)m \qquad \text{or} \qquad x_1 = cm/p_1$$

$$x_2 = [(1 - c)/p_2]m \qquad \text{or} \qquad x_2 = (1 - c)m/p_2.$$

Both the demand functions are rectangular hyperbolas (with unitary elasticity of demand). Note also that the cross price elasticities of demand are zero. (Why?)

Elasticity

If $y = f(x)$, the elasticity of y with respect to x is defined as $(dy/dx)/(y/x)$. Since

$$\frac{d \log y}{dy} = \frac{1}{y} \qquad \text{and} \qquad \frac{d \log x}{dx} = \frac{1}{x},$$

we can express the elasticity as $(d \log y)/(d \log x)$. For example, suppose the demand function is given by $q = c/p$. We have $pq = c$, a constant. pq is also total revenue R. We can write

$$\log R = \log p + \log q.$$

Differentiating both sides with respect to $\log p$, we get $0 = 1 + d \log q/d \log p$. Thus, the elasticity of this demand function is -1 at all points. (It is customary to consider the absolute value for demand elasticity; hence, it is taken to be $+1$.)

Income and substitution effects

We said in the text that the change in demand that results from a change in the price of a good can be divided into an income effect and a substitution effect. We derive the substitution and income effects for the Slutsky method because it is simpler. We omit it for the Hicks method (holding utility constant).

Suppose the original consumption bundle is $(\bar{x}_1, \bar{x}_2)$. The Slutsky demand function tells us what the consumer demands at different prices if the money income given to the consumer is $p_1 \bar{x}_1 + p_2 \bar{x}_2$. Thus, the Slutsky demand function x_1^s, which is a function of $(p_1, p_2, \bar{x}_1, \bar{x}_2)$, is the ordinary demand function at prices p_1, p_2 and income $\bar{m} = p_1 \bar{x}_1 + p_2 \bar{x}_2$. Thus,

$$x_1^s(p_1, p_2, \bar{x}_1, \bar{x}_2) = x_1(p_1, p_2, p_1 \bar{x}_1 + p_2 \bar{x}_2).$$

Differentiating this, we get

$$\frac{\partial x_1^s}{\partial p_1} = \frac{\partial x_1(p_1, p_2, \bar{m})}{\partial p_1} + \frac{\partial x_1}{\partial \bar{m}} \cdot \frac{\partial \bar{m}}{\partial p_1}$$

$$= \frac{\partial x_1}{\partial p_1} + \frac{\partial x_1}{\partial \bar{m}} \cdot \bar{x}_1.$$

Hence we get

$$\frac{\partial x_1}{\partial p_1} = \frac{\partial x_1^s}{\partial p_1} - \frac{\partial x_1}{\partial m} \cdot \overline{x}.$$

This is known as the *Slutsky equation*. The first term is the substitution effect and the second term the income effect.

Chapters 4 and 5

Production in the long run

Consider a production process using two variable factors of production, labour (L) and capital (K). Output is denoted by Q. We can write the production function as

$$Q = f(L, K).$$

In this situation the marginal products of L and K are given by the partial derivatives $\partial Q/\partial L$ and $\partial Q/\partial K$, respectively. To show the link between the production function and an isoquant, we take the total differential of the production function $Q = f(L, K)$. We get

$$dQ = \frac{\partial f}{\partial L} dL + \frac{\partial f}{\partial K} dK.$$

We said in the text that along an isoquant the change in output (dQ) is zero. This implies that

$$\frac{dK}{dL} = -\frac{\partial f/\partial L}{\partial f/\partial K}.$$

This shows that the slope of an isoquant (dK/dL), or the *MRTS*, equals the ratio of the marginal products.

A commonly used production function is the *Cobb–Douglas production function*. This can be written as

$$Q = AL^{\beta}K^{1-\beta} \qquad 0 < \beta < 1$$

For this production function

$$MP_L = \frac{\partial Q}{\partial L} = \beta AL^{\beta-1}K^{1-\beta}$$

$$= \beta Q/L$$

and

$$MP_K = \frac{\partial Q}{\partial K} = (1-\beta)AL^{\beta}K^{-\beta}$$

$$= (1-\beta)Q/K.$$

This shows that the marginal product of L (K) depends only on the ratio K/L and not on the absolute amount of L (K). If we hold K (L) constant and increase L (K),

the MP_L (MP_K) declines, thus satisfying the law of diminishing marginal productivity.

If our production function is of the form $Q = \alpha L + \beta K$, then $MP_L = \alpha$ and $MP_K = \beta$. Both the marginal products are constant, and hence the law of diminishing marginal productivity is not satisfied.

Homogeneous production functions

The Cobb–Douglas production function used above is a linear homogeneous production function in the sense that, if L and K are multiplied by a constant k, then output is multiplied by k. If

$$Q = AL^{\beta}K^{1-\beta},$$

then

$$Q(kL, kK) = A(kL)^{\beta}(kK)^{1-\beta}$$

$$= Ak^{\beta+1-\beta}L^{\beta}K^{1-\beta}$$

$$= kQ.$$

Thus, increasing both inputs by the factor k increases output by the same factor, implying that the Cobb–Douglas function is a linear homogeneous function.

A more general form of the Cobb–Douglas production function is

$$Q = AL^{\alpha}K^{\beta}$$

This function is homogeneous of degree $\alpha + \beta$. If we multiply L and K by a constant k, the resulting output ($Q*$) is given by

$$Q* = A(kL)^{\alpha}(kK)^{\beta} = k^{\alpha+\beta}Q.$$

If $\alpha + \beta = 1$, output is multiplied by k and we have constant returns to scale. If $\alpha + \beta < 1$, output is multiplied by $< k$ and we have decreasing returns to scale. If $\alpha + \beta > 1$, output is multiplied by $> k$ and we have increasing returns to scale.

Output maximization for a given cost

In the text we said that the firm may choose to maximize output for a given total cost or, equivalently, to minimize the total cost of producing a given output. We consider both approaches, starting with output maximization.

Suppose we want to maximize output (Q) for a given total cost (C). Two factors of production, labour and capital, are available. $C = wL + rK$, where w and r are the per-unit costs of the labour and capital inputs, respectively. Our production function is $Q = f(L, K)$.

We begin by forming the Lagrangian Z:

$$Z = f(L, K) - \lambda(wL + rK - C).$$

We set each partial derivative equal to zero:

$$\frac{\partial Z}{\partial L} = \frac{\partial f}{\partial L} - \lambda w = 0$$

$$\frac{\partial Z}{\partial K} = \frac{\partial f}{\partial K} - \lambda r = 0$$

$$\frac{\partial Z}{\partial \lambda} = wL + rK - C = 0,$$

or $MP_L = \lambda w$ and $MP_K = \lambda r$.

Hence we get $MP_L/MP_K = w/r$ at the optimum. This merely says that the $MRTS$ is equal to the price ratio. (The optimal position for the producer is a tangency point between an isoquant and an isocost line.) Also, we can give an economic interpretation to the Lagrangian multiplier as in the case of utility maximization. We have

$$dQ = \frac{\partial f}{\partial L}\, dL + \frac{\partial f}{\partial K}\, dK = MP_L\, dL + MP_K\, dK$$

$$= \lambda(w\, dL + r\, dK).$$

Also, from the cost constraint we have

$$dC = w\, dL + r\, dK$$

Hence we get $\lambda = dQ/dC$ or $1/\lambda = dC/dQ$. Thus, $1/\lambda = $ marginal cost.

Example: We saw above, for the Cobb–Douglas production function, $MP_L = \beta Q/L = \lambda w$ or $\beta Q = \lambda wL$. Similarly, $(1 - \beta)Q = \lambda rK$. So by addition we get $Q = \lambda(wL + rK) = \lambda C$. Hence $1/\lambda = C/Q = $ average cost. Note that in this case we have average cost = marginal cost. Also, $\beta = \lambda wL/Q = Q/C \cdot wL/Q = wL/C = $ share of labour cost in total cost. The MP_L condition $\beta Q = \lambda wL$ gives the demand function for L as

$$L = \frac{\beta Q}{\lambda w} = \frac{\beta C}{w}$$

since $\lambda = \frac{Q}{C}$. Similarly, the demand for K is given by $K = [(1 - \beta)C]/r$. Note that both these demand functions are rectangular hyperbolas (with unitary elasticity of demand). Also note the similarity with the demand functions for goods obtained from a Cobb–Douglas utility function.

Cost minimization subject to an output constraint

We have to minimize $C = wL + rK$ subject to $f(L, K) = Q_0$, a given level of output. We form the Lagrangian

$$Z = wL + rK - \lambda^*[f(L, K) - Q_0].$$

The first-order conditions for a constrained minimum are the same as for a constrained maximum, so we set the partial derivatives equal to zero:

$$\frac{\partial Z}{\partial L} = w - \lambda^* \frac{\partial f}{\partial L} = 0 \qquad \text{or} \qquad w = \lambda^* MP_L$$

$$\frac{\partial Z}{\partial K} = r - \lambda^* \frac{\partial f}{\partial K} = 0 \qquad \text{or} \qquad r = \lambda^* MP_K$$

$$\frac{\partial Z}{\partial \lambda^*} = f(L, K) - Q_0 = 0$$

Again, $MP_L/MP_K = w/r$, as before.

For the Cobb–Douglas production function,

$$MP_L = \beta Q_0/L \qquad \text{and} \qquad MP_K = (1 - \beta)Q_0/K.$$

The demand for labour is given by

$$MP_L = \beta Q_0/L = w/\lambda^* \qquad \text{or} \qquad L = \lambda^* \beta Q_0/w.$$

To find λ^*, we note that

$$wL = \lambda^* \beta Q_0$$

$$rK = \lambda^*(1 - \beta)Q_0.$$

Hence $wL + rK = \lambda^* Q_0$ or $\lambda^* = C/Q_0 = $ average cost. Note that $\lambda^* = 1/\lambda$, where λ is the Lagrangian multiplier from the previous problem. Otherwise, the results are identical.

Total cost of producing a given output

Given the output Q_0 and the factor prices w and r, what is the total cost? To derive this we have to derive the demand for L and K in terms of w, r and Q_0. The demand for labour is given by

$$L = \frac{\lambda^* \beta Q_0}{w} = \frac{\beta C}{w} = \frac{\beta(wL + rK)}{w}.$$

This gives

$$L = \left(\frac{\beta}{1 - \beta}\right)\frac{r}{w} K. \tag{4}$$

Substituting this in the Cobb–Douglas production function,

$$Q_0 = AL^\beta K^{1-\beta},$$

we get

$$Q_0 = A \left[\frac{\beta r K}{(1-\beta)w} \right]^\beta K^{1-\beta}$$

or

$$K = \frac{Q_0}{A} \left[\frac{(1-\beta)w}{\beta r} \right]^\beta \qquad (5)$$

This gives the demand for K. Substituting this in (4), we get

$$L = \frac{Q_0}{A} \left[\frac{(1-\beta)w}{\beta r} \right]^{\beta-1} \qquad (6)$$

Substituting (5) and (6) in the cost function $C = wL + rK$ and simplifying, we get

$$C = k Q_0 w^\beta r^{1-\beta},$$

where k is a constant. Thus, for the Cobb–Douglas production function, the cost function is also of the Cobb–Douglas form.

Chapter 6

Relationship between total revenue, average revenue, and marginal revenue
If R is total revenue, $R = pq$. Average revenue $AR = p$. Marginal revenue $MR = dR/dq$. Furthermore,

$$\log R = \log p + \log q$$

Differentiating both sides with respect to q, we get

$$\frac{d \log R}{d \log q} = \frac{d \log p}{d \log q} + 1$$

But

$$\frac{d \log R}{d \log q} = \frac{dR}{dq} \div \frac{R}{q} = \frac{MR}{AR}.$$

Thus, $MR = AR(1 - 1/\eta)$ where η, the elasticity of demand, is measured in absolute value and, hence is $-d \log q / d \log p$.

Chapter 8

The profit-maximizing condition is derived in the following way. Let q = output, R = total revenue, and C = total cost. Profit is given by $\pi = R - C$. The first-order condition for maximization is

$$d\pi/dq = \frac{dR}{dq} - \frac{dC}{dq} = 0 \qquad \text{or} \qquad MR = MC.$$

The second-order condition is

$$d^2\pi/dq^2 = \frac{d^2R}{dq^2} - \frac{d^2C}{dq^2} < 0.$$

That is, the slope of the MR curve is less than the slope of the MC curve.

Chapter 9

We write the demand function for the monopolist as $p = f(q)$. The total revenue function is $R(q) = pq = qf(q)$. The total cost function is $C(q)$. The monopolist's profit maximization problem is to maximize $R(q) - C(q)$. The first-order condition is

$$d\pi/dq = \frac{dR}{dq} - \frac{dC}{dq} = 0 \qquad \text{or} \qquad MR = MC.$$

The second-order condition is

$$d^2\pi/dq^2 = \frac{d^2R}{dq^2} - \frac{d^2C}{dq^2} < 0.$$

That is, the slope of the MR curve is less than the slope of the MC curve.

Monopoly and taxation: per-unit tax
Consider a monopolist with a total cost function $C(q) = aq^2 + bq + c$. The demand function is $p = \beta - \alpha q$. Consider a tax of t units per unit of output. We show that the tax brings in the maximum return when $t = \frac{1}{2}(\beta - b)$ and that the increase in monopoly price is always less than the tax. The monopolist's total revenue $R = pq = q(\beta - \alpha q)$. The monopolist's output is given by

$$dR/dq = dC/dq \qquad \text{or} \qquad \beta - 2\alpha q = 2aq + b$$

or

$$q = \frac{(\beta - b)}{2(\alpha + a)}.$$

The second-order condition for profit maximization is

$$d^2R/dq^2 < d^2C/dq^2 \qquad \text{or} \qquad -2\alpha < 2a.$$

This gives the condition $\alpha + a > 0$. In order that quantity produced is positive, we also should have $\beta > b$. With a tax of t per unit, the total revenue of the monopolist is $R = pq - tq$. (p is the price buyers pay but $p - t$ is the price that the monopolist gets.) The condition $MR = MC$ now gives $\beta - t - 2\alpha q = 2aq + b$ or $q = (\beta - b - t)/[2(\alpha + a)]$. The tax revenue is tq.

The value of t that maximizes this is obtained by maximizing $t(\beta - b - t)$. This gives $t = \frac{1}{2}(\beta - b)$. Thus, maximum revenue $= (\beta - b)/[4(\alpha + a)]$. To show that the increase in price is less than t with a linear demand function, note that the decrease in quantity produced is $t/[2(\alpha + a)]$. Hence the increase in price is $\alpha t/[2(\alpha + a)]$. If MC is constant, $a = 0$, and the increase in price is $\frac{1}{2}t$. If MC is rising, $a > 0$, and the increase in price is $< \frac{1}{2}t$.

Note that the above result is for the case of a linear demand curve (with variable elasticity). If the elasticity of demand is constant, then the change in MR is equal to the change in MC and the monopolist can pass on the total amount of the tax to his customers.

You can choose different numerical values for a, b, c, α, β, and t and work out the problem. The restrictions on the parameters are provided above.

Percentage tax or sales tax
Consider a sales tax of $100t$ per cent. If the price the monopolist gets is p, the price buyers pay is $p(1 + t)$ and the demand function is $p(1 + t) = \beta - \alpha q$. Hence the total revenue of the monopolist is $R = pq = q(\beta - \alpha q)/(1 + t)$. Equating MR to MC, we now get

$$\beta - 2\alpha q = (2aq + b)(1 + t).$$

This gives

$$q = \frac{\beta - b - bt}{2(\alpha + a + at)}.$$

Again, you can compute the values of q, p, and tax revenue for different numerical values of the coefficients. Also, you can compute the tax revenue for the same level of monopoly output and show that the sales tax raises more tax revenue. You can then go on to compute the maximum tax revenue for the two methods of taxation.

Optimal price discrimination
We can calculate the monopolist's profit under optimal price discrimination. The following example illustrates this. The demand functions in the two markets are:

$$p_1 = 50 - q_1$$
$$p_2 = 25 - q_2/2.$$

$MC = AC$ is constant and $= 10$.

We said in the text that the price-discriminating monopolist maximizes profit by equating the common

MC to both marginal revenues: $MR_1 = MR_2 = MC$. So, $MR_1 = MC$ gives $50 - 2q_1 = 10$ or $q_1 = 20$, $p_1 = 30$. $MR_2 = MC$ gives $25 - q_2 = 10$ or $q_2 = 15$, $p_2 = 17.5$.

The monopolist produces a total output of 35 and charges prices of 30 in market 1 and 17.5 in market 2. The total profit for the monopolist is $p_1 q_1 + p_2 q_2 - C$ where $C = $ total cost. Thus,

$$(30)(20) + (17.5)(15) - (10)(35) = 512.5.$$

If the monopolist charges a single price, what is it? To find the total demand, we have to write the demand functions as

$$q_1 = 50 - p$$
$$q_2 = 50 - 2p$$

Therefore, total demand is $q = 100 - 3p$ or $p = 100/3 - q/3$ (as long as $p < 25$). Now, $MR = 100/3 - 2q/3 = MC = 10$. This gives $q = 35$ and $p = 65/3$. The monopolist's profits are $(65/3)35 - (10)35 = 408.33$. Thus, the total output is unaffected (it it still 35), but profits are higher by 104.17 under price discrimination.

Chapter 11

Duopoly: Cournot's solution
We can derive the properties of the Cournot equilibrium with a little algebra. This requires that we find each duopolist's reaction function. We assume a linear demand function. q_A and q_B are the outputs of the two duopolists. The market demand function is

$$p = a - b(q_A + q_B).$$

For convenience, we assume that marginal costs are zero for both the duopolists. The profit (and total revenue) of the first duopolist is

$$\pi_A = pq_A = q_A[a - b(q_A + q_B)]$$
$$= aq_A - bq_A^2 - bq_A q_B.$$

His marginal revenue is $MR_A = a - bq_B - 2bq_A$. Setting $MR_A - MC = 0$, we get $q_A = (a - bq_B)/2b$. This is the *reaction function* of the first duopolist. It gives his output as a function of the second duopolist's output. Similarly, the second duopolist's reaction function is given by $q_B = (a - bq_A)/2b$. To obtain the Cournot equilibrium, we have to solve these two equations. Since the firms are identical, we can set $q_A = q_B$. We get

$$q_A = q_B = \frac{a}{3b} \quad \text{and} \quad \text{total output} = \frac{2a}{3b}.$$

Note that the competitive output is given by $p = MC = 0$ or $q = a/b$. To determine the monopoly output, we have

$$\pi = R = qp = q(a - bq) = aq - bq^2$$
$$MR = a - 2bq = MC = 0 \quad \text{gives} \quad q = a/2b.$$

Thus,

Competitive output $= a/b$
Monopoly output $= a/2b$
Duopoly output $= 2a/3b$ (Cournot's solution)

The duopoly output under collusion is the monopoly output $a/2b$, and the Bertrand output is the competitive output a/b which is divided equally between the two duopolists.

Stackelberg's solution

In this model one of the firms is a leader and the other a follower. We assume that firm A is the leader and firm B is the follower. In this case, firm A knows firm B's reaction function and uses this knowledge to maximize its own profit. Firm B's reaction function is, as derived earlier,

$$q_B = \frac{a - bq_A}{2b}.$$

This is what firm B produces for given levels of q_A. Firm A takes this into account and maximizes its profit by substituting firm B's reaction function (the value of q_B) into its own profit function:

$$\pi_A = q_A p = q_A\left[a - b\left(q_A + \frac{a - bq_A}{2b}\right)\right]$$

$$= aq_A - bq_A^2 - \frac{a}{2}q_A + \frac{b}{2}q_A^2$$

$$= \tfrac{1}{2}(aq_A - bq_A^2)$$

$$MR_A = MC = 0 \text{ gives } a - 2bq_A = 0 \quad \text{or} \quad q_A = \frac{a}{2b}$$

Substituting this value into firm B's reaction function,

$$q_B = \frac{a - bq_A}{2b} \quad \text{gives} \quad q_B = \frac{a}{4b}.$$

Thus, the Stackelberg output is $a/2b + a/4b = 3a/4b$. These are the results mentioned in Section 11-7.

Glossary

Accounting cost cost concept used by accountants. Accounting cost does not take into account all *opportunity costs*, and can depend on the particular accounting conventions used.

Accounting profit excess of total revenue over total *accounting cost*. Accounting profit generally exceeds economic profit.

Additive utility refers to the case where total *utility* for a bundle of commodities is equal to the sum of the utilities for the individual commodities.

Adverse selection refers to the case where only products of a lower quality remain in a market, or only individuals with greater risk purchase insurance.

Anti-classical revisionist theory (of profit) holds that all markets are competitive and that *economies of scale* are negligible. Profitability differences are due to differences in firm efficiency.

Average cost pricing the setting of price equal to average total cost where both price and output correspond to the intersection of the average total cost curve and the demand curve.

Average product output per unit of factor employed. Average product can be computed for each factor. Average product equals *total product* divided by factor quantity.

Averch–Johnson effect the over-utilization of capital by a public utility as a result of rate-of-return regulation.

Barriers to entry impediments to the entry of new firms into an economically profitable industry.

Benefit–cost ratio rule see *Profitability rate criterion*.

Bilateral monopoly a market where there is a single buyer and a single seller.

Capital-saving technological change an improvement in technology which shifts the production *isoquants* in such a way that the optimal capital–labour ratio declines at the original factor price ratio.

Cardinal theory of utility treats *utility* as measurable with cardinal numbers. The units of measurement are called utils.

Cartel a group of firms acting together to control output and price.

Certainty equivalent the level of wealth offered with certainty that yields the same *utility* as the expected utility associated with a given distribution of uncertain wealth.

Characteristics approach assumes that consumer choice is based on the characteristics of goods rather than on the goods themselves. It is the characteristics that give *utility*.

Classical theory (of profit) holds that profitability differences among firms are due mainly to differences among industries.

Coase theorem holds that under perfect competition, if *income effects* and *transaction costs* are ignored, voluntary agreements among the parties concerned can lead to a socially optimal allocation of resources even in the presence of externalities. Furthermore, the resulting allocation is the same regardless of which party is assigned the property rights to the contestable resource.

Cobb–Douglas production function a production function of the form $Q = AL^\alpha K^\beta$ where A, α, and β are constants, Q is output, and L and K are the quantities of inputs employed.

Collusion explicit or tacit agreement among firms concerning price, output, or other matters.

Compensating wage differential the portion of the wage rate that is necessary to induce workers to accept hazardous or unpleasant jobs.

Complementary inputs a pair of inputs such that an increase in the use of one causes the *marginal product* of the other to rise.

Completeness of preferences the assumption that the consumer is capable of ranking all possible commodity bundles. For any two commodity bundles A and B, the consumer either prefers A to B, prefers B to A, or is indifferent between A and B.

Concentration curve a curve showing cumulative market share for each number of firms where firms are ranked from largest to smallest.

Concentration ratio the proportion of the total market controlled by the largest firms, where n is usually 3 or 5.

Constant-cost industry an industry whose long-run supply curve is horizontal.

Constant returns to scale where a proportionate change in all inputs changes output by the same proportion.

Consumer surplus the difference between the maximum amount consumers are willing to pay for a specified quantity of a good and what consumers do pay to obtain that quantity of the good.

Consumption efficiency requires that the *marginal rate of substitution* (in consumption) is the same for all individuals consuming each pair of goods.

Contestable market a market where both entry and exit are absolutely free.

Contract curve the locus of points in an *Edgeworth box* which represents efficient allocations of goods (in the case of consumption) or inputs (in the case of production).

Convenience goods commodities that are usually purchased without consulting a retailer.

Cost of risk the difference between the expected wealth and the *certainty equivalent* wealth.

Cournot model a *duopoly* model in which firms believe that their rival's output is fixed and simultaneously they decide how much to produce.

Credence goods commodities whose attributes cannot be reliably evaluated by the consumer even after use.

Deadweight loss efficiency loss measured by the sum of the lost *consumer* and *producer surplus*, less government revenue.

Declining industry an industry characterized by exit and very little entry because the demand for the industry's product is continuously declining.

Decreasing-cost industry an industry where the long-run supply curve is downward-sloping.

Decreasing returns to scale the case where a proportionate increase in all inputs causes output to increase by a smaller proportion.

Discounting the act of converting a stream of future returns into a *present value*.

Discrimination the valuation in the labour market (and elsewhere) of personal characteristics that are not related to productivity.

Diseconomies of scale (external) factors beyond the control of the individual firm that cause each firm's average cost curve to shift upwards as industry output is expanded or as new firms enter the industry.

Dominant strategy a *strategy* that is optimal for a player no matter what strategy the other player chooses.

Dual problem the alternative *linear programming* problem which can be solved in order to obtain *shadow prices*.

Duopoly   an extreme case of *oligopoly* where there are only two firms.

Economic cost   see *Opportunity cost.*

Economic profit   the amount by which total revenue exceeds full *opportunity cost*. Economic profit is sometimes called pure profit.

Economic region of production   the downward-sloping portion of all *isoquants.*

Economic rent   the excess of total payment to a factor of production over and above what is required to bring that particular factor into production.

Economic theory of regulation (or intervention)   holds that regulation is like any other commodity, with its price and quantity determined by the forces of demand and supply.

Economies of scale (external)   factors beyond the control of the individual firm that cause each firm's average cost curve to shift downwards as industry output is expanded or as new firms enter the industry.

Economies of scale (internal)   factors that cause long-run average cost to decrease as the firm's output increases. The firm's long-run average cost curve is negatively sloped in the presence of scale economies.

Edgeworth box   a diagram used to describe efficiency conditions and to demonstrate how the allocation of some goods and resources can be improved through exchange.

Elasticity of input demand   a measure of the responsiveness of the quantity demanded of an input to a change in the price of that input. Mathematically, elasticity of input demand equals percentage change in quantity of input demanded divided by percentage change in input price.

Elasticity of substitution   a measure of the responsiveness of the input ratio to a change in the input–price ratio. The elasticity of substitution is equal to the absolute value of the ratio of the percentage change in the input ratio to the percentage change in the input–price ratio.

Engel curve   a curve illustrating the various amounts of a commodity that a consumer (or consumers) is willing to purchase at various income levels, all other things being equal.

Excess capacity   the amount by which *plant capacity* exceeds actual output.

Expected utility theory   argues that individuals behave as if their objective is to maximize expected utility.

Expected value   the average or mean value of a random variable.

Experience goods   commodities whose attributes can be evaluated only after using them.

External benefit   the portion of the benefit associated with an economic decision that accrues to someone other than the party making the decision.

External cost   the portion of the cost associated with an economic decision that accrues to someone other than the party making the decision.

Fair gamble   a gamble with an expected return equal to zero.

First-degree price discrimination   charging each person his or her *reservation price* for a good.

Fixed proportions production process   a production process with an *elasticity of substitution* equal to zero. The *isoquants* in this case are right angles.

Free-rider problem   the problem of *public good* provision resulting from the incentive for an individual to understate his or her preference for a public good in the hope of obtaining the good at a lower cost.

Frontier cost functions   cost functions which measure the technically attainable minimum cost of production at a given scale of operation.

Functional distribution of income   the classification of total revenue into wages, rent, and interest.

Giffen good   the case where an increase in price leads to an increase in quantity demanded. This occurs in theory for an *inferior good* with an *income effect* that is stronger than the *substitution effect*. The *ordinary demand curve* for such a good is positively sloped.

Gini coefficient   an index of inequality in a distribution. A higher value indicates greater inequality. The Gini coefficient is equal to the area between the *Lorenz curve* and the 45° line multiplied by 2.

Growth maximization model   a model of firm behaviour based on the assumption that managers satisfy instincts of power, dominance, and prestige by pursuing growth as an objective.

Herfindahl index a measure of monopoly power in an industry. The Herfindahl index is equal to the sum of the squared market (or employment) shares for all firms in the industry.

Hicks method a method of decomposing a change in quantity demanded into the *substitution effect* and the *income effect*. Under this method, the substitution effect involves a movement along an indifference curve whereas the income effect involves a movement between indifference curves. This is the theoretically correct method of decomposition (see *Slutsky method*).

Homogeneous production function a special type of *homothetic production function* where a proportionate change in inputs causes output to change by a proportion that does not vary with changes in the input bundle.

Homothetic production function a production function such that the ratio of *marginal products* is unaffected by a proportionate change in the inputs.

Human capital skills or knowledge that render workers more productive.

Ideal output the output associated with the minimum point of the firm's *LRAC* curve.

Incentive-compatible mechanism a mechanism by which self-interested individuals are induced to reveal their true preferences for a *public good*.

Income-compensated demand curve a demand curve which reflects only the *substitution effect* of a price change.

Income-consumption curve a curve showing the combinations of two commodities that the consumer purchases at various levels of income, holding prices constant. The curve consists of a series of tangency points between indifference curves and parallel budget lines.

Income effect the portion of a change in quantity demanded that is attributable to the change in *real income* that results from the change in price.

Increasing-cost industry an industry whose long-run supply curve is upward-sloping.

Increasing returns to scale where a proportionate increase in all inputs causes output to increase by a larger proportion.

Independent inputs a pair of inputs such that a change in the use of one has no effect on the *marginal product* of the other.

Independent products products such that the cost of producing one product is unaffected by a change in the output of another product.

Inferior good a commodity such that an increase in consumers' incomes causes a decrease in demand and a decrease in consumers' incomes causes an increase in demand. Income elasticity for an inferior good is negative.

Inferior input see *Regressive input*.

Inflection point a point of change in a function's curvature. Mathematically, the inflection point corresponds to a value of zero for the second derivative.

Initial endowment the original quantities of goods allocated to an individual before any trade takes place.

In-kind subsidy full or partial provision of a particular commodity by the government. Examples include free school meals and housing assistance.

Input monopoly an input market characterized by a single seller of a factor of production with no close substitutes.

Internal rate of return method an investment criterion which ranks projects according to their internal rates of return. The internal rate of return for a project is the discount rate that equates the *present value* of the earnings from an investment to the original cost.

Interpersonal utility comparison the problem of weighing changes in *utility* for two or more individuals. Pareto viewed this problem as impossible to solve.

Intertemporal choice a choice involving time.

Intertemporal exchange the exchange of commodities over time.

Isocost line the locus of points representing all of the combinations of two inputs which the firm can purchase for a given total cost, at specified input prices.

Isoquant the locus of points representing the various combinations of two inputs which yield a specified total output. An isoquant can be constructed for any level of output.

Isorevenue line the locus of points representing the various combinations of two products that yield a specified total revenue at given product prices.

Joint products products that must be produced in fixed proportions, so that a change in the output of one product automatically results in a proportionate change in the output of the other product(s).

Labour-saving technological change an improvement in technology which shifts the production *isoquants* in such a way that the optimal capital–labour ratio increases at the original factor price ratio.

Laspeyres index a cost-of-living index which uses base-period expenditure shares to weight the various price changes (see also *Paasche index*).

Law of diminishing marginal productivity the requirement that, as equal increments of the variable input are added, holding technology and the quantities of all other inputs constant, eventually the increment to output declines. This is also known as the *Law of diminishing returns*.

Law of diminishing marginal rate of substitution in production the requirement that, as one input is substituted for another, eventually the *marginal rate of technical substitution* declines. This law insures that *isoquants* are convex to the origin.

Law of diminishing marginal utility the requirement that, as the consumption of a particular commodity increases, *ceteris paribus*, the *marginal utility* of that commodity eventually declines.

Law of diminishing returns see *Law of diminishing marginal productivity*.

Lerner index a measure of monopoly power which is equal to (price $-$ *MC*)/price.

Lindahl equilibrium a situation where the *socially optimal output* of a *public good* is provided, each individual's price is equal to marginal value, and production costs are fully covered.

Linear programming a mathematical technique which can be used to locate a constrained maximum or minimum value when the objective function and all constraints are linear.

Long-run elasticity a measure of the full responsiveness of quantity after consumers (in the case of demand) or sellers (in the case of supply) have had sufficient time to completely adjust. Long-run elasticities can be computed for price changes, income changes, or changes in some other variable.

Long-run expansion path a curve showing the optimal combinations of two inputs for various levels of output when the input price ratio is held constant and both inputs are adjusted. The curve consists of a series of tangency points between the *isoquants* and parallel *isocost lines*.

Lorenz curve a curve illustrating the cumulative distribution of income or wealth.

Luxury good a commodity with an income elasticity greater than one. As income increases, the demand for a luxury increases more than proportionately.

Managerial efficiency see *Production efficiency*.

Managerial theories of the firm theories of firm behaviour which emphasize the separation of ownership from control in the modern corporation.

Managerial theory (of profit) argues that differences in profitability among firms are due primarily to firm-level efficiency differences based largely on differences in managerial skills.

Marginal cost pricing the setting of price at the level corresponding to the intersection of the marginal cost curve and the demand curve.

Marginal factor cost the increase in total cost resulting from a one-unit increase in the use of inputs, *ceteris paribus*.

Marginal product the increment to *total product* attributable to a one-unit increase in an input, holding other inputs constant. Marginal product can be calculated for any input in the production process.

Marginal rate of substitution the rate at which one commodity is substituted for another without changing total *utility*. The marginal rate of substitution of X for Y is equal to the absolute value of the slope of the indifference curve. Mathematically, it is equal to the ratio of *marginal utilities* for two commodities.

Marginal rate of technical substitution the rate at which one input is substituted for another input in the production process without affecting total output. Graphically, the marginal rate of technical substitution is equal to the absolute value of the slope of the *isoquant.* Mathematically, it is equal to the ratio of *marginal products* for the two inputs.

Marginal rate of transformation the marginal rate of transformation of product *A* for product *B* is equal to the reduction in the output of *B* that is necessary to increase the output of *A* by one unit, holding inputs constant.

Marginal revenue product the change in total revenue resulting from a one-unit increase in the use of inputs, *ceteris paribus.*

Marginal utility the increase in total *utility* resulting from a one-unit increase in the consumption of a particular commodity, holding the quantities of other commodities constant.

Market failure the provision by a competitive market of an output level that is not the *socially optimal output.*

Market-sharing cartel a *cartel* in which the member-firms mutually determine market shares.

Maximin decision rule a decision criterion by which one would choose the *strategy* that maximizes the minimum possible payoff.

Monopolistic exploitation of labour the process by which the *value of marginal product* for labour exceeds the *marginal revenue product* of labour.

Monopsonistic exploitation of labour the process by which the *marginal factor cost* of labour exceeds the wage rate.

Monopsony (pure) the case of a single buyer of a commodity.

Moral hazard the case where an individual's behaviour which might affect expected loss is altered by the quantity of insurance purchased.

Nash equilibrium an equilibrium where each player is choosing the optimal *strategy* given the strategies of the other players.

Natural monopoly the case where the average cost of production declines over the entire range of market demand. This implies that one firm can produce the entire output more cheaply than can multiple firms.

Necessity a commodity with a positive income elasticity less than one. As income increases, the demand for a necessity increases less than proportionately.

Negative externality in consumption the case where consumption imposes costs on parties other than the consumer.

Negative externality in production the case where production imposes costs on parties other than the producer.

Net present value rule an investment criterion that ranks projects according to their net present values and approves only projects with positive net present values. The net present value is simply the *present value* of returns minus the present value of costs.

Neutral technological change an improvement in technology which shifts the production *isoquants* in such a way that the optimal capital–labour ratio is unaffected at the original factor price ratio.

Non-excludability the infeasibility of excluding any individual from enjoying the benefits of a commodity once that commodity is provided.

Nonprice competition rivalry among firms which takes the form of advertising or variation in the production design or quality.

Non-rivalry in consumption a property of *public goods* that allows an additional consumer to enjoy the benefits of a commodity without reducing the availability of benefits to others.

Normal good a commodity such that an increase in consumers' incomes leads to an increase in demand and a decrease in consumers' incomes leads to a decrease in demand. Income elasticity for a normal good is positive.

Normal profit the *opportunity cost* of owner-supplied resources. This is a profit only in the accounting sense.

Oligopoly a market structure characterized by only a few interdependent sellers of a homogeneous or differentiated product and substantial *barriers to entry.* The interdependence commonly leads to intense rivalry.

Opportunity cost the value of a resource in its next-best use. This is the cost concept most relevant to economic decisions and thus is sometimes called 'economic cost'.

Ordinal theory of utility treats *utility* as measurable only on an ordinal basis; in other words, the consumer can rank commodity bundles in order of preference but cannot state by how much bundle *A* is preferred to bundle *B*.

Ordinary demand curve a demand curve which reflects both the *substitution effect* and the *income effect* of a price change.

Output effect see *Scale effect*.

Paasche index a cost-of-living index which uses current-period expenditure shares to weight the various price changes (see also *Laspeyres index*).

Pareto improvement a change in the allocation of resources that renders at least one person better off and nobody worse off.

Pareto optimum a resource allocation for which there are no *Pareto improvements* possible.

Payoff matrix a table showing an individual's returns for various combinations of the individual's and the rival's strategies.

Perfect cartel a group of firms in which each member's output is set at a level that maximizes the group's total profit.

Perfect price discrimination see *First-degree price discrimination*.

Perpetual bond or perpetuity a bond that pays a specified amount of interest each period without termination.

Physical capital the durable manufactured inputs into the production process such as buildings, machinery, tools, etc.

Piece-rate wages a payment method under which workers are paid according to the amount of output produced.

Plant capacity the output corresponding to the minimum point on the average total cost curve.

Positive externality in consumption the case where consumption bestows benefits on parties other than the consumer.

Positive externality in production the case where production bestows benefits on parties other than the producer.

Predatory price cut a reduction in price for the purpose of eliminating rivals by capturing their market shares.

Pre-emptive price cutting a reduction in price for the purpose of deterring entry into a market by potential rivals.

Present value the amount received today that is equivalent in value to a specified future payment or stream of payments.

Price-consumption curve a curve showing the various combinations of goods *X* and *Y* that the consumer purchases for various prices of good *X*, holding the price of *Y* and income constant. The curve consists of a series of tangency points between indifference curves and budget lines where all of the budget lines have the same intercept on the *Y*-axis.

Price discrimination the charging of different prices for the same product when those differences are not cost justified (see *First-degree*, *Second-degree*, and *Third-degree price discrimination*).

Price effect the total change in quantity demanded resulting from a change in price. The price effect is equal to the sum of the *income effect* and the *substitution effect*.

Price leadership a situation such that one or a few firms typically initiate price changes and the other firms in the industry follow.

Price war a situation in which rivals successively undercut one another's prices.

Private cost the portion of the cost of an economic decision which accrues to the party making that decision.

Producer surplus the amount that producers receive for a given quantity of a good in excess of the minimum amount they are willing to accept for that quantity.

Product differentiation the case where consumers perceive similar products to have distinguishing characteristics but to be close substitutes.

Production efficiency requires that the *marginal rate of technical substitution* is the same for (1) all products that a single firm produces using any given pair of inputs and (2) all producers producing the same output. This is also called 'managerial efficiency'.

Production function a statement of the functional relationship between inputs and outputs.

Production possibilities curve a curve showing the various combinations of two outputs that result from efficient allocations of given inputs.

Profitability rate criterion an investment criterion which ranks alternative investments according to their profitability rates and approves only investments with a profitability rate greater than one. The profitability rate is simply the ratio of *present value* of returns to present value of costs.

Public interest theory of government regulation holds that the government responds to a public demand for the correction of inefficient allocations and that the government can correct these inefficiencies at a lower cost than private organizations.

Pure public good a commodity characterized by *non-excludability* and *non-rivalry in consumption.*

Quasi-rent the surplus accruing to factors of production other than land.

Reaction function shows the profit-maximizing output choice of one duopolist as a function of the other duopolist's output.

Real income the purchasing power associated with a specified nominal income.

Regressive input an input such that an increase in output results in a decrease in use at constant input prices. Regressive inputs are also called 'inferior inputs'.

Rent the return paid to an input that is fixed in quantity.

Rent-seeking activity and expenditure for the purpose of maintaining or securing monopoly power.

Reservation price the maximum price a consumer is willing to pay for a good.

Reservation wage the minimum wage at which an individual is willing to work.

Returns to scale see *Decreasing* and *increasing returns to scale.*

Ridge line a line separating the downward-sloping portions of a series of *isoquants* from the upward-sloping portions. Ridge lines bound the *economic region of production.*

Risk-averse a characteristic of an individual who is unwilling to undertake a *fair gamble.*

Risk-loving a characteristic of an individual who is keen to undertake a *fair gamble.*

Risk-neutral a characteristic of an individual who is indifferent between accepting or rejecting a *fair gamble.*

Risk premium the fraction of expected wealth that an individual is willing to give up in exchange for certainty.

Sales maximization model a *managerial theory* of firm behaviour based on the assumption that managers attempt to maximize sales revenue subject to a minimum profit constraint.

Scale effect the portion of the change in input use resulting from the change in output caused by a change in input price. This is also called the 'output effect'.

Screening the evaluation of individual characteristics by direct observation.

Search goods commodities whose attributes can be evaluated by inspection and comparison.

Second-degree price discrimination the charging of several different prices for different ranges or groups of output.

Separation theorem states that, when *intertemporal exchange* is possible, the production optimum is independent of consumption preferences.

Shadow price the change in the value of the objective function which results from a one-unit relaxation of a constraint, without relaxing the other constraints.

Shopping goods commodities for which retailers serve as an important source of information.

Short-run elasticity a measure of the initial responsiveness of quantity when consumers (in the case of demand) or sellers (in the case of supply) have not had time to adjust fully. Short-run elasticities can be computed for price changes, income changes, or changes in some other variable.

Signalling the use of a readily observable characteristic to imply unobservable qualities.

Slutsky method   a method of decomposing a change in quantity demanded into the *substitution effect* and the *income effect*. Under this method, both the income and substitution effects involve movements between indifference curves. Though theoretically incorrect, the Slutsky method is operational (see *Hicks method*).

Social benefit   the sum of private benefit and *external benefit*.

Social cost   the sum of *private cost* and *external cost*.

Socially optimal output   the quantity of output for which marginal *social benefit* equals marginal *social cost*.

Specialization in consumption   the consumption of only one commodity. Specialization in consumption generally results from concave indifference curves but can also occur with convex indifference curves.

Stackelberg model   a *duopoly* model in which one firm is a leader and the other a follower. The leader sets its output first.

Stages of production   based on the behaviour of *average product* and *marginal product*, economists have divided a production process with a single variable input into three stages. The economically meaningful range is given by stage II, with marginal product greater than zero and average product falling.

Strategy   one of several alternative courses of action.

Substitution effect   the portion of a change in quantity demanded which is attributable solely to the change in relative prices.

Sunk cost   a cost that cannot be recovered by selling or renting a resource. This is a cost only in the accounting sense.

Survivor principle   states that firms operating at or moving towards the minimum point on the long-run average cost curve should be the ones that 'survive' over time in a competitive market.

Technological change   a change in the state of the art available for combining and transforming resources into goods and services.

Third-degree price discrimination   the charging of different prices to different groups of consumers. The individuals within a particular group all pay the same price.

Time wages   a payment method under which workers are paid by the hour.

Total product   the total quantity of output that can be produced with a specified input bundle.

Transaction costs   the costs of negotiating a contract or agreement.

Transfer earnings   see *Opportunity cost*.

Transitivity of preferences   the condition that, if bundle *A* is preferred to bundle *B* and bundle *B* is preferred to bundle *C*, then bundle *A* must be preferred to bundle *C*. Transitivity of preferences precludes the intersection of indifference curves.

User cost of capital   the rental cost of *physical capital* expressed as a percentage of its value.

Utility   the satisfaction that a consumer derives from the consumption of goods and services.

Utility maximization model   a general *managerial theory* of firm behaviour based on the assumption that managers attempt to maximize their *utility* subject to a minimum profit constraint.

Valuation ratio   the ratio of the stock market value of a firm to its accounting or book value.

Value of marginal product   the *marginal product* of an input multiplied by the price of the output.

Welfare cost   see *Deadweight loss*.

X-inefficiency   the failure of the firm to maximize the output produced from its given inputs owing to poor managerial motivation and an inefficient market for knowledge.

Zero-sum game   a game where the gains to one party equal the sum of the losses to the other party.

Index

Compiled by Indexing Specialists, 202 Church Road, Hove, East Sussex BN3 2DJ.